W9-CJD-547

ROSEBUD, JUNE 17, 1876

ALSO BY PAUL L. HEDREN

First Scalp for Custer: The Skirmish at Warbonnet Creek, July 17, 1876
(Glendale, Calif., 1980; revised, Lincoln, Nebr., 2005)

*With Crook in the Black Hills: Stanley J. Morrow's 1876 Photographic
Legacy* (Boulder, Colo., 1985)

Fort Laramie in 1876: Chronicle of a Frontier Post at War
(Lincoln, Nebr., 1988); reprinted as *Fort Laramie and the
Great Sioux War* (Norman, Okla., 1998)

(ed.) *The Great Sioux War, 1876–77: The Best from* Montana
The Magazine of Western History (Helena, Mont., 1991)

(ed.) *Campaigning with King: Charles King, Chronicler of the Old Army*
(Lincoln, Nebr., 1991)

Traveler's Guide to the Great Sioux War (Helena, Mont., 1996;
revised, 2008)

*We Trailed the Sioux: Enlisted Men Speak on Custer, Crook, and
the Great Sioux War* (Mechanicsburg, Pa., 2003)

*Great Sioux War Orders of Battle: How the United States Army Waged
War on the Northern Plains, 1876–1877* (Norman, Okla., 2011)

After Custer: Loss and Transformation in Sioux Country
(Norman, Okla., 2011)

(ed.) *Ho! For the Black Hills: Captain Jack Crawford Reports
the Black Hills Gold Rush and Great Sioux War*
(Pierre, S.Dak., 2012)

Powder River: Disastrous Opening of the Great Sioux War
(Norman, Okla., 2016)

ROSEBUD
JUNE 17, 1876

||||||||||||||||||||||||||||||||||||||||||||||||||||||||||||||||||||||||||||||||

PRELUDE TO THE
LITTLE BIG HORN

||||||||||||||||||||||||||||||||||||||||||||||||||||||||||||||||||||||||||||||||

PAUL L. HEDREN

UNIVERSITY OF OKLAHOMA PRESS : NORMAN

LIBRARY OF CONGRESS CATALOGING-IN-PUBLICATION DATA

Names: Hedren, Paul L., author.
Title: Rosebud, June 17, 1876 : prelude to the Little Big Horn / Paul L. Hedren.
Description: First edition. | Norman : University of Oklahoma Press, 2019. |
    Includes bibliographical references and index.
Identifiers: LCCN 2018025526 | ISBN 978-0-8061-6232-4 (hardcover) ISBN
978-8-8061-6616-2 (paper) Subjects: LCSH: Rosebud, Battle of the, Mont., 1876.
Classification: LCC E83.876 .H418 2019 | DDC 978.6/02—dc23
LC record available at https://lccn.loc.gov/2018025526

The p aper i n t his b ook m eets t he g uidelines f or p ermanence a nd d urability o f t he Committee on Production Guidelines for Book Longevity of the Council on Library Resources, Inc. ∞

Copyright © 2019 by the University of Oklahoma Press, Norman, Publishing Division of the University. Paperback published 2021. Manufactured in the U.S.A.

All rights reserved. No part of this publication may be reproduced, stored in a retrieval system, or transmitted, in any form or by any means, electronic, mechanical, photo-copying, recording, or otherwise—except as permitted under Section 107 or 108 of the United States Copyright Act—without the prior written permission of the University of Oklahoma Press. To request permission to reproduce selections from this book, write to Permissions, University of Oklahoma Press, 2800 Venture Drive, Norman OK 73069, or email rights.oupress@ou.edu.

Dedicated to Jerome A. Greene,
lifelong friend, admired historian, lively companion on the dusty roads.
May this never end.

CONTENTS

CONTENTS

ILLUSTRATIONS

MAPS

Cartography by Robert Pilk

PREFACE

The Battle of the Rosebud, which occurred on June 17, 1876, in southeastern Montana, not far from today's Sheridan, Wyoming, may well be the largest Indian battle ever fought in the American West. Custer battle students love to argue the point, insisting that the Battle of the Little Big Horn was the largest soldier-Indian clash in the West. But Little Big Horn devotees struggle to quantify the number of warriors reacting to George Armstrong Custer's charge. We know how many warriors fought on each side at the Rosebud, and the sum was enormous. George Crook's numerical superiority alone may well eclipse Sitting Bull's at the Little Horn. We know, as well, the colossal physical scale of the Rosebud battlefield: the fight at one point amounted to three concurrent disparate clashes playing across a field miles long and miles wide. It simply is a big story, and one that never seems to get its due.

A case is often made that Brigadier General George Crook met his match at the Rosebud, that he was superbly countered by warriors led directly by Crazy Horse and spiritually by Sitting Bull. The debate spills into questions of victory and loss. While all of this is intriguing, it misses, I think, the greater issue of consequence. My views on all this become apparent in the narrative, but let it be said that both sides fought a gallant fight on that hot June Saturday. There can be no question, however, about the interconnectedness of events in this bloody season. The Powder River fight in mid-March incited Sitting Bull's people and all Sioux and Northern Cheyenne Indians in ways that I explore in detail. Those consequences are critical to the Rosebud story. Likewise, comprehending the full Rosebud story is fundamental to grasping the Little Big Horn drama completely. I develop that case carefully as well. Beneath it all is the phenomenon of the great Northern Indian Ascendancy that unfolded that spring and early summer, a marvel central to the story of this Indian war and these engagements and worthy of considerable attention.

I was challenged to take up the Rosebud story by my longtime friend Chuck Rankin, with whom I have worked on projects many times before. Chuck was then the associate director and editor-in-chief of the University of Oklahoma Press. Although now semiretired in Helena, Montana, he keeps his fingers on the pulse of old friends. I had just completed my Powder River book, and Chuck, faster than I did, saw the obviousness of continuing the story. I had other plans and was not particularly enthused at first. But after mulling his encouragement for a few months and talking it through with friends, I bit—and stepped into the most exhilarating project of my writing career.

In *Powder River* I boasted of accessing countless new sources that helped distinguish my work from what had existed before. I certainly can say that here as well. I have used a trove of fresh diaries and reminiscences and an abundance of new scholarship on a variety of topics related to the fight, its personalities, and its contexts. But the most compelling source type for Rosebud proved quite different from Powder River's courts-martial transcripts and Walter Camp interviews. One lone newspaperman participated in the Powder River campaign, and several officers additionally corresponded with newspapers, implying simply that they sent letters to editor friends from time to time. On Crook's Rosebud campaign five full-time newsmen and a full-time illustrator accompanied the general to the field. Most of those reporters sent unique dispatches to not one but several different newspapers. Another half-dozen known and nameless correspondents in Crook's column also filed stories. In June and July 1876 the nation's newspapers brimmed with vital campaign and battle coverage straight from the front. Clearly, the prime sources for Rosebud were those newspaper accounts. I succeeded, I believe, in having at hand virtually every filing by every reporter and also every correspondent that I was aware of and from all of their many newspapers. While a few incidental correspondent's filings may somehow have eluded me, I doubt it will be many. To my pleasure, most of these newspaper stories have never been used in a Rosebud narrative before.

I should note that I overworked Martha Grenzeback, the gracious and ever-efficient interlibrary loan specialist at the W. D. Clark Central Omaha Public Library, who obtained for me dozens of newspaper microfilm rolls (and elusive books). Newspaper work is not entirely tedious, fortunately, thanks to the diligent labors of Marc Abrams, Robert Legoski, James Hutchins, Mary Ann Thompson, E. Elden Davis, and a few others who have enthusiastically collected and published newspaper accounts from and about this campaign. Researchers are aided today, as well, by many marvelous online newspaper sources. What Martha and these fine newspaper sleuths did was largely nonduplicative, so the enormity of the effort is impressive, as my notes and bibliography make clear.

I must say, as well, that in collecting newspaper accounts, I chanced onto something important. Historians before me have consistently assumed that when John Finerty wrote his book *War-Path and Bivouac* he exhausted the worth of his *Chicago Times* newspaper stories. Well, not so, and not even close. Finerty was almost certainly the most prolific reporter in the field that season. His long, detailed accounts of the campaign appearing in the *Times* at least weekly and sometimes more frequently proved a veritable gold mine, even while his book remains an essential source. We already understand the premise, of course. John Bourke's reflective memoir, *On the Border with Crook*, is every bit as vital a source for this story as Finerty's, but not more so than Bourke's now well-published diaries. The same can be said for such related works as John Neihardt's *Black Elk Speaks*; Ray DeMallie's *The Sixth Grandfather*, containing the unfiltered Black Elk interviews; Joe Jackson's marvelous synthesis, *Black Elk: The Life of an American Visionary*; and the collaborations of John Stands in Timber and Margot Liberty. Each individual work is critical to a narrative of this sort.

Campaign and battle reports were obviously essential as well. They are sometimes painfully short and almost always read necessarily sentence by sentence and not as a thoughtful, flowing narrative. But what officers had to say about themselves and their troops, virtually in the moment, was indispensable. Four collections of these reports exist, including the originals in the National Archives and transcriptions by J. W. Vaughn, John M. Carroll, and Neil Mangum. For the sake of convenience, I cite Mangum's transcriptions appearing in his readily available book *The Battle of the Rosebud*, while also acknowledging separately several additional reports inconsistently cited or ignored by others.

I endeavored to the best of my ability also to tell the Indian side of the story fully, in setup, on that dramatic day, and in aftermath. The sources for this perspective are understandably quite different but rich enough to document well the great Northern Indian Ascendancy occurring at that time. It coalesced in part in an extraordinary village at the Forks of Reno Creek on the eve of the Rosebud fight and also in the heroic action playing out on the field during that tense battle. I follow that village from Reno Creek to the Little Big Horn River in the pivotal eight days after the fight. "Eight days," in fact, becomes a story thread linking the Rosebud and Little Big Horn battles. They constitute a revealing period for the Sioux, their allies, and the army, all of which adds distinctiveness to the Rosebud fight on June 17.

Here I pick up the Rosebud story in the spring of 1876, in the days following the Powder River battle. It is well understood that this was an Indian war with deep roots. I chose not to provide such background here, having thoroughly explored that dimension of the Sioux war story in *Powder River*.

Suffice it to say, however, that this was a war about gold in the Black Hills, a northern plains railroad intent on spanning Sioux Country, and the ultimate control of a landscape and people. The battle at Rosebud occurred in the war story's midst and was consequential by many measures. At my story's end I contemplate the repercussions of the decisions made that day and in the several days thereafter. I have also endeavored to narrate the Rosebud story moment by moment, as it played out. I hope that this allows readers ample opportunity to conclude much for themselves. Hindsight, I think, may not always be so black and white.

ACKNOWLEDGMENTS

Many fine individuals lent a hand when I accepted the challenge of writing a new history of the Rosebud battle. Let me say again that I recognize foremost the kindly inspiration provided by Charles E. "Chuck" Rankin, my longtime friend and now mostly retired editor at the University of Oklahoma Press. It was Chuck who suggested this project as I was closing out work on my recent Powder River book. I was prepared to commence something quite different; honestly, Rosebud was not on my horizon. More than providing a strong prompting, Chuck went beyond the call of duty and eventually read every chapter, pressed my consideration of this or that detail, and playfully fretted with me as the manuscript grew increasingly large. This book truly belongs to Chuck.

I have a habit of boring my friends with my work, even prospective work, and I remember repeatedly chewing the Rosebud prospect and project over with the late Jack McDermott of Rapid City, South Dakota; Jerry Greene of Denver, Colorado; Marv Kaiser of Prescott, Arizona; David Wolff of Spearfish, South Dakota; Paul Magid of Vineyard Haven, Massachusetts; Paul Hutton of Albuquerque, New Mexico; Randy Kane of Crawford, Nebraska; and Eli Paul of Kansas City, Missouri. These pals suffer me well. Not surprisingly, they agreed with Chuck on the worthiness of a new Rosebud book, even while despairing over notions of another big project that would capture my attention and spawn more endless chatter. I make no apologies when I call and blurt out, "Did you know this?"

Marc Abrams in Brooklyn was also among the first people that I connected with. Marc is the master of an enormous digital Indian wars newspaper archive. Without hesitation he word-searched "Rosebud" and sent me thousands of transcribed newspaper pages. My first work on the project was simply managing and digesting that incomparably rich download.

Many others offered encouragement and help. I am grateful to Nan Card, Rutherford B. Hayes Presidential Center, Fremont, Ohio; Eric and Patsy LaPointe, descendants of Crook's scout Louis Richard, Chubbuck, Idaho; Joanna Lamaida, Brooklyn Historical Society Library, New York; Tully Thibeau, University of Montana, Missoula; An Bui, Davidson Library—Special Collections, University of California–Santa Barbara; C. Lee Noyes,

Morrisonville, New York; Sandy Barnard, Wake Forest, North Carolina; David Whittaker, Ryan Lee, and Lee Ferrin, Harold B. Lee Library, Brigham Young University; Dennis Hagen and Abby Hoverstock, Denver Public Library, Colorado; Jody Mitchell, Lilly Library, Indiana University, Bloomington; Kat Latham, Pritzker Military Museum & Library, Chicago; Larry Belitz, Hot Springs, South Dakota; Tom Powers, South Royalton, Vermont; John Doerner, Hardin, Montana; Todd Harburn, Mackinaw City, Michigan; Laura Jowdy, Congressional Medal of Honor Society, Mt. Pleasant, South Carolina; Jim Davis, State Historical Society of North Dakota, Bismarck; Dick Harmon, Lincoln, Nebraska; Jessica Michak, Homestake Adams Research and Cultural Center, Deadwood, South Dakota; Martha Grenzeback and Alane Freerksen, W. Dale Clark Main Library, Omaha; Vonnie Zullo, Horse Soldier Research Service, Fairfax, Virginia; Neil Mangum, Payson, Arizona; the late Sandy Lowry and the delightfully present Steve Fullmer, Fort Laramie National Historic Site, Wyoming; Roger Hanson, Parker, Colorado; Michael Her Many Horses, Wounded Knee, South Dakota; Paul Harbaugh, Cherry Hills Village, Colorado; Valerie Schafer, Western National Parks Association, and Dave Schafer, Stonewall, Texas; John Waggener, American Heritage Center, University of Wyoming, Laramie; Keith Werts, Spokane, Washington; Robert Marshall, Corvallis, Oregon; Pat Kalstrom, Ekalaka Public Library, Ekalaka, Montana; Jaeger Held, Broadus, Montana; Vance Haynes, University of Arizona, Tucson; Orville Loomer, Buffalo, Wyoming; Greg Michno, Frederick, Colorado; Tom Lindmier, Hulett, Wyoming; Guy Heilenman, Timothy Hughes Rare & Early Newspapers, Williamsport, Pennsylvania; Nate Skoglund, Pierre, South Dakota; Tracy Potter, descendant of Rosebud Medal of Honor recipient Michael McGann, Bismarck, North Dakota; Michael Donahue, Temple, Texas; Paul Fees, Cody, Wyoming; Kingsley Bray, Manchester, England; Gwen Schultz, Ekalaka Museum, Ekalaka, Montana; the late Jim McLaird, Mitchell, South Dakota; Carla Kelly, Idaho Falls, Idaho; Richard "Dutch" Hardorff, Genoa, Illinois; Raymond Schell, Rosebud Battlefield State Park, Decker, Montana; Robert Utley, Scottsdale, Arizona; Chris Kortlander, Custer Battlefield Museum, Garryowen, Montana; John Woodward and Erin Schock, Sheridan Museum, Sheridan, Wyoming; Kim Ostermyer, Wyoming Room, Sheridan Public Library; Robert Henning, Campbell County Rockpile Museum, Gillette, Wyoming; Judy Slack, Bozeman Trail Museum, Big Horn, Wyoming; Zoe Ann Stoltz and Roberta Gebhardt, Montana Historical Society Research Center, Helena; Margot Liberty, Sheridan, Wyoming; Karl Schug, Delafield, Wisconsin; Callie Raspuzzi, Bennington

Museum, Bennington, Vermont; Mark Miller, Laramie, Wyoming; Jennifer Williams, Rapid City Public Library, South Dakota; Patty Campbell, Enid, Oklahoma; and Adam Scher, Minnesota Historical Society, Saint Paul.

I have a delightful circle of friends in Omaha who are quick with kind words and warm encouragement. I am pleased to recognize Timothy Koester, Jim Kautz, Dennis Anderson, Kyle Eichhorn, Howard Boardman, Tom Richter, Ken Bunger, Hank Vieregger, John Bush, Paul Berg, and Jo Ann Hajek. Jo Ann, I must note, read and commented on a number of chapters and was a courageous companion, twice joining the manly bunch who toured the Powder River and Rosebud battlefields with me during the course of these projects.

Collecting images for the book was its own interesting challenge. Several individuals noted above aided this effort, as did Matthew Reitzel, South Dakota State Historical Society, Pierre; Ellen Keith, Chicago History Museum Research Center, Illinois; Mark Kasal, Lake Forest, California; George Moore, Frontier Army Museum, Fort Leavenworth, Kansas; Robert Smith, Fort Riley Museum, Kansas; Marlea Leljedal, U.S. Army Heritage and Education Center, Carlisle, Pennsylvania; Randy Wise, Lander Pioneer Museum, Wyoming; Luther Hanson, Quartermaster Museum, Fort Lee, Virginia; Karline Stetler, Riverton Museum, Wyoming; Sarah Walker, State Historical Society of North Dakota, Bismarck; Cindy Hagen, Little Bighorn Battlefield National Monument, Crow Agency, Montana; Hailey Woodall, American Heritage Center, University of Wyoming, Laramie; Lorenzo Vigil and Mike Weinstein, Fort Union National Monument, Watrous, New Mexico; John Heiner, Fort Davis National Historic Site, Texas; Jill Reichenback, New-York Historical Society, New York; Marty Miller, Nebraska State Historical Society, Lincoln; Daisy Njoku, Anthropology Archives, Smithsonian Institution, Suitland, Maryland; Susan Lintelmann and Casey Madrick, United States Military Academy Archives, West Point, New York; Marilyn Van Winkle, Braun Research Library, Autry Museum, Los Angeles; Tom Schmidt, Sharlot Hall Museum Library & Archives, Prescott, Arizona; Tempe Johnson Javitz, Menlo Park, California; Cindy Brown, Wyoming State Archives, Cheyenne; and Kim Bultsma, Omaha, Nebraska.

In this effort to collect images, I must uniquely recognize Hayes Otoupalik, Missoula, Montana, possessor of a vintage photograph of Rosebud Medal of Honor recipient First Sergeant John Henry Shingle *and* his Medal of Honor. For two months both objects were in my hands. I am rarely awestruck, but this was over the top.

Doug McChristian of Tucson, Arizona, was especially responsive to a diverse array of ponderables germane to the culture of the Old Army, advising on "Long Tom" Springfield rifles, the Freund Brothers Gunsmiths, army picket pins, and such, and also sharing elusive source material. Similarly, Doug Scott, Grand Junction, Colorado, advised on stray terminology and archaeological explorations on the Rosebud field. Mark Gardner of Cascade, Colorado, presently working his own dual biography of Crazy Horse and Sitting Bull, was a font of unorthodox information on those great chiefs, their mentors, and associated artifacts. Jerry Greene and Jack McDermott freely provided source materials from their voluminous personal research collections, as did B. William Henry Jr. of Eugene, Oregon, who lent me for examination his entire collection of Guy V. Henry Papers, amounting to a lifetime collection of documents and photographs pertaining to this compelling Rosebud character (and coincidental namesake). In turn, and with Bill's encouragement, the entire collection was forwarded by donation to the Case Library at Black Hills State University, where it joins the recently acquired John D. "Jack" McDermott Research Collection, the sums of which are now accessible to all.

Penny Penson Iekel of Sheridan, Wyoming, and Jessie Huffman of Kirby, Montana, owners of private lands surrounding the Rosebud Battlefield State Park, allowed me complete access to the extreme reaches of the field. I can say after many visits that I've about walked it all. What a marvelously complex place it is!

Randy Kane; Gerald "Jerry" Jasmer, Billings, Montana; Ephriam Dickson, Burke, Virginia; and Jerry Greene read with a critical eye some or all of the manuscript and offered constructive, sometimes challenging commentary. I often feared becoming lost in the buffalo grass and somehow missing or flat-out misunderstanding something. These readers know the story. My take in many ways is different from that in the books preceding mine, and I deeply value the thoughtful analyses and consideration offered by these well-read friends. I must note, as well, that Jerry Jasmer accompanied me to the field twice during critical stages of the project. He not only knows the story but also the battlefield's hills and dales.

James Brust, MD, read portions of the manuscript as well. Jim, a practicing psychiatrist in San Pedro, California, offered critical commentary on the medical issues bedeviling Captain Avery Cain, an unheralded hero at Rosebud. Our exchange was robust and insightful.

I again sought out Robert Pilk of Lakewood, Colorado, to produce new maps for the book. Bob has a marvelously clean and effective graphic style. Rosebud is a complicated story, but one marvelously fleshed out in Bob's artful maps.

At the University of Oklahoma Press *Rosebud* fell into the capable hands of a fine pair of book friends that I've had the pleasure of working with before (and specifically asked for again). The ever capable managing editor Steven B. Baker tended production details, the schedule, and me with style and ease. Steven again connected me with Kathy Burford Lewis, my longtime copy editor. Kathy's critical eye and grace with words are wonders. My gratitude is deep. Two other members of the fine staff, Bethany Mowry and Amy Hernandez, also helped mightily along the way.

I acknowledge my girls in all of my books and gleefully do so here. Ethne Denham, Whitney Johnson, Alicia Larrick, and especially my lovely wife, Connie, put up with my obsessiveness when on the project. Of course, any of these girls would blurt, "Well, Dad, er, Paul, when are you not on a project?"

To one and all, thank you very much.

June 17, 2018

ROSEBUD, JUNE 17, 1876

A CHAOTIC SPRING

The young reporter wanted to go with Custer. The newspaper's senior editor wanted a man with Crook. News from the West in the spring of 1876 was spurring both of them. The buzz in Chicago, New York City, San Francisco, and across the land was about gold in the Black Hills *and* Indians. The Black Hills were indeed booming in a rush triggered by George Custer's exploration two summers before. Another army exploration in 1875 confirmed the richness of the new El Dorado, yet only now were the Hills and trails truly alive with prospectors. Offsetting the lure and richness of the gulches was news of the extreme mayhem on the trails, perpetrated by Indians and outlaws. Farther west a major Indian campaign in Wyoming and Montana had gone bust, though now new expeditions were forming to settle issues with the Sioux Indians once and for all. The *Chicago Times* and its senior editor, Wilber Storey, sensed big news, and the paper wanted it firsthand.

The challenge of enlisting an agreeable reporter fell to Clinton Snowden, the city editor of the *Times*. Snowden promptly turned to one of his own staff writers, John Finerty, and asked whether he was open to an adventure in the West. "There is apt to be warm work out there with the Indians," Snowden warned, but if he was up for it, he should go see Mr. Storey. Finerty agreed on the spot but grimaced at the notion of talking with the always brusque, white-haired Storey, the paper's aloof senior man. Storey had built the *Times* into one of the great newspapers of the day. He was a legendary but intimidating character, who once fired a man who wore creaking boots because the noise disrupted others at work in the editorial room.

Finerty's willingness reached Storey even before Finerty did. "How soon can you be ready?" Storey inquired abruptly.

Almost immediately, replied the eager journalist.

"You should have your outfit first," Storey snapped back. "You are going with Crook's column."

"I understood I was to go with Custer. I know General Custer, but am not acquainted with General Crook," Finerty responded.

"That will make no difference, whatever," said Storey. "Terry commands over Custer, and Crook, who knows more about the Indians, is likely to do the hard work. Custer is a brave soldier—none braver—but he has been out there some years already, and has not succeeded in bringing the Sioux to a decisive engagement. Crook did well in Arizona. It is settled that you go with Crook. Report to me when you are ready." Finerty and Storey could hardly know it, of course, but the editor's insistence may have saved the reporter's life.

And so it was that the twenty-nine-year-old Irishman John Frederick Finerty joined George Crook and the Sioux war. A lanky, ruddy-faced Irishman with a thick mustache, Finerty was no stranger to armed conflict. Soon after immigrating to the United States in 1864, he had enlisted in the Union army and fought in the last year of the Civil War. Now he wasted no time in getting ready. Finerty thought first to seek out Lieutenant General Philip H. Sheridan, the army's senior commander in the West and also located in downtown Chicago. From Sheridan he sought a letter of introduction to General Crook. Sheridan happily complied, adding a simple warning: "You will find General Crook a hard campaigner." Finerty purchased arms and a riding outfit, packed a small bag, bade goodbye to friends, and reported back to Storey. "Spare no expense and use the wires freely, whenever practicable," Storey advised. Finerty departed Chicago on the Northwestern line for Omaha on a rainy Saturday morning, May 6, 1876.[1]

Finerty indeed had jumped into an Indian war. As he made his way to Omaha he contemplated the news filling the papers in recent days—stories about Sidney and Cheyenne, the allure of the new Whitewood and Deadwood diggings in the northern Black Hills, the brutal murders of the Metz family and "Stuttering" Brown on the Fort Laramie–Custer City Road, the perplexing if disastrous battle at Powder River, and Crook apparently now quietly at work organizing another movement against the Sioux and Northern Cheyennes.[2]

Upon reaching Omaha on Sunday morning, Finerty sought out General Crook, whom he found at work at his desk in the Withnell Building, headquarters of the army's Department of the Platte, located a few blocks from the railroad station. The department offices were scattered across four floors of the unassuming brick building. A massive American flag flew from a staff off the front. The singular striking feature inside that day was a beautiful buffalo robe collected from the Powder River battlefield and proudly heralded as "one of the finest robes to be found anywhere in this country." Sheridan's letter provided admittance to Crook's office. The two men quickly sized each other up. Finerty recalled encountering a man barely in his forties (in fact, forty-seven), with an athletic physique, distinctive Roman nose, fair hair clipped short, and a beard that seemed to part naturally at the chin. "He looked every inch a soldier," the reporter later remembered, "except that he wore no uniform." Finerty may not yet have understood Crook's preference for casual dress, in the office or in the field.[3]

Crook got straight to the point. "Can you ride and shoot well?"

"I can ride fairly, General," Finerty replied. "I might manage to hit a barn at a couple of hundred yards."

Crook laughed. "You'll need practice then." He told Finerty to make his way to Fort Russell where the expedition was forming, secure messing arrangements with some officer going from there, and purchase a horse in Cheyenne. "There will be some delay yet. I am going to visit the Indian agencies to get some warriors to accompany us. After that I'll go to Cheyenne. Await me there." With that Finerty thanked the general and proceeded to his hotel. The next morning he boarded a Union Pacific train for Cheyenne.[4]

<hr>

News from the northern plains was unusually mixed that spring. Finerty likely carried with him on his travels the current issue of the *Omaha Daily Bee*, one of three newspapers published in the city and the recognized voice of the community and region. Since midwinter the paper had employed special correspondents in the field to report the gold rush, which was the dominant news of the season, even eclipsing reports of Omaha's own Crook and the Indian war. Captain Jack Crawford, the self-proclaimed "Poet Scout of the Black Hills," reported from Custer City in the central hills, while a counterpart, John Harwood Pierce, writing under the pen name "Ranger," rode the rails and filed stories from North Platte, Sidney, Cheyenne, and Laramie. The *Bee* was an ardent advocate of open access to the new gold country, despite the conundrum of the Black Hills lying squarely within the bounds of the Great Sioux Reservation.[5]

The *Bee* particularly championed Nebraska's interests in the rush. Crawford and Pierce penned weekly and sometimes twice-weekly letters describing outfitting opportunities in the various rail towns, the trails northward from the Union Pacific, and the enticing lure of the yellow metal itself, sluiced from French, Spring, Castle, and Rapid Creeks and other watercourses beyond in the central and northern Black Hills. Both correspondents were decidedly circumspect about the many difficulties encountered on the trails, particularly in the proximities of the Red Cloud and Spotted Tail Indian agencies in the Pine Ridge country of northwestern Nebraska. Despite the many incidences that bloodied those roads, the resolute "gold talk" in the *Bee* and the region's other newspapers transfixed readers.

General Crook oversaw the two prime avenues to the gold country. Ironically, the Black Hills themselves lay beyond his official administrative control, which ended at the Dakota border. The two routes originated at communities on the Union Pacific Railroad. Both trails crossed the North Platte River and the one distinctive physical feature between the rails and the Black Hills: the Pine Ridge of far northwestern Nebraska and eastern Wyoming. One of the trails passed the two Sioux agencies in Nebraska in the midst of the Pine Ridge. Jack Crawford and the *Omaha Bee* favored that Nebraska-centric Sidney Road.

Originating at Sidney, on the Union Pacific Railroad, the Sidney Road ran straight north to Red Cloud Agency and nearby Camp Robinson and from there north again to Buffalo Gap, the southeastern entry into the Black Hills, and then on to Custer City. Red Cloud Agency was the home of the Oglala Sioux, the largest body of all Lakotas. Their principal chieftain and the agency namesake, Red Cloud, had masterminded the bloody Bozeman Trail War of the 1860s. Slightly east of there was the Spotted Tail Agency, home of the Brulé Sioux and that tribe's great chief, Spotted Tail. Spotted Tail's followers were much less stridently inclined than the war-prone Oglalas who followed Crazy Horse, He Dog, and others, but some of them also made their way to the warring camps as the looming drama unfolded. From both agencies a great Indian trail stretched westward, generally following the northern margins of the Pine Ridge into Wyoming and continuing to the Powder River Basin. Known as the Powder River Trail or Red Cloud's Trail, this road and these many Oglalas and Brulés were complications to be reckoned with by Black Hillers and soon enough by Crook himself.[6]

The second significant road to the Black Hills in Crook's department ran from Cheyenne, Wyoming, north to Fort Laramie and from there straight north again to the Pine Ridge, where it angled northeast to Red Cañon, the southwestern entry into the Black Hills, and on to Custer City. This road carried significantly greater Hills-bound traffic than all others owing chiefly to the completion (in December 1875) of a three-span iron bridge at Fort Laramie that crossed the turbulent North Platte. This new bridge provided the only safe crossing of this difficult river hazard until the completion downstream of the 3,000-foot, seven-span wooden Clarke Bridge north of Sidney, which unofficially opened to traffic on May 17. No bridge existed upstream, a factor that played directly into Crook's campaign preparations in

May. Like the Sidney Road, the Cheyenne Road also crossed the treacherous Powder River Trail. That intersection was isolated from military protection and became yet another issue that Crook was soon forced to address.[7]

Black Hills traffic on these roads surged as the warmth of springtime transformed the wintery landscapes of Nebraska, Dakota, and Wyoming with emergent grasses and drying roadbeds. The troubles in the region could not be denied. One newspaper editor waxed whimsical about the mysterious connections between grass and warfare on the plains. "When the succulent grass springs up, the wild Indian mounts his pony and starts out in search of the buffalo and the white man." Crook acknowledged that as well. His coming campaign needed dry ground and new grass, without which it would be impossible to maneuver far from a line of supplies. Of course, as the editor noted, those natural elements benefited agency Indians too.[8]

Crook believed that much of the trouble disturbing the Pine Ridge country and Black Hills was directly attributed to agency Indians bound for and or returning from the buffalo country in the Powder River Basin and beyond. The 1868 Fort Laramie Treaty permitted hunting off of the reservation. For that reason alone travel to and from the hunting grounds was steady. Such movement put Indians and Black Hillers on confrontational courses. But there was more. A distinct surliness was palpable in Indian country just then, especially in the Oglala camps. The Indian people had endured in rapid succession the government's attempt to buy the Black Hills in August 1875 (a proceeding raucously brought to failure by the Northern Sioux), severe food shortages during the hard winter of 1875–76 that forced tribesmen into the field to hunt, and most recently news of Joseph Jones Reynolds's aggression at Powder River, which was foisted on Northern Cheyennes and Oglalas alike. As discontented and imposed-upon Indians dealt with such matters, depredations increased dramatically, even locally. On April 26 the cattle corral, slaughterhouse, and scales within a half-mile of Red Cloud Agency were burned. Bitter, hungry, and threatened people were lashing out at those supporting them and at Hillers flooding the roads to Custer City.[9]

Jack Crawford, the *Omaha Bee* correspondent in Custer City, provided his readers with a distinct sense of the dangers on the trails and the underlying fear of Indians disrupting life in the diggings. Foremost he repeatedly warned his audience that people needed to travel in large armed parties. He often colored his letters with examples of those who failed to heed such simple advice, as with the story in April of the man known only as Wood. Traveling alone, Wood was found near Buffalo Gap with a bullet though his heart and an arrow sticking in him, with another arrow lying nearby. "He had a horse valued at $250, which was a big inducement for a northern Sioux to get away with." In another letter Crawford told of a man wounded half a mile from Custer while he and a partner were prospecting and yet another killed at Rapid City and one farther north. "Miners on this creek are working with rifles by their side and revolvers on each hip. These are men who don't scare worth a cent."[10]

Stealing horses was an understood motive for Indian raiding and killing. Traditional plunder beyond firearms—paper money, clothing, metal ware, horse gear—had marginal value to agency Indians, yet Crawford's letters frequently mentioned Indians being sighted as close as the margins of Custer City or down the Sidney Road, especially around Buffalo Gap, always pursuing or running off stock. Some residents of Custer City banded together as the Black Hills Rangers in April and actually responded to a number of those raids, but the successful recovery of stock was never mentioned.[11]

Such prowling plagued ranchers and business owners in the border region as well. In rapid succession in mid- and late April came news of Indians "from the north" (meaning the Pine Ridge country), raiding horses at Coad's Ranch, a few miles below Scotts Bluff on the North Platte River; at Bosler's Ranch on the north side of the North Platte, a few miles below the Sidney crossing; at Harkison and Griffith's Ranch, thirty-six miles west of Sidney, where ten horses were stolen; and from the Government Farm, eleven miles north of Fort Laramie, where stage company stock was run off. Yet another account told of an attack on "embryo miners" on Burntwood Creek, between the Black Hills and the Spotted Tail Agency. They had gone into camp and barely had their bacon half-fried when a party of forty Indians swept down on them and captured all of their horses. Those prospectors put up a good fight, however, and may actually have killed one of their assailants.[12]

Two of the most egregious killings in this bloody spree had the imprints of a single white outlaw and a handful of Indian accomplices who terrorized Red Cañon and the Cheyenne Road just south of there. The first episode was the killing of the Metz party of Laramie City. Charles Metz and his wife had opened a bakery in Custer City in midwinter. As prospecting activity drifted north that spring, particularly toward the fantastically rich Whitewood and Deadwood gulches, the pair sold their business at a good profit and planned on returning to Laramie. On April 16 they as well as their black cook and a driver were murdered in Red Cañon, barely thirty miles southwest of Custer

City. The cook was riddled with arrows. Three others in their party were wounded, two dying later. The killings were inordinately vicious, and Indians were immediately blamed. A more careful investigation also quickly implicated the white outlaw, William F. "Persimmon Bill" Chambers. Persimmon Bill, an ill-tempered, hair-triggered, thirty-two-year-old accomplished horse thief, had killed a soldier near Fort Fetterman six weeks earlier and more recently had been seen loitering in Custer City as the Metzes prepared to depart. In this instance robbery seemed a more probable motive than stock theft. The Black Hills Rangers from Custer City and others responded to the killings, which came to be known as the Metz Massacre, but Chambers and his accomplices were by then long gone.[13]

A second sensational killing occurred just five days later not far from Red Cañon. Henry E. "Stuttering" Brown, superintendent of the Fort Laramie–Custer City leg of the Cheyenne and Black Hills Stage, Mail, and Express Company and late of Omaha, was ambushed and gut shot in a night attack on the road between the Cheyenne River and Hat Creek stage stations. Brown was discovered some hours later and carried to Hat Creek. An army doctor summoned from Fort Laramie could not save the stage man, who died at the station several days later. Brown was a popular figure in Cheyenne and Custer City, and his death was a considerable blow to the company's fledgling business. Persimmon Bill was implicated in this murder too. He and Brown had scuffled at the Cheyenne River station not long before the shooting, where Brown accused the firebrand of thieving company stock.[14]

News of the turmoil in the west had by now come to Crook's attention. Initially, Crook saw the killings in light of the Indians' destitute condition at the agencies, brought on by food shortages. He thought that these were attributable to a "hitch in congressional appropriations." The Oglalas and Brulés were not then visibly leaving for the Powder River country, at least in substantial numbers. Crook viewed that condition as among the wholesome effects of his earlier campaign.[15]

Territorial governor John M. Thayer saw it another way, writing to Crook on April 24 requesting military protection for the road north of Fort Laramie, "owing to the recent outrages by Indians." Crook's response several days later was rather bureaucratic: "Parties of twenty men should be able to protect themselves." Still, he assured the governor that "troops will be sent out to give citizens the best possible protection with the means at hand." Crook knew that Thayer was not a man to be trifled with, especially as these outrages became regional and national news. The *Cheyenne Daily Leader* captured

Wyoming's sentiment rather precisely, observing that the government had permitted these people to enter the Black Hills country so it was now the government's duty to protect them and keep communications open between the settlements there and Fort Laramie.[16]

As if seeking to respond to Governor Thayer in a more personal manner, Crook boarded a train for Cheyenne on April 27, not realizing that Thayer had also boarded a train that day for Omaha expressly to meet with the general. Crook had been summoned as a witness in the general court-martial of Captain Henry E. Noyes of the Second Cavalry, an action emanating from his conduct during the Powder River fight of March 17. Between testimony at the court-martial on April 28 and 29, Crook met with Lieutenant Colonel Luther Bradley, commanding officer at Fort Laramie, and outlined a plan to ensure that civilian traffic north of that fort was well armed and that cavalry from there patrolled the road. Meanwhile Thayer, not finding Crook in Omaha, went straight to the *Bee* newspaper office. His concerns were real, he assured the paper. He plainly outlined his desire that the Black Hills Road and its new stage stations be thoroughly protected, especially in the Hat Creek–Red Cañon area (in that unstated but precise locale where the Indians' Powder River Trail crossed the Custer City gold rush road). It seems not to have been material that the probable perpetrator of the more recent killings was a white man. Death was death, by whatever hand.[17]

Crook was cornered by the *Daily Leader* in Cheyenne for a brief interview. The general assured the reporter that almost immediately a force of cavalry would be dispatched from Fort Laramie to patrol the road to Custer City and would remain on that duty until "all dangers from Indian depredations have passed." A reporter from the *Cheyenne Daily Sun* also caught Crook as he boarded his return train to Omaha. "When will we see you again?" he asked. The ever coy general pleasantly replied: "When least expected."[18]

Within days the lone available cavalry company at Fort Laramie, K of the Second, commanded by Captain James Egan, was dispatched to the Custer City Road. Egan's men had barely returned from the Big Horn Expedition after having endured a hard campaign and suffering four casualties in the Powder River fight. For the next several months the troop was in nearly perpetual motion on what proved to be a summer of sometimes exhilarating but more commonly fruitless duty. Newspapers applauded the deployment. One noted that Egan was soon to be on the gold rush trail and "will also keep an eye on the Powder River trail to prevent Agency Indians from going northward to join the hostile bands." News of Egan's deployment was welcomed in Custer City, certainly, where Captain Jack Crawford otherwise lamented the insufficiency of armaments. "Not one half of our people have rifles," he told his *Bee* readers.[19]

Despite Crook's assurances and Egan's looming departure for the field, Indian raiding and bloodshed only intensified across the region. In central Nebraska a small band of Sioux raiders, likely Brulés, clashed with farmers on the North Loup River on April 28. A detachment of infantry mounted on mules from nearby Fort Hartsuff, a small one-company post in the eastern Sand Hills, responded and engaged the warriors in a distinctive Sand Hills geographic anomaly called a blowout. The episode has been called the Battle of the Blowout ever since. Both sides incurred casualties in the brief fight, including the death of a Twenty-Third Infantry sergeant. The Indians were labeled horse raiders and likely were. But their motive for this incursion into east-central Nebraska may more likely have been horse thieving directed at Pawnee Indians living south of Fort Hartsuff. For generations the Brulé Sioux had held the Pawnees in utter contempt, and such raiding and killing was altogether common and heralded.[20]

A week later Indians boldly attacked the J. D. May and Parrott mule train traveling some eight miles north of Hat Creek, engaging in a running fight that covered more than three miles. Upon reaching a defensive position on a bluff, the outfit corralled its wagons and made a strong stand, fighting from behind wagons and animals. The attackers were driven away, but not before wounding one man, killing fourteen horses, and capturing thirty-five more. Behind them, closer to the Hat Creek station, Indians attacked S. R. Gwinn's oxen train. This party also made a good defense and drove off the attackers with no loss of men or animals. Even the small train bearing the embalmed remains of Charles Metz and his wife was fired upon by Indians as it made its way through the Pine Ridge bound for Laramie City.[21]

Three days later (on May 5) Indians ran off thirty-one horses and mules from the well-known Hunton Ranch on Chugwater Creek, southwest of Fort Laramie. (John Hunton later claimed a loss of thirty-eight animals.) This was the most audacious raid yet, occurring south of Fort Laramie halfway to Cheyenne. One of the Hunton brothers, James, trailed the Indians and his family's stock alone as the raiders drove them eastward. When James's horse came back saddled and bridled but riderless, the ranch hands feared for his fate. And indeed his body was found eight miles east of the ranch. He had been shot eleven times, three times with arrows. Word of the raid and killing spread rapidly. Elements of Company K, Second Cavalry, responded, riding from Fort Laramie eastward into the Goshen Hole hoping to intercept the band, but the Indians managed to circle north, cross the North Platte, and evade the chase.[22]

John Collins, Fort Laramie's entrepreneurial post trader and a well-known Omahan, was in a key position to observe these comings and goings and sent occasional reports to the *Omaha Herald*. In one he told of another well-known Fort Laramie character, Jules Ecoffey, proprietor of a road ranch three miles west of the post, who came in from Custer City on May 4 with four others and told of being attacked by Indians on Indian Creek, midway between the Pine Ridge and Red Cañon. They fought their assailants for five hours, losing one horse and a dog killed and riddling Ecoffey's wagon with bullets. "It is impossible to tell at what point the greatest danger exists," Collins wrote. "Indians are liable to raid on all the ranches within fifty miles of the post. Parties traveling to and from the hills must go in large parties and be well armed." That admonishment had by then become a common refrain.[23]

John Finerty, the intrepid *Chicago Times* reporter, arrived in Cheyenne as these killings were fresh news and chimed in too. "Every day adds yet another crime to the long and bloody record in this territory," he told his readers. Without very well understanding its place on the landscape but capturing its sense of intrigue, Finerty especially fixated on the perils of Red Cañon, emphasizing blood "red." "The red devils have taken up position in the country surrounding what is known as the 'the Red canon'—a pass lying between Fort Laramie and Custer City—the main route from this point to the mining regions among the Black Hills."[24]

The death of young Hunton and the boldness of the continuing Indian attacks on caravans and ranches in the vast outback between the Union Pacific and the Black Hills proved unnerving to most citizens of Nebraska and Wyoming *and* to prospective Black Hillers, the lifeblood of the great gold rush. The *Laramie Daily Sentinel* went so far as to tally the people killed by Indians in the Black Hills region "during the present season," listing the Metzes, their cook, and their driver (all from Laramie), plus Stuttering Brown and eleven more killed and eleven others wounded. A different list maintained in Custer City tallied "fifty-odd" deaths. Meanwhile soldiers at Fort Laramie mocked the witless "pilgrims," as they called the members of the Chicago Mining Company and others as they passed the fort. Another sizable party of prospectors, this one from Pittsburgh, reached Fort Laramie in the midst of the chaos. Despite having come that far, they elected to go no farther and turned for home--at least all but one (Hornberger) did. His story picks up again when Crook's campaign preparations came to dominate the activities of the local military posts and trails.[25]

Not all prospecting parties were as timid as the Pittsburgh bunch. Accounts of activities in Cheyenne, Sidney, and Fort Laramie affirmed the continuing robustness of the rush. Would-be prospectors, the "embryo miners" as one newspaper had labeled them, pushed on in ever increasing numbers, usually consolidating into functional groups that were well armed and led. Some came from different locales entirely. A so-called Powder River Expedition departed Bozeman, Montana, on April 1, intending to travel via Fort C. F. Smith, Goose Creek, Fort Phil Kearny, and Fort Fetterman—the old Bozeman Trail in reverse—as they made their way to the Black Hills, while prospecting every major stream along the way. By any measure this was an intimidating crowd, numbering 202 members, including at least one woman and several Chinese people and trailing thirty-eight wagons. As if reading from Captain Jack Crawford's and General Crook's script, the party was heavily armed, mostly with modern Winchesters and half also with "pistols of the best pattern." The Powder River Expedition reported no difficulties with Indians. Crook's new expedition encountered this crowd's camp debris in the early days of their new campaign.[26]

||||||||||||||||||||||||||||||||||||

Springtime was a puzzling season for General Crook. The failures of his first movement against the Sioux were frustrating enough, resulting in heated bickering among his officer corps, courts-martial charges, and the hurried trial of one of the accused so as to enable his participation in the coming operation. On the political front, the security of the Black Hills gold rush had exploded and while receiving some degree of attention remained largely unresolved. Despite it all, Crook persisted in organizing a second movement against the Sioux. His first campaign had been an embarrassment, but failure was not in his nature and had not marked his operations against Indians in Idaho, Oregon, and Arizona. Crook had at his disposal a vast, well-garrisoned administrative department and proceeded to assemble the largest single force ever mounted against Indians in the American West. This time, unlike his movement in March, he would lead the column personally. The pitiful Big Horn Expedition of March had taught him lessons. The new expedition would be strong, diverse, and well supplied. It would be supported by Indian auxiliaries in the finest emulation of his successful Apache campaigns. And it would operate in the summertime, not in the teeth of a northern plains winter. The disaster at Powder River would not be repeated.

13

ORGANIZING A SECOND CAMPAIGN

The Battle of Powder River on March 17, 1876, had not gone well for General Crook. He was miles away when Old Bear's village of Northern Cheyennes was struck and burned by men under his general command. Contrary to his orders, no meats or robes were saved by the attacking force. No prisoners were taken, and the captured Indian ponies were later lost. Crook may not have been present on the battlefield, but those were his troops and his expedition. Any notions of success or failure reflected as much on him as on the actual commanders on the field. Crook's Big Horn Expedition was the first meaningful movement against the Sioux and their Northern Cheyenne allies in this decisive Indian war. President Ulysses S. Grant had approved of the war, pragmatically viewing it as a necessary measure to eliminate once and for all a perceived and real barrier to settlement on the northern plains. Lieutenant General Sheridan, the war's mastermind, wanted it fought in wintertime, in a quick, decisive action when opposing forces were still on a relative par and when weather's hardships brutalized the Indians (and their ponies) as much as it did the soldiers. Sheridan imagined three separate columns operating in the war zone, but that year's fierce winter had stymied early troop movement from western Montana and northern Dakota. Only Crook's force made it to the field.

Crook returned from this first campaign on March 31, reaching Cheyenne that day and Omaha on April 1. He had a mess to deal with—belligerent officers, courts-martial charges, battle and campaign reports, an inquiring press, anxious superiors. He wasted no time in traveling to Chicago to consult personally with Sheridan, departing Omaha on April 5. No record of the several-day-long visit is known, but the actions in his department in the coming weeks are telling. Surely Crook put his best face on the recent campaign, where, at the least, a sizable Indian village was destroyed. For the longest while he called it Crazy Horse's village. For the most part it was a village of Northern Cheyennes, and he knew it. Almost certainly the two generals discussed the state of the larger campaign. Despite setbacks, Colonel

John Gibbon was finally about to depart Fort Ellis, Montana, with a command of infantry and cavalry and follow the Yellowstone River into the very heartland of the Northern Indians. Lieutenant Colonel George A. Custer would also soon lead a column of cavalry westward from Fort Abraham Lincoln, although the orchestration in Dakota still faced obstructive weather. Certainly Crook assured his senior officer of his own ability to organize a second campaign almost immediately, using forces and other resources within his department. Likely, too, Sheridan expressed a willingness to draw in additional troops from beyond the Departments of the Platte and Dakota, while continuing to believe that Gibbon's, Custer's, and Crook's columns would be of sufficient size to handle whatever Indians they might encounter. These movements were meant to be simultaneous, so if Indians attempted to avoid one column they might well run into another. Sheridan levied no expectation of the columns working in concert and instructed Crook to disregard departmental lines because Indian villages were movable and no objective point could be fixed upon.

Both generals understood that having lost the winter season now meant warmer weather, green grass, and buffalo hunting and, soon enough, predictable movements from the agencies by people driven to hunt in a timeless and treaty-ensured manner. Regrettably for the army, however, now seasonal travel or outright defections from the agencies would almost certainly also aid Sitting Bull and Crazy Horse in a great contest of will and might. The generals knew that a different war was at hand.

In organizing a second expedition, Crook's foremost considerations were the troops and officers available to him within the Department of the Platte. In all, he controlled six army regiments, including all twelve companies of the Third Cavalry; eight companies of the Second Cavalry (with this regiment's other four companies, the heralded "lost tribes of the Second," then serving at Fort Ellis in western Montana in the Department of Dakota); and the Fourth, Ninth, Fourteenth, and Twenty-Third Infantry Regiments, each ten companies strong. All elements were scattered across nineteen forts and camps in the department, dotting Nebraska, Wyoming, Utah, and Idaho. Each post had a core infantry complement, while those in eastern Nebraska, Utah, and Idaho were infantry garrisons alone. Crook and his predecessor deliberately scattered the available cavalry to posts in relative proximity to the several Indian agencies within the department, including not just the

Red Cloud and Spotted Tail Agencies in Nebraska but also the combined Shoshone and Bannock Agency in central Wyoming.[1]

Despite his background as a longtime infantry officer, Crook embraced the conventional wisdom of cavalry mobility and again envisioned an expedition largely composed of mounted troops. So it had been with the Big Horn Expedition, where the accompanying small infantry battalion was reserved as the wagon and camp guard. When meeting with Sheridan, Crook evidently requested that the Fifth Cavalry be made available for this campaign, or perhaps Sheridan broached the notion himself. Either way, the prospect was warmly endorsed. Crook was familiar with the regiment, as the Fifth had contributed to his Apache operations in the early 1870s. Its troops were now scattered at posts in Kansas, Colorado, and the Indian Territory in the Department of the Missouri. Sheridan was amenable to the move, but time simply did not permit the immediate, near wholesale transfer of the regiment from one essential deployment to another (and certainly not as quickly as Crook might have desired). Crook had also wished that no members of the recent Big Horn Expedition be returned to the field, he told the *Cheyenne Daily Leader*, aside from its scouts, guides, and packers, but this too was immediately recognized as an impossibility.[2]

Crook ultimately had no recourse but to order virtually all of the Third Cavalry to the field again, aside from two companies retained at Sidney Barracks, and five of his eight Second Cavalry companies. Of the other Second Cavalry companies, he retained one at Fort Laramie and two at the small posts in the proximity of the Shoshone and Bannock Agency. Four of the five Second Cavalry companies were with him in March. Crook's infantry complement on this campaign would amount to five companies drawn from the Fourth and Ninth Regiments. None of the designated infantry companies campaigned with Crook in March. In all twenty companies of cavalry and infantry would march with him from Fort Fetterman in May, nearly twice as many as he had led north two months earlier.[3]

The new deployment was least welcomed among the cavalry, where nine of the ten companies that campaigned in March were returned to the field. The men of the Big Horn Expedition had suffered brutally. Troops were incessantly buffeted by fierce late-winter blizzards and frigid nightly temperatures and suffered from severe food shortages. The horse stock was also almost wholly consumed owing to shortages of grain and the lack of meaningful grazing. Most troopers were also smarting from the callousness shown on the battlefield by certain officers, not the least the colonel of the Third

Cavalry, Joseph Reynolds, who left behind his unburied dead and actually knowingly abandoned one wounded trooper alive to the enemy. Desertions were consequently rife in both regiments, a matter that would greatly plague the companies when they embarked for the field again in May.[4]

Shortly after returning from Chicago, Crook was interviewed by the *Omaha Daily Herald*. As news of the travails of the Big Horn Expedition filled newspaper columns statewide and nationally, Crook was asked for comment. Reluctant to divulge much, he noted that courts-martial charges were pending and that he did not wish to prejudice the cases. He did regret the loss of the Indian ponies the day after the Powder River battle. More than five hundred had been retaken by Indians from Reynolds's camp at the mouth of Lodge Pole Creek. "The Indians are nothing without their horses," he told the newsman, "and if we could have retained the stock they would have been utterly helpless." He did allow that another campaign was in the offing. "About the middle of May we shall go after them again. . . . There will be grass for our horses, the intense cold will have abated, and our facilities will be enlarged in many ways." Crook did indeed imagine an entirely different campaign, with "enlarged facilities" of all sorts, especially men and equipment.[5]

In mid-April Crook had face-to-face contact with several of the senior officers who would play central roles in the new campaign. Lieutenant Colonel William Bedford Royall of the Third Cavalry, summoned to department headquarters on April 20, discussed with Crook the state of affairs in the regiment: Colonel Reynolds was under charges for the botched Powder River fight, desertions were plaguing the companies, and replacement horse stock was needed to remount each of the troops properly. Royall and Crook likely also discussed a quip that had appeared in the *Cheyenne Daily Leader* at the close of the last movement, alleging that Crook had said that he would soon form another expedition "with experienced officers and men, probably from the 2nd or 5th Cavalry regiments." Royall may have taken this as a slight on the Third Cavalry. Almost certainly, Crook broached his desire for Royall to lead the cavalry brigade in the next campaign. Royall hardly had a choice in the matter, but neither did Crook.[6]

Royall and Crook were acquaintances of sorts, having crossed paths on occasion in Arizona. Remembered as a "blunt, impetuous, old soldier," the fifty-one-year-old Royall was one of the more skilled senior Indian campaigners in the department. He had extensive experience in the West both before and after the Civil War, including most recently on General Sheridan's campaign in the Republican River country of Kansas in 1868 against Tall Bull's Cheyenne Dog Soldiers. He had fought in the eastern theater of the Civil War and was seriously wounded and breveted for gallantry many times. Detached service kept him out of the Apache campaigns in the early 1870s for the most part. Royall was promoted from the Fifth Cavalry to the Third in December 1875.[7]

Crook directed Royall to oversee the important purchase of cavalry horses to replenish the depleted stocks in the Second and Third regiments. Within weeks he and another officer from Omaha Barracks were scouring the city and Saint Joseph and Kansas City, Missouri, purchasing horses, while a second board was convened in Cheyenne to acquire stock there and also in Denver and Pueblo, Colorado. Indeed, the rigors of the Big Horn Expedition had fairly well used up that column's horses. In final tally, nearly twenty-five percent of the mounts of those ten companies were either "lost in action," meaning that they had died or were abandoned on the trail, or condemned afterward and disposed of outright or relegated to draft work.[8]

Also in Omaha was Major Andrew Wallace Evans of the Third Cavalry. Evans was one of Crook's West Point classmates, standing 26th of 43 in the class of 1852 (Crook stood at 37). As with most officers holding a field-grade rank, Evans was well experienced on the frontier and in the Civil War, where he earned several brevets for gallant and meritorious service. He played a prominent role in Sheridan's campaign against the Southern Cheyennes, Kiowas, and Comanches in 1868, leading a column of Third Cavalry from Fort Bascom, New Mexico, and successfully assailing and destroying a Comanche village on the Canadian River on Christmas Day. What distinguished the forty-six-year-old Evans most, however, was his irascible personality. Individuals far and wide remembered him as a dour man, suffering from an old wound, philosophically inclined, devoted to literature, "and having, to all appearance, registered a vow to never smile." Another man in the field with Evans in 1876 remembered him as "the most even tempered man in the Army . . . always cross." But classmates knew how to cut through the cloud. Crook wanted him on the campaign leading the Third Cavalry.[9]

While Crook tended to political matters as well as the Black Hills crisis and traveled incessantly, department staff handled organizational details, issuing orders convening the troops and requisitioning and forwarding munitions, ordnance stores, food stuffs, and even two ponton boats (the press labeled them pontoon boats). Much of this was a great shuffle of wares from the army's principal arsenals and depots, to way depots in Omaha and

Cheyenne, and then to Fort Fetterman, which was again designated as the campaign's point of rendezvous. The thirty-one-foot-long boats constructed of white oak were well caulked, with iron work varnished with asphaltum, transported on distinctive ponton wagons, and equipped with planking, oars, anchors, and tools. They were among the unique facilities provided this time, due to fear of swollen rivers. Two boats went north but rarely get mentioned again. To feed the column, the department's commissary and subsistence chief, Major John P. Hawkins, directed Captain Edwin M. Coates, Fourth Infantry commander of Fort Fetterman, to acquire two hundred head of cattle through local contractors, to be trailed with the column. The Big Horn Expedition had also trailed live cattle north in March, only to lose them all to Indians on the first night out, thus contributing to the food predicament on that campaign.[10]

Hawkins and his staff counterparts in the department also arranged for the shipment to Fetterman of 2,000 pounds of coffee and sugar, 277,000 pounds of grain, and an extraordinary array of ordnance matter: crated firearms, ammunition, saddles, halters, bridles, holsters, and other such wherewithal amounting to another quarter million pounds of freight. The packing of wagons for the campaign occurred in large measure at the Cheyenne Depot, adjacent to Fort D. A. Russell. Some freight was carried from Cheyenne to Fort Fetterman by Crook's vaunted mule train, making numerous round trips in April and May. Since returning from the winter campaign, Crook's revered mules and handlers had subsisted in a rendezvous camp near the depot. News of these shipments by wagon and mule, amounting to many hundreds of thousands of pounds of stores, became local newspaper copy throughout the spring.[11]

One curious exchange occurred as deployment orders flew between Omaha and the commands announced for the campaign. At Fort D. A. Russell, Captain Guy V. Henry, commanding Company D, Third Cavalry, one of Crook's dependables from the Apache campaigns and a seasoned officer if somewhat of a martinet, sought the department's intercession to retain the services of Second Lieutenant William W. Robinson, detached from Company H and presently commanding Henry's outfit. Of Henry's regularly assigned officers, First Lieutenant John C. Thompson presently served on recruiting service and Second Lieutenant John G. Bourke was long detached as an aide-de-camp to General Crook. Henry, meanwhile, was still convalescing from crippling injuries suffered on a wintertime prospector eviction patrol in the Black Hills a year earlier. He and his company lost their way in a dreaded norther. If not for his personal grit, the suffering of his command would have been greater than it was. Henry and his company made their way through blinding snow and wind and returned safely to Camp Robinson. The captain and his subaltern and forty-five of the fifty enlisted men on the ill-fated patrol required immediate medical care, suffering from snow blindness, frostbite, and frozen appendages. All of Henry's fingers were frozen to the second joint. The last digit of the middle finger of his left hand required amputation. Painful inflammation lingered for months, and he was never again able to bend his fingers fully. Lieutenant Robinson's service with the company was not extended, however, and Henry marched at its head in May, alone.[12]

On May 2, 1876, Crook again traveled to Chicago to meet with Sheridan, with much to report. The Henry Noyes court-martial emanating from the Powder River battle had reached its conclusion in Cheyenne. The captain was found guilty of a single charge and sentenced to a reprimand by Crook in general orders. Crook needed Noyes on the new campaign. The Black Hills crisis continued to flare, especially in the wake of the ruthless Metz and Stuttering Brown killings north of Fort Laramie. Troops were being deployed to patrol the roads and intercede. Good strides were being made in organizing the new movement, which by now Crook had dubbed the Big Horn and Yellowstone Expedition.[13]

In what appears to be an entirely chance encounter, though plainly if opportunistically related to the larger campaign against the Sioux, Custer happened to be in Chicago then as well. He was in trouble. The young lieutenant colonel of the Seventh Cavalry had spent much of March and April in Washington, D.C., testifying before a House of Representatives committee in matters related to post traderships and Indian affairs and generally miring himself in partisan politics on the Democratic side. His testimony, largely hearsay and often exceedingly reckless, impugned the recently resigned and politically imperiled former secretary of war William Belknap, Orville Babcock (the president's private secretary), and even the president himself. Grant was furious that an officer of the army would engage in such "self-righteousness, partisanship, and recklessness in insulting the chain of command" and stripped Custer from command of the Dakota column, then organizing for the field in Bismarck and at Fort Abraham Lincoln. When Custer's personal appeals to General Sherman, commander of the army, and President Grant went unheeded, he struck off for Dakota, only to be intercepted in Chicago by General Sheridan.[14]

Crook, Custer, and Sheridan discussed, if momentarily, the status of campaign preparations in the northern departments, though Custer had been away for a while and his sense of it all was not fresh. Meanwhile Crook certainly got a firsthand taste of political theater. Custer was mortified by the loss of command. Sheridan, Custer's foremost patron, was equally horrified because he stood to lose his second prime Indian fighter. By early design, Crook and Custer were to lead the principal forces fielded against the Sioux. The two had exchanged repeated advices in February as Crook planned and embarked on his Big Horn Expedition. At the moment, with Grant's fury and an absent Custer, it was hard to imagine much campaign savvy remaining in the Department of Dakota. Crook returned to Omaha on May 5, doubtless glad to be home.[15]

After personal appeals by Brigadier General Alfred H. Terry, commander of the Department of Dakota in Saint Paul and Custer's direct superior, plus Sheridan, Grant relented and permitted Custer to join the campaign, but only in a secondary role and not in command of the entire expedition. This made big news in Omaha and elsewhere, as did the planning underway in Saint Paul and Fort Abraham Lincoln for the launch of that critical expedition. At the heart of the envisioned Dakota column were all twelve companies of the Seventh Cavalry, led by Custer. The regiment and its de facto commander were well known campaigners in the West and on the northern plains, having faced Sitting Bull and the Sioux repeatedly during the 1873 Northern Pacific Railroad surveys on the Yellowstone and served as explorers guiding the very expedition that discovered gold in the Black Hills in 1874.[16]

Turning his attention to final planning matters in the Department of the Platte, Crook issued a stream of orders and follow-up directives during the next several days. The medical staff of the Big Horn and Yellowstone Expedition had yet to be identified, but orders on May 8 and 10 settled that. Captain (and assistant surgeon) Albert Hartsuff was appointed medical director of the expedition and ordered to Fort Fetterman with the companies originating at Fort Laramie. The required medical stores for the expedition were to be largely drawn from Fort Laramie stocks and augmented upon reaching Fetterman. Similarly, Captain (and assistant surgeon) Julius Herman Patzki was ordered to accompany the troops originating at Fort Fred Steele, Wyoming, while acting assistant surgeon Charles R. Stephens, a citizen physician, was ordered to proceed from Fort McPherson, Nebraska, to Fort D. A. Russell and accompany the troops from that point to the rendezvous. Additionally, hospital steward Samuel W. Richardson from Fort Russell was also ordered to accompany the troops from that point.[17]

This was an experienced medical staff. Hartsuff, the senior physician and at the time the post surgeon at Fort Laramie, had served the army through the long course of the Civil War and was breveted for meritorious service. Patzki was a Civil War enlisted veteran and later also a wartime surgeon. Less known is Stephens, an 1874 graduate of the Bellevue Hospital Medical College in New York City, whose army service until then was mostly limited to Fort McPherson, east of North Platte and private practice in Omaha before that. Stephens had served with the Big Horn Expedition in March but remained with Crook on Otter Creek and was not present on the Powder River battle-field, although he tended its wounded a day later. Even less is known about Richardson, but as a class such hospital stewards after the Civil War were an admired and valued lot, all competent, all medically inclined, and sometimes medically trained. Stewards' assistance to post surgeons included working as pharmacists, performing minor surgery and simple dentistry, record keeping, and managing post hospitals. Having such a highly skilled assistant on the campaign was a distinct asset.[18]

Crook also ordered to the field a number of staff officers and assistants. Captain William Sanford Stanton of the Corps of Engineers, chief engineer of the department, officially joined the campaign on May 8. It was almost certainly because of him that ponton boats trailed with the wagons, along with a wheeled odometer. Stanton also maintained a valuable day-to-day journal during the campaign, which was published a year later. Captain Azor Howitt Nickerson of the Twenty-Third Infantry and Second Lieutenant John Gregory Bourke, Third Cavalry, both aides-de-camp to Crook, were also officially ordered to the field. Both were widely respected men who would play critical roles in the campaign (and forthcoming battle). Of the two, Bourke had the more intimate relationship with his patron and mentor. They were rarely apart, and the lieutenant was one of the very few in Crook's intimate circle who was privy to his every thought. Bourke, too, was a dedicated diarist whose meticulous and often lengthy day-to-day jottings were ultimately transformed into an essential history of Crook's western campaigns. One final indispensable staff officer ordered to the field was Captain John Vincent Furey of the Quartermaster Department, at the time the depot quartermaster in Omaha. Crook's wagons would soon carry northward an extraordinary array of war materiel, all of it accountable and in Furey's charge. Of this administrative crowd, only Bourke had participated in the Big Horn Expedition. Nickerson, however, was well familiar with Crook's direct and forceful campaign style, having experienced it in Arizona.[19]

Upon completion of the various preparations needed to reopen the campaign, Crook left Omaha for Cheyenne on May 9, accompanied by Bourke and Major Elisha H. Ludington, inspector general of the department. A reporter from the *Omaha Bee* happened to be trackside and in a unique moment caught a sense of the general. "Gen. Crook, in his top boots and carrying a double barrel shot gun, looked every inch an Indian fighter as he walked the platform at the depot, waiting for the train. He will visit Red Cloud agency and do a little hunting before his expedition is ready."[20] Crook certainly loved to hunt and filled his life with it, but in the coming weeks he did not find any time for a pleasurable diversion. The same reporter noted that all the companies in the Department of the Platte had received their orders to move, even some from the nearby Omaha Barracks who were not destined for the campaign directly but dispatched as backfill for other troops ordered into active service. For that purpose, on the afternoon of May 10, four companies of the Twenty-Third Infantry marched the four miles from the barracks to town and boarded a special train bound for the west, one company detailed to Fort Hartsuff, one to Fort McPherson, and two to Sidney Barracks. The regimental band led the procession as townsfolk crowded the streets. Many flew flags. "It reminded one of war times," quipped a newsman.[21]

On Crook's journey west Chicagoan J. P. Hart, who was traveling to Salt Lake City, openly engaged the general. On a layover in Cheyenne, Hart jotted down the essence of their conversation in an open letter to the *Chicago Inter-Ocean*. The two mostly discussed Black Hills gold and of course the Indians, Hart observed. Crook spoke from personal knowledge of the gold rush, having explored the Black Hills the previous summer and panned for gold and talked with miners. "There is no question but that there is plenty of gold in the hills," he assured Hart, "but it will require large companies with plenty of capital to get it," suggesting that profitable placer mining required massive sluices, long canals carrying water great distances, and manpower, while stamp mills required an even greater financial outlay. As for the Indians, Crook espoused the core tenets of the recent treaties without exactly attributing it that way. Indians should be put on reservations, he said, with easy access to railroads and steamboats, where the soil is good, and where they would be protected. There they would be encouraged to cultivate the soil and acquire ownership in their own land, houses, barns, cattle, and horses and "will thus entirely become self-sustaining." This tidy summation of President Grant's Peace Policy apparently rolled from Crook's tongue easily, in all likelihood because he knew its precepts intimately and believed in them.[22]

Crook was frequently in Cheyenne, the key point of transfer from the Union Pacific Railroad to the campaign trails and forts to the north, plus the two agencies in the Pine Ridge country as well as the Black Hills gold fields. He and Bourke may have become inured to the gold rush bustle by now, but most newcomers found the city a sensory overload. In an earlier moment Bourke had predicted that Black Hills gold would cause Cheyenne and cities like it "to hum like a swarm of angry bees." Storekeepers had plenty of gold to show. Everyone had an opinion, though it was "rank treason in Cheyenne to say aught about the Black Hills country." No one was listening anyway. Moreover, as John Finerty of the *Chicago Times* put it, the town had "the smell of gunpowder in the air." The most flourishing place in Cheyenne may well have been the Converse and Warren mercantile, though most everyone better remembered the saloons and dancehalls that closed at 8 A.M. daily, if only momentarily, and during church hours on Sundays. The center of town was Seventeenth and Eddy Streets, with McDaniel's Theater on one corner, restaurants to the right and left where customers washed down oyster suppers with French champagne, and the Freund Brother's Wyoming Armory and Pioneer Gun Store down the street. The killings on the Black Hills Road deterred no one. The business of the day was surviving Cheyenne, assembling a miner's kit, joining a prospector's train, and making way for Custer City or the new town of Deadwood. Finerty noted that "it was a quiet kind of hell."[23]

Crook was all business. When in the city he often seized a moment to visit with Frank Freund at the popular Freund Brother's gun shop. Frank and brother George were German-born gunsmiths renowned on the frontier as purveyors of nearly every pattern of American firearm and especially for modifying Sharps and other high-grade rifles with improved breechblock actions, distinctive sights, and other patented enhancements. On the coming campaign, in addition to a shotgun for hunting small game, Crook planned on carrying an army issue Model 1873 Springfield .45–70 rifle, but with Freund modifications. Whether Crook picked up his rifle at that point or had recently had one serviced, the Freunds had modified the weapon by contouring its stock, adding double triggers and an ornate trigger guard, modifying the rear sight, and mounting a thin copper blade front sight. In a day when officers often carried personal weapons to the field, Crook's choice of a standard-issue infantry rifle was a statement unto itself.[24]

Crook also ventured to Fort D. A. Russell and the Cheyenne Depot to visit with officers who would soon march north with him and with his old friend from Arizona days, Captain James Gilliss, commanding officer at the depot. While making his rounds, Crook quickly sensed the demoralization evident among the officers and men of the post. This was headquarters for the Third Cavalry, the regiment particularly sullied at Powder River. Many believed that Colonel Reynolds and Captain Alexander Moore, officers facing courts-martial charges for their actions in the battle, would never be brought to trial because both had sufficient political influence in Washington, D.C., to prevent it. Indeed, Reynolds was a West Point classmate and intimate friend of President Grant and even now was seeking intercession on his behalf. Crook would have nothing of it and ordered Lieutenant Colonel Royall, also freshly arrived in the city, to arrest his own colonel and see to his confinement to the limits of the military reservation (which did not extend to Cheyenne).[25]

Campaign-bound newsmen were also swarming the city. Two competing newspapers served Cheyenne's news interests, the *Daily Leader*, founded originally as a weekly paper upon the establishment of the city in 1867, and the newcomer, the *Daily Sun*, which printed its first issue in March 1876. Both papers devoted considerable column space to military news, acknowledging a voracious readership at nearby Fort Russell and the quartermaster depot and also at Fort Laramie, eighty-eight miles north, and Fort Fetterman, eighty-one miles beyond that. The distant posts received their papers by regular mail or, at least to Fort Laramie, on a newly established stage line. Neither paper had the financial wherewithal to dispatch its own reporter to Crook's Big Horn Expedition in March, although both had abbreviated campaign news gleaned from secondary sources. This time, however, the *Daily Leader* boasted to its readership that it had contracted with a national reporter and would feature fresh news from the general's new expedition. Both papers also covered the spectacle of outside reporters arriving in the city and outfitting for the campaign.[26]

Only one reporter went north with Crook in March, and he was eager to join the general again. Robert E. Strahorn, writing principally for Denver's *Rocky Mountain News* and incidentally for several other newspapers, relished military news and the adventures of field service. The year before he had befriended Major Thaddeus H. Stanton, the Department of the Platte's Cheyenne-based paymaster, and traveled with him on one of his pay circuits. Both local newspapers followed Strahorn's comings and goings, noting, for instance, the day when he also purportedly signed on as a reporter for the *Chicago Times* and even the occasion when he "patronized a tooth carpenter." Strahorn wrote under the pen name "Alter Ego." In March his reports from the field provided a careful chronicle of the day-to-day movements of Crook's column and then the Powder River battle itself, which he was in the thick of. On that campaign he shared Crook's and Bourke's mess and had their trust. Strahorn turned twenty-four years old on May 15.[27]

The principal *Chicago Times* man, John Finerty, was also in Cheyenne, having arrived just ahead of Crook and Bourke. Finerty immediately penned a colorful report on the boisterousness of the town and the campaign preparations underway at Fort Russell. In Omaha several days earlier Crook had advised Finerty to obtain a horse and secure a messing arrangement with an officer at Fort Russell, which he set about doing. But the inquisitive newsman also sought out and interviewed Colonel Joseph Reynolds. The white-haired senior received him cordially and spoke pleasantly enough of the approaching campaign and regretted that he would have no part in it. He dodged the reason why, but Finerty understood perfectly, knowing that he and Crook were not on good terms. Before parting, Reynolds offered sage advice: "As you have not been out after Indians previously, allow an old soldier to give you this piece of advice—Never stray far from the main column, and never trust a horse or an Indian."[28]

Reuben Briggs Davenport of the *New York Herald* and Thomas C. Mac-Millan of the *Chicago Inter-Ocean* were now also in Cheyenne. Davenport's arrival in Omaha was noted on May 13. Two days later he and MacMillan chanced to meet when overnighting in one of that city's hotels. The two were acquainted, both having accompanied Lieutenant Colonel Richard I. Dodge's surveying expedition to the Black Hills in 1875. Like Strahorn, both men were young, Davenport twenty-four and MacMillan twenty-six. In his private journal Dodge remembered them both, recalling MacMillan as "very gentlemanly, hard to stuff, and with excellent good sense" and Davenport as a good writer with "the regular reporter knack of pumping people" but "green as a gourd." Davenport's personality invited teasing and the men in Dodge's camp pleasured in doing so, in one instance suggesting that a hooting night owl was really an Indian signal and always "predicting a hard fight today." Obsessively fearing an Indian encounter, Davenport told one of the scientists on the 1875 expedition that "he intended to put his 'Herald Flag' over his tent so that the Indians would know he was a non-combatant." Despite it all, Davenport knew his way around and his stories from the front were lengthy and filled with commendable detail.[29]

Upon reaching Cheyenne, Davenport and MacMillan, like Finerty, sought out good horses and field kits and messing arrangements at Fort Russell. Here

Davenport distinguished himself from his colleagues and earned a rather cutting quip from Strahorn of the *Rocky Mountain News*. Davenport was an excessively proud New Yorker and a boastful *Herald* man and conspicuously marked his saddle, bridle, blankets, haversack, and canteen with the name *New York Herald*. Strahorn wrote: "He has not branded his horse '*Herald*,' but he has got him so he looks like a *Herald* horse. In fact, everything about him goes to herald the fact that he represents the *Herald*," providing touches of overstatement and understatement at the start of a great campaign.[30]

A fifth full-time newsman was still en route. Joe Wasson, sometimes writing under the penname "Jose," was a Crook crony of sorts. The affable red-haired reporter was thirty-five years old, making him the eldest among the newspapermen. He and his brother John had wandered the Far West as prospectors, editors, and correspondents and encountered a younger Crook in Idaho during his campaigns in the Great Basin. The Wassons then owned the Silver City *Owyhee Avalanche*. The prospects of the desert Southwest in the early 1870s lured the pair to Tucson, where they founded the *Arizona Citizen* and again frequently chanced upon Crook when covering and lauding his campaigns. By 1876 Joe had drifted to San Francisco and now reported for the *Daily Alta California*, principally covering the coming Big Horn and Yellowstone Expedition while also writing for the *Philadelphia Press* and *New York Tribune*. Unlike Davenport's and Finerty's stories, which were detailed and wordy, Wasson's filings typically evinced an economy of words as well as some extraordinary prose. Coming from the West, Wasson joined the campaign at Medicine Bow, a rail stop west of Laramie City, where a considerable number of campaign-bound troops were concentrating.[31]

Yet a sixth man, sketch artist Charles St. George Stanley, employed by *Frank Leslie's Illustrated Newspaper* of New York City, was also making his way to the campaign. An urbane Englishman, Stanley resided of late in the mining camps of the Colorado high country. Educated at the Royal Academy of Art in London and some fifty-four or fifty-five years old, Stanley was soon providing compelling illustrations from the field that filled *Leslie's* pages several times in the summer. Stanley also sent *Leslie's* insightful if only occasional written copy and also maintained a detailed private journal during the campaign that he published serially in the *Georgetown Colorado Miner* two years later. Stanley uniquely messed with the expedition's packers, a convenience because as an artist he had additional baggage in tow.[32]

With a sketch artist, five full-time newsmen, two intentionally identified correspondents (who were not professional journalists), and at least four more unidentified correspondents, most but not all drawn from the officer corps, Crook's Big Horn and Yellowstone Expedition was destined to become the most fully reported Indian campaign in the history of the American West. Crook was never averse to such attention and generally enjoyed the company of journalists, but on this occasion he did nothing at all to induce it. As Finerty's senior editor told him before leaving Chicago, Crook knows how to fight Indians. As this Indian war was heating up, with Custer and Crook soon in the field and Gibbon already wending his way down the Yellowstone, the enticement was plain enough.[33]

Crook's hope of employing Sioux Indian auxiliaries on this campaign was perhaps his greatest remaining challenge. Finding and relentlessly following Indian trails was central to his manner of campaigning. In his experience no one did this better than full-blood and mixed-blood Indians of the same tribe being pursued. Such people knew the habits, haunts, mindsets, and languages of their fellow tribesmen. Crook reckoned with a parallel lesson gained from his winter expedition. Nowhere in his experience in Indian campaigning had he encountered anything on the order of the sweeping vastness of the northern plains, with its daunting distances and obscuring landscapes that rose and fell and funneled and hid. Sherman once called finding Indians there a matter "worse than looking for a needle in a hay stack, rather like looking for a flea in a large clover field."[34] Reporter Joe Wasson, experiencing the northern plains for the first time, expressed it another way: "The immensity of this vast region cannot be described in words: one must travel over it on foot and horseback to fairly realize the overwhelming character of the vacuum."[35] Crook needed allies who knew not only the Indians but also the land. He had been unable to enlist full-blood Sioux scouts on his winter expedition, but his column was still well tended by a sizable corps of mixed-blood scouts from Red Cloud Agency and white Plainsmen from the agencies, nearby forts, and beyond. He needed twice that many now.[36]

On one of Crook's visits to Chicago, General Sheridan talked up the prospect of hiring Shoshone Indians recruited from their reservation in Wyoming. This notion was inspired by a visit to Camp Brown in 1874, when he witnessed the successful muster of a sizable contingent of Shoshones led by their great chief, Washakie, who worked cooperatively with a Second Cavalry company to drive off Sioux and Arapaho hunters prowling the Big Horn Basin. Crook listened intently but still wanted Oglalas at his side in this war.

In late April the *Omaha Bee* told of a similar spectacle in the Ute country. A white interpreter there proposed organizing two or three companies of Ute Indian soldiers to assist the army in subjugating their hereditary enemies, much in the manner of Major Frank North's well-known Pawnee Scouts operating in Nebraska. Again Crook took in the information, but he still wanted Oglalas. Publicly Crook had hoped to enlist as many as three hundred Indians at Red Cloud Agency. The *Omaha Republican* quipped that such reinforcements would certainly "add variety and spice to the movement." The *Cheyenne Daily Leader* noted, however, that Crook had better act quickly or those much desired warriors would go north instead and he would "have three hundred extra to fight." Despite Crook's desire for Oglalas, the pragmatist in him reconciled hiring Shoshones and Crows if his efforts at Red Cloud failed, an option understood at department headquarters before he left Omaha.[37]

Crook did not tarry in Cheyenne. After visiting with friends at Fort Russell and Cheyenne Depot and effecting the arrest of Colonel Reynolds, he and Bourke set out for Red Cloud Agency to enlist Indian scouts. Bourke found the road north this time both long and tedious—a trail that they knew too well. Aside from its "new spring dress of green" to the right and left it was a tiresome succession of sandy ruts, treeless waste, and clayey bottom streams. The pair traveled the first leg without an escort, ignoring the general's own advice to Black Hillers to gang up, and overnighted en route at the Phillips Ranch on Chugwater Creek. At Fort Laramie Crook greeted the officers there who would soon join the campaign and also found his friend Frank Grouard waiting. Grouard had proved himself an indispensable guide on the first campaign and was now one of the few scouts from that expedition willing to join Crook again. Crook, Bourke, and Grouard resumed the trail to Camp Robinson the next morning, this time accompanied by a small infantry escort riding along in wagons. The party camped on Rawhide Creek that evening.[38]

Bourke thought that the bloom of the gold rush had passed because trail traffic seemed to have slackened. Still, he recorded in his diary viewing some handsome coarse gold nuggets, including one valued at $6.20 and another from Deadwood Creek worth $120.54 (weighing at the prevailing worth of gold at some 6 pennyweights and 6 troy ounces, respectively). Bourke reflected on Crook's demeanor on the trail, eyeing a man in full: "a clear-headed thinker, a fluent conversationalist, and a most pleasant companion." Crook was sure that the Sioux could never stand the same punishment that the Apaches had suffered. The Sioux had accumulated too much property in ponies and other things, and those losses would be felt most deeply. Crook also confessed his concern over his chances of enlisting Indian trackers and feared that Chief Red Cloud would not heed his request.[39]

Crook's colleague and confidant Major Thaddeus Stanton of the Pay Department, Ludington (the department's inspector general), and Stanton's pal Robert Strahorn of the *Rocky Mountain News* traveled to the agencies on business ahead of Crook and were on hand to welcome him when he reached Camp Robinson on May 14. A short while before, Stanton had opportunistically interviewed Chief Spotted Tail at his agency. The charismatic old Brulé had offered a sarcastic assessment of the affairs of the day, particularly in light of the mess at Powder River. He admonished the paymaster that "if you don't do better than you did the last time, you had better put on squaws clothes and stay at home." Spotted Tail's scolding was troubling. He was perhaps the wisest and most accommodating of the many chiefs at the Pine Ridge agencies, and his candor plainly reflected the prevailing anxiety in that country. A white resident at the Spotted Tail Agency expressed similar sentiments in a letter to the *Omaha Bee* dated May 8, telling how Indians there "would be contented if Crook had been less ambitious and kept the soldiers out of the country. There were no murders committed until he burnt up their village and the stragglers got to Crazy Horse's camp and made their report of the attack."[40]

Crook found the state of affairs at the agencies disturbing but set out immediately to talk with the chiefs at Red Cloud Agency and learn where they stood on the question of peace or war. He still hoped to enlist a contingent of scouts, though perhaps not three hundred. Crook arranged for a formal meeting with Red Cloud and other Oglala headmen on Monday, May 16, on the Camp Robinson parade ground. Meanwhile on Sunday several headmen came to him, eager to parley. Red Cloud agent James S. Hastings was absent that day. An underling attempted to keep the chiefs away. Sitting Bull (the Oglala often called Sitting Bull of the South), Three Bears, and Rocky Bear brushed the subordinate aside and were conducted into the adjutant's office. There Crook, Bourke, Stanton, Grouard, and the commanding officer at Robinson, Captain William H. Jordan, Ninth Infantry, greeted them. With Louis Richard interpreting, Crook detailed his plans for the coming campaign, explaining that it was the president who had ordered the Northern Indians to go to the reservation and that troops would stay after them until they did. (Richard was another of the scouts from the Big Horn Expedition willing to join Crook's next movement.) Crook particularly spoke openly about wanting Sioux from the reservation to come along and acknowledged that the Crows had sent word that they would join the campaign. He preferred, however, to have Sioux.[41]

Sitting Bull spoke for the three Oglalas, lamenting how Sioux land was getting smaller and the buffalo scarcer. "Soon the Indians must all come to live on the Reservations set out for them or be killed off." Crook again acknowledged the war. "If all the soldiers now in the country were to be killed off, others would come to take their places. I talk as [a] friend." Sitting Bull told how he had tried to bring his sons in as he knew the soldiers were coming. He and the others expressed a willingness to join the campaign. He then asked Crook whether he was going to Spotted Tail Agency, but the general said no. The conversation ended there. The chiefs withdrew to talk among their followers. Crook was heartened by their apparent willingness to join the expedition.[42]

Later that evening agent Hastings returned to the agency and summoned Crook. Hastings and the general were on frosty terms. Crook had publicly declared barely weeks earlier that it was the fault of Hastings and Spotted Tail agent Edwin A. Howard that the Indian village at Powder was crammed with ammunition and other supplies received from the agencies. Hastings vigorously denied this publicly, and Howard declared that there had been no trade in arms and ammunition at his agency for the past two years. (In fact, no Brulés were in the Powder River camp.) Still, Hastings told the general that he would not object to any Red Cloud Indians going out with him but would not recommend it. That was simple political cover: when things went bad the next day, Crook and Bourke were both immediately convinced that the chiefs "had been tampered with."[43]

The morning-long meeting on May 16 began with abundant handshakes, "How! Colas," and the traditional smoking of the pipe (what Bourke collectively called the "necessary preliminaries") but went poorly from there. Seven chiefs were present. Foremost among them was Red Cloud, along with Old Man Afraid of His Horses, American Horse, Little Wound, Sitting Bull of the South, and two others. Hastings and Howard sat with the Indians. The same men from the day before sat with Crook, plus Strahorn of the *Rocky Mountain News*. Again Louis Richard interpreted. Red Cloud was openly interested in who had started this war: the president or the secretary of the interior? Crook said that it was both. Red Cloud then proceeded to harangue. "The Government sent ten commissioners here to hold a council with us on the White Earth River below here. The Sioux have been thinking of that Black Hills Council all winter. Since they left we had no trouble. But an expedition went out and whipped some Cheyennes and now we have trouble and here is the man who made all this trouble." Red Cloud was staring straight at Crook.[44]

Red Cloud's rant turned ever more strident. "The Gray Fox must understand that the Dakotas, and especially the Ogallalas [sic], have many warriors, many guns and ponies. They are brave and ready to fight for their country. They are not afraid of the soldiers nor of their chief. Many braves are ready to meet them. Every lodge will send its young men, and they will say of the Great Father's dogs, 'Let them come!'"[45]

When Crook attempted to dodge the verbal assault, Little Wound continued the berating. "I have been twice to Washington. The Great Father told me not to go to War anymore; not to fight enemies anymore." It became plainly apparent that the chiefs did not want their young men to go with Crook and neither did the agents. Grouard later found out that the agents had indeed joined Red Cloud in persuading their charges to stay home. There simply was little or no support for the notion of Sioux warriors fighting fellow tribesmen. Hastings later took Sitting Bull of the South severely to task for speaking freely with Crook the day before without first consulting him.[46]

Equally troubling, Crook came to comprehend the seriousness of the recent defections more fully during his visit and even in the days immediately preceding his arrival at Camp Robinson. Midwinter intelligence had suggested that the Sitting Bull and Crazy Horse factions, the Northern Indians as they were so commonly known, numbered fewer than three hundred warriors in camps tallying perhaps a thousand people collectively. These were Indians who had not signed treaties, were not collecting gifts and annuities, had not accepted the reservation or the agencies, and remained steadfastly committed to a traditional buffalo-hunting lifeway. Sheridan and his commanders well understood that opportunities for a meaningful wintertime campaign were gone. The land was greening up, and the Red Cloud Agency people were heading north. Some went for buffalo, but many more appeared headed for the Northern Indian camps, especially the circle of the Oglala leader Crazy Horse. The notion of an all-out war had come home to these people. The bloodying of the countryside between the Black Hills and Union Pacific Railroad, spurred in part by the unstoppable gold rush and the prick of the Powder River battle, had fomented calamitous conditions across the Pine Ridge.

Various reports hinted at how great the defections were. Agent Hastings and Captain Jordan estimated that some fifteen hundred to two thousand Indians had left the Red Cloud Agency in early May. Eighty lodges took flight in a single day. No Water and Little Big Man, traditionalists like Crazy Horse, departed with ten lodges as Crook was coming in, despite a stiff remonstrance from Hastings. Fifty lodges had defected from Spotted Tail Agency. The agencies were far from deserted, but these numbers were disconcerting and in hindsight foreboding. Crook saw enough of it firsthand. The newspapers locally and nationally were also sounding the alarm. Sheridan received the reports, read the papers, and lent the issue an even broader perspective, understanding that three other major Sioux agencies on the Missouri River were in circumstances identical to those in the Pine Ridge. The refrain hurt. The generals knew this to be a different kind of war.[47]

When Crook's meeting with the chiefs ended at about noon on May 16, he and several of his party dined with John W. Dear, one of the two licensed Indian traders at Red Cloud Agency and an individual with broad business interests across the region, including a stake in the fledgling stage lines running from Sidney and Cheyenne to Custer City. Dear had witnessed troubles of all sorts in his several years at Red Cloud and now related the sense of anxiety gripping the agency and adjacent army camp. Such episodes as the burning of the agency hay scales the week before, the ugly behavior exhibited by many Indians when coming to trade, and the constant running off of stock were bad omens.[48]

Intent on reporting to Sheridan, Crook and his party departed the agency and Camp Robinson in the early afternoon bound for Fort Laramie, the nearest telegraph station. Crook's escort had grown, which undoubtedly saved his life, and now included the various attendants who had accompanied Crook, Stanton, and Ludington when they came to Robinson, plus a handful of citizens, guides, and discharged soldiers—in all about sixty-five men. The trail to Fort Laramie from Camp Robinson and the agencies followed the White River, a shallow stream that coursed straight west some eighteen miles to its headlands in the wide-open prairie beyond the breaks and pines of the ridge. For three or four miles from the start Crook's party passed through scattered Indian villages. That was the nature of such agencies, which provided a central focus. The agency headquarters and its associated trading posts were surrounded for miles by Indian tipi camps dotting the water courses and open grassy glades that sheltered the people and sustained their substantial pony herds.[49]

Crook and others noticed Indians on prominent points along the trail, looking attentive and expectant. Shortly afterward a big smoke went up from one of the white clay outcroppings in the rear of the column, which Crook and others interpreted as a signal. As the caravan neared the high end of the White River canyon where the valley's pine, ash, and cottonwood timber gave way to the prairie, Crook and the others passed Charlie Clark, the Fort Laramie–Camp Robinson mail carrier, driving a wagon and team, alone. They exchanged hellos. Clark dutifully continued his eastward course, disappearing in the swales of the well-defined road. Crook's party, meanwhile, continued its westerly journey for a few more miles to one of the small springs whose water formed the White River and paused there for a cold meal. Bourke speculated that, "had our sense of hearing been a little more acute, we might have heard the death cry of the poor mail driver." Crook's entourage continued to a night camp on the Niobrara River.[50]

At about midnight a courier from Captain Jordan reached Crook with a dispatch reporting the death of Charlie Clark. Earlier that afternoon three herders driving oxen to a ranch on the Niobrara had heard shots and found the mail carrier lying dead in his wagon, his body riddled with six bullets. In the distance they saw four Indians driving off Clark's horses. Later that afternoon John Dear, his brother Dick, and fifteen friendly Indians attempted to track the culprits, but the murderers escaped. Separately, Jordan sent a small party to recover Clark's body and the wagon. The mail had not been disturbed.[51]

Crook, Bourke, Strahorn, and almost everyone in the party took the news of Clark's killing as an assassination attempt meant for the general, not the hapless mailman, and believed so contemporaneously, not in hindsight. The ugly meeting that morning, Crook's visibility in the many Indian camps that he passed through and by when departing, the Indian lookouts on hill tops, and the plainly visible smoke signal all equated in their estimation to an ambush intent gone awry, owing simply to the strength of their party. While the sources are silent on this point, these officers surely recalled the assassination in 1873 of Brigadier General Edward R. S. Canby by Modoc Indians while engaging in a peace negotiation in California's lava beds. Crook was Canby's direct-line successor in the corps of brigadier generals. Poor Clark fell victim because of simple proximity and vulnerability. Crook reported the event as such in a letter to Sheridan written immediately upon reaching Fort Fetterman three days later. So did the newspapers. Bourke learned long afterward that the smoke was a signal to conspirators that Crook and his party were leaving the post.[52]

Even as Crook was bound for Fort Laramie, news of another large band of Sioux Indians fleeing Red Cloud Agency was making the rounds. They were intercepted on May 7 while harassing a Black Hills–bound freight train on Sage Creek, north of the Hat Creek stage station. The episode occurred in that deadly intersection where the gold rush trail crossed the heavily trodden Powder River Trail. The Indians' foolhardy act was interrupted by the timely appearance of Captain James Egan and Company K, Second Cavalry. Egan's unit had been in near perpetual motion all month in response to Wyoming governor John Thayer's pleadings with Crook for protection on these roads. Egan did not press the tribesmen, but his arrival hastened their disengagement and flight. The captain estimated the size of the band at six hundred to eight hundred people and was sure that Crook would encounter them again. The captain could not know that the band was led by the Oglala chief Big Road (also known as Long Road, Wide Road, or Wide Trail) and was being guided by Little Big Man, Crazy Horse's friend. It included Red Cloud's own son, Above Man (commonly known as Jack Red Cloud by the agency whites), as well as No Water and Black Elk and his twelve-year-old son of the same name. Egan's company numbered merely fifty-five men. In his report of the episode he stated that he "did not think it prudent to attack and they did not molest him." In its own unique way, Egan's decision acknowledged even at this early juncture of the Sioux war that not all Indians were recognized as enemies. That would change soon enough.[53]

Crook reached Fort Laramie on the afternoon of May 17 and gave no time for ill omens or reflection. Communiqués from Sheridan and Sherman awaited, and he dispatched his own reports to division and department headquarters. Crook's report to the department's assistant adjutant general told how "matters at Red Cloud have a bad look." He proceeded to detail the defections, the continuing depredations, his inability to enlist scouts, and the slaying of Clark. Crook learned from Sheridan that General Terry's column had departed Fort Abraham Lincoln on May 16 (actually 17). He learned from Sheridan that a panel of officers had been decided upon to try Colonel Joseph Reynolds for the debacle at Powder River. Crook gave that issue no time, aside from commending that the court-martial start date be set back from July, the intended start date.[54]

The issue of scouts vexed Crook most. He may not yet have fully comprehended the depth of the Indian auxiliaries accompanying Gibbon and Terry, each column supported by substantial bodies of Crows and Arikaras, respectively. But he fully understood the inherent necessity of Indian trackers. His winter campaign had given him a front-end appreciation of the bedeviling northern plains countryside. At Fort Laramie he wired the commanding officers at Camp Brown, Wyoming, and Fort Ellis, Montana, inviting them to enlist Shoshone and Crow scouts on his behalf, to meet his column in the field. He also charged Frank Grouard with enlisting willing mixed-blood scouts and Plainsmen from the surrounding area to form a cadre similar to the one serving with the Big Horn Expedition. He knew that he was blind in the field without scouts thoroughly familiar with the landscape and wiles of the Sioux. With this final matter put to an uneasy rest, Crook and Bourke prepared to depart for Fort Fetterman early the next morning, May 18. The general was anxious to be in the field. The elements of a great campaign were in motion, obstructive Red Cloud Oglalas notwithstanding.[55]

3

FORT FETTERMAN

Campaigns led by George Crook had several distinguishing characteristics, not the least of which was a robust cadre of supporting Indian auxiliaries. Despite the discouraging results of his recruiting effort at Red Cloud Agency, Crook remained hopeful as he and John Bourke made their way from Fort Laramie to Fort Fetterman on May 18. The general presumed that his appeals elsewhere would bring him useful contingents of Shoshone Indians from the Wind River country and Crow Indians from their agency in south-central Montana. Both tribes regarded the Sioux as mortal enemies and knew the buffalo country. The Crows were especially familiar with it because their traditional lands overlapped the same lower Yellowstone countryside occupied by the Sioux and Northern Cheyennes, the obdurate tribes at the heart of this war.

A second distinguishing characteristic of a Crook campaign was his warm embrace and advocacy of a fully developed mule train service, enabling him to extend movements beyond the confining limits of supply wagons. Crook was already acknowledged in the army as "the father of the modern aparejo train." On earlier campaigns he had developed an affinity for mules, mule handlers, and the business of packing, which was elevated to an art form in the hands of experts. Moreover, Crook openly enjoyed the company of packers. He loved their stories and plain talk. He appreciated their common sense and keen ability to handle stubborn animals and often messed with them. As Bourke later expressed it, mules and mule handling became the great study of Crook's life. The Department of the Platte had no mule service before Crook arrived in 1875. As he set about planning his first campaign, he invited two veteran packer friends from Arizona, Thomas Moore and David Mears, to Cheyenne to organize pack transportation for that movement. Moore and Mears were legendary mule handlers and in turn imported three organized trains for the Big Horn Expedition, complete with mules, bell horses, cargadors, horseshoers, cooks, packers, and unique form-fitting leather and straw-stuffed pack saddles known as *aparejos*.[1]

Upon the completion of that first expedition in March, Moore's mule train returned to Cheyenne and took up a home-in-the-field at the quartermaster

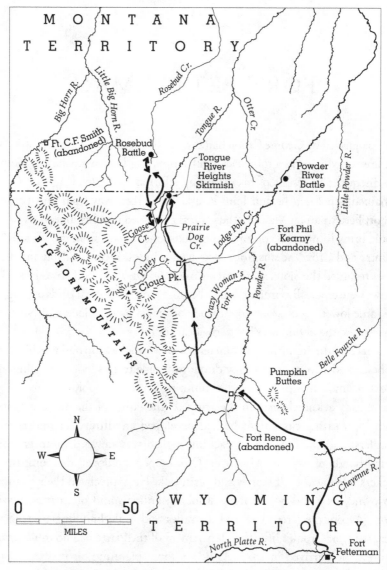

1. **Big Horn and Yellowstone Expedition, May 29–June 23, 1876**

depot, a place providing stockpiles of hay and grain, corrals and yards, and available pasturage in addition to its orderly array of warehouses. Charles St. George Stanley, the *Leslie's* artist, found himself in the packers' camp on the eve of the campaign and marveled at his surroundings, with its scattering of tents, flickering watch fires, long lines of *aparejos*, tinkling bells announcing the proximity of pack mules, the braying of an occasionally restless animal, and passing sentries. But then Stanley's dreamy serenity was abruptly interrupted by the ringing notes of reveille. In an instant, he wrote, all was life and activity. Fires blazed again as cooks prepared the morning meal, tents were lowered, files of mules were brought into position, blinds were placed over their eyes, and then all were rapidly saddled and packed with an astonishing efficiency. Five trains of seventy-five mules were handled simultaneously in less than fifteen minutes, Stanley marveled, with the handlers bolting breakfast in between. It was indeed an art form.[2]

Since receiving orders in early May, the twenty companies detailed to the Big Horn and Yellowstone Expedition had undertaken an array of organizational and outfitting duties and preparations unique to their circumstances and points of origin. Drafts of recruits were welcomed to the ranks, and most regiments and companies received some. Replacement horses were outfitted and introduced to cavalry service. Some posts had the wherewithal in their own quartermaster and ordnance storehouses to dress and equip their campaign-bound men fully, but some companies like those from Fort Sanders were ordered to Fort Russell to complete their outfitting. Meanwhile officers were also detailed to or excused from field service. Many who went north with Crook in March conveniently finagled their way out of doing so again in May. Captains passed command of their companies to lieutenants, and an occasional captain assumed command when a junior officer had been in charge on the earlier expedition. Captains Henry E. Noyes, Company I, Second Cavalry, and Anson Mills, Company M, Third Cavalry, who both had played conspicuous roles in the Powder River fight, returned to the field in May. Of the twenty companies bound for the field, only Mills's outfit went to active service with its full complement of three officers. Five companies went to the field with only one officer.[3]

While Fort Fetterman was designated as the campaign's point of rendezvous, some companies were ordered to interim stations for consolidation before continuing northward. Fort D. A. Russell, headquarters of the Third Cavalry and home of five of the participating companies, was one such station, soon welcoming the two Second Cavalry companies from Fort Sanders at Laramie City. Medicine Bow Station on the Union Pacific, west of Laramie City and directly south of Fort Fetterman, served as the second consolidation hub, where the three Third Cavalry companies from Sidney Barracks, the two Third Cavalry companies from Fort McPherson, and the single Second

Cavalry company from Fort Fred Steele assembled. The McPherson and Sidney Barracks units traveled by rail to that point. Lieutenant Colonel William Royall and Major Andrew Evans were sent from Omaha to Russell and Medicine Bow, respectively, to command the assembling battalions. All of this was in motion as Crook and Bourke attempted to recruit Oglala scouts at Red Cloud Agency.[4]

Departures from home stations were always melancholy events. The wife of the post surgeon at Sidney Barracks lamented the parting of their resident cavalry companies and the arrival of two Twenty-Third Infantry companies as summer replacements in a letter home. While the new officers were all gentlemanly enough, they did not bring along their wives. She was as much alone as ever. This same woman had an uncomplimentary view of Crook, whom she blamed for this unfortunate circumstance. "It was very sad to see them all go from here & seemed like old war times. I wish Genl. Crook had been left quietly in Arizona. He has just stirred up a hornets nest here for nothing."[5]

The departures from Fort D. A. Russell occurred in several phases and were preceded by a farewell ball held at the post on the evening of May 17. It was attended by the field-bound officers of the Second and Third regiments, the few officers remaining behind, wives, several of the visiting newsmen, and other guests. The reverie was short lived. Five companies marched from Russell the next morning, followed by two more on May 19, escorting Lieutenant Colonel Royall and First Lieutenant George A. Drew, the Third Cavalry quartermaster. Both movements were accompanied by a martial air provided by the Third Cavalry regimental band, with the ladies of the garrison waving kerchiefs and throwing heartfelt wishes for victory and a safe return. The mule train with its grizzled handlers and the long caravan of wagons departed the depot on May 16 as well, all generally following the well-trodden road north, with mules in the fore, the wagons following, and the cavalry companies keeping to the flanks—all of it rather nonchalant.[6]

Meanwhile, as troops were departing from the nearby post, the newsmen Finerty, MacMillan, and Davenport in Cheyenne were still scurrying about outfitting for the campaign. Horses and kits were readily acquired, but the most pressing need was the securing of messing arrangements with someone at Fort Russell. Crook had instilled that notion in Finerty in Omaha ten days earlier. MacMillan and Davenport, veterans of the Black Hills expedition the previous summer, understood the need plainly. The three were ultimately invited into Captain John Alexander Sutorius's mess. Finerty called Sutorius the "soul of hospitality" and bonded with the worldly, Swiss-born, thirty-nine-year-old almost immediately. Sutorius was something of a character in the Third. He enlisted in the Mounted Rifles in 1854, serving as its chief bugler, and campaigned in the American Southwest in the prewar years, principally against Apaches. A dependable soldier, Sutorius was commissioned a second lieutenant in the Third Cavalry in April 1863 (the Mounted Rifles was redesignated the Third Cavalry in 1861) and in succession served four years as regimental adjutant and two more years as regimental commissary and subsistence officer, and regimental quartermaster, all positions of great responsibility. The witty officer and his Company E were in the thick of business on the campaign. Finerty clearly enjoyed the captain's friendship, quoting him often in his regular reports.[7]

The first day on the trail was a torment for the leading Fort D. A. Russell complement, accompanying although hardly squiring the expedition's mule train and wagons. They all wended their way headlong into a cold springtime deluge. It so soaked the trail that they held over for a day at their first night's camp on Lodge Pole Creek. The weather was only half of the dismay tormenting battalion commander, Captain Mills. In the continuing rain and gloom sixty-five men deserted the camp, taking with them their horses, equipments, and arms. Both cavalry regiments were affected. Most of the deserters headed for Cheyenne and were followed in quick succession by several lieutenants, who scoured the city but apprehended only a few. When Royall heard of this a short while later, he declared that he'd shoot such men deserting almost in the face of the enemy. The episode had a demoralizing effect on the column and caused some to worry: if desertions were such a predicament now, when troops were still so near to civilization, what would be the troopers' dispositions when actually confronting Indians? "That is the general question," noted Finerty. A deserter captured in the sweep by the lieutenants explained that "the men left their colors because it is reported among them that in the event of a battle and defeat the wounded are to be left in the hands of the Indians." This was another of the bitter legacies of the Powder River fight, where a wounded trooper was knowingly abandoned on the field by the commanding officer.[8]

On May 19 Royall and the last of the Fort Russell companies reached the same Lodge Pole Creek camp occupied by Mills's battalion, held over by the inclement weather the day before. Finerty, MacMillan, and Davenport arrived together but separately from the troops, traveling the nineteen miles from Cheyenne on their own. They were warmly welcomed by Sutorius as they entered camp. He introduced the reporters to the two officers of the

Second Cavalry who had accompanied him that day, Captain Elijah R. Wells and Second Lieutenant Frederick W. Sibley of Company E. In Wells Finerty saw a gruff Civil War veteran who had risen from the ranks and was covered with honorable scars. Sibley, Wells's subaltern, was an affable twenty-three-year-old West Pointer with an expressive face, already recognized for heroics on the Powder River battlefield. "It does not take very long to become thoroughly at home with soldiers, if they take a liking to you," remembered Finerty. Around a dinner "of plain military fare" that evening the conversation easily turned to the campaign. Wells was sure that the Indians were stronger than anyone imagined, not the least Crook, "who was accustomed mostly to the southern Indians." Wells noted that Finerty and MacMillan had cropped their hair short and joked that they were cheating the Sioux out of their scalps. After a smoke and strong toddy, Sutorius, "Mac," and Finerty bedded down in blankets and buffalo robes in the captain's wall tent. Finerty's slumber was occasionally disrupted by MacMillan's eternal cough and the captain's profound snore. "Thus opened, for me, the Big Horn and Yellowstone campaign," he wrote.[9]

Five more desertions occurred that night, but on May 20 the principal agenda for Royall's seven companies and the mule train and wagons was advancing on Fort Laramie. On Crook's direction, Royall's column marched by way of Fort Laramie instead of the alternative and slightly shorter cut-off route so that they might cross the North Platte River on the new iron bridge. The North Platte was in its springtime rise, but the new route eliminated a problematic crossing at Fetterman. These were break-in marches of sorts. Many horses were new, and men and mounts unaccustomed to the saddle and trail needed hardening. Reporters needed hardening too, including Finerty. He had unknowingly ridden that first day with short stirrups before discovering that cavalrymen rode with long stirrups that lessened the bump and slap on their rears. Yesterday's mud quickly became today's dust and heat. The men learned to husband water, replenish canteens at every opportunity, and when necessary suck on pebbles to produce saliva. For some the cavalcade was an exhilarating sight. Sketch artist Charles Stanley, riding with the packers, was taken by the casual dress of the troopers, especially in the heat of the day when few wore their blue woolen blouses or much else of a uniform. But for their belts and eagle belt plates, an observer might not have known that these were "members of the cavalry arm of the United States service." Stanley also thought that the gaiety of the column might lead an observer to believe that "there was no thought of care or anxiety in the world."[10]

ııııııııııııııııııııııııııııııı

At Medicine Bow Station, a windy rail stop roughly midway between Laramie City and Fort Fred Steele in south-central Wyoming, other troops began
assembling on May 14. A "summer route" from Medicine Bow connected the
Union Pacific with Fort Fetterman, eighty-five miles directly north by way of
a gentle pass through the Laramie Mountains. The consolidating companies
of the Second and Third Cavalry and Fourth Infantry idled at Medicine Bow
for six days awaiting the arrival of Major Evans from Omaha, plus recruits
and remounts for the cavalry companies. Captain William Stanton, the
department's engineer officer, traveled separately from Omaha to Medicine
Bow. He was accompanied by three infantrymen detailed for the reconnaissance, Privates Henry Kehl, Charles Holtes, and Stephen Bowes, plus
Rochus F. Koehneman, a civilian draughtsman from headquarters. These
otherwise unnoticed assistants tended Stanton's wheeled odometer and other
instruments utilized throughout the early campaign. Captain Azor Nickerson, Crook's chief aide-de-camp, and Private Robert H. Reynolds, another
otherwise unsung individual noted simply as a messenger for Crook and his
aides, also traveled separately from Omaha.[11]

The lone voice recording this assembly and Evans's movement north from
Medicine Bow was Private Louis Zinser of Captain Frederick Van Vliet's
Company C, Third Cavalry. An inquisitive twenty-one-year-old in his first
enlistment in the army, Zinser maintained an extraordinary diary throughout the campaign that focused less on the mundane features of the trail—the
heat of the day, the rivers and waterholes—and much more on the wonders of
geography and the great Indian campaign in which he was now participating.
This fascination is easily apparent when reading his description of the wintery
allure of Elk Mountain, a prominence straight south of their Medicine Bow
camp. He vividly captured, as well, the soldiers' apprehension when shipping
their extra clothing and blankets to Sidney Barracks, when "our trouble will
now begin"; the daily struggle crossing swollen creeks en route to Fetterman
and beyond; and his friends' fear of Indians and relief at finding themselves
in the midst of fifteen companies of cavalry and five of infantry when the
campaign began. Zinser was one of the expedition's exceptional enlisted
men.[12]

Evans's column took four days to make its way from Medicine Bow
Station to Fort Fetterman, where it arrived on May 25. Crook, Bourke,
paymaster Thaddeus Stanton, and Frank Grouard, meanwhile, arrived on
May 21 after leaving Fort Laramie on the eighteenth. Royall's command

had not yet reached Fort Laramie. Major Stanton, traveling with Crook, was working a pay circuit. His small entourage provided security for the general's contingent. The paymaster finished his business at Fetterman and returned to Cheyenne. He had participated in the Big Horn Expedition in March but was not joining this campaign at that time. Unlike Crook's route recommended to Royall, his own route from Fort Laramie followed the North Platte's right (looking downstream) or south bank directly to Fetterman. For the most part the road was open and the many creeks encountered safely crossed, although Bourke noted that waters were almost always high and swift. A storm on May 20 had downed Fetterman's telegraph line, hampering Crook's ability to communicate with the department and division for five days. Still, he busied himself interviewing officers, promulgating orders, overseeing and dispersing troops as they arrived, and superintending the ferrying of stores from the post to the expedition's burgeoning camp on the river's north bank. An impatient Bourke thought it all terribly dull. "I was sensible each day of the oppressiveness of waiting at a frontier post for the arrival of the slowly moving columns and supplies coming up from Fort Laramie and from Medicine Bow."[13]

This was the second occasion (barely months apart) when a great Indian campaign overwhelmed this unpretentious three-company post. By most measures Fort Fetterman was one of dreariest forts in the Department of the Platte, in one reporter's estimation: "in summer, hell, and in winter, Spitsbergen." Established during the closing days of the operation of the Bozeman Trail, which angled northwest from there to the Big Horn Mountains, the fort's humble adobe and log structures sat on a high bench overlooking the confluence of La Prele Creek and the North Platte. Absent a bridge, which never existed in the army's day, crossings of the river relied on a ferry located at the base of the hill or the use of a ford at the mouth of the La Prele. Both were problematical when the river was in its springtime rise. Despite its isolation, the generals recognized Fort Fetterman for its strategic importance because it lay much closer to the heartland of the Northern Indians than Forts Abraham Lincoln and Buford in northern Dakota and Fort Ellis beside Bozeman in western Montana. General Sheridan had long wanted forts in the very heartland of Sioux Country, but that ambition was still a year and several disasters away.[14]

While Crook awaited the arrival of his command and staff, he dispatched Sergeant John Carr and twelve men from Fort Fetterman's lone mounted unit, Company A, Second Cavalry, northward on May 21 to assess stream crossings as far as the Powder River, an issue of concern in this time of heavy spring runoff. Frank Grouard accompanied them. Grouard and Carr were also told to watch for Crow Indians, Crook's much anticipated auxiliaries. The small outing became an instant ordeal. Grouard later explained that the detachment came under Indian surveillance when barely five miles from the North Platte. At the first night's camp they felt so threatened that they devised a ruse to escape, building a big fire, fabricating dummies with their blankets, and slipping away in the dark. Later they heard Indians firing into the dummies. The detail continued on to the Powder, keeping to ravines and hoping to avoid being discovered again. The detachment never reached the river. Again sensing that they were being watched, Carr turned his detail toward Fetterman and rode as quickly as their horses allowed. Grouard followed at some distance and watched Indians trail the soldiers nearly all the way to the fort. "I have always considered that trip as close a call as I ever had," he later told his biographer. Carr found no better route than the old road.[15]

After Crook's departure from Fort Laramie but before Royall's arrival, Laramie's infantry contingent ordered to the campaign (Companies C, G, and H, Ninth Infantry, commanded respectively by Captains Samuel Munson, Thomas B. Burrowes, and Andrew S. Burt) departed on May 22, accompanied by the expedition's medical director, post surgeon Albert Hartsuff. Noyes's Company I, Second Cavalry, followed the next day. As with the departures from Fort D. A. Russell half a week earlier, this was a despondent time. Elizabeth Burt, wife of Andrew Burt, expressed a nearly timeless sentiment: "We wives who were left behind knew the inevitable danger to all in the field. With aching hearts we watched the soldiers march away while the band played 'The Girl I Left Behind Me.' So many times have I listened to that mournful tune played when a command marches out of garrison to take the field. This time we knew so well there was to be fighting to the death."[16]

Meanwhile Royall's slow-moving column of cavalry, pack mules, and nearly one hundred supply wagons reached Fort Laramie early in the afternoon of May 23 and camped along the Laramie River midway between the post and North Platte bridge. Their march was repeatedly hampered by thundershowers that bogged the wagons. Stanley marveled at Fort Laramie, for so long one of the strongest posts in the Department of the Platte, with a reputation, sprawl, and garrison depth dating to the days of the overland migrations to Utah, California, Oregon, and Montana. It was a place of treaty signings and now had renewed importance owing to the Black Hills gold rush. But little of its ordinarily large garrison was present at that time. Four companies had just departed for Crook's camp, Egan's company of cavalry was protecting Black Hills traffic, one of the fort's remaining infantry companies was encamped in the Hat Creek Breaks north of the post, and its lone surviving infantry company divided itself between household chores and escort service. The bustle and sprawl of the post was impressive. But one wag in Royall's column, a sergeant in Company E, Second Cavalry, thought that the neighborhood looked rather bleak, with the soil mostly gravel and growing only prickly pears, rattlesnakes, and prairie dogs.[17]

During Royall's overnight stay much of consequence occurred, some of it immediately evident and more that would unfold as the campaign played out. Interpreter Louis Richard arrived that day from Red Cloud Agency. Richard had interpreted for Crook when he attempted to enlist Oglala scouts for the campaign and was now one of the few mixed-blood participants in the Big Horn Expedition willing to take the field again. Richard carried difficult news from the agency. In all some three thousand Sioux and Cheyenne had defected from there and were preparing to fight Crook. They were well armed, he noted, "with the choicest rifles, and plentifully supplied with ammunition furnished by post-traders." They were gathering, he learned, at a place called Blue Stone, a geographical anomaly in southeastern Montana in the high divide between the Powder and Little Missouri drainages. Others knew the destination as the well-forested Blue Mountains, with the Chalk Buttes on their western margins. Confirming these details was impossible, but by any measure the news as received and forwarded was foreboding.[18]

Royall's arrival brought another round of commotion to the post. Ernest A. Hornberger, a Pittsburgh bookkeeper and would-be Black Hills prospector, was quietly intrigued by it. The twenty-year-old had gone west intent on exploring the new El Dorado, traveling with the sizable so-called Pittsburgh Black Hills Expedition. The party's passing was noted in Cheyenne on April 20, as was its arrival at Fort Laramie, coming in the midst of the bloodletting plaguing the Custer City Road. That chaos was proving too much for the Pittsburgh miners, who elected to abandon their quest at Fort Laramie and return to Pennsylvania. Hornberger was one of the few exceptions. Enthralled with everything he saw and undeterred by the mayhem, he apparently grew infatuated with the martial bustle, with officers and men coming, going, and tending business of every sort. In a letter home later that summer, he commented on the hustle at John Collins's post trader's store, where soldiers and civilians alike filled their kits with necessities and niceties for use on one or another of the trails. He noted reporters darting from Royall's sprawling army camp to John Ford's telegraph office, posting stories to newspapers throughout the land. At some moment during Royall's pause Hornberger changed courses and joined the Indian campaign, perhaps encouraged to do so by one of the newsmen. He had no entrée to the soldier's world but evidently learned that by posing as a newspaper correspondent he might quietly fit in. The similarly uninvited but inquisitive and self-anointed "Captain" Jack Crawford had done precisely the same thing the year before when quietly joining the Dodge Expedition in the Black Hills. Two bona fide newsmen from that affair were now in Royall's camp and may have been Hornberger's counselors. However induced, Ernest Hornberger went to the Indian war and ultimately penned one of the most erudite if brief accounts of the campaign and its great battle on record.[19]

Royall returned to the trail at 6 A.M. on May 24, leading his troops across the North Platte bridge and west on the Old Utah Route, an "unfrequented path" as Finerty remembered. Many in the column believed that in crossing the North Platte River they had entered "hostile ground," a throwback to the days of the 1868 Fort Laramie Treaty that defined, among many things, the vast sweep north of the river as a no-man's-land reserved only as a hunting ground for the Sioux. The trail to Fetterman for the most part was a tortured one, a succession of sandy ruts, difficult hills, monotonous badlands, and long waterless reaches, broken only by the continual sight of the majestic Laramie Peak on the western horizon and occasional Mormon emigrant graves. Elements from the command, including scouts, mail carriers, and several newsmen, advanced ahead of the column and reached Fetterman on May 26. The main force with the mules and wagons arrived at the post the next day and immediately spread onto the plain north of the river. Evans's command from Medicine Bow and the Fort Laramie contingent were already encamped there, having arrived the day before.[20]

The camp of Crook's Big Horn and Yellowstone Expedition was a marvel to behold. No finer description exists than the one penned by the chance correspondent, Ernest Hornberger. Soon after departing Fort Laramie in the traces of but not among the body of Royall's column, Hornberger chanced onto Sylvester Reese, riding alone except for the company of two donkeys and a pony. Reese, a prospector, also intended on joining Crook's command, hoping to prospect the Big Horn country under the expedition's cover. The two agreed to travel together and worm their way into the campaign. They reached Fort Fetterman on May 27 slightly behind Royall's column.

Hornberger crossed the river and climbed his way into the fort. Looking back, he was astounded at what lay off to the north below him:

> I stood upon the hill on which the fort is situated, and had a fine view of the whole scene. Below at the base of the hill on which I was standing rolled the noble Platte river, creeping like a silvery serpent through the green banks on either side. Stretched along the stream, on the other side of the river, in rows, were the white tents of the cavalry and infantry, gleaming and glittering in the bright sunlight. Out on the plains in separate herds were the cavalry horses, wagon and pack mules and beef cattle grazing. Away on the right was the wagon train, corralled, the canvas covers making it look like a white ring lying in the green grass. Near the train was the circle of *aparejos* for carrying the cargo of the pack mules. All through the extended encampment soldiers were hurrying to and fro, making active preparations to leave. On the left was the ferry boat crossing the river at regular intervals laden with freight for the expedition and propelled back and forward by the current of the river. This was run night and day until everything for the expedition had been crossed.[21]

Owing to Sergeant Carr's and Frank Grouard's failure to make a satisfactory survey of the route to Fort Reno on the Powder River and perchance meet up there with the Crow auxiliaries presumably en route or arrived from Montana, Crook on May 27 ordered a second foray in that direction. Carr and Grouard complained of encountering Indians all the while they were afield, so this time Crook dispatched a much stronger squadron, Companies C and G, Third Cavalry, commanded respectively by Captain Frederick Van Vliet and First Lieutenant Emmett Crawford. Both companies were newly arrived with Evans's battalion, having originated at Sidney Barracks, Nebraska. Rations for eight days were carried on mules, and the outfit was guided by Baptiste "Big Bat" Pourier and accompanied by the *Frank Leslie's* sketch artist Charles Stanley. Van Vliet's sole mission was to link up with the Crow allies.[22]

Pourier was the third and final of the Plainsmen from Crook's Big Horn Expedition in March willing to join him again. Crook had thirty such guides on that campaign. The shortage now was a matter of grave concern and drove his obsession with meeting the Crows. Some in the command were already worrying that the Sioux had turned the Crows back. Although Crook at the moment did not know this, Pourier inflamed those fears when Van Vliet's column was barely five miles from the Fetterman camp, informing the captain that there were Indians ahead (implying Sioux) and that they were *immediately* ahead and not a distant abstraction. How do you know this, the captain asked? "Colonel," he replied, "I smell them." But no Indians were encountered. At their second night's camp Van Vliet's troops occupied the same site that Crook's Big Horn Expedition had used on the evening of March 2. Private Zinser of Company C observed that the camp was strewn with soldier clothes and looked like a battleground. In fact, that camp had been attacked by Indians in the wee hours of March 3. The Sioux raiders had successfully driven off the expedition's cattle herd, seriously complicating the rationing of that column for the remainder of its time in the field. For the most part now, however, Van Vliet's sortie was uneventful. No Crows awaited them at old Fort Reno.[23]

At Fort Fetterman Crook and his staff made final preparations for the advance. The Fetterman ferry proved vexatious: its guide cable broke often. Local operators and soldiers detailed from Royall's camp worked tirelessly making repairs and keeping the service on-line. Horses, stores, and men crossed as conditions allowed. The operation was supervised by the post quartermaster, Second Lieutenant Henry E. Robinson, Fourth Infantry, assisted by the post's ordnance sergeant, William McLaughlin, and the expedition's own quartermaster and commissary officers, Captain Furey and First Lieutenant John W. Bubb. Bubb was a line officer in the Fourth Infantry but had served a recent stint as the regiment's quartermaster and knew the role. According to Robert Strahorn of the *Rocky Mountain News*, on May 27 some sixty thousand pounds of commissary stores and forage awaited transfer from the south bank, although six hundred thousand pounds of supplies had already crossed. Army livestock was simply driven into the river and forced to swim to the north bank, but at the cost in one such crossing of a teamster and many animals who drowned.[24]

Ferry crossings served the needs of both banks, of course. By sundown on May 27 most of the stores meant for the campaign were across and either loaded on wagons or shunted to the *aparejo* circles for loading on mules. Once all troops were present, company inspections occurred. Countless personal effects belonging to officers and men were returned to the fort's quartermaster storehouse. Every pound that could be shed was left behind. Trunks and heavy "packages," nineteenth-century parlance for satchels and valises, were not permitted on the trail. Curry combs and brushes were not allowed to the cavalry. As an officer of the Second Cavalry remembered, "the supply of clothing, blankets, and equipage was closely scanned and reduced by an inflexible rule." What remained was packed into wagons, twenty-five of which were allotted to the fifteen cavalry companies and six to the five infantry companies. Emblazoned on canvas tarpaulins in large letters were "D C⁰ 4ᵀᴴ INF," "C C⁰ 3ᴿᴰ CAV," and so forth. Newsman Thomas MacMillan expressed the restrictions another way. He had come from Cheyenne to Fetterman with an array of "traps" and was comfortable, he wrote. But then came the order to cut things "ornamental, useful, and necessary": "with a Colt's revolver in one hand, and a match-box full of clothing in the other, we took the field for the centennial summer campaign against the hostile Sioux." Shedding all but the most essential gear was another quiet dimension of a Crook campaign.[25]

The newsmen seized opportunities to cross the river too, variously introducing themselves, ingratiating themselves with Fetterman's telegrapher, J. A. Steele, on whom they would depend as the campaign progressed, and feeding wire copy to their respective newspapers. The reporters were keenly aware that they were on the brink of a great campaign, as their early stories suggested. Their simple narratives recounting time on the trails from Cheyenne and Medicine Bow, the great camp sprawled across the north bank of the North Platte River, and the bustle of orchestration were already newsworthy and welcomed by their papers. On the fort grounds Finerty of the *Chicago Times* and MacMillan of the *Chicago Inter-Ocean* encountered Crook. The commander was in high spirits, Finerty recalled, and laughed heartily at the reporters' rough and miserably tanned appearance, with stubble beards, dirty clothes, and peeled noses. "This is only the prelude," he teased. Crook invited the pair to dinner but they preferred a meal at Ephraim Tillotson's post trader's store and the general had an orderly guide them there.[26]

Joe Wasson, a Crook acquaintance from Arizona and Oregon now writing for the *Philadelphia Press* and several other newspapers, also found an opportunity to engage the general. Wasson's opening story for the *Press* recounted the larger scheme of the war: with Terry's, Gibbon's, and Crook's combined forces of thirty-one companies of cavalry and about half as many of infantry, Sheridan was fielding the largest regular army force on "one set of Indians" in many years. He allowed, too, that Crook was not particularly optimistic about a successful expedition and already foresaw continued fall and winter campaigning.[27]

Even as Crook invested himself in the organization of the Big Horn and

Yellowstone Expedition, he issued orders deploying additional troops to the Fort Laramie–Custer City Road. Companies of infantry from Fort Bridger and Omaha Barracks were to proceed to Fort Laramie for deployment by Major Edwin F. Townsend, Ninth Infantry, the post's new commander. Townsend in due course sent both companies north, directing one to encamp at the head of Sage Creek, adjacent to the Hat Creek stage station, and the other to establish a camp at the mouth of Red Cañon. With Captain Egan in the field as well, this tripled the army's full-time presence at that treacherous juncture of the Black Hills Road and Indians' Powder River Trail.[28]

Early on May 28 Crook summoned Royall to the quarters of Captain Edwin M. Coates of the Fourth Infantry. Coates, a veteran of the Big Horn Expedition, commanded the post and welcomed Crook as his house guest. There the two senior officers of the new expedition surveyed the composition and general structure of the force and the few remaining details yet to be tended to before a departure on the morrow. Crook was about to issue General Orders No. 1, formally announcing the organization of the Big Horn and Yellowstone Expedition and a prescriptive administrative confirmation of an array of special orders and verbal instructions emanating from the Department of the Platte throughout the month. In the order Royall was announced as commanding the fifteen-company cavalry brigade, while Andrew Evans commanded the ten companies of Third Cavalry and Henry Noyes commanded the five companies of Second Cavalry. Major Alexander Chambers of the Fourth Infantry was announced as commanding the five-company infantry battalion drawn from the Fourth and Ninth Regiments. Nickerson and Bourke were confirmed as aides-de-camp. Captain George M. Randall, Twenty-Third Infantry, was announced as chief of scouts; William Stanton as chief engineering officer; John Furey as chief quartermaster; John Bubb as commissary and subsistence officer; and Albert Hartsuff as medical director. Each of these officers, in turn, had personal staff or access to orderlies and couriers. In due course Evans branched his sizable Third Cavalry command into three battalions, each with its own commander. Neither Brigadier General Alfred Terry marching from Dakota nor Colonel John Gibbon coming from western Montana fielded a comparably strong force. This was distinctly the largest command in the field by May 29.[29]

Officers all along had seen to the proper outfitting of their companies. Access to the quartermaster and ordnance storehouses at Fetterman provided a last opportunity to ensure completeness, as Crook reminded them. *Leslie's* artist Charles Stanley caught an impression of the troops early in the march from Fort D. A. Russell, mentioning belts and eagle belt plates, blue blouses, canvas jackets, "wide rimmed gray sombreros," and trousers decorated with "foxings of heavy ducking." The articles of clothing on campaign—trousers, blouses, pullover shirts, underwear, boots, overcoats—were typically as issued by the quartermaster department or commonsense substitutes accepted by company officers who understood matters of practicality and functionality in the field. In addition to standard-issue wear, old pattern uniforms, civilian shirts, and a variety of wide-brimmed hats were always acceptable and available, as were issue kersey trousers reinforced with heavy canvas duck. An individual's equipment amounted to a single blanket, shelter half, poncho, haversack, canteen, tin cup, simple utensils, cartridge belt or box, and for cavalry also a carbine sling, holster, and pistol box, all standard issues from the Quartermaster and Ordnance Departments. In reality this was a rather uniform army, perhaps not quite as flashy as John Ford's Hollywood cavalry would one day be or quite as nonconforming as Stanley suggested.[30]

In matters of weaponry, troops carried standard-issue firearms without exception. Infantrymen handled single-shot breech-loading .45 caliber Springfield rifles, while mounted troops carried comparable .45 caliber Springfield carbines and .45 caliber Colt revolvers. Oddly, on the Big Horn Expedition in March, only one of ten cavalry companies carried a revolver, a situation grounded in worries at the start over the unwieldiness of pistols buried in cumbersome winter wraps. That was not an issue on this campaign, although grumblings about revolvers persisted. William C. Rawolle of the Second Cavalry, a veteran of Crook's first two campaigns in 1876, groused some years later that revolvers should be abandoned by the cavalry. A soldier would do better "to carry its weight in carbine ammunition," he wrote. "I look upon it as a useless weapon liable to do much mischief." No infantryman carried a bayonet, no cavalryman carried a saber, and no infantry officer but one is known to have carried a sword. Furthermore, no national or regimental flags fluttered in the breeze, and Crook and Royall had no designating flags. Some evidence suggests that Crook's cavalry may have carried guidons, but whether for company or battalion designation is unclear. That small detail aside, for Crook, cutting baggage meant packing and leaving behind the superfluous of every sort.[31]

Early in the morning of May 29 Crook received a troubling telegram from Townsend at Fort Laramie informing him of Egan's brush with seven or eight hundred Indians on May 7 along Sage Creek, in the shadows of the Hat Creek Breaks. Crook had come close to that crossing when returning from Camp Robinson. Egan continued on to Robinson and learned there that nearly a thousand young warriors had departed from the two Pine Ridge agencies. That comported closely with news delivered by Louis Richard to Fort Laramie on May 23, which in turn was hand carried by Royall to Crook at Fetterman (the telegraph line was then down) and confirmed subsequently in a face-to-face meeting with Richard on May 28. It must have appeared to Crook and his staff that the entire Sioux Nation had abandoned the agencies and was making its way to the camps of Sitting Bull and Crazy Horse, a situation more fatefully true than Crook could possibly grasp.[32]

May 29 was departure day for the Big Horn and Yellowstone Expedition. Organized chaos overcame the already bustling camp as harness mules were hitched and supply wagons aligned for the road. Tents were struck and stowed along with other camp gear on assigned company wagons, which also then joined the train. In all the expedition tallied one hundred wagons driven by as many teamsters and pulled by six hundred mules. The train carried some 350,000 pounds of stores and ordnance matter, including 300,000 rounds of .45 caliber carbine and rifle ammunition, .50 caliber rifle ammunition, and a large store of revolver ammunition. The wagons were in the charge of Charles Russell, the expedition's master of transportation, who was assisted by ten wagon masters. Three ambulances carrying hospital stores, the two ponton boats loaded with tackle, and several smaller vehicles, including a wheeled odometer in engineer Stanton's charge, also joined the train, driven by enlisted men. Separately Thomas Moore and five assistant packmasters managed five pack trains of 320 mules loaded with 64,000 pounds of freight, with their own distinctive corps of handlers, seventy-five strong. An officer corresponding with the *Cincinnati Commercial* told his readers that Crook's wagons and mules carried subsistence enough to ration the command until August 1 and grain enough to sustain the expedition's animals until about June 15.[33]

Also supporting the new expedition were a few civilian auxiliaries beyond the teamsters and packers. While Crook's cadre of scouts was limited initially pending the arrival of Crow and Shoshone auxiliaries, three stalwart veterans of the Big Horn Expedition had agreed to join him again. Several had been of assistance already. Foremost among them was Frank Grouard. Crook first met Grouard at Fort Laramie on February 25 when interviewing prospective scouts for his initial campaign. Grouard was a Plainsman of the first order. His mixed-blood, dark-skinned heritage allowed him to pass as an Indian (although he was in fact a Pacific Islander). He wore his hair braided, was perfectly fluent in the Sioux language, and had long lived in the northern Sioux camps, including with Sitting Bull himself and also with He Dog, one of Crazy Horse's closest friends. The Sioux called him Grabber. Grouard knew the people and the land. This familiarity endeared him to Crook, who embraced the talkative twenty-four-year-old as one of his most trustworthy advisors. The entire story of the Powder River battle on March 17 turned on intelligence provided by Grouard, whose role had been critical.[34]

Crook also retained the services of Louis "Louie" Richard, a true mixed-blood interpreter of French and Oglala parentage. The thirty-year-old had already figured widely in affairs between the government and the Sioux, interpreting at Fort Laramie during the treaty proceedings there in 1868 and during the fractious Black Hills purchase negotiations in 1875, serving among the scouts of the Big Horn Expedition in March, and most recently interpreting at Camp Robinson when Crook attempted to recruit Oglalas. Richard's open participation in the first expedition had so irked Red Cloud Agency Sioux, however, many of whom already despised him for his part in the Black Hills business, that he relocated his family from the Pine Ridge to Fort Laramie following that campaign. Moreover, Grouard and Richard were competitive. On the Tongue River before the Cheyenne village was discovered in March the two nearly came to blows when arguing the locations of Indian camps. In fact, both men were correct in their views, but Crook sided with Grouard. Still, when Crook challenged Grouard at Fort Laramie to hire local scouts, he immediately turned to Richard, "one of the best men [he] knew."[35]

The third scout engaged with the new expedition was "Big Bat" Pourier, another veteran of the Big Horn Expedition. Born and educated in Saint Charles, Missouri, of French parentage, the thirty-two-year-old had come west in 1857, eventually making his way into the employ of John Richard Sr., scion of the sprawling Richard clan. Pourier married one of Richard's daughters, making him Louie's brother-in-law. Freighting for Richard Senior took Pourier up the Bozeman Trail to the Montana goldfields in the 1860s. Later he worked as a hunter at Fort C. F. Smith on the Big Horn River and was among those engaged in the infamous Hayfield Fight in 1867. More recently Pourier had been employed as an interpreter at Fort Laramie. His fluency in the Crow, Sioux, and Cheyenne languages and his familiarity with the Montana Road endeared him to Crook and explains why he accompanied Captain Van Vliet's squadron to old Fort Reno on May 27 to rendezvous with the anticipated Crow auxiliaries.[36]

Several additional civilians with the expedition are noted, including Dick Simmons and Ben Arnold, both signed on as couriers. Each was familiar with the Montana Road and regularly carried mail between Fetterman and Crook's camp once the expedition started. Maintaining reliable communications between the post and field was both a desired condition and a significant challenge almost from the start.[37]

One individual who did not make it to Fort Fetterman in time for the commencement of the campaign was Doctor Valentine T. McGillycuddy, a citizen physician. McGillycuddy had accompanied the Dodge Expedition to the Black Hills in 1875, where he was chiefly employed as a topographer. He spent the winter in Washington drawing maps for the War Department. On May 25 the army's surgeon general, Brigadier General Joseph K. Barnes, ordered him to Crook's command. By then, of course, the troops of the Big Horn and Yellowstone Expedition were nearly fully assembled at Fort Fetterman. Despite McGillycuddy's diligence in traveling from Washington to Omaha, Cheyenne, and Medicine Bow, he did not reach Fetterman until June 13. By then it was prudent to await conveyance to the expedition in a subsequent movement of supplies or troops. Meanwhile McGillycuddy was the houseguest of Captain Joseph R. Gibson, Fort Fetterman's post surgeon. Both would play critical roles in coming events.[38]

One individual chose the campaign over exercising four months' leave, with permission, as the military commonly expressed it, "to go beyond the sea." First Lieutenant Henry Seton of Captain Avery Cain's Company D, Fourth Infantry, nominally stationed at Fort Fred Steele, Wyoming, joined at the last minute and served as adjutant for Major Chambers's infantry battalion.[39]

Before departing, Crook had one final exchange with Sheridan, passing on the essences of Egan's report on the defections from the Pine Ridge agencies and announcing the imminent departure of the expedition. Nickerson relayed this same information to the department. Sheridan, in turn, announced his intention to order the Fifth Cavalry into the war, sending them to duty in Wyoming to stem Indian traffic on the Powder River Trail. At the least Sheridan could finally be comforted knowing that the three offensive columns that he had so long visualized as waging this war against the Sioux were finally afield, intending, he presumed, to bring this Indian war to a swift and satisfactory conclusion.[40]

THE NORTHERN INDIANS
AND THE GREAT ASCENDANCY

From afar the smoldering Indian village on the Powder River represented nothing but chaos and death. Before the soldiers rode away that afternoon of March 17, they had toppled and set ablaze all but one of the 105 smoke-stained skin and canvas tipis and brush wickiups scattered across that timber-mantled floodplain. Nearly everything was destroyed: lodges, robes, blankets, meats, clothing, cultural finery, gunpowder, fixed ammunition. Anything that might burn, even items lying randomly about outside the lodges (saddles, meat racks, firewood piles, spare tipi poles propped in the crooks of cottonwoods), was thrown onto the flames. All was reduced to ashes. Only one tipi remained standing when the soldiers rode away, the lodge of a blind old woman. Somehow the soldiers had not killed her. They knew that she was there and a few had even talked with her but then simply went away.

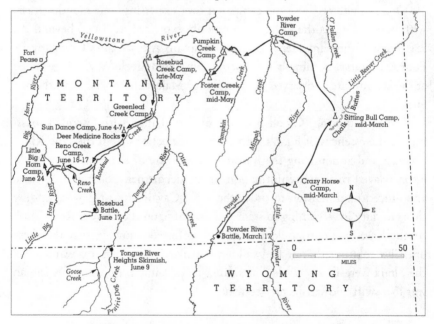

2. Northern Indian Ascendancy, March–June 1876

During the attack that morning, the people driven from Old Bear's North-ern Cheyenne camp did what was necessary to survive. Women, children, and old people fled the scene, mostly rushing north across the snowy bottoms and then into the high breaks west of the river. Warriors protected their flight and then returned to the margins of the village, where they took advantage of high ground to the west and poured a continuous desultory fire onto the bluecoats until the soldiers gave up the fight. After the white soldiers had gone away, many of the people returned to the smoldering camp and scoured their burned-over homesites for anything that might somehow have survived. They found little. The people camped nearby that night, hungry, cold, and destitute.

The next morning the camp's Cheyenne elders (Old Bear, Box Elder, and Black Eagle) led their people north, guided by the Oglala He Dog, whose people were also in the camp and who knew the way to Crazy Horse's vil-lage. Almost everyone walked. A few old people rode horses, but most of the camp's ponies had been driven off by the soldiers. For three days He Dog led the impoverished Cheyennes north following the Powder and then veered to the Little Powder River, an eastern tributary. On the morning of the fourth day, March 21, they made their way into Crazy Horse's camp, located on a bench above the Little Powder. The venerable warrior was shocked. His peo-ple streamed forth to greet the cold, gaunt, and half-clothed refugees, calling out: "Cheyennes, come and eat here." Soon in every tipi women were roasting fresh meats or boiling nutritious broths, while families distributed clothing, blankets, and robes. "The Oglalas received us hospitably, as we knew they would," remembered the Cheyenne warrior Wooden Leg. But in truth the Oglalas had little to spare. It was a small camp with many forlorn people, but this was also no time for parsimony.[1]

On the evening of the Cheyennes' arrival, Crazy Horse hosted a coun-cil of headmen and listened intently to stories of the distress brought on at Powder River. Less than a week earlier these people had been heeding the government's call to come to an agency and thus stay out of this war. Their declared home was the Red Cloud Agency in the Pine Ridge, alongside their Oglala friends. But they had made it only as far as that place on the Powder where they were attacked. When the Cheyennes had said their piece, the great war chief offered a careful response: "I am glad you are come. We are going to fight the white man again." Cheyenne Kit Fox Society chief Two Moon, a spokesman for this people, agreed. "All right, I am ready to fight," he said. "I have fought already. My people have been killed, my horses stolen; I am satisfied to fight."[2]

The assembled Oglalas and Northern Cheyennes agreed that their combined bands did not possess sufficient food, weaponry, and munitions to withstand another attack by soldiers and that they must travel together to Sitting Bull's Hunkpapa camp and achieve a much larger and more sustaining alliance. Kate Big Head remembered that the Cheyennes rested for several days before Old Bear's and Crazy Horse's people set off together for help. War had come to the Northern Indians, in a day of infamy at Powder River and a day of resolve on the Little Powder.[3]

<hr />

Inherent to an understanding of the origins and outlook of the so-called Northern Indians is a simple grasp of the geography of Sioux Country in the mid-nineteenth century. By the time of the great Fort Laramie Treaty of 1851, sometimes called the Horse Creek Treaty because it was actually signed along the banks of that little stream thirty miles east of the fort, the notions of southern Teton tribes and northern Teton tribes had great currency, especially in the world of the fur traders. Unlike treaty commissioners, the fur traders lived among and cultivated lasting relationships with the plains tribes with whom they were engaged, including the Sioux. Traders knew who lived where, tribe by tribe, band by band, in the vast Sioux Country, at its greatest extent spanning from the Missouri River westward to the Big Horn Mountains and from the Platte River in the south all the way north to Canada. Central to the Sioux universe were the Black Hills and the great northern buffalo herd (and for some Sioux the herd on the central plains as well).[4]

When government commissioners negotiated the 1851 treaty they outwardly acknowledged lands occupied by the Sioux (at least as they understood such matters), defining a Sioux homeland that included the Black Hills and the prairielands adjoining to the east, west, and south. Their definition rather neatly described the lands of the southern Tetons, particularly the Oglalas, Brulés, and Sans Arcs, people for the most part participating in the treaty proceedings that summer. But the commissioners failed to acknowledge as Sioux Country the prairielands north and northwest of the Black Hills, in part because the Hunkpapas and Blackfeet Sioux who occupied that range were not engaged at Fort Laramie. These were people of the north, before the notion of Northern Indians had any currency. The Fort Laramie proceedings amounted to an affair of the south. The treaty commissioners rather blindly labeled most of the landscape of the northern Sioux as the country of the

Crows, a smaller tribe that shared and contested that enormously rich buffalo range.[5]

The northern Sioux were consciously detached all along. Their relationships with the traders were never good. A generation of conservative chieftains like the Hunkpapa leader Little Bear outwardly despised white people. The traders knew that it was never safe to enter their camps or establish wintering houses near them. The southern Tetons, meanwhile, contended with the manifestations of contact, the ultimate objective of the 1851 treaty. They grappled with soldiers, overlanders, diseases, and conflict, and all in plain view of the northern people who contemplated this price of interaction.[6]

By the mid-1860s a new generation of Lakota headmen contended with the actions and decisions of their forbearers. By then other conflicts had spawned yet another great treaty, but many of the northern Tetons ignored that one too. They rejected participation in the proceedings again convened at Fort Laramie and every notion and aspiration of the document—a Great Sioux Reservation, agencies, schooling, husbandry—while ever more zealously embracing a traditional lifeway centered on buffalo and occurring as far from whites as possible.[7]

When war came in 1876, the homeland of these tradition-bound Tetons was the remote center of the greater Sioux Country of old, spanning the Little Missouri River in Dakota west through the Lower Yellowstone Basin to the Big Horn River. Included also was the land immediately north of the Yellowstone: the so-called Big Open, nestled between Montana's Musselshell, Yellowstone, and Missouri Rivers and itself inherently rich in buffalo. So were the drainages of the Powder, Tongue, Rosebud, and Little Big Horn Rivers. If this subsection of Sioux Country, the homeland of fervent, tradition-minded Indians, had a stronghold, it was the Powder River, particularly its lower extent. For the Indians who embraced it most, the Powder River country was rich. The river flowed through the heart of the game country. It offered reliable water and wide bottoms for camping and safety and was crowned by timber in its high country. The geographic center of this unique Indian universe would be today's Broadus, Montana, and everything surrounding it for 150 miles or more. This was the location of the Northern Indians in the late 1860s and early 1870s and most certainly during the long course of the Great Sioux War.[8]

It would not be correct, however, to suggest that all traditionalists were averse to visiting the agencies from time to time, particularly when arms and munitions were dispensed to enable the buffalo hunting sanctioned by the

1868 treaty. Some traditionalists even wintered at the agencies, eating white people's food and collecting arms, tobacco, blankets, and other utilitarian wares. But they also flocked to the Powder and Yellowstone countryside whenever they saw fit. Gall, the well-known Hunkpapa, was typical. He and his people were at the Standing Rock Agency in midwinter of 1875–76 when he learned of the government's ultimatum to the Northern Indians to submit at an agency by January 31, 1876, or be turned over to the army, which would force their submission. Gall quietly traded agency rations for metal cartridges and led the majority of his people, some eighteen or twenty lodges, west to join Sitting Bull. Variations of this held true for many others. Summer roamers, people more consciously bound to the agencies, traveled west to the buffalo country, too, to hunt or join the traditional summer gatherings at Sun Dance time. Reservation agents were well familiar with this back and forth travel and for the most part paid it little heed. In any case as the Indian Office understood it in early February 1876, the die-hard Northern Indians numbered only a few hundred warriors and were not united.[9]

Upon learning of the Interior Department's ultimatum to the Northern Indians, the chiefs and headmen in the Powder and Tongue River camps questioned or scoffed at the notice. Many simply rejected it out of hand. Few were treaty people. Instead they were Indians deeply committed to the old ways. They saw themselves as living a good deal better than the agency people. They were healthier, were better fed, suffered no epidemics, and lived at no expense or seeming consequence to the government. Some were wary of the couriers, certainly, viewing them as nothing but spies for the army. Others were puzzled, allowing that they were in the north hunting buffalo, a right guaranteed by treaty. Some, however, were threatened and wanted no part of the army or a war and concluded among themselves that complying with the summons was a prudent measure. Old Bear, himself a fervent traditionalist and a Northern Cheyenne Old Man Chief, along with Box Elder, Black Eagle, and other leading chieftains, decided to come in. They were leading their people from their wintering place on a middle reach of the Tongue River to Red Cloud Agency when Reynolds found them on the Powder on March 17. That day the war came to the Northern Cheyennes.[10]

The land of the Northern Indians that winter was speckled with camps, not very many in all and none particularly large except perhaps one. A small band of Miniconjou Sioux under Lame Deer spent the winter on the lower Tongue, part of the time harassing the small Fort Pease trading post, constructed in June 1875 on the Yellowstone opposite the mouth of the Big Horn

River chiefly to engage the Crow Tribe. The white occupants, mostly from Bozeman, fell under a relentless Indian siege almost from the start, eventually necessitating relief by troops from Fort Ellis just as Crook's first column was making its way north from Fort Fetterman. For some in the northern camps, this direct military intervention into the Lower Yellowstone country, coming so immediately in the wake of the Interior Department's ultimatum, foreshadowed the coming war.[11]

Not all of the Northern Cheyennes aligned with Old Bear when he left the Tongue for Red Cloud Agency. Most of the Cheyenne traditionalists had spent the early part of the winter on Otter Creek, a principal tributary of the Tongue, before moving downstream and camping alongside the Oglalas, their traditional allies. Others wintered near the mouth of Prairie Dog Creek on the Tongue. Wooden Leg remembered how Cheyenne people were always coming and going, their camps varying from thirty or forty lodges to two hundred or more. Some eighty Cheyenne lodges followed Old Bear to the Powder River. Most of the others remained near the Oglalas, with a few joining the Miniconjous as they bedeviled the traders at Fort Pease. When Crook's troops crossed into Montana in mid-March and began their descent of the Tongue, they encountered abandoned Indian camps seemingly at every bend of the river, a detail that comports well with accounts of Indian movements during this time.[12]

Crazy Horse and his ally Black Twin, another prominent Oglala war leader and a Bad Face Shirt Wearer, also received the summons. In midwinter they led their followers toward the Black Hills. The influential Black Twin had offered Red Cloud agent James Hastings an assurance that his people would come to the agency in the spring, but for now snow blocked their trail. The combined bands for a while camped in Wyoming along the Belle Fourche River near Bear Lodge Butte, which white people knew as Devil's Tower. Then an ominous event befell the Oglalas. Black Twin died. He was a proud and forceful traditionalist who had never visited an agency. Of late, however, his views were moderating, much in the vein of Chief Red Cloud, another Oglala who had done much the same in the years since the Bozeman Trail War. With Black Twin's death, a voice of pragmatism and influence was stilled, and Crazy Horse was freed from the prospect of appearing at an agency, if that indeed was their true course. Whatever their intentions may have been, Crazy Horse now turned his people north, away from the agency, and led them across the divide between the Belle Fourche and into the valley of the Little Powder.[13]

The combined camps of Old Bear's Northern Cheyennes, He Dog's Oglalas, and Crazy Horse's adherents spent three days making their way to Sitting Bull's village, located directly north in the lee of the Chalk Buttes, a striking white columnar sandstone formation on the high divide east of the Powder. Their movement was ordered and deliberate from the start: the Cheyennes, a people wronged and asking for help, were in the lead, followed by the Oglalas, supporting and protecting the beleaguered.[14]

That winter Sitting Bull and the Hunkpapas had camped at the mouth of the Powder until early in the new year. There they received the threatening ultimatum from a Standing Rock courier. Four other small Indian bands were scattered up the Powder, including Black Moon's small camp of Hunkpapas, and four more bands on the Little Missouri River, the next major drainage to the east. In late February or early March Sitting Bull led his followers to the Little Missouri, likely intent on aligning those camps with his own. He almost at once returned to the west, eventually reaching the striking pine-timbered highlands known to some as the Blue Mountains, with the Chalk Buttes framing its western side. There Crazy Horse, He Dog, and Old Bear found the great Hunkpapa spiritual leader Sitting Bull, "a philosopher among Indians." It was then about April 1.[15]

Sitting Bull's Hunkpapas in the Chalk Buttes "more than lived up to the cardinal virtue of generosity." They had a prosperous village of about 150 lodges and provided every critical comfort that the Cheyennes needed, feeding and clothing them, providing robes, tipis, and horses, and even offering one a medicine pipe. "Oh, what good hearts they had," remembered Wooden Leg. "I never can forget the generosity of Sitting Bull's Uncpapa Sioux on that day."[16]

The chiefs and headmen of the growing encampment, which nearly doubled in size with the coming of the Cheyennes and Oglalas, counseled often over the next several days and came to several momentous decisions. At one gathering Two Moon, again speaking for the Cheyennes, told the Hunkpapas of the attack at Powder River, where the women and children were driven into the hills to go hungry and cold, homes were burned, and ponies were stolen. He implored his hosts to "give us arms and horses and we will fight." With little demur, the chiefs agreed to stay together and fight the *wasicu* (big talkers, the Sioux name for white people). Crazy Horse, normally reserved, was outspoken as well. "This is it," he declared in council. He "had never made war on the white man's ground, but . . . he would now strike a blow that would be remembered by those who invaded his country."[17]

The gravity of the moment was unmistakable, and Sitting Bull grasped it. At Powder River the soldiers had mounted an offensive directly threatening the Sioux and Cheyennes in their homeland. This was quite different from the situation when soldiers came to the Yellowstone country with the railroad explorers. This time they had attacked the people themselves. From this camp Sitting Bull sent runners to the scattered camps in the Powder and Tongue River countryside to meet him on the Tongue for a council. He also sent messengers to the agencies to hasten the return of the Northern Indians who had gone there for the winter. He needed their strength in numbers. He knew that the agency people would join him soon enough, coming out as they always did as soon as winter ended. This year they were doubtless inspired by news of the blow at Powder River as well.[18]

It was a desperate time. Many years later Wooden Leg remembered the great Hunkpapa chief's resolve and generosity. "Sitting Bull had come into notice as the most consistent advocate of the idea of living out of all touch with white people," he recalled:

He would not go to the reservation nor would he accept any rations or other gifts coming from the white man government. He rarely went to the trading posts. Himself and his followers were wealthy in food and clothing and lodges, in everything needful to an Indian. They did not lose any horses nor other property in warfare, because they had not any warfare. He had come now into admiration by all Indians as a man whose medicine was good—that is, as a man having a kind heart and good judgment as to the best course of conduct. He was considered as being altogether brave, but peaceable. He was strong in religion—the Indian religion. He made medicine many times. He prayed and fasted and whipped his flesh into submission to the will of the Great Medicine. So, in attaching ourselves to the Uncpapas we other tribes were not moved by a desire to fight. They had not invited us. They simply welcomed us. We supposed that the combined camps would frighten off the soldiers. We hoped thus to be freed from their annoyance. Then we could separate again into the tribal bands and resume our quiet wandering and hunting.[19]

The rest and recovery at the Chalk Buttes lasted about a week, after which the combined camp meandered slowly northward, remaining in the high ground east of the Powder. Wooden Leg deliberately mentioned staying in the "upper regions" before swerving consciously to the northwest. Again the procession was orderly, with the Cheyennes leading, the Oglalas following, and the Hunkpapas now trailing. Cheyenne scouts went far in front looking forward from high points, while young Hunkpapas kept well to the rear, watching for enemies who might be following. The simple duty of the Cheyennes was to locate places with early grass for the ponies. There was no haste in the movement. The daily journeys were short, driven by good grazing opportunities and chances to hunt buffalo. Overnights lasted from a day to sometimes as many as three.[20]

Crazy Horse apparently departed the camp about that time and made his way toward the Black Hills, apparently accompanied by his close friend Little Big Man. Occasions for self-reflection marked Crazy Horse's life. It is questionable whether he traveled as far south as Red Cañon, in the very southwestern margin of the Hills, and enmeshed himself in the Metz party killings, as alleged by his principal biographer. The Metz outrage was plainly associated with Persimmon Bill Chambers, a white outlaw, and his band of cut-throat Indian allies. Crazy Horse's name is never mentioned in that context or anywhere else in that land of mayhem. Still, some time away from the group was entirely in keeping with Crazy Horse's introspective nature, whatever the motive. Little Big Man, however, was not an unknown at Red Cloud Agency and would surface there again very soon.[21]

While still east of the Powder, the allied tribes encountered Lame Deer's band of Miniconjous and then a band of Sans Arcs. Both joined the aggregation, traveling with the procession just behind the Oglalas and ahead of the Hunkpapas. The Miniconjous and Sans Arcs swelled the number of lodges to at least 380. According to Wooden Leg, 50 to 70 of these lodges were Cheyenne, 60 or 70 lodges each were Oglala, Miniconjou, and Sans Arc, and 150 lodges were Hunkpapa. By any measure, this was still a modest collective: 380 lodges by one reckoning or 430 by another, with an aggregate population of some 2,400 to 2,730 people, including 560 to 630 men and not all of them fighters. No wintering traditionalists or summer roamers from the agencies had yet joined these committed Northern Indians.[22]

On today's Sheep Creek the bands "swerved to the northwest," as Wooden Leg recalled, heading to the Powder but still traveling very deliberately. New green grass was beginning to appear. The tribes' ponies, searching greedily for it, were growing stronger by the day. The tribal herds were kept separate, Wooden Leg remembered, with young boys from each tribe guarding their own bands' animals.[23]

Soon after they reached the Powder River, a sixth distinct band of Indians, a small circle of Blackfeet Sioux, joined the assembly. The newcomers camped separately but close to the Hunkpapas and were remembered because of their many extra horses, which they shared generously with the other bands.[24]

While still in the valley of the Powder, a straggle of Santee Sioux also attached themselves to the camp. These followers of the charismatic sixty-one-year-old Inkpaduta, were wandering refugees from an earlier day in Indian-white strife on the northern plains. In recent years this destitute Dakota band had been living in Canada, but perpetually harsh conditions there led to their return to Montana in the fall of 1875, expressly to hunt buffalo. The Santees were a hungry and ragged lot without horses. Instead they relied on dogs, "big dogs," to drag their lodges and few possessions from camp to camp. The Sioux and Cheyennes called the new arrivals the "no clothing people" because of their astonishing impoverishment. Inkpaduta may or may not have intended to join in the war, but one source suggests that these Santees may have been among the Lakotas and Dakotas who had received a runner from Sitting Bull's camp. However motivated, these fifteen small lodges of Santees aligned with the Northern Indians who welcomed them and assisted in their well-being, as they had with the others. The Santees did not constitute a separate camp circle in the growing alliance but folded in with the Hunkpapas.[25]

While the growing village camped on the Powder, small scatterings of Assiniboine Indians and Brulé Sioux, apparently not more than a lodge or two of each, joined the throng. The Assiniboines folded in with the Hunkpapas and the Brulés with the Oglalas. Five Yanktonai Sioux also joined the camp there: Thunder Bear, Iron Bear, Long Tree, Medicine Cloud, and Medicine Cloud's wife. They had come from Old Fort Peck and may have traveled with the Assiniboines. Most notable of the continuing arrivals was Lame White Man and some ten lodges of Southern Cheyennes, who had come out late in the winter from the White River in the Pine Ridge expressly looking for Old Bear's people. In their search they wandered along the Powder and the headlands of the Tongue and Rosebud then doubled back and found the trail on the east side of the Powder. Lame White Man and his followers had long aligned with the Northern Cheyennes but had not yet heard of the Powder River battle. Lame White Man, a chief in the Elkhorn Scrapers warrior society, was regarded as a fierce warrior. He and his people joined the Northern Cheyenne circle.[26]

The arrival of the small band of Blackfeet Sioux, fifteen humble lodges of Santees, the scattering of Assiniboines and Brulés, and ten lodges of Southern Cheyennes added nearly another thirty-five lodges to the growing camp, which now swelled to at least 415 tipis. Determining the camp's population is challenging. The record is silent, for instance, on the number of Blackfeet lodges that joined, remembered for delivering a surplus of horses and forming an independent camp circle. For reckoning purposes ten Blackfoot lodges are counted. There is no firm sense of how many Santees accompanied Inkpaduta, although the number of fifteen small lodges occurs repeatedly. Likewise, it is unknown how many Assiniboines and Brulés joined the camp, but their numbers appear trifling. Accepting the tally of 415 lodges, the camp's population now approached 2,640 people, with some 610 men, although again not all of them were fighters. It was near the end of April.[27]

With grasses in the bottoms and hillsides greening in the increasingly warm days and the ponies growing ever stronger, the camp commenced a slow movement westward from the Powder through rolling uplands until it reached and followed Pumpkin Creek to its confluence with the Tongue. The village camped two or three times en route, with individual circles established at each place. "It was the taking down, moving and setting up again every day of a little city," Wooden Leg later remembered.[28]

The village camped in the broad open Tongue River–Pumpkin Creek confluence for several days, a location barely thirteen miles from the Yellowstone. The place was of particular note because raiders, likely from the village, stole horses in the wee hours of May 3 from Colonel John Gibbon's infantry and cavalry camp sprawling in the vicinity of Fort Pease. The loss of an American horse and mule and thirty-two Crow ponies was a perplexing blow for the soldiers, who had not yet encountered any Northern Indians and did not do so then, aside from discovering telltale evidence after their animals disappeared. Sitting Bull and the headmen in the Indian camp were well aware of the presence of these soldiers on the Yellowstone. Wooden Leg remembered that the young men in the camp were anxious to fight them. Instead the chiefs and elders urged all to keep away from the *wasicu*.[29]

While in the Pumpkin Creek camp twelve lodges of Blackfeet Sioux and fourteen lodges of Hunkpapas joined the growing alliance, having come west together from Standing Rock Agency. Much is known about this particular group, including the names of each of the principals in the individual lodges, because the leader of the band, Kill Eagle, a Blackfeet Sioux chief, was interviewed later that summer when returning to Standing Rock. Versions of his story appeared almost immediately in newspapers throughout the land. Kill Eagle was adamant that he had not gone west in response to Sitting Bull's summons to rally and fight but only to hunt buffalo and collect robes and skins for moccasins and lodges. He chanced onto Sitting Bull's encampment, however, which put him in the midst of the growing fury over the independence of the traditionalists and the looming all-out war. Kill Eagle apparently found these matters uncomfortable if not outright distasteful. Nonetheless, the new people were warmly received, feasted, and given presents. How many of the fighting-age men in these twenty-six lodges joined in the battles to come is unclear. But Kill Eagle did not do so, which became a matter of great consternation a month later on the Forks of Reno Creek.[30]

The requirements and security needs of the growing camp kept it in motion. The presence of soldiers on the Yellowstone may have dictated its turn to the south, up the Tongue, where the camp paused for several days at the mouth of Ash Creek and several more days at the mouth of Foster Creek. Both were small affluents entering the Tongue from the east but offered broad confluences that featured scatterings of timber and excellent grazing. Again Wooden Leg provides a clear and nearly unique narrative recounting these day-to-day travels and overnights (one sleep here, two sleeps, three sleeps), accounting for the movement of the Northern Indians well into the middle of May.[31]

At the Foster Creek camp the largest band yet of Northern Indians aligned with Sitting Bull's village. There Black Moccasins, or Dirty Moccasins as Wooden Leg remembered him, led some thirty lodges of traditional Northern Cheyennes into the village. Black Moccasins was another of the tribe's venerable Old Man Chiefs, like Old Bear. His people had come from the Pine Ridge country, traveling the Indians' Powder River Trail straight west to the Powder then down that river through Old Bear's ruined village, over the broad divide separating the Powder and Otter Creek, down Otter to the Tongue, and down the Tongue another thirty or forty miles to this camp. His arrival was noteworthy not only because his nearly thirty lodges plus those of Lame White Man and other stragglers nearly doubled the size of the Northern Cheyenne circle but also because he arrived bearing ammunition, sugar, coffee, and tobacco, welcome staples that were shared with the tribe.[32]

With Kill Eagle's 26 lodges of Blackfeet and Hunkpapas and Black Moccasins' 30 lodges of Northern Cheyennes, Sitting Bull's Northern Indian camp had now grown to nearly 470 lodges, with a population of some 2,995 people, all scattered across six independent tribal circles.

Lured by the news of herds of buffalo west of the Tongue in the broad highlands between that stream and Rosebud Creek, almost certainly delivered by the wolves (scouts) and horse thieves aligned with the traditionalists' village who watched and raided Gibbon's camp on the Yellowstone, Sitting Bull turned the northern people west from Foster Creek toward the Rosebud. They did not move far before encountering buffalo in the headlands of what Wooden Leg called Wood Creek, the first stream of importance west of the Tongue. This small rivulet flows northward to the Yellowstone and is known today as Graveyard Creek. The village camped there for four or five days before continuing on to Sioux Creek (Sweeney Creek today), camping there for one more day. These rolling highlands provided superb grazing for the pony herds and equally splendid hunting. According to Kate Big Head, "We women tanned many skins and stored up much meat." The Cheyennes in particular made a concerted effort to collect a supply of buffalo skins for fabrication into new tipis to replace those lost at Powder River.[33]

In the evenings the chiefs and elders at these camps regularly counseled. The young men remained anxious to run off and fight the soldiers, but the chiefs consistently cautioned against doing so. Fighting wasted energy, they admonished, when instead the camp should be focused on food and clothing, the essences of summer work for Indians caring for themselves. Wooden Leg remembered the moment in treaty terms, telling his biographer: "We were within our treaty rights as hunters. We must keep ourselves so." But few if any treaty people were present, and the traditionalists' caution was probably motivated primarily by the needs for safety and food.[34]

The camp had been discovered, although its inhabitants may not have sensed this. Gibbon's Crow Indian scouts and their dutiful chief of scouts, First Lieutenant James H. Bradley of the Seventh Infantry, had been probing the country south of the Yellowstone River since the time of the horse raid on May 3. Indians presumed to be Sioux were observed watching the soldier camp from time to time. Bradley's probes discovered occasional moccasin tracks and hunting shelters and for a moment the trail of the stolen mule, but nothing substantial came of this until a foray on May 16. Riding into the highlands between the Rosebud and Tongue, the Crows discovered the presence of the Indian village, unseen in the distance but discerned by smoke rising in different columns and hanging as a cloud over the valley far ahead. In between buffalo in constant motion filled the broad foreground for miles. The Crows were sure that Sioux hunters were stirring the animals. Bradley wanted to advance after nightfall and observe the camp close-up, but the Crows convinced him that that would be foolish. Instead, they returned to Gibbon's camp on the Yellowstone, which by now had moved downstream to just above the mouth of Rosebud Creek. Bradley and the Crows had seen only smoke and agitated buffalo, but the news was sobering.[35]

Continued travel interspersed with nearly a week of successful hunting brought the Northern Indians to the Rosebud Valley, where a sprawling camp was established on the creek's east bank barely seven or eight miles below the Yellowstone. The Indians were keenly aware of the nearness of the soldiers on the Elk River, across from and now slightly below the mouth of the Rosebud, but the camp's prime focus remained buffalo hunting. Another great herd dotted the hills west of the creek. There another small band of Northern Cheyennes led by Charcoal Bear, one of the tribe's medicine men and the keeper of its medicine lodge and sacred Buffalo Hat, joined the sprawling village. Charcoal Bear had with him some ten lodges of followers.[36]

The Northern Indians remained at this camp for seven or eight days, hunting buffalo, gathering berries, tanning robes, and fabricating new skin lodges. In the midst of this long pause, the ever-spiritual Sitting Bull departed the camp to pray. From the top of a nearby butte he communed with Wakan Tanka, the Great Mystery, the animating force of the universe. For four days Sitting Bull prayed and meditated, slept and dreamed. In his meditation he saw a great cloud and a coming storm, with high winds, thunder, lightning, and sheets of rain. The storm passed, leaving the cloud intact, then the cloud drifted away too. Sitting Bull returned to camp and told the chiefs of his dream. He was sure that the storm represented soldiers and the cloud represented the Sioux and Cheyenne village. The soldiers would attack, but they would fail. He was sure of it. The Indians would win a great victory.[37]

Indian accounts are generally silent about the soldier camp on the Yellowstone, barely nine or ten miles below their Rosebud village. The Hunkpapa chief Rain in the Face remembered the exuberance of the young warriors, who "were delighted with the prospect of a great fight!" But the elders consistently dissuaded the young men from aggressively striking the soldiers, at least en masse. Even so, wolves from the village paid the *wašicu* careful, even annoying attention, a matter well documented in white sources. The most daring episode occurred on the morning of May 23 when two soldiers and a teamster, hunting without permission several miles upriver from the soldier camp, were ambushed and killed. The teamster's body was found riddled with bullets, one of the soldiers was scalped, and the other had two butcher knives buried deeply in his skull. Two companies of Gibbon's cavalry pursued the attackers, said to be Sioux numbering as many as forty, but the Indian trail vanished.[38]

On other occasions Indians visibly taunted the soldiers from hilltops across the Yellowstone. In one instance a warrior took off his immense feather bonnet and shook it at the soldiers defiantly. In another instance Indians were observed attempting to cross the river, perhaps intent on stealing horses. These sightings so unnerved the troops that the column's twelve-pounder cannon was rolled to the riverbank to repel an attack everyone assumed was eminent, with one infantry company manning the gun and riverbank nightly and the other soldiers ordered under arms from 2 A.M. until broad daylight. Suddenly the Indians completely disappeared.[39]

Sitting Bull's vision of soldiers attacking the Northern Indian village prompted a move up the Rosebud away from Gibbon's camp. These camps were almost always linear in nature. Wooden Leg remembered that the new Hunkpapa circle was some twelve miles from the previous camp and that the Cheyenne circle was a mile and a half south of that, with the other four circles in between. Gibbon's scouts observed this village too. Intent on understanding what had become of the taunting but now nonexistent Indians, Lieutenant Bradley on May 27 led a small contingent of mounted soldiers and Crows in the direction of his previous foray. They quickly came upon the carcasses of freshly killed buffalo and numerous pony tracks sometimes were so dense that they "left a beaten track like a traveled road." Bradley followed that road, keeping more or less to the same high ground from which he had seen the telltale evidence of the camp eleven days earlier. This time peering up the Rosebud Valley, he again spotted the village. Bringing binoculars to bear, Bradley and the Crows plainly observed the camp, with smoke curling from the tops of tipis, entire lodges plainly visible, and black specks—horses—dotting the plain above. Bradley hastened to report his findings to Gibbon, but the colonel made no movement in that direction. Bradley offered no estimation of the village's size, only calling it "immense." Another scout viewing the abandoned camp two weeks later estimated that it held some 400 lodges and from 800 to 1,000 warriors (a modern tabulation suggests perhaps 700 hundred warriors). Gibbon's column then tallied about 350 men.[40]

The Indians spent only one night at this camp and kept moving, first overnighting at a place near what Wooden Leg called Teat Butte and then at Greenleaf Creek, a clean water affluent entering the Rosebud from the south (in this locale Rosebud Creek ran in a northeasterly direction). There Wooden Leg and ten other Cheyennes set out for the Tongue River to hunt and also keep an eye out for soldiers, while many Sioux hunted the hills west of the Rosebud. The Northern Indians remained at this camp for five or six days.[41]

While at Greenleaf Creek, Sitting Bull again wished to pray. He called together his nephew White Bull; Jumping Bull, an adopted brother of Assiniboine blood; and a son of Black Moon, who came along as witnesses. After all four participated in a careful pipe ceremony, Sitting Bull again prayed to Wakan Tanka, asking for food enough for his people and for the safety of his followers. "Do this for me," he prayed, "and I will sun dance for two days and two nights and will give you a whole buffalo." When all had smoked again, he wiped his face with sage and set out for camp. Sitting Bull went hunting and immediately shot three buffalo. The fattest one he staked out for Wakan Tanka, making good his vow, and then began preparations for a Sun Dance.[42]

While the Northern Indians were camped at Greenleaf Creek, the first substantial group of agency Indians joined them. This was a significant development in many ways. For one thing, this group was indeed a sizable body numbering some six hundred people in perhaps ninety or one hundred lodges. For another, they had come straight from Red Cloud Agency in direct response to Sitting Bull's call at the Chalk Buttes camp for the traditionalists to join him, a message carried to these people by Little Big Man, Crazy Horse's friend. Wooden Leg remembered that the new arrivals included some Cheyennes, maybe ten lodges, but were mostly Oglalas and a few Brulés, all following Oglala chief Big Road. This is the same party that included Red Cloud's eldest son, Jack Red Cloud. Also with them were Black Elk and his twelve-year-old son of the same name. Jack Red Cloud was remembered at the agency for having taken his father's engraved Winchester presented to his father by the president at the White House in 1875. These were also the people that Captain James Egan encountered on Sage Creek in early May about when General Crook was attempting to enlist Oglala scouts at Red Cloud Agency. They carried substantial arms and munitions and, more important, brought the dire word that "lots of soldiers are being sent to fight the Indians," a disquieting note plainly remembered years later by the Oglala leader Short Bull, who was there.[43]

The arrivals of Charcoal Bear's 10 lodges of Cheyennes and Big Road's 90 lodges of Oglalas and Cheyennes expanded the camp to at least 570 lodges, bringing its population now to some 3,630 people. By the accepted calculation, the adult male population of the Northern Indian village had swelled to some 840. A few were very old, but most were boys and men of fighting age. It was very early in June.

The arrival of Big Road's Oglalas was a significant moment in the Northern Indian Ascendancy—the coming together of the Sioux people and their allies in this time of war. Sitting Bull's summons of the traditionalists and news of the army's strike at Powder River had a chilling affect among the agency people, whether they were wintering traditionalists or summer roamers. Tempers were already frayed after the unsuccessful Black Hills purchase negotiation the preceding fall, followed as everyone could plainly see by the continued invasion of the gold country by miners. Systemic food shortages at the agencies and the paucity of local game contributed to the anxiety. So did the agency traders' embargo on the sale of arms and ammunition, much-needed commodities if agency people were to hunt to support themselves when issues of government cattle and flour fell short. Agents who in the past had paid little heed to the outflow of people from the agencies now watched and reported with concern, sometimes understanding the circumstances and sometimes obfuscating.[44]

Each of the principal reservation agents reported these circumstances quite differently that year. Henry W. Bingham, agent at Cheyenne River, explained it plainly in his annual report to the commissioner of Indian Affairs—as he saw it anyway. "It must be remembered that the whole Sioux Nation is related," he wrote, "and that there is hardly a man, woman, or child in the hostile camp who has not blood relations at one or the other of the agencies. It is therefore not at all surprising that a certain amount of sympathy should exist between the two parties, and that they should feel anxious to visit each other."[45]

Standing Rock agent John Burke acknowledged the departure of Kill Eagle for the "hostile camp" in his report and conceded that a few others, not more than a hundred, had also gone west, chiefly "for the sake of trade, novelty, and curiosity, without any hostile intentions." He may only have been deluding himself. Sitting Bull and Gall were Hunkpapa, and this was the Hunkpapa agency. But neither chief registered in Burke's sensibility. In the case of the recalcitrant Sitting Bull, Burke's obfuscation was perhaps understandable. In the case of Gall, Burke was being coy. Gall was reasonably visible at Standing Rock. Burke's report, like Bingham's, reflected the patent unease at his agency, which he described as a place of utter helplessness, hopeless farming, and the constant influence brought to bear on local residents from the Sitting Bull camp.[46]

Agent Edwin A. Howard at the Spotted Tail Agency in the White River country conceded that a number of "dissatisfied Indians have quietly disappeared from here" but went on to write in his annual report that the Brulés were peaceable and open to the progress of civilization. Howard could not bring himself to acknowledge that this condition was largely attributable to the influence of the leading Brulé chief, Spotted Tail, a pragmatic Indian in this most difficult time.[47]

Agent James Hastings at the Red Cloud Agency was the frankest of them all and also the most irascible. His annual report described the agency as a hotbed of discontent, the center of unease over the Black Hills question, with failures in agriculture and problems associated with managing three tribes (the Sioux, Cheyennes, and Arapahos) at one agency. Hastings did not help his cause by persistently advocating the removal of his charges to the Indian Territory, a notion utterly abhorrent to these three tribes. Hastings's report for 1876 was the shortest of all those originating on the Great Sioux Reservation that year. He was also the least willing to acknowledge the departures and defections under way, even when others around him saw them so plainly. After Captain Egan's encounter with Big Road's Oglalas in early May, he continued on to Camp Robinson and learned from the commanding officer there that the Red Cloud Agency was nearly deserted. This situation was confirmed by Lieutenant Colonel Wesley Merritt, Ninth Cavalry, who personally investigated the matter for General Sheridan. In a report on June 7 Merritt told Sheridan that between fifteen hundred and two thousand Indians had left there since May 10. "The agent is inclined to under estimate those who have gone," he asserted.[48]

If the reservation agents were circumspect about departures from their agencies, local and regional newspapers told a different story. A note coming by way of Sioux City told of Miniconjous around Fort Sully "leaving the reservation daily, ostensibly to hunt game, but really to go on the war path and hunt for the scalps of Black Hills pilgrims." The *Cheyenne Daily Leader* and *Laramie Daily Sentinel* also highlighted such news, informing their readers in mid- and late May of eighty lodges that left Red Cloud "in the past ten days," ten more "three days ago," and three thousand ready to fight it out and presently rendezvousing on the Blue Stone, a stream emptying into the Yellowstone in Montana. While scrambling the numbers and Sioux War geography somewhat, the newspapers outlined the rudiments of the Great Ascendancy without realizing it.[49]

||||||||||||||||||||||||||||||||||

Several days after Big Road's Oglalas joined the Northern Indians, the village moved up Rosebud Creek another eleven miles, close to a place renowned ever after as the great Sun Dance camp. This locale was noted for its scattering of white sandstone monoliths dotting the side hills of the Rosebud Valley. One of them was the Deer Medicine Rocks, known as the Written Rock by the Hunkpapas, the Painted Rocks by the Cheyennes, and the Rock Belonging to the Black Tail Deer by the Miniconjous. Deer Medicine Rocks had numerous Indian etchings in stone of birds, animals, and spirit beings memorializing and interpreting the Indian cosmos. The valley was wide here. The Northern Cheyennes again led the procession from Greenleaf Creek to this place, spreading their circle on the west side of the Rosebud about a mile below the Deer Medicine Rocks. The Hunkpapas were again last in the procession and camped on the east side of the creek a mile below the Cheyennes. The other four tribal circles filled the gap.[50]

Fulfilling his vow for the favor asked of Wakan Tanka, Sitting Bull organized his Sun Dance here. The Hunkpapas laid out a dance circle on a bench alongside the creek near their circle and pitched a sacred medicine lodge just north of their camp. They cut a straight cottonwood tree and planted it at the center of the circle, with its trunk peeled to a high fork and its leafy top branches left entwined. Rawhide cutouts of a buffalo effigy and a human were tied to branches along with other sacred objects and offerings. A brush arbor made of willows encircled the dance ground, providing shelter from the sun for observers and others involved in the elaborate rituals associated with the ceremony and dance. This was a Hunkpapa Sun Dance only, but people from every camp watched and prayed during the course of preparation and the days that followed.[51]

Usually candidates for the Sun Dance ritual were tethered by rawhide ropes tied high in the tree. This time Sitting Bull meant to sacrifice his flesh in a different manner. After purification in a sweat lodge he entered the dance circle and sat facing the sun, with his back leaning against the pole and his legs outstretched. At the appropriate moment Jumping Bull came to Sitting Bull's side and began lifting and cutting pieces of flesh the size of match heads from his forearms, fifty pieces from each. Bleeding profusely, with his arms swelling painfully, Sitting Bull cried out in supplication and sacrifice. And then he danced for two days, with neither a morsel of food nor a drop of water passing his lips. Observers were mesmerized. The ritual came to an end on the morning of the third day, when Sitting Bull stopped his dance and stood facing the sun. It was as though he had fainted, although he did not drop to the ground. His helpers White Bull, Jumping Bull, and Black Moon eased him down. One sprinkled water on him. In a while he opened his eyes and told of a dream.[52]

In a quiet voice Sitting Bull described for Black Moon the vision that had come to him while he faced the sun. Black Moon in turn relayed it to the thronging observers. Sitting Bull had seen soldiers and horses, numerous as grasshoppers, bearing down on an Indian village. Both men and animals came upside down, with their feet in the sky, their heads to the earth, their hats falling off. "These soldiers do not have ears," the dream proclaimed. "They are to die, but you are not supposed to take their spoils."[53]

Word of Sitting Bull's vision passed quickly through the camps and made a powerful, if disturbing, impression on all who heard it. The vision was interpreted as an impending fight that the Indians would win against an enemy that did not listen, that had no honor. It further outraged the Northern Indians who had been gathering since Old Bear's refugees descended on Crazy Horse's camp in March, and they in turn descended on Sitting Bull. Soldiers were already known to be on the Yellowstone River. Big Road, Little Big Man, and others foretold of soldiers organizing again from the south. Kill Eagle may well have reported on soldiers organizing on the Missouri River. The great prophesy carried compelling immediacy. Blue coats would fall upside down into an Indian camp. But this, Sitting Bull assured them, would not be another Powder River.[54]

THE ROAD NORTH

By all measures George Crook organized an impressive campaign. The new Big Horn and Yellowstone Expedition officially departed from Fort Fetterman at 1:30 P.M., on Monday, May 29. The infantry battalion had marched somewhat earlier. No one questioned the general route north—the supposedly abandoned, though never really dismissed or forgotten, Montana Road. Earlier that year Crook's first expedition had traveled this same avenue north to Forts Reno and Phil Kearny, heralded old posts now in shambles. In March both places were buried deeply in snow. Telltale evidence of that trek was plainly evident, particularly in the deeply scarred track (usually parallel ruts in fact) that snaked across the rolling prairie.

Crook's aide-de-camp John Bourke painted a vivid word picture of the outbound column at its start: "The long black line of mounted men stretched for more than a mile with nothing to break the sobreness of color save the flashing of the sun's rays back from the arms of the men. A long, moving streak of white told us our wagons were already well under way and a puff of dust just in front indicated the line of march of the Infantry Battalion." Every component of the expedition had its place, the infantry in the van on this day, the cavalry following, and the wagons in line. The mules moved in file on the lee side of the column "so the troops wouldn't get our dust, but we got theirs," a muleskinner joked. They were followed by a small horse remuda and substantial cattle herd. In the days to come these elements sometimes rotated positions, especially when the livestock required greater security. But not on this hot, sultry day, when the fine dust thrown up by the hooves of more than two thousand animals rose like a ground fog all the way to the first day's camp on Sage Creek, twelve miles from Fetterman. Perhaps the oddest element came at the end: prospector-turned-correspondent Ernest Hornberger, his new pal Sylvester Reese, Reese's donkeys packed with two months' worth of provisions, and four other obscure miners, William Wyatt, Charles Calderbaugh, Frederick Smith, and H. C. Meyers, all from McKeesport, Pennsylvania, nonchalantly bringing up the rear.[1]

At the last minute before marching, Major Evans's ten companies of

Third Cavalry were formally segmented into three manageable battalions. Captain Van Vliet's two companies, C and G, were already well ahead of the column, having been ordered to the field by Crook on May 27 to Fort Reno to await the arrival of the Crows there. Van Vliet's companies would remain a separate squadron throughout the weeks to come. The other eight companies were divided equally between Captain Mills and Captain Henry, made up of battalions generally equivalent in size to Captain Noyes's five companies of Second Cavalry and Major Chambers's five companies of infantry.[2]

Crook remained behind at Fort Fetterman that afternoon, exchanging last-minute telegraphic advice, particularly with Sheridan. He took the trail at the end of the day, escorted by aides and orderlies. Upon reaching the Sage Creek camp that evening, the reporters sought him out. He had little to report, except perhaps the news of Egan's encounter with Indians several weeks earlier, which reached Fetterman that same day. The ever-cordial Crook seized the occasion, however, to introduce the reporters to one another. Before that time Robert Strahorn and Joe Wasson, who had come to Fetterman from different directions at different times, apparently had not yet encountered Davenport, MacMillan, and Finerty. Sketch artist Charles Stanley, rarely mentioned at all in these contexts, was two days ahead of the command, having accompanied Van Vliet's squadron sent in search of the Crows.[3]

Early on May 30 Crook ordered forward Companies B and L, Third Cavalry, under Captains Charles Meinhold and Peter D. Vroom to explore the lands to the right and perhaps locate a better place to cross the Powder than the one lying directly ahead at old Fort Reno. Frank Grouard guided. At a pause on Meinhold's advance while his men prepared coffee in the rough breaks at the head of Seventeen Mile Creek, another of the dry forks of the Powder, Private Francis A. Tierney of Company B accidentally shot himself. While gathering kindling Tierney had removed his pistol belt and carelessly tossed it to the ground. His revolver struck a rock and discharged a bullet into his right thigh that passed upward into his abdomen and rested near his left kidney. Although the ball missed all major blood vessels, this was nonetheless an agonizing wound. After a rider hurriedly returned to the column, medical director Albert Hartsuff rushed forward with an ambulance and attendants, but to no avail, as the bullet could not be found. The wound proved fatal within a week. They could not return to Fetterman, and the hapless Tierney was carried forward in the ambulance.[4]

The expedition encamped on the South Fork of the Cheyenne that evening, a location remembered by some for its "shockingly bad" water, strong with alkali, and by others as the place where Indians ran off with the Big Horn Expedition's cattle herd on March 3, critically wounding a herder in the sneak attack. The loss of the cattle, which were never recovered, seriously crimped the provisioning of that command. The episode quickly became the talk of the camp and also brought some caution for the first time. Pickets were doubled, men slept with arms close at hand, and "we all felt that we were on dangerous and hostile ground." The episode also prompted a touch of whimsy. Second Lieutenant James E. H. Foster of Captain William H. Andrews's Company I, Third Cavalry, a young man with a dry wit, penned this couplet at his campfire:

> If Sitting Bull doth steal our meat,
> What shall we do for grub to eat?

Whereupon someone else at the fire echoed a plaintive refrain: "half rations of bacon," which was the pathetic fate suffered by the men of the first expedition.[5]

The third day on the trail was remembered chiefly for a drastic change in weather. As happens on the northern plains in winter (and its shoulder seasons), abominable cold and pitiless winds occasionally swept out the north, on this day blowing alkaline dust that perfectly tormented everyone on the trail. The route this day crossed the headwaters of the several forks and main channel of the Cheyenne River. At one of the high divides in a moment of sunshine the men caught a unique Wyoming view: the imposing Laramie Peak to the distant south, the snow-clad summits of the Big Horn Mountains in the distant front, and the distinctive Pumpkins Buttes in the right foreground. The vistas offered little pleasure, however, as the men hunkered down in greatcoats and endured the day and the lurking storm. With every soldier in a service greatcoat, one wag noted that the command looked more uniform than usual.[6]

The weather only got worse. After a tormentingly cold night with incessant howling winds, a snowstorm struck the command on the morning of June 1. (This was the same storm that pummeled General Alfred Terry's column, obliging it to hold over in camp in the Little Missouri Valley in Dakota.) Between the duststorm the day before and the snow today, one trooper in Company D, Second Cavalry, remembered laconically: "We were getting some early lessons in how to be physically tough." Undeterred by the inclement weather, Crook pushed on. By noon the norther had abated, and by midafternoon the temperature again became comfortable. That afternoon an officer in the van thought that he detected Indians on the distant horizon. Captain Henry's Company D, Third Cavalry, was advanced in a rush. Word passed through the column to "Close up, close up!" in the event that the command indeed faced Indians. Soon enough, however, Henry encountered Meinhold's and Vroom's companies returning to the column. "What a fuss about nothing!" boomed Crook as he closed his telescope and resumed his place at the head of the line. Meinhold and Vroom encountered no Indians and located no better crossing of the Powder. The expedition reached the Dry Fork of the Powder that afternoon, having marched eighteen miles that day and some sixty-nine miles since departing Fort Fetterman.[7]

Besides the difficult weather on June 1, many of the column's diarists and reporters noted having passed a litter-strewn campsite in the headlands of the Dry Fork that had been used quite recently by Montana miners bound for the Black Hills. The place was in fact a standard campsite used by several mining companies heading that way. In early May the well-publicized 202-member Powder River Expedition may well have paused there. Their journey was memorable in part for having found at Fort Reno a soldier's blood-stained shirt and the travois that that man had been brought in on, discarded, they presumed, by Crook's first campaign.[8]

A more recent sixty-five-member party, variously identified as "Captain St. John's Command" and "Tony Pastor's Opera Troupe," was also noted, their names and the date, May 27, 1876, penciled on a board left behind in the camp. Scattered about were freshly emptied tin cans, recent fire pits, and several well-formed rifle pits. In the coming weeks the Big Horn and Yellowstone Expedition frequently encountered the evidence of prospectors, some bound for the Black Hills, others bound for the Big Horn Mountains, and some soon welcomed into the soldiers' midst. The expedition already had the little Hornberger-Reese party lurking on its margins, though at the moment the soldiers ignored them entirely.[9]

From the Dry Fork camp on June 2 the expedition had relatively easy travel to the Powder River and old Fort Reno, one of the three posts abandoned in 1868 in the closing days of the strife-torn Bozeman Trail. Captain Van Vliet's squadron awaited, their horses grazing and his two companies neatly hutted in a small line of shelter tents on the east side of the river. No Crow auxiliaries had come in. Fort Reno itself sat on a table above a hard-bottom crossing of the river, the only such crossing for miles upstream and down. Crook's first expedition parked its wagons at Reno for several weeks in March, where the wounded soldiers from the Powder River battle reached the warmth of tentage and stoves. They traveled comfortably in ambulances to Fetterman (thus the discarded travois and bloody shirt). While the expedition camped on the plain just below the post on the west side of the river, some officers and reporters explored the remains of the fort. Debris of an endless sort littered the place—crumbling adobe walls, chimneys, stoves, axles, iron bedsteads, gun carriages—enough metal, Finerty figured, to "make a Chicago junk-dealer rich." The real curiosity of the place was its cemetery, a forlorn "Sacred Field" in Bourke's words, with headboards upended and broken, its surrounding fence in tatters, and a brick monument dismantled and now a heap of rubbish at the entrance. Private William Magill of Captain Samuel Munson's Company C, Ninth Infantry, knew the cemetery from earlier days. "They [Indians] had cut out the headboards from the graves and we found part of my old company named Slagle six miles away."[10]

Crook was openly dismayed that the Crows had not yet joined his column. Without Indian auxiliaries he knew that he was virtually blind in any meaningful attempt at closing with Sitting Bull. The effort at recruiting Oglalas at Red Cloud Agency had failed, but thus far his reach to the Crow Agency for help had showed promise despite this failed appearance. The Crows certainly knew the land, were acknowledged as natural trailers, and likely also knew the whereabouts of the Sioux. In hindsight, assuming that Crows might somehow be waiting at Reno seems unrealistic, particularly given the considerable distance between their agency on the Stillwater River (southwest of present-day Columbus, Montana), some 150 miles through Sioux Country, and also the simple dilemma of marshalling sufficient help after a comparably heavy recruitment by Colonel Gibbon, commanding the war's Montana column. Still, Crook determined to track down the Crows and have them led to his command. That evening Crook's only guides, Grouard, Richard, and Pourier, were dispatched from the camp to meet these friendlies or even travel as far as Stillwater and recruit them personally at their agency. Each guide was provided a second horse drawn from the led mounts of Royall's cavalry brigade. By nightfall they were off. Crook and Grouard planned to rendezvous on the Tongue in about a week.[11]

Dispatching his only guides was a bold move for Crook. Grouard was not familiar with the Crows but was the first man that Crook turned to for help in this somewhat overthought dilemma. When offered the assistance of as many men as he desired from the column to get through, even as far as the Crow Agency, Grouard picked only Richard and Pourier. Both had freighted through Crow Country in the days of the Bozeman Trail. Pourier, having lived for a while at Fort C. F. Smith, knew the language. But their departure left Crook blind. The Montana Road was obvious enough, and he had officers along who had been with him in March and also several who had served on the Bozeman Trail during that era. It was the unforeseen that caused hesitation.[12]

As the expedition made its way from the Powder River northward on June 3 to the next night's camp on Crazy Woman's Creek, Finerty offered his readers a careful description of the column. "I shall never forget the beauty of that scene," he wrote. All twenty companies were together for the first time. The infantry, the "walk-a-heaps" as Finerty hailed them, started early, around 5 A.M., remembered Gerhard Luhn of the Fourth. Two hours later the wagons started, followed by the cavalry riding by twos, the Third in the van and the Second bringing up the rear, with just enough of an interval between companies to define each unit. The mules paraded next and the entire column was followed by a single cavalry company in the extreme rear. From head to tail the line of troops, wagons, and mules extended from four to five miles. Crook, now taking on the role of guide, and his staff rode well ahead on a trail that needed no particular defining and an expedition at best still only approaching the dangerous homeland of the Northern Indians.[13]

By now pet names for the soldiers were appearing in the reporter's and correspondent's file copy, which they succeeded in forwarding by courier to Fort Fetterman from time to time. Finerty embraced the name "walk-a-heaps," which he first used in his dispatch written in the camp on Crazy Woman's Creek, suggesting that it echoed the name bestowed on the infantry by Indians.[14] Lieutenant Foster of the Third Cavalry, corresponding anonymously for the *Chicago Tribune* and *New York Daily Graphic*, favored the term "doboy," a name already long popular for the infantry.[15] Robert Strahorn, reporting principally for the *Rocky Mountain News* and also for other papers, preferred the name "boys in blue," referring to the men of both branches now in the field.[16]

Other impressions were gained on the march north of Fort Reno. All of the reporters invariably disparaged the wide-open prairies that they traveled through in getting to this point but marveled at what lay ahead. "Mac," Thomas MacMillan of the *Chicago Inter-Ocean*, wrote:

> The Powder River Valley seems to be the dividing line between the sterile, unattractive lands of Central-eastern Wyoming and the richer, better-watered, and finer country of the northern third of the

Territory. The entire face of the country to the north of Old Fort Reno undergoes the completest transformation. With an overshadowing range of hills we observe the difference; the surroundings are pleasant; the atmosphere is humid, and the general effect on the climate and productions is apparent on every knoll, in every valley, along every watercourse.

MacMillan's reverie was well balanced, however, with careful descriptions of the fragility of the human condition. He also regaled his readers with accounts of the persistent terror and death in this same reach in the days of the Bozeman Road.[17]

Crazy Woman's Creek afforded the discrete little party of miners trailing the expedition, the Hornberger-Reese outfit, its first chance to prospect a cold mountain stream. To everyone's pleasant surprise, probably including theirs, the fledgling prospectors successfully panned placer gold. It was not much, but it was gold all the same. Charles Stanley, the *Leslie's* illustrator, had befriended Hornberger and learned that the results amounted to about eight cents to the pan. MacMillan was eyeing this as well and was told by the miners that enough gold was taken out to "make it pay to average placer miners." By comparison, Deadwood and Whitewood Gulches in the northern Black Hills were yielding from ten cents to twenty-five cents and as high as $1.30 to the pan, with some side gulches yielding as much as $5 to the pan in March 1876. The U.S. Treasury's fixed price for gold was $20.67 per troy ounce. In the mining camps the conventional discounted value was $18 per troy ounce. Clearly, optimism reigned on Crazy Woman's Creek, especially in streams that had not yet been well prospected.[18]

With the Pumpkin Buttes fading from view in the rear, the verdure of the mountainscape to the left and increasingly lush prairie to the front continued to enthrall observers on June 4, especially participants of the winter campaign. Robert Strahorn of the *Rocky Mountain News* had been with Crook in March and called the seasonal transformation "almost miraculous." The destination that day, twenty-three miles ahead, was Clear Fork Creek, a prominent tributary of the Powder and the "first good water since leaving Fetterman," remembered First Lieutenant Thaddeus Capron of the Ninth Infantry. The road was often hilly, however, and washouts were common, requiring pioneering labor performed by a cavalry company assigned the duty. Buffalo tracks were seen for the first time as well, and hunters brought in small numbers of antelope and deer for consumption in the officers' messes.[19]

The members of the column did not yet seem to have any sense of apprehension or angst as they slowly entered the Northern Indian country, although Crook was cautious. A dense column of smoke seen in the east all afternoon was interpreted as Indians firing the prairie, but the column did not encounter any Indians or travois trails. The scene mesmerized Stanley, who sketched it for his *Leslie's* audience. Already bugle calls had been abolished; all orders were transmitted through the officers of the respective staffs. Deployment of evening pickets was strictly adhered to. The careful dispersal of pickets was a lesson learned on the Big Horn Expedition, where inattention to that detail was a major if not the sole contributor to the successful theft of that column's cattle herd. Now mounted pickets encircled the nightly bivouacs. Imposing buttes and bluffs a mile or more away were occupied by entire mounted companies sent out with the purpose of holding in check any Indians who might attempt to rush down and drive off the expedition's horses, mules, and cattle.[20]

In camp that afternoon an episode occurred that would be repeated often in the coming days and weeks. An Indian scaffold grave was observed on a hill above the creek. It was the first seen, Finerty remembered, and became an instant curiosity. Finerty and Stanley set off to examine the burial. Before they could reach it, however, they watched as some Ninth Infantrymen pulled it to the ground. Finerty grimaced as the body was stripped of blue blankets, a beaded jacket, and moccasins and casually tossed into the creek. The doughboys then uprooted the cottonwood poles and cross pieces, broke them into kindling, and hauled the sticks to their camp. "Thus the relationship of all men to each other in point of savagery was established," Finerty concluded. "The Sioux defaced the white graves at Reno. The whites converted the Sioux funeral pedestal into kindling-wood. It was all the same to the dead on both sides."[21]

Mining again dominated the newsmen's attention in some quarters and now also Crook's. The Hornberger-Reese party prospected the Clear Fork and again found gold, this time worth $4. Lieutenant Foster, writing anonymously for the *Cincinnati Commercial* (the third paper that he corresponded with), called the party a "queer looking outfit, consisting of an ordinary farm wagon, covered, drawn by two mules, and two . . . donkeys that are used as pack animals." This late awareness of the miners in the cavalry camp suggests their continuing relative obscurity in the sprawl of the expedition. Two new rough-looking characters entered the camp that evening and sought out the general. Led by John Graves, they represented a party of sixty miners who were coming from the Black Hills expressly to explore the Big Horns, having given up on the Dakota diggings. The party was a day behind the expedition. The two miners confessed that the smoke seen in the afternoon was a prairie fire accidentally ignited by their own party. The miners also told Crook of having seen no Indians but having crossed a number of large trails, all heading north.[22]

Graves's miners joined Crook's expedition on June 5 as the column wended its way northward in the direction of Fort Phil Kearny. Miners departing the Black Hills became a relatively common circumstance at this stage of that rush, where prime spots in prime gulches were claimed-out and the future beheld expensive mechanical operations. In the days to come Graves's miners formed their own camp circle and for the most part overtly ignored the military routine. They prospected streams along the way and offered news copy from time to time by their simple presence—in a day when gold was always good copy—but seemed quite content to operate in the shadows of Crook's troops. The roles of some would change in coming days as this column ultimately faced its enemy.[23]

The distance traveled on June 5 was short, barely fifteen miles. Crook was content to reach old Fort Phil Kearny, the second of the great Bozeman Trail posts abandoned and promptly destroyed by Indians in 1868. Ten miles north of the Clear Creek camp the column passed within a mile and a half of Lake DeSmet, a deceivingly attractive body of cold, clear water two miles long and a half-mile wide. An oddity on the landscape, DeSmet had no outlet and was highly alkaline and worthless as a water source, as it remains today. Five miles beyond, the column reached the forks of Piney and Little Piney Creeks and encamped early that afternoon.[24]

All of the chroniclers commented on some aspect of the old fort. A few ridiculed its vulnerability. Lieutenant Foster observed that it was "admirably situated to be harassed by Indians, as it can be approached on almost any side, under good cover, to within easy rifle-range." Nothing more remained than portions of the charred stockade, scattered chimneys, and the same profusion of broken metallic debris that littered Fort Reno. Chroniclers explored the post's brickyard, with its huge pile of broken brick. Some climbed "Picket Hill," the prominence commanding the southern margins of the fort where soldiers were stationed to signal to the garrison the movement of Indians. Others lauded the sheer attractiveness of the area, with lush grasses, the inviting waters of Piney and Little Piney Creeks, and dense stands of cottonwoods and ash, all amounting to "a landscape never to be forgotten." Some like

Captain Samuel Munson and Lieutenant Thaddeus Capron of Company C, Ninth Infantry, seized the occasion to bathe in the creek. After "donning clean clothes, we felt like new beings," Capron wrote. Several writers remembered the discovery of a small Indian hunting camp on the Piney, apparently hastily abandoned when the troops came: campfire embers still smoldered and an axe lay nearby covered with fresh blood stains, evidently having just been used in butchering an animal.[25]

The greater attraction was the fort's cemetery, which drew inspection throughout the afternoon and evening. Like the cemetery at Fort Reno, the place was in ruins and for some was a sheer disgrace. In the farthest reach of this "God's Acre" was the long mound containing the bodies of the eighty-one men killed with Captain William J. Fetterman on December 21, 1866. The grave was marked with a decaying shaft of brick. The trench was not disturbed, but elsewhere human bones lay unburied, bleaching in the sun, having been exhumed by coyotes, according to Foster. Noted one observer: "The grave-yard at old Phil Kearney [sic] is but one more sad commentary on the gratitude—or absolute want of it—of this our model Republic." This humble scene was carefully sketched by Leslie's artist Charles Stanley and appeared in that publication's August 12 issue.[26]

As the column resumed its general march northward on June 6 it passed the already renowned Massacre Hill, a hallowed landscape observed that morning by all and studied carefully by some. Everyone knew one version or another of the horrendous Fetterman story, a tale repeated in camp and again now as troops marched by. A cluster of rocks and the long ridge over which the fighting occurred were distinguishing features. Stanley sketched the scene, notably placing Crook and several staff officers in the midst of his drawing.[27]

Some assumed that Crook's destination on June 6 was Goose Creek, an inviting trout-filled tributary of the Tongue, along a north-by-northwesterly course from Fort Phil Kearny on what was then referred to as the Fort C. F. Smith Road (the next leg of the Montana Road). Crook anticipated rough travel in the morning, particularly through a succession of long hills and cutting arroyos that would slow the wagons. On the afternoon of June 5 at the Little Piney camp he ordered Royall to advance a cavalry company in the morning to serve as pioneers to smooth the road. Adding some to the confusion over the intended course this day, Captain Noyes, who shared Crook's obsession with hunting and fishing, sought permission to advance ahead of the column to fish in Goose Creek. The general allowed the side trip, advising the captain to take an escort. Noyes evidently did not discuss with Crook the day's intended orientation but assumed that the column would follow him to Goose Creek. Noyes and ten men from Company I were off ahead of the infantry, which itself marched at 5:00 A.M., minutes after dawn. But in the breaks beyond Massacre Hill the day's general course diverted from the C. F. Smith Road, a detail that has perplexed observers ever since.[28]

Crook and his entourage of aides and orderlies were often the first on the trail, leading or passing the infantry battalion, which itself was consistently the initial organized element of the column to march each day. On June 6, however, Crook spent time investigating Fetterman's battleground. In the jumbled country ahead, the foot troops matter-of-factly headed in a northerly direction and crossed onto Peno Creek, in the headwaters of Prairie Dog Creek. In due course the rest of the expedition followed the infantry and in doing so challenged contemporary and later-day assumptions about the general orientation of the column. Without question, Crook instructed Major Chambers to orient northward to the Prairie Dog. But Crook's general silence on the detail undergirded the confusion. Among those commenting on this puzzling point (including Bourke), only Finerty believed that Crook made the course change consciously. The rest were not so sure, particularly when the ground ahead yielded little more than profusions of rattlesnakes, mosquitoes, and prairie dog villages and the stream bore no trout. Historians analyzing the day's movement leveled an even greater charge, asserting that Crook got lost. Crook was characteristically silent on the matter in his autobiography, as if to say that there was no issue at all. Fortunately, Crook's trusty scout Frank Grouard sets the record straight, confirming in his autobiography that "the command was to be camped at the mouth of Prairie Dog and was to wait for me until my return."[29]

Aiming for the mouth of Prairie Dog Creek also made sense for other reasons. The adopted course was the same one traveled by the Big Horn Expedition in March and thus familiar to Crook and Grouard when they agreed to a point of rendezvous while still together at Fort Reno. And it was the most direct route to the Tongue, itself a principal entrée into the realm of the Northern Indians, just as it had been on the first campaign. Crook fixated incessantly on his Indian allies and was confident that he would meet them there, if they did not come to him beforehand. Crook knew perfectly well what he was doing and was thinking aggressively. Buffalo were spotted in the valley of the Prairie Dog as well, which added to the luster of the day's travel. Thus far only the tracks of buffalo had been seen, no animals. Many in the column were mindful of the old refrain on the Great Plains that "where you find the buffalo there you find the Indians too."[30]

The day was not without other tribulations. While the column was traversing the rough breaks, an accident befell a man of the Ninth Infantry. Sergeant Andrew J. O'Leary of Munson's Company C, driving one of Hartsuff's ambulances, overturned while descending Massacre Hill. The lone casualty was O'Leary himself, who injured his back and broke an arm. Despite all "soldierly pride" this doughboy who "had walked every step of the way until this unlucky morning" was ordered into that same ambulance. Later that afternoon a heavy two-hour thundershower drenched the column. Camp that day was on Prairie Dog Creek, eighteen miles from the forks of Piney Creek. Dinner for a handful of officers and newsmen was enlivened with a feast of roasted buffalo from the six or seven killed during the day. Sadly, after midnight Private Tierney of Company B, Third Cavalry, the soldier who accidentally shot himself on May 30, expired, a victim of blood poisoning.[31]

Captain Noyes's fishing party rejoined the column as the expedition resumed the trail on June 7. By noon on June 6 it had been apparent to the captain that Crook was not following his course. Undeterred, he continued fishing well into the afternoon. Mindful of Indians, he hid his detachment in a dried-up beaver swamp that night, huddled around small fires as they cooked and ate their fish. Among the chroniclers, only Bourke called attention to the captain, dismissing him as the "benighted" fisherman.[32]

Captain William Andrews's Company I, Third Cavalry, served as the pioneering corps on June 7 and left camp two and a half hours ahead of the infantry. For the most part the trail in the morning was a new one for wagons and proved winding and difficult, requiring tedious excavating, embanking, corduroying, and grading to prepare a suitable passage. This labor, moreover, occurred in a drenching rain. Fortunately for the laborers, the valley widened by noon. The pioneering burden eased some as the trail passed alternating stretches of good grass and thick sage. In its final ten or twelve miles Prairie Dog Creek was some ten feet wide but much obstructed with beaver dams. In the van, attention focused on a small herd of buffalo sighted within the last mile near the creek's juncture with the Tongue. Crook and his entourage characteristically closed on them and killed three, noting the locations of the carcasses so that camp attendants could again bring in the meat. Other buffalo might have been killed, but *Leslie's* artist Charles Stanley explained a prevailing condition at the time, mockingly noting that "everybody seemed possessed of the 'buck fever' at about this time, and to this malady the buffalo owed their escape."[33]

Camp on June 7 was established in the broad confluence of Prairie Dog Creek and the Tongue River. The Tongue, a major tributary of the Yellowstone

River, emerged from the Big Horn Mountains far to the southwest of there and in this area flowed in a gently sweeping easterly direction before bending sharply to the north and entering Montana. The river was some 160 feet wide and 3 feet deep. On the south bank a heavy growth of mature cottonwood trees lined the bottoms. In that level, open plain the expedition's wagons were circled into a large corral, which served as a confinement for the wagon stock at night. As the troops arrived they established camps on the bench surrounding the corral, with the cavalry occupying ground to the left and Crook's headquarters and the infantry taking ground to the right. Tall rocky bluffs on the north side of the river rose almost perpendicularly for several hundred feet, limiting long-range views in that direction. Thick growths of prickly pear cactus on that side lined the scant few feet of ground between the water's edge and the rising bluffs. Scaling the heights was not particularly inviting. Some officers saw the bluffs as a vulnerability and found fault with the camp's placement. Others treated the feature lightly. Anyway, Indians had yet to be seen. Meanwhile fishing in the Tongue was superb. For the most part the confluence of the Prairie Dog seemed an idyllic campground.[34]

After settling in on June 7 the expedition's first order of business was the burial of Private Francis Tierney, whose body was carried forward in one of the ambulances. As Tierney was prepared for the grave, Doctor Hartsuff examined the gruesome death wound. As he noted in his report, the pistol bullet had entered in the upper third of Tierney's right thigh, tracked upward and across the abdomen, passed near femoral vessels, and lodged near his left kidney. The cause of death was peritonitis or blood poisoning as Private Zinser noted in his diary. While a grave was prepared in the low hills south of the cavalry camp, Tierney's body was wrapped in his blue overcoat and gray blanket.[35]

Tierney's burial occurred with military honors at evening "retreat," normally the second to final bugle call of the day when roll was taken and orders were published. Sometimes that occurred at sunset, but on this campaign it was at 6:30 P.M. (While bugle calls had apparently been abolished earlier, they clearly flourished now.) Tierney's body was escorted from Hartsuff's camp to the grave by eight men drawn from his unit, B of the Third Cavalry, in the charge of a noncommissioned officer. The formal procession included every off-duty man from the ten companies of the regiment. Nearly every other available man in the sprawling camp, infantry and newsmen alike, also witnessed the interment. With nearly palpable emotion Bourke wrote in his diary that the procession "acquired magnificent proportions, fully 600 persons being present" from General Crook on down.[36]

The ceremony was simple but impressive. Captain Guy Henry, commander of the battalion in which Tierney had served, read the burial service from the Episcopal *Book of Common Prayer*. He provided a comforting doxology of praise and remembrance drawn from the Bible that began with "I am the resurrection and the life, saith the Lord; he that believeth in me, though he were dead, yet shall he live: And whosoever liveth and believeth in me, shall never die." The whole affair took fifteen or twenty minutes and drew to a close with three volleys fired over the grave and massed cavalry bugles sounding taps. Captain Meinhold, Tierney's commanding officer, shoveled the first spadeful of earth onto the remains. The grave was then rapidly closed. The assembled companies quick-stepped back to their camps. Afterward a large flat stone requiring the united strength of ten men and horses was placed atop the grave, etched with Tierney's name, age, and date. "He was a good soldier," wrote Joe Wasson of the *Philadelphia Press*, "and it was like burying him at sea to leave him thus." Writing for the *Chicago Inter-Ocean*, Thomas MacMillan noted: "Poor fellow, he came a long way to find a grave!"[37]

The column did not move on June 8. The Big Horn and Yellowstone Expedition had thus far traveled some 188 miles from Fort Fetterman, so the layover was welcome. It was a "long, lazy summer day," remembered Stanley, with the men variously reading, writing letters home, fishing, bathing, and washing clothes. For the most part the command was in good health, though "sunburnt and ragged." Many in camp believed that Crook intended on establishing his permanent camp here or at least remain at this place until his Indian allies arrived. Couriers had come from Fort Fetterman from time to time since the expedition's departure on May 29, but the general still had no news about the Crows and Shoshones. Grouard, Richard, and Pourier had been away since June 2. Grouard and Crook had an understanding that they would rendezvous on the Tongue. Surely Crook worried, but his natural reticence masked any outward concern.[38]

Crook's innate reserve was always puzzling. During the day the ever-inquisitive young Lieutenant Foster asked Crook whether he intended this to be his permanent camp. "Nobody knows but Gen. Crook," Foster wrote, "and he won't tell." Crook had a way with such questions. The general "looks pleased at the interest manifested in affairs by the inquiring officer," Foster continued, "and sometimes gives him an answer which leaves the querist more completely in the dark than before, but generally simply says 'I don't know,' which answers the purpose just as well."[39]

Oddly, thus far the expedition had encountered neither Indians nor meaningful Indian signs, aside from the trails that the miners observed when exiting the Black Hills and the smoldering fire and bloody axe discovered in a hunting camp on Piney Creek several days before. Yet, seen or unseen, Indians were in the area. On the afternoon of June 8 men from Noyes's Company I, Second Cavalry, who were hunting buffalo above the camp encountered the fresh trail of five Indians crossing the Tongue. The soldiers followed the trail in the bottoms and came upon a sore-backed pony abandoned by these suspected prowlers. The troopers took the pony to their camp and proudly paraded it about. In another episode that may or may not have been related to the one involving Noyes's men, fifteen Indians were supposedly seen around sunset. To the embarrassment of some, a careful examination with field glasses exposed clumps of sage, not warriors. But it was dusk. The first episode was news enough for Crook to order a company of cavalry, Dewees's A of the Second, to cross the Tongue and camp on the opposite bank in the cottonwood grove west of the bluffs. For a third time that day Indians were spotted. At about 10 P.M. shots reverberated through the camp. Jittery pickets had opened fire on suspected skulkers. Upon closer examination, it was discovered that the pickets had fired on a clump of sage. The camp was awakened, but nothing more came of the incident.[40]

Yet it is entirely possible that fifteen Indians had been seen and that Dewees's pickets had truly detected Indians, although perhaps not Sioux or Northern Cheyenne warriors as everyone feared but Crows. Finerty vividly described a fourth episode involving Indians that day. At around 11 P.M. he was awakened by the loud and persistent howling of what he thought were coyotes—animals, he wrote, that Indians often imitated when approaching an encampment. Captain Sutorius, Finerty's tent mate, heard the howling too and then the voice of someone shouting down from the bluff. "That sounds like the voice of an Indian," Sutorius exclaimed. Grouard, Richard, and Pourier, Crook's principal interpreters, were away, so Ben Arnold (or Ben Connor as he was sometimes known) was summoned from the packer camp. Arnold, employed as a courier, had not yet been called upon to carry messages to Fort Fetterman. Now he was one of the few men in the camp, maybe the only man, conversant in an Indian language: Sioux. The exchange with the individual on the hill was halting. Arnold recognized the "Crow dialect." The man shouted down, "Any half-breeds there—any Crows?" Arnold made a reply that was not understood by the other, who shouted down again, "Have the Crows come yet?" When Arnold replied in the Sioux language, the individual on the bluff turned silent and then disappeared. Arnold later told his biographer that he had wished it had been daylight so that he could have talked in sign language. Learning of this incident soon afterward, Crook grew angry, fretting that the Crows were expected momentarily but might now have been frightened away.[41]

The next day, June 9, the story of the Indian on the bluff made the camp rounds and soon had a dozen variations. Some speculated that perhaps the Indian was indeed a Sioux showing his bravery by taunting the soldiers and warning them to go home. Perhaps Crook's scouts had been captured and this Indian had come to brag of it. Perhaps he was a friendly Indian but got scared off when the Sioux language was spoken. A great deal of anxiety was felt for Grouard and his companions, Lieutenant Foster remembered. Joe Wasson of the *Philadelphia Press* expressed a similar sentiment: "We feel sort of lost here in the absence of all the scouts."[42]

A measure of relief came before sunup, when two couriers (one known simply as Harrison) from Fort Fetterman reached camp. The two carried eagerly anticipated dispatches for Crook and a large mail for the command. Couriers usually traveled by night and hid out by day. From Lieutenant Colonel Robert Williams, assistant adjutant general in Omaha, Crook learned that eight companies of the Fifth Cavalry had been ordered from the Department of the Missouri to the Platte to join the greater campaign. Crook and Sheridan had discussed that prospect while this expedition was organizing, and Crook had encouraged the move. For the time being, the regiment would take station at Red Cloud Agency. Williams also reported that a great mass of three thousand or more Indians had departed from the lower agencies for the northern camps and that "military authorities," doubtless meaning Sheridan and Sherman, were of the opinion that Crook would be hard pressed to manage the Northern Indians. By now, of course, this was a familiar refrain. Sheridan, meanwhile, advised that 120 Snake Indians under the command of two white men were en route to Crook's camp and were expected to reach Fort Phil Kearny by June 8. This was especially gratifying news, Bourke recalled, as was Sheridan's admonition that "no Indians should be allowed to return to Red Cloud until whipped."[43]

After the commotion of the preceding night, it rained most of the morning, but June 9 passed as another recuperative day for nearly everyone. The general "cleaning up" of clothing, persons, and weapons continued, as stock was groomed and horses and mules were shod. Captain Dewees made out well with the mail, receiving from his wife both a letter and a bundle of oranges. Charles Stanley wandered eastward beyond the infantry camp and came upon an Indian grave in the high branches of a cottonwood. As he drew closer he noticed three infantrymen in the tree working to tumble the body down and rob it of its blankets and beadwork. "It strikes me that this sort of thing ought to be made a serious offense," he later wrote.[44]

In the afternoon several horse and foot races relieved the monotony of the day, seemingly inspired by the good-natured ribbing long suffered by Captain Andrew Burt, commanding Company H, Ninth Infantry. Burt rode forth from Fort Fetterman with several horses, including a prized white pony, and had such a penchant for riding his pony about the countryside hunting for game and signs that the men in the command called it "Burt's cow." Robert Strahorn remembered it as the "apple of his eye." The men teased Burt relentlessly, saying that one day the Sioux would get him, but he dismissed the notion, claiming that Indians could never catch his pony. On this particular afternoon Burt created no small amusement by challenging any other pony and rider in the command to run against his own. Men and mounts came forth. Major Chambers's horse was viewed as the fleetest. Money being scarce, the prime wager in the first race was a can of corn. Burt and his pony handily won the race and another one too, earning the reputation, as one news wag put it, "of being the 'liveliest cow' in the herd."[45]

Despite this calm day of horse and foot races, many of the chroniclers noted that the chief topic of conversation during this momentary lull was the prospect of the campaign. Most of all, the men asked themselves, where were the Sioux? Captain Luhn expressed the concern succinctly in a letter to his wife written in camp that afternoon: "I do wish that Mr. Sitting Bull would come and give us battle, we are all ready, and if we could get one good fight out of him we would soon be back to Fetterman." In the eyes of some Crook had conducted a more aggressive campaign in March, and some of those officers were with him now. By the time he reached this location during that campaign, Crook had been regularly feeling to his front, advancing his corps of mixed-blood and Plainsmen scouts into the drainages of the Rosebud and Tongue in search of Indians. But the opposite was occurring now. Crook was waiting for his Indian auxiliaries to find him. The greater question of the day, and the campaign, remained unanswered. Where were the Indians?[46]

TONGUE RIVER HEIGHTS

By June 9 Crook had advanced his sizable Big Horn and Yellowstone Expedition to the very doorstep of the Northern Indians. He had come to the right place, yet he was stymied. Without the services of mixed-blood or Indian trackers or deliberate explorations by his own cavalry, he was blind to the whereabouts of his foe. History reveals that this war's great opponents, Crook's substantial column and Sitting Bull's ever-expanding village of Northern Indians, were barely fifty miles apart. And yet while Crook pensively awaited the arrival of his overdue Crow and Shoshone allies—his eyes on this campaign—his enemy knew precisely where he was and was not the least bit apprehensive about telling him so.

In the earliest days of June Wooden Leg and ten other Northern Cheyenne wolves set out from Sitting Bull's camp, then located on lower Rosebud Creek near Greenleaf Creek, to hunt buffalo. They ranged first to the Tongue River, a familiar stream a mere nine or ten miles east of the Rosebud through a low pass. Not finding many buffalo on the Tongue, the Cheyennes kept moving, southward at first and then east again into the Powder River valley. Their travels kept them moving south until they nearly reached Lodge Pole Creek (known as Clear Creek to white people). This was abundantly familiar ground for Wooden Leg, particularly because he had been on that same reach of the Powder in mid-March when he and a handful of other Cheyenne and Sioux wolves trailed the pony herd that Colonel Joseph Reynolds had taken from them after the Powder River fight. Wooden Leg and the wolves stole back their ponies at Reynolds's camp at Lodge Pole Creek, which caused pronounced embarrassment for the colonel and brought enormous jubilation to the trailers.[1]

A member of the current hunting party, Lame Sioux, who was exploring the countryside northwest of the Lodge Pole-Powder confluence, was the first to spot the soldiers coming from the south. He summoned the others, and soon all could see evidence of a large army camp in the distance. Wooden Leg remembered dressing for a fight. That night the hunters closed on the camp, getting near enough to have a broad view and see burning campfires. When the Cheyennes awakened the next morning, the soldiers were gone. Wooden

Leg and the hunters explored the abandoned campsite and discovered among other things a beef carcass that had on it many slivers of meat and also a box for hard crackers. According to Wooden Leg, "We ate what we wanted of them. We cooked pieces of the beef in the fire coals. We enjoyed a fine breakfast. Then we set out on the trail of the soldiers." This was Crook's campsite of June 6, in the headlands of Prairie Dog Creek.[2]

The soldier trail led down the Prairie Dog. Wooden Leg and the hunters followed from a careful distance and watched as the soldiers again went into camp, where the creek emptied into the Tongue. They skirted around the camp and crossed the swollen river upstream and hid among cottonwoods until morning. Through the day they watched from a cliff, as soldiers walked about their camp and splashed in the river. Some soldiers rode away from the camp. Maybe they were Crows, the Cheyennes speculated, but they did not know. Among themselves they talked about attacking those that had ridden away or trying to steal soldier horses. "We were anxious to do something warlike, to get horses or to count coups," Wooden Leg recalled. All agreed that that was too risky. "We considered it most important that we return and notify our people on the Rosebud."[3]

That afternoon Wooden Leg and five others started for the hills between the soldier camp and the headlands of Rosebud Creek. Five other Cheyennes remained behind to see where the soldiers might go, but the next day they hurried to join the others. All eleven made their way down the Rosebud. The hunters were uncertain where the great Indian village might now have moved but knew it to be somewhere ahead.[4]

Wooden Leg and the others found the camps strung out along the Rosebud at the mouth of Muddy Creek, a short day's travel upstream from the great Sun Dance camp. Wooden Leg said: "We wolf-howled and aroused the people. Cheyennes flocked to learn why we had given the alarm." He and the others reported what they had seen. Soon the word spread to all the camp circles, and councils were called. Young men wanted to ride out and fight the soldiers, but the chiefs and elders urged restraint. Only the Cheyennes, the upriver camp circle, had a different response. The Cheyenne chiefs appointed Little Hawk, Crooked Nose, and two or three others to return to the area and keep track of the soldiers. A few Sioux warriors might have gone along, Wooden Leg recalled, but for the most part this action involved the Cheyennes. Ultimately as many as fifty warriors, maybe a few more, rode south to Crook's camp. "I think they depended upon the Cheyennes to do the work," said Wooden Leg.[5]

Little Hawk provided Cheyenne historian George Bird Grinnell with an account of the Indian movement:

> A good many young men who were brave and strong and able to make a quick trip . . . started after night and travelled all next day going a little way and then stopping. Scouts sent ahead had discovered that soldiers had come as far as Tongue River and had stopped there. [We] went close to Tongue River and waited, having determined to make a night charge thinking that [we] could stampede the soldier horses. When night came and [we] thought soldiers were sleeping, [we] slipped up close and charged and began to shoot but the soldiers must have been sitting up with guns in their hands for a rain of bullets met [us].[6]

It rained bullets!

IIIIIIIIIIIIIIIIIIIIIIIIIIIIIIIII

Captain Gerhard L. Luhn remembered the opening salvo distinctly. It was 6:30 P.M. He had just gone on duty as officer of the day in the infantry camp and was inspecting his own company when infantry pickets on the ridge east of them commenced firing. First Lieutenant Henry Seton, the battalion adjutant, heard the shots first and brought them to Luhn's attention. Then "like a flash," the captain wrote, fifty or more Indians appeared on the high bluffs of the Tongue and "let loose on us." (Luhn thought that the Indians numbered seventy-five. The consensus among the chroniclers suggests that it was closer to fifty.) Across the broad confluence in the cavalry camp "stable call" had just sounded. Troopers were grooming their horses on the line, having just led them in from grazing minutes before. Finerty remembered a single shot from an infantry picket, a succession of volleys, and then "the peculiar whistle and scream of bullets around our ears." It was as though hell had "broken loose in the bluffs," he wrote. Charles Stanley, the *Leslie's* artist, remembered the moment vividly as well. He and his mess mates had just settled in for a dinner of bacon and beans "when a sharp report broke upon the evening air, followed by the vengeful hiss of a bullet. Then another and another report and finally a regular volley. 'Indians!' was the cry and away we dashed to secure our weapons."[7]

Moments passed before the camp fully grasped the threat, and during that time it was a scene of general confusion. Infantry pickets on the right had opened the fight, then Second Cavalry pickets on the left also began firing. Lieutenant Capron, when hearing the shooting, looked about the infantry

95

camp to discern the direction of the threat. He quickly grasped that the pickets were firing to the north and turned and saw the attackers on the bluff across the river. He watched as eight or ten Indians would show themselves in bold relief, fire down upon the camp, then drop back. Then others would come up and "treat us to a like dose, and so it continued." Captain Avery Cain's Company D, Fourth Infantry, joined the fray, leveling heavy fire on the hilltop. And so did the packers and teamsters, who opened such a perfect fusillade on the rocks and crevices across the river that one wag called it "a first-class foundation for a lead-mine in the face of the cliff."[8]

Within minutes Crook grasped the predicament. He and his headquarters staff were camped with the infantry. He first ensured that the pickets on all sides of the camp were strengthened and that the herds were well secured and then put a halt to the indiscriminate shooting, worrying about the needless waste of ammunition. To protect his right flank, Crook ordered Major Chambers to advance his battalion's three Ninth Infantry companies eastward to secure the approaches from that direction. He simultaneously dispatched an orderly westward through the camp in search of Lieutenant Colonel Royall at cavalry brigade headquarters with orders to secure that sector and advance a cavalry battalion across the river to disperse the attackers. Crook's movements to protect the flanks proved more valuable than was immediately grasped, because when the fray began Indians were seen in several directions. Half a mile west of the camp warriors attempted to cross the river, only to be driven back by pickets, men of D Company, Second Cavalry. One of them knocked an Indian from his pony. Indians were also seen south of the camp but remained a good distance away.[9]

East of the camp the Ninth Infantry companies deployed in good order, with Captain Samuel Munson's Company C taking the center and the advance, Captain Andrew S. Burt's Company H taking Munson's right and rear, and Captain Thomas B. Burrowes's Company G advancing on Munson's left and rear. "We anticipated an attack from our front but it did not come," Lieutenant Thaddeus H. Capron noted in his journal. The men of the Ninth took and occupied the heights east of the creek and from that position had a commanding view of the whole affair. These infantry officers later estimated that the attackers numbered from one hundred to two hundred. "As the position which they occupied overlooked the whole ground, they are better able to judge than any one [sic] else," commented one chronicler.[10]

Royall handled Crook's order expeditiously, calling out Captain Mills: "Gen[eral] Crook desires that you mount your men instantly, colonel, cross the river and clear those bluffs of the Indians." It took a short while for Mills's battalion to saddle and the men to gather revolvers and carbines from their individual camps. But the four companies, in all some 230 men, were quickly mounted with proud efficiency. The captain cried out "Forward," and "forward we went." Two of the expedition's chroniclers accompanied the movement, the apparently fearless Finerty of the *Chicago Times* and Lieutenant Foster of Company M, the *Chicago Tribune* correspondent. "In a minute our charging companies were half wading, half swimming through [the] Tongue river, which is swift and broad at that point," Finerty recorded. It was a necessary if short ride. Mills directed the battalion toward the cottonwood grove on the far west end of the bluffs where Captain Dewees's A Company, Second Cavalry, was encamped, providing the sole measure of security in that quarter.[11]

Mills directed Dewees to reposition his men farther to the left to cover his battalion's staging and assault. In the cottonwoods Mills dismounted the companies, drew off the horses in the care of every eighth man, and prepared to scale the bluffs as skirmishers. All the while the shooting from the top continued, with discernible direction and effect. Through nearly all of the demonstration at least two Indians were mounted, seemingly drawing purposeful attention to themselves. Some of the men below thought that these two warriors directed the shooting of the others. One of the mounted Indians drew unique attention. Riding a white pony, he wore a distinctive, brightly burnished headdress that several of the chroniclers thought resembled a tin helmet with a horsehair plume; he earned the name "the man with the Tin Hat." Another of the Indians wore a distinguishing feather bonnet. Nearly all of the soldiers below believed that the attackers were exceptionally well armed but also quickly came to appreciate that their firing was indiscriminate and seemingly directed at the now empty white canvas tents that filled the bottoms. Still, for those under fire, especially for the first time, the scene was gripping. "I must confess that the horrible whizzing of rifle balls was most demoralizing, and I for one, managed to keep well behind a large cottonwood tree," Stanley confessed in his journal.[12]

Mills formed the battalion into a broad front, with his own Company M taking the right center, commanded now by its First Lieutenant Augustus C. Paul, with First Lieutenant Joseph Lawson's Company A taking the extreme right, Captain Alexander Sutorius's Company E taking the left center, and Captain William Andrews's Company I taking the extreme left. Scaling the bluff was exhausting and perilous because the hillside was slippery and steep, and the Indians above continually laid down a scattering fire. By the time the troopers were halfway to the top, however, the Indians had abandoned their original crest-line positions and retired to a ridge a thousand feet to the north and east. Upon reaching the top Mills wheeled his line to the left and charged the Indians, who were now mounted and easily retired to the next crest beyond, where they turned and fired at the soldiers. Their bullets sailed harmlessly above Mills's line. The warriors retreated again to a bluff farther back, where, as Finerty described it, "they appeared to take delight in displaying their equestrian accomplishments" and "nothing less than a long range cannon could reach them." As to any effect of Mills's charge, Finerty summarized it frankly: "To say the truth, they did not seem very badly scared, although they got out of the way with much celerity when they saw us coming in force." After that the attackers simply disappeared. Thus ended the brazen, hour-long episode that has come to be known as the Tongue River fight or by some troopers as the Tongue River Heights fight.[13]

The camp took a while to calm down. The men on the heights held their ground until relieved by First Lieutenant William Rawolle and Company B, Second Cavalry, which had been ordered to "garrison the bluff." The men could not bring their tents along and had to endure "in the open" a pitiless rainfall throughout the night. The rain tormented everyone. "I had a rough night of it posting pickets," infantryman Luhn groused in his diary. Meanwhile, the men in the camp assessed the damages. Three troopers were wounded slightly by spent balls: Sergeant John C. A. Warfield, Company F, Third Cavalry, in the right arm; Private Emil Renner, Company D, Second Cavalry, a flesh wound in the left thigh; and Private John E. Collins, Company I, Second Cavalry. The men returned to duty. This was a time when such wounds were "of no consequence," or so Bourke dismissed them. These three men were not noted by Doctor Hartsuff in his medical report. One Indian was believed to have been killed, shot at the river.[14]

Elsewhere a hefty toll was noted in splintered tent poles and wagon bodies and perforated tentage and stove pipes, mostly scoffed at but also taken as evidence that the attackers had imagined a great punishment being inflicted on the soldiers by shooting at the place where they slept. Three horses and a mule were seriously wounded, including the mount of Second Lieutenant Edgar B. Robertson of Burt's company and Captain Burt's prized white racing pony, picketed at his owner's tent. Burt, having deployed east of the camp during the fight, quickly noticed his charger's shattered leg when returning at 8 P.M. "Burt's heart was well-nigh broken when its suffering had to be ended by a merciful shot," Robert Strahorn wrote. Adding an unnecessary jolt to an evening of surprise, as Second Lieutenant Henry Lemly (cavalry brigade adjutant) was about to retire, he found a rattlesnake coiled in his blankets. "Lemly had the intruder banished from his bed."[15]

The expedition laid over another day at the mouth of Prairie Dog Creek, quietly "reciting the events of yesterday," as Lieutenant Capron expressed it. In a letter to his wife, Captain Luhn of the Fourth Infantry told how the attack "reminded me of old times to hear the bullets go by zip." The affable, German-born Luhn, at age forty-five, was one of the remarkable "old men" of the expedition. He had enlisted in the Sixth Infantry in 1853, fought at Blue Water Creek, Nebraska, in 1855 with Harney's Expedition, marched with the Utah Expedition in 1858, was commissioned from the ranks to the Fourth Infantry in 1863, engaged at Chancellorsville and Gettysburg, and served largely on the plains in the postwar years. He knew something about zipping bullets.[16]

Crook remained characteristically stolid. He told several of the newsmen that he believed the demonstration was the work of one village of Indians, who meant it as a distraction that would allow the people of their village to break camp and distance themselves from the soldiers. As he told his old friend, Joe Wasson, he feared that "the hostiles are going north, across the Yellowstone." Without scouts or any aggressive movement on his part, Crook could not know that Sitting Bull's village was then barely thirty-seven miles north and actually moving closer and not farther away.[17]

In his diary Bourke captured one benefit of the encounter: it helped transform young soldiers into veterans. When under fire, he noted, young troops "learn the importance of implicit obedience to authority, of keeping constantly in readiness for instant attack or defense and above all things of saving their ammunition. Pickets and sentinels display more vigilance; officers become more zealous and energetic. Loose ends are gathered up; animals are herded with care and wakefulness and a general air of soldierly discipline is infused."[18] Joe Wasson echoed much the same sentiment: "This little brush was a cheap lesson. It will serve to teach our men to obey orders, save their powder and lead, and be constantly alert. A few hostile shots every twenty-four hours would serve a good purpose."[19]

Acknowledging the limitations and vulnerabilities of the Prairie Dog–Tongue confluence, Crook dispatched a party on the morning of June 10 to locate a more agreeable long-term camp. The expedition had all but consumed the available grazing on the Prairie Dog. Much better grass was known on Goose Creek, some fifteen miles to the southwest. The exploring party returned that evening, confirming a suitable location at the forks of Big Goose and Little Goose Creeks. Orders were passed announcing a movement in the morning. Meanwhile the command endured a day of continuing rain. Captain Peter D. Vroom's Company L, Third Cavalry, succeeded Rawolle's Second Cavalry company as the picket en masse on the bluff overlooking the Tongue. Many in the camp feared the Indians' return, though unnecessarily as it turned out.[20]

As the expedition prepared to move on June 11, Company E, Third Cavalry, temporarily commanded by Second Lieutenant Foster of Company I, crossed the Tongue and relieved Vroom's outfit so that it might pack its baggage. Company E held the bluff-top position until the last soldiers marched from camp and then joined another company as the expedition's rear guard. Thomas MacMillan of the *Chicago Inter-Ocean* called the journey to Goose Creek a "retrograde movement." This has been interpreted as a judgmental term by several historians who adhere to the belief that Crook's travel down Prairie Dog Creek was a mistake all along. The objective on June 11 was the Forks of Goose Creek, a distance of slightly less than eighteen miles. The trip was partly a retracing of the expedition's trail down the Prairie Dog then across a low divide to the Fort C. F. Smith Road and down that road until it reached Goose Creek at the mouth of its south branch. The term "retrograde," of course, can also mean simply a backward movement, with no critical judgment implied.[21]

Crook still fumed over the whereabouts of the Shoshones and Crows. He had learned from Sheridan that the Snakes, as white people also called the Shoshones, were supposedly closing on his camp and might already be as near as old Fort Phil Kearny, an easy ride south of the new camp. As for the Crows, Frank Grouard and Crook had agreed to rendezvous on the Tongue when the scout had left the expedition nine days earlier. Crook still had no way of fully understanding the strange encounter with a Crow-speaking Indian on June 8 at the mouth of the Prairie Dog. Perhaps the movement to the Forks of Goose Creek addressed not only the need for fresh grazing but also an attempt to position the command in the fore of the one band of badly needed auxiliaries that Crook knew to be coming.

No one complained about Goose Creek. Goose and Little Goose were clear, cold affluents draining from the Big Horn Mountains, which served as a backdrop across the western horizon. Wood was scattered in abundance, and excellent pasturage swathed the adjacent hillsides. Robert Strahorn of the *Rocky Mountain News* considered it the most beautiful and enticing camp that he had ever seen. As the day's rain abated that afternoon, attention turned to the intended dispatch of mail to Fort Fetterman that evening. The courier Harrison, who had delivered official communications and a general mail on June 8, was making ready for a return. Word had passed through the command earlier in the day of Harrison's imminent departure. Despite the limitations imposed (one letter from each officer and only a few permitted from private soldiers), a heap of letters and small parcels quickly accumulated in Captain Nickerson's tent at headquarters. Loose envelopes were bundled, and the packages were strapped to the courier's pack animal. After dark Harrison and his companion sallied forth on a perilous journey, again riding by night and hiding by day. Buried in the mail was a bevy of dispatches from the newsmen and correspondents providing updates on the expedition's movement to this point and also a brief report from Crook to Sheridan. Crook expressed his continued concern with the overdue Indian scouts, wrote several dismissive lines about the demonstration against his camp on the Tongue, and shared the belief that the Indians' main camp was on the "Little Rosebud or Tongue River." Crook did not predict any imminent advance.[22]

Small knots of officers congregated at headquarters to ponder the non-appearance of the promised Shoshones and Crows and the future of the campaign. For some, even ardent Crook cronies, the idleness was frustrating. "We are compelled to fritter away much valuable time: instead of hunting the Sioux and engaging in action with them, we have only routine duties to occupy our time," Bourke penned quietly in his diary. Crook's silence on all things continued to baffle his officers. The animated Foster again quietly mocked the general, telling his *Chicago Tribune* readers that "everybody again supposes that we are to leave the infantry and wagon-train here, and start out with pack-mules; but nobody knows anything about it but Gen. Crook, and he has a faculty for silence that is absolutely astonishing. There is only one thing very certain: none of the General's plans will ever be discussed until after they are executed, a priceless quality in a commanding officer. Grant is loquacious when compared with him." The reference to Grant reflected an common impression of the day where the president was sometimes called "Grant the Silent" or "the quiet man." Americans saw Grant as a man of deeds, not words.[23]

Over the next several days the Big Horn and Yellowstone Expedition indeed frittered away its time. Any advance against the Sioux hinged on the arrival of Indian auxiliaries, an element that Crook inflexibly embraced as central to his manner of campaigning and without which he would not move at all. Employing Indian trackers was a well-known feature of a Crook campaign. Adding pack mules extended his range. The combination was a manner of campaigning he had perfected long ago, which had earned him accolades from the president and nation. Doubtless now he felt the need ever more acutely as he faced not only the unique vastness of the northern plains but also the incomparable wiliness of his foe. These Northern Indians were proving unafraid of him and were not dodging his advances but were willing to bring the fight straight to him. Moreover, by all accounts thousands of Sioux were massed somewhere down the Tongue or Rosebud or even Powder. Having knowledgeable Indian auxiliaries at his side and following him gave Crook an advantage, and his very silence suggests that he sought every advantage he could muster.

Meanwhile the command demonstrated its perfect knack for killing time, especially in such an idyllic setting as Goose Creek in the lush front country of the Big Horns. Officers and civilians, unlike those in the enlisted ranks, enjoyed near perfect freedom of movement. Many embarked on hunting and fishing forays. Anson Mills was the most visible among them, leading a hunting adventure that netted a large cinnamon bear, a variant of the American black bear. Henry Noyes and Captain Elijah Wells of the Second Cavalry took to fishing. Wells himself hooked nineteen, including one weighing two pounds eleven ounces. First Lieutenant William L. Carpenter of the Ninth Infantry collected ornithological specimens. Andrew Burt and Robert Strahorn joined prospector-turned-correspondent Ernest Hornberger and several other miners in the foothills exploring for gold. When the yields were paltry, they returned to the Goose and caught forty-five large trout. Lieutenant Foster, an accomplished artist as well as an extraordinary correspondent, sketched points of interest, intending to send them to *Harper's Weekly* for publication.[24]

Uncharacteristically, Crook did not stray far from camp, welcoming a few officers to his tent to play whist and otherwise generally minding the business of the expedition directly and indirectly. The Tongue River Heights episode was telling. In addition to the usual line of pickets established on the summits of buttes and bluffs, entire companies of cavalry were thrown out at greater distances by day to hold in check any attackers until the herds could be secured and the various battalions saddled and able to respond. On June 12 alone Captain Guy Henry's Company D, Third Cavalry, took station up one branch of Goose Creek, while Second Lieutenant Bainbridge Reynolds and Company F, Third Cavalry, advanced up the other. Downstream Mein-hold's and Vroom's companies of the Third Cavalry occupied the high bluffs above the Goose. Aside from squads kept on continuous observation, the horses of the deployed companies remained saddled all the while, although not bridled. On June 13 Crook dispatched First Lieutenant Samuel M. Swi-gert and D Company, Second Cavalry, to Fort Phil Kearny to rendezvous with the expected Shoshones. Swigert returned that evening, having encoun-tered no auxiliaries. Despite the momentary lull, Bourke remembered that the officers and men were always on the alert and that considerable anxiety existed throughout the camp, particularly at headquarters.[25]

The expedition's unusual respite continued into June 14. The predawn silence that day was broken when a sentry accidentally discharged his carbine when about to go on duty. The shot reverberated throughout the camp and was instantly noticed and viewed with suspicion, especially in the predawn among men who had already been attacked in twilight hours. Quiet was quickly restored, but this was a jittery camp in some quarters. For their part, the camp's sportsmen again went about their callings, delivering among other comestibles several elk and a buffalo bull.[26]

∥∥∥∥∥∥∥∥∥∥∥∥∥∥∥∥∥∥∥∥∥∥∥∥∥∥∥∥∥∥

The oddest side note in the history of the Big Horn and Yellowstone Expedi-tion's Rosebud campaign occurred on June 14 when Martha "Calamity Jane" Canary was discovered in the army camp. Calamity's comings, goings, and associations have long been interesting fodder in the history of the American West. It is an absorbing element of her story that she or any woman could somehow worm her way into the testosterone-filled world of a major military campaign. In her own day Calamity proudly boasted that she was "bearer of important dispatches" for General Crook in 1876. Biographers expanded on that notion, claiming that she also scouted for Crook's command. Carrying dispatches and scouting were two distinct roles in the campaign. Many of the expedition's contemporary chroniclers noted Calamity's presence, mostly upon reflection, however, as if they had heard of her but never actually encountered her. Most historians of the campaign also note her unique pres-ence without delving into any specifics, particularly her own timeline. For-tunately, it is possible to piece together primary and circumstantial evidence that reconciles the various confirmed dates in Calamity's history with one of the several inferred dates of her intersection with Crook's column. In fact Calamity rather remarkably appeared at Goose Creek on June 14.[27]

By 1876 "Calamity Jane" Canary was a well-known character on the northern plains. All of twenty years old, she had an unquenchable thirst for adventure, soldiers, and drink. The year before she had wended her way into the Black Hills while Dodge's Expedition was there sizing up the new El Dorado for the government. A soldier in Dodge's camp suggested that she wear cavalry clothes so as to blend in. She was photographed by the expedition's photographer in soldier clothes and may have met General Crook or at least stood in his presence when he visited in July and August and talked with miners. When not assaulting army expeditions, Calamity Jane lived among the ever-drifting flotsam of Cheyenne, Fort Laramie, and Custer City. She was a hard drinker and an occasional brothel worker at Cuny and Ecoffey's Three-Mile Ranch west of Fort Laramie.[28]

Women flitting about Crook's army camp are hinted at while the expedition was still organizing at Fort Fetterman. Thomas MacMillan, reporter for the *Chicago Inter-Ocean,* alluded to such hijinks in a dispatch he wrote at the fort on May 29:

> The other evening after we went into camp a lad of 15 or 16 knocked at the tent-door, and wanted to know if we could see him through the expedition. His voice and face were feminine, but his clothing was unmistakably that of the soldier-citizen. We gave him (or her) some supper, and promised to see him (or her) to the end of the expedition. When the meal was done our visitor had some calls to make in the other companies, and has forgotten to return, although he (or she) said he (or she) would come back the next morning. Many mornings have come and gone, and yet he cometh not, she said. Such is life in the West.[29]

In all likelihood MacMillan encountered a young sporting woman from a road ranch operating quietly south of the fort on La Prele Creek. Establishments of the sort were always located apart from the military reservation and were thus beyond army control. This place was known simply as Fisher's and had three or sometimes four prostitutes in residence. MacMillan's reference is often cited as introductory proof of Calamity's connection with the expedition. In fact, however, she had been continuously incarcerated in Cheyenne on charges of grand larceny since May 22. A jury eventually acquitted Calamity, but she was not released until June 8. By then Crook's expedition had reached the mouth of Prairie Dog Creek and stood on the verge of its night-time encounter with the Crow-speaking Indian. Ironically, the interpreter during that episode was Ben Arnold, who figures in the Calamity Jane story more than is plainly understood.[30]

Ben Arnold accompanied the expedition in the capacity of a courier, just one of many cogs in a communications system that had messengers departing respectively from Fort Fetterman and the expedition every three or four days, often meeting midway. Maintaining this system became a challenge as the season wore on, but in the expedition's earliest days couriers stood ready on both ends to serve Crook's needs and also those of the newspaper correspondents, who occasionally drummed their own riders. Arnold's "told-to" biography related his fitful experience communicating with the Crow Indian and how on the next day, June 9, he was engaged to carry dispatches to Fetterman. (In fact, separate newspaper dispatches datelined June 8 and June 10 support Arnold's statement, implying as well that his courier services were provided to newspapermen, not the army.) Such rides for a courier were of two or three days' duration, depending on distances and obstacles—chiefly Indians—encountered along the way. In this particular instance Arnold described actually encountering a small band of Indians, exchanging shots with them, fleeing against all odds, but ultimately reaching Fort Fetterman. That element of the tale reads rather fancifully.[31]

Upon Calamity's release from the Cheyenne jail, she promptly went on a several-day drinking spree. She then, for reasons unclear, rented a horse and buggy from James Abney's stable in Cheyenne, ostensibly for a ride to Fort D. A. Russell three miles away. Instead Jane bounded north on the Fort Laramie–Custer City Road. Her spree continued at road houses along the way and finally ended upon reaching Fort Laramie on June 10. The county sheriff trailed her all the way but rather than arresting here only reclaimed Abney's outfit. Calamity seems to have been fully aware of Crook's campaign, which was continuous news in Cheyenne during her incarceration and spree. At this point her principal biographers momentarily lose her. It seems entirely conceivable, however, that she secured a horse at Fort Laramie or the nearby Three-Mile Ranch (where she worked from time to time), made her way to Fort Fetterman in time to connect with Arnold there late on the evening of June 11, and then joined him on his return trip to the expedition.[32]

Ben Arnold described having a companion on his return to Crook's camp. He did not mention Calamity Jane but instead implied that his riding partner was a soldier provided by Captain Edwin M. Coates, Fetterman's commanding officer. Perhaps that was so, and Jane merely hid among the shadows of this several-day-long trip to Goose Creek. It is just as likely that she was Arnold's companion. His own description of this individual suggests this, even as he conveniently and understandably perpetrates a ruse on his contemporaries and on history:

> My companion sent by the post commander to keep me company, was a sort of a nuisance. He tired easily, would lag behind, then shout to me at a distance if he had anything to say. He could not realize that we were going through a dangerous country where quietness was necessary to safety. Sometimes he would whistle and sing. Finally I told him I didn't want to advertise myself to the Indians, whatever he preferred, and that we would part company if he persisted in his noise making. I was entrusted with important papers and wanted to get them through. After that my companion was more subdued, and we got though without mishap.

In Arnold's description we can just as easily read an under-the-weather whippersnapper instead of a proffered indifferent soldier. Importantly, Arnold confirms the delivery of dispatches and mail on the morning of June 14.[33]

Many of the campaign's chroniclers mention Calamity Jane's appearance in the army camp, but only two do so inside the tight timeline central to Canary's chronology. She had a very short window, front and back, in which this distraction could possibly have occurred. Her jail time and drinking spree already set the front date. John Bourke directly confirms the date of June 14 for Jane's arrival in the Goose Creek camp—not in his diary but in his classic history of Crook's Indian campaigns, *On the Border with Crook*, published in 1891 on the occasion of the general's death: "It was whispered that one of our teamsters was a woman, and no other than 'Calamity Jane,' a character famed in border story; she had donned the raiment of the alleged rougher sex, and was skinning mules with the best of them." Robert Strahorn, reporter for the *Rocky Mountain News*, also confirms this date, rightly placing her appearance immediately ahead of the reappearance of the long-lost scout Frank Grouard on the same day.[34]

Strahorn confirms that Jane quickly blended in with the teamsters, and mule packer Henry Daly recalled her driving a six-mule team through the entire campaign. Many years later Private Frank Foss of Company I, Second Cavalry, snarled: "We had half our bewhiskered, unwashed teamsters that were prettier than she was." These accounts twist some details and appeared late in life: Strahorn's reminiscence written in 1942, Daly's story published in 1926, and Foss's recollection set down in 1930. They plainly drew on deep reflection but nonetheless capture the essence of Calamity Jane in the Goose Creek camp.[35]

Captain Anson Mills also remembered Calamity and later recollected one of the more vivid encounters, although he places the episode at Fort Reno on the expedition's outbound journey. In an account of the campaign prepared in 1917 as an after-dinner talk for the fraternal Order of Indian Wars, he recollected how the wagon master unintentionally employed a female teamster at Fort Fetterman. When discovered she was immediately arrested and placed in improvised female attire. "I knew nothing of this," Mills told his audience, until "I was going through the wagon master's outfit when she sprang up calling out 'There is Colonel Mills, he knows me,' when everybody began to laugh, much to my astonishment and chagrin, being married." In fact, Mills was in the Black Hills in 1875 when such a previous encounter could well have occurred. He only later learned that this was Calamity Jane and then endured endless ribbing from his friends. "I denied any knowledge of her or her calling, but no one believed me, and I doubt whether they all do yet."[36]

Crook had no time for such tomfoolery. He had Calamity arrested and kept under guard in Captain Furey's wagon corral (he was the expedition's quartermaster and she was a pretend teamster). Keeping her far from the expedition's headquarters may explain why Bourke did not set this episode down in his daily diary and only wrote of it upon reflection. Crook also ordered that Jane be dressed as a woman. Mills simply called her new outfit "improvised female attire." Private Foss more particularly described it as "skirts made from flour sacking over her trousers." In due course she was returned to Fort Fetterman.[37]

In the end the episode was of minuscule significance to Crook's Big Horn and Yellowstone Expedition and its Rosebud Campaign. Calamity Jane's appearance in the general's camp on Goose Creek made no difference at all to the army and caused no undue stress, concern, or embarrassment, except perhaps for Anson Mills, who dismissed it with a laugh. Yet inside Calamity's world, where many things played big to a fragile if outsized ego, delivering "important dispatches" to Crook enhanced her self-worth and budding stature. She may have been a slight nuisance to the army, but for her this was a really big deal.

George Crook, Azor Nickerson, and John Bourke
in San Francisco, April 1875

Brigadier General George Crook poses in San Francisco with his two principal aides, Captain Azor H. Nickerson, Twenty-Third Infantry (standing) and Second Lieutenant John G. Bourke, Third Cavalry (left). The three were en route from Arizona to Crook's new assignment as commander of the Military Department of the Platte in Omaha, facing the looming Black Hills crisis and an out-and-out war with the Sioux. Bradley and Rulofson photograph. (Sharlot Hall Museum Library & Archives, MIL-225P-2991)

John Finerty, *Chicago Times*

Of the five full-time newsmen accompanying Crook's Big Horn and Yellowstone Expedition in June, Irish-born John F. Finerty of the *Chicago Times* was the most effusive, penning lengthy, thoughtful accounts of the column's day-to-day movements, its puzzling pauses, and the day-long battle at Rosebud Creek. Finerty was then twenty-nine years old. He went on to report other Indian campaigns, was the first American newsman to interview the long-serving and controversial Mexican president José de la Cruz Porfirio Díaz, served a stint as the *Times* political correspondent in Washington, D.C., and was elected to a term in the House of Representatives. Charles D. Mosher photograph. (Chicago History Museum, ICHi-173518)

Captain William Stanton, Corps of Engineers, 1882

Dapper William Stanton, an 1865 West Point graduate, served as Crook's engineering officer in the Department of the Platte from 1874 to 1881. He was a dutiful if seemingly reluctant participant in the Rosebud campaign, authoring a useful day-to-day journal but taking no particular role in the engagement. He is well remembered on the northern plains for superintending the construction of a stout iron bridge at Fort Laramie and conducting detailed surveys of the roads connecting the department's scattered military posts. Stanton enjoyed a long career in the Corps of Engineers, retiring in 1906. (Author's collection)

"General Crook at the Scene of the Fort Phil Kearney [*sic*] Massacre, June 6th"

Crook and his entourage spent time on the morning of June 6 examining the Fetterman Massacre site directly north of Fort Phil Kearny. The place had a haunting lure, much like the fort's cemetery, which most of this same crowd had explored the day before and seen the humble interment of Fetterman and the other casualties of that fight. Charles St. George Stanley sketch for *Frank Leslie's Illustrated Newspaper*, August 12, 1876. (Author's collection)

**"Indians Attempting to Surprise General Crook's Camp
at Tongue River, June 9th"**

In a complete surprise to the men of the Big Horn and Yellowstone Expedition, on the evening
of June 9 fifty Northern Cheyenne and Sioux warriors openly taunted these hated *waśicu* at
their camp at the mouth of Prairie Dog Creek. Several soldiers were slightly wounded, and the
expedition's tentage was pock-marked. The demonstration was meant as a warning: the hunting grounds north of the Tongue River belonged to the Northern Indians: interlopers entered
at their own peril. Charles St. George Stanley sketch for *Frank Leslie's Illustrated Newspaper*,
August 12, 1876. (Author's collection)

Frank Grouard, January 1877

As he had done on the Big Horn Expedition in March, Frank Grouard provided indispensable service to General Crook on the Rosebud campaign. In addition to leading 175 Crow scouts to the general's Goose Creek camp, Grouard provided vital intelligence on Sitting Bull's whereabouts. It was this information, reflecting an understanding gained directly from the Crows, that led Crook straight to Rosebud Creek. Grouard remained a visible figure on the northern plains through the close of the century. He lived in Saint Joseph, Missouri, where he died in 1905 at the age of fifty-four. D. S. Mitchell photograph. (Missouri History Museum, Wikimedia Commons)

Ben Arnold

Frontier roustabout Ben Arnold was something like Hollywood's Jack Crabb (*Little Big Man*). A deserter in Wyoming from his Ohio volunteer cavalry unit during the Civil War, Arnold placer mined in Montana and labored as a bullwhacker, wood hawk, and wolfer in Montana and Dakota. Counted among the flotsam at Fort Fetterman in the mid-1870s, he connected with Crook's campaign, where he served as a courier, misinterpreted a critical exchange with the Crows at the mouth of Prairie Dog Creek, and in all likelihood delivered Calamity Jane to the general's camp. (State Historical Society of North Dakota, A0370–00001)

Old Crow (Crow)

When Frank Grouard traveled to Crow Country in June 1876 seeking to enlist local tribesmen to scout for Crook, he encountered Old Crow at the onset. Old Crow listened to Grouard's plea and agreed to help enlist allies, eyeing an opportunity for fellow tribesmen to whip old enemies. He fought valiantly in the Rosebud battle but subsequently was among Crow headmen who refused to lead Crook down the Rosebud Narrows, a critical turn-of-events that brought to a close the day's fight and ended Crook's hope of attacking Sitting Bull's village. David F. Barry photograph. (Denver Public Library, Western History Collection, B-19)

Plenty Coups (Crow) and Bull Snake (Crow), ca. 1908

Plenty Coups (left) and Bull Snake (right) were among the 175 Crow chiefs and warriors who joined Crook on the Rosebud campaign. All were eager to fight hereditary enemies. In 1876 Plenty Coups was a band chief among the Mountain Crows, a role that grew ever more prominent through the years and endured until his passing in 1932 at the age of eighty-four. Bull Snake was unhorsed at Rosebud and seriously wounded in the leg. He was dramatically rescued from certain death by two other Crows, Finds Them and Kills Them and The Other Magpie, shown on page 331. . Richard Throssel photograph. (Richard Throssel Papers, ah02394_0813, American Heritage Center, University of Wyoming)

Wesha (Shoshone)

Wesha was a Shoshone headman prominent in tribal affairs in the late nineteenth century. On the Rosebud campaign he and Chief Washakie's sons, Dick and Bishop, led contingents of warriors, all under the general command of Texan ex-Confederate cavalryman Tom Cosgrove. The Shoshone complement was a mirror of the widely respected assembly of Pawnee Scouts operating at the same time in Nebraska. (Author's collection)

Dick Washakie (Shoshone) and Edmo LeClair (Shoshone)

Dick Washakie (left) and Edmo LeClair (right), two veterans of the Shoshone contingent scouting for Crook on the Rosebud campaign, returned to the Rosebud Battlefield in June 1926. Here they pose at the Rosebud X4 Ranch at Kirby, several miles north of the field, with Finn Burnett, another individual with long historical ties to the region. LeClair, a mixed-blood scout, was among the Shoshones rallying to save Guy Henry from sure death. Jessamine Spear Johnson photograph. (Tempe Johnson Javitz, X4 LLC Collection)

"Grand Council Held at General Crook's Headquarters on Goose Creek"

General Crook held two councils of war on June 14. News of the whereabouts of Sitting Bull's village had just been received. That evening Crook summoned the headmen and chiefs of the newly arrived Crows and Shoshones. Around a crackling fire at headquarters he detailed his plans for an assault on Sitting Bull's camp and listened as the chiefs expressed their willingness to help and a feverish desire to take this war to the Sioux. Soldiers and newsmen remembered a solemn and enchanting spectacle. Charles St. George Stanley sketch for *Frank Leslie's Illustrated Newspaper*, September 2, 1876. (Author's collection)

**"A Crow Warrior in General Crook's Command
'Crying for Scalps,' June 15"**

In a display that soldiers found both enthralling and mysterious, on the morning of June 15 a Crow warrior rode through Crook's Goose Creek camp pleading, praying, and exhorting the empty air. He was seeking courage in the coming fight and particularly asking for many scalps, in a supplication remembered as "Crying for Scalps." Charles St. George Stanley sketch for *Frank Leslie's Illustrated Newspaper,* August 26, 1876. (Author's collection)

"Issuing Arms and Supplies to the Friendly Indians in General Crook's Army, June 15th"

Crook allowed one day for the men of his expedition to prepare for the advance. While Major Chambers's infantry battalion was introduced to its mules, everyone else in the command, including the Indian auxiliaries, gathered at the quartermaster and commissary corral of John Furey and Lieutenant John Bubb to receive requisite allowances of rations and ammunition and issues of new Springfield carbines for some auxiliaries. Charles St. George Stanley sketch for *Frank Leslie's Illustrated Newspaper*, October 14, 1876. (Author's collection)

121

Major Alexander Chambers, Fourth Infantry

Alexander Chambers commanded Crook's infantry battalion on the long summer campaign of 1876. An 1853 West Point graduate and classmate of Phil Sheridan, John Grattan, and Elmer Otis, he was a veteran of repeated combat on the prewar Indian frontier and throughout the Civil War. He was wounded several times and frequently breveted for gallant and meritorious service. He commanded the Seventeenth Infantry at the time of his death in 1888 at the age of fifty-five. Chambers is buried in Owatonna, Minnesota. (MOLLUS-Mass Civil War Photograph Collection, Volume 69, United States Army Heritage and Education Center, Carlisle Barracks, Pennsylvania)

Captain George Randall, Twenty-Third Infantry

On the Rosebud campaign George Randall served as Crook's chief of scouts, a role entailing more coordination than actual command. A veteran infantry officer many times breveted for gallantry in the Civil War, Randall became friends with Crook while they were serving together in the Twenty-Third Infantry and again during the Apache campaigns in the early 1870s. Here he is seen as colonel of the Eighth Infantry about 1898. (Author's collection)

Captain Samuel Munson, Ninth Infantry

Aside from brief service with a Maine infantry regiment in the opening days of the Civil War, Samuel Munson and the Ninth Infantry (the regiment that he joined in August 1861) spent the war at posts in the San Francisco Bay area. Munson commanded a portion of the initial skirmish line at Rosebud, joined in the charge on Conical Hill, and later escorted the wounded to Fort Fetterman. He died in service in 1887 and was buried in Portland, Maine. (Author's collection)

Captain Henry Noyes, Second Cavalry

Henry Noyes, seen here as lieutenant colonel of the Second Cavalry in the mid-1890s, graduated with the second West Point class of 1861 and counted George Armstrong Custer as a classmate. For an indiscretion in the Powder River battle, Noyes was court-martialed in May but immediately returned to duty. At Rosebud he joined Major Chambers in establishing a critical skirmish line when the battle opened, thereby providing essential cover for other troops as they saddled and prepared for action. (History Colorado, 10044650)

Major Andrew Evans, Third Cavalry

The ever-stoic Andrew Wallace Evans was a West Point classmate of General Crook and a veteran field commander many times breveted for gallant and meritorious service during the Civil War and on the Indian frontier. For much of the Rosebud campaign, however, he seemed to be an officer without a purpose. At a critical juncture in the battle, with Royall's command facing seemingly inevitable destruction, Evans withheld the support of his own cobbled-together detachment, despite pleas from subordinates and gunfire crescendoing across the battlefield. He may simply have been following orders. Evans retired in 1883, died in 1906, and is buried in Elkton, Maryland. (Creative Commons and the Elkton, Maryland, *Cecil Whig*)

Captain Frederick Van Vliet, Third Cavalry

Frederick Van Vliet commanded a Third Cavalry squadron on Crook's Big Horn and Yellowstone Expedition. During much of the Rosebud fight his two companies occupied a critical position on the south side of the field, where they witnessed much but engaged lightly. Here he is seen as a major of the Tenth Cavalry, circa 1882. (RG641s-MOLLUS-PA11.26, United States Army Heritage and Education Center, Carlisle Barracks, Pennsylvania)

Sitting Bull (Hunkpapa Sioux)

Whites demonized the great Lakota chief Sitting Bull and often referred to the Indian war of 1876–77 as Sitting Bull's War. In truth, few other northern plains Indians of the day engendered the same charisma as this venerable Hunkpapa traditionalist. Sitting Bull's Sun Dance vision of soldiers falling upside down into an Indian village, foretelling an astounding Indian victory, spurred followers to great valor at Rosebud and Little Big Horn and deepened a mystique that survives to this day. David F. Barry photograph. (State Historical Society of North Dakota, 00051–00007)

Little Big Man (Oglala Sioux), 1877

Standing barely five feet tall, the barrel-chested and muscular Little Big Man was a fervent Lakota traditionalist. He opposed the Fort Laramie Treaty of 1868 and the sale of the Black Hills in 1875. After the Powder River battle in March 1876 he was among those carrying word from Sitting Bull urging agency traditionalists to rally and fight the *wašicu*. In May he guided one of the largest groups of agency Indians—Big Road's confederation—to the northern camp, arriving on Rosebud Creek just days ahead of the great Hunkpapa Sun Dance. Little Big Man is also remembered for switching allegiances after the Oglalas surrendered at Camp Robinson in 1877 and was complicit in the death of Crazy Horse that September. He is thought to have died about 1887. D. S. Mitchell photograph. (Nebraska State Historical Society, RG2955-PH-25)

Big Road (Oglala Sioux)

Big Road was a fervent traditionalist and chief of a Bad Face band of Oglalas. In May 1876 he led his White River agency followers to Sitting Bull's camp. Big Road was among those who fled to Canada in 1877 but then surrendered at Fort Keogh in 1880. Big Road remained a staunch nonprogressive in the early reservation years. He did not sign the controversial land cession agreement of 1889 and was a ghost dancer in 1890. His date of death and place of burial are unknown. (Braun Research Library Collection, Autry Museum, Los Angeles; P.36977)

Kill Eagle (Blackfeet Sioux)

While not a participant in the Rosebud Battle, Kill Eagle and his Blackfeet Sioux followers were present in Sitting Bull's camp on Reno Creek. They had come west from their Missouri River agency to hunt buffalo, not to fight. When returning to Standing Rock later that fall, Kill Eagle provided a lengthy interview that was widely reprinted in American newspapers and provided compelling insights into the Northern Indians who defeated Crook and destroyed Custer. W. R. Cross photograph. (Nebraska State Historical Society, RG3730–38)

Little Hawk (Northern Cheyenne)

Little Hawk was twenty-eight years old at the time of the Rosebud Battle. While scouting with other Northern Cheyenne wolves for *wasicu* who had been seen on the Tongue River days earlier, on the afternoon of June 16 he spotted soldiers in the highlands of Rosebud Creek advancing northward. Riding feverishly through the night, he delivered the ominous news to the great Northern Indian camp on Reno Creek. Little Hawk was remembered ever after by the Cheyennes and Sioux as the man who discovered Crook before the Rosebud fight. (Nebraska State Historical Society, RG3730-PH0–24-detail)

Wooden Leg (Northern Cheyenne)

Wooden Leg, a member of the Northern Cheyenne Elkhorn Scrapers warrior society, was eighteen years old at the time of the Rosebud battle. His compelling personal narrative was collected by Thomas B. Marquis, a long-serving agency physician among the Cheyennes, and preserved in the book *A Warrior Who Fought Custer*. Wooden Leg's story provides a vital recounting of the early battles of the Great Sioux War and the Northern Cheyennes in the late nineteenth century. Thomas Marquis photograph. (Thomas Marquis Collection, PN.165.1.48, Buffalo Bill Center of the West)

South Fork of Reno Creek

While most of the warriors from Sitting Bull's Reno Creek camp who engaged Crook traveled to the Big Bend by way of Rosebud Creek itself, Little Hawk, Wooden Leg, and a smaller group of Northern Cheyenne and Sioux warriors traveled by way of the South Fork of Reno Creek, seen here. That route was considerably shorter from point to point but doubly challenging when crossing a length of the Wolf Mountain highlands seen on the distant horizon. The Reno Creek camp sprawled across this view right and left, occupying another of the bucolic mid-June landscapes characteristic of southeastern Montana. (Author's photograph)

FATEFUL INTELLIGENCE

By dawn of the third day at the Goose Creek camp, June 14, the hand-wringing over the whereabouts of Frank Grouard, Louie Richard, and Big Bat Pourier dominated all other conversation. Officers and war correspondents alike wondered why fishing and hunting was again filling their time instead of aggressively moving against the Sioux. The ever stoic Crook had fretted over Grouard for nearly two weeks, his anxiety compounded after the puzzling encounter with the Crow-speaking Indian at the mouth of Prairie Dog Creek six days earlier. The expedition's only scouts had been absent since June 2, off to Crow Country to bring back or even recruit if necessary a contingent of Crow allies for the campaign. Crook had assurances from Sheridan that Crows were available and had been on the lookout for them daily, illogically in the first days of the campaign and fearfully now. "A few go so far as to imagine that evil may have befallen them," Bourke confided in his diary. "Yet it would be a relief from doubt and anxiety to have them back that we might commence in dead earnest the work of the campaign," he continued, "which up to this time has been nothing but a picnic without exploit or advantage."[1]

The doldrums, "the throes of anxiety" as Joe Wasson put it, disappeared early that afternoon. Pickets posted in the far north of the camp, "I being one of them," remembered Private William Miller of Company E, Third Cavalry, "discovered a large cloud of dust about 3 miles [out] on the plains. We notified the officer of the day; he reported to General Crook. One of the officers in the command had a pair of field glasses and made out that they were Indians and white men."[2]

It was not a large group, barely more than a dozen Crows led by Grouard and Richard. Soldiers swarmed them as they entered camp. Grouard rode ahead to headquarters seeking out the general. When Grouard dismounted, Crook eagerly grasped his hands within his own and blurted: "Frank, my boy, I began to think you were lost." Behind him, Richard and an old Crow man (a chieftain, some thought) and a handful of warriors came on. Grouard quickly explained that many others were ten miles back and reluctant to come in, fearful that this was not a safe camp. Scout Baptiste Pourier remained with them. Quickly a hearty meal was dished up—hot coffee, sugar, biscuits, butter, venison, jam, and stewed apples—the sumptuous fare at headquarters so long as wagons were still at hand. Grouard, meanwhile, had much to explain.[3]

<hr/>

Enlisting Crow scouts proved to be a trial for the Sandwich Islander and the others. In later days Grouard related the story to his biographer in careful detail, likely repeating all that he told Crook that afternoon. After leaving Fort Reno on June 2, Crook's three scouts followed the Montana Road as best they could, mostly traveling by night and laying over by day. They killed a buffalo on Crazy Woman Creek and cooked all the meat they needed for the trip, not intending to make any more fires that might betray their presence. On the second day the trio was jumped by a bear. "I had to kill it," Grouard explained, as there was no other way. Surmounting a hill a short while later they discovered an Indian camp below them. The Indians did not hear the shot, "which was lucky for us," but it forced the three into the mountains for the day. They came down on Piney Creek after dark but again encountered a camp of Indians, which kept them moving. "I could not travel very fast," Grouard confessed. As they neared the Little Big Horn River the scouts encountered even more Indians, and the next morning they were sure that they were being followed. The three kept moving. When they reached the Big Horn River, they peered across and again saw Indians on the far hills. Believing now that they were Crows, Grouard signaled to them. The Indians saw the signal but rode away. When two more Indians appeared, Grouard signaled again. They too saw the flashes but rode away in the same direction as the others.[4]

Thinking nothing of the Indians on the far banks of the Big Horn, with the river in its spring rise, Grouard and Pourier set about fashioning a raft for use in crossing, while Richard built a fire and prepared a meal. Barely had the three begun to eat when Grouard was startled to see great bodies of Indians behind them *and* across the river, Sioux perhaps on one side and Crows on the other. Bat Pourier was the first to make sense of it. Recognizing Crow acquaintances in the band behind them, he began crying aloud "Left Hand." The Crows knew him as "Left-Handed." As soon as they heard the name, they stopped what Grouard took to have been an aggressive move, rode up, shook hands, and asked about their business. With Pourier interpreting, Grouard explained that they had come from General Crook's camp and were headed for their village, hoping to lead many of them back to Crook. "They did not seem much in favor of going with us," Grouard admitted.[5]

Four days passed while Grouard and the others held a council with the chiefs and elders in the Crow camp and made sense of it all. First Lieutenant William Quinton of the Seventh Infantry from Fort Ellis assisted with negotiations. "They were very changeable about the business," Grouard observed, as if "a little afraid of the Sioux or something." Only on the spot could he fully understand the demands for help already levied on the tribe and the reluctance of some chiefs to support this war. Gibbon had similarly counseled with the Crows and their agent in early April soon after he had taken the field. He too wanted Crow scouts. Successfully enlisting twenty-five, he induced others to probe eastward to find and fight the Sioux on their own. On the fourth day a man by the name of Old Crow, "who seemed to be one of the headmen," asked Grouard when it was that he intended to start back. The next morning, Grouard told him. "All right, I will go with you," the old man said. He got on his horse and went about haranguing the camp, telling his people that he was going along and asking what they were afraid of. Plenty Coups, a young pipe bearer of the tribe, joined in as well, admonishing his followers: "Let us help this man. His wolves here say he has many soldiers in his camp and with them we shall whip our old enemies." Before nightfall, Grouard recalled, "we had 159 Indians ready to start back the next morning."[6]

If the trip to the north was complicated for Grouard, the return journey held unique challenges and delays as well. In all the contingent numbered 176 people. Three of the chiefs brought along their wives. Also in the band were a scattering of "young boys learning their first lessons of war." Almost all trailed extra horses. With a dangerous reach of Sioux Country to cross, Grouard and Old Crow kept scouts well in the advance. It was several of those wolves who had encountered Crook's camp at the mouth of Prairie Dog Creek. But after attempting to communicate with the camp and hearing responses in the Sioux language, the Crows fled, uncertain of the camp's friendliness. Soon after crossing the Little Big Horn the Crows encountered a buffalo herd and started a hunt. "The next morning we were killing buffalo; could not travel very far on account of airing the meat," Grouard explained.[7]

Assuming a rendezvous with Crook on the Tongue at the mouth of Prairie Dog Creek, Grouard led the Crows in a southeasterly direction into the Wolf Mountains. After discovering that Crook's camp had been abandoned, Grouard and the Crows followed the expedition's plainly visible trail to the divide between the Prairie Dog and Goose and finally observed the general's camp at the forks of the Big and Little Goose Creeks in the distance. Even then they felt a strong reluctance. This was the same outfit that Crow scouts had attempted to communicate with at the mouth of Prairie Dog Creek. Some still believed that this was a Sioux camp and that Grouard and the others were luring them down to have them killed. Shaking the notion was difficult. Left Hand (Big Bat) Pourier was, in fact, a Sioux squaw man. Richard was a mixed-blood Sioux. Grouard was simply unknown to the Crows. "I told them that what they saw were the tents of the troops, [and] that if they would wait there, I would leave Bat and Louie with them and would go into the camp and send an officer out to meet them." When the Crows consented to this, Grouard hurried on, with Richard riding along. Pourier remained behind. So things stood as Grouard sought out the general as quickly as possible.[8]

After a brief exchange Crook directed Richard and Captain Andrew Burt to return to the Crows and lead them in. Old Crow went along. He knew Burt and had also seen Captain Thomas Burrowes in the camp. During the days of the Bozeman Trail, Burt and Burrowes served at Fort C. F. Smith on the Big Horn River and both enjoyed the tribe's friendship and confidence. At the rendezvous ten miles from the soldier camp, Burt told the Crows that the Sioux had not defeated Crook, as some had come to believe after encountering the general's trail leading away from the Tongue. By 6 P.M. the members of the great Crow contingent, their reluctance dissipated, entered the Goose Creek camp, as Plenty Coups remembered, with a great "Crow war-whoop, firing our guns in the air, [and] dashing down the hill." Among the chiefs present, in addition to Plenty Coups and Old Crow, were Medicine Crow, Good Heart, and Feather Head.[9]

In short order the Indians erected wickiups (war lodges as Bourke called them): saplings covered over with blankets and pieces of canvas. Ponies were sent to graze alongside the army herds. Fires were built, and every one feasted on comestibles provided by the commissary (and later five cattle thieved from the expedition's herd). The Crow camp was an immediate lure, with a curious crowd of officers, soldiers, and teamsters milling about, studying the Indians' every move and especially their colorful dress, with ornately trimmed leggings of cloth and skin, an abundance of eagle feathers decorating braids and bonnets, and elaborately adorned moccasins. Nearly all of the Crows were well armed with an array of modern weaponry as well as lances, knives, tomahawks, and bows and arrows. The variety of firearms astounded the gawkers.

They were good arms, wrote Joe Wasson, "mostly Sharps carbines, with a few Springfield needle-guns and other breech-loaders, besides revolvers." By needle-guns Wasson chiefly meant .50–70 Springfield breech-loading rifles and also a few .45–55 and .45–70 Springfield carbines and rifles of current army issue. On this account alone, Crook's wagons carried crates of .50–70 ammunition, anticipating the needs of his Indian allies, although Wasson noted that the Crows were already well supplied.[10]

iiiiiiiiiiiiiiiiiiiiiiiiiiiiiii

Crook spent much of the afternoon of June 14 grilling Grouard for news of the Sioux. He learned much, and it all changed the trajectory of the campaign. Grouard had old news and new from the Crows. They had tribal members with Gibbon and were aware of the colonel's movements along the Yellowstone, Grouard said. He told also of Sioux raids on Gibbon's camp and fruitless cavalry pursuits (matters more clearly known to history as episodes of Sioux horse thievery and the killing of three whites from Gibbon's camp in the third week of May). These details were nearly a month old, "stale" as one account put it. Much more startling, however, and as fresh as yesterday, Crook heard news from Grouard that Sitting Bull and seven hundred lodges were camped on the Rosebud, within forty-five miles of his own Goose Creek camp. This information was almost certainly obtained from recent Crow forays into that country, perhaps even by the scouts fronting Old Crow, Grouard, and this Crow contingent as it made its way to Goose Creek. The detail was jaw-dropping. Sitting Bull was the central bogeyman of this war. Now he and all of his followers were two days away, due north on the first drainage west of the Tongue.[11]

History confirms the intelligence that Grouard offered. For the second time on consecutive campaigns Grouard provided Crook with information that spurred his expedition to battle. On March 16 he had spotted two Cheyenne hunters ranging down Otter Creek, a Tongue River tributary. The Cheyennes fled, but Grouard had a keen sense of their direction and origination. He had assured Crook that he could lead troops straight to that village and then did just that, which led to the battle of Powder River. Now Crow wolves had gained a firm sense of the whereabouts of Sitting Bull's village. In the days since the great Sun Dance on Rosebud Creek, from June 4 through 7, that massive encampment had continued its inexorable drift up Rosebud Creek. When Northern Cheyenne wolves harassed Crook's troops at the mouth of Prairie Dog Creek in the early evening hours of June 9, the great village was then located about where Muddy Creek joins the Rosebud. By June 13, when Grouard and Old Crow were leading Crow auxiliaries across the southern Wolf Mountains, heading for the Tongue River and the mouth of Prairie Dog Creek, Sitting Bull's encampment had moved again, upstream beyond today's Busby, Montana. As always it was a sprawling village, with the Northern Cheyenne circle reaching the mouth of Davis Creek, a Rosebud Creek tributary. Davis Creek and the Forks of Goose Creek are scarcely fifty-five miles apart. Grouard and the Crows knew where to find Sitting Bull's village on June 14, and now so did Crook.[12]

It was as simple as that. The notion of destroying a major Indian village was central to the army's canon for Plains Indian warfare. As frustrating as Crook's first campaign otherwise had been, a village had been destroyed and its occupants (Crazy Horse's people, he wrongly believed) impoverished, losing every capacity to sustain themselves in the traditional way. Furthermore, those people on the Powder River had not fought particularly well. In a parallel way, Crook thought that the tribesmen on the Rosebud would not coalesce and fight now, at least not vigorously, as the demonstration at the mouth of Prairie Dog Creek affirmed. Crook was sure that these Plains Indians would not stand and fight. Instead they would flee: necessity dictated that they protect women, children, and old people. For Crook, the village was the key. Deprive Indians of their lodges, foodstuffs, clothing, blankets, robes, and ponies, and they would have no recourse but to submit at a reservation agency. This was army doctrine. Crook was no mere subscriber to it but one of the army's most innovative, exemplary, and experienced practitioners. What mattered most now, however, was not what the Northern Indians would do but what he himself would do.[13]

Calling an immediate council of war after evening retreat, Crook summoned his battalion commanders and staff to the open field in front of the headquarters tents. Other officers crowded around, and newsmen hovered on the margins. Bourke detailed the assembly carefully in a long diary entry. Crook's remarks, he said,

> were characteristically terse and soldierly. The command would cut loose from wagon and pack-train on the morning of the 16th, taking four day's rations in the saddle bags. One blanket to each man and officer, either the saddle blanket of ordinary issue or a bed blanket, to be

used as such. No extra clothing whatever for officers or men. One hundred rounds of ammunition to each person with the expedition, to be carried in the saddlebags. Lariats and side-lines, but no extra shoes and no picket ropes for horses. The wagons were to be parked and mules to be corralled in a defensible position up the valley of the Tongue, there to be guarded by a detachment left for the purpose. All the available force that could be mounted and equipped to accompany the General. Men from the Infantry companies who could ride and shoot and who so desired to be detailed; the same rule to be applied to volunteers from among the teamsters and packers, mounts to be obtained from extra cavalry horses, team and pack mules; saddles from the wagons and in case of deficiency, blankets and surcingles to be used.[14]

The driving point that Crook impressed upon all was his intent to make a quick, bold strike. Sitting Bull was on the Rosebud barely two days away. A fully mounted corps with four days' rations, guided by Indian auxiliaries who knew the way forward, would lead the expedition straight to Sitting Bull. Probably they would return to the wagons, but foodstuffs in the village would be saved, enabling further maneuvering as the situation might dictate. Alternatively, the corps might even advance to the Yellowstone and combine with Gibbon or Terry. The details—issuing, packing, securing, mounting—would be spelled out in the morning. "It was evident the General meant business," Bourke crowed.[15]

Crook's newfound energy took many in the expedition by surprise. Some had expected that a base of supplies would be established on Goose Creek and that the wagons would return to Fort Fetterman for resupply. By one chronicler's estimation, the column had departed Fetterman with grain enough to last until the middle of June. Instead the wagons would be corralled on Goose Creek in Quartermaster Furey's charge, guarded by teamsters and packers. Everyone else was going forward, mounted, including citizen volunteers and the infantry. Doubtless the business of mounting the infantry was the greatest surprise of all. Thaddeus Capron of Munson's Ninth Infantry company put it rather laconically in his diary: "The order will be out in the morning mounting the infantry on mules, and we are to form part of the command for the execution of the grand movement of the expedition. I trust that we shall do our part and do it well."[16]

Scarcely had Crook's conference ended when pickets raised an alarm on the south side of the camp. Quickly the ruckus was understood to be the arrival of the general's other anticipated corps of Indian allies, the Shoshones from the Wind River country of west-central Wyoming. Eighty-six resplendent warriors rode proudly into camp, cavalry style in a column of twos, many wearing feather headdresses and nearly all with colorful pennons flying from atop long lances. Two American flags fluttered at the column's head. John Finerty thought that the Shoshones looked like Cossacks of the Don, referring to the renowned cavalry mercenaries active on the Russian frontier who sold their military services to different powers in Eastern Europe. Crook dispatched a scout to lead them to headquarters. Commanding the contingent was Tom Cosgrove, a colorful Texan and ex-Confederate cavalry captain, assisted by two fellow Texans, Bob Eckles and Nelson Yarnell, and a mixed-blood named Louissant. Among the Shoshones were two chiefs, Wesha (Wisha, Weshaw) and Nawkee, plus Coo-coosh and Conna-yah (Dick and Bishop Washakie, sons of the venerable Shoshone chief Washakie). Edmore "Edmo" LeClair, a mixed-blood Shoshone, interpreted.[17]

Like the renowned Pawnee Scouts of Nebraska—another dedicated corps of expertly trained Indian auxiliaries led there by Frank North and active on the plains from the 1860s onward—these Shoshone scouts and their leader, Cosgrove, were a similarly well-drilled troop operating in the Wind River country. Cosgrove's scouts played a notable role in the Snake Mountain or so-called Bates fight between Shoshones and Arapahos on July 4, 1874, supported by soldiers from Camp Brown led by Captain Alfred E. Bates of the Second Cavalry. That episode caught the attention of General Sheridan, who commended these men to Crook in April. When Crook was unable to enlist Oglala Sioux auxiliaries he turned to the Crows and Shoshones. The Shoshones needed little inducement. Like the Crows, they viscerally hated the Sioux. Additionally, particularly for the Shoshones, such service afforded young men a chance to pursue a traditional activity in a day when the tribe, like most other reservation people, dealt with intense pressure to give up the old ways and accept a sedentary agricultural life. Here the Shoshones not only had a chance to fight old enemies but were well fed, their wives and children were cared for at their agency, and they were uniquely armed with the latest pattern .45 caliber Springfield carbines—the current regulation carbine (a point noted by many astonished chroniclers). Crook greeted the newcomers, who in turn saluted him, circled his headquarters area, and turned to make a camping place of their own alongside the Crows. The meeting between the tribes was boisterous, warriors from both camps united in their "desire to give the Sioux a final and fatal blow."[18]

Crook allowed his new allies several hours to get their bearing and then at 9 o'clock summoned the chiefs and headmen of both tribes to a grand council of war at his headquarters. In a campaign already marked by graphic spectacle, including the magnificence of the army column marching north from Fort Fetterman, Crook and others in deep study at the mournful Fetterman Battlefield, and Indians firing wildly from the bluffs at Prairie Dog Creek, this night-time assembly on Goose Creek was another great scene for the ages. In the inky darkness with a sliver moon, around a huge fire ablaze in the center of the headquarters area, battalion and company officers, Crows, and Shoshones assembled in conference, their faces and bodies illuminated in the crackling hues of yellow and red. The officers, Indians, correspondents, teamsters, and other civilians formed a broad double circle around the fire, with the Shoshones filling one quadrant and the Crows another. Everyone in the fore sat on the ground or squatted. Behind them other soldiers and civilians crowded about. The group had an "imperturbable calmness," remembered Bourke, no one wishing to miss a word. Joe Wasson remembered it all as a "very impressive and gratifying scene, and one I can never forget."[19]

Crook stood at the center of the circle near his allies, along with Captain Nickerson, the interpreters Grouard, Richard, and Pourier, and the chiefs. Each tribe had a designated spokesman who repeated aloud to his people Crook's words as they were made known through the interpreters. Crook opened with the customary expressions of goodwill and then repeated the same message that he had given to the first of the Crows when they came in and to the officers when they gathered in this same place after evening retreat. Now, however, Crook's words were delivered in segments, interpreted, then repeated to the Indians. A low guttural "Ugh! Ugh!" was the usual response. Bourke was sure that nothing was lost. The process might have been "tedious," wrote MacMillan of the *Chicago Inter-Ocean*, but for so many "novelties in the scene." Charles Stanley sketched the action for *Leslie's*, serving up a vivid impression of the solemnity of the occasion.[20]

When Crook finished, elders of the bands asked the general to be allowed to scout in their own way, a privilege that he easily conceded. Then two of the Crow chiefs in turn stood and expressed their views. Crook stood all the while, his hands in his pockets. At his side was Captain George M. Randall, Twenty-Third Infantry, his designated chief of scouts. Like Crook's remarks, the Crow chiefs' statements were translated sentence by sentence. Good Heart's utterances were plainspoken. The Sioux had long robbed and killed Crows, and now they wanted to get even. The Crows and Shoshones would lead the soldiers to the Sioux. They would run off their horses. Without horses the Sioux could not run off, and the soldiers could destroy their village. The Crows and Shoshones would help them do it.[21] Old Crow's remarks were much more strident. "The face of the Sioux is red, but his heart is black. The scalp of no white man hangs in our lodges. They are thick as grass in the wigwams of the Sioux. Our war is with the Sioux and only them. We want back our lands. We want their horses for our young men, and their mules for our squaws. The Sioux have trampled upon our hearts—we shall spit upon their scalps."[22]

Old Crow's exhortations drew the night's loudest approvals—a "storm of 'Ughs' and yells," wrote Finerty. Crook's response was simple enough. "All they were expected to do was find the villages of the common enemy; he would attend to the fighting; they might have the ponies." Old Crow and Crook shook hands and the council ended. Several hours had elapsed, but Crook continued shaking hands with most of the prominent chiefs as they retired.[23]

Bourke was sure that the newly arrived auxiliaries needed rest, particularly the Shoshones, who had ridden some sixty miles this day. But to everyone's surprise, the two bands returned to their camps and spent most of the night dancing, singing, and exhorting valor. It was a "fearful racket, beating their tom-toms, and howling in a manner calculated to aggravate the most even-tempered individual," wrote one reporter. All night long the snorts of buffalo bulls, the whines of wildcats, and the howls of wolves emanated from the camps. "Our young soldiers appeared to relish the yelling business immensely, and made abortive attempts to imitate the Indians," greatly to their amusement, Finerty wrote. "I fell asleep dreaming of 'roystering devils' and lakes of brimstone." Stanley both sketched the scene and described it carefully in his transmittal to *Leslie's* and in his private journal: "All night long the Indians kept up a drumming and singing, and sleep was banished by their infernal noise, although we had to look at it in a charitable light, as these children of nature had offered us their arms, their services, and their lives." It was a memorable day and night on Goose Creek.[24]

"With this wild requiem ringing in his ears," Private William Nelson of Company L, Third Cavalry, died in the early morning hours of June 15, a victim of chronic diarrhea. Nelson had taken ill two days earlier, and the ministrations of Doctor Hartsuff had been of no avail. Except for two accidents on the trail and several cases of mumps and digestive ailments earlier on the campaign, the health of the Big Horn and Yellowstone Expedition was noticeably sound. Nelson's burial was planned for later in the day.[25]

ELEVENTH U.S. DRAGOONS

June 15 dawned clear and warm. The incantations emanating from the Indian camp had barely subsided by daybreak, not yet at all in one instance. Captain Nickerson remembered being awakened at headquarters by an old Crow warrior riding through camp at dawn, nearly naked, carrying a rifle that he would swing in the air from time to time, all the while with tears rolling down his cheeks. During his ride the Indian was seen pleading, praying, and exhorting "the empty air." The sight was both enthralling and mysterious. Nickerson learned from one of the interpreters that the Crow ally was going through a supplication known as "crying for scalps," a pleading with the spirits that in the coming fight he would be granted many scalps. Charles Stanley remembered seeing such episodes in the Indian camp the night before and sketched such a scene for his *Leslie's* audience.[1]

The expedition braced for one final day of intense preparation before embarking for the Rosebud. News running the camp that morning had it that a large Sioux village—700 tipis, upward of 2,500 warriors—had been spotted on Rosebud Creek, barely forty-five miles due north. It was said that the command would march at 5 A.M. tomorrow "and finally settle [this] business for the Sioux Nation." Every sector of the command was in motion, especially early in the wagon corral. There Captain Furey, nominally the expedition's quartermaster, doubling as its ordnance officer, oversaw the continual streaming of ammunition to the command, grounded in commanding officers of each of the respective infantry and cavalry companies, ensuring that their men carried the requisite one hundred rounds of rifle or carbine ammunition and each cavalry trooper fifty rounds for his Colt revolver. When the troops went to the field they had already been allotted ammunition, carried in looped leather waist belts or belt boxes and some stowed in haversacks or saddle bags. But this initial supply had also been used over the past seventeen days. Throughout the camp, men cleaned their individual arms in readiness for another round of hard marching and the prospect of a fight.[2]

First Lieutenant John Bubb, the expedition's commissary officer, handled repeated calls for rations and labored to ensure that prescribed allotments of coffee, sugar, hard bread, and bacon were in the hands of company cooks, who in turn put individual rations in the hands of every soldier. On Crook's order, on the morrow every man in the command would carry a complete four-day ration. The bacon was to be fully cooked. Only preparing coffee would be permitted on the trail, nothing more. The officers—some of them anyway—and the newspaper correspondents and accompanying civilians (those with connections) enjoyed a bit of latitude, quietly augmenting the same basic soldier fare with provender obtained from three days of hunting on Goose Creek. Nickerson recalled how he and others "took the precaution to carry in their saddle pouches, or fastened to the saddle, by 'hook or by Crook,' a good sized piece of dried elk meat." Nickerson was referring to meats available to some from drying racks in the packer camp that brimmed with deer, antelope, elk, bear, and buffalo.[3]

Horses and mules were examined and reshod as necessary in the cavalry and packer camps, and across all camps officers and noncommissioned officers ensured that individual baggage was reduced as Crook had ordered. The night before, Crook had specifically mentioned carrying single blankets but no extra horseshoes, lariats and side-lines but no picket ropes. What was unsaid becomes intriguing fodder for historians.

Nickerson and Stanton both mentioned that the officers and men also carried greatcoats, important pieces of apparel easily strapped to saddles. This surely would have been problematical otherwise for infantrymen, who were normally obliged to carry everything across their shoulders when apart from their assigned wagons. But now even the foot troops were going forward mounted. Crook mentioned single blankets and may have meant that literally, but Strahorn, in a *New York Times* story, specifically mentioned "one blanket besides a saddle blanket." The army's rubber poncho was not mentioned, although in another account Strahorn tells of donning his light rubber overcoat on the evening of June 16. Such gear was also easily strapped to saddles. No one mentioned the commonplace: canteens, yes; shelter halves, almost certainly no; tin cups, mess tins, issue knives, forks, and spoons. With cooked rations, mess ware was largely superfluous, aside from the ubiquitous army cup and perhaps the spoon. Extraneous matter was stowed in the wagons, making room in saddlebags and haversacks only for rations and boxes of ammunition. Remembered one participant: "We traveled in light marching order, taking as little with us as possible—much less than we needed." Crook had ordered a stripped-down army.[4]

In the Indian camp the Crows and Shoshones were provisioned much like the soldiers. Captain George Randall, the expedition's chief of scouts, oversaw the outfitting and contended with several unique problems. Most of the auxiliaries arrived bearing good personal arms, in the case of the Shoshones new .45–55 Springfield carbines. But not everyone. From within the wagon stock Indians drew standard-issue carbines as needed. Ammunition was also provided so as to achieve the requisite allotment per man. The patriarchal Crow chief Plenty Coups described the scene:

> The soldiers gave us boxes of cartridges, cans of powder, and more balls than we could carry. I had never before seen plenty of ammunition. My own people were always out of either powder or lead. We could make arrows for our bows, but we could not make powder or lead for our guns. But now everybody had more than he needed, more than he could use. And besides cartridges and powder, the soldiers gave us hard bread and bacon—too much of it. They had wagons filled with such things, and the soldiers were generous men. We had everything we wanted and we were in good condition to fight.[5]

Randall's foremost challenge was ensuring that his charges could be distinguished in the field, especially in the smoke and chaos of battle. The auxiliaries were provided strips of red flannel cloth meant to be tied across a shoulder to distinguish a friendly Indian from a foe. Some of the scouts tied the red cloth about their heads. In hindsight, while well intended and necessary, the adopted cloth only added to the coming confusion. As Second Lieutenant Henry Lemly of the Third Cavalry and Royall's cavalry brigade adjutant noted, red "is a favorite color among all our Western tribes." Likewise, Luhn, of the infantry, remembered that the red cloth "did not answer at a distance." Ironically, Luhn reflected in another letter later that summer on the ease with which Indians distinguished one another and the difficulty whites had in doing so, implying a cultural ease and bias when distinguishing friend from foe.[6]

At the camp's hospital Doctor Hartsuff and his colleagues also prepared for the advance and the prospects of battle. Hartsuff was allowed the use of two pack mules—the only designated pack mules accompanying the movement. From stores carried in his ambulances he packed one with an array of medical supplies and the other with a set of pioneering tools, including tent flies, shovels, picks, and axes, not for use in traditional pioneering but for use at a field hospital. The Rosebud sources say no more about medical supplies, but Hartsuff's counterpart on the earlier Big Horn Expedition, assistant surgeon Curtis E. Munn, faced a similar predicament when Crook abandoned his wagons in March and the command advanced with mules. Explaining in good detail how he covered his needs, Munn, who also was allotted two mules, reported packing a surgical kit of instruments, dressings and chloroform, a well-stocked medicine pannier, and two blanket cases, each with twelve blankets, plus a rubber bed cover and bottles of brandy and turpentine. One of Munn's assistants, Doctor Charles R. Stephens, accompanied Hartsuff now, and in all probability the packing of medical supplies on Goose Creek was virtually the same.[7]

||||||||||||||||||||||||||||||||

The ordinary bustle of the camp included the commotion at the wagon corral with the dispensing of foodstuffs and munitions, shoeing horses in the cavalry camps and packing and stowing for the advance, and also packing for an aggressive movement at the hospital and headquarters. Almost certainly all this was a sideshow on June 15 to the business of putting the infantry battalion on mules. Nearly every chronicler had something to say about the foot troops and their predicament, mostly in passing or in a sharp quip about the undertaking's circus atmosphere. Only a few grasped the enormity of the challenge. Fewer still understood Crook's aim, beyond simply accelerating the movement of foot troops in the accompaniment of a predominantly cavalry command. Yet there was precedent for the action and a reasonably well-conceived capacity within the expedition for such an undertaking, suggesting that Crook had considered the option of putting infantry on mules long before the expedition embarked from Fort Fetterman.

Crook's affinity for mules was well known. He packed with mules on his Oregon and Arizona campaigns and cultivated intimate friendships among the West's packing elite. He often rode mules when in the field (although not on these Sioux campaigns). And he imported packers, mules, and their impedimenta from Arizona for use in the Sioux war and then greatly expanded the service before commencing his first campaign. Crook's high regard for the animals and their handlers led one of his long-time packer friends, Henry Daly, to observe that "General Crook may well be called the 'father' of [the] modern pack service in the United States Army." Lieutenant Bourke reflected similarly, labeling Crook's embrace of the packer's world "the great study of his life." But packing mules and riding those same brutes were distinctly different challenges.[8]

Crook had previously put infantry on mules. As a junior officer in the Fourth Infantry before the Civil War, he led mule-mounted infantrymen against the Rogue River tribes of California and Oregon. He did so again in the immediate postwar years, putting elements of the Twenty-Third Infantry on riding mules. He was then lieutenant colonel of that regiment. His mounted doughboys joined First Cavalry companies in the Paiute campaigns in central Oregon. All along, he may simply have been emulating a commonplace practice in the rugged mountains of Oregon. A story written by Robert Strahorn appearing in the *Rocky Mountain News* indicated that Crook had been thinking of such a move. It reported that the prospect was freely discussed well before he ordered it on June 14 at his officers' assembly on Goose Creek: "Crook has quite a fancy for infantry, and told me the other day that it was quite likely that a company or two of the 'long guns' would be mounted on mules this summer and kept right up with the cavalry." Keeping up with the cavalry was but one element of the gain. Having the infantry's "long guns" in action was an even greater asset, a point well appreciated by this former lieutenant colonel of foot.[9]

The ignominious task of mounting the doughboys largely fell to battalion commander Major Alexander Chambers. Like most of the infantry officers on the expedition, Chambers was already mounted on a horse and apparently a skilled rider, as he was among those racing horses in the Prairie Dog Creek camp on June 9. Anson Mills of the Third Cavalry remembered that Chambers and other officers of the infantry battalion protested when learning of their assignment but that Crook was "obdurate and compelled him to do so suddenly but very reluctantly." Crook may have been reluctant not to achieve the intent but to force the issue on a friend. Crook and Chambers had a long history. The two attended West Point together, although not in the same class. Crook was among the class of 1852 and Chambers in the class of 1853 with such comers as James McPherson, John Schofield, and Phil Sheridan as well as John L. Grattan, killed by Sioux Indians near Fort Laramie in 1854.[10]

Chambers, now forty-three, was a consummate infantryman and respected Plainsman. Reporter Strahorn recalled Chambers as an officer with excellent executive abilities and "a thorough education in the art of frontier warfare." Upon graduation from the academy, Chambers served with the Fifth Infantry, including as regimental adjutant from 1857 to 1861. Promoted to captain in the Eighteenth Infantry in 1861, he was immediately drawn into the Civil War, serving as colonel of an Iowa infantry regiment and then as a brigadier general of volunteers. He was twice wounded at Shiloh, wounded again at Iuka, and earned four brevets for gallant and meritorious service, including during the siege of Vicksburg. After the war Chambers transferred to the

Twenty-Seventh Infantry during the expansion of the Regular Army and was promoted to major in 1867. In 1870 he was assigned to the Fourth Infantry, then stationed in the Department of the Platte, and served at Camp Robinson and Fort Fetterman. He also served on the army's Equipment Board at Watervliet Arsenal in 1874, inventing a small double-barred brass buckle for canteens and haversacks renowned ever after as the Chambers buckle. Chambers commanded Fort Fetterman during the course of Crook's Big Horn Expedition and got unwittingly enmeshed in that outfit's postcampaign squabbles, which was playing out even now as several of those officers faced courts-martial. In many quarters he was remembered simply as a methodical soldier. One doughboy serving with him in 1876 quipped that when on the trail his default command was "Route Step, March," meaning a straight-forward uncadenced march that earned him the nickname "Route Step Chambers."[11]

Chambers immediately tackled several issues. Nearly all of his command—180 men, according to Captain Luhn—was going forward. That meant acquiring 180 sets of equipment—lead straps, ropes, surcingles, and saddles or extra blankets—and corralling that number of pack mules willing, somehow, to be saddled and ridden. Some chroniclers implied a relative ease in securing available animals, with nearly a thousand mules within the column, counting harness and pack animals. Others clearly understood that the prospective mounts intended for Chambers's use were pack mules only, which narrowed the pool to some 320. Fortunately, the pack train already included a goodly number of riding mules because many of its personnel—cargadors, horseshoers, cooks, and packers—rode the animals, although some of those men intended on accompanying Crook's advance.[12]

Gathering the necessary riding gear proved considerably more complicated than having mules to choose from. While Furey's wagons necessarily carried a measured stock of replacement saddles, bridles, bits, halters, sidelines, picket pins, and lariats, assembling the needed sets was a challenge. Captain Dewees of the Second Cavalry described the predicament, calling it something of a "skirmish" as doughboys scrounged about the camp gathering available gear. Furey provided all that he had. A good number of sets were available within the pack train because not every handler planned to join the advance. Nearly all of the teamsters' saddles were turned over to the infantry, as was everything that could be spared in the cavalry camp. In due course, Chambers had what he needed.[13]

With riding gear secured, packers brought prospective mules to a flat, grassy staging area along the creek, several hundred yards from the infantry camp, where they were tied to a conventional cavalry picket line. On the line the doughboys were introduced to their mounts, coached by Chambers, Burt, and Luhn of the infantry battalion, and assisted by officers from Crook's staff, a handful of veteran infantry sergeants who had seen mounted service before, and Tom Moore and his packers. For a few men, particularly farm boys in their prearmy days, the challenge of bridling and saddling animals was second nature and the task went well enough. Likewise, some mules accepted their fates calmly. For the most part, however, the majority of the infantrymen "had never before straddled anything more formidable than a fence rail." Green mules and men were stubborn alike, and there was little calm. Mules were forced to have unfamiliar saddles or blankets placed on their backs and doubly secured by girths and surcingles. Animals brayed and snorted and iron-shod hooves flew.[14]

Newspapermen Finerty and Strahorn were amused by it all. After a rough go at first, the mules were allowed to quiet down some. Then, as doughboys attempted to mount their wary steeds for the first time, "the circus commenced," as Luhn put it. Some animals fought and kicked on the line. Some loosened their ties and attempted to run off, rearing uncontrollably, with men tugging on reins. Only the deep soft grass of the creek bottom prevented bones from breaking as soldiers shot into "the air like rocket[s]" and landed with "dull thud[s]." Cackled Strahorn: "Slow, momentous mountings and quick disgraceful dismountings were the order of the hour." Fortunately there were plenty of mules to choose from. Utterly unmanageable animals were changed out and did not hinder the show.[15]

Adding to the general discomfort, the unsought challenge and embarrassing scene along Goose Creek quickly became a public spectacle. Indian allies were particularly drawn to the mêlée and laughed openly at the "discomfiture of the battered and disgusted infantry." Some young warriors even seized runaway mules and effortlessly jumped on their backs, gleefully demonstrating their own natural-born equestrian skills. As Grouard later put it, soon the valley was "filled with bucking mules, frightened infantrymen, broken saddles, and applauding spectators," amounting to "the first circus Goose Creek Valley ever beheld." But the cagey scout also noted the story's predictable end. As comical as the ordeal had become, "the average soldier is as persevering as the mule is stubborn, and in the end, the mule was forced to surrender."[16]

The great ruckus ended at about noon with no serious mishaps and well-earned praise accruing to the doughboys. Bourke thought the morning's "experience with the reluctant Rosinantes equaled the best exhibition ever given by Barnum," abstruse references to *Don Quixote*'s awkward, past-his-prime horse and P. T. Barnum's popular traveling circus. John Finerty labeled the persevering foot soldiers with the long guns the "Eleventh U.S. Dragoons," harkening back to a long-gone day in American military history of unique horsemen and armament. Strahorn, one of the gawkers at the morning picket line may have expressed it best: "night found every man ready with his mule and little bundle, anxious for the start that the end might sooner come." After all, these were proud *infantrymen*.[17]

Elsewhere in the camp civilians came to their own conclusions about joining Crook's advance. The general's friend Tom Moore, chief of the train of packers, organized a contingent of twenty volunteers from his ranks, "every one a fine rider and as near being a dead-shot as men generally get to be on the frontier." Likewise, seventeen of the miners among the several parties flitting about the margins of the Goose Creek camp (sixty under the general sway of John Graves and six others in the Hornberger-Reese party) chose to tag along with Crook, including Graves and Hornberger, the adventuresome prospector-correspondent. He recollected: "I instantly made up my mind to go along, as I heard that the general was going to attack a village and I wanted to see the Indians badly whipped."[18]

At headquarters Crook seized a moment in the afternoon to communicate with Sheridan. In a hastily written telegram dispatched by courier that evening he reported on the arrival of the Crows and Shoshones. The entire command would march tomorrow, aside from one hundred men, mostly civilians and a few sickly soldiers, remaining behind to guard the camp. The Indians, he told Sheridan, were reportedly on the Tongue near Otter Creek, another of the bits of information gleaned from the Crows when they came in. To what degree Crook second-guessed his destination, Rosebud Creek or Tongue River, is unclear. He apparently would allow the trail on the morrow to reveal itself, guided certainly by advice from his scouts.[19]

Intelligence gained from Crook's Indian auxiliaries was never more important. This morning the general summoned Plenty Coups to headquarters and asked that he select a handful of good men and begin scouting the way to the Rosebud. Crook told the chief that he intended to march in that direction the next morning and would march without resting from sun to sun. Plenty Coups picked eight men besides himself and headed north immediately. At a high point well north of the camp the old chief looked back. "The village of Three-stars [Crook] was pretty to look at and made my heart sing. 'We can whip all the Sioux, all the Cheyenne, all the Arapahoe on the world,' I thought, wishing we might begin the fight at once."[20]

As evening fell, the somber note of death again gripped the camp when Private William Nelson was buried on the high inner bench overlooking the Big Goose and Little Goose confluence. Nelson had died at the hospital in the wee hours of the morning. As with Private Tierney's burial on June 8 at the Prairie Dog Creek camp, all available men in the command again turned out, with the companies of the Third Cavalry forming the funeral cortege that escorted Nelson's body from the hospital to the grave and the music of four bugles providing appropriate processional air. Again the Episcopal burial service was read, shots were fired over the grave, and the buglers played the last call of the camp. The Crows and Shoshones watched the proceeding with great curiosity.[21]

Tomorrow Crook would move boldly. He at last had his eagerly anticipated and utterly essential Indian allies and had learned from Grouard the whereabouts of Sitting Bull's village, in all probability as near as forty-five miles directly north. For the advance he had fully mounted every available man in his command. Each soldier, civilian, and scout was well armed and issued ammunition enough for a big fight. But mounting his infantry had a consequence. Without a conventional pack train loaded heavy with additional rations and ammunition he had limited his capacity for any follow-up on this presumptive direct and hurried hit on the enemy. In Crook's estimation mobilizing the infantry was a fair trade. Only time would tell whether the general's haste and sacrifice were justified.

Hindsight tells us that Crook still plainly underestimated his enemy. He remained convinced that the Sioux would flee either when attacked or if the element of surprise was somehow lost. And yet, in the general's view, boldly striking a major Indian village, capturing its foodstuffs and ponies, and destroying the lodges would be paramount accomplishments. They would cripple the Indians and lead directly or indirectly to their submission. Even if they mostly fled, Gibbon and Terry patrolled the Yellowstone Valley and would in turn willingly engage anyone coming toward them. The Yellowstone could well be Crook's own destination too, if circumstances led him there. On Goose Creek the conditions and decisions seemed right. Optimism was universal. Crook was ready for a fight.

TRAIL TO ROSEBUD CREEK

The men of the Big Horn and Yellowstone Expedition rose early on June 16, most of them around 3:30 A.M., when noncommissioned staff began pushing their slumbering charges to a hurried breakfast. The fare was skimpy this morning, little more than a tin of soldier coffee, a hardcracker, and perhaps a bite of fried bacon. It was a soldier's challenge now to eat sparingly and make four days' rations last. A howl emanated from the Indian camp about then. Finerty believed that medicine men and head soldiers of the Crows and Shoshones were exhorting their eager warriors with recitations of the cruelties of their enemies and stimulating their valor for the coming fight. The haranguing lasted about an hour. Elsewhere across the camp no bugle calls spurred the soldiers. After their meager repast the men gathered arms and gear and made for the picket lines. The canvas in the camp remained in place, to become the work of teamsters and others left behind with Furey when the column marched away. Finerty wrote that "everything worked like magic," although the sky was ominous with heavy clouds tinged a foreboding salmon color.[1]

The order of the command's departure was unique, though chroniclers hardly noticed. As was the norm, the daily marching order was governed by some prescription, such as infantry or pioneers on the trail first, the cavalry next, mules and wagons following, and a trailing company or two closing the rear. On June 16 the chroniclers noted simply that the cavalry marched first, at 5, the infantry at 5:30, with the Indian auxiliaries initially following them but then hurrying to the flanks and front. Lieutenant Capron reflected on the newly mounted infantrymen: "Men doing very well, and contrary to antici-pations we had none thrown upon starting out." Crook and his staff followed all, departing from Goose Creek at 6 A.M., accompanied by the packers and miners who had adopted the role of bodyguard for the general. The marching order was of little consequence on June 16 but much more important the next day when placement on the trail figured in the unfolding story. The order may have been the same on both days, especially among the Third Cavalry, where senior captains commanded battalions and seniority dictated order.[2]

By any measure this was a sizable force, twenty companies in all plus hundreds of auxiliaries. Lieutenant Colonel Royall and his staff of aides and orderlies led the fifteen-company cavalry brigade. In due course, under the immediate command of Major Evans, came Captain Mills's four-company battalion of Third Cavalry, Captain Henry's four-company battalion of that regiment, and Captain Van Vliet's two-company squadron of the Third. Captain Noyes commanded his company and the five-company Second Cavalry battalion. Separate but not actually the last to leave the Goose Creek camp were Major Chambers's five companies of mounted infantry. The soldier combatants alone numbered some 975, including officers. Captain George Randall commanded the Crow and Shoshone auxiliaries, numbering another 250 friendly Indians, all now conspicuously visible with strips of scarlet cloth tied about their persons as bandannas, brassards, or sashes. Some of these scouts were already well ahead of the column, having departed the camp long before daybreak. Then trailed an array of tag-alongs and incidentals: thirty-six packers and miners; eight or ten men with Doctor Hartsuff, including Doctors Patzki and Stephens, a hospital steward, and attendants; and Captain Stanton and two of his four engineering office attendants from Omaha. Stanton trailed alongside him his odd two-wheeled odometer pulled by a mule, the only wheeled vehicle to begin the advance. The headquarters complement added another ten or twelve men to the force, counting Crook, Nickerson, Bourke, and a small corps of couriers and orderlies. Grouard, Pourier, and Richard rode with Crook. The varied Indian and white auxiliaries raised the count of combatants to nearly thirteen hundred men. Even the medical staff went armed.[3]

From a hilltop along Goose Creek General Crook and his staff reviewed the force as it passed by. He was intent on seeing that "everything was in perfect order." Nearly everyone understood that their objective was a strong Indian village situated on Rosebud Creek, some said in or just beyond a deep canyon through which that stream flowed. Morale was high. The column was in readiness for active work at a second's warning. And it was supremely confident. Lieutenant Foster of Company I, Third Cavalry, riding in the midst of Mills's battalion, captured a sense of the élan. "It was a favorite remark," he wrote, "when we could come on a hill where the long, snake-like column could be seen for miles, 'Lord, what *will* "old Sit" think of this outfit when he sees it?' '*Won't* he skin out?'"[4]

The column crossed Goose Creek immediately upon setting forth and followed its course north for some seven miles. The route at first extended through the lush valley of the creek and then ascended to the high, rolling ground of the Tongue River valley when the Goose veered to the east. A crossing of the Tongue was not immediately possible, so the route turned nearly eastward and persisted in the broken ground of the river bluffs until approaching the mouth of Goose Creek.

The troops then crossed the Tongue about a mile above the Goose's mouth on a hard-bottomed ford and again immediately ascended to the high ground north of the river. The trail was unimpressive and rough, a succession of barren ridges, cactus, and sagebrush until reaching the narrow valley of today's Spring Creek, an intermittent tributary of the Tongue emerging from the northwest. One officer thought the landscape resembled Mauvaises Terres (badlands) similar to the area in the vicinity of the Black Hills. Spring Creek flowed directly from the Wolf Mountains in the general direction of the Rosebud Creek headlands.[5]

In the broken ground north of the Tongue one of the wheels of Stanton's rig shattered. It crumpled to the ground. Stanton lamented having to abandon the cart, but he had almost anticipated it, having left behind with Furey many of the delicate instruments that it normally carried plus two of his men who would keep up the meteorological observations at the quartermaster camp. Essential measurements continued on the trail now, however, as attendants used a compass to document courses and a watch to record distances in lieu of the odometer that one hapless aide carried. Some in the command ridiculed Stanton and his conveyance because the engineer also used the little vehicle to transport many of the same necessities that everyone else obligingly carried on their persons.[6]

Rain drenched the command at midday, but the men slipped their folded rubberized ponchos from beneath pommel straps and pulled them over their heads easily. The army poncho was perfectly suited for such circumstances. Most civilians had their own versions, usually rubber raincoats specifically designed for use on horseback. When on the trail, ponchos were customarily put on while mounted so as not to retard the march. Regrettably for Robert Strahorn, the *Rocky Mountain News* reporter, doing so proved horrific. "While my arms were helplessly entangled in the garment, the flapping of its ample folds scared my horse and he bucked me off ingloriously into the midst of the headquarters staff, with one foot, however, still clinging to the stirrup. Then, with increasing fright, he started to run, bucking and kicking, dragging me face downward through a patch of thickly growing prickly pear cactus." General Crook and others surrounded and rescued the reporter, whose face and arms were punctured with cactus barbs. "It took weeks," Strahorn lamented, "with all the help of the surgeons, very painfully to extract those barbs whose sharp spearlike forms drew them persistently inward."[7]

Bourke remembered how the command "kept right along." After some twenty-seven miles, Crook's route turned up the Spring Creek valley and continued with few pauses until it reached the foot of the long divide separating the Tongue and Rosebud drainages. The difficult barren ground of the Tongue gave way to good grass and evidence of buffalo everywhere. Then buffalo were seen in the distance in thick droves. At the head of Spring Creek scouts returned to report that the herd was agitated, meaning that the Sioux must be in the vicinity. Plenty Coups later told his biographer that he encountered several Sioux hunters and he made signs with them. He felt good-natured toward his natural enemy, believing that Crook would soon give them a deserved whipping. Crook dismounted the column and allowed the animals to be unsaddled and graze and the men to make coffee. The pause lasted nearly two hours.[8]

News of a buffalo herd ahead, supposedly running away from a suspected Sioux hunting party, excited the auxiliaries. Crook counseled with the chiefs, anxious to learn more about the enemy, but the friendly Indians were much more interested in hunting buffalo. This put Crook at odds with the various elders, yet he knew he had little recourse. Two days earlier Crook had assured his allies that they could scout in their own way, so he called upon them to send men forward to explore the land ahead. The few who were willing advanced under the leadership of Frank Grouard and Tom Cosgrove even as the march resumed to gain the Rosebud, whose headwaters were still some eight miles away.

The column quickly surmounted an undulating tableland blanketed with a rich carpet of buffalo grass, profusions of wild roses, and blue phlox. Then it rode straight into buffalo, "not rejected old bulls, but fine fat cows with their calves following close behind," in bunches of ten and twelve and sixty and seventy. The animals sometimes ran straight through the column. The Indian allies were crazed. Despite Crook's annoyance and worry that hunting would alarm the Sioux, with the Crows on the west side of the trail and the Shoshones on the east, thirty buffalo were killed in short order. Choice cuts of hump, tenderloin, tongue, heart, and ribs were packed on the horses, including the mounts of a few timorous officers. "They all wasted ammunition—only 100 rounds per man—with true Indian improvidence," wrote Finerty. Crook seethed, but he could ill afford a falling out with his scouts. Quietly, some officers joined the spontaneous hunt. Ernest Hornberger, riding with Andy Burt and the infantry, watched the captain kill a young buffalo cow and acknowledged that it made for a good supper. To others in the command, the sight of so many buffalo was foreboding. "There will be music in the air now, sure," Captain Andrews told Sutorius as they rode along in Mills's battalion. "Wherever you see buffalo, there, too, you will find Indians." It was an echo from the march on Prairie Dog Creek.[9]

The day was getting long when the command finally crossed into the Rosebud Creek drainage. The firing of friendly Indian guns still crackled, and another shot was heard, quite unexpectedly and nearly fatally. At the evening halt as Finerty was fidgeting with his horse (remounting, as he recalled) the muzzle of his carbine struck the hammer of his revolver, which he had carelessly let down upon a cartridge. The pistol discharged. It "felt as if somebody had hit me a vigorous blow with a stick on the right rear of my pantaloons, and my horse, a neat little charger, lent me for the occasion in order to spare my own mount, reeled under the shock." It was a big scare. Captain Mills and others rode up, inquiring into Finerty's well-being. The reporter dismounted sheepishly. The bullet had blown away a portion of his saddle's cantle and lodged in the ground. Amazingly, no one was hurt. Lloyd, Captain Sutorius's servant, said simply: "You were not made to be killed by bullets, or that would have fixed you."[10]

Interestingly, in his telling of the episode in *War-Path and Bivouac* Finerty provides the first mention of a manservant accompanying an officer in the field. Hired men, invariably camp attendants and cooks and also invariably black, were not uncommon on these campaigns although they were almost always socially invisible. An accomplished black chef, Jefferson Clark, accompanied Major Thaddeus Stanton to the field on the first expedition. His going afield proved something of a curiosity, and he was subsequently interviewed by several local newspapers. This would not be the last mention of manservants on the Big Horn and Yellowstone Expedition.[11]

Camp was established that evening in what Finerty called an "amphitheatrical valley," a place commanded on all sides by steep but not lofty bluffs on the Rosebud's South Fork. Mills recalled coming to a lake or swamp some 500 yards in diameter in the creek's headlands. Engineer Stanton also wrote of steep hills but not a lake or swamp and instead described a scattering of small miry streams and excellent grass. Pickets were posted on high points. The command bivouacked in a great hollow square. The cavalry occupied three sides and the infantry the fourth, with the horses and mules herded to the center. Chambers's doughboys were the last battalion to arrive. A proud soldier, the major attempted to exude an air of dignity on coming in, barking the command "Left front into line" in military style as he took his place in the camp square. The lead company went into line, but no sooner had the mules halted than they began braying as loudly as they could. The attempt at showmanship faltered as the other infantry companies came on. Cavalry officers watching the spectacle thought it all hilarious, laughing and snorting uproariously. Chambers, Mills recalled, "lost his courage and with oaths and every evidence of anger threw his sword down on the ground and left the command to take care of itself as best it could," glad to have this sorry day behind him.[12]

The few scouts who went forward under Grouard and Cosgrove returned at dusk with foreboding news of other Indian signs straight ahead, including having come upon a camp freshly abandoned, with buffalo meat on a fire, burnt to a crisp. Lieutenant Daniel Pearson of the Second Cavalry called the news "electrifying in the extreme." For Crook, it confirmed what he already believed. The direction of the hunter's flight was down the Rosebud. Grouard remembered: "I was satisfied the camp was on the Rosebud, down the stream." Crook had steadfastly held to this notion since first hearing of it when the Crow allies arrived on June 14.[13]

News of an abandoned Indian wickiup and half-burned buffalo meat lying in campfire ashes spread throughout the camp. Many were sure that the soldiers had been discovered and that the village ahead was forewarned. Plenty Coups told Crook as much. The old chief did not like camping so near Crazy Horse. Crook ordered that no fires should be lit, fearful that such light would further betray his presence in the lair of the enemy. Again his auxiliaries ignored him (and apparently many of his soldiers as well), forcing him to concede to their actions as they raised fires throughout the camp. They not only roasted fresh buffalo meat well into the night but also unleashed "indescribable war chants, of which they never seemed to tire." It had been a grueling day. The expedition had traveled some thirty-five or forty miles from its Goose Creek camp, and much of the route was difficult. Rain had complicated the movement at midday. Now the evening meal for most was little more than coffee, hardtack, and cold bacon. Then everyone bedded down in the chill of a very cold night. Captain Sutorius, wrapped in his blanket and with his saddle for a pillow, remarked to Finerty, who was lying on the ground next to him: "We will have a fight to-morrow, mark my words—I feel it in the air."[14]

"'Reveille at 3 o'clock. We march at 4:30 in the morning,' was gallant old Royall's order on the night of the 16th," Finerty told readers in a dispatch written several days later. Finerty and Stanley both reported that bugle calls stirred the camp in the predawn of Saturday, June 17, the veil of silence apparently lifted. Many remembered the dawning of day as the anniversary of the Battle of Bunker Hill in 1775 in the earliest days of the Revolutionary War. A few men also remembered that it had been "three months today since the Powder River Fight with Crazy Horse." Those involved at Powder River consistently believed that they had fought Crazy Horse on that day. The men were heavy with anticipation and weary still from the long ride of the day before, made no easier by the numbing chill of the night. Low cooking fires were permitted, and men huddled to boil coffee in their well blackened tin cups. Horses and mules were then saddled with dispatch. The men readied themselves for the order to move. On the lines some men joked, some enjoyed a cut of chewing tobacco, and a few rested their heads on saddles to catch last-minute catnaps.[15]

At that predawn hour Crook, through his three scouts from Fort Laramie (Grouard, Pourier, and Richard), marshaled a contingent of allies, particularly Crows, to explore the Rosebud ahead. "They knew the country and the Indian customs, and were good trailers," remembered courier Ben Arnold. In their preparations before departing, the Crows and Shoshones demonstrated a healthy respect for the Sioux and the prospects of a fight ahead, getting their war horses ready and tending weapons carefully before riding straight down Rosebud Creek before dawn.[16]

By 4:40 A.M. the sun was breaking across the eastern horizon. Although nestled in an amphitheater of sorts, the camp was in high ground. From any hillside the vistas were dramatic: the snow-clad peaks of the Big Horn Mountains to the south, the surrounding breaks of the Wolf Mountains, and the simple awe of a summer sunrise. The moment was deceiving. "The sun rose red, heralding an unusually warm day, rich in dust," remembered one chronicler. Crook's aide, Captain Nickerson, recalled the dawning almost poetically: "The sky, clear and cloudless, the air, soft, balmy and fragrant with the spicy perfume of the juniper trees that fringed the banks of the little stream. Nature seemed unusually calm and peaceful."[17]

The command moved at 5 A.M. The men of the infantry on their mules departed first, followed immediately by the cavalry. To shorten the column's length, troops marched on both banks of the stream, with the mounted infantry and Second Cavalry on the left bank, Royall and the Third Cavalry on the right, and Captain Mills's battalion in front. Shortly after departing the Second Cavalry overtook Chambers's infantry and thereafter led the column on that side. Other auxiliaries combed the front and covered the flanks. The march, recalled Finerty, had the "regularity of a machine, complicated, but under perfect control."[18]

The trail on June 17 followed the South Fork of Rosebud Creek in a northeasterly direction. In that high reach the branch was a sluggish little stream, although the valley was well defined and wide enough for easy marching. Pines and junipers speckled the highlands on both sides. The only curiosity noted on the early march was the sight of the several dead buffalo killed by Indians that had caused such a ripple of excitement when reported by scouts the day before. In about five miles the column met the North Fork of the Rosebud, a shorter affluent flowing straight out of the west from the rugged spine of the Wolf Mountains, the distinctive highlands that separated the Rosebud and Little Big Horn valleys. Comparable highlands on the far right, which some called the Rosebud Mountains, separated the Rosebud and Tongue River drainages. The North and South Forks formed Rosebud Creek, a heralded if diminutive tributary of the Yellowstone River, itself seventy-seven miles straight north on a bee line. At the point where the forks merged, the Rosebud curved slightly and flowed straight east for nearly three miles before turning abruptly north again. The sharp curve at the far end was widely known as the Big Bend of the Rosebud.[19]

The column was well along on this easterly stretch, almost at the Big Bend, when Crow scouts galloping in interrupted travel at about 8 A.M. Finding Crook, they reported seeing Sioux to the left (meaning to the north), down the Rosebud. Some of the Sioux, the scouts added, were driving ponies. In his autobiography Crook wrote that the scouts had asked him to halt while they reconnoitered farther. The news was ambiguous. Robert Strahorn, riding with Crook, believed that only a small hunting party was discovered. Crook anticipated a village somewhere ahead. If it was near, and if his approach had not been detected, perhaps his best option would be to stay where he was for the day and night and make a swift march in the overnight to attack that village at daybreak. This was conventional wisdom in Indian warfare, and precisely what Reynolds did at Powder River on March 17. When they halted, many in the command (officers and enlisted men alike) assumed that this was Crook's intent. But other scouts were still out. There was much yet to learn.[20]

While Crook waited, a "strong line of pickets" was thrown out along the ridge north of the creek. These apparently were Crows and Shoshones loosely scattered under the guidance of Captain Randall. At the same time orders were passed to unsaddle and picket the horses and "brevet horses," as the cavalrymen jocularly called Chambers's mules. Crook was buying time. Many officers mentioned this unsaddling action in their battle reports, as did some newsmen. It meant literally dropping the McClellan saddle and blanket from the horse's back during a prolonged pause or rest. Unsaddling during the course of a day's travel was a near effortless action among veteran cavalrymen, as the column had done just the day before. More interesting, perhaps, was the telling order to picket the horses, a point that only one officer and one newsman mentioned specifically. Lieutenant Foster described it as lariating the horses, a step in picketing. Robert Strahorn mentioned picketing explicitly in stories written for the *Rocky Mountain News* and *New York Times*. His three words "picket the horses" add critical weight to a subtle detail that surfaced early in the twentieth century with the discovery of a welter of physical evidence on the eastern portion of these bottoms.[21]

As part of a cavalryman's basic horse equipment, every trooper carried a fourteen-inch iron picket pin and thirty-foot-long hemp lariat tied to a ring on the McClellan saddle. The pin, to be pounded into the ground, had a swiveling lariat ring fitted around its neck that was twisted into the shape of a figure 8. Picketing a horse enabled an untended animal to graze a sixty-foot circle of grass, but doing so necessarily scattered a unit's horses to avoid entanglements. Picketing during this halt on Rosebud Creek strongly indicates that Crook intended to stay a while. He knew that the scouts had spotted Sioux Indians but was apparently not at all fearful of his enemy. This picketing episode had an additional context, as would soon play out.[22]

Not everyone in the column embraced Crook's decision to dismount. Little Mountain Sheep, a Crow scout traveling with the troops that morning, told Bat Pourier to tell Crook not to dismount the men on account of the Sioux, who would charge the horses and attempt to drive them off. But the dismounting proceeded. The soldiers called it "going into camp."[23]

The irony of the order no doubt struck Captain Henry Noyes the hardest. After scrutinizing the field from a distant hill, on his own volition he had unsaddled his company on the Powder River battlefield and permitted his men to make coffee. Hearing only scattered gunfire beyond the village, he thought that the decision was logical for the well-being of his company. But in the acrimonious aftermath of that mismanaged battle, Colonel Joseph Reynolds, commander on the field that day, brought court-martial charges against Noyes for this unseemly if mostly misunderstood action. Noyes was court-martialed in April and found guilty of an indiscretion. Crook reprimanded him in orders. Noyes was particular to note in his Rosebud battle report that the battalion's horses were unsaddled and allowed to graze "in obedience to orders received."[24]

Some soldiers seized the interlude on the Rosebud to enjoy a morning pipe. Others stretched out in the soft green grass to doze in the warm summer sun. A few preferred resting in shade and cut willows from along the creek to fashion small arbors. Many led horses to water. Second Lieutenant Henry Lemly, Royall's adjutant, just loosened the girth of his saddle and allowed his horse to nibble grass while he held onto the reins. Finerty simply gazed about, extolling the thick growth of wild roses seen abundantly along the stream and on the hills rising abruptly on both sides. No fires were permitted, however, and men were not allowed to climb adjacent crests and hills. Captain Gerhard Luhn and Company F, Fourth Infantry, stopped opposite of Captain Frederick Van Vliet and Company C, Third Cavalry. After unsaddling his horse, Luhn crossed the creek and sat down with Van Vliet, First Lieutenant Emmet Crawford, and Second Lieutenant George Chase. Wondering why Crook had ordered a halt so early in the day, the four officers could only imagine that they were staying put for a while.[25]

As the unsuspecting soldiers relaxed, the Crows and Shoshones, according to Lemly, gathered behind the infantry in an excited state, stripping themselves and their ponies in preparation for a fight. Even that commotion stirred little interest or alarm among the troops. Lemly quipped: "We were getting accustomed to such demonstrations upon the part of our Indian allies."[26]

Upstream and down, men of the expedition sprawled casually. On the south side (right bank) of the Rosebud, half a mile short of the Big Bend, Mills's First Battalion of the Third Cavalry, Companies A (Lawson), E (Sutorius), I (Andrews), and M (Paul), unsaddled and picketed their mounts. Royall and the cavalry brigade's staff officers rode with Mills at the head of that line. Behind Mills on the south bank stretched Captain Guy Henry's four companies: the Second Battalion of the Third or Henry's battalion, consisting of Companies D (Henry), B (Meinhold), F (Reynolds), and L (Vroom). Major Evans rode with Henry; Henry commanded his own company as well as the battalion. Closing the column on the Rosebud's south bank was Captain Van Vliet's squadron of the Third, Companies C (Van Vliet) and G (Crawford), with Van Vliet commanding his own company and the squadron.[27]

Drawn out along the left or north bank of the Rosebud, opposite Mills's companies, was Captain Noyes's battalion of the Second Cavalry, Companies

A (Dewees), B (Rawolle), D (Swigert), E (Wells), and I (Frederick W. Kingsbury). Behind or west of Noyes on the north bank was Major Chambers's battalion of mounted infantry, consisting of Companies C (Munson), G (Burrowes), and H (Burt) of the Ninth, and F (Luhn) and D (Cain) of the Fourth. On the trail that morning Crook and the headquarters contingent rode with Chambers. Stanton and his small cadre of field engineers, plus the medical staff, and the thirty-six packers and miners brought up the rear. When the first of the Crow scouts returned from down valley (the appearance that triggered this halt), the contingent of remaining Crows and Shoshones under the general oversight of Captain George Randall gathered to the west beyond the infantry line and commenced their spiritual ablutions. Randall carefully maintained close contact with Crook. The general, meanwhile, gathered several officers and engaged in a game of whist at the rear of the column. Officers remembered how Crook could pull a deck of cards from an inner coat pocket at a moment's notice. When other Crow and Shoshone scouts came pouring in from down the valley, Royall, Mills, and Noyes were positioned at the head of the column, while Crook was nearly two miles to the west at its tail. Oddly, however, the quirky geography of this Rosebud locale and the broad approach of Indian warriors out of the north made these head and tail placements almost irrelevant.[28]

The expedition's newsmen were well scattered among the troops. Finerty spoke for all in one of his dispatches to the *Chicago Times*: "There is virtually no such thing as 'rear,' unless with the reserve, which is generally called into action before the fight is over. Besides, if the journalist does not share the toil and the danger, his mouth is shut, for if he presumed to criticize any movement, some officer would say to him, 'what the devil do you have to say about it? You were skulking in the rear, and got everything by hearsay.'" Hearsay factors into the story naturally, however, because the events of the day unfolded across an uncommonly broad field.[29]

To history's benefit, reporters were in nearly every sector of the column. MacMillan, riding with Captain Lawson and Company A, Third Cavalry, in Mills's battalion, was presently near the head of the line. Finerty rode with Sutorius and Company E, Third Cavalry, likewise in Mills's battalion. Davenport accompanied Royall and the cavalry brigade staff throughout the day and at the moment was also at the head of the column. Wasson and Strahorn aligned with Crook, while Stanley rode with Tom Moore and the packers. Even Ernest Hornberger, the self-proclaimed correspondent for the *Pittsburg Leader*, got a distinct eyeful. Not aligning with the other miners, he instead rode with Captain Burt in Chambers's battalion. The odd nature of Hornberger's involvement was revealed in an aside in a letter to his parents, which they in turn shared with the *Leader*: "I was, of course, independent of the military, but I stayed with Major Burt and his company, and did the same as they did, although I rode wherever I pleased." On this day Hornberger indeed saw and told plenty.[30]

The dismounted column lazed along the creek for half an hour or more before firing reverberating from down the valley broke the morning reverie. It began simply enough. Officers and others at the head of the column heard three or four distinct shots coming from well north of the Big Bend. Another participant described them as coming from "behind the northern bluffs in the direction of the canyon." The references are to the same place, shaped by the listener's position in the line, with the Rosebud Cañon being a pronounced feature directly beyond the Big Bend. Some individuals dismissively assumed that the scouts had again encountered buffalo and hoped simply that they would have a good hunt. "They are shooting buffalo over there," Sutorius remarked to Finerty. But the shooting increased, and the alternate rise and fall of the reports plainly suggested that the guns were not all being fired in the same direction. Foster called the shooting a "dropping skirmish fire" that kept "coming nearer and nearer, until at length our allies break over the ridge."[31]

Crook heard the firing as well. The command had not been resting long, he acknowledged in his autobiography, "before the scouts came back as fast as their ponies could carry them, followed closely by the hostiles, both yelloing at the tops of their lungs, giving the war whoop that caused the hair to raise on end." Everyone along the sprawling line had some sense of this. Mills's nameless manservant heard shouting. "His ears were better than mine," Mills conceded. The captain climbed part way up the hillside lining the south side of the creek and could plainly see on the crest some two miles away great numbers of moving objects silhouetted on the horizon. "I soon came to the conclusion that they were Indians in great numbers." The scouts confirmed this dire fix as they raced toward the soldiers, shouting at the tops of their voices, "Heap Sioux! Heap Sioux!"[32]

The great Battle of the Rosebud, one of the most complicated and misunderstood engagements of the Great Sioux War and almost certainly the largest Indian battle in the whole of the American West, was exploding across the scene.

ON RENO CREEK

Sitting Bull's Sun Dance vision of soldiers and horses bearing down on an Indian village—upside down, feet in the sky, heads to the earth, hats falling off—electrified the great camp of Northern Indians. The village had grown substantially since the terrible blow at Powder River in mid-March, as tradition-minded bands from throughout the heartland of Sioux Country aligned with the venerable chief in a defense of independence and the old ways. Like-minded agency traditionalists had joined the camp in recent days, and soon the summer people would additionally swell its numbers. Word at the agencies about war was dire. The Indians knew that the buffalo country would soon teem with soldiers. Already the Northern Indians had toyed with the army camp on the Yellowstone near the mouth of Rosebud Creek. What most of the people wanted, however, was simply to be left alone. This was the buffalo hunting season. Meat needed to be dried and robes tanned. But the Northern Indians were also prepared for whatever might come. Sitting Bull's dream had empowered them. The people in the great camp would handle whatever surprises awaited them.

As always, practical considerations dictated the camp's movement. The Sun Dance camp near the sacred Deer Medicine Rocks was occupied for four days, from June 4 through 7, exhausting local grazing and hunting. On June 8 the village of some 570 lodges in six great camp circles, tallying as many as 3,625 people and untold thousands of ponies, moved seven miles up the Rosebud to the mouth of Muddy Creek. The Muddy was a short affluent draining the rugged pine-covered highlands south of the Rosebud. Elders urged careful vigilance, particularly by the camp's hunters and wolves as they ranged beyond the great assembly. Moreover, the latest arrivals foretold of soldiers coming from the east and south. This was no time to be lax.[1]

Wooden Leg knew of the soldiers coming from the south. He and ten other Northern Cheyennes had departed the great camp before the Sun Dance and ranged through the Tongue River and Powder River countryside hunting buffalo. On June 6 one of the party, Lame Sioux, discovered Crook's campfires in the headlands of Prairie Dog Creek. Wooden Leg and the hunters carefully trailed the soldiers and watched them encamp at the mouth of the Prairie Dog. They lingered, watching soldiers coming and going and debating among themselves whether to raid horses, but concluded that it was more important to notify the camp of the nearness of these *ve'ho'e*, who were moving toward them. Wooden Leg and the hunters reached the Indian camp on the afternoon of June 8 and spread the word: "Soldiers have been seen. They are coming in this direction." Councils were called. Most elders urged restraint, but in the Cheyenne circle the chiefs appointed Little Hawk, Crooked Nose, and several others to keep a watch on the soldiers. As many as fifty warriors rode south, including a few Sioux, and openly harassed Crook's camp on the evening of June 9.[2]

Rains beset the Indian camp for the next several days, making it much easier to stay put than to move. Crazy Horse and others debated the threat posed by the soldiers on the Tongue and were equally wary about those in the north, where the other soldier camp was last seen. Good news came late on June 11 that the soldiers in the south were moving away, as if abandoning the Tongue. With the only overt threat now seemingly from the Yellowstone, the people resumed their slow drift up Rosebud Creek on June 12, away from the Yellowstone. Again the Cheyennes, the uppermost camp circle, led the way, stopping at Davis Creek, some twelve miles from the day's start. The Cheyennes established camp on the Rosebud's east side, directly across from the mouth of the little tributary. The sprawl behind them was impressive: the other five camp circles were strung out one by one as far downstream as Busby Creek, where the Hunkpapas spread their circle two miles away.[3]

While they were paused at the mouth of Davis Creek, some twenty lodges of Two Kettles Sioux under Runs the Enemy joined the camp, adding nearly 130 people to the assembly. A small number of Cheyennes, some 57 people in 8 or 9 lodges, likely including Weasel Bear, a later-day informant, also joined the encampment. They had come from the Black Hills, traveling with Runs the Enemy's Two Kettles. These new arrivals enlarged the count in the great village to nearly 600 tipis and 3,800 people.[4]

Wooden Leg remembered that this camp remained in place for several days. On June 15 it moved again, dictated as always by the quest for grazing and hunting. This time the procession turned west from the Rosebud Valley and ascended the shallow Davis Creek drainage, a well-traveled avenue leading directly to the Little Big Horn River. Camp that evening was on the east side of the divide at a place with no water but many coulees filled with wild plums.[5]

Although the soldiers in the south were riding away, the camp's elders agreed to shadow them and aggressively fight them if they came within a day's ride of the village. That evening the Northern Cheyenne warrior Little Hawk and four others (Yellow Eagle, Crooked Nose, Little Shield, and White Bird), all members of the Elk Society military band, returned to the Rosebud, partly to scout for enemies and partly to hunt. Little Hawk had led the raid on the army camp at the mouth of Prairie Dog Creek, and Crooked Nose was with him then. Perhaps this time the warriors would get some horses from the white people. That had been Little Hawk's desire in the earlier fray. Their travel took them southward in a beeline through the Wolf Mountains before dropping into the Rosebud Valley. By noon on June 16 they reached the Big Bend. The five Elks followed the Rosebud from that point, westward at first to the forks and then south up the South Fork. On the South Fork the wolves ran headlong onto a small herd of buffalo bulls. Little Hawk told his followers that they should kill one of the bulls and roast some of its meat. Little Hawk shot at one and broke its back. The animal dragged itself down to near the creek, where it was shot again and killed. The bull lay close to a good spring. With fresh water at hand, the warriors began skinning the animal. One of them started a cooking fire.[6]

Little Hawk later described the particular location to Young Two Moon: "Pretty near to the head of Rosebud where it bends to turn into the hills." The specific point can be found today and is critical.[7]

As Little Hawk and his friends roasted their meat a large group of buffalo cows came into view farther up the South Fork. Wishing to kill a fatter animal, Little Hawk and three others set out after them, leaving Crooked Nose behind to tend the roasting meat. The four had barely headed out when Crooked Nose was seen motioning for them to return. When they hurriedly did so, Crooked Nose told of seeing two men on a far hill looking straight at them. Each led a horse. "They rode out of sight toward us," he said. Thinking perhaps that the two men on the distant hill were friendly Sioux, Little Hawk urged the others to join him: "We will have some fun with them," meaning sneaking out and frightening them. The five Elks rode forward, keeping carefully out of sight in the side hills. As Little Hawk neared a distant crest, he dismounted and crept to its brow. Peering ahead, he was astounded and shocked by what lay below him, not buffalo, not the two supposed Sioux, but "the whole earth . . . black with soldiers." If, indeed, the soldiers had ridden away from the Tongue as those in the great camp believed, they were coming back now.[8]

Little Hawk crept back to his friends and told them what he had seen. He spoke softly, fearing that they were close enough to the soldiers to be heard. Little Shield urged his friends to go back to where they were roasting the meat. "There is timber on the creek and there we can make a stand," he insisted. Little Hawk ignored the suggestion. He jumped on his horse and began riding hard, and the others followed. They were headed to the Rosebud but over a more direct highland route. At a high point three miles above the soldiers, they stopped and looked back. They could plainly see the soldiers coming down the hill. Their only urge then was to return to the great camp and report the news. The awe of the moment also struck them: not at having seen soldiers but at being in the midst of buffalo. Remembered Little Hawk: "If they had not killed that buffalo they would have kept on and ridden right into the soldiers. The buffalo bull saved their lives."[9]

It was a long ride for Little Hawk and the others. They knew the camp had moved from the head of Davis Creek and maybe had reached the Little Big Horn. They rode through the night, crossing the Wolf Mountains and reaching the South Fork of Reno Creek. In the morning twilight they found the camp, sprawled along Reno Creek. As they neared, they howled like wolves. Some early rising Sioux came out to meet them and inquired as to who they were, Sioux or Cheyenne? When learning they were Cheyenne and that soldiers had been seen, the Sioux left them alone but passed word to their own people that soldiers were in the upper reaches of Rosebud Creek. In the Cheyenne circle Young Two Moon heard the howling too and rode out to meet the scouts as they came in. Little Hawk's news was terrifying. He and the Elks reached their own circle "just at good daylight."[10]

On a beeline twenty-four miles southeast in the headlands of the South Fork of Rosebud Creek, "just at good daylight," or at about 4:40 A.M. by soldier watches, a red hot sun was breaking across the eastern horizon. The *wašicu* had had their coffee and were preparing to ride north. Opposite them, on Reno Creek, among the Cheyennes and Sioux, Little Hawk was remembered ever after as the man who discovered Crook and those soldiers before the Rosebud battle of June 17, 1876.[11]

||||||||||||||||||||||||||||||||||

While Little Hawk and the Elks were away on June 16, the great encampment crossed the divide from Davis Creek and came to a stream known then by several names and today as Reno Creek. Whether called Spring, Sun Dance (or Great Medicine Dance), Ash, Move, Trail, or Reno Creek, this was a thin but reliably watered tributary of the Little Big Horn and a natural link through a shallow divide with Davis Creek and the Rosebud. For the Sioux and Cheyennes this easy avenue was a prime entrée to good buffalo hunting country in the Little Big Horn and Big Horn basins. It was also Crow Country. Indian sources make it very clear that the camp was established on the second fork of the creek, meaning where the South Fork of Reno Creek joins the main stem. The primary channel, Reno Creek, runs nearly east-west on its near ten-mile course, with the South Fork entering slightly more than four miles up from Reno's mouth. The South Fork drained from the highlands to the southeast and was a natural pathway to Rosebud Creek at about its Big Bend. White Bull, a Northern Cheyenne, remembered that the camping place also featured white bluffs, referring to a prominent rocky escarpment north of the main stem. The Oglala leader He Dog also recalled that particular bluff and the pines on its crown, as did Shave Eagle (alternatively known as Thomas Disputed), an Oglala in Big Road's band. These details are timeless. Fixing the location with certainty is critical both to the Rosebud story and to Custer's movement to the Little Big Horn a few days later.[12]

The enormous village was well scattered along the creek, as it had been at most of its recent camps. The Reno Creek valley in this locale is another of the endlessly alluring landscapes dotting the Sioux and Cheyenne heartland. The creek bottoms are scored with ash trees, and its benches are speckled with sagebrush and carpets of lush grass. The grasses of the Great Plains would cure and tan by midsummer, but this was still late spring. The June 16 landscape was a verdant green.

The six tribal circles filled the Reno valley: the Cheyennes about a mile below the confluence with the South Fork and the Hunkpapas about a mile above, with the Oglala, Sans Arc, Miniconjou, and Blackfeet Sioux camps in between and in that order. The Sans Arc camp circle stood closest to the confluence, so Little Hawk probably encountered Sans Arcs when he and the Elks arrived after their long ride from the Rosebud headlands.[13]

Little Hawk's news was stirring. Heralds in all the circles rode about reporting the nearness of the soldiers. The camps erupted with anticipation and motion. Women, fearing an imminent threat, gathered personal possessions. Some began taking down tipis, preparing to flee if necessary. Additional watchers were sent out among the ponies grazing the open slopes beyond the camps. Men of fighting age went out for their war ponies, brought them to their lodges, and began dressing for a fight. Among the Cheyennes especially, memories of devastating army attacks on Cheyenne villages at Sand Creek, the Washita River, and Powder River reminded the people of what could happen if soldiers found their camp.[14]

Little Hawk's news also brought the chiefs and headmen to council, not separately in each of the circles but in one great gathering. "There was excitement among the people, and a great council was held," Rain in the Face remembered. "Many spoke. I was asked the condition of those Indians who had gone upon the reservation, and I told them truly that they were nothing more than prisoners." No one doubted the threat was ominous. Even Crazy Horse, normally reticent, was highly visible and may have been so animated as to warn the elders that "we must make this a war of killing, a war of finishing, so we can live in peace in our own country." The elders remembered Sitting Bull's vision of soldiers attacking an Indian village, upside down, hats falling off. But the talks bogged down. This was indeed a sudden appearance of the enemy, but some fretted that it might simply be a decoy. There were other soldiers in the field. Was this the most imminent threat? The consensus among the elders swung against premature action. Perhaps this was not Sitting Bull's vision. The gathering, which lasted perhaps an hour until 5:45 A.M., then adjourned, with the elders instructing the heralds to announce to the circles: "Young men, leave the soldiers alone unless they attack us."[15]

This time, no one listened.

The young men in the camps had been repeatedly restrained before, as when the people first learned of soldiers on the Yellowstone when the Northern Indians themselves were making their way west to Rosebud Creek. They had been restrained again when soldiers were discovered at the mouth of Prairie Dog Creek barely ten days ago. They could not be held back now, with so sizable and ominous a threat as described by Little Hawk—the whole earth black with soldiers. Rain in the Face captured the essence of the fervor, telling an interviewer years later: "It was decided to go out and meet Three Stars at a safe distance from our camp." Runs the Enemy similarly remembered the frenzy: "Almost at once everybody who could ride a horse or hold a gun mounted his horse and [prepared] to meet the troops." In each of the camps the younger war leaders rallied their followers, and the response was frenzied and beholding. Warriors prepared for a big fight, eating a quick meal, assembling weapons and the scant necessities for a long day on the trail and a great battle, painting their faces with sacred colors and symbols, and dressing in the best war clothes, including for some lavish feather bonnets and artfully beaded vests, leggings, and moccasins. "Fine war clothes made a man more courageous," remembered twenty-six-year-old White Bull, a Miniconjou and nephew of Sitting Bull. White Bull himself donned an eagle-feather bonnet, blue woolen leggings decorated with broad strips of blue and white pound beads, a long red flannel breechcloth, and a buckskin war shirt.[16]

Foremost was the need to prepare spiritually. Indian accounts speak to the many ways in which individual warriors invoked the animating and protective powers of the spirit world—for themselves and for their ponies. Many warriors wiped themselves with sage, sweet grass, or another spiritual fragrant. Most tied war charms (*wotawe*) to their belts or hair or to thongs suspended around necks or across chests. Some had war whistles fashioned from eagle wing bones suspended on leather thongs. Everyone prayed fervently for strength, honor, and protection, for themselves and their respective brotherhoods. Many warriors tended these essential rites before departing. Others bundled their war apparel, bonnets, and charms, and dressed for battle when nearly upon the enemy. No one neglected these critical spiritual rituals.[17]

Crazy Horse's unique preparations are especially well described. This highly visible and charismatic defender of the sprawling camp was watched and emulated by many. In such times Crazy Horse was rarely apart from his spiritual mentor and friend Horned Chips or simply Chips. Chips was perhaps the most powerful thunder dreamer of all the Oglalas and a mentor to countless young men. He alone interpreted Crazy Horse's complex dreams and prepared for him unique *wotawe*, including a small medicine bag tied to his belt that contained the dry seed of the wild aster, mixed with the dried heart and brain of an eagle. These elements Crazy Horse tasted and rubbed on his body. Chips also instructed Crazy Horse to make a zigzag streak of red earth from the top of his forehead down to one side of his nose and to the point of his chin. Also at Chips' direction, the great war chief wore but one eagle feather and most importantly a tiny ear stone behind his left ear, its leather tie woven through his free-flowing hair. A smooth white quartz heart stone was carefully cradled in rawhide and suspended by a thong across his chest and under his left arm. Crazy Horse then anointed his horse similarly, enabling both horse and rider to be invisible to the enemy. These stones and varied medicines possessed magical powers embodying the destiny of his dreams. If they were properly applied, Crazy Horse would be protected and strong, empowered by Wakan Tanka. This would be a good day for a fight.[18]

An abundance of functional weaponry also made these warriors strong.

Some chroniclers tend to minimize the profusion and adequacy of the weaponry carried by the warriors who descended on Crook and his Big Horn and Yellowstone Expedition, suggesting way too many worn-out and nearly worthless trade muskets and smoothbore long arms in Indian hands and too few modern repeating weapons. The opposite is much more nearly the case. These were people who understood and valued fine weaponry and had access to the latest and best through trade networks. White Bull explained it bluntly: traders, in his case at Fort Bennett on the Missouri, sold many guns to Indians who had goods enough to pay the price. Certainly some warriors carried bows and arrows, evidenced by oral accounts and a few iron arrowheads collected on the field over the years. And some carried aged weaponry. In no way were the warriors uniformly armed, as with the army and its Springfields and Colts. But this was a lethal force, to be sure.[19]

Agents questioned Kill Eagle exhaustively about Indian weapons and other things when he returned to his agency in mid-September. He was the Standing Rock Blackfeet Sioux chief who went west in May to hunt buffalo, not participate in Sitting Bull's war. He did not participate in the Rosebud fight but saw much and spoke freely. Standing Rock agent John Burke was especially interested in the armaments of the Northern Indians. "Did they have plenty of arms and ammunition?" he asked.

"All the Indian soldiers who were guarding me had splendid arms," Kill Eagle said.

"Did they have needle guns?" Burke specifically asked, referring to army Springfield breechloaders of old and new pattern, with their distinctive long firing pins. Indians also called these guns "open and shoot" weapons.[20]

"They had all kinds of arms: Henry rifles, Winchester, Sharps, Spencer, muzzle loaders, and many of them two or three revolvers apiece; [and] all had knives and lances," Kill Eagle detailed.

"Did the soldiers guarding you have plenty of ammunition?" Burke asked.

"Yes, their belts were full, and the best kind of arms, fixed ammunition, metallic cartridges," Kill Eagle replied.[21]

White Bull recalled carrying his seventeen-shot repeating rifle purchased from an agency Indian at Fort Bennett. He was describing a seventeen-shot Winchester .44 caliber rifle (or a dangerous eighteen-shot weapon if a cartridge was chambered). Wooden Leg recalled carrying his "six-shooter," likely referring to a six-shot Colt revolver and just as likely a captured weapon from a dead soldier in the Powder River battle. Cheyenne warriors captured other Colt revolvers and Springfield carbines at Powder River and almost certainly carried them now. Above Man (Jack Red Cloud) carried the Winchester rifle that he had taken from his father, given to Red Cloud by President Grant the previous summer. White Wolf, a thirty-year-old Cheyenne, had a repeating rifle. Expended cartridge cases collected from known Indian positions across the Rosebud Battlefield in the many decades afterward confirm the regular use of .44 caliber Henry and Winchester carbines and rifles, .50 caliber Sharps carbines and rifles, .44 and .45 caliber Remington and Colt pistols, .50 and .56 caliber Spencer carbines, .45 and .50 caliber Springfield carbines and rifles, and .58 and .69 caliber muskets and trade guns. The list is not exhaustive but suggestive enough to foretell of the devastating lethal capacity of these warriors rising to the threat discovered by Little Hawk.[22]

Many accounts suggest that groups of warriors began streaming from the camps in the darkness, implying that some, perhaps many more than will ever be known, did not await any counsel from the elders but simply gathered, tended personal affairs, and struck out directly through the hills for the enemy. As each individual circle disgorged warriors, single fighting men and small groups soon converged. The larger of the two initial bodies departing that morning rode first in a near easterly direction, diverting from Reno Creek through a high country divide and descending onto Rosebud Creek a few miles above the mouth of Thompson Creek. This put this group some twelve or fourteen miles below the Big Bend. Little Hawk had reported that the soldiers were descending the Rosebud and the warriors wished to be well in front of them. This initial body counted as many as 200 men, 50 or 60 of them Cheyennes, including the newly arrived Weasel Bear and 11 others of his band. Uniquely, a Cheyenne woman, Buffalo Calf Road Woman, the sister of Chief Comes in Sight, was also acknowledged in the group. Two Moon, his namesake Young Two Moon (the son of his half-brother), and Spotted Wolf guided. In the main the people in the Northern Indian camp again respected the Cheyennes' general knowledge of the landscape and its watercourses and trails. Two Cheyenne and two Sioux wolves were hurriedly advanced ahead of the band, carefully scouting and anticipating the enemy.[23]

When barely in the Rosebud Valley, this first group of warriors encountered a small circle of other Cheyennes and Sioux camped at the mouth of Trail Creek. This was a small bunch, not more than fifteen or twenty lodges and remembered as belonging to the Cheyenne chief Magpie Eagle. Its fighting men quickly joined the warriors as they continued up the valley.[24]

On the heels of this first party another large band of Oglalas and Hunkpapas rode forth. Crazy Horse was the most visible warrior-chieftain in this trailing group, which also included Rain in the Face and Lone Wolf of the Hunkpapas. Crazy Horse rode at its head, surrounded by many close friends: He Dog, Bad Heart Bull, Short Bull, Little Shield, and others. Scattered warriors from every other Sioux tribe were also in the mix, including Spotted Eagle, Iron Star, and Fearless Bear of the Miniconjous and Sans Arcs.[25]

Sitting Bull, still weak from the tortures of the Sun Dance, also attached himself to the second group and rode to the threat. He went armed with his repeating rifle and wore feathers in his hair, but he was in no condition to fight. On the trail and field his voice was loud, however, urging warriors to a good fight. His nephews One Bull and White Bull and friend Old Bull stood with him throughout the day, engaging as they could but foremost ensuring Sitting Bull's safety and well-being. White Bull's horse gave out on the long ride and limited his capacity to engage in the battle.[26]

Meanwhile Little Hawk led another small group of warriors directly up the South Fork of Reno Creek, traveling a south-by-southeasterly direction more or less in the reverse of the route that he and warriors of the Elks Society had ridden in the hours before daylight. The great storyteller and esteemed warrior Wooden Leg traveled with this group. Their course took them through the Wolf Mountains on a beeline straight for the Rosebud just above the Big Bend. Some accounts suggest that they were aiming for Sioux Pass, a prominent gap descending straight through to the east-west reach of the creek. Others called the location simply the Gap. After leaving the South Fork these warriors followed no natural watercourse but were always able to affirm their orientation from intermittent high ground. This group may have numbered no more than thirty or forty warriors initially, though other stragglers followed in due course, as occurred with the other groups simultaneously ascending Rosebud Creek.[27]

From a safe distance Little Hawk and his followers were the first to see the *ve'ho'e* stopped on Rosebud Creek above the Big Bend, eight or ten miles downstream from the highlands where he had spotted them the day before. The warriors had traveled quickly to cover the nineteen miles separating the Reno Creek camps and this vantage point. The great mass of soldiers was still some two or three miles away.[28] These warriors had not slept much that night, and their horses were jaded. Little Hawk held them back so that the ponies and men could rest. He knew well that other warriors were somewhere east of him, in the valley of the Rosebud below the Big Bend.[29]

By full daylight the great camp on Reno Creek was nearly emptied of fighting men. Shave Elk, an Oglala who fought at the Rosebud, recalled that a few men and boys of fighting age remained behind to guard the villages from any threats from soldiers on the Yellowstone. Young Black Elk, then thirteen years old, had wished to go south with the warriors but was held back by an uncle, who urged him to stay and look after the helpless. Kill Eagle and his Blackfeet Sioux followers also remained in the camp, closely watched by Indian soldiers and later denounced as traitors for their unwillingness to fight. He and his people only wished to hunt buffalo, despite the pressure and admonishment to do otherwise. In all, some 750 to 800 warriors were now closing on the enemy on Rosebud Creek: 80 or 90 were Cheyennes and the rest Lakotas.[30]

The warriors guided by Two Moon and Young Two Moon rode hard on Rosebud Creek until they passed Trail Creek, where they stopped to rest their horses and dress for battle. Some in this leading band of warriors had fully prepared themselves before leaving the village that morning. For others, this was their opportunity to don war shirts, feathers, and other finery, fix personal talismans, anoint themselves with earthen paints, and properly daub their ponies. Older warriors and military society chiefs watched out for and counseled their younger followers and prayed for blessings and courage in the fighting ahead. These arrangements took time. Warriors rode on as they finished their preparations, stringing the group out some. This was not a structured U.S. Army command. Individual warriors followed society and war chiefs, fathers, uncles, and mentors. Some allied with friends. Some followed individual tendencies. It may have appeared ragged to some, but on that day the resolve among the bands riding on Rosebud Creek was fearsome. The massing swarm was utterly unimaginable to those lounging with their picketed horses on the banks of this same stream, twelve or thirteen miles straight ahead.[31]

Twenty-nine-year-old Two Moon, Young Two Moon, and White Bird, one of the Elks who brought news of the *ve'ho'e* the day before, were among six scouts that the chiefs sent forward after this pause near Trail Creek. Somewhere ahead lurked the soldiers or their scouts. Two Moon remembered that he and the others kept to the west side of the Rosebud. They climbed hills from time to time and peered over and also glanced back to see the main war party of Cheyennes and Sioux following carefully.[32]

A few miles after their pause, perhaps no more than three, Two Moon and the scouts crossed Corral Creek. Barely two miles beyond that minuscule dry tributary a prominent hill juts out on the west side of the Rosebud. Its top affords long views up and down the valley. As Two Moon and the others rode up its side, they were startled by enemy scouts coming over the crest straight toward them. The wolves fired at each other. A Sioux horse was wounded. The enemy scouts charged down the hill and turned back the Cheyenne and Sioux wolves, who luckily evaded the chase. But the Crows and Shoshones also saw other Indians coming up, drawn by the firing. The enemy Crow and Shoshone scouts turned heel and ran. Apparently these enemy wolves had been watching the approaching Sioux and Cheyennes for some while. Some of them carried word of this to Crook, announcing that Indians had been spotted down the Rosebud. This chance encounter occurred some nine or ten miles below the Big Bend or some three or four miles north of the Rosebud's deep canyon, where important events were to unfold that day.[33]

Hearing the exchange of fire, the leading Sioux and Cheyenne band rushed up the valley and soon commenced a running fight with the enemy wolves. In a few miles the enemy retreat took them into the high ground on the west side of the Rosebud, perhaps in the vicinity of Indian Creek, another short intermittent drainage coming out of the west, or more likely into the draw immediately south of there. The enemy wolves knew that the soldiers were on the Rosebud's east-west reach, which avoided the right angle of the Big Bend. That path carried them squarely onto the high ground on the east side of the Gap and brought them to the attention of Little Hawk's warriors, who themselves were resting in the far end of that distinctive funnel. Little Hawk's warriors had already heard the intermittent shooting in the Rosebud Valley, which now was coming so plainly their way. With a crescendo of firing rising in the high ground north of the east-west reach, Crow and Shoshone scouts charged down on the resting soldiers screaming "Heap Sioux! Heap Sioux!" Young Two Moon, on the tail of the army scouts, remembered the moment when he first peered onto the east-west reach. "The soldiers were pretty strong," he told an inquisitor in 1908. With shooting around and below him, the great Battle of the Rosebud had begun.[34]

NOTES ON ROSEBUD GEOGRAPHY

In his seminal book *On War* the Prussian officer, historian, and military theorist Carl von Clausewitz famously observed that "geography and the character of the ground bear a close and ever-present relation to warfare. They have a decisive influence on the engagement, both as to its course and to its planning and exploitation." The description is timeless. Clausewitz's view was forward. Historians might add that geography also helps us to understand the complexities of campaigns, battles, and battlefields in hindsight.[1]

Landscapes tell stories and are as vital to storytellers as primary documents. In our story, soldiers and Indians often moved where they did and behaved as they did because geography led them to do so. Those natural guiding features remain on the field as critical elements helping to bring clarity to it all. Nowhere in the compelling saga of the Great Sioux War is the landscape more complex than on the Rosebud Battlefield, with its monumental boulders, rocky strewn ledges, sweeping grassy swales, imposing ridges, cross-cutting crests, deep coulees, connecting drainages, blind corners, and intriguing prominences and vistas. Geography is indeed telling.

By any measure, Rosebud Battlefield is enormous. If we accept the area of General Crook's original pause along Rosebud Creek at 8 A.M. on June 17 as the relative focus or center of the field, that heart alone amounted to nearly two square miles of bottomland and benches. Fighting around that focus sprawled nearly another mile east, more than three miles west, and two miles north, encompassing a battlefield spanning no less than fourteen square miles. In addition troops maneuvered another near four miles down Rosebud Creek before returning to the field cross country, cutting the angle from their farthest advance to the backside of the Gap. By comparison, the Little Big Horn, another enormous battlefield of this Great Sioux War, encompasses an area of nearly twelve square miles (counting the footprint of an Indian village as well, but not so at Rosebud). No other Indian wars battlefield in America is quite as diverse and expansive as Rosebud Creek, Montana.

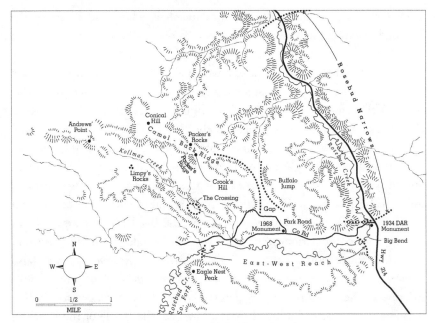

3. Rosebud Battlefield Landmarks

Central to understanding the story of the Rosebud battle is grasping the distinctive look of the field. Most of its draws, ridges, gullies, and prominences have names, some contemporary, some bestowed in the battlefield's homesteading era, some given by battle aficionados. For the purposes of this study, names are used carefully. Legacy names are embraced. Names bestowed yesterday are employed sparingly, if at all.

Rosebud Creek itself forms where the south fork and north fork of the stream converge just west of the area occupied by the Big Horn and Yellowstone Expedition during its initial pause on the morning of June 17. Some sources describe that place as the stream's *West Bend*, a slight misnomer because the Rosebud's North Fork already flows in a relative easterly direction. But the troops coming onto the field followed the south fork, which coursed in a northeasterly direction and turned east where the waters merged: thus the notion of a bend.

From the confluence of the two forks, Rosebud Creek flows in an easterly direction for some three miles to the Big Bend. In the present narrative this critically important locality is labeled the *east-west reach*. Crook's expedition paused there around 8 A.M., picketed its horses, and generally idled while Crook awaited further intelligence from his Crow and Shoshone scouts.

From Crook's perspective the east-west reach is where the Battle of the Rosebud began, a literal ground zero in a day-long drama of well-scattered action.

At the easternmost end of the east-west reach, the Rosebud turns abruptly north at a corner long understood by Indians and whites alike as the *Big Bend*. Well before the battle in 1876, Indians knew of and even revered the Big Bend. The place is critical to the Rosebud battle story for several reasons. As a matter of simple geography, Rosebud Creek turns at the Big Bend and adopts a straight-line northerly course for more than eighteen miles until it passes Davis Creek, where it changes direction again and continues through the area of the 1876 Hunkpapa Sun Dance camp and beyond, on its slow meander to the Yellowstone River. The Big Bend is noteworthy as well because battle action occurred at the inner angle of the turn. Beyond the corner to the north is the start of the distinctive *Rosebud Narrows* (also known in the sources as the *Deep Cañon* and *Rosebud Cañon*), a discernible stricture in the valley through which the stream flows for some four miles. By some measures, including the day's timeline, the Battle of the Rosebud ended in the fore of those narrows. What was feared there and what actually occurred has been a source of intrigue ever since, a matter discussed carefully at the close of this narrative.

The valley of the east-west reach was grassed and open. While the stream's bottomland was not particularly wide, it easily accommodated Crook's troops, who during their initial halt sprawled across the flats on both sides of the creek, grazing and watering horses, sunning themselves, and in Crook's case playing cards. Soldiers mentioned cutting willows to frame small shade structures during the pause, but such brush was not particularly common or intrusive along the stream's banks. At the time a person could look east or west and scan virtually the entire reach without obstruction. This same condition holds to the present. Only Elmer "Slim" Kobold's ranch buildings and a few mature trees surrounding them gently intrude on the scene. Kobold homesteaded a portion of the battlefield and expanded his holdings greatly over the years. His modest buildings are now the headquarters for today's Rosebud Battlefield State Park.[2]

Looking south from the east-west reach a visitor's view is cut short by abruptly rising bluffs leading to timbered highlands spanning the horizon. These nameless highlands dominate the battlefield's entire southern margin, although at the time of the battle the prominence featured many fewer trees. That was the day of sporadic wildfires and grazing buffalo, which both limited the treescape, making today's notions of timbered abundance misleading. Troops maneuvered on that high ground on June 17, accessing it from an obvious notch starting on the valley floor at the center of the east-west reach. The westernmost end of this high ground is a vast plateau with a distinctive cone-shaped feature at its west end known as *Eagle Nest Peak*. Shooting occurred in this locale in the proximity of the peak. Little Hawk and fellow Northern Cheyenne Elk Society warriors also crossed this high ground, south to north, after initially encountering Crook's troops on June 16.

Looking north from the bottomland of the east-west reach, the extent of the view would have depended upon the viewer's position in the column, east or west, and position on the north or south side of the creek. Nearly everyone on the left bank (north side) suffered a view obstructed by rising bluffs, an encompassing visual barrier running from the column's head west to the mouth of Kollmar Creek. On the other hand, Royall, Mills, and Henry, positioned on the south side of the creek on land that rose slightly, had longer views to the north. Thus it was that Mills, alerted by his cook, could see Indians on the distant northern horizon when the shooting began.

The initial rise north of the stream is easily surmounted. From that crest it is possible to see more of the field but still not all of it. A newsman with Crook described that vantage perfectly, calling the view to the front, right, and left a fine grassy amphitheater several miles each way, with sparse hills and broken, rocky gullies perfect for secreting warriors. Straight north was a long sparsely timbered bluff. The Rosebud Battlefield had three distinct planes: the valley floor, this broad bench or seeming amphitheater, and the critical northern heights.[3]

On the east end of the field at the setting of today's park entrance and wayside exhibits, the *Gap* is easily visible straight north. The initial shooting and subsequent first formal action of the engagement played through the Gap, triggered after Crook's scouts, chased by Sioux and Cheyenne warriors, spilled southwestward from the Rosebud highlands between the Gap and the Rosebud Narrows. The Gap was a distinctive wide notch, a literal wide-bottomed, U-shaped feature with pronounced high ground on its east and west shoulders. The farthest extent of the Gap, a simple crest, opens to tumbling highlands beyond that reach northward to Indian Creek, the next substantial if intermittent drainage north of the battlefield. This rugged landscape in the depths of the Gap was contested ground and the most difficult and complex terrain on the entire battlefield.

Rosebud Battlefield, 1929

This general view of the Rosebud Battlefield taken from the east side of the Gap in 1929 looks south upon Rosebud Creek and the imposing heights beyond. Van Vliet's Third Cavalry Squadron maneuvered on the distant high ground during much of the battle. The openness of the landscape is striking, with only a few trees visible on the distant ridge's eastern end and in the draw leading to its crown. That same ridge is well timbered today. Jessamine Spear Johnson photograph. (Tempe Johnson Javitz, X4 LLC Collection)

The Gap's shoulders, right and left, figure prominently in the story, with warriors and soldiers contesting and successively occupying this dominant ground. Centrally located on the shoulder's right is a long rocky ledge known as the *Buffalo Jump*. While the root story of the Buffalo Jump is of no consequence to the battle, the ledge and the rocky terrain above and below were fiercely contested early in the fight.

The long shoulder to the left of the Gap is the most imposing feature on the entire battlefield, amounting to a sometimes narrow-topped, continuously rising plateau extending to the northwest for several miles. A newspaperman on the scene in 1876 labeled the feature the *Camel-Back Ridge*. Along this gradient lie a succession of features figuring directly in the story. One location, the incongruity known as Crook's Hill, served as the general's command post during the fight. By some measures, that place is a puzzle. From the valley floor and first bench Crook's Hill indeed resembles a prominence dominating the northern horizon. This simple impression almost certainly lured Crook to it. But the position at the top is little more than a wide spot on the gradient, a grassy flat on the continually rising plateau. From various vantages, Crook could indeed command portions of the field but not all of it at once. From its southwestern brink Crook was certainly in an advantageous position to observe Royall's maneuvering along Kollmar Creek. But when doing so at that point Crook was blind to Mills's maneuvering east and north of him in the Gap. If Crook walked or rode to the Gap side of this position, a distance of more than a hundred yards, he was blinded to Royall's actions behind him. Attendant headquarters staff, orderlies, infantry, and horses and mules further cluttered and confused the position. The point worth remembering, however, is that Crook took high ground and commanded the battle from there. This may have been an imperfect command post, but there was no better or more practical place on the field. Clausewitz reminded his readers that a wide view is a strategic benefit in battle, and Crook made the best of this one.[4]

On the shoulders of Crook's Hill, north and south, are distinctive rocky outcroppings that served as natural breastworks initially for the Indians occupying this high ground and later for the packers and miners who made themselves bodyguards for Crook and protectors of Hartsuff's hospital. The long, intermittent rocky ledge on the south side of Crook's Hill came to be known as *Packer's Ridge*, while a large jumble of rocks on the northwest side of Crook's position are known as *Packer's Rocks*. Packer's Rocks overlook the northern extent of the Gap. As defensive works, these positions in the north and south had no equal.[5]

The broad Camel-Back Ridge extends in a northwesterly direction for another mile and a half, ultimately reaching the dominant feature on the entire battlefield, *Conical Hill*. Warriors occupied this hill throughout much of the morning until infantry drove them away and occupied the same place at midday, remaining there until they were withdrawn in the afternoon. While providing a commanding view of much of the battlefield, Conical Hill is nearly 2.5 miles from the battle's start (ground zero) in the east-west reach and too far removed to serve any meaningful military purpose (such as a command post for Crook). Still, the place had tactical value to the army and drew military action. We can also imagine Little Hawk's Cheyenne and Sioux followers eyeing soldiers from this distinctive feature before the battle unfolded. North of Conical Hill, in the direction that Little Hawk's followers had come, the land is a succession of grassy and timbered high-lands and gorges characterizing the encompassing Wolf Mountains. Conical Hill provides the finest sweeping vistas on the field, including to the south. That location and Crook's Hill offer spectacular views of the snow-clad Big Horn Mountains in the distance and their central dominant feature, the 13,167-foot-tall Cloud Peak. But dramatic views of snow-clad mountains were of little relevance to the warriors of 1876.

When the battle began, Crook was playing cards near a spring at the mouth of *Kollmar Creek*, an incised, invariably dry streambed entering the Rosebud's east-west reach from the northwest. While Royall paused at 8A.M. at the head of the column, Crook paused at its rear, surrounded mostly by staff, the packers and miners, and Indian auxiliaries. When the shooting began, his view of the field was severely limited by the first line of bluffs north of the creek and east of Kollmar's mouth. Crook's initial reaction was to surmount the hill in his immediate fore, a distinctive nameless knob in its own right, from which he directed the initial response. From atop this knob, however, Crook's view was limited by the long crest dominating his entire northern front, the Camel-Back Ridge. Crook soon spotted the misnomered hill on that rise that became his headquarters. While Crook maneuvered to the high ground, to his left lay Kollmar Creek, the deep declivity dominating the battlefield's entire left-center. Kollmar factors into the Rosebud story repeatedly. Indians used it in part to gain initial access to Crook's command and its horses. Royall was dispatched along its course to drive off those Indians. And a dramatic Indian episode occurred at its midpoint: the rescue of a Northern Cheyenne warrior at a place called *Limpy's Rocks*.

During the attempted consolidation of troops near the end of the battle, the fiercest fighting of the entire engagement played out along Kollmar's entire southern shoulder and at the *Kollmar Crossing*, a shallow swale through which Royall crossed the drainage on his withdrawal. The place was a tortured hell for Royall's command. Nearby was the *Led Horse Ravine*, a momentary haven for the colonel's horses during this retirement and remounting. Both positions are directly south of Crook's Hill. From that prominence the general watched in abject horror the bloodiest fighting of the day.

Historians, landowners, and Indians have physically marked key locations on the field over the years, some with concrete pylons and in one instance with rock slabs. Such features are occasionally acknowledged in the endnotes. The battlefield has been memorialized as well, and those several distinctive vintage monuments are also recognized. The Rosebud Battlefield has also gained its share of extemporized place-names. While these efforts are often well intended, there is no consistency or consensus or any direct historical derivation to them. The present study chooses to ignore such ephemeral nomenclature.[6]

OPENING SALVOS

The Sioux and Cheyenne attack was brazen and unforeseen. Crook's Big Horn and Yellowstone Expedition had reached the Rosebud fully assuming that any offensive movement belonged to them. Somewhere ahead lay Sitting Bull's village. Grouard and the scouts would key the advance, whether by day or night, presaging a presumptive devastating and campaign-ending attack on the morrow. The first shots heard from downstream, coming around 8:30 A.M. according to many sources, were misinterpreted. "They are shooting buffalo over there," Captain Sutorius remarked to John Finerty, reminiscent of circumstances the day before. The word quickly spread among the soldiers. "'They are firing at buffalos,' said the recruits." But the shooting increased and kept coming on.[1]

Whatever their position in the long line, officers, enlisted men, reporters, and auxiliaries alike were certain that the opening volleys of the great battle came directly at them. In reality, the action spilled from right to left, east to west, high ground to low ground, as frantic Crow and Shoshone scouts raced pell-mell from the timbered highlands above the Rosebud Narrows, aggressively pursued by Sioux and Cheyenne warriors. Crook's Indian scouts knew precisely where they were headed, beating a path straight southwest across the descending hills, bound for their own people and their horse remuda, which they could plainly see on the column's heel in the far west of the valley. A horse remuda, containing mostly the led horses and war ponies of the auxiliaries, was a burden fit only for the end of a column, not for its front or anywhere in between. Intuitively, Crook was there too. The scouts were his eyes and ears and sources of critical advice and counsel in a land entirely foreign to him.

The sharp yells from the auxiliaries—the frantic and oft repeated "Heap Sioux! Heap Sioux!"—resonated across the rolling hills as the Crows and Snakes scrambled to the bottoms. Grouard remembered one of the criers' names, a "little hunchbacked" Indian named Humpy, whom he mistakenly identified as a Sioux when in fact he was Shoshone. Between their shrieks, sharp reports of carbine and rifle fire echoed across the bluffs. The scouts

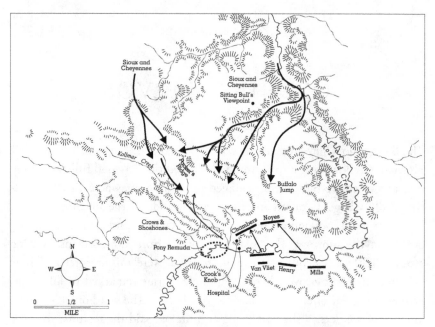

4. Opening Salvos, 9:00 A.M., June 17, 1876

from time to time turned and fired at their pursuers, and pressing warriors shot straight at them (and thus seemingly straight at the soldiers unhorsed and scattered along Rosebud Creek).[2]

For many the bluffs immediately fronting the valley floor obscured the unfolding drama. Noyes, Chambers, and Crook were sprawled along the Rosebud's left bank. Their battle reports and subsequent reminiscences plainly indicate that they heard plenty but saw much less. Royall, Mills, Evans, Henry, and Van Vliet, in contrast, were extended along the south side of the stream, the Rosebud's right bank. Their view of the first line of bluffs to the north was much less restricted. What they saw was nothing less than astounding. Finerty stood with those men of the Third Cavalry and plainly saw "the enemy swarming in crowds upon the higher range of the bluffs in every direction on a line of at least two miles. They were all mounted and fired with wonderful rapidity." "A perfect blaze of musketry made the hills seem on fire," he added later. Private Oliver C. C. Pollock of Mills's Company M remembered the hills as a "mass of humanity."[3]

The frantic commotion coming headlong at the soldiers spurred immediate action across the entire front. These were battle-hardened officers fully anticipating the challenges of an imminent fight. Foremost, they put their companies at the ready. Cohesion was the watchword, especially in so sizable a command. In the accounts of the day the existence of a chain of command and an adherence to it must sometimes be intuited from battle reports and accounts. Contemporary writers invariably assumed the point to be general knowledge, while later writers have missed it all too often. No one on the field that morning doubted or misunderstood that this was Crook's fight.

One of Finerty's several accounts of the unfolding action provides a keen sense of the expedition's command structure in play. Crook, he wrote, apprehending the situation, ordered companies of the Fourth and Ninth Infantry forward as skirmishers, leaving their mules behind with holders. Chambers, who was likely among those playing whist with Crook at the mouth of Kollmar Creek, elaborated on this initial movement in his battle report. "I sent, as ordered, two companies, dismounted, to the edge of the bluffs to protect that point: posted as skirmishers." A key element, offered casually, was the statement that the movement occurred "as ordered." Both the sense of command and anticipation are evident at the company level. At the sound of the firing, Captain Luhn of Company F, Fourth Infantry, recalled that "our men were ordered to stand to horse," a cavalry expression meaning standing beside their mounts, halter and reins in hand, prepared to mount when directed to do so. In his report Captain Samuel Munson, commanding Company C, Ninth Infantry wrote: "I immediately formed my company as previously directed and waited for orders. The first order I received was to take my men dismounted up the bluffs and report to General Crook."[4]

At the other end of the line Anson Mills similarly prepared his command for deployment, shouting to his company and battalion: "Saddle up, there— saddle up, there, quick!" Men scrambled from sunshades and grassy bowers and sought out their horses (if they had wandered at all); saddled, cinched, and mounted; and assembled in company order. The extreme haste of it all is telling. Mills's horses were picketed. Driving picket pins in hard earth was work. Grazing horses moving about on their tethers only further cemented the pins in that hardpan. Pulling pins became its own chore for the men. It was better just to leave them. Alternatively, releasing picket ropes from figure-8 swivels occurred with the flick of a snap hook. Under duress, putting personal kits in order, throwing saddles, cinching girths and surcingles, and coiling picket ropes was labor aplenty. An untold number of picket pins were unearthed from this eastern position when some of that ground was turned early in the twentieth century to create alfalfa meadows, attesting to the adrenaline rush and need for haste consuming these soldiers when under fire and preparing for action.[5]

Crook's scouts commenced their own preparations. When the first news was received at 8 A.M. that Sioux warriors were spotted downstream, the remaining Crow and Shoshone auxiliaries still attached to the column (amounting to the majority of both groups) drew in their war ponies, stripped away finery, including the feathers and streamers adorning the Shoshone lances, and gathered in large circles around elders and spiritual leaders. Sketch artist Stanley, at the west end of the line with the packers and miners, and Nickerson, huddled among Crook's staff, had splendid views of it all. As on Goose Creek several days earlier, these animated allies sang war songs, danced, and invoked along with the elders and spiritualists "good medicine to fight." The ruckus only intensified when harried scouts returned to their respective tribal circles screaming "Sioux! Sioux!" and reporting on early morning encounters with their enemies. These incoming weary riders wasted no time, hurriedly exchanging jaded ponies for fresh mounts and joining the others as they prepared to meet the enemy head-on.[6]

Lost in the initial commotion is a sense of time. Battalion and company reports and newspaper columns seem to indicate that everything in the valley occurred seamlessly and relatively instantly, when in fact the business of assessing, scrambling, saddling, mounting, gathering, and waiting took reasonable time. Stanley thought that as many as ten minutes passed between the first crackle of gunfire—Sutorius's supposed buffalo hunting—and the appearance of scrambling Crow and Shoshone scouts chased from the hillsides by Sioux warriors. Grouard estimated that as many as twenty minutes passed before soldiers appeared "over the hill," meaning out of the bottoms. Plainly put, preparation and movement consumed time.[7]

The least encumbered in the valley was General Crook himself. Hearing gunfire and the oncoming ululations of the scouts at his respite near the mouth of Kollmar Creek, Crook was instantly animated. He ordered Major Chambers (or the major himself volunteered) to place his infantry on the northern crest to strengthen the pickets while the cavalry companies went about saddling horses. He then set off afoot to the top of the first hill in his front. In his autobiography Crook recalled that "some of the infantry" went up with him and took possession of the bluff-line overlooking the Rosebud. Crook's initial vantage was a point immediately north and east of Kollmar, a scramble of nearly two hundred yards from his start. Nickerson and Bourke went along, as did Grouard, a scattering of orderlies, and also Robert Strahorn, the *Rocky Mountain News* reporter, and Joe Wasson, writing for New York, Philadelphia, and San Francisco papers.[8]

From the crest Crook and his aides saw their enemy for the first time. The commotion was widespread. Crook later detailed the initial dispositions that he made on the bluff top but not the awe of the moment. Nickerson and Strahorn, however, were immediately struck by the enormity of the threat breaking upon them. Wrote Nickerson: "When we reached the crest of the plateau, there appeared in our front a formidable band of those justly celebrated Sioux and Cheyenne warriors, magnificently mounted, and in all the splendor of war paint and feathers. Every hill appeared to be covered with their swarming legions, and up from every ravine, and out of every little vale more seemed to be coming."[9]

Strahorn was comparably spellbound. "At this moment the eye could not cover a single mountain . . . without resting upon a band of approaching savages. Right, left, front and rear alike were faced by the incoming braves, and it seemed as though the whole surface of the country for miles around was one vast skirmish line. It was a general uprising."[10]

Bourke's first impression was unadorned. "From the crest of the little ridge . . . , the long line of advancing Sioux could be seen moving towards us seemingly confident they had but to attack to succeed. The Sioux had, it seemed almost conclusively, made up their minds to seize our stock first and with this end in view had pushed down two little ravines, coming in from the west."[11]

Bourke's "two little ravines" were the plainly visible span of Kollmar Creek to the left and a shorter, nameless forked ravine straight north of him that reached to the bluff on the horizon, the imposing high ground that Wasson called the Camel-Back Ridge. Clearly the attack was general, with Sioux and Cheyenne warriors taunting and spilling from all of the northern ridges, through the wide conduit on the skyline's right, a feature soon renowned as the Gap, and also on the left, down Kollmar's branches and main stem.

By now other soldiers and civilians had surmounted the first ridge and were astonished by the enormity of the attack. Descriptions and reminiscences of the depth and whirl of Sitting Bull's Indians buried in diaries are vivid, some almost storybook-like. Oliver Hanna, among the knot of civilians hanging close to Crook, reached the ridge at about the same time as the Crows and Shoshones did in their renewed attack and watched them engage the enemy. "The firing was fast and furious," he wrote. "The Indians seemed to be as thick as blackbirds. If one of them fell from a shot a dozen were there to take his place." Another observer embraced much of the same wording: "In front of them to the right, the left, the low bluffs inclosing the plain, were ringed with Indians in full war-gear. They looked like swarms of blackbirds, there were so many of them and in such rapid motion. They kept coming and coming into view, and as they dashed up to the brink of the hills upon their war ponies they opened a long-range fire upon the soldiers." David Mears, among the packers, likewise remembered how the Indians "were in front, rear, flanks, and on every hilltop, far and near. I had been in several Indian battles, but never saw so many Indians at one time before, at least not when they were on the war-path."[12]

On the soldiers' far left the Crows and Shoshones were the first to fully engage. Crook's silence on this initial movement is telling, suggesting that the auxiliaries' attack was almost entirely self-driven, although the influence of Cosgrove and the mixed-blood Louissant among the Shoshones and Plenty Coups and Old Crow among the Crows cannot be dismissed; nor can the encouragement and leadership of Captain George Randall, Crook's chief of scouts, who charged with them. At one point in the opening mêlée, scouts and Sitting Bull's warriors caught each other's eyes. A Sioux warrior spat out: "You go home! We want to kill only white men!" But the Shoshones and Crows were loyal, another of the packers remembered, and were hotly engaged in supporting the troops. "The troops were not ready to meet the attack," according to Grouard, who was huddling with Crook, "and had it not been for the Crows, the Sioux would have killed half our command." For a while the fighting between bitter enemies turned hand-to-hand as the scrape spilled across the entire broad bench between the first rise and the distant skyline ridge and on both sides of Kollmar Creek. "The coming together of the Sioux, Crows, and Shoshones was the prettiest sight in the way of a fight that I have ever seen," Grouard continued. "They were all mixed up, and I could hardly distinguish our allies from the hostiles."[13]

The onset of the tussle had a toll. Particulars on injuries suffered by Indian warriors at Rosebud, friendly or foe, are thin, although unique instances stand out. As Grouard moved about before the troops fully engaged, he recalled passing a Crow Indian sitting on the ground, not acting a bit hurt but intently watching the fight between Indians. Every once in a while he would "yell like a madman," Grouard said. "He was unable to get on his feet, having been shot just above the knee, and the bone was terribly shattered. His horse was lying dead by his side." The Crow warrior was identified as Bull Snake, who was shot making a bravery run in front of the enemy. Bull Snake later told his own version of the episode: "I raised my coup stick to strike a Sioux and he shot me, hitting my horse and we fell together. I found that I was badly wounded and could not stand up. I raised up as far as I could and fired three shots at the Sioux. There the battle ended." Fox Just Coming over Hill remembered Bull Snake as the toughest individual he ever knew. As Bull Snake was being taken home two days later, with his leg bound in a splint and fastened to his pony's neck, the injured limb would sometimes get twisted in underbrush so hard as to grind the ends of the broken bone. When this happened, Bull Snake would remark, supposedly cheerfully, "there goes another piece of bone into fine meal." Fox Just Coming over Hill was keenly aware of the trials of the injured for he, too, was seriously wounded in the fight.[14]

The Bull Snake story had a sequel. Several Crow women rode with their tribe's warriors that day. One of them, The Other Magpie, had a hand in slaying the Sioux man who wounded Bull Snake. She sought revenge for her brother, who had been killed by the Sioux the year before. Long afterward the Crows remembered The Other Magpie well. She was courageous and pretty, one source claims. She wore a woodpecker skin on her head, painted her forehead yellow, and rode a black horse. Seeing Bull Snake badly wounded and shot from his horse, Finds Them and Kills Them and The Other Magpie dashed in and brought down the Sioux warrior who was threatening Bull Snake's life. The two killed the warrior and scalped him. Later that scalp was cut into pieces and passed out among the women of the tribe and tied to willow poles and waved during the scalp dance. The Other Magpie was among those who tended Bull Snake on his painful journey home.[15]

With the Crows and Shoshones fully involved on the bench in what became for the moment a scattered desultory fight, the first of the infantry companies appeared on Crook's right. At the morning halt Chambers's Infantry Battalion occupied the Rosebud's left bank behind Noyes's Second Cavalry and ahead of the headquarters detachments, including Stanton's engineers and Hartsuff's doctors and hospital attendants. Details on this initial infantry deployment vary slightly. Chambers himself reported sending two companies forward immediately, with the other three companies following and not necessarily referring to the Fourth and Ninth in respective regimental cohesion. Luhn and Burt recollected that all five infantry companies deployed relatively simultaneously, holding back about ten men from each of the units with the mules. Strahorn described the movement as three companies immediately thrown forward as skirmishers and the other two following quickly. Minus the mule holders, some 152 officers and enlisted men were scrambling up the bluff in the first formal movement of the engagement.[16]

The advance, whether by two, three, or five companies, was slightly staggered. The two Fourth Infantry companies were the trailing units in the battalion that day. The second of them and the last in line, Company D, commanded by Captain Avery Cain, was the first to surmount the ridge and open fire on the Sioux. Cain did not pause on the crest but fired and charged and fired and charged again, slowly but deliberately creeping his way north across the open bench in the direction of the Camel-Back Ridge. After every volley, which Strahorn remembered as a "perfect rain of bullets," the Sioux retired to the next higher rise. This persistent sparring, with rushes and repulses, soon characterized the day's battle.[17]

Among the officers engaged in this initial deployment, Avery Billings Cain's coolness "under the hottest fire" was widely acknowledged. The dapper, mustachioed thirty-six-year-old infantry captain fought valiantly that day. But his courage and evident fearlessness came at a considerable personal cost, as revealed more fully later and in the immediate injuries suffered by two of his men. Company D's casualties were the first incurred by troops in the Battle of the Rosebud. Probing Cain's background is problematic but worthwhile. A toughened Civil War veteran, he bequeathed to history an insightful body of papers from that time but very little from his service on the frontier. He was married and fathered one daughter, who died at a tender age. Cain's battle report for that day is lamentably short. So, too, is his official record, though reading between lines reveals that he was hardened to combat and bloodshed. In fourteen years of service, he had seen plenty of blood and carnage.[18]

Cain's Company D suffered the battle's first wounded men, Privates James A. Devine, with a serious gunshot wound to the head, and Richard Flynn, with a slight gunshot wound to the left shoulder. Both were carried to the creekside for ministration by the medical officers. The battle had barely begun.[19]

In due course all five infantry companies were engaged, scattered along a skirmish line established slightly above the ragged first crest north of the valley floor. Their line shielded the cavalry as it went about mounting and deploying. Chambers's initial alignment, left to right, can be discerned from Luhn's diary entry and a newspaper account: Cain was positioned on the extreme left, Luhn and Company F, Fourth Infantry, on Cain's right, Captain Samuel Munson and Company C of the Ninth in the center, Captain Thomas Burrowes and Company G of the Ninth on Munson's right, and Captain Burt and Company H of the Ninth on the far right.[20]

The scrap between the warriors and doughboys lasted nearly three-quarters of an hour and at times was exceedingly hot. The bluff above was particularly threatening, swarming with mounted tribesmen who seized the immense rocks and ledges on the southern shoulders of the Camel-Back Ridge, creating what one observer called a stronghold from which they poured heavy fire upon the troops. When the battle was over, Robert Strahorn and several other newsmen explored this fortress-like stony ground and recalled finding "nearly a peck of freshly fired cartridge-shells. Many of them were of the pattern used in a celebrated sporting rifle, which is far superior to the Government arm." Later in the day the packers also occupied this ground. Strahorn could well have been referring to their firearms or to .44 caliber Winchester rifles and carbines, whose expended shells are the ubiquitous cartridge cases found in Indian positions across the battlefield.[21]

The infantrymen on the line below fixated on those warriors and worked their long-range rifles to good effect. Despite the unjustified notoriety of Winchester and Henry repeaters, the army's Springfield rifles were the finest weapons on the field that day. Years later George McAnulty, a private in Captain Munson's Company C, Ninth Infantry, remembered this nerve-wracking predicament and also the calm assurances rendered by First Lieutenant Thaddeus Capron, who managed McAnulty's section of the line. "I shall never forget his brave action at that time and his quiet 'Steady—men—Steady,' as those naked painted hordes rode down upon us—it was a terrible moment. I believe nothing in civilized warfare could equal it for chilling horror. We stood our ground well and after a sharp fight the Indians withdrew."[22]

The Third Cavalrymen lined up on the opposite side of the Rosebud directly below the doughboys, Companies C and G of Captain Frederick Van Vliet's squadron, were fully conscious of the cover afforded by the Eleventh Dragoons. Private Zinser of Company C confided in his diary that "the Infantry cannot be praised enough for the excellent service . . . rendered in keeping them [the Indians] at bay while we got to our horses, but the Infantry kept them at bay, and their charge was repulsed."[23]

Meanwhile, on Chambers's immediate right, Captain Noyes also attacked, leading four of his five Second Cavalry companies, dismounted, out of the bottoms and over the northern ridge. His battalion thus far had only received the simple command to saddle up and await further orders. Hearing considerable gunfire straight north, suggesting the threatening proximity of the Sioux, Noyes took it upon himself to lead his companies forward, leaving Captain Dewees's Company A in charge of the battalion's horses. Noyes advanced in skirmish order and fired several volleys that scattered the enemy. Noyes particularly noted in his battle report that he undertook this movement "without awaiting further orders," an obvious tip to his action at

Powder River, where his initiative was questioned and his lack of discretion led to a court-martial and reprimand from General Crook. Noyes was a solid officer. His initial charge in the lower end of the Gap was spirited. Sioux warriors contested the ridgelines right and left and particularly availed themselves of rough, rocky ground on both sides that afforded good cover. While slow to yield, the advance effectively drove the Sioux from the mouth and front sides of the Gap. Having achieved that much, Noyes posted First Lieutenant Samuel Swigert and Company B on a knob to the right and Captain Wells and Company E on high ground to the immediate left. Additionally, on Wells's left First Lieutenant William Rawolle with Company B and Second Lieutenant Frederick Kingsbury with Noyes's own Company I occupied the ascending ridgeline of the Camel-Back.[24]

Exercising a good deal of self-initiative, elements of Crook's command successfully checked the opening Sioux attack at the Rosebud. Captain Randall and the Crow and Shoshone scouts were ably sparring with Sioux and Cheyenne warriors on the far left, in the drainage of Kollmar Creek and particularly its mid-ground, therewith effectively occupying, if momentarily, the enemy in that quarter. In the center Chambers's infantry battalion held firm on a skirmish line stretching across the first bench immediately north of the Rosebud's east-west reach. Chambers's line of foot soldiers roughly attached to Noyes's line of dismounted Second Cavalry, which itself covered the lower ascent of the Camel-Back Ridge and secured the mouth of the Gap east of there. Meanwhile, behind them, ten companies of the Third Cavalry were still responding to deployment orders that would soon scatter that regiment's two battalions and squadron north, west, and south as the battle intensified.

While Crook's troops and allies seized and dutifully held their ground, the general as yet had no control of the field. Strahorn saw it plainly. "For the first time it was really evident against what fearful odds our brave officers and men had to struggle, while the field was not yet half won." Crook did not bring on this engagement and was only beginning to grasp that Sitting Bull, Crazy Horse, and their vast avalanche of warriors were not this time making a showy demonstration, as at Tongue River Heights, only then to melt away. Crook, one of the nation's ablest Indian fighters, had never seen anything like it before.[25]

SWEEPING THE GAP

As Crook stood on the bench immediately above the small confluence of Rosebud and Kollmar Creeks, he could only have watched in utter amazement and alarm the fiery onslaught of warriors engaging his soldiers and auxiliaries. The emerging battlefield already spanned several miles right and left. Indian warriors were challenging his entire line and still plainly gathering, taunting, and pouring off the top and sides of the enormous long ridge on the northern horizon, a mile or more away. Crook quickly grasped the importance of that broad ridgeline commanding his entire front, and maybe the entire battlefield, but he had no way of getting there so long as the rolling foreground and those very heights were controlled by Indians. To his right he may not yet have fully appreciated the nature of Noyes's engagement at the far end of Chambers's line. But he almost certainly understood those to be men of the Second Cavalry, who stood ahead of Chambers's infantry in the valley during the morning pause and now were rightly defending that adjacent sector of the field. Behind them, still in the valley, he could see the ten companies of Third Cavalry scrambling to order.

Crook could also see the vulnerabilities of the emerging battlefield. To his left the fighting was spilling continually westward and southward, as if the enemy was curling around his feebly set flank and threatening his left and rear. The distant view east down the Rosebud was less clear, but the chance of being flanked there by swarming warriors seemed equally probable. Robert Strahorn, the reporter who endlessly shadowed the general throughout the day, likely articulated Crook's thinking when he said: "We were practically surrounded and had stern business on all sides." Crook and his command were on a field where "there was no rear."[1]

Crook's initial orders addressed each of those predicaments. A courier carried word to Crook's old academy classmate, Major Andrew Evans, who directly commanded the Third Cavalry and would guide its initial deployments. Finerty labeled the messenger an "aide-de-camp." As Bourke was elsewhere on the field at the time, the messenger was almost certainly Nickerson. Crook wanted Third Cavalry companies placed on the imposing heights south of Rosebud Creek to check any threat of attack from the rear and also downstream to thwart any flanking movement from that direction. He wanted the remainder of the regiment to cross to the left side of the creek and there engage the attackers flowing through the Gap, where the fight at the moment appeared heaviest. This courier or another—the sources do not distinguish—continued on to Royall, who later acknowledged receiving orders. His course also took him to the left bank, where the Second Cavalry, aside from Dewees's company, was already engaged.[2]

Evans reacted swiftly, ordering Van Vliet's squadron, mounted, to advance to the commanding ridge south of the creek. A natural funnel-shaped swale opened about where those companies, C and G of the Third, paused that morning and provided an opportune pathway straight to the top and then westward to a point later known as Eagle Nest Peak. Crook was correct in surmising the vulnerability of that position. As Van Vliet's companies reached the top and continued to that farthest west point, they encountered warriors also "striving hard for it," the captain reported. The squadron drove the Indians from the ridge, incurring no casualties, and held that critical position until late in the morning. Private Louis Zinser of Company C noted finding five dead Indians on the hill, doubtless meaning older scaffold or tree burials. This long ridge was loftier than any other on the field. First Lieutenant Emmet Crawford, commanding Company G, later told John Finerty that it afforded them a "splendid view of the fight."[3]

Meanwhile Evans also immediately advanced two companies forward to occupy appropriate ground at the Big Bend to preclude any flanking action from that direction. Captain Guy Henry personally led the detachment, composed of his own Company D, and Company F, commanded by Second Lieutenant Bainbridge Reynolds, the son of Colonel Reynolds. The pairing of Henry and Reynolds was almost certainly intentional. The seasoned Henry was the third-ranking captain in the regiment; Reynolds was the second lowliest second lieutenant in the Third. Reynolds was also, as he proudly proclaimed later, the youngest officer commanding a company on this expedition. He would see much this day. The movement, however, tore apart Henry's battalion, a point of chagrin to the captain. They advanced eastward, sticking to the south side of the creek to the place where the stream makes its pronounced turn northward. Henry and Reynolds encountered no Indians. Upon reaching their assigned position the captain "reconnoitered personally" and observed warriors at "some distance to my right on the bluffs." If he was scanning to the north or more probably to the northwest, in the direction of the shooting, he almost certainly was referring to warriors on bluffs over-looking the west side of the Rosebud Narrows, where the main thrust of the attack commenced and now was especially heated.[4]

Major Evans then directed Captain Mills to lead his battalion, mounted, across the creek and "charge and drive the Indians from the opposite hills." Mills's four companies were the lead battalion in the Third Cavalry column that morning. Evans's sequence of deployment plainly flowed simply from the rear to the front—Van Vliet, Henry, and now Mills. Mills promptly led his four companies across the Rosebud and into the shallow gradient at the open end of the soon infamous Gap. They formed for their advance behind the dismounted men of the Second Cavalry, who held a thin skirmish line thrown across the mouth of that distinctive funnel-like feature. Mills recog-nized that he would soon hold the battlefield's "extreme right."[5]

Meanwhile, on the far left, Bourke rushed orders from Crook to Captain Randall, riding among the scouts, encouraging him to renew the fight in that sector. In the preceding half-hour the clash between Indians along Kollmar had reached a stalemate, even while Sioux warriors continued streaming onto the battlefield to occupy advantageous high ground, from which they invariably pinned down their lifelong enemies. Randall rallied the Crows and Shoshones and pressed an attack, but heavy Indian fire almost immediately checked the assault. "Randall's Redskins" again took cover in the tumbled ground of the Kollmar drainage. They faced overwhelming numbers of Sioux, here as elsewhere firing volley after volley into the allies and then disappearing, only to reappear at some other point.[6]

Aside from Dewees's Company A, Second Cavalry, some fifty detached infantrymen, all holding their respective battalions' horses and mules, and the two remnant companies of Henry's battalion, temporarily commanded by Royall, the entire Big Horn and Yellowstone Expedition was now engaged. The field was vast and the action unpredictable, stretching from where the Crows and Shoshones sparred with the Sioux in the west across the middle ground of Kollmar Creek and eastward to the other great doorway for the Sioux, the open saddle of the Gap. Van Vliet covered high ground to the south. Henry stood watchful for a flanking movement in the proximity of the Big Bend. The men of the Fourth and Ninth Infantry and Second Cavalry held a thin skirmish line on the wide bench above and parallel with the entire length of the original soldier line in the bottom. Young Crow and Shoshone boys and other camp attendants among the auxiliaries corralled the led ponies of the auxiliaries near the mouth of Kollmar. Just east of them, also in the valley, the medical staff tended the several wounded men carried down from the initial skirmish line and likely also the Crow scout Bull Snake, although that detail is unconfirmed. From the mouth of the Gap, Mills prepared to sweep northward. Crook's first important offensive action was soon to begin.

—————

Crook remained animated during these opening maneuvers. With orders flying, attendants brought up the horses belonging to the headquarters detachment and the general and his entourage of aides, orderlies, and packers rode eastward along the undulating crest, easily threading their way behind Chambers's and Noyes's skirmishers. Crook soon encountered Mills, who had just crossed the Rosebud and was now momentarily dismounted behind the line of skirmishers. That Mills had dismounted is yet another reflection of the manner in which time eludes dated and summary narratives. The fluidity in combat suggested by live-action reports and accounts in truth meant successions of movement and pause. By one account it was now about 9:30 A.M. Crook and Mills consulted. The captain reported his observations that morning and how Indians could still be seen roaming the highlands and here and there coming onto the field from due north, mostly meaning straight through the Gap or by way of its margins. Crook made it clear that those Indians needed to be checked. He pointed to two prominent features deep in the Gap that were swarming with warriors, a rocky ledge on the right and a crest in its apparent farthest depths. Crook wanted them cleared.[7]

Royall, who now personally led the two remaining companies of Henry's battalion, appeared on the scene as Crook and Mills finished their business. Crook affirmed that the colonel should charge and occupy the hills to the left, meaning not the rising Camel-Back Ridge to the northwest but the rolling ground between the infantry line and the southern flanks of the long Camel-Back, where the Sioux were "hotly pressing our steady infantry." Crook and Royall both conceded that it was a tall order for two companies, so the general permitted the withdrawal of Henry and Reynolds from the Big Bend. He ordered Royall also to withhold Captain Andrews's Company I from Mills's battalion, then positioning for its attack. These decisions meant the concentration of a suitable offensive force. (Many accounts of Mills's charge in the Gap imply that Andrews's company participated in that action. But Royall, Andrews, and Mills make clear in their respective reports that Company I was withdrawn and added to Royall's force before that initial charge.)[8]

In a moment all attention turned to Mills, whose battalion was again mounted and moving. As the captain told an audience many years later, he ordered his soldiers "front into line." With soldierly precision, the men of Sutorius's Company E, Lawson's Company A, and Mills's own Company M, commanded now by First Lieutenant Augustus Paul, spread unit by unit, platoon by platoon, soldier by soldier, into a north-facing line that spanned much of the bench below the mouth of the Gap. After the command, numbering some 179 officers and men, carefully threaded its way through Noyes's dismounted ranks, Mills "sounded the charge." With pistols drawn and officers riding in advance of platoons, the soldiers spurred their horses into a spirited attack, "driving," as one observer put it, "the enemy like chaff before the winds of heaven." The charge was in full keeping with one of the gallant traditions of the United States Cavalry, albeit one of the most uncommon maneuvers in Indian warfare, despite the great John Ford and John Wayne Hollywood Westerns. Mounted charges with pistols drawn through Indian villages on the plains occurred from time to time, most recently at Powder River. But this was a charge against a comparably aggressive mounted foe, *mano a mano*, warrior against warrior. Myth and reality were converging on a Sioux war battlefield.[9]

John Finerty, riding with Sutorius during the charge, strove to capture the drama and pure glory of the action in several penned descriptions. "Rising in his stirrups," Finerty wrote, Mills shouted "Charge!"[10]

> The order was executed with a brilliancy and celerity seldom equaled, under a sweeping, hostile fire, which made a volcano of the plateau between the lower bluffs above our camp and the higher ones occupied by Sitting Bull. The battalion charged at full gallop with fierce ringing cheers, halted for a moment to pour in a withering volley, and then galloped up the ascent to the crest of the ridge. Despite their great numbers and splendid position the Sioux center broke and ran like a pack of wolves, taking shelter on other bluffs, 1,200 yards behind, for this battle-ground is a succession of ridges for miles on miles. The battalion then dismounted and deployed as skirmishers along the position they had carried.[11]

Finerty rewrote a portion of this memorable newspaper passage in his 1890 campaign reminiscence, *War-Path and Bivouac*. While again describing a stirring cavalry charge, he changed one particular detail worth noting. "We were going too rapidly to use our carbines," he observed in the rewrite, "but several of the men fired their revolvers, with what effect I could neither then, nor afterward, determine." Both halting and pouring in a withering carbine volley and advancing and firing revolvers were conventional cavalry assault tactics. Maybe both actions occurred as Mills swept the Gap.[12]

The targeted ridge was some eight hundred yards from Mills's start. The distinctive sandstone feature consists of a conglomeration of rocky ledges and enormous boulders stringing the right side of the Gap. When he reached that initial objective Mills dismounted his companies and fanned them into a loose skirmish line across the floor of the Gap and into the hillside. This, too, was a standard tactical maneuver, with three of four troopers advancing on the line and every fourth man withdrawing the horses to some point of relative safety. Mills described the fight at this initial pause in close detail to his Order of Indian Wars audience in 1917: "When I reached the first ridge the leading Indians were there but gave way. There were large boulders at its foot, some large enough to cover the sets of four horses. I dismounted and directed the horse holders to protect them behind these rocks." Mills then led his men onto the ridge, where he confronted warriors in close quarters, most of them mounted, all gaudily dressed and painted, and demonstrating equestrian skills that earned the captain's warmest praise in hindsight. "The Indians proved then and there that they were the best cavalry soldiers on earth." His captive audience of aged Indian war campaigners in Washington, D.C., must have been enthralled.[13]

Mills pressed forward into the rocky, pine-strewn ground above a feature later recognized in part as the Buffalo Jump. Large chalk rock knobs, or boulders as Mills called them, dotted the southern margins of the precipice and provided cover for the battalion's horses, while smaller rocks and outcroppings above provided other cover as his soldiers maneuvered northward. "We met the Indians at the foot of this ridge, and charged right in and through them, driving them back to the top of the ridge." Mills's men were ascending the high ground between the Gap and Rosebud Cañon, a critical vista at its highest and one of the central points of attack earlier that morning. Remembered Mills: the warriors "refused to fight when they found us secured behind the rocks, and bore off to our left."[14]

Behind Mills, Crook meanwhile reengaged the dismounted battalions of infantry and Second Cavalry still holding the initial defensive line, ordering both to draw up their mounts and prepare to support the first battalion's action in the Gap. Even while Mills advanced on the far right, warriors vigorously contested much of the Gap's left, especially along the northern margins of the Camel-Back Ridge. Companies E, B, and I of the Second occupied the initial ascent of the ridge, with Company I being the farthest exposed. Facing sharp fire from warriors secreted behind the jumbles of rock scattered along the ridge (including a cluster soon renowned as the Packer's Rocks) Crook's aide John Bourke interposed himself. Observing a detachment of Company I under concentrated fire and otherwise without an officer, he led the men in a successful charge of the "rock-breasted, steep bluff on whose summit the Sioux had taken post." The warriors fled. In his diary that evening Bourke noted no "deficiency of courage" in those men of Company I. Behind them Dewees and Company A brought up the Second Cavalry's horses. Noyes recollected that nearly an hour passed before the captain reported, at about 10:30 A.M. For the moment Noyes's battalion, with horses now at the ready, was held in reserve as Crook assessed conditions generally and strategized an attacking movement that could well turn this fight from a purely defensive one to an offensive action.[15]

Noyes's independent advance that morning was costly. During the attack and occupation of the lower swales at the mouth of the Gap and the Camel-Back, Sergeant Patrick O'Donnell of Company D and First Sergeant Thomas Meagher of Company I both received gunshot wounds in their right forearms. Meagher was wounded in Bourke's impromptu charge into the rocks.[16]

One particular moment during Noyes's regrouping was awkward, at least for one officer. Second Lieutenant Daniel C. Pearson of Dewees's Company A, an 1870 West Point graduate, had not yet been in the fight. He remembered "the strange and unaccustomed sensation when the bullets kept whizzing close to my firing point," as he came up with the horses, likely referring to the same incoming fire that Bourke had noted. Pearson recalled how "at one time, more than my share of bullets apparently struck the ground near by, and afterward discovered that the motion of my horse had inverted my open cartridge box and pitched a large percentage of my cartridges upon the ground." The incident was embarrassing at the least but not enough to keep him from revealing it in his memoir. Pearson did not mention retrieving the cartridges.[17]

Chambers's battalion likewise went about securing its mules. With all five companies on the skirmish line, and a segment of this front still hotly contested, the major detailed his units to the camp one by one. They saddled and in due course returned to the bluff. When they reappeared, the respective companies were directed to the cover of one of the hillocks at the south-eastern end of the Camel-Back, just west of the assembling Second Cavalry. Captain Burt's Company H, Ninth Infantry, was the last unit relieved from the skirmish line. In the bottoms while saddling, First Lieutenant Henry Seton, Chamber's adjutant, directed Burt to ensure the safe relocation of the hospital and its wounded. Thus far those men had been huddled in the valley near the mouth of Kollmar Creek. But with the assistance of Burt's dough-boys they were now carefully ushered forward, ultimately to a secure flank of the Camel-Back Ridge. An hour elapsed before Burt joined Chambers. As with Noyes's movement, it was about 10:30 A.M.[18]

By mid-morning only the replacement ponies of the Crows and Shosho-nes remained circled in the valley under the watchful eye of a few boys and dependents. Above them on the imposing rise south of the Rosebud, in the vicinity of the Eagle Nest Peak, Van Vliet's Third Cavalry Squadron secured that quarter. The south side of the field had grown quiet.

At this midmorning hour, the principal action on the battlefield centered on the Gap, the conduit that brought warriors onto the field from several points beyond and ultimately connected directly with the Indian village on Reno Creek, twenty miles northwest. That circumstance was utterly unimag-ined by Crook and the men of his expedition. The Gap was indeed a funnel of sorts, narrowest at its mouth and continually widening before opening broadly beyond a mid-length crest. On the right Mills still contested the fea-ture's delineating shoulder and high ground, although most of the warriors in his front had retreated to other vantages farther north. While the Gap was well defined at its mouth and mid-reach, in its depths it tumbled in a succession of rocky and boulder strewn crests and vales, all perfect ground for desultory fighting and protected movement. Private James Forristell of Swigert's Company D, Second Cavalry, captured the essence of the fight in this sector in a reminiscence recorded many years later. "We struggled back and forth, here and there, on the small plateau valley and its neighboring hillsides. It was impossible to bring the Indians to a steady and settled battle. They dodged in and dodged out, from all sides of us, as was the old-time Indian mode of warfare." While the Second Cavalry succeeded in clearing the lower ascent of the Camel-Back Ridge, Indians visibly hovered behind the rocks and ledges beyond its mid-length. Crook, a canny observer, wanted the Gap cleared entirely.[19]

That challenge on the left fell to Chambers's infantry. On Crook's direc-tion, the major began a formal ascent of Camel-Back Ridge. He initially led three mounted companies—Munson's, Burrowes's, and Luhn's—along its broad crown, headed at the moment for the mid-rise feature so plainly seen from the first bench above Rosebud Creek and soon remembered as Crook's Hill. Cain's and Burt's companies followed as quickly as they were saddled and off the bottoms, with Burt shepherding the hospital cadre. The lead companies met only slight resistance.[20]

While Chambers advanced along the lower crest of the Camel-Back Ridge, Mills's first battalion of the Third renewed its sweep of the high country on the far right. The Indians across his front fought well but when pressed consistently withdrew to the next prominence beyond Mills's immediate reach. Finerty, never far from Sutorius, described their "boldness and impudence," riding up and down the hillside six hundred yards to the north, "wheeling in circles, slapping an indelicate portion of their persons at us, and beckoning us to come on." The newsman was certain that Crazy Horse himself was directing the fight, even signaling with a pocket mirror. Perhaps so, but of course to these men every prominent warrior was Crazy Horse or Sitting Bull. Mills glanced back and saw the Second Cavalry forming at the toe of the Camel-Back, ready to support him if needed.[21]

Mills called up his horses and within minutes remounted his companies. His charge on the next rise was less of a show this time but every bit as effective. Mills again led his troopers forward and then, at an appropriate moment, wheeled sharply to the right and rushed straight at the scattered hillocks from which warriors challenged his flank and front. Again the fighting was fleeting but vigorous, with Sioux warriors pouring in several heavy volleys. At the toe of the increasingly broken ground, Mills dismounted his men, withdrew the horses to cover, and advanced on foot. As before, the Sioux abandoned their positions when pressed, this time noticeably fleeing westward in the direction of the "the cone shaped mount," Conical Hill. As Finerty put it, "when we got there [meaning the crest in their immediate front], another just like it rose on the other side of the valley." And there, too, he noted, numerous warriors, "as fresh, apparently as ever." Mills assumed that this cat-and-mouse chase would proceed in that direction, but for the moment he focused on those warriors challenging his front. It was also becoming apparent, as Finerty observed, that the weight of the fighting was shifting away from this sector of the field.[22]

Mills's second advance lasted fully half an hour before the warriors broke to the west. From the start, aside from Mills's consecutive charges on the Gap's floor, his engagement mostly sprawled through the highlands across the feature's right. Rarely did fighting spill onto the floor, although several instances are recounted elsewhere. The battlefield, moreover, had a clear limiting delineation on the extreme right, an observation aptly noted by Mills. Mills's farthest eastern perimeter was protected by the jagged high ground above Rosebud Cañon. When the action shifted yet again, Mills assumed that he would regroup and turn his attention toward Conical Hill. But while still engaged on this front he received an order to scatter dismounted skirmishers and hold the position.[23]

A trooper in Sutorius's Company E, Private Thomas Lloyd, was in the midst of Mills's fight in the hills and had his own view. Several months later at Fort Laramie Lloyd wrote a letter to his cousin telling of the Rosebud Battle:

> It was one of the hottest places I ever was in. The company was surrounded by Indians and only that we stuck together and give them the best in the shop, they would have got away with our scalps. They stood and fought us within 100 yards until we got 6 volleys into them and commence to drop them and their ponies. Then they took a tumble and fell back into the hills and trying to coax us to follow but we knew too much of Mr. Sitting Bull for that.[24]

Mills's battle on the far right took a toll. In his report afterward the captain tallied one man wounded, Trumpeter Elmer Alanson Snow of his own Company M. Additionally his command suffered one horse killed and four wounded. The Snow episode was particularly beguiling and earned the trumpeter a Medal of Honor and a complicated and often messy life thereafter.[25]

Many soldiers and civilians scattered across the eastern sector of the Rosebud battlefield witnessed the Elmer Snow spectacle. An inordinate number chose to write about it, some perceptively and others fancifully. Like everyone else in Snow's battalion, the twenty-four-year-old trumpeter of M Company participated in Mills's second charge in the Gap. He almost was certainly among those blowing the shrill notes of charge that precipitated the attack. According to Lieutenant Paul, Snow was positioned on the extreme advance of the line. This second movement covered some six hundred yards from the place where the companies mounted in the vicinity of the Buffalo Jump to the second ridge, where warriors took refuge after the first assault. This was the second prominent Indian position that Crook and Mills had observed earlier in the morning, which Crook wanted cleared. Snow's dilemma befell

him when the battalion wheeled to the right and bore straight into the retal-
iatory fire of Sioux warriors.[26]

A shot from one of those defenders struck both of Snow's wrists simultaneously. The trumpeter's hands went limp instantly, bones severed. He could
not conventionally control his headstrong horse, which bolted or perhaps
simply continued its straight-away charge even after other troopers were
halting. The hapless Snow was carried directly into the midst of surprised
warriors, who continued to fire. Whether because of reverberations from the
front or Snow using his knees to maneuver his horse, it gradually turned in a
wide circle. Snow barely escaped immediate death.[27]

By that time many were watching Snow's predicament in abject horror.
Bourke's version of the story mixes up some details but vividly depicts the
miserable trumpeter's horrific ride, "badly shot through both arms, near
the wrists." First Bourke and then Frank Grouard, who was near Crook at
the time, joined in chasing Snow and attempting to grab the horse's reins.
Grouard closed on the frightened animal but could neither grab the reins
nor get ahead of it. All the while he was shocked to see Snow's hands dan-
gling from the wrists. Grouard screamed at Snow to throw himself off. "He
gave me one look that I will never forget. I got up close as I could to the
horse and hit it on the side of the head. The blow turned the horse some
. . . , and the wounded man threw himself off." Help came immediately.
Snow was shepherded to the hospital. The wretched trumpeter was crippled
for life.[28]

A good deal of after-the-fact credit for saving Snow accrued to Bourke,
who in his diary wrote brilliantly of the episode and placed himself at center stage in the heroic scene. He toned the recollection down some in his
1891 memoir. Lieutenant Henry Lemly, Royall's adjutant, not a witness to
the affair, similarly acknowledged Bourke's heroics, perhaps having read his
book. At the 1917 annual dinner of the Order of Indian Wars he declared
that if his regimental mate had been a British soldier he ought to have been
awarded the Victoria Cross. Snow likewise credited Bourke for having saved
his life at Rosebud. A problem arises, however, because Bourke was nowhere
near center stage as the affair played out, although he was an eyewitness and
involved to a degree, perhaps the first one riding to Snow's aid. Grouard's
account, in contrast, rings with an authenticity virtually impossible to con-
trive. Alas, the odd, mixed-blood scout was but an ephemeral character in the
larger saga of Third Cavalry heroics at Rosebud Creek. Memory, we should
allow, has a way of twisting things.[29]

|||||||||||||||||||||||||||||||||||||||||

Mills's fight also had a toll of another sort. In the immediate wake of the battle soldiers and newsmen began to banter over a perceived weakness with the
cavalry carbine, particularly a problem encountered over ejecting expended
cartridge cases. Fault was found with the carbine's lone shell ejector, a small
spring-driven device wedged in the hinge of the breech. When the breech
was opened after a discharge, the ejector sometimes tore through the heads
of the army's soft copper cartridge cases, leaving "the soldier at the mercy of
his enemy." Finerty pointedly exposed the problem but apparently misunderstood the central issue. The newsman rode with Mills's battalion and was in
the heat of the action in the Gap. "I saw, at [the] Rosebud fight," he wrote,
"not less than half a dozen soldiers in my immediate neighborhood punching
and swearing at their carbines, all of which had 'stuck.' Is not this a nice time
to be finding out the weak-points of our firearms?"[30]

Finerty's tirade chastised the army's "delicate" cavalry carbine while
extolling the worthiness of the infantry rifle. "Even if the shell of the infantry
soldier should stick, he has still his iron wand wherewith to punch it out."
Finerty was referring to the practicality of the rifle's ramrod, an appendage
that carbines did not feature until the modifications of 1879. He also praised
the general merits of the infantry rifle, which was deadly at greater ranges and
feared by Indians. "Crook always carries one on his saddle," he noted. At the
least "a double ejector would much improve the arm and save trouble from
inextricable shells." Finerty entirely missed the extraction problem's central
issue, that of waxy green verdigris forming when copper cartridges came in
contact with leather for any length of time. This was a day when a soldier's
preferred accoutrement for carrying cartridges in the field was a homemade
all-leather thimble belt worn around the waist. Verdigris-encrusted shells
shoved into hot, often dirty breeches during combat frequently cemented
in the weapon's chamber. Not everyone was oblivious to the problem, fortunately, and some officers addressed the issue forthrightly during the course
of the campaign by instructing their men to "clean cartridges." Solving the
problem was nearly as simple as that (clean breeches helped too), although the
army gyrated over the issue for years thereafter, repeatedly investigating the
matter and eventually authorizing canvas cartridge belts.[31]

|||||||||||||||||||||||||||||||||||||||||

As the fighting raged across Mills's front a tremendous roar arose from down
the Gap. Captain Randall and a band of Crow and Shoshone auxiliaries

joined the fray, having broken away from their stalemated fight in the Koll-mar drainage and drawn now perhaps by the thunderous gunfire in this direction. By then a palpable cacophony rose above the battlefield when action intensified and proved a lure for fighting men more than once that day. The friendly Indians could plainly discern the action in the high ground and promptly rode in that direction. The Sioux, aware of this new challenge, rose to the charge of these hereditary enemies and engaged vigorously, just as others had done on Kollmar Creek. The soldiers near the mix held their fire because they could not differentiate the Sioux from friendly Indians. The red cloth badges, sometimes barely distinguishable, were nearly unrecognizable in the smoky fog of battle. As on Kollmar, the Sioux again proved themselves aggressive fighters, forcing the Crows and Shoshones to halt their charge and fight from cover. This manner of fighting in the Gap between the soldiers and Sioux and the auxiliaries and Sioux offered unique examples of aggressive and passive action. The soldiers were virtually tireless in their efforts, while the auxiliaries, with quite different values at stake, often proved much more hesitant. In both instances, however, the majority of Sioux warriors slipped out of their entanglements, riding southwest behind the folds of the distant ground, plainly bound for Conical Hill.[32]

Among the knotted fighters at the far end of the Gap was First Sergeant John H. Van Moll of Lawson's Company A, Third Cavalry. The thirty-two-year-old first sergeant, a Gettysburg veteran and widely respected soldier, was on Mills's left when the battalion charged the second ridge. In turn, Van Moll fought on his company's far left, where the Shoshones, Crows, and Sioux were mixing it up. One of the several *Chicago Tribune* correspondents with the expedition, likely Captain Andrew Burt of the Ninth Infantry (the *Tribune* stories were invariably unsigned), observed the episode from afar. He noted how Van Moll and a few others from Company A were drawn into the tumult between the rival tribes and had advanced a good distance from the security of their own lines. The Sioux and the scouts fought to a draw. When the auxiliaries had had enough, they quietly withdrew, carrying away several wounded tribesmen. Van Moll was abandoned in this reversal, alone and some four hundred yards from his own line. Sioux warriors, eyeing his predicament, rushed out to kill him.[33]

Comrades in the soldier lines saw Van Moll's dilemma, and several started to his rescue. The sergeant turned and attempted to flee, firing as he went. The soldier liberators would have been too late but watched in amazement as a solitary Indian, a "small, misshapen Crow warrior, mounted on a fleet pony," dashed boldly among the Sioux and rescued the sergeant. The individual was later identified as the Shoshone warrior Humpy. Bullets flew as Humpy reached the sergeant, motioned for him to jump on the back of his pony, and then raced toward the soldier lines "amidst the cheers and shouts of those who witnessed it, and the disappointed yells of the enemy." "It was one of the most thrilling episodes of the Sioux war," recalled an observer.[34]

By late morning the army controlled the Gap. The battle's earliest fighting had spilled from its rocky ledges as Sioux and Cheyenne warriors chased the army's Indian scouts from the highlands on the far right all the way to Kollmar Creek in the west. Early on, Noyes's Second Cavalry plugged the mouth of the Gap but remained vulnerable to warriors holding dominant high ground on the right and left. Spirited cavalry charges ultimately broke that hold and pushed those tribesmen into ever higher countryside. By late morning most of them had relocated to more advantageous positions elsewhere on this sprawling battlefield. The fighting in the Gap was a struggle, with individual and group heroics of many sorts, plus narrow escapes and outright tragedies. Most important, early in the fight Crook grasped the significance of the Gap and seized control. Even now he was making his way to a hilltop that, as seen from the bottom, appeared to offer commanding views of the whole field—the dominating high ground of Clausewitz's "wide view." But this battle was far from over. Newsman John Finerty expressed the moment best. He and others could plainly hear "the volume of fire, rapid and ever increasing, from our left. The wind freshened from the west, and we could hear the uproar distinctly." The Battle of the Rosebud was merely spilling onto new ground.[35]

COMMANDING THE FIELD

By midmorning the battle on Rosebud Creek still greatly perplexed General Crook. This was not a place or fight of his choosing and was certainly no minor demonstration such as the one at the mouth of Prairie Dog Creek. If anything, the battle was intensifying. Sitting Bull's warriors were demonstrating no sign of retreat. Instead, their vigor was exploding with emotion and rage even as Crook worked to take command of the fight. Already he had directed countering offensive maneuvers of his own and now contemplated a grand shift that might well change the course of the day. But first he needed to assess conditions across the entire field.

From his vantage near the foot of the Camel-Back Ridge, Crook could plainly measure Mills's second engagement that morning and watched intently as the captain attacked ever deeper in the highlands on the right of the Gap, again driving the Indians from that sector of the field. Relatively close to Mills, Captain Randall and a strong contingent of Crow and Shoshone allies had joined the fray and were challenging warriors across the Gap's deepest central recesses. Crook could also plainly see warriors navigating the broken landscape that generally concealed them to the north and west of his troops as they in turn made their way to the distinctive knob at the far end of the Camel-Back Ridge. Perhaps most perplexing of all, the general and his entourage plainly discerned the escalating gunfire reverberating from the left, across the southern downsides of the Camel-Back Ridge and in the margins of the Kollmar drainage. It could only be Royall, and Crook especially needed to understand the engagement ensuing in that remote quarter.

|||||||||||||||||||||||||||||||||||||||

Crook and his staff and followers kept pace with Chambers and the infantry battalion as they advanced up the crown of the Camel-Back. The ridge then and now has a broad open top with occasional scatterings of pines and scrub oaks dotting its shoulders. Resistance was slight as the infantrymen pushed their way to the feature's mid-length and the point known ever after as Crook's Hill. The sources are vague but suggest that Crook, exposed,

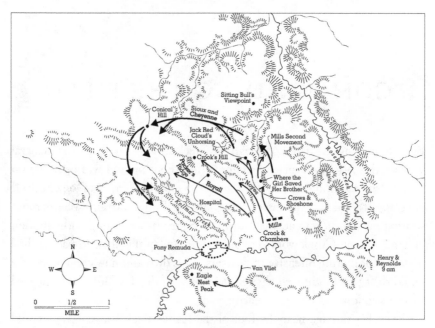

5. Crook Attacks, 10:30 A.M., June 17, 1876

advanced alongside his old West Point friend, Major Chambers, rather than safely shield himself behind the advancing infantry line. It may have been on this very ascent that the general's black charger was shot from beneath him. Many sources confirm this detail, but only Bourke and the *Sidney Telegraph* provide any substance, meager as it is. They also tell of strikingly different outcomes. In his diary entry for the day Bourke noted that the general's horse was shot in the leg but not mortally wounded. Finerty confirmed the detail, similarly noting that the horse was wounded.[1]

Another report portrayed the incident as more dire. The *Telegraph*, in its Rosebud Battle EXTRA edition published on June 24, reported Crook's horse was killed but that "the general was not long in remounting, and came out of the fight without a scratch." Three Third Cavalry companies originated at Sidney Barracks: Van Vliet's E, Crawford's G, and Andrews's I. While the newspaper correspondent was unnamed, it was almost certainly Lieutenant Foster, who also corresponded for the *Chicago Tribune* and *New York Daily Graphic*. After returning to Omaha in late June, Captain Nickerson added one other minuscule note, labeling the episode "a close call."[2]

Whatever the case, Tom Moore's packers and miners advanced with Crook and Chambers. This motley crew of thirty-six "old seeds," as Robert

210

Strahorn characterized them, shadowed Crook closely. They trailed him from the bottoms to the first bench then to the toe of Camel-Back Ridge, where the general conferred with Mills and Royall. On this initial ascent they moved like a mob behind the headquarters contingent of aides and orderlies. Upon reaching their destination (the perch aptly named Crook's Hill), the general invited Moore to disperse his well-armed marksmen to the two natural breastworks overlooking the battlefield. One, a jumble of rocks on the north shoulder slightly west of Crook's Hill, would soon be remembered as Packer's Rocks (the objective of Bourke's sortie with the detachment from Company I, Second Cavalry). The other was a lengthy rocky ledge straddling the south shoulder of Crook's position that was soon branded Packer's Ridge. Armed with Sharps and Remington sporting rifles and government-issue Springfield rifles, the men in both positions became opportunistic snipers through the remainder of the day. Not thirty minutes earlier, both positions had been occupied by warriors who had used those rocks to similar good advantage.[3]

Crook's attention turned immediately to the action exploding south and west of his vista. When he and William Royall conferred near the mouth of the Gap around 9:30 A.M. immediately after Mills received his orders to attack in that sector, Crook consented to the consolidation of Captain Henry's battalion of the Third. He also approved the redeployment to Royall's command of Captain Andrews's Company I from Mills's battalion. Royall immediately dispatched an orderly to Henry, who under earlier orders from Major Evans had taken two companies to the Big Bend of the Rosebud, nearly 1.75 miles east of the mouth of the Gap, ostensibly to turn any flanking attempt at that far end of the battlefield. Easily half an hour elapsed before Henry and Reynolds came on, at about 10:00 A.M.[4]

Royall's command now totaled five companies under his personal leadership: Henry and Company D; Captain Charles Meinhold with Company B; Second Lieutenant Bainbridge Reynolds and Company F; Captain Peter Vroom with Company L; and Andrews and Company I—about 290 men counting Royall's headquarters complement. Crook's specific orders, as Royall repeated them in his battle report, were plain enough: "deploy as skirmishers, [and] charge and occupy the hills in the possession of the enemy." Another account put it even more bluntly: "attack Sitting Bull's right." Sitting Bull's right at the moment was Crook's and Royall's left. The objective, albeit obtusely described in the accounts, was easily comprehended on the field: it simply meant moving aggressively westward against the mass of warriors swarming the flanks of Kollmar Creek and the highlands across that drainage's north side, conceivably to the farthest extent of the Camel-Back Ridge.[5]

In his own battle report Captain Meinhold offered a clear sense of this initial movement. He and Vroom had remained with Royall in the bottoms during the initial deployments and followed him when he crossed Rosebud Creek, surmounted the bluff, and encountered Crook. When Henry and Reynolds came on, Royall was ready to advance. Meinhold and Vroom formed frontal lines, with Meinhold in the fore and Vroom following. They advanced, mounted, to the west, into the "open space to the left and front of the camp," across the level plain previously contested by the dismounted skirmishers of the Second Cavalry and infantry battalion when the fight opened that morning. Meinhold allowed that Royall and his escort led the entire movement, implying that he rode ahead of Company B but almost certainly suggesting that the colonel and his aides rode alongside or behind Company B and exercised control from there. Beyond them, Meinhold's men could plainly see warriors occupying successions of knolls and hillocks across their front. As Mills and others had discovered elsewhere on the field, when facing troopers advancing and firing, warriors invariably returned that fire and fell back. "Firing from their ponies, their shots were generally a little too high . . . fortunate thing for us," noted one of the correspondents.[6]

As Royall progressed, Crook and the others with him on the ridge appreciated the colonel's objective, although no one grasped the depth and vigor of the resistance baiting and challenging the battalion. Already a third of a mile separated Royall's right and Crook's Hill. The colonel now "occupied a very important and dangerous position, one which if held by the enemy would have rendered Crook's line on the bluff untenable." The Indians "seemed to divine his mission," moreover, and the fighting escalated. Sioux and Cheyenne warriors consistently held advantageous ground on the scattered hillocks, ridges, and ravines lying between the Camel-Back Ridge and the roughly parallel Kollmar Creek, which plainly compounded Royall's task.[7]

Second Lieutenant Henry Lemly, Royall's adjutant, rarely strayed far from the lieutenant colonel and had his own keen grasp of the situation at this early stage of the advance. As the five companies pushed westward and passed through the forked draw directly below Crook's Hill, the undulating plain widened. The companies trailing Meinhold and Vroom—Henry's D, Reynolds's F, and Andrews's I—spread themselves on Meinhold's left, with Henry and Company D on the extreme left of this staggered line. Although the entire front was under scattered fire all the while, Lemly sensed that it was most intense on the center and right, with the Indians occupying a prominent ridge across their fore, a spur off the Camel-Back. As Royall pushed on, the warriors retreated. Each time they seized another advantageous position behind them, where they threw themselves to the ground and fired at the troops "while their well-trained ponies grazed or stood fast at the extremity of their lariats." This steady if hazardous advance continued westward across the plain until it reached what Lemly called "a high and wooded crest." Reuben Davenport of the *New York Herald* labeled it more descriptively as "the top of a ridge adjacent to the highest crest, but separated from it by a deep ravine." Both chroniclers referred to the same place: one more nameless spur off the Camel-Back Ridge, this one tying to Kollmar Creek, southwest of Crook's Hill.[8]

At the moment the warriors seemed simply to be playing with Royall and his command. Yielding ground grudgingly, preserving their own strength and capacity, and making the troopers pay as dearly as possible was an acknowledged manner of Indian warfare. It was conceivably dangerous to push too far, becoming exposed and in this case exposing the men on Crook's Hill. But Royall, experienced in Plains Indian warfare, sensed none of that. He pushed on and then pushed some more.

<hr>

The Battle of the Rosebud had by now become general, a battlefield expression meaning that fighting was occurring virtually everywhere. The Sioux on that day, Saturday, June 17, had found General Crook's army and were proving themselves. John Finerty called them "the best fighting Indians that ever fired a shot." Mills remained under fire on the far right. Royall was advancing under concentrated fire onto Kollmar Creek. Van Vliet's squadron, occupying the critical hilltop on the south side of the field across Rosebud Creek, had also deflected warriors and was soon enmeshed again. Crow and Shoshone auxiliaries were scattered, some fighting in the depths of the Gap and others huddled in the lee of the Camel-Back Ridge, well behind Royall's command. Chambers's infantry battalion had advanced to Crook's Hill. Three of its companies were preparing to resume an attack on Conical Hill, the most vexing position on the field. Only the Second Cavalry was momentarily paused. After retiring from its initial skirmish line and drawing up horses, Noyes's five companies were held in reserve on the toe of the Camel-Back Ridge, perhaps already sensing their next movement.[9]

On Crook's Hill attention turned to Major Chambers, who had consolidated his battalion and fixated on the farthest reaches of the Camel-Back

Ridge. Crook, Chambers, and those around them could plainly see warriors teeming on the ridge's distant shoulders and crown—as they had done all morning. Crook understood that this battle could not be won so long as Sitting Bull's warriors held such a dominant location. They not only taunted their enemies from that distant landmark but used its recesses to full advantage in concealing movements on the western half of the battlefield. Chambers divided his command for the advance, withholding Burrowes's and Burt's companies as a reserve on Crook's Hill. Not unlike versatile chess pieces, those two companies could conceivably support, as needed, the movement of the battalion's other half, or Royall on the plain, or the packers and miners securing Crook's immediate north and south flanks, or the hospital on the southeastern flank. Chambers, for the moment, remained behind with Burrowes and Burt.[10]

The duty of assaulting Conical Hill fell to the ever-dependable Captain Cain, supported by Captains Luhn and Munson. Evincing a proud doughboy élan, the disciplined (if emotionally teetering) Cain advanced the 109 officers and men of Companies D and F of the Fourth and C of the Ninth, mounted, and dispersed into a frontal line. Their gleaming rifles provided a splendid spectacle in the midday sun. The ride took them northwestward along the Camel-Back's wide crown. Cain aimed for its farthest extent, the point that Luhn called "the round bute on the far end of the hill from where the Indians were annoying us very much." By his own reckoning, Cain began the advance at about 11:00 A.M.[11]

As the movement started, the Sioux delivered brisk defensive fire from the rocky ledges abounding on both sides of the ridge and also eventually from the off side of Conical Hill itself. In his diary entry for the day Lieutenant Thaddeus Capron of Munson's Company C noted how the three units "drove the Indians from our front, skirmishing a distance of nearly two miles." When the doughboys reached within four or five hundred yards of the hill, the warriors fled. The full distance by all measures was exposed and dangerous. Luhn noted that the "entire length of this hill [meaning the whole of the Camel-Back Ridge] was about 2½ miles." In fact, it measures nearly three miles from toe to head, and this advance starting from Crook's Hill alone spanned half that distance. Upon reaching Conical Hill, Cain dismounted his companies, drew off the mules and holders to a dimple southeast of the hill's crown, and scattered the remaining eighty-odd men in a broad semicircle around the downside of the crest, establishing a stout infantry redoubt in what was a strategic and still highly vulnerable sector of the battlefield.[12]

Cain's companies held Conical Hill and dispensed disciplined desultory fire from their long-range infantry rifles until circumstances changed that afternoon. By now, the psychology of infantrymen and their "Long Toms" (contemporary slang for these government-issue Springfield rifles) was appreciated on both sides. These were formidable weapons, firing a cartridge that packed a walloping seventy grains of powder and with an effective range of eleven hundred yards (versus a cavalry charge of fifty-five grains and a conventional range of five hundred yards). As John Finerty noted, "the long infantry rifle is the thing to lift the Indian off his feet." Jerry Roche, reporting for the *New York Herald* on Crook's third Sioux campaign, similarly extolled the worthiness of the infantry rifle: "It would seem that the Indians' favorite method of fighting is to surround the enemy as they would a herd of buffaloes, and in this style of fighting a long range gun is of inestimable advantage."[13]

The Northern Indians had their own candid perspective on this threat. Red Horse, a Miniconjou Sioux participant in the Little Big Horn battle eight days later, told an interviewer in 1881 of the final hours at that place. The massive village on the Little Big Horn (fully a third larger than the Reno Creek camp) broke and moved when a "Sioux man came and said many walking soldiers were coming near. The coming of the walking soldiers was the saving of the soldiers on the hill [meaning Major Reno's entrenched command]. Sioux can not fight the walking soldiers, being afraid of them, so the Sioux hurriedly left." It will be remembered, as well, that Crook's personal weapon of choice on this campaign was also a standard issue .45–70 Springfield rifle, although there is no evidence that he fired a shot in the Battle of the Rosebud.[14]

During the advance on and occupation of Conical Hill, Cain's command suffered one man wounded, Private John H. Terry of the captain's own Company D. At some point during the assault Terry was shot in the left leg, fracturing his tibia and fibula. Luhn noted that the wound was inflicted by someone in the soldier's own company, although he offered no particulars. He also reported that Corporal Ludwig Roper of Company F received a bullet hole through his hat. The infantry battalion had already suffered two men wounded on the initial skirmish line but incurred no other casualties during the battle.[15]

–––––––––––––––––––––

Captain Nickerson on Crook's Hill captured a fine sense of the ebb and flow and precariousness of the battle at this late morning hour:

Our efforts were directed toward closing in with the enemy by a series of charges, and theirs to avoiding close contact until, by the nature of the ground, our forces began to get scattered, and then their tactics changed from the defensive to an offensive. Each separate detachment was made the objective of terrific onslaughts; the warriors charging up to them, careening on their horses, and firing from behind them, while exposing as little of their own persons as possible. All the time they were whooping and yelling, hoping thereby to strike terror into the hearts of their adversaries and, if possible, stampede them. And woe to the officer or soldier who, at such a moment, lost his presence of mind. Let him turn to seek safety in flight, even for an instant, and immediately a score of warriors would pounce upon him.[16]

While Cain's command moved with a certain innate infantry precision, attention increasingly returned to Royall's engagement. The colonel's generally western line of advance and the slight northwesterly orientation of Kollmar Creek were converging. As Royall assessed conditions across his front, he discerned a distinct threat along the crest to his left and ordered Captain Andrews to lead Company I in that direction and drive those Indians from the ridge. Royall was referring to the ever rising southern shoulder of Kollmar Creek, which all along had been providing a particularly advantageous perch for Indian warriors. The landscape to the front and right, meanwhile, had widened and shallowed as the drainage reached its headlands. Royall intended on continuing his westerly course, which would soon enough carry him through Kollmar's thin swale. But he first dismounted his command. Horses and holders were held in the open creek bottom. The enemy on the immediate right and left had been pushed westward and at the moment only threatened from the west, where Andrews was now maneuvering and Royall intended to follow.[17]

Royall had commenced this advance with some 280 officers and men and a handful of staff. By detaching Andrews his total strength was diminished by 55 men. In the four remaining companies every fourth man was drawn off, linking horses and circling the mounts in the Kollmar swale. Removing every fourth man reduced the effective capacity of the dismounted force to some 170 men. Only Royall, his immediate staff, the company officers, and a few select noncommissioned officers remained mounted. The colonel then led his dismounted force out of the crossing and directly westward, aiming for an obvious notch on the near horizon. The troopers were well spread out, not in a traditional skirmish interval of ten or fifteen feet apart but still showing a distinctive line of blue. Andrews was clearing this front in his own advance, but Indian fire persisted and disturbingly heightened on the left, behind Company I. In due course Royall's four companies reached the crest in their front, taking a position on the high ground to the right of the swale or notch that had been their guide, having advanced some seven hundred yards from the crossing. Davenport, who rode in the midst of the action, noted that the men took prone positions on the "friendly crest of Kollmar" and "pour[ed] into the Sioux a hot answering fire." The advance was conducted with "an ardor and enthusiasm that found vent in cheers," he added. The colonel held this crest, commonly referred to as Royall's "first position," for more than an hour.[18]

The Third's momentary enthusiasm quickly soured, however. Davenport described the troubling situation: "Seeing the long gallant skirmish line pause . . . , [the Indians] dashed forward . . . and in an instant nearly every point of vantage within, in front and in the rear . . . was covered with savages wildly circulating their ponies and charging hither and thither, while they fired from their seats with wonderful rapidity and accuracy." Adjutant Lemly saw the matter similarly. "At first the fighting was most severe upon the right and in the center, but the Sioux, in giving way, retired by our left, where they occupied a high wooded crest." The warriors had found yet other advantageous ground offering opportunities for enfilading fire, particularly now on the left.[19]

||||||||||||||||||||||||||||||||||||

Sioux and Cheyenne warriors, largely retiring by the left as Lemly described it, not only took new positions on knobs and crests in the Kollmar highlands but also began circling widely south in the direction of Rosebud Creek. Sitting Bull's followers had eyed another prize there. A substantial herd of Crow and Shoshone ponies had been circled and held near Kollmar's mouth since the start of the fight. The Crow contingent, initially 176 strong and all mounted, led a similar number of extra ponies to Crook's camp. Almost certainly, the Shoshone scouts came with extra ponies as well, although particulars are vague. When Crook's scouts scampered out of the Rosebud highlands around 8:30 a.m., screaming "Heap Sioux! Heap Sioux!" and reached the general and fellow tribesmen, they immediately traded their jaded ponies for fresh mounts. Their mixture of replacements remained along Rosebud Creek, watched over now by young herders, mostly sons and nephews of friendly warriors confronting Sioux and Cheyenne enemies across the field. Pony herds were always enticing targets, especially a herd so sizable and plainly visible from Conical Hill and other lofty Indian positions on the battlefield.

Apparently the chief horse raiders, as Finerty later learned, were a small band of Cheyennes who rode the back side of Kollmar straight to its mouth, emerging near the spring where Crook and Bourke first heard shots as the day's events unfolded. The attack on the auxiliary herd was quick, a mere swoop that cut out and drove off a small bunch of ponies. One luckless Shoshone boy was killed outright by a gunshot through the back. Bourke later recorded that the boy's slayer paused long enough to dismount and take the child's scalp, a gruesome slice from "the nape of the neck to the forehead, leaving his entire skull ghastly and white." The boy's name is not recorded, but he was the first fatality on Crook's side in the Battle of the Rosebud.[20]

Van Vliet's squadron saw it all. Since the start of the fight his two companies had occupied the plateau south of Rosebud Creek, sent there by Major Evans to secure that quarter of the field. Aside from driving off a few warriors when they reached the crest, the officers and men until then had been mere observers of the action's ebb and flow to the north and west across Rosebud Creek. Lieutenant Emmett Crawford's Company G occupied the westernmost point of the summit, holding a position near Eagle Nest Peak opposite and slightly southwest of the mouth of Kollmar Creek. Some of Crawford's men in fact threw up a breastwork there. Those soldiers were well situated to observe the horse raiding episode playing out below them, and some troopers opened fire on the raiders. Later in the day Finerty overheard men boast of such sharp marksmanship that the raiders abandoned some of the stolen horses and fled, leaving one dead warrior whose body was found the next day and several wounded. One figured in the story on the morning of June 18.[21]

By that time three significant independent fights were underway simultaneously on disparate sectors of the sprawling Rosebud battlefield. Mills's battalion and Randall's scouts remained engaged in a desultory exchange with warriors in the vigorously contested Gap. Cain's doughboys had skirmished their way to Conical Hill and were holding a redoubt of considerable tactical importance on a distant corner of the field. The soldiers of Royall's command, the largest concentration now actively engaged, were pushing Sioux warriors straight west, up the swales of Kollmar Creek. Added to the commotion were the doctors, attendants, and wounded men laid out at a field hospital near Crook's Hill, Royall's skittish horses and holders circled on a Kollmar flat well behind the colonel's skirmish position, and a discernible hubbub straight south in Van Vliet's quarter. The Rosebud had become a battle of incomparable complexity and challenge.

In the midst of it all, Robert Strahorn overheard an odd exchange between Crook and Captain Andrew Burt of Company H, Ninth Infantry, which spoke volumes about human emotion on a sensory and adrenaline overload. The general, Chambers, Nickerson, and others stood on the brink of Crook's Hill watching and discussing Royall's movements below when Burt approached to convey some detail critical to the moment. Battlefield noise nearly obscured the exchange, prompting this unexpected remark. "General," Burt said, "many say that they get so hardened to this sort of thing that they don't mind it, and I often wonder whether you feel like I do in a position of this kind?"

"Well how do *you* feel?" asked the general.

"Why," answered Burt, "just as though, if you were not in sight, I'd be running like hell."

"Well," said Crook, "I feel exactly that way myself."[22]

‖‖‖‖‖‖‖‖‖‖‖‖‖‖‖‖‖‖‖‖‖‖‖‖

As Crook studied the field and parried the challenges thrown at him by Sitting Bull's warriors, he never once shied from his determination to strike the village from which these tribesmen had come. This had been his overriding ambition since learning of this village three days earlier on Goose Creek when Grouard and the Crows arrived and told the general about Sitting Bull's camp, supposedly located somewhere along Rosebud Creek. Crook pushed hard to get to this point. Despite the surprises of the morning, he still believed that an aggressive offensive movement on his part might well alter the course of this difficult fight and perhaps the whole of the Sioux war. He might even achieve the ultimate objective of driving the Northern Indians from this hinterland. As always, when analyzing the day and attempting to understand and assess Crook's mindset more completely, his own relative silence on most matters is utterly frustrating. In Crook's several battle reports and his regrettably unfinished autobiography, he wrote sparingly of his tactical maneuvering on the Rosebud field. And he was perfectly silent on matters of strategy, aside from a note in one report to Sheridan declaring that he "did not believe that any fight we could have would be decisive in its result, unless we secured their village supposed to be in close proximity. I therefore made every effort to close the command and march on their village." But then again, in Crook's inimitable way, perhaps that said it all.[23]

Certainly some chroniclers on the field grasped Crook's overarching intent. In the midst of Mills's first charge in the Gap around 10 A.M. "some of the scouts came in and informed Gen. Crook that there was a large Indian village in sight." It is unclear whether Crows or Shoshones had actually seen any tipis that morning—perhaps the fringe of Cheyenne chief Magpie Eagle's small camp—or were merely speculating in light of the magnitude of the battle playing out. Yet the notion of a massive Indian village somewhere nearby, presumably down the Rosebud as Grouard and the Crows had foretold, was reinforced. Strahorn, nearly always within earshot of Crook, again is helpful. "The General believed that it [Rosebud] was only a fight made to prevent our advancing upon the village until it too could be put on wheels of Sioux invention and silently stolen away," he told his readers. Crook "determined to sweep the field and then make a bold dash at full speed for the tepees of the warriors, which could not be far off." Davenport echoed elements of Strahorn's observation, suggesting that it was Grouard who told Crook that a village was near, a mere six miles from the battlefield. Grouard himself seems to support this sequence, recalling that when he returned to Crook's side after having been involved with the Elmer Snow rescue "the General had sent all of his aides out with orders to the different commanders." That can only foretell a massive redeployment.[24]

By late morning it had become apparent to some that Crook's interest in this fight was shifting. When calling up the horses for Noyes's command, the general saw no need to dispatch those troopers to support Mills's movements in the Gap or augment Royall's command as it advanced west into the Kollmar drainage. As a reserve force, Noyes's five Second Cavalry companies were certainly available for any contingency, but the battle (to this point anyway) never beckoned. Likewise, Mills was stopped in place when he achieved the objective of his second charge—the confrontation and dispersal of the warriors holding high ground deep on the Gap's right—and watched those Indians retreat westward toward Conical Hill. Had he not been checked, Mills was fully prepared to continue the chase. Straight south, Van Vliet's squadron had thus far seen little action, at least as Crook discerned matters.

By linking Mills's, Noyes's, and perhaps even Van Vliet's commands, Crook immediately had ten companies available to march on the Rosebud village. Almost certainly Crook believed that the warriors challenging him now would break from this fight when they saw the looming threat to the young and old in their village and make for their defense. Thus was Crook's sense of "follow[ing] the Indians in the direction of their retreat," as he declared in one statement. Doing so would free five more companies of cavalry and five of infantry who in turn would then also march on the Indian village on the direct heels of the advancing column. Twenty companies of cavalry and infantry, thus far only lightly damaged in the morning battle, joined by 250 auxiliaries, would do their duty. No Indian village could withstand such an assault. The people would flee. Many ponies would be captured. Hundreds of lodges would be destroyed, and with them robes, meats, and the necessities and fineries of life. The essences of Powder River—a damaging assault on a village—would again be served, this time on the grandest of scales.[25]

All Crook needed to do was reassemble his forces and turn them toward the ultimate goal: Sitting Bull's Indian village.

SOWING THE WIND

On Crook's Hill the general and others could plainly see that Royall was heavily challenged. The lieutenant colonel had unhorsed his battalion and continued his attack west along Kollmar Creek, following simple orders to strike the Indians there. The situation on Royall's front, while not dire, evinced a certain truth about this remarkable battle, which was fully apparent among the headquarters staff and observers nearby. Wherever the Sioux were countered—and it was always the Sioux being countered, whether in the Gap, along the Camel-Back Ridge and Conical Hill, or on Kollmar Creek—they invariably fought well but then fled to the next ridge or hillock behind. Occasionally they disappeared en masse, only to reappear elsewhere on the battlefield and often in greater numbers. Crook, a novice in fighting Plains Indians, may not have seen this before, but Chambers, Evans, and Grouard would have comprehended this style of warfare immediately. Crook waged an offensive fight to the best of his ability, taking the battle to Sitting Bull's warriors right and left, but the Indians were never driven from the field. Royall's steadfast advance changed nothing. Fully provoked, Sitting Bull's warriors merely brought on a new fight elsewhere on this enormous landscape.

Captain Azor Nickerson, Crook's senior aide-de-camp, grasped the general's motive for dispatching troops down Rosebud Cañon in direct pursuit of the Indian village. In a reminiscence written years after the battle, and with ample time for reflection, Nickerson put the decision foremost in tactical terms: it was a maneuver aimed at winning the fight at hand. "Seeing so many [Indians] occupied in the attack upon Royall, Crook hurled nine [sic, eight] companies under Colonel Mills down the canon to attack and, if possible, capture their village with their surplus horses." Joe Wasson, a reporter like Strahorn who never strayed far from Crook during the fight, put the matter in practical terms: Crook "had concluded to change the order of battle."[1]

When Crook halted Anson Mills deep in the Gap and ordered him simply to throw out skirmishers and advance no farther, Mills immediately rode off to find the general. Mills could plainly see that the enemy had escaped to the west in the direction of Conical Hill. In his battle report and later reminiscence he suggested that Crook came to him, though perhaps meaning simply that the general rode to the Gap side of Crook's Hill as Mills was coming on. Crook spoke plainly. He did not want this battle pressed any more but intended to assemble the whole command and move toward the village. Mills, the senior captain on the field this day, would lead the first battalion in the advance and generally command the attack until Crook himself arrived on the scene. (Ironically, Mills was the senior captain on the Powder River battlefield as well and led the withdrawal—not an advance—from the field that day, with reprehensible consequences.) Crook told Mills that he was to advance down the Rosebud as fast as his stock would permit and that he should pay no heed to any harassment or assault coming from the Sioux on his flanks. Friendly Indians, Crook assured him, would support the first battalion in the highlands and shield his movement. Upon reaching the village, Mills was to pitch in immediately, take the camp, and hold it until Crook and the rest of the command came to his support.[2]

The friendly Indians offered by Crook were some or all of the Crows and Shoshones generally commanded by Captain Randall, who still occupied the center of the Gap. The coming and going of these auxiliaries is not well documented in the sources. Randall did not pen any known battle report or reminiscence, so little information is firm about this specific diversion. Mills, however, noted that twenty men from Captain Lawson's Company A, commanded by a noncommissioned officer, were "detailed to accompany the friendly Indians and keep up communications." Lawson was oddly silent on the matter in his own report, aside from complimenting the efficiency and bravery exhibited by his own men throughout the engagement. Lawson had no subaltern serving with him on this campaign.[3]

Crook also told Mills that Captain Noyes and the Second Cavalry battalion would report to him and join the advance. Even then Bourke was carrying orders to Noyes to "withdraw from the crest," meaning from the lower Camel-Back, and follow Captain Mills down Rosebud Creek. Mills did not tarry in assembling his three companies and in due course led them to the mouth of the Gap. The battalion paused there, awaiting the arrival of several key individuals from Crook's headquarters contingent.[4]

While Mills's companies were regrouping, one man in Sutorius's Company E was seriously wounded. During the fighting in the Gap, Sioux warriors were repeatedly swept from the highlands on the right. When Mills's troopers withdrew from their positions, however, Indian warriors quickly infiltrated that same ground. In fact Indian fire became "audacious," as Finerty put it, as warriors were emboldened by notions of soldiers retreating. Mills and Crook comprehended this phenomenon. Thus Crook offered assurances that the first battalion's flank would be protected when it turned north in Rosebud Cañon. Private Horace Herold was returning this fire when an aggressor's bullet passed along the barrel of his carbine, glanced off his shoulder, penetrated the skin of his neck, and lodged in the point of his lower jaw. The shock laid Herold low. He picked himself up and reached for his weapon, as if preparing to fire again, but then collapsed. Troopers scrambled to him and escorted him from the field. Herold never relinquished the grip on his carbine. This was the second first battalion man wounded in the Battle of the Rosebud.[5]

||||||||||||||||||||||||||||||||||||

By the reckoning of one Third Cavalry officer on the field, Mills's advance commenced "before Royall's first position had been abandoned." This is a key marker and the only such specific reference known in the literature. Importantly, it comports with abundant circumstantial evidence that points to this critical movement occurring in the very midst of the Battle of the Rosebud rather than as a concluding episode, as if an afterthought in a long, eventful, and complicated narrative. In certain ways presenting the story of Mills's movement at the end of the Rosebud story fits a simplistic outline that allows the Royall episode to carry through, from start to finish. But the Rosebud battle did not occur that way. In fact Mills's episode contributed significantly to the very manner in which the battle escalated on Royall's front.[6]

Understanding Mills's movement in proper sequence, occurring before Royall abandoned his first position, further affirms Crook's sense that this battle could yet be won by moving aggressively toward the Indian camp. Surely Crook believed that the Indians would withdraw from the field once they grasped that their village was imperiled. To that point Crook plainly sensed no jeopardy in Royall's engagement. He would learn soon enough, of course, that this battle did not follow expectations. Clausewitz called the condition "friction in war": the simplest thing is difficult, thoughts and exaggerations of theory are exposed, things go wrong, and battles, like wars, are filled with unique episodes. Sitting Bull's warriors did not abandon the field but instead turned the Rosebud into a bloody quagmire almost immediately after Mills and Noyes departed.[7]

Among those attaching themselves to Mills's advance were Lieutenant Bourke, who apparently joined out of sheer audacity more than in any official capacity from headquarters, and Frank Grouard. Bourke is puzzlingly silent in his otherwise detailed and verbose writings about abandoning his aide-de-camp duties to join the movement, saying only: "I went with Mills." Clearly Bourke loved adventure. At Powder River he also wiggled away from Crook and joined Reynolds when the colonel separated from his commander and commenced his nighttime advance on that Indian village on March 16. Grouard's participation, in contrast, was deliberate. All along it had been Grouard's counsel that had planted the notion of an Indian village on Rosebud Creek. Crook specifically attached the scout to Mills's column to guide the two battalions down the creek to "find out whether the village is at the other end of the canyon or not."[8]

Mills had an impetuous streak and did not wait for Noyes to arrive before leading his battalion from the mouth of the Gap east toward the Big Bend. The two officers were veteran cavalry captains in rival regiments, Mills forty-one and Noyes thirty-six. As with Mills in the Third, Noyes was the senior Second Cavalry captain on the Big Horn and Yellowstone Expedition, though only the second senior captain in his regiment. Little warmth apparently existed between the two. In their respective writings neither says much about the other. Oddly, both men played decisive roles in the Powder River fight, where their paths critically crossed in the episode of the abandonment of Lorenzo Ayers. Ayers, a private in Mills's Company M, was abandoned alive on the line established at the north end of the village. At the close of the engagement Noyes commanded the covering line at the south end of the camp, behind which troops assembled preparatory to withdrawing. He learned of Ayers's abandonment but did nothing in response, even rather coolly telling fellow officers that he believed it was a "general principle of warfare for each organization to take care of its own wounded," meaning that it was Mills's burden to retrieve the hapless soldier and not his own. At Rosebud Noyes followed Mills in due course. Finerty remembered that the leading companies could see Noyes's dust in their rear.[9]

Mills's departure created a momentary vulnerability on the east end of the battlefield. Despite apparent Indian infiltration, Crook had no intention of relinquishing to the Sioux this important sector of the field, especially an area with critical high ground in its recesses. In addition to the redeployment of Mills and Noyes at that time, Crook withdrew Van Vliet's squadron from its perch on the high ground south of the battlefield. He may have considered adding the two companies to Mills's complement but instead chose to position them on the margins of the Gap, where Mills had charged earlier that morning and where Indians were again being seen. Major Evans assumed command of the squadron when Van Vliet and Crawford arrived. Aside from deploying the two Third Cavalry battalions and lone two-company squadron at the onset of the battle, Evans was a senior officer with no particular cause or duty until that point, always shadowing Crook and conveying orders but commanding nothing. As Evans put it in his report: "I was ordered to hold another portion of the ridge [meaning Mills's sector of the Gap] with Capt. Van Vliet's squadron, where, however, no firing worth mentioning was encountered." Van Vliet reported his departure from the hill south of Rosebud Creek as occurring at "about Eleven o'clock."[10]

Mills returned to the valley floor as he commenced his march and held to an easterly course for more than a mile until reaching the Big Bend. Reflecting a sense of the landscape, Mills's battle report called attention to the narrowness of the high ground between the upper reaches of the Gap and the Rosebud Cañon, which offered an advantage and safety for his command. South of there the high ground broadened nearer the east-west reach of Rosebud Creek and provided ample maneuvering space and cover for Indian warriors now situated on that ground. Just when men in Mills's formation first observed warriors on the heights above their left flank is unclear, but by the time the troops reached the Big Bend they were under fire.

Despite Crook's admonishment to disregard such demonstrations, Mills could hardly ignore a direct threat and ordered Captain Sutorius and Company E, which at the moment led the column, to charge the west side of the cañon at its mouth, a maneuver executed with alacrity. First Lieutenant Adolphus H. Von Luettwitz, Sutorius's lone subaltern, was particularly singled out for his heroics in the aggressive assault. The gregarious Prussian-born officer, who had been educated at the Artillery and Engineering School in Berlin, with a generous blonde mustache, thick German accent, and "huge dragoon boots," was a favorite of the newsmen. The charge cleared the bluff. "The Indians, however excellent as skirmishers, have not yet learned the art of standing a cavalry charge," Finerty told his *Chicago Times* readers. "After this," he added, "our march began in earnest."[11]

With Sutorius sweeping the Indians from the hills on the left, Mills and the other two companies turned north and rode into Rosebud Cañon, descending a reach of the creek that ever since has been steeped in the mystique of this great battle. The four-mile-long narrow cañon had an ominous look, and many saw it as a perfect place for an ambush. When Mills entered the run, the sun was at its meridian and the cañon was fully illuminated. Soon, however, the high bluffs again threw long shadows across its narrow, winding course. Straight walls of sandstone and projecting rocky knobs dotted its length, and its sides and crests were thickly strewn with pines. It was "a measly-looking place," Bourke recalled.[12]

The men were almost immediately struck by what they first took to be countless "trails made by buffaloes going down stream," only to realize soon that those tracks instead were hoof prints "made by the thousands of ponies belonging to the immense force of the enemy here assembled." The dawning made a powerful impression on the men. Mills, Grouard, and Bourke rode at the head of the small column. One company rode on the east side of the creek and the others on the west side, with each prepared to cover the other if fired upon. Finerty wrote: "We began to think our force rather weak for so venturous an enterprise, but Lieutenant Bourke informed the colonel that the five troops of the 2d Cavalry, under Major Noyes, were marching behind us."[13]

Somewhere ahead, whether six miles as Grouard estimated or seven, eight, or ten miles as Finerty and others reported it, lay Sitting Bull's village. This was a battle yet to be won and an audacious move in the face of a dangerous foe.[14]

|||||||||||||||||||||||||||||||||||||||||||

Reuben Davenport, the *New York Herald* man, shadowed William Royall and the headquarters detachment of the cavalry brigade throughout the fight. A year earlier on Dodge's Expedition to the Black Hills, at the age of twenty-three the newsman had professed a deep aversion to the notion of fighting Indians. Now, clinging to Royall and his assembled five companies of Third Cavalry as they advanced westward along Kollmar Creek, the young reporter found himself enmeshed in some of the most difficult Indian fighting ever to bloody the plains. Davenport's carefully detailed accounts of the Rosebud action and the eventual carnage on Kollmar Creek filled several long newspaper dispatches and are the stuff of legendary eyewitness battlefield journalism. No other dedicated reporter accompanied Royall's troops on this advance, although one other individual, Lieutenant James E. H. Foster of Company I, also corresponded with a slate of newspapers. Foster, like Davenport, penned his own detailed accounts of the action. Each man witnessed the worst of this great battle and bequeathed to history unequaled tales of the duty, honor, and selfless sacrifice shown by these soldiers in their most trying if gloried hour on Rosebud Creek.

In these moments before midday Royall could not know the consequence of Crook's decision to disengage Mills and Noyes and send them down the Rosebud to strike Sitting Bull's village. Crook's motives were straightforward and logical. By attacking the village from which these many warriors had come, the battle along the sprawling east-west reach of Rosebud Creek above its Big Bend would fade to a close. All effort could then be redirected against an always vulnerable Indian camp, presumably overflowing with defenseless people and the essentials of life. Crook had been assured many times that that village was within easy striking distance downstream. In addition, most though not all of the attacking warriors came from downstream. History, of course, reveals the rest of the story. Sitting Bull's village was not located down Rosebud Creek at all but instead to the west across the Rosebud/Little Big Horn divide on Reno Creek, on an entirely different heading from this battlefield. And it was not in the least bit threatened. The warriors challenging Crook were astounded when battle lines were abandoned and seemingly half of the enemy force rode away in a direction posing no threat to anyone, not the least the family members of the warriors on this field. This was an opportunity to crush the soldiers who remained. The 750 or 800 warriors confronting Crook this morning, their own numbers barely diminished in the battle thus far, fixed their resolve on the outnumbered soldiers fighting on their right, on Kollmar. This was Sitting Bull's battle to win, and his Sioux and Northern Cheyenne warriors seized the opportunity.

<hr />

As Royall advanced, the situation across his front grew ever more complicated. A few tribesmen were recognized as Crows and Snakes, crossing from right to left and in all likelihood reacting to the continuing threat posed by enemy warriors who had flanked the advance and charged the auxiliary's horse herd in the creek bottom, killing a young Shoshone herder in the assault. The troopers momentarily held their fire as the friendly Indians passed their line. But not all was as it seemed. Meinhold remembered the situation just then when a party of some hundred Sioux warriors also passed within several hundred yards of his company. The men had seen a great deal of red among them—"a scarf of red flannel being the mark of our allies"—and did not fire, thinking that the Indians were friendly. "The troops never mistook Shoshones or Crows for Sioux," one participant remembered, but every point beyond

Royall's line appeared crowded with warriors. Davenport remembered that hundreds were massed on a main ridge to the west, where they held their ground and poured in murderous fire.[15]

The horse-raiding episode caught Royall's attention, although he most likely knew it only as robust action on his left and perhaps even a deliberate attempt at flanking his line. He therefore advanced Captain Andrews and Company I to check those warriors. Fifty-four-year-old Andrews was another of the seemingly countless unassuming officers in the Regular Army of whom virtually nothing is known today other than the three or four lines accorded them in Heitman's *Historical Register*. Andrews fought steadily through the Civil War with a New York infantry regiment, earning a brevet for meritorious service. He received an appointment to the Regular infantry in 1866 and was assigned to the Third Cavalry in 1870, where he was promoted to captain in May 1875. Here perhaps was his moment. In Andrews's report afterward, he expressed the situation simply. He was ordered to "carry the ridge on our left," meaning the long, pronounced, generally west-running ridge separating Kollmar Creek and the next shallow nameless drainage south of it. Andrews's company struck off boldly. The captain ordered his troop into line and charged the Indians at a trot. Successfully surmounting the ridge, he redirected the assault westward along an ever-narrowing crest. The warriors reacted boldly as always, defending themselves and firing aggressively when the situation was advantageous and then withdrawing to safe ground in their rear, both southward and westward.[16]

Andrews's advance carried him farther and farther west. At a momentary halt he observed a strong body of Indians to his left and ordered his lone subaltern, Lieutenant Foster, and the eighteen men of the company's second platoon to "clear those people on the left . . . who threatened to enfilade our line." Foster detached the platoon and turned it south. (Davenport later learned that Foster's purpose might also have included cutting off the Sioux and recapturing ponies taken from the Crows and Shoshones.) Andrews, meanwhile, resumed his advance along the ridgeline. A strong challenge awaited both officers.[17]

Foster's platoon made a left half-wheel and plunged down the side of the hill, "charging as foragers," he wrote, meaning in a swarm. His course took him off the crown of Kollmar's south side and onto a parallel crest straight south, all the while driving warriors pell-mell from that ridge. Maintaining this same southward axis, the lieutenant charged the next ridge to the south, again carrying it easily. There he wheeled the platoon to the right "to conform to the general direction of the main line," meaning Andrews and the remainder of Company I in plain sight on the Kollmar crest straight north of him. Foster then swept the next plateau in his front, "giving them [the Sioux] the pistol as they rode." Warriors in superior numbers fled, firing from their ponies as they gave way. Spurred by adrenaline, opportunity, and bravado, Foster charged again, making his way to a rocky knoll, while taking sharp fire from a timber-clad point several hundred yards beyond. On the knoll he momentarily halted the platoon and dismounted, taking cover behind its crown, and "issued some of the best shots fired on the enemy occupying the point."[18]

Foster was not yet through. "With an abiding faith in his men and horses," the lieutenant mounted and carried the timber-clad point held by the warriors challenging him now. He followed the retreating enemy along the crest behind the point, "pursuers and pursued firing rapidly as the movement was executed." At the end of this ridge he again halted, determined now to await Andrews's advance. Only then, apparently, did Foster come to appreciate the precariousness of his position. His successive charges had led him on a course carrying him farther from and not parallel with his captain's own advance, which in any case had veered in the near opposite direction. In Davenport's estimation as he watched from afar, Foster had dashed alone some two miles beyond Royall's line on Kollmar Creek. Making the situation worse, Foster watched warriors circling his right flank, moving in the swales between his own line of advance and Andrews's natural course. Foster was sure that the enemy intended to intercept his paltry nineteen-man platoon.[19]

With the enemy springing up thickly around him and fearing for his own ability to fight his way back, Foster changed course and ordered, in his own word, a "retreat." Warriors immediately sensed an opportunity and charged from all quarters, delivering heavy fire. Foster's men returned that fire and kept the attackers at a "respectful distance" while they retreated to a plateau south and east of the timber-covered point where this final advance had started. Foster hoped to hold this position while awaiting support from Andrews but had only barely arrived when two orderlies, one from Colonel Royall and the other Private Herbert Weaver from Company I, came up, having run a gauntlet of sharp enemy fire to reach him and carrying positive orders to fall back at once and as rapidly as possible. From the distance Royall and Andrews could both plainly see warriors circling about and attempting to cut off Foster's isolated platoon. Weaver's heroics on a gray horse named Rover were later singled out in a newspaper story. "Without this timely warning," the account chronicled, "one officer and eighteen men would have been added to the list of killed, already large enough."[20]

When eyeing the line of retreat before the return began, Sergeant John Sullivan, remembered as one of the "oldest and best soldiers in the regiment," chanced to see an Indian "skulking" in a pile of rocks that the platoon would have to pass by to regain Royall's line. The threat was too much for Sullivan. Keeping under cover, the sergeant crept out, watched until the warrior exposed himself in aiming at the platoon, and sent a carbine bullet through his throat, killing him instantly. As Foster related it, a Crow scout who had seen the Sioux warrior fall later secured his scalp.[21]

Starting at a trot down the hill, the platoon reached the bottom but then slowed and struggled to cross a wide, steep-sided gully. As the men continued up the opposite slope, Foster's predicament turned grave. Barely had they begun their climb out when pursuing warriors reached the crest just abandoned and poured in a heavy volley. Foster ordered "the charging gait" as the platoon reached the crest and rode hard in the direction of Royall's line. In riding toward Royall, the platoon crossed what Foster called a "broad valley," meaning simply the final long, wide divide separating the drainage where the lieutenant had now been maneuvering and the distant southern shoulder of Kollmar Creek. Remembering the scene, an eyewitness on Royall's line said: "At last we saw the little party coming over the brow of a hill over 2,000 yards away, at a trot, while we could also see the Indians coming down from the ridges on either side and to the rear of him, with the evident intention of wiping out the second platoon of 'I' Troop, Third Cavalry 'without benefit of clergy.'"[22]

The final run was costly. Two men in the platoon were wounded severely. Private James O'Brien received a gunshot wound in the left forearm, and Private Charles W. Stewart received a gunshot wound in his left wrist and chest. One horse was also wounded in the hock joint. In due course the platoon rejoined Company I, which by then had withdrawn from its own precarious advance. O'Brien and Stewart were ushered to the hospital directly. Foster's final ride might have been even costlier but for the army's astonishingly poor marksmanship, a point much discussed before the day was through. Remembered Davenport: "In rejoining the left wing he [Foster] rode through a series of ravines, and in emerging from them at full gallop was unfortunately mistaken for a party of the enemy and three volleys were fired at him by the troops. No damage was done to his men." Davenport later qualified this original statement, which was much repeated in newspapers. He attributed this hot fire to Andrews, while allowing that it was covering fire that turned back Foster's pursuers. The marksmanship lingered as a separate issue.[23]

|||||||||||||||||||||||||||||||||||||||||||

After dispatching Foster to chase Indians threatening Andrews's left, the captain resumed his own advance to the west. As he later expressed it, they moved "at a sharp gait with the remainder of the Company." He was dutifully complying with Royall's order to clear the ridge on the colonel's left, meaning the distinctive shoulder framing Kollmar's south side. As Andrews advanced, he drew galling fire from a rocky point on his right. Following the natural curvature of the ridgeline, which at that point swept in a northwesterly direction, he charged and cleared that rocky prominence and held it, although under continual fire. This location, a distinctive outcropping of boulders along the southern headlands of Kollmar Creek, quickly became known as Andrews's Point. From this prominence Andrews could see Foster chasing warriors from knob to knob far to the south.[24]

Royall by then had surmounted the same crest that Andrews occupied, although well behind him and to his left. He could see Foster as well and wanted nothing of it. Royall dispatched a courier to the captain ordering the lieutenant's return. In recalling the young officer, Andrews, in turn, added a second man, Private Weaver, and the two riders struck off to the south to catch the fearless young cavalier. Andrews, meanwhile, continued to hold his distant position until he too was ordered back. As had happened when Foster retired, warriors immediately reoccupied the ground yielded by Company I and spewed heavy fire on the retiring Andrews and on Royall's line. Andrews reached Royall safely without incurring casualties in his advance or withdrawal. He then dismounted the company and assumed a position on the crowded line.[25]

Even with the added strength, Royall's consolidated force was enduring intense enemy fire. His men were reasonably well situated on a protected crest and defended themselves well, but the colonel could plainly see warriors advancing and occupying every point of advantage across his front and flanks. Andrews recalled that warriors charged the line three times but were consistently repulsed. Royall sensed a growing threat on both his right and left. In the vast openness on his right between the end of his line and across the Kollmar swale Indians were plainly seen on crests and knobs all the way to the Camel-Back Ridge. Davenport also sensed that some men on the right were "beginning to feel a panic." On the left warriors continued to sweep that flank and rear, especially eyeing Royall's led horses held on the Kollmar slopes behind the line. To check any flanking movement in that direction, Royall refused his line, repositioning Captain Henry and Company D on a rocky ledge to the left and rear of the colonel's position. Plainly the Sioux were not yielding the field but were massing and becoming ever more aggressive. Royall's immediate instinct, as Davenport put it, was not to hold this precarious position but instead to charge the heights and dislodge the Sioux. Then Crook intervened.[26]

Crook had watched the evolution on Royall's front with growing concern. From his vantage over the last half hour he plainly saw the odd dispersal of troops below him. One unusually small mounted contingent was operating alone farther and farther to the southwest and often dipping from view. Another independent mounted unit hardly any larger than the first was also moving alone straight west of Royall's main line, which sprawled across a distant high southern crest of Kollmar Creek, with its horses having been withdrawn. None of these commands was nearer than a mile from Crook's Hill, and the remotest one was more than two miles away. Most concerning of all, Crook, Nickerson, Chambers, and others could plainly see Sitting Bull's Indians swarming like bees from protected back slopes across this ever-widening field. The smoke from their guns betrayed their positions on too many vantages. Ominously, all of this suggested the potential for enveloping Royall's five companies. Crook now had at his immediate disposal the barest of support, only two companies of Chambers's infantry. Chambers's other three companies, under Cain, had pushed off in an entirely different direction that had taken them a mile and a half to the northwest to Conical Hill. Cain was alone and a long way from support but had a contingent of self-assured infantrymen with deadly Long Toms. Meanwhile Evans and two companies of the Third Cavalry held ground on the eastern sector of the field, out of Crook's sight. He knew nothing of their circumstance.

Crook reacted immediately. He wanted his scattered lines reconnected as the first step in withdrawing those troops for the movement down Rosebud Creek. The substance of Crook's several messages delivered to Royall in relatively quick succession suggested to some a measure of confusion in the transmittals. But in fact the general's successive orders and their intent were clear enough. The most telling recorder was Royall himself. In his battle report written three days after the fight, he acknowledged having received

233

word that "a charge would be made upon the enemy's left flank by the Battalion of the Second Cavalry." This somewhat puzzling statement, in the clarity of hindsight, was almost certainly a reference to the Mills and Noyes movement, which would have been an action on the Indians' left. That advice was received shortly after Andrews, Foster, and Company I rejoined Royall's line on Kollmar. Crook's first specific order, according to Royall, was delivered by an orderly. It directed him to "extend my right and connect with the left of the main body occupying a remote portion of the highest crest," meaning Crook's position on the Camel-Back Ridge. There was no confusion or misunderstanding of this communiqué. An unnamed correspondent with the *Army and Navy Journal* reported it plainly, describing the orderly's message as "orders for Colonel Royall to retire or connect his line with General Crook's." Davenport understood the order in the same manner, noting how Royall "obeyed his order to extend his line in that direction by sending Captain Meinhold's company of the Third Cavalry around by such a route as saved it from much exposure."[27]

Royall, indeed, promptly detached Meinhold and Company B with instructions to extend the line in Crook's direction. But a more abstruse if well intended order is hard to imagine. Meinhold judged the distance to Noyes's Second Cavalry at about eight hundred yards. In fact it was almost two miles away. He certainly had to have understood that his movement would not achieve an actual connection, although, as Davenport wryly noted, it did save Company B from much exposure. Meinhold struck off for the bluff. He came under "a very severe sweeping fire" from Indians concealed on one of the perpendicular ridges jutting from the Camel-Back, killing a horse and injuring Private Henry Steiner, who received a severe gunshot wound in the left shoulder. In due course the captain joined Noyes, whose battalion was on the verge of following Mills. Noyes ordered Meinhold to join him, but Major Evans appeared in their midst and ordered the captain to follow him instead. Meinhold subsequently joined Evans and remained with him until the entire command concentrated later that afternoon.[28]

Once again that morning Sitting Bull's warriors watched soldiers react in ways suggesting that this great battle was playing out in their favor and not that of the soldiers. As they viewed it, warriors had repulsed Foster's and Andrews's paltry commands. Now a considerable mass of soldiers was retreating from the line on Kollmar Creek. These actions and the general disappearance of soldiers from the Gap inspired heightened courage among the Sioux and Northern Cheyennes, who crept ever closer to Royall's thinning line.

And in truth this was a dangerously thin line, even with the return of Andrews's company. After drawing off horse holders, the colonel's command at this first position on the far southern crest of Kollmar numbered some 212 officers and men. The departure of a handful of troopers (4 or maybe 6) from Andrews's company to assist Foster's 2 wounded men to the hospital thinned the line a bit more. Now the departure of Meinhold's company (64 enlisted men and an officer: the largest unit in the battalion) seemed crippling, reducing the line to barely 157 enlisted men, plus 6 company officers mounted behind them and commanding the action. So obviously vulnerable had the front become that Captain Vroom, commanding Company L, and Lieutenants Henry Lemly and Charles Morton of Royall's staff took places on the skirmish line and used their carbines to good effect. Even Reuben Davenport, who was later commended by Morton for his coolness and bravery, dismounted several times and fired alongside the skirmishers. Every carbine was essential.[29]

To fill the void when Meinhold rode away, the men of the four remaining companies merely extended themselves even while facing increased Indian fire from the front and flanks. At one point a number of men on the far right started to fall back but were intercepted by the officer in charge of that sector. Rather than callously barking at them, he instead "strongly appealed" for them to return to their place. An empathetic tone was the correct approach. One of the men turned about and said: "All right, Lieutenant, if you say stay, we'll stay." The men returned to their places on the line and remained without a murmur until the whole command was ordered to abandon the position.[30]

Crook's order to close the lines was followed quickly by another order. Throughout the morning Crook had used his aides-de-camp, Nickerson and Bourke, to carry critical orders to battalion commanders. With Bourke now advancing with Mills, the general turned to Nickerson with instructions to carry a directive to Royall to withdraw completely. Royall plainly understood the order and immediately carried it out.[31]

Nickerson did his duty but did not linger. Several individuals in Royall's midst described the captain's in-bound ride from Crook's Hill. Davenport particularly noted how the captain's course carried him down the steep side slope of the Camel-Back Ridge to the west of Crook's Hill and in a broad sweep through the wide hollow between the general's headquarters and Royall's line. Sioux warriors quickly caught sight of the captain and showered him with concentrated fire, "bullets making the dust fly under his horse's hoofs." The *Army and Navy Journal* correspondent described the ride as an act undertaken at great personal risk. The *Omaha Herald* offered a similar appraisal later, when welcoming Nickerson home from the campaign, reminding readers of his selfless heroics "through the storm of bullets on the Rosebud." What was doubly astonishing was Nickerson's prompt turnaround. Royall assured him that he would delay his own movement to allow the captain to "get out of the way" then watched the seemingly fearless rider strike off on Meinhold's trail toward Crook's Hill. Still, the captain's heroics, already stellar, were not yet finished for the day.[32]

Captain Anson Mills, Third Cavalry

In 1876 Anson Mills was the senior captain of the Third Cavalry and a spirited officer, repeatedly breveted for gallantry. In the Powder River battle he commanded the most exposed position on the field. At Rosebud his repeated charges cleared the Gap of attacking warriors. Here he is seen in 1892 after promotion to colonel of the Third Cavalry. Mills retired in 1897 and earned a considerable fortune inventing cartridge belts and other equipments for soldiers and sports enthusiasts. Bradley and Rulofson photograph. (Vincent Mercaldo Collection, P.71.759, Buffalo Bill Center of the West)

Rosebud Battlefield, The Gap

This panoramic view taken near the mouth of the Gap may have been all that Crook and Mills saw before Mills attacked. Crook motioned to two rocky positions swarming with Indians. The elongated ledge on the right is obvious, a position later known as the Buffalo Jump. The second Indian vantage point is likely the treed prominence on the center horizon. Both positions were contested heavily, including when the Cheyenne warrior Chief Comes in Sight was unhorsed in the vicinity of the rocky ledge only to be rescued by his sister, Buffalo Calf Road Woman. (Author's photograph)

Lieutenant Colonel William Royall, Third Cavalry

Aside from George Crook's, no other officer's conduct in the Rosebud battle has been more thoroughly scrutinized than William Royall's. Along Kollmar Creek his command suffered the majority of the battle's casualties and all of its fatalities. Royall followed orders dutifully and fought gallantly, but his involvement occurred in the most dynamic moments of the battle, where the unforeseen and unimagined nearly destroyed him and ever after colored the story. Here he is seen as colonel of the Fourth Cavalry, circa 1882. In 1890 Royall was breveted a brigadier general for gallantry at Rosebud. He died in 1895 and is buried in Arlington National Cemetery. (RG641s-MOLLUS-PA11.12, United States Army Heritage and Education Center, Carlisle Barracks, Pennsylvania)

**Henry Seton, Gerhard Luhn, and William Andrews at Fort Fetterman,
September 1877**

On a sunny day in the fall of 1877 three Rosebud veterans and one other Sioux War officer
posed on the south porch of Fort Fetterman's commanding officer's quarters. Left to right:
First Lieutenant Henry Seton (Major Chambers's Infantry Battalion adjutant on the Rosebud
Campaign); First Lieutenant George Webster; Second Lieutenant Henry Robinson (standing);
Captain Edwin Coates (commanding Fort Fetterman and a participant on Crook's Big Horn
Expedition in March 1876, seated); and Captain Gerhard Luhn, all of the Fourth Infantry;
and Captain William Andrews, Third Cavalry, for whom Andrews's Point is remembered at
Rosebud. Charles Howard photograph. (Sub Neg 13427, Wyoming State Archives)

"Sioux Charging Colonel Royall's Detachment of Cavalry, June 17th"

While the perspective in this first-ever depiction of the Rosebud Battle is skewed, viewers are provided a fair sense of the intensity of the fighting at midday. Here Sioux warriors assault Royall's first position in the headlands of Kollmar Creek. *Leslie's* artist Charles Stanley placed his perspective behind the Indian line and facing Royall's command, which is dismounted in the right foreground. In fact Stanley was huddled then with Crook and viewed this episode from the distant ridgeline, well behind these Third Cavalrymen. Charles St. George Stanley sketch for *Frank Leslie's Illustrated Newspaper*, August 12, 1876. (Author's collection)

Rosebud Battlefield, Looking West from Crook's Hill

This broad swale, with scrub vegetation marking its shallow course, is the Kollmar Creek drainage at its western limits. Andrews's Point is the timbered rocky ridge immediately below and to the left of the peak on the right horizon. Royall's first position stretched across the ridge to the left of Andrews's Point, beginning at the dirt scallop and leftward. Royall's horses were initially held in the depths of the drainage below that scallop. These landmarks are fully a mile beyond Crook's Hill. General Crook could plainly hear Royall's carbine fire and see ever-coiling white smoke, but the position was too far away to comprehend conditions there. (Author's photograph)

Captain Guy Henry, Third Cavalry

When Guy Henry was shot in the face on the hillside south of the Kollmar Crossing, the tide of battle was turning against Royall's beleaguered command, which had yet to reach its horses and thereby enable an extrication from the contested drainage. Watching an officer fall from his horse (Henry, one of few soldiers still mounted) was its own impulsive trigger for the descending chaos. Henry survived the battle and is seen here in 1879, as a captain of the Third Cavalry, facially scarred but proud. (MOLLUS-Mass Civil War Photograph Collection, Volume 24, United States Army Heritage and Education Center, Carlisle Barracks, Pennsylvania)

Rosebud Battlefield, Where Henry Was Shot

Guy Henry was shot and fell from his horse on the southern crest of Kollmar Creek opposite the Led Horse Ravine. Royall's beleaguered command was about to descend into the shallow swale, aiming for their horses and an escape to the northern crest. The place where Henry fell was well remembered, first by Northern Cheyenne tribesmen who placed three flat stones there and later by local landowner Slim Kobold, who positioned a concrete pillar on the site. These landmarks can be seen today. (Author's photograph)

Second Lieutenant Henry Lemly, Third Cavalry

Henry Lemly, seen here in 1872 upon graduation from the Military Academy, was Royall's cavalry brigade adjutant during the course of the Big Horn and Yellowstone Expedition. In the thick of the Rosebud fight Lemly carried Royall's frantic plea to Crook for help in extricating his command from the Kollmar Crossing. Lemly transferred to the Third Artillery in 1878, served with Guy Henry in Puerto Rico during the Spanish-American War, retired in 1899, and was recalled to duty during the First World War. He was also a prolific writer and wrote a fine account of the Rosebud battle. (United States Military Academy)

Captain Thomas Burrowes, Ninth Infantry

Thomas Burrowes was one of several officers on Crook's Big Horn and Yellowstone Expedition who was familiar with the Powder River and Big Horn Mountain countryside, having served at Forts Phil Kearny and C. F. Smith during the heyday of the Bozeman Trail. During the Civil War, Burrowes was severely wounded in the Battle of Jonesboro, Georgia, on Sherman's Atlanta Campaign. The wound suppurated for the remainder of his life and ultimately led to his retirement in 1879. Burrowes died in 1885 and is buried in Lancaster, Pennsylvania. (National Archives)

Captain Andrew Burt, Ninth Infantry

Andrew Burt was another of the officers with Crook's expedition who was familiar with the local countryside, having served at Forts Phil Kearny and C. F. Smith during the Bozeman Trail years. At Rosebud Burt and his company were among the first to respond to the morning attack and later joined Burrowes in covering the extrication of Royall's command at the Kollmar Crossing. Burt enjoyed a long and successful career, including service in the Spanish-American War. He retired in 1902, a brigadier general. (RG77S-ASB-17, United States Army Heritage and Education Center, Carlisle Barracks, Pennsylvania)

Captain Peter Vroom, Third Cavalry

After long and conspicuous company duty during the Civil War and with the Third Cavalry in the West, including a stint as regimental adjutant, Peter Vroom was promoted to the Inspector General's Department in 1888. He retired a brigadier general in 1903. Vroom and Company L of the Third suffered terribly at the Kollmar Crossing at Rosebud. For unexplained reasons, he prepared no known report recounting this horrendous action and never told of it in later years. (Wikimedia Commons)

Rosebud Battlefield, Looking South from Crook's Hill

This was Crook's view looking south from his battlefield command post. Cloud Peak and the Big Horn Mountains command the distant horizon. Early in the battle Van Vliet's squadron occupied the ridge on the middle horizon. The deadly Kollmar Crossing sits in the center of the view, near enough for Crook plainly to see and hear the devastation engulfing Royall's command. (Author's photograph)

Rosebud Battlefield, Led Horse Ravine and the Kollmar Crossing

The bloodiest action on the Rosebud Battlefield occurred in this reach of Kollmar Creek. Ahead of Royall's withdrawal eastward along Kollmar, his horses were pushed into the ravine on the left. The action at this point was one of utter mayhem, as men scrambled under heavy fire from the southern shoulder of the drainage into the depths of the swale, sought out their horses, and ascended to the right, all the while with Indians swarming from behind and down the trough from the left. Often the fighting was hand-to-hand. Crook's Hill is the treed high ground on the center horizon. The hospital was located on the fore slope of the trees on the right horizon. (Author's photograph)

Two Moon (Northern Cheyenne)

Two Moon, seen here about 1907, was a leading figure in the challenging transitional era of the Northern Cheyennes. He was prominent in the Powder River, Rosebud, and Little Big Horn battles but later scouted for the army in the closing action of the war. He often told his story, which is an essential one. This venerable and accessible warrior died in 1917 at the age of seventy. His grave is marked by an imposing scoria obelisk along U.S. Highway 212 at Busby, Montana. (Richard Throssel Papers, ah2394_0862, American Heritage Center, University of Wyoming)

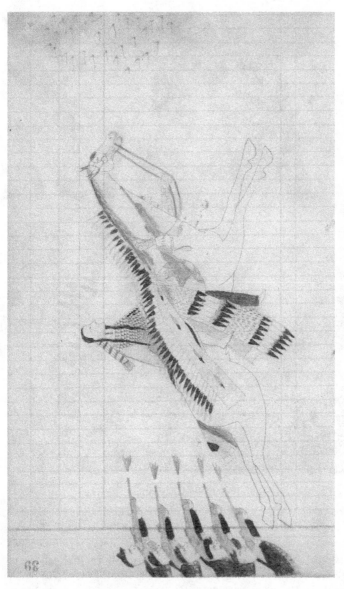

Buffalo Calf Road Woman Rescuing Her Brother

This vivid ledger book drawing by Yellow Nose, a Ute captive and adoptee of the Northern Cheyennes, dating to about 1889, shows Buffalo Calf Road Woman rescuing her brother, Chief Comes in Sight, early in the Rosebud Battle. Crook's troops were firing wildly, but the pair escaped unscathed. Buffalo Calf Road Woman fought valiantly at the Little Big Horn eight days later and survived several late-war Northern Cheyenne catastrophes, only to die in 1879 at the age of about twenty-nine. (Smithsonian Institution, MS 166,032, INV 08704700)

Jack Red Cloud (Oglala Sioux)

Jack Red Cloud, son of the great Oglala chief Red Cloud, doubtless would have preferred to forget his day in the Rosebud battle. Wearing his father's flowing feather headdress and carrying his engraved Winchester carbine, he was unhorsed early in the battle and run-down by a Crow scout, Bull Doesn't Fall Down. Rather than killing the feckless eighteen-year-old, the Crow warrior harangued and humiliated Jack Red Cloud for wearing honors that were not his and for abandoning his horse's bridle, unforgivable acts in a warrior society. Jack lived it down and met his assailant again in 1926, before dying in 1928. He was by then a chief. (Nebraska State Historical Society, RG2845-PH-11–4)

Two Moon (Northern Cheyenne) and Bull Doesn't Fall Down (Crow)

On opposite sides in 1876 but friends in 1898, Northern Cheyenne warrior Two Moon (left) and Crow scout Bull Doesn't Fall Down (right) stand elbow to elbow on a wintery day in Montana. Bull Doesn't Fall Down counted coup on Jack Red Cloud and humiliated him during the Rosebud battle and counted coup on him again in 1926 during an Indian convocation at the fiftieth anniversary of the Little Big Horn battle. Enemies one day could be friends fifty years later. Fred E. Miller photograph. (National Park Service, Little Bighorn Battlefield National Monument, LIBI_00268_07955)

Limpy (Northern Cheyenne)

Limpy was an eighteen-year-old warrior at the time of the Rosebud fight. Here he poses in 1929 at the age of seventy-two. His unintended heroics on the battlefield are forever immortalized at a cluster of sand rocks on Kollmar Creek that bear his name. Like Wooden Leg and John Stands in Timber, he was another valuable informant who ensured that the Northern Cheyenne legacy at Rosebud was remembered. Limpy died in 1935 and is buried in the Busby community cemetery. Thomas Marquis photograph. (National Park Service, Little Bighorn Battlefield National Monument, LIBI_00012_01921)

REAPING THE WHIRLWIND

Crook's order to Royall to withdraw from his tenuous hold at the head of Kollmar Creek triggered a convergence of forces that crippled and nearly destroyed this command of some 210 men. At that moment most of them held a thin line on a crest at the far end of this otherwise inconsequential dry watercourse on the western half of the Rosebud Battlefield. One participant in the succession of charges on the enemy that took the troopers to this point was quoted in the *New York Sun* as lamenting that nothing much was accomplished by it, "beyond driving the Sioux from one crest to immediately reappear upon the next. Casualties ensued among them, of course, as with us; but beyond a probable continued equalization of them, nothing further was to be gained. We had won the crest, but no especial advantage was to be obtained by occupying it." Crook by then, of course, imagined something different anyway.[1]

Indeed many in these companies were puzzled by the notion of retiring. Despite the intensity of the fight, the men had held their own. Casualties were few. "Neither the officers nor men in 'Royall's Line' knew why this order had come, and, knowing full well that they had not been beaten, the thought naturally possessed them that disaster had overtaken us in the right of the line."[2]

The natural curvature of the Kollmar Creek ridgeline in its headlands dictated Royall's retirement move. For the past hour soldiers had occupied a forward line that afforded very little maneuvering ground. Retiring to the right or alternatively simply about-facing would have immediately exposed Royall's command to an Indian onslaught from the very high ground just abandoned plus the many knobs, knolls, and creases across the headlands itself. The vulnerability on the right had been proved just minutes before when warriors raked Meinhold's withdrawing company with harsh flanking fire. Foster had similarly endured harsh Indian fire as he abandoned high ground and traversed open fields and chasms when withdrawing from his chase south of this position, with Indians hot on his heels. Enemy warriors were fighting in even greater numbers now.[3]

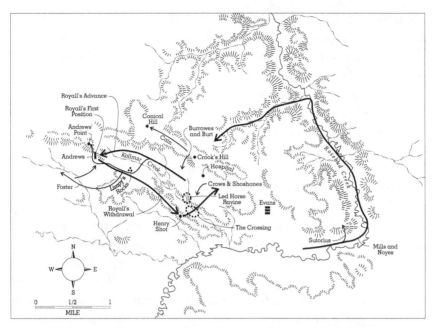

6. The Crescendo, Midday, June 17, 1876

Retiring by the left was Royall's only option. It was also a sound move tactically. Doing so kept him on high ground along Kollmar's southern shoulder. The top there was narrow, but it widened continuously to the east, on Royall's intended pathway back. Such a move also kept warriors in sight and at bay. A short while earlier the colonel had already advanced Captain Henry and Company D in that direction to check a movement by the Sioux that threatened his flank and the led horses, still curbed on the Kollmar slopes behind the forward line. Company D now occupied a rocky ledge on Royall's near left and rear.[4]

Protecting the led horses was Royall's initial challenge. By themselves they made an inviting target and were especially vulnerable to a storming from the right. (These cardinal orientations can be confusing. Royall's focus remained westward and his right was still northward, the Camel-Back Ridge side of the field.) While still holding his forward line, Royall directed that the horses be led onto the streambed and then to the east. Protecting that rear, Royall withdrew Captain Peter Vroom and Company L, deploying them as skirmishers across the low end of the drainage on the trailing end of the horses. In due course Vroom's line would link with the rest of the command but not initially. While the remaining two companies could not use this same

257

direct course in their own withdrawal, these men did provide essential cover for Vroom as he commenced his move. Indian warriors to the north quickly perceived the nature of the shift and subjected Company L to annoying if momentarily ineffectual flanking fire.[5]

With these several elements in motion, Royall ordered a retreat or, as Foster branded it in fashionable and correct military parlance, a retrograde movement. A trumpeter riding with the colonel sounded the call lower on the swale and then rode to the crest and sounded it again. This effected "a sort of left about wheel" movement wherein the scattered men of Companies F and I still holding the forward line swung to the left and pulled back, clinging to their ever-tenuous hold on Kollmar's southern crest. Companies F and I connected with D in due course. The three commenced a cautious pull-back, attaching to Company L directly and always conscious of Indian movements on their right and rear. (Royall's cardinal directions have now changed.) In the Kollmar swale ahead and to the left, the soldiers could plainly see their horses being led eastward, with the four companies shielding them and retaining a sense of a tight skirmish line as the mass of blue withdrew southeastward.[6]

Sitting Bull's warriors plainly construed Royall's pullout as an out and out retreat. Encouraged by notions of the complete defeat, even annihilation, of these soldiers, warriors singly and in groups demonstrated greater resolve and aggression than the soldiers had already seen. As Lemly later told it, the Indians felt that "they had inflicted a severe loss upon us. From every ridge, rock and sagebrush, they poured a galling fire upon the retiring battalion, encumbered with its led horses. They seemed, indeed, to spring up instantaneously as if by magic, in front, in rear and upon both flanks. Our casualties, comparatively slight until now, were quickly quadrupled."[7]

Royall's course took him southeastward along the southern shoulder of Kollmar Creek. Lemly noted that the ground being traversed was difficult, a high bank variously open but also bisected by occasional cross-cutting ravines, and all under harassing Indian fire. The officers and scattered non-commissioned officers riding among the troopers were conspicuous targets for enemy rifles. From time to time the line halted, faced about, and fired directly at warriors pressing the movement. The retrograde turned increasingly ominous. In Foster's words, "the affair now became serious, and the men were cautioned to husband their ammunition and to fire only when they had a fair assurance of hitting their man." But husbanding ammunition was a distinctive challenge. Troopers normally carried on their persons barely more than forty carbine rounds, usually in homemade leather thimble belts. Two days earlier all had started on Goose Creek with one hundred carbine rounds each. The balance was in cardboard boxes of twenty buried in saddle bags on troopers' horses, which were being led away—yet another reason why the soldiers paid careful heed to the whereabouts of their mounts.[8]

Only a few minutes had elapsed before warriors again dashed toward the line. The soldiers received them steadily and poured in scattered volleys, driving the attackers to cover in the rocks and ravines beyond the sweeping margins of the crest. The Indians' relentless onslaught was taking a toll, however. With every fourth man leading horses, and details from time to time separating and carrying wounded men to the hospital, Foster estimated that no more than sixty or seventy troopers held this front, while facing an enemy "estimated to number about seven hundred warriors, and admittedly the bravest Indians on the plains." Even if Foster's points about the thinness of the soldier line and the strength of the enemy are exaggerations, the odds were nevertheless daunting. Allowing for officers on horses, horse holders, and men shepherding off wounded soldiers, the straggling thin line may have numbered 145 men, while Indian numbers were multiplying. Again Royall refused the outer line, hoping to derive some benefit on this most vulnerable edge. Officers close to the action cried out: "Steady, men; show them what you can do." For some it became a question of adrenaline and sheer fright. Unusually large numbers of live carbine cartridges were collected from this long line of retreat in the immediate wake of the fight, and recovery of dropped live rounds has continued in the ensuing years.[9]

Royall's withdrawal was a step-by-step ordeal stretching for nearly half a mile along Kollmar's southern crest, until he reached what he called in his battle report "the last defile which separated me from the main command." He was referring simply to a dimple in the crest leading to the first suitable place along Kollmar Creek where a crossing seemed possible (the dry streambed having no name at the time). There Kollmar's shoulders on the south and north sides were shallow and the bottom rather wide and flat. Up slightly from the envisioned crossing, on the opposite side, the bottom scalloped northward into its bank, forming a large high-sided notch offering some protection for the horses. Already the holders had pushed the troopers' mounts into the area, anticipating Royall's call to remount. Although the landscape appeared propitious for an easterly crossing and eventual remounting, Royall also anticipated an inevitable surge of warriors who were hounding his flanks and rear and seemingly awaiting an opportunity to rush. The company officers—Henry, Reynolds, Vroom, Andrews, and Foster—worked the line, mounted as they had been all morning, urging caution while anticipating the inevitable Indian charge.[10]

With the tide of warriors barely contained and their fire intensifying, Royall, anxious to get to the horses and remount as safely as conditions might allow, directed Vroom and Company L to realign itself along the immediate lower margins of the swale. The hope was to offer a measure of cover while the men sought out their animals. Vroom's advance merely triggered the surge that Royall feared the most. Barely had the captain begun his shift when the entire front exploded in a rage of Indian fire. Royall ordered the battalion to make for the horses. The word had just spread along the line and the men were starting for the creek bottom when all hell broke loose.[11]

John Finerty, in a summary of the Rosebud battle and Sioux war written later that summer, used the phrase "Reaping the Whirlwind" aptly to describe the bloodletting that befell Royall's small command at the Kollmar Crossing. This phrase often used by military chroniclers is borrowed from a biblical passage in the Book of Hosea, "They that sow the wind, shall reap the whirlwind." To that moment in the battle, Royall had fought a good fight. He was an experienced, cool-headed campaigner who followed orders, was obsessed with the well-being of his commands, and demonstrated sound tactical decision-making in combat, including there. But, as the cautionary passage suggests, at times one reaps the whirlwind. Royall could not have fully anticipated the maelstrom rising up and descending upon him.[12]

From the moment Royall commenced his pull back, Sitting Bull's warriors had brutally dogged the beleaguered command, using to their continuous advantage the same succession of ridges, coulees, shoulders, and rocky outcroppings bypassed by the four companies on their withdrawal. The warriors particularly favored the paralleling deep draw south of Kollmar (Foster had fought his way through the same draw farther west when advancing and retiring from his jaunt). There warriors found successions of natural firing positions, a detail affirmed by artifact recovery from Indian positions along the colonel's line of retreat. Royall refused his line several times in that southerly direction to fend off continual pressure. But then came that moment when the natural inclination for self-security was thrown aside, when the opportunity for glory in fighting an enemy overcame all hesitancies. The battlefield erupted.[13]

Several fine descriptions captured that crucial moment. In one of Foster's several accounts of the day's fighting, he recalled in a story in the *Chicago Tribune* the "'Yip! Yip! Hi-yah! Hi-yah!' [as] the [Indians] dashed at the line at a gallop. The skirmishers gave back a few paces, but, instantly returning, poured a withering volley into the rascals, repulsing them with considerable loss. The horses were about 100 yards farther back, in a ravine, and the enemy, getting on the right flank, poured an enfilading fire into the troops, and threatened the safety of the animals."[14] The Indians' continuous fire and the zipping of the balls were "like the whir of a threshing machine in full operation," he added in another story.[15] "The death's grip was upon every man's throat," remembered Captain Henry. "The Sioux thought we were at their mercy."[16] Charles Stanley, who observed the action from Crook's Hill, recalled that "for a moment, every rifle volleyed in answer to the wild yells of the hideously painted and charging savages, and the drifting smoke gave an indistinctness to the scene that made it appalling."[17]

For a moment in the initial Indian rush it looked as though Royall's companies were doomed, but officers and noncommissioned officers dashed forward. First Sergeant John Henry Shingle (known then simply as John Henry), riding among the men of Company I, was heard shouting in a clear, stentorian voice, "Face them men! Damn them, face them!" Sergeant Shingle's courage throughout the morning earned him Crook's plaudits and later a Medal of Honor. Soldiers turned on the line and fired into the charging enemy, some shots loosed at such short range that they nearly burned the noses of the Indian ponies. The volley drove many warriors back over the slope of the ridge, buying a moment's lull in the fury.[18]

As the fighting at the crossing intensified, Captain Randall and a body of Shoshone and Crow scouts swept onto the scene, aiming directly for the mêlée along the creek. Randall and these auxiliaries had last been fighting Sioux warriors in the depths of the Gap. As that confrontation trailed off and fighting shifted to Kollmar, the auxiliaries threaded their way south. Some of the group may have splintered and remained in the high ground above the Rosebud Narrows, to be utilized by Crook when Mills's battalion struck off for the village. Many more, nearly all, turned their attention to Royall's fight. Crow chief Plenty Coups told of watching the colonel's horse soldiers backing up, as Sioux and Cheyenne warriors pressed them hard. "I saw many a soldier go under, before the horse-soldiers began to run, so mixed up with Indians and plunging horses we dared not shoot that way. The enemy was clubbing the soldiers, striking them down, with but scattering shots speaking, when we charged." The Shoshone mixed-blood Louissant remembered their attack similarly: "There was a headlong rush for about two hundred yards which drove the enemy back in confusion; then there was a sudden halt, and very many of the Shoshones jumped down from their ponies and began firing from the ground. Then, in response to some signal or cry which . . . I did not understand, we were off again, this time for good, and right into the midst of the hostiles."[19]

||||||||||||||||||||||||||||||||||

When Royall's soldiers focused their attention eastward to the Kollmar Crossing, they for all intents turned their backs to the enemy. In the retirement to that point the command had maintained a semblance of a broad skirmish line and constantly faced the enemy as it withdrew. But this was different. Sitting Bull's warriors grasped the moment immediately and delivered another heavy fusillade. One shot hit Guy Henry in the face. It was later determined to be a Winchester .44 caliber bullet that struck him in the left temple and exited beneath his right eye. One of the attending surgeons later called it a "dreadful wound." (A government round, whether a .45 Colt, .45–55 Springfield, or anything larger, would have blown Henry's face away.) In the long story of the Battle of the Rosebud the wounding of Captain Henry resonates in countless ways, not merely because he was the only officer injured in the fight but also because of the heroics surrounding his rescue and his own deadpan stoicism while bleeding profusely on the field and during his treatments in the hospital that afternoon and evening. It was simply the "most exciting incident of the battle of the Rosebud," wrote *Leslie's* reporter Charles Stanley, echoing a distinctive refrain heard widely on this vast battlefield.[20]

Second Lieutenant Charles Morton, brigade quartermaster and acting Third Cavalry adjutant, was at Henry's side, along with an orderly, when the near-fatal shot occurred. The best description of the moment, uniquely, is from Henry himself. "I felt a sharp sting as of being slapped in the face, and a blinding rush of blood to my head and eyes. A rifle-bullet had struck me in the face, under my left eye, passing through the upper part of my mouth, under the nose, and out below the right eye. I retained my saddle for a moment, then dismounted and lay on the ground." The soldiers around Henry, distraught at the frightful and seemingly fatal injury to such a brave and dignified soldier, gave way, as the Sioux charged right over the captain's prostrate body. He was lucky, noted one chronicler, not to have been struck by the hoofs of galloping horses.[21]

Elsewhere, as Shoshone and Crow scouts swept along the northern flanks of Kollmar Creek, Captain Randall saw the perilously close fighting consuming the cavalry on the opposite side and turned his followers straight toward it. As friendly warriors passed through Royall's bewildered and frightened soldiers, several of them almost immediately grasped that an officer had fallen. They rushed to overtake and scatter the enemy warriors hovering about him. It is uncertain whether any Sioux or Cheyenne warrior also sensed that Henry was clinging to life, but surely to some the captain would have represented a coup and scalp to be collected. As Davenport described the moment, one of the allies "stood and protected him until the soldiers made a dash and bore him off." Henry, blinded by the uncontrolled flow of his own blood, likewise remembered a friendly Indian "fighting over my body."[22]

But just who was this savior? Crow chief Plenty Coups told his biographer that "our war-whoop, with the Shoshones, waked the Echo-people! We rode through them [meaning through the Sioux], over the body of one of Three-stars' chiefs who was shot through the face under his eyes, so that the flesh was pushed away from his broken bones. Our charge saved him from being finished and scalped." The Crow chief's statement is broadly correct. The scouts' charge confronted and helped drive off enemy warriors from Henry's bloody corner of the field.[23]

The Shoshones, meanwhile, tell a different story. In several of their accounts Henry's savior was identified as an individual named Tigee (or Taggee). When Tigee came on the scene, he galloped to the spot where the captain had fallen, threw himself from his horse, drew his knife, and "fought off the enemy in a hand-to-hand encounter, until other soldiers and Shoshoni[s] had re-formed and . . . dashed to their assistance." Davenport suggested that Louissant rescued Henry, and he may have been with Tigee or among those arriving moments later. Davenport's assertion was made in hindsight, because the newsman was no longer on the immediate scene. Other chroniclers, Stanley included, suggested that Henry's rescuer was the Crow Indian Humpy (actually a Shoshone), but that identification reflects an inherent confusion surrounding several of the heroic rescues occurring that day. Sorting out such details is not particularly difficult, fortunately. It is simply a matter of noting who was where, particularly by unit, at the time of the specific episode. Humpy was already plainly identified as First Sergeant Van Moll's rescuer in the Gap. (The Van Moll episode is sometimes mistakenly placed on Kollmar Creek when in fact the man was a trooper in Lawson's Company A in Mills's first battalion.) Grouard, meanwhile, asserted that a Shoshone known as Ute John saved Henry, but Grouard was riding then with Mills. The Tigee claim is a simple but sound one. An oddity in the Henry saga is that neither Morton nor Henry's nameless orderly is mentioned as hovering over and saving the esteemed officer, although they may have come on the scene moments later.[24]

John Finerty, at that time riding with Mills in Rosebud Cañon, gathered important details later in the day that help reconstruct the continuing story. One of Finerty's best informants was the captain's orderly. That now all but forgotten attendant confirmed that Henry sat his horse for a few moments after being shot but then fell to the ground. The orderly rushed to his sprawled captain and saw that he was blinded and "throwing blood from his mouth by the handful." Finerty noted how the orderly may have been hit by gunfire about then too, although no man from Company D is listed on Hartsuff's official report of men wounded in the fight.[25]

Some sources debate whether Henry actually fell to the ground. Several in fact declare that "the gallant fellow never lost his seat in the saddle but rode slowly back to the field hospital." Yet the account of Sweet Mouth, one of several Crow women riding with their menfolk that day, disagrees. She witnessed the episode. "Sweet Mouth did not attempt to tell anything about the battle, except that part which she personally witnessed," her interviewer, Tom LeForge, remembered. She described the wounding of one officer. "He was one officer she was willing to admit was brave—as brave and courageous almost as a Crow. She says this officer was on his horse . . . , and while he was shooting with his revolver, a bullet struck him on the side of the face, coming out the other side. She told how the blood spurted and how the officer spit it out, but still kept on shooting until finally he fell off his horse."[26]

Other soldiers were not long in returning to Henry's side and joined the scouts in stanching the flow of blood blinding and suffocating him. Edmo LeClair, a mixed-blood Frenchman and Indian riding with the Shoshones, noticed Henry lying on the ground, saw his arm move, and rushed to help. "I took the white cloth I wore around my waist and wiped the blood from his mouth and head," he remembered. Henry later recalled that one of his sergeants put a kerchief about his face and assisted in getting him back onto his horse (either he had clung to the reins all the while or the animal had not strayed far in the tumult). With his eyes closed and face swelling terribly, Henry was led to the hospital, located nearly straight north near Crook's Hill, all the while barking "remonstrances against leaving his men."[27]

||||||||||||||||||||||||||||||||||||

In the midst of this chaos and bloodshed, Royall knew he was overmatched and in desperate need of help. He dispatched his brigade adjutant, Lemly, to Crook, requesting assistance as quickly as possible. The colonel knew by now that Crook had forwarded troops in the direction of the supposed Indian village, although he may not have been told or comprehended the full extent of that departing force, particularly that it included Noyes's companies. Royall likely assumed the availability of at least Meinhold's company and perhaps other troops holding with the general. Davenport noted that Royall specifically asked for the support of the infantry. Lemly noted this detail as well, acknowledging that Crook was asked "to station two companies of infantry with their longer range rifles upon the crest in front." The colonel may have learned of these companies from Nickerson or another of the couriers, or perhaps this small but critical detail was understood only in hindsight. The accounts are not clear.[28]

Royall watched with enormous concern as Lemly rode the half-mile north to Crook's Hill, dodging a "storm of bullets" along the way. Although the colonel hoped for timely assistance, circumstances were no longer in his favor. Henry's fall and rescue had been nightmarish but heartening. Despite it all, Foster noted what he called Royall's "utter recklessness": the colonel exposed himself carelessly to the dangers across his front, challenging "death with a laugh and a passing joke." Already the colonel had had a horse shot from beneath him that morning. The lieutenant, when reflecting on the scene later, was plainly refuting the "slanderous assertions" appearing in major national newspapers, not least the *New York Tribune,* over alleged (though real!) fecklessness exhibited by officers of the Third Cavalry at Powder River. The slights cut deeply at the honor of the regiment and were undeserved, he charged, as plainly evidenced by the bravery exhibited by officers and men against odds "ten to one."[29]

iiiiiiiiiiiiiiiiiiiiiiiiiiiiiiiiiiiiiiiiiii

As the fighting surged along Kollmar Creek, Lemly reached Crook's Hill and delivered Royall's plea for help. Already keenly aware of the tenuousness of the colonel's contested withdrawal, Crook easily grasped the precariousness of his situation, which had been in plain sight from the start. A pall of dust and smoke hanging over the action drifted eastward along Kollmar Creek, perfectly scoring Royall's retiring movement and intensifying in a frightening crescendo straight to the south. Nickerson also had reported on the stiff resistance encountered at Royall's farthest position. The situation greatly perplexed Crook. These Indians had not withdrawn from the field as he had presumed would happen once they grasped the imminent threat to their village posed by Mills's and Noyes's advance. Instead they had merely scrambled about, skirted Conical Hill, and regrouped with their entire might on Royall's four companies, which were not engaged in an orderly withdrawal but were instead now fighting for their own survival. It was apparent to everyone at headquarters that dividing the cavalry had put all commands in unforeseen peril.

Lemly's arrival with news of Henry's fall and Royall's appeal changed everything. While still anxious to move on the Indian village, Crook needed Mills and Noyes on the field immediately. He again turned to his faithful aide, Nickerson, and directed him to take an orderly and race down the Rosebud with an urgent call for Mills's return by the shortest route possible. Time was of the essence. Crook then addressed Royall's predicament. At the moment he had only two companies to give, just the infantry reserve retained at headquarters. Major Chambers was at hand and at Crook's nod immediately directed his adjutant, Henry Seton, to deploy Captain Burrowes's Company G and Captain Burt's Company H of the Ninth to the ridge jutting into the valley below them, several hundred yards west of Crook's Hill. "We dismounted and moved forward at double time," remembered Burt, and "stopped the Indians quickly and decisively without loss on our part." In his battle report written later Burt compressed some details but expressed satisfaction with the effort played by these two companies. They had stemmed the warriors' advance to skirt the northern shoulder of Kollmar. The Indian attackers would otherwise have further imperiled Royall's crossing and escape. Captain Luhn, then fighting with Cain on Conical Hill and gleaning his understanding later that day from comrades who were on the scene, echoed Burt's boast: "It is my candid opinion had it not been for Burt & Burrows Cos who poured in there [sic] fire by the Volleys Royall would have a different story to tell." Davenport acknowledged the point as well. "A line of infantry was all that kept [the Indians] from sweeping the whole ridge."[30]

Ernest Hornberger, the would-be Black Hills miner from Pittsburgh, was with Burt on the deployment (as he had been throughout the campaign). "I was through the whole fight," he wrote home. "The bullets were whistling around us like hail. I got a fine view of the whole thing from the top of one of the bluffs where the heavy fighting was. I stood there holding my pony, which was eating grass, and shooting whenever I had a chance. The Crows and Snakes were all around us, fighting desperate."[31]

Oddly, Major Evans now controlled three companies of the Third at the eastern end of the battlefield, Van Vliet's C, Crawford's G, and Meinhold's newly arrived B. Crook seems not to have considered making these units available to Royall, apparently believing that the infantry support was sufficient for the time being and that the return of Mills and Noyes would ultimately turn the tide. To this end Evans had been tasked simply to hold the ridge in this eastern sector of the field, which had witnessed intense fighting earlier in the engagement but was quiet now. Not drawing Evans into the fray suggests that Crook still intended to use this place and these companies as rallying points for an assault on the Indian village, a plan that he was not abandoning but merely delaying.[32]

Some in Evans's makeshift battalion rankled at their predicament, however. Van Vliet and Crawford readily comprehended the fierce fighting to the west, which was confirmed when Meinhold joined them. They both wanted in. Thus far these two company commanders had not seen much action, aside from the horse-stealing episode nearly two hours earlier. In the midst of the rising din both officers approached Evans and asked his permission to take their troops to Royall's aid.

"What for?" was Evans's curt reply.

"The troops are catching the very devil," answered Crawford.

"I am ordered to occupy this hill," Evans snapped back, abruptly ending the conversation. Private Louis Zinser of Company C witnessed the exchange. "Our captain volunteered to go to their assistance, but was ordered back and told that if his services were wanted, he would be called for. We all thought hard of our commander for that, for we may have saved many lives with a little aid." Zinser's reflection was more prescient than he could possibly know.[33]

IIIIIIIIIIIIIIIIIIIIIIIIIIIIIIIIIIIII

At the Kollmar Crossing Royall's troopers could hear the firing reverberating from the hill above them. Foster recognized infantry volley firing. It was a bit "late in coming," he said, but helpful in checking the main body of Indians who were still advancing out of the west along the northern crest. But the doughboys could do nothing to stem the attack also pouring straight down to the depths of Kollmar Creek. The bloodiest fighting of the day was descending upon these companies. From that moment on, the Kollmar Crossing earned a number of frightful names: Death Hollow, the wide hollow, the exposed hollow, the Valley of the Shadow of Death. The horrors were real. The officers present who had been through the Civil War—Royall, Henry, Morton, Foster, Andrews, Vroom—"say that they never in their experience saw anything hotter."[34]

As Royall's soldiers closed on their mounts, Vroom's Company L continued to hold the precarious southern crest opposite the ravine where those animals were bunched: a final thin line between the assaulting Indians and the remainder of the battalion. Indians tore through the company, inflicting five fatalities and wounding three others in desperate, often hand-to-hand fighting. Among the casualties were a sergeant killed and another sergeant wounded. The record is skimpy about some of this. Vroom, an otherwise seasoned thirty-four-year-old twice-breveted Civil War cavalryman, was among a small handful of officers who did not file any known official report. That is regrettable, because no other company on the field suffered comparable casualties that day. Royall gave the company a solid mention in his own report. "For protection in the passage I had directed Lieutenant [*sic*, newly promoted captain in May] Vroom and company to precede and line a crest which covered it; but by this time every Sioux in the engagement was surrounding this battalion and the position assigned to it was too exposed to be even temporarily occupied."[35]

One of the soldiers who paid dearly was Private Richard W. Bennett of Vroom's unit. Bennett, a recruit, was among several men in the company who was surrounded by warriors and shot at nearly point-blank. Badly wounded, Bennett fell to the ground but lay obscured among some rocks as warriors charged by. When those same Indians retreated under fire from the soldiers, Bennett mistook them for passing Crows and emerged from his hiding, only to confront the enemy. Sioux warriors struck him repeatedly with tomahawks, disemboweling him and cutting off his hands and feet.[36]

One unnamed soldier wounded in the Kollmar mêlée was positive that the Indians were chiefly interested in the horses, perhaps because of the munitions carried in the saddle bags. That miserable soldier, who, remarkably, survived the day, was awestruck by the many bows and arrows being used by the warriors—sure evidence, he thought, that they were out of ammunition. In fact the soldiers' own supply was being exhausted as well.[37]

Sergeant Daniel Marshall and several others from Reynolds's Company F, while still some distance from their mounts, did run out of ammunition and began clubbing the attacking warriors with their carbines, frantically fighting to escape. Marshall, an esteemed veteran of nearly twenty-five years of service, was shot through the face. Other comrades watched in horror as yet another F Company man, Private Gilbert Roe, a recruit, suffered a similar horrid fate. "With an insane idea of salvation or because he preferred a fatal bullet from his own piece to the torture of being pierced by spears and arrows, [Roe] calmly surrendered his carbine, handing it to the nearest Sioux, and immediately his skull was broken by a blow from a loaded whip [a long-handled war club] or tomahawk."[38]

Other soldiers displayed magnificent courage across the hollow. Men charged by Indians from the rear and flanks ran a few steps and turned and delivered sharp volleys. Farrier Richard O'Grady of Company F, with three men, charged the enemy and captured back the bodies of their comrades, Marshall and Roe, intent on saving them from the scalping knife. The bullets came "thick and fast," remembered one of the men. Another soldier remarked to a comrade, "Jack, it's only a question of cartridges," while an officer blurted coolly to another, "Well, I guess we're done for! Better die right here, facing the rascals, than give way an inch, and go down with a lance in the back." But the soldiers' disciplined fire again repulsed the Sioux, affording a slim pause in the action.[39]

Trooper Phineas Towne of Company F watched his comrades retrieve Marshall and Roe and lent a hand, but the lull lasted only a moment as warriors again charged over the hill. "Quick, here they come!" Towne screamed to the others. Marshall and Roe were dropped as the men made for their horses but Towne, sensing a gasp of life in the wounded sergeant, picked him up again. "I am dying. Don't stay with me," the sergeant pleaded, yet Towne carried him a few more yards "until it was useless to carry him any farther, for he was dead. I then laid him down and left him and hurried to get away."[40]

Towne's predicament only worsened moments later when he received a gunshot wound in the abdomen. As he reeled and fell to the ground in agony, a charging warrior jumped on him, stripped away his carbine, and struck him unconscious. He awakened moments later. A lariat had been snagged about his feet: he was being dragged away by a pony, its hooves barely missing the writhing soldier. Towne's comrades rescued him almost as quickly as the event unfolded. He survived the wound and near-death humiliation. Towne told his story often in later years and at least twice saw it recorded. He received no medal, although he thought he deserved one, but retained his sense of humor. At one point he wrote to the *Winners of the West* newspaper, the organ of the National Indian War Veterans Association, that if the Indians had gotten away with him, "well, I guess that the pension office would not have to pay me a pension now."[41]

Royall edged closer to the horses, consciously refraining from allowing an out-and-out run for them, which he was sure would trigger its own tumultuous fight. But now that moment had come. Royall spread the word to make for the horses, mount in the coulee, and fall back to the north toward the infantry line. One officer's voice was heard above it all. "Great God! men, are you going to go back on the Old Third? Forward!" A gallant cheer rang out on the field, and the movement was executed at once. Warriors reacted predictably, surging through the coulee or "head of the hollow" as Davenport labeled it. It was a long, dangerous run for the beleaguered men of the battalion, for some stretching from the southern crest two or three hundred yards to the mouth of the ravine where the skittish horses were being held by jittery holders.[42]

Remounting became mass confusion as men scrambled to find their mounts. Some horses bolted, galloping madly away and "leaving their troopers at the mercy of the Sioux who now swarmed the ravine." Private William W. Allen of Company I met his end just after remounting. His horse was shot twice, throwing him to the ground, where he was charged by several warriors. Allen, an old soldier with more than twenty years of service, fired coolly with his carbine until the Indians, coming at him from two sides, shot him down. Still fighting, Allen drew his pistol and was attempting one more shot when a warrior clubbed him in the head and killed him. Sergeant Andrew Grosch, also of Company I, witnessed Allen's death. Grosch also was wounded but was spared a similar fate by the timely arrival of several friendly scouts and then a corporal and other men from his own company, who carried him to the hospital.[43]

Three of the first sergeants, John Henry Shingle of Company I, Michael A. McGann of Company F, and Joseph Robinson of Company D, exhibited extraordinary leadership and exemplary courage at that point. Shingle watched as men around him wavered when Private Allen of their company was killed while remounting. The first sergeant in turn mounted, rushed into the thickest fighting, and rallied the breaking ranks. McGann, the next most senior ranking man in Company F (the company commanded only on this campaign by its second lieutenant, Bainbridge Reynolds), likewise rallied his company during these frantic moments, fending off warriors as the men sought out their horses and mounted. Robinson of Company D rendered especially valorous service. This was Guy Henry's outfit. Like Lieutenant Reynolds, Henry went to the field without the support of a subaltern. With Henry now en route to the hospital, with his face virtually shot away, Robinson assumed command of the company and demonstrated conspicuous gallantry and conduct under heavy fire. Shingle's exemplary action was singled out for mention in Andrews's battle report, and he, McGann, and

Robinson were each later awarded Medals of Honor for gallantry in action in these final desperate moments of the Rosebud battle.[44]

Davenport escaped the murderous fighting at the end, riding ahead of Royall's force and gaining the infantry line, plainly conscious of his narrow escape as he rode away from Indians firing and yelling to his left and rear. As he surmounted the heights and looked back, he watched with delight as Tom Cosgrove, Louissant, and the Shoshones made one final charge to the south, sweeping the southern crest beyond Vroom's crumbled position, and driving the Sioux away. Little did Davenport realize that he was witnessing the end of the Battle of the Rosebud.[45]

The Shoshones and Crows proved themselves perfect allies that day. As the Shoshones swept the southern ridge, Edmo LeClair saw a Sioux warrior turn back and stick his knife into the temple of a wounded soldier. "Captain Cosgrove yelled at me to 'get that Indian.' I rode after him, and I got him. I thought I'd scalp him, but somehow, well my heart failed me and I gave it up." LeClair's story had an odd twist. "I stole a horse that day, an' I didn't intend to either," he told an interviewer. "During the worst of the fighting, the rope on an Indian's horse got tangled around my waist and I just rode off with him trailing along behind. I gave him to another scout who had his horse shot from under him. Always after that he called me 'brother' because he said I had saved his life."[46]

Behind these scouts, Vroom's men, now under the cover of auxiliaries, were the last of Royall's command to reach their horses. Mounting quickly, they galloped forward to gain Kollmar's northern crest and distance themselves from the murderous Valley of the Shadow of Death, aptly dubbed by Captain Henry, a never-to-be-forgotten corner of the Rosebud Battlefield.

At 1 P.M. the shooting on Royall's front withered to an end. The colonel's four companies had been engaged for three full hours. Slowly they made their way northward, first passing Burrowes's and Burt's infantry line, which itself had descended from its initial perch and was still volley firing into lingering warriors. Moments earlier the infantry line had knocked several Indians from their ponies and killed a number of horses as they helped check the harassing assault behind the retiring cavalry. Burt and his cronies crowed long afterward about having rescued Royall's cavalry from a massacre. Evidently even Royall agreed; it is always easier to extend graciousness in the calm of hindsight. Even Captain Henry, barely restrained in Doctor Hartsuff's field hospital on the hillside, complimented the two infantry companies, which saved the battalion from further loss. This "I personally observed," he added, if with but one blurry eye. The line of Royall's final retirement angled eastward, skirting the hospital and continuing along the lower shoulder of the Camel-Back Ridge to the location where Major Evans awaited.[47]

The last to ascend the slope from the Kollmar bottom was Colonel Royall himself. He was calm and not perspiring, Lemly recalled, chagrined at the chaos surrounding the retreat yet all along obedient to orders under very difficult circumstances. "Those instructions were doubtless the only ones that should have been given at the time," Lemly observed candidly in hindsight to an Order of Indian Wars audience in 1917. By then he knew well the circumstances surrounding Crook's orders and the bitter criticism in the intervening years, particularly in regard to Royall's costly withdrawal and ultimately the battle itself.[48]

As Royall passed the hospital, he paused to check on the well-being of Captain Henry and the regiment's other casualties. Henry's condition was grave but stable. The surgeons presumed that he would recover. Lying in the baking sun nearby were eighteen enlisted casualties from the fight. Thirteen of the men were from the Third Cavalry. Eleven had been with Royall on Kollmar Creek. Royall then tended to one final but critical detail. He directed Foster, Andrews, and Vroom to return to the Kollmar Crossing and retrieve their dead. Nine soldiers were killed in the Battle of the Rosebud. All were from the Third Cavalry and perished at the crossing. Royall's concern for the dead may reflect an innate personal trait. But we should also remember the unconscionable callousness exhibited by the Third Cavalry's full colonel, Joseph Jones Reynolds. He abandoned one man alive *and* his dead at Powder River, to the utter horror of the men of the Second and Third regiments who had a stake in those lives. That sordid fact was among the current court-martial charges against Reynolds. In due course eight of the nine soldiers who died at Kollmar Crossing were delivered to the hospital and placed along one of its outer margins. A ninth trooper was so badly hacked to pieces that his remains were not immediately transportable.[49]

iiiiiiiiiiiiiiiiiiiiiiiiiiiiiiiiiii

Royall's withdrawal had been devastating. His movement westward had started as a simple attack on the left aimed at driving the Sioux from that sector of the battlefield, much as Mills had driven the Sioux from the Gap. Both movements were necessary checks while Crook assessed conditions and formulated an offensive movement to counter this general attack by the Sioux. Royall's persistent advances indeed successfully pushed the enemy farther and farther to the west, as ordered and expected. Contemporary and modern chroniclers alike assert that the relative ease with which this occurred was more directly attributable to a ploy devised by Crazy Horse, aimed at luring this small command farther and farther from support and ultimately to its doom. That is certainly possible, but it is hard to confirm from critical sources. Royall's continual advance appears logical, controlled, and completely intended, if perhaps not particularly supportable at its farthest extent (especially in light of what hindsight tells us of Crook's ultimate ambition and of Sioux aggressiveness in this phase of the battle). Royall's advance to its farthest extent, his so-called first position and even Foster's and Andrews's sallies still farther out were achieved at negligible costs. These maneuvers were occurring before Mills and Noyes rode away, which freed countless other warriors to ride west to bolster the challenge across the colonel's front.[50]

Royall's story at Rosebud changed when Crook intervened. Presuming the presence of Sitting Bull's village near enough down the Rosebud to warrant a full-drawn offensive maneuver, Crook ordered Royall's withdrawal so that his five companies might consolidate with Evans and Van Vliet's squadron and follow Mills and Noyes to that village under Crook's personal leadership. Crook's presumption that Sitting Bull's warriors would melt away from the Rosebud battlefield once they realized the precariousness of their village proved to be faulty thinking, of course, which he came to comprehend only when the resistance on Royall's front did not diminish but instead exploded with enormous rage.

Royall's position weakened measurably when Meinhold's company withdrew toward Crook, ostensibly to connect lines somehow. Matters worsened on Royall's front when the pull-back began. Tribesmen, perceiving no threat to their village at all, consolidated their numbers and seized the opportunity to wipe out these soldiers. Every retirement step was challenged, and Royall began taking casualties. Before he pulled out of his first position, the battalion had suffered only two men wounded. By the time he successfully crossed Kollmar Creek and gained the full cover of Burrowes's and Burt's infantry rifles, twenty men of the Third were dead or wounded, the only soldier fatalities and the greatest concentration of casualties in the entire fight. To everyone's credit, there was no immediate carping over these events and consequences. Crook's and Royall's decisions were logical and thoughtful at the time. But the Rosebud story was about to take a momentous turn, which prompted second guessing and criticism around evening campfires almost immediately.

WARRIORS HEROIC

In the early twentieth century a surprising number of interviews and narratives were collected from Indian participants in the Rosebud and Little Big Horn fights, the two momentous events interconnected in the story lines of many Lakota and Northern Cheyenne men and women. Anniversary events, especially those on the Little Big Horn battlefield, prompted much of this documentation, and a spillover to the Rosebud story was inevitable. The accounts not only place individuals on these respective fields but also provide contexts and associations and sometimes delightful surprises. In a spontaneous side note, for instance, coinciding with the fiftieth anniversary gathering at the Little Big Horn in 1926, two Crow and Sioux survivors of Rosebud confronted one another again and acted out one of the dramatic episodes on that field, much to the surprise and delight of former enemies. As late as 1934, on the fifty-eighth anniversary of the Rosebud battle, a reporter for the *Billings Gazette* gathered original stories from four elderly but spry Cheyenne men who had fought there. Another Cheyenne man, not yet born at the time of the fight, John Stands in Timber (1882–1967), grew to be a renowned tribal historian who took a special interest in the Rosebud battle and listened, collected, and passed forward the reminiscences of other Cheyennes who were there. Their voices were thereby not lost but instead bolstered the Indian record.[1]

There was a time in the twentieth century when scholars of the Rosebud and Little Big Horn battles, indeed all of the clashes of the Great Sioux War, paid little heed to the Indian perspectives on these events, asserting that warrior narratives were so individualistic and disjointed that almost nothing could be made of them. No reasonable story line, it was believed, could be woven to tell and memorialize the countering sides of these great combats. That misbegotten rejection is regrettable and could not be farther from the truth, evinced again and again in modern scholarship. Indian voices lend compelling perspectives, subtleties, and enrichments to the retelling of these stories of northern plains conflict, whether the Grattan fight of 1854, the Bozeman Trail saga of the mid-1860s, the long and transforming Great Sioux

War, the astonishing and tragic Cheyenne Exodus in 1879–80, or the horrible massacre at Wounded Knee in 1890.

The Rosebud story breaks into episodes. Fights across that sprawling landscape above the Big Bend often occurred concurrently, adding to the confusion and turmoil of the day but also making the Rosebud battle so utterly fascinating. Beneath the surface of most known Indian narratives are countless revealing keys, anchors of a sort, such as mentions of physical landmarks, distinctive movements, or recognizable associations. These help bind reminiscences, narratives, and oral histories with time, place, and action. Weaving diverse individual narratives into a plausible story is not impossible at all. Doing so reveals a righteous account of sweeping scale, extraordinary personal valor and heroics, and common cause, told warrior by warrior, band by band, people by people.

|||||||||||||||||||||||||||||||||||||

Most of the Sioux and Northern Cheyenne warriors confronting Crook's scouts on Rosebud Creek poured onto the battle landscape through the high ground between the Rosebud Narrows and the Gap. A nameless natural avenue above Indian Creek provided simple access for most of the warriors arriving from the Rosebud Valley. One and all left behind a silent but telling footprint in the soft earth, actually countless pony hoofprints. Soldiers riding the valley floor many hours later initially interpreted them as evidence of a passing buffalo herd, only to be shocked when they realized that this was telltale evidence of masses of warriors who had ascended the Rosebud and were fighting them now. This simple detail of hundreds of warriors coming onto the field from down the Rosebud was a contributing factor that led Crook to believe that the village from which these people had originated was somewhere *down the Rosebud*.

The high ground on the far right of the field, the crest line above the Buffalo Jump, and the even higher prominences farther north were not mere access ways for warriors crossing over from the Rosebud Valley. They were also critical vistas for the chiefs and others. Sitting Bull, still terribly weakened from his Sun Dance ordeal eleven days earlier, made the ride from the Reno Creek camp, surmounted this key ridgeline to a prominent and still obvious knob. From there he watched the action occurring across that side of the field. "His voice was loud in urging on his warriors," a biographer wrote. "Steady men! Remember how to hold a gun! Brace up, now! Brace up!" Sitting Bull took no part in the actual fighting, but his presence on the field was a powerful omen providing immeasurably valuable encouragement. In the soldiers' view, Sitting Bull was the bogeyman on this battlefield. They barely comprehended who they fought this day, other than nameless Sioux and Northern Cheyenne Indians, but everyone there understood that these were Sitting Bull's warriors.[2]

These Indian combatants took a long time to arrive on the battlefield, coming in two sizable waves by way of Rosebud Creek. Another, smaller group, mostly Cheyennes, traveled up the South Fork of Reno Creek. Crossing over from that tributary's highlands through the rugged Wolf Mountains, they appeared in the depths of the Gap near Conical Hill, the dominating point on the west side of the field. Young Two Moon was among those coming from the Rosebud side. He remembered pausing on the high ground above the Narrows and looking southward into the east-west reach of the Rosebud Valley. "The soldiers were pretty strong," he recalled, but he and his riding companions "did not stop long on the divide but charged down on the soldiers, who stopped their pursuit and fell back." Young Two Moon was probably referring to the opening salvo with the army's scouts. He and others had chased them out of the eastern highlands and across the bench immediately north of the stream's east-west run in the opening moments of the engagement. It was a give-and-take like many others all day long, from time to time with consequences. Wooden Leg remembered a young warrior who, as he put it, "foolishly charged too far, and some Indians belonging to the soldiers got after him" and shot and crippled his horse. "I took the young man behind me on my horse, and we hurried away to our main body of warriors."[3]

The first significant fighting of the morning occurred in the Gap, below and west of the pronounced high knob from which Sitting Bull watched the action. The Cheyenne warrior Dog (Louis Dog in a later day) told how the cavalry horses and mules grazing in the creek bottom were inviting lures as more and more of Crazy Horse's followers poured onto the field. Horses and mules were timeless attractions. More interesting is Dog's mention of Crazy Horse. Many Indian accounts, whether Northern Cheyenne or Sioux, acknowledge Crazy Horse as the battle's preeminent war chief, while white accounts almost blindly identified Sitting Bull as the dominant Indian tactician on the field. Storytellers need objective characters, but creating them sometimes brings an unwarranted focus on individuals that invariably clouds their own actions and those of others.[4]

Frank Grouard saw the matter much as Dog did and also linked much of the control on the battlefield to Crazy Horse. As one of the newsmen with

Crook put it, while "none of the half-breed or Indian scouts who were with us were able with certainty to recognize the chief warriors of the enemy," Grouard was positive that Crazy Horse was not merely one of them but the most prominent of them. "His dress is well remembered by Frank Grouard, as well as the appearance of his favorite war pony," the *New York Herald* later reported. Grouard had outspokenly provided Reynolds and Crook with a similar positive identification on the Powder River battlefield, labeling that place Crazy Horse's village and thereby clouding that critical identity for months. Some of Crazy Horse's Oglala friends, including He Dog, were present at Powder River, but not the great war leader himself. The army's chief of scouts, George Randall, meanwhile, drew his own conclusions and also assumed that Crazy Horse was on the field and influenced the action of others, which at least was subtler. "Noticing his prominence and audacity, [Randall] directed several of the Crows to turn their fire against him. This attention he seemed to defy, and rode harmlessly among the bullets."[5]

The nature of Sioux and Northern Cheyenne leadership and tactical maneuvering on the Rosebud battlefield has vexed the story from the start. George Hyde, who interviewed Indian warriors in later years, asserted that "it is perfectly clear that the [Indians] had no plan and no real leadership. Groups of warriors charged here and there, as they pleased. Crazy Horse was there, but he was only a warrior taking part in the general mêlée. Sitting Bull was there, so badly crippled from his torture in the recent Sun Dance that he could hardly ride. He took little part in the battle, but his voice could be heard encouraging the warriors."[6] The Hunkpapa warrior Bear Soldier (from Standing Rock) expressed the matter similarly: "Chiefs have little influence after battles start."[7] Yet words of encouragement floating above the din invariably worked to good effect. Wooden Leg lauded the leadership of Lame White Man, the Southern Cheyenne war chief long aligned with his northern kin: "He called to us for brave actions. Our young men had high regard for him . . . , and went flocking to him." Lame White Man's courage extended to the Little Big Horn battle as well. He was killed there by soldiers.[8]

Many individuals on the field rightly remembered Crazy Horse's powerful influence, whether in his personal feints and charges or with allies like Bad Heart Bull, Black Deer, Kicking Bear, Low Dog, Iron Hawk, and others who emulated the great Oglala's resolve and added their own coercive persuasion to the action. It was perhaps early in the fight when Crazy Horse shouted above the din a never-to-be-forgotten challenge that came to be one of the memorable hallmarks of the battle. Deep in the high ground of the Gap early in action, with his Winchester thrust high, Crazy Horse was heard crying aloud:

> Hold on, my friends!
> Be strong!
> Remember the helpless ones at home!
> This is a good day to die![9]

On the *wasicu* side of the line Crazy Horse's heroics were remembered another way. Aside from the notion of Crazy Horse being everywhere, others besides Grouard recognized him. Bat Pourier had crossed paths with the great chief before this day and spotted him on the field. Interviewed late in life, he told of Crazy Horse's medicine man, Chips, the medicines that Chips prepared for his friend, and the associated consequences that day. "You can call it medicine or anything you want to, but I saw Crazy Horse at the Rosebud Creek charge straight into Crook's army, and it seemed every soldier and Indian we had with us took a shot at him and they couldn't even hit his horse."[10]

In the battle's earliest moments the army's Crow and Shoshone allies bore the brunt of the Indian assault. Cheyenne and Sioux warriors had chased them from the highlands, but then the army scouts charged the warriors again. White Shield, riding among the Cheyennes arriving from the west on the broad bench west of the Gap, saw a man wearing a large feather bonnet who had been shot. Several Cheyennes attempted to count coup on the victim. White Shield closed to within three or four yards of the individual, but army scouts fought to protect him. White Shield turned his horse and rode away. His account may refer to the wounding of the Crow scout Bull Snake and his rescue by Finds Them and Kills Them and The Other Magpie, who dashed in and fought off Bull Snake's assailants. This encounter occurred above the mouth of Kollmar Creek.[11]

Many Sioux and Northern Cheyenne warriors remembered the army's charges in the Gap, the enemy's first aggressive movement on the battlefield. White Shield plainly described cavalry troopers galloping toward them but not yet shooting. This first charge became something of a rout. When the soldiers began to fire, the warriors retreated to the hills. "The soldiers made a strong charge, and were right behind the Cheyennes and Sioux, who were forced to whip their horses on both sides to get away. It was a close race."[12]

One episode in the Gap that occurred sometime between the soldiers' first and second charges is remembered by the Northern Cheyennes as the tribe's defining action in this nearly day-long battle. Louis Dog and many others, Crazy Horse among them, witnessed the discordant swirl of action on the open plain of the Gap. "Only the bravest were fighting down in that gap," Dog remembered. "White Shield, Comes in Sight, Scabby, White Bird, and some Sioux, Red Cloud and Low Dog. It's pretty hard in a battle to come to an open place and have hundreds shoot at you." Warriors rode across the Gap, plainly intending to lure soldiers to fire at them. They were engaging in the custom of "emptying their guns" or "playing with them," conspicuous acts of bravery meant to earn honors and panic the soldiers. When touring the battlefield many years later, John Stands in Timber marveled at the notion of warriors riding wildly, seeking only to be shot at. "It sounds like it is foolish the way they did [it] but it is customary, they say it was a great thing for a warrior to be shot at."[13]

One of those bravery runs drew visible attention and gunfire from cavalrymen concealed along the bluff and rocks above the Buffalo Jump. Two Cheyennes and a Sioux were riding noticeably down the Gap toward a "big pile of rocks," perhaps on a bravery run or just as likely drawn by the many soldier horses being held behind those stony monoliths. As the three were turning back in the face of harsh enemy fire, Chief Comes in Sight, a valiant Cheyenne, was thrown when his horse suddenly somersaulted. Its hind leg was broken by a bullet. Chief Comes in Sight landed on his feet and started running, zigzagging to avoid the shooting. Soldiers started down the hill to kill him. Another Cheyenne, White Elk, had also been riding nearby and attempted to draw the soldiers' fire and help his friend escape. Suddenly White Elk spotted a slender figure racing down from the Indian lines, heading straight for the running warrior. When she reached him, she wheeled her horse about and came up behind him. He jumped on, then the two rode away. Only then did White Elk recognize Buffalo Calf Road Woman, wife of Black Coyote and the sister of Chief Comes in Sight. With bullets flying as thick as falling hailstones, sister and brother escaped unharmed. But for the woman's brazen courage, Chief Comes in Sight would surely have been killed on the field.[14]

Chief Comes in Sight's rescue was as honored as it was startling. Buffalo Calf Road Woman was the only Northern Indian woman who rode from the Reno Creek village that morning. The twenty-six-year-old mother of two was an excellent horsewoman and fearless woman-warrior. By virtue of her presence in Old Bear's village at Powder River the previous March, she, Black Coyote, and Chief Comes in Sight were already victims of this Great Sioux War. Moreover, as Crook's army had Charles St. George Stanley of *Frank Leslie's Illustrated Newspaper* capturing scenes from this campaign, the Cheyennes visually documented this dramatic episode in a distinctive piece of contemporary color ledger art created a few years after the battle. The artist is thought to have been Yellow Nose, a Ute captive adopted into the Northern Cheyenne tribe. His rendition is preserved today in the collections of the Smithsonian Institution as part of a folio known as the Spotted Wolf–Yellow Nose Ledger. The painted figures of Buffalo Calf Road Woman on her bounding pony, Chief Comes in Sight, and cavalrymen spraying them with bullets present a striking scene. Rosebud was Buffalo Calf Road Woman's stellar moment. To this day the Northern Cheyennes remember this victory over Crook's soldiers as the Battle Where the Girl Saved Her Brother.[15]

The army horses massed behind the tall stony monoliths were a sweet lure for others too. Barely had the brother and sister escaped when six other riders, among them Two Moon and Black Coyote, charged again and nearly cut out a set of four horses (cavalry horses were held by fours, their halters snapped in unison with short link straps). When the soldiers comprehended the threat, they charged and almost overtook the warriors, "shooting at them fast," but then turned back.[16]

The fighting in the Gap divided the Indians. With sweeping gestures, Louis Dog showed an audience on the field many years later how the warriors separated: half of them turned to the right and rode onto the crest bordering the west side of the Gap, while the others veered left and climbed the slopes on the east side where Sitting Bull watched the fighting from a distant hilltop. On the west side was another dominant feature on the field, labeled Camel-Back Ridge by one of Crook's newsmen. The warriors on both sides soon became the objects of soldier attention.[17]

Louis Dog's narrative places another dramatic episode that morning in the Gap. It was considerably humbling for its central character, Above Man, who was known as Jack Red Cloud in agency circles in Nebraska. While the elder Red Cloud took no part in this war, his eighteen-year-old son joined Big Road's band of Oglalas when they fled the agency in May and joined Sitting Bull's confederation just before the Sun Dance.[18]

Jack Red Cloud's horse was shot and killed from beneath him in a skirmish with Crow scouts. The young man was conspicuously, if foolishly, wearing his father's flowing feather headdress, which he had no right to wear. He carried his father's ornately engraved Winchester rifle, presented to him at the White House the year before. Thrown to the ground, Jack Red Cloud did not pause to remove the bridle from his dead horse. That was an act of righteousness expected of warriors "according to the Indian way," even in the face of deadly enemy fire. Instead the inexperienced and scared young man started running as quickly as he hit the ground, with his flowing eagle feather bonnet drawing inordinate attention to himself. Several Crow scouts spotted the boy, drawn by the feather bonnet. Bull Doesn't Fall Down singled him out as an enemy worthy of a coup. When he saw that Jack Red Cloud did not stand and fight but kept on running, and furthermore had not taken the bridle from his dead horse as a proud warrior should have, Bull Doesn't Fall Down ran the young man down. Instead of killing him, however, Bull Doesn't Fall Down flogged him severely with his riding quirt, berating him as a coward and telling him that he was a boy and ought not to be wearing a warbonnet. When Jack Red Cloud wept and begged for mercy, Bull Doesn't Fall Down and another Crow, Along the Hills, took the young Oglala's bonnet and rifle and, in an "eloquent expression of contempt," let him go. It was an act of humiliation worse than death.[19]

Crazy Horse and two others charged the Crows and saved Jack Red Cloud. The war chief's close friend He Dog, the elder Red Cloud, and Jack were members of the influential Bad Face band of Oglalas, people deeply committed to preserving the old ways. Caring for one another, even in this humbling circumstance, was a critical attribute. Still, none of Jack Red Cloud's saviors would look at him afterward, shaming him for his behavior in crying before his enemies. For all its lasting embarrassment, this escape was memorialized in ledger art too, just as Buffalo Calf Road Woman's heroic episode had been. By the turn of the twentieth century, however, when this particular drawing was created, many details had been softened. The episode had the look of a manly running fight, "a more favorable version" in the words of one chronicler.[20]

The *wašíču* were astounded by the surprising spirit and reckless behavior of the attacking warriors. Describing the roar of gunfire, pounding hooves, and shrieks of eagle-bone whistles, one renowned chronicler of the Oglalas observed that "the old method of hovering, circling at a safe distance, and taking little risk was gone; a new spirit had been born." Warriors came on with their ponies at a dead run, "often breaking in among the troops and fighting hand-to-hand encounters. Many of the warriors rode up and down very near the line of troops, insulting the soldiers with gestures and daring them to come out and fight." Elsewhere Indians dashed out from behind rocks, hugging the necks of their ponies as they half bounded, half tumbled down vertical banks after a bold Crow, Shoshone, or white skirmisher. They delivered a shot or two and then disappeared in a flash. A contemporary was astounded by the warriors' abilities "to take advantage of every knoll, rock, tree, tuft of grass and every aid the topography of the country affords." It was a style of fighting perfectly suited for these rolling, half-broken plains. "One thing was an absolute certainty," remarked an observer, "and that is the fact that the Sioux staked a great deal on this battle and that their fighting was consequently little less than savage frenzy or the fighting of demons."[21]

And still the heroics continued. White Bull, Sitting Bull's nephew who accompanied the great spiritualist to the field, confronted a Shoshone scout deep in the Gap. "He came charging at me, but I stood my ground. When he saw that I was doing this, he became afraid and turned back, but just then I shot and hit his horse. The man stood by his horse and then retreated to his own lines, where his friends gathered around him." White Bull was remembered from that day on as "the man who lamed the Shoshoni." Years later White Bull learned from the Crows, enemies who had become friends, that this had been a particularly brave Shoshone warrior.[22]

The disjointed nature of the Rosebud battle soon became apparent as the action spilled from the Gap across the Camel-Back Ridge and onto Kollmar Creek. Early in the Kollmar fight a boy maybe thirteen or fifteen years old whose name may have been Without a Tepee met a tragic fate. The Cheyenne warrior White Shield watched this young Sioux boy riding with a band of Cheyenne warriors, among them Yellow Black Bird and Chief Comes in Sight. The soldiers were fighting desperately along Kollmar. As opportunity allowed, Chief Comes in Sight rode close and fired into the soldiers with his pistol. When the army's Crow and Shoshone allies charged these pressing warriors, Chief Comes in Sight, Yellow Black Bird, and four others turned back to the hills, but the young Sioux boy was overtaken by the army scouts, pulled from his horse, and killed outright. John Stands in Timber later assembled much of this boy's story and learned that the young man's brother, filled with remorse, took a suicide vow and was killed in the Custer fight eight days later. Indians later marked these respective places of death on the Rosebud and Little Big Horn battlefields with cairns of stones.[23]

As in the Gap, the action on Kollmar had many distinctive episodes, perhaps none more thrilling than the escape of the eighteen-year-old Cheyenne warrior Limpy. The young warrior had experienced a crippling leg injury some years earlier—hence his name—but had survived, walking with difficulty because his leg bones had been poorly set. Like most Sioux and Cheyenne warriors that day, Limpy fought fearlessly. In the swirl on the south side of Kollmar Creek, as the soldiers moved eastward on foot, Limpy rode with Yellow Black Bird, Chief Comes in Sight, Young Two Moon, White Bird, and Louis Dog, the same six warriors linked to the death of the Sioux boy. As these fighters pressed the retreating soldiers, they came to a cluster of sand rocks. Most of the stony monoliths were as tall as a man, some as tall as a horse, and all of them provided cover on an otherwise exposed shoulder. But the warriors paid no heed to their left flank and were startled when soldiers came at them from that side, firing as they advanced. The six warriors were almost trapped. For a moment matters looked grim. They then decided to make a run for a hill rising some two hundred yards behind them. Young Two Moon argued that they should not ride away together, however, and the others agreed. They rode off, one by one, and safely evaded the soldiers. All escaped readily, except Limpy.[24]

Limpy was the youngest in the group and obligingly started last. He had barely begun riding when his pony went wild, kicking and jumping and finally bucking him off, and then dropped dead from a bullet. The young warrior ran back to the sand rocks but thought immediately of his horse's bridle. It was a fine one, mounted with silver dollars that an uncle had given to him. Not wanting to bear the shame of losing it, he ran to his dead horse and started untying and pulling at the headpiece amid a shower of bullets striking rocks beside him, barely missing as they ricocheted. They "were flying on top of my head," Limpy remembered.[25]

From a distance, Young Two Moon saw Limpy's plight and that army scouts were rushing toward him, aiming to kill and count coup. Young Two Moon shouted to Limpy to be ready to jump on his horse and rode out. Whizzing bullets shied the horse. Young Two Moon closed on Limpy, but the boy was too crippled to jump on the pony's back. With soldiers still coming, Limpy hobbled over to a sand rock and climbed onto it. When Young Two Moon rode out for a second time, Limpy jumped on the pony's back. The two Cheyennes escaped together, with Limpy clutching his weapon and the prized bridle tightly in hand. Sioux warriors rode out and drove the soldiers and scouts toward the pocket where the army horses were held. Reflecting on his narrow escape years later, Limpy said: "When you are in a tight pinch like that it seems like you don't have no feelings. It seems like your feet don't even touch the ground." Before the fighting ended, Limpy was given a new horse, not a led animal but one captured in the battle. He and his five companions then joined another body of Indians, mostly Cheyennes, coming from behind them and charged again into the fight.[26]

The jumbled nature of the battle is apparent in the accounts of Louis Dog and Limpy. Late in life Dog related a version of his story to a newsman from the *Billings Gazette*. "Scouts and soldiers come toward us. We shoot and run. Then more Indians come and we make a charge. Soldiers go back down valley." Louis Dog waved his arms wildly to indicate many men. "Valley full," he exclaimed. "Three fights going on. We follow soldiers until they meet other soldiers," indicating that this was at the amphitheater at Rosebud Creek's western bend. "All go back to this place," he said. "Here we fight very long." Limpy told a similar story: "Three fights. My war chief is Little Hawk. We ambush soldiers between big bunch and scouts. They split up badly. We charge. They come together by and by and push us back to hills. Then we go downstream."[27]

The intensity of the fighting along Kollmar Creek and its odd consequences are reflected in many Indian accounts, including one revealing statement that John Stands in Timber shared in one of his many interviews:

> Some of these old-timers that were there . . . said the soldiers never stopped to take aim at you; they just shoot here and there and the same time running. They saw many horses run over them and run over each other; it was quite a mess—really hand to hand. Some say they would rather be in a fight like that than at a distance; there was more danger because they were shooting most any old way but they were not shooting at you. After they [the soldiers] emptied their pistols there was no time for them to reload them. When they fight that way they say most of the warriors had clubs or hatchets; both sides had no time to load the guns—the Indians had a better chance because they had more of those weapons. The soldiers just had guns; instead of using the point of the arrow they took one end to knock the Indians down.[28]

The notion of soldiers "shooting most any old way," but "not shooting at you," resonates on this battlefield in countless ways and is worth remembering.

The warrior Ogallala Fire offered a slightly different version of the frenzied nature of the fighting at the last. He had already had one narrow escape and was slightly wounded. Two feathers in his bonnet had been clipped by bullets. An experienced fighter some fifty years old, he happened to be with two young men, Wakute-Mani and Jack Red Cloud. Wakute-Mani's horse was worn out and Jack's was wounded, so Ogallala Fire shouted out, "'Dismount and stand by your horses! Sell your lives dearly; there is no hope!' Just then help came from One Bull and Rain in the Face with their respective followers, who rode between them and the Shoshones."[29]

Officers and noncommissioned officers were the only *wašicu* mounted during the long retreat along Kollmar Creek, so some warriors were aware when an officer had been shot. White Shield watched as the soldiers tried to hold the Indians back after that soldier (Henry) fell from his horse, but the mass of warriors was too great. The troopers ran. At almost the same time, in the Kollmar bottoms, White Shield witnessed a soldier struggling to mount his horse. He rode between the man and his mount, pulled the reins from the trooper's hands, and killed and scalped him. White Shield remembered that this man had a bugle.[30]

The mix-up and confusion as the soldiers were mounting provided many opportunities for warriors to close on those men at a vulnerable moment. The consequences were as deadly for the warriors as for the soldiers. Scabby, a Cheyenne, and five or six Sioux came on the scene through the Kollmar draw and rode directly into the mêlée. While White Shield was scuffling nearby, Scabby jumped from his horse and attacked another soldier. He knocked the man over, but the trooper jumped up quickly and shot Scabby through his body. Scabby managed to crawl away and was discovered and carried away when the shooting ended. He was later taken to a small Cheyenne camp located between the Tongue and Powder Rivers and died at the mouth of Prairie Dog Creek two or three days later. When shown Scabby's grave in the rim rocks in 1905, John Stands in Timber remarked that he was the only Cheyenne warrior killed in the Battle of the Rosebud.[31]

A *wašicu* on the long hill north of Kollmar observed a different episode involving the many sand rocks that speckled the field and learned more of the story later when he lived among the Hunkpapas. In the fighting between Crow and Sioux warriors near the end of the battle, Yellow Ear Rings was seen firing his gun until it jammed and the breech broke. "Thinking his time had come and wishing to inspire his companions he mounted a large stone in plain view of the enemy . . . , and began his death chant in a far-reaching falsetto." Instead of having inspired his followers, however, one of his fellow warriors rebuked him, screaming at him that he was too brave to die. Yellow Ear Rings' friends put the Crows to flight and saved themselves as well as their friend. "His death chant saved his life."[32]

The shooting on the battlefield all but ended when the soldiers escaped from the Kollmar bottoms, yet none of the warriors immediately rode away. Some counted coup on the bodies of the many dead soldiers at the crossing. Others gathered abandoned army carbines and revolvers, collected live cartridges, and scrounged through army saddlebags, looking especially for boxed ammunition. Some helped remove wounded and deceased tribesmen from the field. One of the *wasicu* on the hill above the Kollmar Crossing watched as warriors removed kith and kin, "slung over the backs of ponies and carried off." Wooden Leg remembered finding a "good white hat and a good pair of gloves" as well as a package of coffee. "My heart was glad. I had something good to take as a gift for my mother." Two Moon remembered collecting a "soldier gun" and "heap soldier cartridges off of soldiers' saddles," which he later boasted of using to good effect at the Little Big Horn.[33]

Recalling the terror and confusion on the field, the Hunkpapa warrior Iron Hawk said: "I don't know whether I killed anybody or not, but I guess I did, for I was scared and fought hard, and the way it was you couldn't keep from killing somebody if you didn't get killed, and I am still alive." The Miniconjou White Bull, Sitting Bull's nephew, remembered Rosebud as "a hard fight, a really big battle. I lived up to my good name and counted five coups."[34]

"It had been a pitifully long stretched-out battle," remembered one young Hunkpapa fighter. But Two Moon recalled the day joyously. "Many soldiers were killed—few Indians. It was a great fight, much smoke and dust."[35]

EVENING ON THE ROSEBUD

For Crook's soldiers, the blood-soaked horror of the Kollmar Crossing was not the only sacred ground on the Rosebud battlefield that day. Just below Crook's Hill on a swale to the southeast, Doctor Hartsuff and the medical staff gathered and tended the battle's wounded all day long. Captain Burt and Company H of the Ninth Infantry had helped deliver the captain and his attendant staff and the initially wounded soldiers to the hillside, carrying them from the Rosebud streamside when the battalions scattered in the opening hour of the battle. Only the Crow and Shoshone horse remuda and handlers remained in the bottoms then. Hartsuff cared for two soldiers almost from the start, privates from Company D, Fourth Infantry, who were gunshot on the battle's initial skirmish line. Hartsuff's retinue was small, consisting of two other physicians, Julius Patzki and Charles Stephens, one lone hospital steward, Samuel Richardson, several enlisted attendants, and two heavily laden mules.

As the day unfolded, wounded soldiers dribbled into Hartsuff's care. Some came on horseback led by a comrade or two. Others, particularly from Royall's fight, were helped in on foot or carried on blankets manhandled by fellow troopers who hauled them the long distances from the colonel's various skirmish lines. Near the end of the fighting, Robert Strahorn, the *Rocky Mountain News* reporter hovering close to Crook, visited the scene and penned a vivid description of Hartsuff's difficult predicament. The spot was a grassy little nook just below the brow of the Camel-Back Ridge. "On one edge of the pretty basin a cluster of small but rich green bushes gave to the place an air of refreshment as the hot June sun added heat to over heated brows." Scattered about were nearly twenty "poor sufferers," arranged around a common center, with horses close beside to afford "a little precious shade." The heat on the hillside was brutal, and shade and water were in short supply. So was advanced medical care beyond basic battlefield triage. Lamented Hartsuff: "The wounded were all collected together and their wounds hastily and rudely dressed, neither time nor circumstances allowing us to give them the necessary care and attention."[1]

Strahorn, present when Captain Henry was delivered into Hartsuff's care, noted: "His wound [was] a very dangerous one through the face." Henry himself described his predicament in a story penned in 1895 for *Harper's Weekly*, an illustrated tabloid competing in the marketplace with *Frank Leslie's Illustrated Newspaper*. While Henry was lying on the ground south of the Kollmar Crossing with friendly Indians and orderlies hovering about, "one of my sergeants put a handkerchief about my face, and with his assistance I mounted my horse, and with both eyes closed, my face badly swollen and black, representing I have been told, a most horrible appearance, I was led to the surgeon, who put his hand in the upper part of my mouth to see how much had been shot away, and who then told me to lie down."[2]

Thirty-seven-year-old Henry was in a precarious condition. Upon arrival he could neither speak above a whisper nor see anything at all, could scarcely hear, and had great difficulty breathing. Doctor Julius Patzki examined the wound closely and likely was the one who probed the wound with his hand, as Henry grimly remembered. Patzki diagnosed that Henry had been hit by a Winchester bullet, a smaller-caliber projectile "shattering both upper maxillae & the intermediate structures," meaning the bone matter of the upper jaw, roof of the mouth, and floor and lateral walls of the nasal cavity, "causing a free hemorrhage resulting in great impairment of vision, especially of the left [eye], the floor of its orbit receiving the wound." Another account described the mangled injury in plain terms: "A Rifle bullet struck him under the left eye, passed through the upper part of his mouth under the nose, and came out below the right eye." All versions are dire enough.[3]

Descriptions of Henry's demeanor while on the hillside may be overdrawn, perhaps even apocryphal, but they were also in character. Hardly breathing, flowing blood barely stanched, Henry is alleged to have challenged Patzki to "fix me up so that I can go back." On his ride from the crossing to the hospital, he similarly purportedly barked "remonstrances against leaving his men." Henry was revered by the troopers of Company D, and such bravado may have been meant to resonate. The words, fact or fancy, were remembered long afterward, along with an even more memorable utterance later in the day. Henry had experienced tough fixes before, most recently in a Dakota blizzard seventeen months earlier when his limbs and face were severely frozen and a part of a finger on his left hand consequently amputated. Importantly, he led his men to safety then. Kollmar Creek had been a terrible bloodletting where nine men of the Third Cavalry were killed and eleven others wounded, although none from Henry's outfit. Patzki and Hartsuff, practical men, would hear nothing of the captain's protestations and forbade his return. "Lie down," said Patzki.[4]

The intense sun and open exposure of the field exacerbated the difficult condition of the afflicted. Henry remembered that there was no shade aside from the shadow cast by his own horse, kept in the necessary position by the captain's faithful orderly. A few other horses were similarly used. Whether the men were shaded or not, their thirst was intense. Flies buzzed about annoyingly, drawn to bloody wounds and dressings. Hartsuff recollected that "not a drop of water could be obtained during the day for we were on the hills and the nearest water (Rosebud, a miserable little stream) two miles away." David Mears, one of Tom Moore's packers ensconced on the stony ridge above the hospital, responded to the abysmal plight of the wounded by striking off with canteens for the creek, a full mile away. Almost certainly others joined Mears, who followed a ravine forking off the hillside that led straight to the stream, emerging beside the mouth of Kollmar Creek. Indians still lurked on the battlefield, so he kept well out of sight and encountered only a lone Shoshone searching for a saddle lost along the creek bed.[5]

ɪɪɪɪɪɪɪɪɪɪɪɪɪɪɪɪɪɪɪɪɪɪɪɪɪɪɪɪɪɪ

During the worst of Royall's fighting at the Kollmar Crossing, Crook dispatched his senior aide, Captain Azor Nickerson, to recall Mills from Rosebud Cañon—hard duty for the thirty-nine-year-old. Long possessed of a frail constitution and perpetually suffering even these many years later from nearly fatal wounds received at Antietam and Gettysburg, Nickerson had already endured a long and dangerous ride carrying Crook's recall order to Royall when the colonel was well up Kollmar Creek. The ride undertaken now was many times that length on a course where Indians might still lurk at every hillside and bend. Nickerson was the most vital man at headquarters, and this message to Mills was an essential communiqué, occurring while the fate of the battle swayed in the balance. Mills was accompanied by a lone unnamed orderly, perhaps the same Robert H. Reynolds, noted at the onset of the campaign as traveling with Nickerson from Omaha. They rode the three miles from Crook's Hill to the Big Bend and three more miles down the Rosebud to Mills.[6]

Mills at the moment had paused his battalions at a cross canyon that opened plainly on the left, an unnamed drainage already well used by warriors that day. The men in the column were tightening girths. As Mills saw it, a great Indian village and a desperate fight were not far ahead. The battalions had increased their pace when Noyes joined Mills a mile or two back. Fresh signs of Indians were everywhere. "We began to feel that the sighting of their village must be a question of a few miles further on," remembered Finerty. Grouard and Mills noted gunfire plainly echoing through the draw. They could not know that they were a mere two miles from the back side of the battlefield and were hearing the cacophony of Royall's fight reverberating across the field. Mills and his entourage at the head of the column discerned two horsemen galloping toward them from the rear. They saw a rider in buckskins and long black beard, now gray from the dust, and instantly recognized Nickerson.[7]

"Mills," Nickerson screamed out, "Royall is hard pressed, and must be relieved. Henry is badly wounded, and Vroom's troop is all cut up. The General orders that you and Noyes defile by your left flank out of this cañon and fall on the rear of the Indians who are pressing Royall." Finerty, mounted nearby, overheard the exchange. Another onlooker remembered Nickerson also telling Mills that Crook could not move out on account of the wounded, meaning that he could not support Mills's own attack.[8]

The order was unwelcome and flustered Mills momentarily. "Are you sure he wants me to go back?" he questioned. Nickerson's reply was a simple but firm "yes." Officers from the lead battalion came forward and argued against the move. "We have the village," they blurted, "and can hold it." Mills silenced the objectors and studied the canyon to his left, then obeyed Crook's order.[9]

Mills and Noyes defiled up the draw in parallel columns, skirting boulders and fallen pines and maintaining a near westerly course for about a mile and a half until emerging in open country. The final ascent passed through loose rock and scraggly pines rimming the drainage's crest. The top was "a sort of plateau," one chronicler remembered. The battalions were farther to the northwest of where they had fought in the headlands of the Gap earlier in the day, but the rolling countryside was instantly familiar: key landmarks—Camel-Back Ridge, Conical Hill—were plainly visible. Mills turned straight south, aiming for Crook's Hill, less than a half-mile away. To the far right troopers could plainly see scattered Indians, mostly boys, tending the led horses of Sioux and Cheyenne warriors. Seeing the troops advancing, they fled immediately westward out of harm's way. Grouard was positive that Indians had been watching Mills's movement all along and had deliberately withdrawn from his front just before the troopers reached the plateau. Finerty echoed the notion. "We dashed forward at a wild gallop, cheering as we went, anxious to avenge our comrades of Henry's battalion," he wrote, but the Indians quickly broke to the northwest. Noyes and others watched the exodus. "I saw a large party of Sioux, leaving the field, a mile or more to our right and rear," he remembered.[10]

The arrival of Mills and Noyes achieved the desired effect. Royall's self-managed extrication of his command from Kollmar Creek coupled with a final assault on the Sioux by the Shoshone and Crow allies stemmed the battle in that quarter. That attack, coupled with the return of the recalled battalions who had otherwise disappeared down Rosebud Cañon, proved a final statement to any lingering warrior. Crook's command was whole again. This battle was over.

When Mills found Crook, their exchange had a tone of consternation, as the captain later described it to an audience of Indian war veterans. Crook might have sensed arrogance. "General, why did you recall me? I had the village and could have held it," Mills remembered saying. "I never saw a man more dejected," he continued.

Crook replied: "Well, Colonel, I found it a more serious engagement than I thought. We have lost about fifty killed and wounded, and the doctors refused to remain with the wounded unless I left the infantry and one of the squadrons with them. I knew I could not keep my promise to support you with the remainder of the force."[11]

Crook's responses were telling on several counts. When the general dispatched Nickerson to withdraw Mills from the cañon, Royall's forces were engaged in a desperate fight and safely extricating that battalion looked problematic. Crook held back Evans and Van Vliet's squadron as his only viable reserve, to advance on Royall or even toward Mills, as the situation demanded. Properly shielding the wounded was an equally legitimate concern. Hartsuff now tended Captain Henry and eighteen frightfully wounded enlisted men. No officer, and certainly not Crook, willy-nilly neglected a battle's casualties. At the moment Crook simply did not have men enough to meet these scattered challenges.[12]

Also apparent, however, was Crook's continued ambition to charge the Sioux village. By now, Royall's fight was over. Mills and Noyes were directed to move their battalions through the Gap to the Rosebud streamside where the action had begun that morning and prepare for a general advance down the watercourse. Evans and Van Vliet's Squadron were already there. Royall and Henry's Battalion, still rather shaken from their brawl on Kollmar Creek, were also making their way down, as were Crook and the headquarters staff plus Randall and the Crow and Shoshone auxiliaries. Crook had achieved reconsolidation. Tom Moore's packers and Burrowes's and Burt's Ninth Infantry companies remained behind momentarily to anchor the field and provide security for the hospital.[13]

At the farthest end of the sprawling battlefield, Captain Cain on Conical Hill could also sense the fight diminishing. Since midday Cain's three companies had proven themselves a steady annoyance to Sitting Bull's warriors, who rode a wide circle in the west to avoid coming within range of the infantry's Long Toms. But with attention shifting to the assembling cavalry, Major Chambers and Lieutenant Seton set off from Crook's Hill when the general and his headquarters detachment went east. Chambers was intent on redirecting Cain's companies. Upon arriving on Conical Hill, the major ordered a general cease-fire. Cain complied, barking out the command in a loud voice, all the while openly encouraging his soldiers in an undertone to keep on firing, especially when ripe targets presented themselves. Charles Stanley rode out with Chambers and captured the quixotic scene, with Cain calmly encouraging his doughboys to "Keep it up! Keep it up! Damn them, give them hell!" Stanley remembered how Cain's soldiers idolized him. In due course the three companies were consolidated, but only after complying with one final order, likely from Cain, to flatten spent cartridge cases to render them valueless to the warriors. Chambers led the assembled companies, mounted on their mules, to Crook's Hill, where they joined Burrowes and Burt in holding that place and safeguarding the hospital. In the consolidation of the infantry battalion Crook's Hill was transformed from a command post into an infantry redoubt even sturdier than Conical Hill had been during much of the fighting on the western half of the battlefield.[14]

As soon as Crook's mounted detachments were assembled, he personally led the horse soldiers east to the Big Bend, intent once again on marching upon the supposed site of the Indian village located somewhere beyond the Rosebud Narrows. The allied Indians rode with the general in the van, while Van Vliet's and Crawford's respective companies of the Third were thrown out as flankers right and left. That was "the only time during the entire campaign when such disposition was made," remembered Lemly. But Crook's feint came to an abrupt halt almost immediately. Upon reaching the Big Bend and facing north, the Crows and Shoshones stopped suddenly and refused to proceed. The circumstance confounded Crook. In a rising bluster he encouraged their advance into the Narrows. When the attempt faltered, with Grouard at his side and Bat Pourier interpreting, Crook quizzed, prodded, and attempted to understand his allies' newfound reluctance.[15]

At times the words exchanged were simply "unquotable," according to Lemly. Crook's urgings were rebuffed. Some of the Crows and Shoshones replied with the few English words in their vocabulary, "which were more emphatic than polite." White Face of the Crows was a principal spokesman, telling Pourier that they did not want to get killed, as they all would be if they entered the canyon. Grouard interjected, telling Crook how the Crows on another occasion had been enticed into this very defile and were "massacred almost to a man" by the Sioux. Accordingly they called this place the "Valley of Death." A headman named The Crow wondered why Crook had not let the Crows fight back at the Kollmar Crossing, implying a continuation of the fight after Royall had crossed. This forced the general to explain that he wanted the battle taken to the Sioux village. White Face told Crook that thus far he had only been fighting a "little war party," but if "you go to the village you will find as many Indians as the grass." Furthermore, the canyon ahead was a trap. He and the others were sure of it: the soldiers would all be killed. Rubbing the palms of his hands together in imitation of grinding stones, the Indian sign meaning complete destruction, White Face told Crook that he and the Crows were turning back and going home. They had wounded men to care for. The Crows and Shoshones then withdrew to the hillside behind the column's head to consult.[16]

As White Face finished with the general, Bat Pourier told Crook of his own concerns about ammunition. Earlier in the day he had watched men leave great numbers of cartridges on the ground. Infantrymen on the initial skirmish line would lie down or kneel to fire and in doing so would draw handfuls of cartridges from their belts and place them on the ground beside them, handy for use. When advancing, however, they did not pick up those cartridges, thus leaving them behind. The Indians, Bat told Crook, had seen the same thing. Chiming in, Grouard questioned the ammunition now available to the command. The scouts had only a little, he said, and many of the companies were running short as well. Concerned, Crook dispatched an orderly to the officers to inquire about the ammunition reserves among the companies.[17]

Other officers soon joined in the exchange. Nickerson, for one, was aghast at the prospect of advancing into the Narrows. "I had just been there," he penned in his reminiscence, and "was vividly impressed with the danger of such a movement. I stated my opinion very strongly." Mills and Grouard confirmed that the canyon was a veritable cul-de-sac, with broken ground, vertical walls rising closely on the sides, and the "lower part ahead . . . closed by a dam and abatis of timber." Without having seen conditions personally, Strahorn shared in his news report an echoing refrain that the canyon was "just long enough to comfortably admit the whole column in regular line of march," providing a perfect place for the Indians to roll down rocks and "shoot us down in detail."[18]

Whether Sitting Bull's Indians planned a trap in or beyond the Narrows is unknown and has clouded the Rosebud story ever since. Two Moon and Crazy Horse both later asserted that they had hoped to lure Crook into the canyon, where the existence of barriers and timber breastworks would have made it impossible for the troops to escape. It was also common chatter among soldiers and packers that night that the "gulch was . . . favorable for an ambush." Cargador Joseph A. Fontaine recollected that the Indians "had partially felled trees and expected to finish them behind us and cut off retreat, but we did not get into their ambush." Crazy Horse admitted to the notion of a trap when being interviewed at Camp Robinson shortly after his surrender in May 1877. But he may simply have been suggesting the presence of a sizable number of warriors biding their time in the proximity of the Narrows. They might be willing to resume the fight if an opportunity arose or otherwise just ride off for Reno Creek if no soldiers appeared. Anyway, many Indians scoffed at notions of formal barricades. As one Cheyenne historian noted, no one had axes, no one had time, and, furthermore, cutting trees was women's work. Mills, Noyes, Nickerson, Bourke, and Grouard had just traveled through some of the canyon barely an hour before, safely and with eyes wide open.[19]

Whatever the Indian preparations for and probability of an ambush, the prospect of trapping the command in the canyon's straits was ruined when Crook's Indian scouts refused to advance beyond the Big Bend. The auxiliaries' unwillingness to continue the fight and reports coming back from the column about ammunition expenditures and reserves undid Crook's resolve. Ammunition consumption varied by squadron and battalion, to be sure, in a day when cavalry fire discipline was a concept not yet imagined. While no on-the-spot accounts are known, several later reports help flesh out the situation. Noyes's summary was likely the most heartening. He suggested an average expenditure of twelve rounds per man (referring to carbine rounds), with eighty-five or ninety rounds per soldier thus remaining. His battalion's principal encounters with the enemy occurred only on the initial skirmish line, however, as the battle opened. Reports of high consumptions appeared as well. An unnamed correspondent for the *New York Times* opened his account of the fight with the note that "we had but fifty rounds of ammunition . . . left per man." Private Zinser of Van Vliet's Company C noted that "after dark, we took an inventory of our ammunition and found we had only five rounds to a man left." Another soldier, Corporal John P. Slough of

Company I, Second Cavalry, recollected many years later that after the battle the men had only eight rounds each. Zinser and Slough must certainly have been reflecting on column-wide expenditures and not their own condition personally or that of their respective companies.[20]

Summary reports and estimates available that evening became critical and more clearly reflected the situation on the field at the end of the fight. Lieutenant Chase, acting adjutant of the Third Cavalry, told Thomas Mac-Millan of the *Chicago Inter-Ocean* that Crook's command had fired ten thousand rounds during the engagement. Strahorn reported that number as well. Lemly noted that the friendly Indians alone fired ten thousand rounds. In his initial battle report Finerty suggested that "between 15,000 and 20,000 rounds of ammunition were fired by this command," echoing that judgment in a follow-up dispatch penned eleven days later, which stated that "nearly 20,000 rounds of cartridges were expended." That number rose in his 1890 reminiscence, *War-Path and Bivouac*, becoming the startling and subsequently oft-quoted expenditure of 25,000 rounds, roughly one-quarter of the ammunition carried in the column. Davenport's assessment was the most startling of all. He told his *New York Herald* readers that "the ammunition, only 100 rounds to the man, was half exhausted." That figure comported with the identical assessment appearing unattributed in the *New York Times* on June 28 (which perhaps was merely an outright echo of Davenport).[21]

Whether 10,000, 15,000, 20,000, or 25,000 carbine and rifle rounds were expended in the battle or the implausible 48,000 rounds in Davenport's estimation (half the soldiers' supply), ammunition expenditure was but one consideration vexing Crook. Nothing that day had gone according to plan, to the extent that Crook had a plan. He had paused in the east-west reach of the Rosebud early that morning believing that Sitting Bull's village was somewhere ahead, even around the proverbial next bend. He advanced his scouts that morning plainly presuming that he would receive intelligence from them that would trigger his own instant rush upon the Indian village or a covert overnight advance and morning attack the next day. Instead Sitting Bull's warriors brought this battle to Crook. The general consequently spent the day parrying their every assault, holding his own to be sure, but barred from making any aggressive advance on the village. An advance proved impossible even now, after a long heavy fight, with his cavalry command again fully assembled. Crook had not lost this battle but was losing daylight, and the full weight of this great engagement had yet to be reckoned with. It was now about 4:00 P.M.[22]

Noyes's field report captured the deflated end of Crook's final movement. "After rejoining the command [meaning following Crook's and Mills's sortie down the Narrows], we marched a short distance toward the front, halted a short time, and countermarched to a camp near where we had been resting when the affair commenced." It was an ending so simple, so short, and for Crook so disappointing. The respective battalions soon reoccupied virtually the same ground as they had that morning, although their alignment was different or Mills's men would simply have recovered and used their buried picket pins, which they did not. Finerty described the appearance as "a circle around our horses and pack train, as on the previous night" in the highlands of the South Fork. The configuration was more nearly an elongated rectangle, with battalions occupying the stream's right and left banks from beneath the mouth of the Gap westward to beyond the mouth of Kollmar Creek. Horses were watered and allowed to graze both inside and beyond the lines. Soldiers gathered wood from the nearby hillsides and lit fires for evening coffee. The command had started from Goose Creek with four days' of cooked bacon, but there had not been much time for bacon and hard bread that day. The men were especially eager for a cup of coffee. Security, not much needed but not neglected either, was provided by the infantry battalion holding Crook's Hill.[23]

As soon as order prevailed in the Rosebud camp, Hartsuff began relocating his hospital from the ridge to the valley. Henry recalled being carried in a blanket on a mile-long zigzag by four men and that he had to stop two times en route "owing to nausea from swallowing too much blood." Tom Moore's packers served as blanket bearers as they too relocated from the ridgelines north and south of Crook's Hill to the valley floor. As at the start, Hartsuff's hospital occupied flat ground on the north bank of the Rosebud, slightly downstream of the mouth of Kollmar Creek. The hospital's whereabouts is important because later that evening the battle's fatalities were delivered for interment close by. Bourke confided to his diary a brutal reference to those left on the Powder River battlefield: "There was no leaving of dead and dying and no Alex. Moore skulking, this trip."[24]

Relocating the wounded was time consuming. Hartsuff had nineteen men in his care, including Henry, with gunshot wounds to heads, limbs, shoulders, chest, and abdomen. In two instances bullets were not extracted. Most men suffered from considerable blood loss, and all were exhausted from the "great heat of the day." Hartsuff's orderlies threw up a rude structure in the valley using willow boughs and rushes. The wounded were placed beneath it on blankets as examinations and treatment continued. The medical staff dressed and redressed wounds and made the soldiers as comfortable as limited means allowed. Tending the men was a constant strain for the three doctors and lone steward. In his report Hartsuff commended the members of the staff heartily for their great skill and humanity. Oddly, he made no mention of the assistance rendered by Second Lieutenant Frederick Schwatka of Mills's M Company. Schwatka was another of the army's young renaissance men, a West Pointer of multiple scholarly interests, and a one-time student at Bellevue Hospital in New York City, a noted medical college. At Bellevue Schwatka had acquired, as Bourke noted, "knowledge of therapeutics." Hartsuff observed that it was about 6:30 P.M. before all was in order in his rustic ward on the Rosebud Battlefield.[25]

Hartsuff's official count of nineteen wounded men did not include soldiers whose injuries were not considered serious enough to restrict them from duty and require hospitalization. Bourke noted fifty-seven casualties of all sorts, including "many of no significance." Stanley acknowledged forty-six wounded and nineteen additional men with lesser wounds. Finerty noted "about fifty" casualties, including friendly Indians and the deceased. Strahorn recorded another dozen or more who were "slightly scratched with spent bullets, battle-axes, lances and arrows. The latter are already fit for duty and are not reported in the official list." He later counted a total loss of fifty-seven killed and wounded. Lieutenant Foster's reckoning agreed in part with Hartsuff's report but added "33 slightly wounded and not reported at the hospital."[26]

Four days later Crook provided the adjutant general with his own obligatory report on the day's casualties, tallying twenty-one wounded enlisted men by name, two more than Hartsuff. In addition, Crook's list included Private Otto Broderson of F Company, Third Cavalry, with a slight bullet wound and "Not in Hospital, Not treated by Surgeon"; and Corporal Tobias Carty of Company I, Third Cavalry, also with a slight gunshot wound and not carried on the sick report. Most of the casualties were men of the Third, "which bore the brunt of the fight." This sad epitaph was widely comprehended in the camp. Hartsuff and many of the newsmen separately counted the casualties among the Indian allies, generally agreeing on one killed (the Shoshone boy) and seven or eight wounded (three Shoshones and four Crows). Hartsuff brusquely dismissed the medical needs of the auxiliaries, declaring that "none of the [Indian] cases are of especial interest." Bull Snake, the Crow Indian with the bullet-shattered leg, might have disagreed.[27]

The plight of Guy Henry drew considerable attention as the expedition settled into camp that late afternoon and evening. When Anson Mills visited the hospital inquiring about the wounded from his battalion, Henry recognized his voice and called him over. Henry was an appalling mess, Mills remembered, his coat covered with clotted blood, his eyes swollen shut, and both cheeks bearing ghastly wounds. Shocked by the picture, Mills blurted out, "Henry, are you badly wounded?" Henry replied: "The doctors have just told me that I must die, but I will not." The doctors did not in fact expect Henry to live through the night. "Nine out of ten under such circumstances would have died," Mills told his audience in 1917, but Henry defied the odds and lived. "Henry and I were rival captains in the same regiment," Mills added, "but always friends."[28]

John Finerty visited with Henry that evening as well, giving rise to one of the most memorable battlefield exchanges in all of American military and Indian wars history. Attempting to console the battered and frail officer, Finerty heard Henry exclaim in a low but firm voice: "It is nothing. For this are we soldiers." Finerty recorded the line in his book *War-Path and Bivouac*, published in 1890. Perhaps the captain's heroic words were contrived, for the reporter's newspaper dispatches from the field do not contain anything of the sort. Henry's words were repeated verbatim in 1891 in the *Army and Navy Register*, although they were unsourced and perhaps merely pulled from Finerty's book. They appeared again, nearly verbatim, in 1904 when Cyrus Townsend Brady included them in his *Indian Fights and Fighters* book. Brady and Finerty were acquainted and were perhaps even personal friends. Still, the line was wholly in character for Henry and became embedded in Rosebud lore. As film director John Ford had one of his characters in *The Man Who Shot Liberty Valance* observe, "When the legend becomes fact, print the legend." In the field hospital that June night in 1876 Henry also advised Finerty "to join the army!" Guy Henry had much to say that day, all of it characteristic and believable.[29]

Later that evening Henry Lemly, the cavalry brigade adjutant, visited the captain and found him suffering from an intolerable thirst. There were no provisions for invalids at hand, Lemly regretted, but in scrounging about in the nearby camps, he obtained some red currant jelly from First Lieutenant William Rawolle, commanding B Company, Second Cavalry. Although nearly insoluble, the jelly was watered down enough to "furnish a grateful relief to the wounded officer."[30]

There were other small acts of kindness as well. Thomas MacMillan, the

Inter-Ocean reporter remembered by some for his "eternal cough," likely an annoying asthma, rode alongside Captain Lawson throughout the day, including the fighting in the Gap. MacMillan and Lawson had befriended one another on Dodge's Expedition to the Black Hills in 1875. "My health was quite indifferent," MacMillan later wrote, "and he was as thoughtful as a father and as gentle as a mother. Never shall I forget his care of me after the fight on the 'Rosebud,' when exhausted with the day's work, we camped on the banks of the stream the Rosebud. I had ridden with him at the head of the company, all through that tedious day."[31]

Guy Henry is an ironic critical voice for another episode that occurred near Hartsuff's hospital: the burial of the day's dead. In his reminiscence of the battle, Henry recalled dryly that "during the long hours of that most weary night preparations could be heard for the burial of our dead, among whom we might be numbered by morning." Hartsuff's medical packs contained the only available picks and shovels in the camp. Before nightfall soldiers were detailed to excavate a long, deep trench for the common burial of the Rosebud fatalities, all now lying like cordwood in the lee of Hartsuff's camp.[32]

For many, burying the Third Cavalry's nine fatalities was one final moment that obliged friends and associates to confront one of the sickening realities of the day, whether digging the trench, handling the remains, offering a quiet prayer, or remembering touching moments on the field. The deceased were carried from the hillside hospital to the valley floor on the backs of horses. Most had bloated from the heat of the day. Private George Potts had no less than a dozen Indian arrows sticking in his body. One trooper was found with a butcher knife buried in his forehead. Another had two knife blades broken off in his breast. The thirty-year-old quartermaster sergeant of Company L, Anton Newkirchen, a clerk from Cologne, Germany, in a former life, had barely two months remaining in his current five-year enlistment. Newkirchen was found hacked to pieces and was delivered to his burial in a saddle blanket. Private Richard Bennett, also of Company L, was disemboweled, with his hands and feet cut off. He was delivered to the grave in a sack. The bodies of others were apparently untouched by the enemy.[33]

The precise location of the burial trench is unclear. One account places the excavation "at the base of a cut bank along the edge of Rosebud Creek," a place, readily recognized today. Another adds a small detail: "in the vicinity of . . . wild rosebushes," which were ubiquitous. Bourke confided to his diary that the trench was dug in the muddy banks of the stream, near the water-line. One of Strahorn's newspaper dispatches specifically locates it near the hospital, which would be consistent with Henry's memory of the burial being within earshot. Nearly all accounts agree that a long, deep trench was excavated and that all nine deceased soldiers were laid in a row, mostly wrapped in blankets, covered with stones, mud, and earth, and packed down. Some say that horses were led back and forth over the top after the grave was closed to tamp down the loose soil. Many accounts mention that a great fire was built atop the burial to conceal it further. Bourke noted additionally that the entire command marched over the grave the next morning, hoping to obliterate its every trace. Oddly, only one account by Strahorn in a latter-day reminiscence mentions a burial ceremony. It seems inconceivable that this touching and traditional detail was neglected, even if it occurred without massed witnesses and trumpets.[34]

Oliver C. C. Pollock, of Company M, Third Cavalry (serving under the name of John E. Douglass), believed that one of the day's fatalities, likely Bennett, was not removed from the field at all owing to the miserable condition of his remains. He was "left in a ravine covered with logs and stones." Although he wrote an otherwise compelling personal narrative, Pollock was with Mills throughout the fight and in no particular position to know directly of the recovery of remains at the Kollmar Crossing. This detail, recorded in 1940, runs counter to the generally consistent accounting of nine sets of remains interred in the streamside trench. Sergeant George L. Howard of Captain Elijah R. Wells's Company E, Second Cavalry, likewise believed that one man was "so badly cut up that he could not be brought away." But Howard, like Pollock, was in no position to know of the actions on Kollmar during and after Company L's bloodletting.[35]

The last soldiers to return to the valley that evening were Major Chambers and the infantry battalion, withdrawn from their position on Crook's Hill around 7 P.M. It was nearly dark when the doughboys watered their mules and settled into camp. Although the distant outpost was no longer manned, the security of the camp remained a concern. Captain Luhn of Company F, Fourth Infantry, was detailed as officer of the day. Under his supervision squads of four to eight men were drawn from the foot battalion and scattered across the wide margins of the camp, which never much settled down all night long. Luhn remembered a long and troublesome night, with his pickets imagining Indians in the darkness.[36]

As had occurred that morning, the Crows and Shoshones again circled up at the western end of the sprawling troop camp, returning their ponies to the massive remuda that filled the narrow valley floor west to the stream's forks. Because of their late-afternoon refusal to lead Crook and the cavalry into the Rosebud Narrows, Crook was worried about their demeanor and outlook. These friendly Indians had fought well. They engaged enemy warriors in the Kollmar drainage in the earliest moments of the fight, allowing troops precious time to assemble and embark on their own initial deployments. Later in the morning they battled alongside Mills in the deepest recesses of the Gap and elsewhere. As the *Inter-Ocean* put it, they "succeeded in annoying and diverting the Sioux during the progress of the battle." Almost single-handedly they challenged and repulsed the warriors who were overwhelming and nearly annihilating Royall's command and particularly the beleaguered men of Companies F and L when they broke for their horses at the Kollmar Crossing. Despite such vigor and heroism, all indications now suggested that the Crows had had enough and wanted to go home and that the Shoshones were ready to break off as well.[37]

During the dinner hour Crook's auxiliaries huddled among themselves on a hill south of their camp. In the fading light the general, Pourier, Richard, Grouard, and Randall joined them. Still clinging to the belief that what mattered was not what the enemy would do but what he himself would do, despite the obvious realities and consequences of the day's fight, Crook spoke to the headmen about a night march on the Indian village and an attack at daylight. To that moment Crook was the self-driven aggressor, longing to pursue his enemy to the fullest extent of his capacity, regardless of the day's issues and in full keeping with his own reputation as a determined Indian campaigner.

The Crows and Shoshones would hear nothing of it. They told him that they had taken thirteen scalps during the day and were well satisfied. Again the Crows spoke of their wounded and their need to return to their village. They had discovered many Crow ponies in the possession of the Sioux, they said, concluding that their enemies might have attacked their own villages in the absence of the warriors who now rode with the expedition. In truth an astonishing body of enemy warriors had come to this field, which meant trouble as long as the enemy had the capacity to fight on such a scale. Crook also heard from some of the allies who expressed their dismay with the day's manner of fighting. They referred not to the general's tactical maneuvering but to the vulnerabilities of being friendly Indians on a smoky field where it was sometimes impossible to distinguish friend from foe, notwithstanding the red headbands and long red streamers. Red, Crook heard in a scolding tone, was a favorite color among all Western Indians.[38]

So it was that Crook comprehended that he was losing his Indian allies. The Rosebud story turns at the very moment he did. Only then did he decide upon the safe course of returning to Goose Creek to protect his own wounded and resupply. Crook did not bring this battle on but won the field after a long, hard day of fighting and occupied it still. Had he retained these Crows and Shoshones—his critical eyes and ears in a challenging land—he almost certainly would have pressed the hunt for Sitting Bull that same evening or on the morrow. Issues of food, munitions, and the wounded were manageable and momentarily secondary to this driving ambition but were now upended when his allies abandoned him. Sitting Bull's Indians did not defeat Crook at the Rosebud: the reluctance of his own friendly Crow and Shoshone allies did. Despite their stellar service all day long, their refusal to remain with Crook for a renewed advance on Sitting Bull's village, however justified in the Indian view, did this campaign in.

Crook's hand was forced. Only then, apparently, did the realities of his situation settle in. This was day two of a four-day issue of rations, meager as they were. Crook had not sacked an Indian village where he could have resupplied with buffalo and other wild meats from enemy food stocks. The matter of ammunition consumption, whether feared or actual, might well have been handled by simple redistribution if the campaign had been pressed. Now that detail was among the factors rising to doom Crook's plans. If the auxiliaries had agreed to stay with Crook for an advance, the wounded might well have been evacuated on the morrow under a minimal infantry or packer guard or even left in place on this east-west reach of the Rosebud, again under a minimal guard. Now, however, proper care of the wounded became an obsession. How well Crook had thought these considerations through beforehand is unclear. Now that the prospect of continuing the campaign was moot, however, these details became the focus of his attention.

The normally effusive and introspective Bourke was silent on Crook's momentous decision in his diary. In his 1890 reminiscence he observed simply that "as we had nothing but the clothing each wore and the remains of the four days' rations with which we had started, we had no other resource [*sic*, recourse?] but to make our way back to the wagon trains with the wounded." Lemly remembered it much the same way: "Handicapped by short rations and ammunition, and the necessity of caring for the wounded, [Crook] determined to return to our permanent camp and await reinforcements. The Sioux had proved more numerous than he had expected." Nickerson mentioned nothing at all about this critical turn of events in his own reminiscence. Crook's confidant among the scouts, Frank Grouard, said merely that the general "found he would have to wait until he got more ammunition from the wagons before taking the offensive."[39]

Crook attempted to explain himself to Sheridan in back-to-back reports written from Goose Creek. In a hurried telegram penned on June 19 and dispatched by courier to Fort Fetterman he described in a few words a vigorous fight with an enemy strong enough to defeat his command. The Indians, he assured Sheridan, were driven back in great confusion, but he suffered badly, with nine killed and twenty-one wounded, including Captain Henry. He had no recourse, he continued, but to return to his train and properly care for his wounded. In his official report written the next day Crook expanded on the nature of the battle and noted that continuing the offensive would have meant following the retreating Sioux without rations, dragging the wounded on rough mule litters, or returning to the train where the wounded could be cared for, "the latter being the course adopted." We can never know what other options Crook might have quietly contemplated or discussed with friends and confidants. Ultimately the general's silence is itself telling and allows historians enormous latitude in exploring the what-ifs of General Crook and this pivotal moment in the still unfolding Great Sioux War.[40]

Interestingly, Crook was also silent in these reports on the lack of sustained support from his Crow and Shoshone allies. Other than acknowledging their arrival on June 14, he said no more. Perhaps this silence was an intentional deflection of blame or burden away from them and onto himself. If so this was a magnanimous gesture. After all, the use of Indian auxiliaries was a fundamental dimension of a classic Crook campaign. On the other hand, perhaps Crook did not wish to show any undue deference to his friendly Indians for any successes, shortcomings, or failings thus far. This operation was not yet doomed: success remained attainable, at least for a few more days.

The newsmen were quick to grasp the enormity of the new course. In their initial battlefield dispatches one by one they noted matters of rations, munitions, and the day's wounded. But Finerty suspected something more. Crook, he asserted, "was also convinced that all chance of surprising the Sioux camp was over for the present, and perhaps he felt that even if it could be surprised, his small force would be unequal to the task of carrying it by storm. The Indians had shown themselves good fighters, and he shrewdly calculated that his men had been opposed to only a part of the well-armed warriors actually in the field." This dimension of the assumed, the actual, and the invariably awesome strength of the enemy soon pervaded nearly every conversation.[41]

|||||||||||||||||||||||||||||||||||||||

The night of June 17 was "an unquiet and busy time for everybody," Bourke remembered. Across the scattered camps the day's battle was fought "a thousand times by the light of the camp fires." The scene harkened back for some to a refrain from the days of Arthur Wellesley, Duke of Wellington, at Waterloo: "nothing except a battle lost can be half so melancholy as a battle won." Nearly everyone had something to say about Royall's near disaster on Kollmar. In fact, of course, everyone had been under fire, all had stories, and most everyone knew someone who was wounded or killed by an Indian. Opinions flew and were not always favorable. Sergeant Howard of the Second Cavalry was particularly grim, unburdening himself in his diary of his personal angst over giving up the advance. "The Fighting was so poorly conducted that the Enemy came in our rear and stole everything left back where we were when the fight commenced. The soldiers have lost all confidence in General Crook. Fine weather." While an element of Howard's private rant is incomprehensible, part of it is straightforward, unsolicited, and doubtless reflective. Such chatter about Crook intensified in the days to come, much of it outright hostile.[42]

No one questioned the valor of the troops, however. One newsman wrote: "It must be said that braver men never faced an enemy. They would charge the Sioux to the gates of hell had they been allowed."[43] For others the stigma of Powder River weighed heavily. One unnamed correspondent, whose observations appeared in the *New York Times*, put it this way:

> There were many narrow escapes and thrilling adventures during the contest, and to say that they were met with surprising courage, and that every incident had its worthy hero, is language none too strong. Many of the file were recruits of but a few months standing; others had been well-nigh disheartened by the management and result of the battle of Powder River, which closed last winter's campaign; and there were still others who had never heard the terrifying whoop of an Indian or the whistle of leaden missiles. Yet such men were heroes in the broadest acceptance of the term. Look back to it when they may, their work on this occasion will bring only the flush of true pride.[44]

Almost as quickly as the various camps were reestablished every reporter in the field prepared copy for his primary and secondary newspapers. The initial reports, most of them datelined June 17, were consistently straightforward accounts of the day's fighting, accentuated with personal experiences. Of the five dedicated newsmen, Davenport, Finerty, and MacMillan rode with officers on the front lines. Davenport in particular was in such hot fighting on Kollmar Creek that he wielded a carbine alongside the troopers. Such action made for vibrant copy. The foremost dilemma that these newsmen faced was getting their accounts to a telegraph line. Their business was competitive and did not encourage cooperation. Davenport told how he engaged Louis Richard that evening to carry his dispatch to Fort Fetterman. The scout's initial attempt was thwarted. Having been discovered and pursued by Indians, he hurried back to camp. Several days passed before another attempt was made. Davenport also later sent duplicate dispatches with the Crows, bound ultimately for Fort Ellis and the public telegraph office in Bozeman. That secondary copy met a sorry fate when the scrawled papers got soaked in a river crossing. "The dispatch to the New York *Herald* was written in a small condensed hand, and being wet and faded, could not be read very well by the Post Traders to whom it was directed; nor was it dispatched." Nor were the Crow messengers paid, to their ultimate chagrin. In the end, only Joe Wasson's primary battle dispatch failed to reach its intended paper, the *Alta California* in San Francisco, although a parallel report reached the *New York Tribune*. Crook and Wasson were old friends, and the general wildly speculated that the *Alta California* dispatch was suppressed in the telegraph office at Fort Fetterman. It might just as easily have drowned in a river crossing.[45]

A great game at the campfires that evening was estimating the strength of the enemy combatants who fought and died on the battlefield. On-the-spot estimates captured in diaries and initial newspaper dispatches typically overestimated the number of Sioux warriors challenging the command. (The enemy was always Sioux. Aside from discerning Crows, Shoshones, and Plainsmen like Grouard, Pourier, and Richard, the others had only the barest comprehension that Northern Cheyennes were also a notable body of opposing warriors.) Of the reporters, Joe Wasson offered up the most conservative estimation, suggesting that Sitting Bull and Crazy Horse were present "with at least a thousand warriors." One unnamed correspondent likewise concluded that "the Sioux numbered about one thousand." Bourke recalled that Royall estimated the number at not less than fifteen hundred, maybe more. MacMillan repeated that number in his initial battle report, as did Finerty.

By the time Finerty's book appeared in 1890, however, the opposing force had grown to no less than twenty-five hundred, an estimation that he claimed to have gotten from Crook. Luhn mentioned fifteen hundred in a letter to his wife written two days later, although the number rose to two thousand in his unpublished autobiography written many years after the fight. Strahorn fudged the detail, suggesting from twelve hundred to two thousand warriors. Davenport's on-the-scene estimation topped the lot, reporting no less than twenty-five hundred Indians opposing the troops.[46]

Simply put, Rosebud was a baffling engagement: pervasive gunsmoke, dashing, darting, and fleeting Indians, with an enemy popping up here and there and disappearing just as quickly, concurrent action across an expansive field, and massed warriors suddenly appearing. Under these circumstances the enemy could well have appeared to be a thousand, fifteen hundred, or even twenty-five hundred Indians strong, even if modern-day tallies do not support such lofty estimates. Oddly, Crook was silent on the point in his own initial battle reports.

Interestingly, in estimating warriors on the Rosebud field, James Foster almost in passing noted that "from five to seven hundred Indians" challenged Royall in the Kollmar Creek fight. Of all the estimates, so many of them terribly wide of the mark, the young lieutenant actually got this fact about right. Royall's troopers indeed faced the general mass of Sioux and Cheyenne warriors who had come to the field from Reno Creek and barely escaped death. Royall's command incurred all of the army's fatalities and a disproportionate number of the day's wounded.[47]

For all the variability in reporting Sioux combatants at Rosebud, there was relative consistency in reporting Sioux casualties. Finerty remembered: "Thirteen dead bodies of the enemy remained on the field, and through field glasses we could see their wounded and such dead as they had picked up strapped to their horses and borne away. Clots of blood all along their trail showed the extent of their loss." Captain Andrew Burt of the Ninth Infantry estimated that "about fifty [Indians] were knocked off their ponies and carried off the field." In Strahorn's estimation, the bodies abandoned on the field, wounded and dead carried away, and blood amounted to a loss of more than one hundred killed and wounded, perhaps even one hundred and fifty. Crook was cagey in his assessment, writing that it was "impossible to correctly estimate the loss of the enemy as the field extended over several miles of rough country, including rocks and ravines, not examined by us after the fight. Thirteen of their dead bodies being left in close proximity to our lines."

Bourke's calculations were conservative. He confided to his diary that eleven scalps were taken by the scouts and that no less than fifty Indians were killed and wounded in all. "Of our own losses we can speak authoritatively; of the enemy, of course, not so much is known." Truer words were never written. To be sure, of course, mothers, fathers, brothers, sisters, wives, and children in the Sioux and Cheyenne camps on Reno Creek comprehended well the toll of fighting warriors at Rosebud, a matter yet to be explored.[48]

The loss of cavalry horses was noted as well. Finerty reported nineteen mounts killed outright and the same number more or less injured. MacMillan expressed it another way, hinting at the sorry task of mercy killing badly wounded animals. Sixteen horses were thus shot. An early settler hauled several wagonloads of horse bones from Kollmar Creek, and all the hooves had iron shoes. Even in the early 1950s horse skulls were unearthed in the area of the led horse ravine, one with a bullet hole in its side.[49]

The day's events closed with one last ruckus in the Shoshone camp. In their midst lay the dead young boy, slain by Cheyennes that morning while tending the tribe's pony herd. Their sad rite of mourning, which Bourke described as "an infernal caterwaul," lasted well through the night before the boy was buried along the stream. As with the soldier burial, caution drove the mourners to obscure the grave. Warriors on horseback rode over it several times to blend the interment in with its surroundings.[50]

At Hartsuff's hospital Tom Moore and his packers yet again quietly lent the doctors and wounded needed assistance, working through the night to fashion a horse litter and five travois for use in evacuating the invalids to Goose Creek. Among Moore's crowd was Tom Cooper, who remembered his services on the Rosebud with a deferential acknowledgment of Guy Henry and the other casualties. Putting his packer experience to efficient use, Cooper joined others in cutting young box elder trees from along the creek for use as litter and travois poles and rigging two suitable cavalry horses as litter bearers. These field expediencies were new to Hartsuff, who described them in lavish detail in his report.[51]

For Crook's soldiers, June 17 began at 3 A.M. in the headlands of the South Fork of Rosebud Creek. The men had experienced a long and terrifying day seared evermore in memory. Yet in the eternal nature of army field service the command would soon rise again and turn its attention and direction to Goose Creek. For these men, the Battle of the Rosebud was over. On Reno Creek, twenty-four miles away, an entirely different story was unfolding.

RETURN TO GOOSE CREEK

The men of Crook's command were predictably edgy the night after the battle, but the time passed quietly and without incident. Colonel Royall's adjutant, Lieutenant Henry Lemly, remembered that some in the scattered camps were certain that the Sioux would return and attempt to stampede the animals. No threats of any sort materialized, however, and no shots were fired, although Captain Gerhard Luhn remembered that his pickets were skittish. Trumpets sounded reveille at 3 A.M. (Finerty remembered it as 4 A.M.). The men of Crook's bruised command awakened to a heavy frost. But the breaking sky above was cloudless and immaculately blue, portending another blisteringly hot, sunny day in Montana. Breakfast was hurried. Tin cups of steaming soldier coffee broke the chill and washed down powder-dry hardcrackers and four-day-old fried bacon.[1]

The jaded animals had recuperated considerably, and by 6:30 A.M. the column was in motion, retracing its route up what engineer William Stanton called the left bank of the Rosebud, meaning simply the stream's south fork, until it reached the same headlands near where it had camped on the evening of June 16. Stanton's diary entries are puzzlingly blasé, offering only simple reflections from an unduly focused field engineer. His subsequently published paragraphs for June 17—the day of the great battle—were half the length of his reports of movements on June 16 and 18, themselves straight business with scarcely any color. The battle itself warranted a mere three sentences in Stanton's journal, although he never strayed far from General Crook at the epicenter of the action. Perhaps he was overwhelmed by the action and had no desire or capacity to put into words what he had seen.[2]

Finerty rode with the Third Cavalry in the van and described the marching order. The cavalcade of wounded, some riding horses and others borne on litters and travois, trailed the Third, while Noyes's battalion of the Second Cavalry followed Hartsuff, and Chambers's mounted infantry brought up the rear. Crow and Shoshone scouts worked in all directions—front, right, left, and rear—to cover the movement. Finerty and others discerned small parties of Sioux along Camel-Back Ridge, watching the departing soldiers intently but posing no threat. No effort was made to challenge them. The persistently dour Sergeant George Howard of Captain Elijah Wells's Company E, Second Cavalry, captured the melancholy of the movement. Their withdrawal to Goose Creek, he confided to his diary, was "another disastrous retreat with nothing accomplished." Howard remembered too well the Powder River fiasco three months earlier and gave quiet voice to the parallels he was sensing.[3]

Properly transporting the wounded was a principal challenge at the start of the movement. The men in Doctor Hartsuff's care had passed a good night. Their condition, Bourke noted, "was all that could be hoped for." During the evacuation, thirteen men rode their own mounts, with five others placed on travois pulled by single mules. Captain Henry rode in a two-mule litter. Tom Moore's packers had fashioned these "extemporized" contraptions the evening before: poles and cross-pieces cut from young, flexible trees, rope lashings interwoven to form beds, and canvas sheets or woolen blankets providing covers. To further soften the mattresses, green leaves were strewn beneath the covers, with greatcoats arranged as pillows.[4]

Six enlisted men were detailed to each of the conveyances, and Sergeant John Warfield of Company F, Third Cavalry, was put in charge of the entire detail. The trail was rocky and broken, with steep hills and deep canyons. On many occasions attendants carried the ends of the travois poles, performing the duty, Bourke acknowledged, without a murmur. Hartsuff took a particular interest in these conveyances, which were devices entirely new to him, but grew rightly critical almost from the start. The travois were fine on smooth surfaces, he observed, but otherwise so troublesome and uncomfortable that he had them all thrown away when camping that evening and had litters made instead.[5]

Guy Henry suffered his own unique travails. Barely had the movement begun when Henry's mules balked when crossing a bog. The Rosebud from its head to the Big Bend had a continuous muddy bottom with scattered adjacent wetlands. In a struggle the rear mule of Henry's litter struck the captain across the face with its jaw. Almost as quickly the litter upended, throwing Henry to the ground. Fortunately, Henry joked in a retelling, it was soft earth. To avoid being struck in the face again, Henry's placement on the litter was then reversed. He now endured the swooshing tail of the lead mule. Kicking was possible—and feared as well—but never occurred. The Crow chief Plenty Coups watched when Henry was thrown from his litter. "He did not complain at all. I liked that man," he told his biographer. Henry did voice one complaint. Sometime early in the morning the captain learned apparently for the first time that Crook was retreating on account of the wounded. In characteristic Henry bluster, he protested, sending word to Crook that the wounded should not be a consideration if such concern in any way interfered with the success of the campaign. Although Henry's appeal was acknowledged by some, the withdrawal to Goose Creek continued apace.[6]

Barely had the movement begun again when gunshots drew attention to a draw some distance to the west. A Crow ally discovered a Cheyenne warrior in the dewy tall grass, but somehow still alive. Late in the fight the warrior had been shot, scalped, and left for dead by one of the Shoshones. Hearing the pounding of horse's hooves, the blood-smeared, blinded Indian thought that these were Cheyenne or Sioux ponies and friends. He crawled from a gully and called out *mini, mini,* meaning "water, water." Instead of a friend responding, however, a Crow answered with a murderous yell and six shots from his needle carbine. Davenport, Finerty, and others rode over and watched in horror as the Crows dismembered the warrior, digit by digit, limb by limb. Private Hermann Ashkey of Company I, Second Cavalry, also caught sight of the episode as his company rode by. "I saw our Indians take one wunded Sue Indian by the legs & take their tomehack & split him in to [*sic*]." "The scene . . . beggars description for bloodthirsty cruelty and savage joy," wrote Charles Stanley in abject disgust. The disconcerting episode on that Sunday morning was yet one more gruesome act on an already ghastly field.[7]

The nature of the episode touched Captain Anson Mills in another way. Mills told his Order of Indian Wars audience in 1917 that when they scanned the vast landscape fully twenty-four hours after the battle erupted, after yet one more killing, that "we then all realized for the first time that while we were lucky not to have been entirely vanquished, we had been most humiliatingly defeated." For Mills, Rosebud was stigmatizing. Marching away was a welcome relief.[8]

The expedition's course followed the Rosebud's south fork to its head. There the incoming trail that the troops had followed on June 16 veered southeastward toward the Tongue. Crook and his scouts at this point sought a more direct route to Furey's camp on Goose Creek and maintained a south by southwesterly course, aiming straight for the snow-capped Big Horn Mountains on the far horizon. Cloud Peak, at the heart of the range, may well have served as a beacon. Meanwhile, in the difficult high ground of the intervening Wolf Mountains, the troops followed buffalo trails that Bourke remembered being "as conspicuous as a wagon road." They encountered rivulets in the divide that flowed to the Rosebud behind them, the Little Big Horn to the west, and the Tongue, straight south, "impart[ing] a charming diversity to the country."[9]

At the divide the column paused for an hour to allow the slow-moving wounded and trailing infantry battalion to catch up. There the Crows formed a close circle and performed a war or scalp dance, holding the black locks of the Sioux and Cheyenne warriors killed in the fight aloft on willow poles and lances. Some members of the command found the profusion of buffalo seen in the high country more interesting. Buffalo were again common (as on the ascent into the Wolf Mountains on June 16), both live animals and the detritus of a recent Indian hunt. A few hunters now secured fresh meat as the column descended onto the headlands of what Bourke presumed was Ash Creek, an innocuous tributary of the Little Big Horn. This identification may have been mistaken, as today's Ash Creek is a tributary of the Tongue. Bourke may well have been referring to a branch of Owl Creek, which others referred to as Rotten Grass Creek.[10]

At about 2 P.M. Crook halted after having advanced some twenty miles from the battlefield. The early halt was chiefly for the sake of the wounded, who had suffered considerably in the day's heat and in crossing the torturous Wolf Mountains highlands. The entire command was well worn and welcomed the stop. Finerty and others remembered the place as a perfect camping site, abundantly supplied with wild flowers of every hue, good water, and a few trees. Sergeant Howard again groused, confiding in his diary that the campsite had poor water and no wood, although the road that day had been good. Perhaps he and the Second Cavalry were assigned a camping place on the dry margins of the sprawl.[11]

In the early evening the Crows left the expedition, striking west for their home country by way of old Fort C. F. Smith on the Big Horn River. Despite Crook's strenuous appeals the day before, the Crows held firm in their intent to return to their families. They too had wounded men and were tired. Of greater concern, the Crows feared that the Sioux were headed in that same direction or perhaps had even already marauded in the Crows' home country (Crow ponies had been found with the enemy the day before). The parting was cordial. Frank Grouard, instrumental in bringing the Crows to Crook, noted simply that "nothing we could do or say would stop them." "We shook hands," Plenty Coups remembered. "We had ten enemy scalps, a good many horses, saddles, and blankets. And we still had plenty of ammunition for our guns, a thing we were always short of before we met those soldiers. We believed we had helped the white men and felt proud of it." The Crows promised to return within fifteen days. Reporter Thomas MacMillan, writing for the *Chicago Inter-Ocean*, openly doubted that probability.[12]

Again the night was cold, one of the coldest summer nights that Bourke had ever experienced, with frost covering the ground at daybreak. Henry remembered that ice had formed but believed that the frigid fresh air helped stanch bleeding and generally aided in his own recovery and that of those suffering with him. The night's rest was disrupted at about 1 A.M., however, when pickets fired on supposed Indians crawling up a deep ravine. An actual threat was not substantiated, but the shots were disruptive all the same. Finerty surmised that they might have been "supposed" Sioux.[13]

The trip to Furey's Goose Creek camp resumed just after sunrise on June 19. The route to the forks of Goose Creek was as much a beeline as the rugged undulations of the landscape permitted. Engineer Stanton called the descending terrain to the Tongue "devious," due to both its strenuous nature and its sparse vegetative cover, consisting mostly of cactus and thick sage. The troops again hunted buffalo early in the day. They forded the Tongue, not more than three or four feet deep, without difficulty and resumed their south by southeasterly course until they reached the old Fort C. F. Smith Road. The column turned onto the well-beaten track and within several miles passed the expedition's campsite from four days earlier at the forks of Goose Creek, the site of the rendezvous with the Crow and Shoshone auxiliaries and the uproarious if humiliating mounting of the infantry battalion. In another two and a half miles Crook reached Furey's wagon corral, nestled within a grassy bend of the South Fork of Goose Creek (known today as Little Goose Creek). It was noon.[14]

Crook paused through the noon hour, allowing the column momentary rest and a meal while he conferred with Captain Furey. The supply base needed reconfiguring. Wagons had to be offloaded and readied for an abrupt return to Fort Fetterman. But not at that locale, which was grazed off. A place with fresh grass two miles upstream was agreed upon. One thing was certain. In Crook's short absence Furey had fortified his camp heavily and could easily have withstood a Sioux assault. Tucked within the curves of the South Fork, with its waters providing protection on several sides, Furey's teamsters, packers, and invalid soldiers—some 190 capable defenders—had created a veritable fortress. Ropes and chains were stretched from wheel to wheel to form a corral for the wagon stock, and breastworks of earth and logs were thrown up to command the approaches. Furey's crew was not idle by day. Some men tended grazing stock, while others hunted buffalo and elk, portending activities that would soon become commonplace on Goose Creek.[15]

Early in the afternoon the entire command, now including Furey's teamsters and wagons, moved two and one-half miles up the South Fork and established a new camp. Strong pickets were immediately thrown out to commanding ground surrounding the place. Horses and mules were unsaddled and turned out to graze and drink, and details set up hospital tents for the wounded. With access to camp baggage again, a few officers with lemons and limes remaining in their satchels dug them out. There were barely a half dozen in all, Bourke recalled, but enough to make a pleasant glass of lemonade for each patient. "The eagerness of their drinking was a most welcome token of their gratitude and improving condition," he observed.[16]

Crook seized a moment in the afternoon to prepare an initial telegraphic report for General Sheridan, dated June 19. In this one he was nonjudgmental. He matter-of-factly reported to Sheridan that he had been attacked on the morning of June 17 by an enemy force strong enough to defeat his command, but he repulsed the attacking Indians in great confusion. He had returned to Goose Creek on account of his wounded, whom he enumerated and specifically mentioned Captain Henry, shot in the face. Most importantly, he advised Sheridan that he was ordering up five additional companies of infantry. "I expect to find those Indians in rough places all the time," he observed. Little could Crook, Sheridan, or anyone with the Big Horn and Yellowstone Expedition know then how this small detail, the ordering of additional infantry, sealed forevermore the reputation of this accomplished field commander and his sizable expedition, as events elsewhere would soon make clear. Crook dispatched Ben Arnold to Fort Fetterman that evening. Arnold traveled alone, reaching Fetterman on June 22. That day and the next Fetterman's telegraph wires hummed nearly nonstop as Sheridan and the nation learned of the Battle of the Rosebud.[17]

Crook clarified his interest in additional infantry in a separate telegram on June 19 to Lieutenant Colonel Robert Williams, assistant adjutant general at department headquarters in Omaha. He wanted three companies of the Fourteenth Infantry from Camp Douglas at Salt Lake City and two from Fort Laramie (or one company from Camp Robinson if necessary). Thus far the Fourteenth Infantry, then mostly scattered across Utah, had not been drawn into the war. Williams ordered forth the requested number of companies, although they were not quite sourced as Crook initially imagined.[18]

Officers wrote letters that day and the next. For the most part such correspondence was bundled for shipment with the ambulances and wagons, destined to leave Goose Creek for Fort Fetterman shortly. In addition to a lengthy letter to his wife, Captain Gerhard Luhn also packaged a Sioux headdress collected on the battlefield by his friend Baptiste Pourier. Luhn told his wife that he assumed he would be among the infantry companies escorting the wagons when they departed. Captain Andrew Burt penned two brief telegrams, a few words to his wife at Fort Laramie assuring her that all in the company were well and that a letter was coming by mail and another to the *Cincinnati Commercial* newspaper, with whom he corresponded from time to time. That particular communiqué, a short paragraph reporting on the fight, concluded with the observation that "the campaign so far proves the ability of General Crook to accomplish in time against the Sioux what he has done with the Apaches." Apparently there was little or no disgruntlement in the infantry camp over the handling or outcome of the great battle, at least not at that point.[19]

The five dedicated newsmen traveling with the command, each with a unique perspective, finished writing initial or follow-up dispatches for their papers. John Finerty of the *Chicago Times* and Thomas MacMillan of the *Chicago Inter-Ocean* rode with Mills and were in the thick of the action in the Gap and then trailed into the Rosebud Narrows with Mills and Noyes before Crook recalled those battalions. Robert Strahorn, writing for Denver's *Rocky Mountain News*, and Joe Wasson of San Francisco's *Alta California*, attached themselves to Crook and observed the battle throughout from headquarters. Of the five reporters, only Reuben Davenport, covering the campaign for the *New York Herald*, rode with Royall and experienced the worst.

All of the newsmen's initial stories were straightforward accounts of the fight, shaded only by their personal experiences on the scene. Invective came later from some, certainly, but not initially. Attempts to engage couriers on the night of the battle were unsuccessful. No account from these reporters appeared in their respective newspapers before June 24, often augmenting Crook's own report to Sheridan, which received wide and immediate circulation as well. Ben Arnold carried these communiqués as well, but Crook's report had priority in the telegraph office at Fort Fetterman because the army controlled the courier, the operator, and the wire. Strahorn had faced the same predicament at the conclusion of the Big Horn Expedition in March.[20]

On Tuesday, June 20, Crook moved the camp seven miles up the South

Fork of Goose Creek. Engineer Stanton bestowed a name on the place for the first time: Camp Cloud Peak. Abundant grass, water, and wood dictated the move as always. Here the Little Goose was a "prattling brook" with a boulder bottom, some thirty feet wide and two to four feet deep. Bourke and Wasson both thought the Goose a lovely mountain stream, doubtless containing coveted trout. Wounded comrades were cared for immediately, Henry remembering a welcome grassy mattress and a canvas drape overhead. It turned into a sweltering day, with the temperature at 3 P.M. reaching 103 degrees F in the shade. These men were operating in a land of temperature extremes. Two nights earlier and barely thirty miles away, water had frozen in canteens and cups. Now the temperature was topping 100 degrees F. The swings were excruciating and exhilarating at once.[21]

The day's principal business was preparing the wagons and ambulances for a return to Fort Fetterman. All but one of the supply wagons were thoroughly emptied, and remnant food stocks, munitions, weaponry, and equipment stockpiled under canvas. One month's rations remained. Two of Hartsuff's three ambulances were similarly readied for the trip. These vehicles were capable of transporting two or four recumbent men comfortably, depending on configuration, or eight men sitting, plus a driver and two attendants. To soften the ride, cushions and mattresses were additionally stuffed with fresh clean grass.[22]

While subalterns and sergeants tended to the business of the camp, battalion and company commanders responded to a circular order requiring their preparation of written reports accounting for their action in the Rosebud battle. Compliance was spotty. Major Chambers and each of the five company commanders in the infantry battalion submitted individual reports that became part of the official record. Cavalry brigade commander Royall filed a report, but Captain Noyes was the only officer of his Second Cavalry battalion who did so. If any of Noyes's five company commanders complied, which seems doubtful in hindsight, none of their reports have survived. Regimental, battalion, and squadron commanders Evans, Henry, Mills, and Van Vliet of the Third Cavalry complied, as did four additional company commanders, but four others did not. (Mills wrote for his battalion; First Lieutenant Augustus C. Paul wrote for Mills's Company M; and Van Vliet wrote for his squadron and Company C.) Regrettably, Captain Peter D. Vroom and Second Lieutenant Bainbridge Reynolds (commanding Companies L and F respectively) evidently did not prepare reports. Both companies were mauled at the Kollmar Crossing. Their perspectives and reflections on that critical action are thus sadly missing from the historical record. Captain Charles Meinhold dutifully took down Guy Henry's report, direct "from Col. Henry's lips." Hartsuff and Stanton prepared separate reports that were passed through medical and engineering channels. Hartsuff's report included a formal tally of those killed and wounded in the fight.[23]

On June 20 Crook prepared a second report for Sheridan, considerably more elaborated than his shorter telegram the day before. This account opened with the arrival of the Crow and Shoshone Indian scouts on June 14 and recounted the march to the field of battle, the deployments, the nature of the physical landscape, and the difficulty of joining the scattered battalions once the fight opened. In this report Crook obliquely explained and justified his ambition of following the retreating Indians to their village and expressed great regret in his inability to do so. He commended the gallantry and efficiency of the officers and men of the command, singling out Royall and Chambers particularly, who "have given me great strength by the able manner in which they commanded their respective columns." Crook dripped with magnanimity. As we shall see, he would view this matter quite differently in 1886 when he lashed out at Royall and Captain Nickerson for what by then he deemed their imagined failures on the battlefield.[24]

Also originating at headquarters were orders detailing the escort for the hospital and quartermaster train on the morrow. The duty fell to Major Chambers, who, as senior officer of the assigned complement, would command. Assistant surgeon Julius Patzki would accompany the ambulances and tend to the welfare of the expedition's wounded. Furey, the expedition's chief quartermaster, would have general charge of the train. Remaining stores would be stockpiled and dispensed under the oversight of First Lieutenant George Drew, regimental quartermaster of the Third Cavalry, and First Lieutenant John Bubb, the expedition's chief commissary of subsistence. Crook's force would be entirely resupplied. Two of Chambers's infantry companies, Luhn's Company F, Fourth Infantry, and Captain Samuel Munson's Company C, Ninth Infantry, would guard the train. First Lieutenant Henry Seton, Chambers's battalion adjutant, and First Lieutenant Thaddeus Capron of Munson's company rounded out the service detachment, which in this instance would ride wagons, not mules.

Unsettling rumblings were being heard in the Shoshone camp. Like the Crows, these warriors wished to return to their agency to display enemy scalps and ensure the security of their villages. On June 20 three Shoshones left the Goose Creek camp for Camp Brown, across the Big Horns in west-central

Wyoming. Their purpose was simply to report on the results of the war. On June 21 all but ten of the Shoshones abandoned Crook, all bound for Camp Brown. Among those remaining behind were five with wounds and five others to help the doctors care for them. Like the Crows, the Shoshones promised to return. Crook was generous, writing to James Irwin, Indian agent at the Shoshone and Bannock Agency, to assure him that this detachment under Tom Cosgrove performed with "more than ordinary discipline and behaved with marked bravery during our late engagement with the hostile Sioux." Regrettably, however, aside from those few remaining Shoshones and Crook's three original Plainsmen—Grouard, Richard, and Pourier—the general was again hamstrung before an enemy whose land and wiles he barely knew.[25]

At 4 A.M. on June 21 the wounded were placed in ambulances and an hour later began their 169-mile journey to Fort Fetterman. "It was a painful sight to observe Capt. Henry, his whole face covered with a cotton plaster, unsupported on either side, feel his way into the ambulance," reported Robert Strahorn. John Finerty similarly noted a sadness in the departure: "We all turned out and gave Colonel Henry and the other wounded three hearty cheers as they moved out of camp. It was the last we were to see of them during that campaign."[26]

In addition to Chambers, Furey, Henry, and the other wounded, a number of campaign notables accompanied the caravan. Captain Nickerson, for one, departed on the stern commendations of Doctors Hartsuff and Patzki. His exertions in the saddle at the Rosebud had reopened a Civil War chest wound that now had nearly finished him (he had been shot through an arm and both lungs at Gettysburg). His cover, if somehow he needed one, was a mission from Crook to recruit Ute Indian scouts at their agency in eastern Utah. (Davenport understood this differently, informing his readers that Nickerson was sent to Nebraska to secure the services of Pawnee scouts.) Captain Stanton and his complement of enlisted engineers left the campaign as well. In his subsequent report Stanton offered no explanation for the departure beyond implying that his mission—a simple geographical reconnaissance of the sort that he commonly made for the Department of the Platte—was complete. At best, Stanton was a reluctant participant in the Rosebud battle anyway. No one in the command succeeded him in keeping an official itinerary. Also departing with the wagons was Louis Richard, specifically dispatched by Crook to the Red Cloud Agency to organize a contingent of mixed-blood agency Indians—not full-blooded Indians—willing to join the campaign. Crook was grasping at straws. After his experience at Red Cloud in May, he knew the odds were against him. But in light of the Crow and Shoshone departures every prospect was worth a second chance.[27]

Thomas MacMillan, reporter for the *Chicago Inter-Ocean*, Charles Stanley, artist for *Frank Leslie's Illustrated Newspaper*, and the oddball prospector-turned-correspondent Ernest Hornburger and his traveling companion, Sylvester Reese, departed from the expedition as well. Like Nickerson, MacMillan had a frail constitution. The cumulative day-by-day grind in the saddle and the exhausting hours on the Rosebud battlefield had thoroughly consumed him. The column's doctors vigorously recommended his return to Chicago. Second Lieutenant Frederick Schwatka of Company M, Third Cavalry, would continue to supply the *Inter-Ocean* with news from the front. Stanley cavalierly dismissed his own departure, noting simply the difficulty in placing his drawings in the hands of couriers and that he "determined to be the bearer of [his] own papers." In Hornberger's lone story appearing in the *Pittsburg Evening Leader* he acknowledged that he had "had enough of the Sioux county" and intended to travel southward into Colorado, New Mexico, and Arizona. Stanley and Reese were both Coloradans and perhaps had sparked Hornberger's interest. Not the least of the departees, though apparently only of interest to people of another era, was Calamity Jane Canary. Her confinement with Furey in the quartermaster corral since June 14 had passed without mention. She would next be seen at Fort Laramie at the end of the month, where she quietly joined the Hickok train bound for Deadwood.[28]

With the departure of the train, including the several ambulances and ponton boats, life at Camp Cloud Peak quickly assumed a new normal. Bathing, grazing and stock watering, fishing, and fighting black flies filled the daylight hours. "Luckily, the nights are so very cold, sleep is not disturbed at all and everyone is refreshed and rested," Bourke recalled in an oddly disturbing reflection. An Indian war was fully underway, with other army columns in the field. Prospects of another momentous engagement were ever present and almost literally just over the hill.[29]

Captain and Assistant Surgeon Albert Hartsuff, Medical Department

At the time of the Rosebud battle, Captain Albert Hartsuff was the senior medical officer on Crook's Big Horn and Yellowstone Expedition and before that a Fort Laramie physician. He promoted to the rank of major on the day following the Little Big Horn fight. Hartsuff retired in 1901, having risen to the rank of colonel and assistant surgeon general of the army's Medical Department. He died in 1908 and is buried in the Elmwood Cemetery, Detroit, Michigan. (National Library of Medicine)

Captain and Assistant Surgeon Julius Patzki, Medical Department

The historical record on Prussian-born Julius Patzki (1838–1930) is thin. The army acknowledged his service in the enlisted ranks and as a surgeon during the Civil War. He attained the rank of captain and assistant surgeon in 1867, was promoted to major and surgeon in 1889, and retired in 1892. On the Rosebud battlefield he joined two other physicians and a steward in administering to casualties and also tended the wounded on their evacuation to Fort Fetterman. (National Library of Medicine)

Hospital Steward Samuel Richardson

When Samuel Richardson enlisted in the Fourth Infantry in 1869 his occupation was recorded as a druggist, reflecting an aptitude if not actual education as a pharmacist. Two years later Richardson received an appointment as hospital steward, a position he retained with the army and later the Public Health and Marine-Hospital Service well into the twentieth century. At the time of this photograph in 1909 Richardson was a senior pharmacist with the Public Health and Marine-Hospital Service. (South Dakota State Historical Society)

"Killing of a Sioux Warrior on the Morning after the Rosebud Battle, June 18th"

Many in Crook's column witnessed the horrific killing and dismemberment of a Cheyenne warrior by the Crows as troops left the battlefield the next morning. The battered, nameless warrior had been left for dead when the fighting ended. Hearing horses pass, the blinded Indian cried out for water. His killing was one more gruesome act on an already ghastly field. Charles St. George Stanley sketch for *Frank Leslie's Illustrated Newspaper*, October 21, 1876. (Author's collection)

Camp Clouds Peak Stone

Contemporary memorials scoring the comings and goings of Crook's Big Horn and Yellowstone Expedition of 1876 are exceedingly rare. This unique gem, a flat-faced piece of sandstone etched by Frank Grouard six days after the Rosebud battle, was discovered along Little Goose Creek, Wyoming, decades later. Today the stone is a centerpiece exhibit in the Bozeman Trail Museum, Big Horn, Wyoming. (Hillman Collection, Bozeman Trail Museum, Big Horn City Historical Society)

Brigadier General George Crook, Department of the Platte

George Crook posed for this picture in San Francisco in April 1875 when changing stations from the Department of Arizona to Omaha. The army's wunderkind Indian fighter had not yet faced the tribesmen of the northern plains. In the coming months he was taught an abject lesson in tribal dynamics as he, Sheridan, Terry, and Custer warred against a people unwilling to yield a homeland and way of life. Bradley and Rulofson photograph. (Mark Kasal Collection)

First Lieutenant Thaddeus Capron, Ninth Infantry

Thaddeus Capron fought valiantly at Rosebud, helping manage the initial skirmish line as the battle opened and during the assault on Conical Hill. He was better remembered that season, however, for the ill-advised words that he shared with fellow officers at Fort Laramie weeks later when on a hurried visit with his wife after evacuating the Rosebud wounded. Capron's thoughtless chatter impugning Crook's leadership on the battlefield drew national attention and Crook's quiet but steaming ire when the lieutenant returned to Goose Creek. (National Park Service, Fort Laramie National Historic Site)

Captain Avery Billings Cain, Fourth Infantry

Avery Cain, seen here late in the Civil War, served exclusively with the Fourth Infantry from 1861 until his untimely death in 1879. He led troops valiantly at Rosebud Creek, charging on the initial skirmish line and then capturing Conical Hill. Five weeks later he was evacuated from the war zone after attending surgeons declared him insane. Within months Cain recovered and returned to duty. In another day his affliction would be characterized as post-traumatic stress disorder (PTSD). Charles D. Fredericks photograph. (Bennington Museum, Bennington, Vermont)

Trumpeter Elmer Snow, Company M, Third Cavalry

At Rosebud twenty-four-year-old Elmer Snow was struck by an Indian bullet during Mills's second charge in the Gap. The projectile shattered both arms, rendering them virtually useless thereafter except with the assistance of a wire apparatus. Snow received a Medal of Honor for his heroics. Here he is seen in September 1879 when examined and photographed at the Army Medical Museum in Washington, D.C. Snow surmounted his disability, becoming a successful attorney, marrying, and fathering five children. (National Library of Medicine)

Bull Snake (Crow)

With a long-suffering warrior's stare and wearing warrior's paint and dress, Crow scout Bull Snake posed in 1909 beside a stately cottonwood tree along the Little Big Horn River. Bull Snake's left leg was shattered early in the Rosebud fight. The severity of his injury is plainly apparent thirty-three years later: his left thigh was badly mangled and his left foot barely touched the ground (and only when his right leg was cocked). Bull Snake's hobble was extreme. His case came to the attention of Congress in 1910 in a pleading for a pension earned honorably at Rosebud. Joseph K. Dixon photograph. (Author's collection)

First Sergeant John Henry Shingle, Company I, Third Cavalry

Civil War veteran John Henry Shingle enlisted three times in the Third Cavalry, consistently using the alias John Henry, a simple shortening of his name. By the time of the Rosebud campaign he was first sergeant of Company I, commanded by Captain William Andrews. In acknowledgment of Shingle's heroics on the Rosebud battlefield, particularly in the mêlée at the Kollmar Crossing, he was awarded a Medal of Honor in 1880. He posed at Fort Sanders, Wyoming, shortly before receiving his medal. Shingle spent his final years at the National Home for Disabled Volunteer Soldiers in Leavenworth, Kansas, where he died in 1907. He was buried in the adjacent Leavenworth National Cemetery. Charles Howard photograph. (Hayes Otoupalik Collection)

John Henry Shingle's Medal of Honor

First Sergeant John Henry Single received this Medal of Honor on June 1, 1880. His citation reads simply "Gallantry in action." The pattern is the first style of medal authorized in 1862, featuring within a five-pointed bronze star the standing figure of Minerva, the Roman goddess of wisdom and war. The star is suspended from an eagle with outspread wings perched upon two crossed cannon barrels, a cavalry saber, and a cluster of cannonballs. The eagle in turn is suspended from a red, white, and blue ribbon representing the flag of the United States. The pin brooch features a federal shield flanked by cornucopia. Engraved on the planchet's plain back are these words: "The Congress to 1ˢᵗ *Sergeant John H. Shingle*, TROOP I, 3ᴿᴰ CAVALRY, FOR BRAVERY AT ROSEBUD FOR BRAVERY AT ROSEBUD MOUNTAIN M.T., JUNE 17, 1876." (Hayes Otoupalik Collection)

Finds Them and Kills Tem and The Other Magpie (Crows)

Early in the fighting along Kollmar Creek, Finds Them and Kills Them (left) and The Other Magpie saved the badly injured Crow scout Bull Snake from certain death. Finds Them and Kills Them, known also among the Crows as *Osh-Tisch* and Squaw Jim, was a berdache or two-spirited person, a biological male who adopted a female lifestyle. Dressed in male clothing during the battle, she shot a Sioux charging in to kill Bull Snake. The Other Magpie then scalped the enemy—the first coup achieved by the Crows during the battle. Photograph by John H. Fouch at Fort Keogh, M.T., circa 1879. (James S. Brust Collection)

Rosebud Monument

A sizable crowd of Montanans, including a reporter from the *Billings Gazette* and four aged Northern Cheyenne veterans of the fight, attended the 1934 dedication of this imposing scoria and bronze Rosebud Monument overlooking the creek's Big Bend. The battlefield is a mile west, while this monument sits prominently astride the Busby-Decker highway. (Author's photograph)

John Stands in Timber (Northern Cheyenne)

The affable John Stands in Timber (1882–1967) was an ever-eager, ever-helpful Northern Cheyenne historian, generous with his time and knowledge. Here he poses on the Rosebud battlefield in the mid-1950s, having accompanied the battle's first historian, Jesse W. Vaughn, to the field. Stands in Timber devoted his life to collecting and preserving stories of Cheyenne battles, valor, and cultural heritage and was for Vaughn a generational link connecting the past and present in a manner impossible to repeat. (Jesse W. Vaughn Papers, ah003573, American Heritage Center, University of Wyoming)

EIGHT DAYS

The departure of the Rosebud wounded on June 21 for proper medical care at Fort Fetterman was an enormous relief for General Crook. Largely on account of those stricken men, he had withdrawn his command from the war front in the Rosebud Basin to his base camp on Goose Creek, some forty beeline miles straight south. Barely a week earlier on Goose Creek Crook's newly arrived Crow allies had told of the existence of Sitting Bull's village on Rosebud Creek. The general had been close, so very close.

Crook had other reasons for withdrawing. When he left the Goose Creek camp on June 16, each man in his command carried a full allotment of ammunition, one hundred rounds, and four days' rations. To buy time on the chase, he mounted his five infantry companies on the expedition's pack mules, service animals that otherwise would have been burdened with additional rations and reserve munitions to prolong his time away from the supply train as necessary. The enemy village, Sitting Bull's camp no less, was so near that these odd decisions appeared to make sense at that moment. But in the four ensuing days Crook's command had fully consumed its rations, used up a good measure of its ammunition, and struck no village.

Other things had changed too. Most critically, Crook lost his Indian scouts in the immediate wake of the battle. They were savvy and necessary in a strange land. Detachments of Crows and Shoshones numbering collectively some 250 fighters chose to depart Crook's campaign, seeking solace and recovery in their home country. The Sioux and Northern Cheyennes had proven themselves a formidable enemy. More importantly for the Crows, this same enemy posed a dangerous threat to the well-being of their home villages. Both bands promised to return, but Crook and others in the command doubted them. The general had already dispatched Azor Nickerson and Louis Richard to recruit replacements—whether Utes, Pawnees, or agency mixed-blood Indians.

Plentiful stores of munitions and foodstuffs were at hand, stockpiled on the South Fork of Goose Creek under canvas tarpaulins. All but a handful of teamsters remained to guard the cache, but that might have been immaterial.

If all of it could not be packed on mules, some could be left behind in the care of those teamsters and several packers. Tom Moore's crew of muleskinners had proven themselves capable fighters at the Rosebud. Mounting the infantry on those same mules on June 15 proved to be a folly that had lost its charm. But the value of infantry in combat against the Sioux was an eye opener for Crook. As a longtime infantry officer he surely knew this intuitively. While he no longer needed foot troops on mules, he instinctively saw the need for additional foot soldiers employed against this enemy. On June 19 he ordered five additional companies to the front. That order might already have reached Fort Fetterman, spurring companies at Camp Douglas and Fort Laramie into motion.

What was clear at Crook's Camp Cloud Peak headquarters on June 21 was that this command had faced a formidable enemy. Though Crook had lost his Indian allies and, for the moment, two of his infantry companies, he had three other foot companies at hand, plus all fifteen original cavalry companies. How the general reacted from that day forward would become clear. How he might have reacted in the eight critical days between his Battle of the Rosebud and the great calamity crowding the horizon on the Little Big Horn becomes rich fodder for counterfactual history.

||||||||||||||||||||||||||||||||||||||

Crook's first thought was to go hunting. On June 22 he, Captain Frederick Van Vliet, Captain Andy Burt, and a few others struck off for the mountainside to hunt and fish. Hunting was a lifelong passion for Crook, a recharge of sorts that found expression on most of his campaigns, from his earliest service in California to his recent trip to the Black Hills in 1875. Already on this campaign he had rousted some buffaloes on Prairie Dog Creek and was remembered for having taken along a shotgun for bird hunting. Still, he had devoted no time yet to a private hunt. As he awaited the return of his wagons and the additional infantry, however, he made time. Colonel Royall commanded the camp while Crook was away.[1]

For those whose orbit was limited to Camp Cloud Peak, a sense of odd leisure overtook the command. While pickets continually manned the heights surrounding the camp's sprawl, the basic chores of tending men and horses were discharged easily. In idle hours soldiers played cards, washed and mended clothes, bathed, and fished so continuously that in some circles fried trout became standard fare. Some men were granted permission to hunt, and buffalo and elk steaks were also introduced to the general diet. The daily temperature moderated slightly, but men still built willow shelters to shield themselves from the oppressive sun. "Loafing hangs heavily upon us," remembered Finerty.[2]

If anyone with the Big Horn and Yellowstone Expedition had momentarily lost focus, reality returned soon after sunrise on June 23 when First Lieutenant Walter S. Schuyler and two couriers (plus several orderlies, a packer, the miner-turned courier John Graves, who knew the country, and several heavily laden pack mules) arrived from Fort Fetterman. These were the first in-bound couriers to reach Crook in more than a week, bringing critical news from Omaha and Chicago and the first mail since May 29 but no newspapers. The men had had a difficult four-day ride from Fetterman, traveling some of the distance by day and some by night. East of old Fort Reno they encountered a fresh trail of some fifty Indians. They hid out in rocks that day and continued their journey after dark. North of Reno on the old wagon road they accidentally started a grass fire. When these men were passing Furey's supply train and the ambulances, Nickerson provided directions to the Goose Creek camp and suggested that they complete their ride at night. They did so and arrived in the morning.[3]

Among the other news, Schuyler (who was detached from the Fifth Cavalry as an aide-de-camp to Crook) reported that eight companies of his regiment under Lieutenant Colonel Eugene A. Carr were transferring from posts in Kansas to Wyoming to join in the interdiction of Indian traffic between the Nebraska Sioux agencies and Sitting Bull's camp. As Schuyler understood matters, the regiment was traveling with supplies for six weeks and might scout the country west of the Black Hills, perhaps as far north as the area where Terry was supposedly operating. Vagueness over the operation of other field commands, whether Gibbon's, Terry's, or Carr's, is reflected in Schuyler's news and plainly apparent in contemporary sources. This was by design. Sheridan meant to flood Sioux Country with troops, in plain emulation of his successful campaign on the southern plains the year before. While the various commands generally knew of one another, no direct communication was expected. Communicating by way of division headquarters in Chicago would suffice. Crook's several telegrams to Sheridan on June 19 and 20 met this obligation. Schuyler and his companions quickly settled in and especially came to enjoy pan-fried trout three times a day. Schuyler wrote to his father that his only regret was not having been with Crook in time for the big fight. "However we shall hit them again in a week or two, as soon as the supplies come, and we expect to wind the matter up by the first of September."[4]

Yet not all was as it seemed. A day earlier Reuben Davenport, nestled in Royall's camp, had finished a long, detailed accounting of the Rosebud fight. Crook had just struck off on his hunt. Davenport had seen the worst of the battle and was not without strong opinions. His emerging views were almost certainly reflections of the attitudes and perspectives roiling at Third Cavalry campfires. His story contained three explosive paragraphs in a section subtitled "What Might Have Been" (possibly a segment title contrived by his editors and not by the writer). Davenport lamented that the prolonged exposure of the left "without assistance was the disaster of the day." He was plainly referring to Royall's involvement on Kollmar Creek and Crook's order to withdraw when the colonel was so close to winning the "palisades" and "hollow on the west," meaning the Indian-held high ground at the far head of the drainage. Royall's turnaround became a demoralizing and disastrous "retreat." Royall had borne the brunt of the fight, suffering the only fatalities and a disproportionate share of the wounded, and all of this smarted. Davenport's comments were meant to deflect the handling and consequences of this end of the battle onto Crook, not Royall or the Third Cavalry. The Third was a besmirched regiment in the wake of the Powder River affair. The attack on Crook by the newsman was but the beginning of what became an avalanche of vitriol flowing from his pen, and his Democratic-inclined newspaper, that summer.[5]

Forty-two-year-old blacksmith Heinrich Glusing, a veteran soldier in Captain Van Vliet's Company C, Third Cavalry, wrote home to his father in Germany a while later. He expressed his own views of the costs and missed opportunity of the Rosebud. "I have to excuse myself for not writing such a long time," he wrote:

> We were out with a General Crook, after a bad enemy Sitting Bull, who is more than 1,200 men strong and who kills every white man he gets. We met him at a place called Rohe Buth, on the right side of the big hills, and fought from 05:00 A.M. until 03:00 P.M. We lost nine men and had 18 men wounded. The Indian losses were big. Most of them took their dead away with the ponys. We wanted to take their village, but were too weak and didn't have canons with us. We trekked back to our camp.

The sturdy blacksmith was not the only individual in the camp who imagined the worth of artillery in this war. Finerty assured his readers that the reinforcements coming from Fetterman, chiefly infantry and cavalry, would also include mountain howitzers. Crook in fact never asked for such guns.[6]

One additional small piece of business occurred that day, unremarkable by itself but of considerable note in the decades since. Frank Grouard and Baptiste Pourier etched a stone that has forever acknowledged this place and time. Apparently the two scouts had noticed or discovered a suitable flat sandstone rock some two and a half feet across by six inches thick that was perfect for their purpose. On the stone's smooth face Grouard scratched the simple legend: "CAMP CLOUDS PEAK GOOSE CREEK CROOKS COM. JUNE 23, 1876." Along the base Grouard additionally etched their names, "GROUARD" and "B. POURRIER BAT" (the misspelling of Pourier's name suggests that it was Grouard who did the scratching). The two no doubt presumed that someday someone might notice the effort and remember the place.[7]

The expedition spent most of June 24 relocating its camp. After three days at the wagon departure camp the grazing was again all but consumed, not only by the present cavalry horses and pack mules but also by the now departed teamster animals. Perhaps the fishing was exhausted as well. A new Camp Cloud Peak was established for all but the infantry, who remained behind, on a broad plain four miles south, closer to the mountainside but still on the Little Goose at a point where it rushes from a pronounced gorge. Bourke, Finerty, and Strahorn extolled the lushness and beauty of the place, the plain carpeted with grass and flowers, and groves of shade trees fringing the emerald banks of the stream. Strahorn wrote: "If we were compelled to be banished nearly five hundred miles in any direction from Denver's enlightened sphere—about our present distance from the plains' Queen City—there would be one quick decisive choice for the scene of our isolation, and that would be Camp Cloud Peak." The simple burden of moving baggage from one camp to another, with the mules doing most of the heavy work and the few remaining wheeled vehicles hauling the rest, was more than compensated for by the astounding beauty of the Big Horn Mountains and the prospects of an unfished reach of the stream. Even the hunters were immediately satisfied. "Already a bear or two and several buffalo have been killed almost within the limits of the camp," Strahorn remembered. And all this was on the fringes of a war zone.[8]

A courier from Fort Fetterman reached the camp on Sunday morning, June 25, bearing welcome mail and the first newspapers from the East to come to the camp since the campaign started. Accounts of the Rosebud fight were then filling the nation's newspapers, but those pages would not reach

Camp Cloud Peak for many days more. Still, as Strahorn reflected on it, "many of us are somewhat surprised at the over-anxiety seeming to possess the good people East as to our safety and the safety of the commands under Gen. Terry and Col. Gibbon, seeming to imply that, if we are caught out alone, the warlike Sioux will 'gobble' us up at a mouthful." His words seem remarkably prophetic in hindsight.[9]

The only activity of note in the vast army camp on Little Goose Creek that Sunday seems to have been officers openly sparring not with any meaningful enemy and not with weapons but with words. For some "the monotony of camp, despite the beauty of the surroundings, became more intolerable than ever," Finerty observed. "Officers, who, in time of excitement, would take no notice of trifles, became irritable and exercised their authority over their subordinates in a decidedly martinetish manner. This, as a matter of course, produced friction and occasional sulking." Two episodes played out in plain view of the camp. One has no specifics but is highly suggestive. "One field officer became particularly morose, and another, criticizing him, used to say 'Major —— is the most even tempered man in this own brigade—he's always in a bad humor.'" Major Andrew Wallace Evans was remembered as a man in perpetually bad humor.[10]

The second episode has an unusually detailed contemporary paper trail. Difficulties between Royall and Noyes over the execution of various orders and instructions had apparently been brewing since the start of the campaign. The matter came to a head on the morning of the June 25, when the colonel issued orders for the cavalry battalions to exercise their horses. Noyes dutifully promulgated an order for his battalion to drill their horses *tomorrow*, as Royall had not specified a time. That evening Noyes appeared at Royall's mess and was unceremoniously dressed down for not having obeyed the order. Royall, Noyes noted, demanded that it be done *now* or he would have the captain arrested and his command taken from him. Royall's admonishment occurred, according to Noyes, with "clenched fist in the air and oath on lips," in the "presence of staff and a citizen, Mr. Davenport." Noyes put an explanation and complaint in writing to Crook. A line in his note added a compelling detail pertinent to the Rosebud story: "With experience of last campaign, started out on this determined to do exactly as ordered and as little as possible on personal responsibility." Royall subsequently refuted most of what Noyes alleged. Crook weighed in the next day and sided with Royall, writing to Noyes: "The Brigadier General commanding does not perceive the necessity of making this complaint and further believes that promptness and alacrity in obeying orders are the essentials for securing harmony and efficiency in the command."[11]

This was an explosive time. Other pressing matters were erupting in the war zone on June 25, barely seventy-five miles due north, eight days after the great Battle of the Rosebud. But in Crook's camp on Little Goose Creek officers were not fighting Indians but one another.

|||||||||||||||||||||||||||||||||||||||

For the Sioux and Cheyenne tribesmen who engaged valiantly across the Camel-Back Ridge, in the highlands and recesses of the Gap, and along the broad shoulders of Kollmar Creek, the Rosebud battle was a brawl unlike most had ever participated in or even heard of before. The demonstration that had taken place at the mouth of Prairie Dog Creek against these same soldiers was a simple statement by some of these warriors, the taunting of an enemy daring to enter the people's revered homeland. Days later that whole army had marched openly into the hunting grounds. The response at Rosebud was no mere demonstration this time but an enormous bout. The Sioux had participated in other outsized battles before—Whitestone Hill in the Coteau Prairie of Dakota in 1863 and Killdeer Mountain west of the Missouri River a year later. These clashes involved not hundreds but thousands of people on vast landscapes, where villages were invested too. But few in the Reno Creek camp knew of those episodes except by word of mouth. Although stirring, the great fights along the Bozeman Trail in 1866 also barely compared, although one of them (the Fetterman Fight) was astoundingly devastating for the soldiers involved. The Powder River fight in March 1876 was different as well, and not remotely on the same scale as Rosebud.

As the Sioux and Cheyenne warriors viewed it, they had many good reasons for quitting the fight that day. While the *wasicu* had fought valiantly, chasing the tribesmen wherever they appeared, the warriors had fought heroically too. By midafternoon many believed that they had done enough for one day. Some were taken aback by the presence of good Crow and Shoshone scouts. They were "afraid [that the] Crows and Shoshones would get at our village," remembered He Dog, the great Oglala warrior and ardent friend of Crazy Horse. Ironically, the Crows, fearing the vulnerability of their own villages at the hands of these Sioux, had an almost identical view. More importantly, by the midafternoon the people simply were hungry and their ponies worn out. It had been a strenuous fight through a long hot day. Most of the warriors had ridden from their Reno Creek camps well before sunrise and had eaten little or nothing since then. It was time to quit this fight and go home.[12]

A few lingered and scrounged about the field when they could before riding away, particularly looking for weapons and ammunition and finding some of both. More significantly, the dead were retrieved where possible. Sadly, at least thirteen bodies were left behind because they lay dangerously close to the *wašicu* camp, yet five or six others were put on the backs of ponies and carried away. The others would be gathered another day. Countless wounded were also helped away.[13]

In some minds the day was ambiguous. The Hunkpapa warrior Iron Hawk saw no finish to the fight. "We were afraid that Crook's army was too much for us so we decided it was better to go back." Kill Eagle, the Blackfeet Sioux chief who had come to Sitting Bull's camp intent only on hunting and refused to fight at the Rosebud, told an interviewer several months later that it was a common belief, at least that night as warriors returned to the Reno Creek camps, that the Sioux had been whipped. They had captured no horses and their own ponies had given out. Many had been killed and wounded. The Miniconjou warrior Standing Bear, cousin of the later famous Black Elk, likewise remembered that emotions ran high that evening. "The fighters came back in the night and everyone was excited . . . and no one slept."[14]

Four warriors lingered, Lost Leg and Howling Wolf of the Cheyennes and two others. The wolves took obscure high ground and watched the soldiers gather up their dead and carry them near the creek. The next morning the wolves watched intently as the soldiers took up their trail to the south. Only then did these Northern Indians begin to grasp the meaning of this fight on the Rosebud. This great battle had stopped these soldiers in their tracks.[15]

On the morning of June 18 twenty men returned to the Rosebud battlefield from the Reno Creek camps. One of them, Standing Bear, later provided a vivid description of the field that partly belies one critical point in the soldiers' own reflections of their closing deeds there. "The first thing we saw was a dead horse," Standing Bear remembered. "The next thing we saw was a horse with shoes on [a cavalry horse]. The next place we went was where the horses were standing when they fought. Here and there were horses all over dead and rocks were all over. Where the cavalry horse was lying there was a man lying near who was full of arrows." Standing Bear was describing the Kollmar Creek crossing, a bloodied landscape where cavalry horses were held momentarily in a northern draw. Sheer pandemonium and death had struck both men and horses there during frantic moments of remounting. In describing an unburied soldier, Standing Bear may have been referring to Private Richard Bennett, of Company L, Third Cavalry. Several soldier accounts suggested that one horribly mutilated man was not taken off the field.[16]

Standing Bear's narrative turned even more gruesome. "We got to where General Crook camped and there was a place where the dirt was fresh and they had built a fire up there and this is where they buried the dead. We all got down on our hands and knees and dug into the ground. . . . The first thing we saw was a blanket. The blanket was wrapped around a soldier and it was tied around his legs and waist and neck. We got ahold of him and pulled him out." One by one, Standing Bear and his comrades pulled dead men from the grave and took their blankets. Then "one of the men scalped a white man and started home with it on a stick." The fate of the unearthed dead soldiers on the Rosebud battlefield is unclear, although one army account suggests that these remains were reburied when Crook passed near this ground again in August.[17]

After plundering the soldier graves, the warriors rode to the top of the southern ridge, where soldiers during the battle had fired upon Cheyennes as they attempted to run off with the Shoshone horses. The warriors could see the soldiers in the distance, retreating to the south. "There was dust flying and of course we did not want to go there, as it was just a small bunch of us. We went home." No one expected any more fighting from those *wasicu*.[18]

<hr />

In the camp circles on Reno Creek any jubilation emanating from the day-long fight was tempered by family grief for the deceased and the needs of the wounded, some of whom were clinging to life. Accounting for Indian casualties in the Rosebud battle is perplexing, and most of the summary reflections miss their marks widely. In Two Moon's many recollections of the fight, for instance, he variously stated that three Sioux and one Cheyenne were killed and later asserted that three Cheyennes were killed, including Black Sun and Scabby. The wife of the Hunkpapa warrior Spotted Horn Bull recollected that seven Sioux were killed that day. Kill Eagle asserted that four warriors were killed and left on the field, where they were mutilated by the Crows, and that twelve more died in the camps. "It was impossible to say how many were wounded," he added, but he noted that 180 Indian horses were killed. "They numbered them at the Statesman's lodge after the battle." Wooden Leg's recollection was a similar generalization: "One Burned Thigh Sioux was killed during the battle, and one Minneconjoux died after arrival at the camps. I do not know how many other Sioux were killed, but some Cheyennes said there were twenty or more. I think the Uncpapas lost the most warriors." Soldiers in Crook's camp, of course, repeated a refrain that thirteen Indian dead had been left on the field and other fatalities were seen being carried away.[19]

In spring 1877, during the avalanche of surrenders at the Nebraska agencies, Indian informants offered a number of Rosebud-specific casualty assessments (Little Big Horn was of common interest then too). Second Lieutenant William P. Clark at Red Cloud Agency, Crook's intercessor during the proceedings, learned that eight Indians were killed in the Rosebud fight, including two Cheyennes, two Hunkpapas, one Sans Arc, one Miniconjou, and two Oglalas. A newsman at nearby Camp Robinson was told that thirty-six Indians were killed at the Rosebud and another sixty-three wounded. Captain George Randall at Spotted Tail Agency, chief of scouts on the Big Horn and Yellowstone Expedition and a key figure in the battle, was told that the Indians lost 118 or 120 killed and wounded at the Rosebud: "fourteen were killed outright, on the field, eight died of their wounds that night and four died next morning; and there were besides these eighty-six wounded badly."[20]

A few enticing particulars surface in Indian accounts. White Bull asserted that four Sioux were killed, naming Little Crow, Black Bird, Sitting Bear, and Little Wolf, and one Cheyenne, Scabby, known to the Sioux as Alligator. Scabby, remembered by Two Moon for his valor in the fighting at the Kollmar Crossing, was wounded there and carried off to the south, not north. He died several days later in a small Cheyenne camp on the Tongue River. Black Sun, also mentioned by Two Moon, sustained a gunshot wound in the spine. He was carried back to Reno Creek on a travois and died that night in his home lodge. He was dressed in his best clothing, swaddled in blankets and robes, and buried in the rimrocks overlooking the place. The Cheyennes preferred burying their dead in the ubiquitous rimrocks of the Powder, Tongue, and Rosebud countryside. Many Sioux and Cheyenne men remembered the death of the young Sioux boy, perhaps a Sans Arc named Without a Tepee, early in the fighting along Kollmar Creek. The story was made doubly remarkable when his grieving brother, Long Road, made a suicide vow and was killed at the Little Big Horn eight days later.[21]

Stories of painful wounds also abound. Thunder Hawk, wounded in the left hip, was carried to Reno Creek and joined the others in the movement to the Greasy Grass. He witnessed but took no role in the coming fight there.

Horse Runs Ahead was wounded in the heel at Rosebud and likewise witnessed but did not take part in the coming battle. Rattling Hawk was shot through the hips at the Rosebud. For a while it appeared as though he would not recover. Four days later, however, after the massive camp had moved from Reno Creek to the Little Big Horn, he underwent a bear medicine ceremony and in due course fully recovered.[22]

On June 18 the encampment moved down Reno Creek. Slightly above its mouth the people turned south. They came to a massive bench on the east side of the Little Big Horn and established a new camp. As always, the Northern Cheyennes led the way and occupied the ground farthest to the south, with the trailing Hunkpapas spreading onto the ground northernmost at this new place. A death pall clung to the Reno Forks campsite behind them. Besides, the grass was mostly consumed. Traces other than clipped grass, tipi circles, and fire rings also scored the place now abandoned. In the midst of the old Sans Arc circle located directly opposite the mouth of the South Fork of Reno Creek, a tipi was left standing. Inside lay the body of Old She Bear, a Sans Arc warrior shot through the hips and bowels. Slightly downstream in the remnants of the Oglala circle were three more tipis, each shrouding one or more deceased and generally nameless Sioux. Young Two Moon recalled the identity of one, a warrior named Plenty Bears, shot in the guts.[23]

The encampment remained at this new place along the Little Big Horn for six nights, through June 23. Grass, water, and firewood were abundant, as were buffalo, always a lure for the hunters and in high demand in so large a camp. There news was received from the wolves trailing the *ve'ho'e* that the Rosebud soldiers had ridden away, far to the south. They were in a "bad fix," Tall Bull recalled. As word of the soldier retreat reached the tribal circles, the lingering woefulness of the previous night quickly dissipated. "Our runners had discovered that Crook had retraced his trail to Goose Creek, and we did not suppose that the white men would care to follow us further into the rough country," Rain in the Face later recounted. At Rosebud, "the Great Spirit was with us," remembered Cheyenne warrior Weasel Bear. "We whipped the white soldiers and drove them back south." Turning the soldiers back, driving them south, became a joyous refrain that spread widely in the circles. This was cause for a great celebration. Singing, dancing, and feasting commenced and continued for four nights.[24]

Some warriors in the camps considered charging off and fighting those soldiers in the south again, but that never occurred. The enemy was now a long distance away and no longer presented an imminent threat. The villagers were also aware of other soldiers to the north on the Elk River, but they likewise posed no particular threat. Besides, "if there were any, they now would be afraid to come," remembered Wooden Leg. For the first time, the Northern people in the six circles fully grasped the enormity of their accomplishment at the Rosebud. It was a decisive victory. The Indians basked in the heroic display of the People's powerful unity. The most conspicuous threat had been met and repulsed. "We knew we had defeated him because he turned back," He Dog remembered of the enemy leader. Neither he nor anyone else in the great Sitting Bull village then knew his name.[25]

In the Hunkpapa camp Sitting Bull and his immediate family and counselors pondered the nature of this victory over the *wašicu* and whether it was fulfillment of his extraordinary vision three weeks earlier during the great Sun Dance on middle Rosebud Creek. In his dream he saw soldiers and horses, numerous as grasshoppers, bearing down on an Indian village, upside down, hats falling off. After much deliberation and introspection Sitting Bull concluded that the Rosebud fight was not what he had foreseen in his vision. An even greater victory was coming.[26]

Yet another reason for celebration made the camp joyous in these days following the Rosebud battle. At last the agency people began arriving in significant numbers. The first to appear were a puzzling band of five Arapaho men from Red Cloud Agency, including Waterman, Yellow Eagle, Yellow Fly, Well Knowing One, and Left Hand. They were greeted skeptically, and many Sioux and some Cheyennes viewed them as scouts for the white soldiers. The Sioux at first confiscated their guns and horses and made them prisoners. But Two Moon interceded: "These Sage People are all right. They have come here to help us fight the soldiers." The men were set free. "The Cheyennes and the Arapahoes have always been brothers," Waterman remembered. The Arapahos fought steadfastly alongside the Cheyennes in the days to come.[27]

In the coming days the camp swelled in size. The marvel of summer roamers was a well-known and anticipated phenomenon among the Northern Indians. For the most part, since the time of the Fort Laramie Treaty in 1868, the summer people were otherwise near year-round agency residents. These Sioux and Northern Cheyennes generally accepted agency life but were also beholden to buffalo hunting and tribal gatherings at Sun Dance time. The normal prompt for these migrations was the emergence of spring grasses, but that growth was late in coming this year. It had been a hard winter. This year was different in other ways as well. Sitting Bull's call to arms and the Powder River battle had imparted a heightened sense of urgency and anger in

Sioux Country. All Lakota people were called to rally with their northern kin in the cause of tribal sovereignty.

Notable newcomers included Gall, leading some sixty lodges of Hunkpapas, and Crow King, with eighty warriors in another fifty-four lodges of Hunkpapas. These two highly visible chiefs from the Standing Rock Agency on the Missouri River traveled together. Near the end of their journey they followed Sitting Bull's deeply scored lodgepole trail up Rosebud Creek and across the Davis Creek-Reno Creek divide. "Our trail during all of our movements throughout that summer could have been followed by a blind person," Wooden Leg remembered. Unknown to Gall and Crow King, they traveled barely ahead of an entirely different army column that was following that same distinct path, wide-eyed and deeply impressed with the trail's width and freshness.[28]

Hollow Horn Bear, a Brulé Sioux traveling with twenty Two Kettle warriors, also reached Sitting Bull's camp during this pause. They had been chasing horses south of the Yellowstone River and observed soldiers heading west. They shadowed these *wašicu* for several days and then determined to join Sitting Bull.[29]

Foolish Elk and a band of Oglalas also arrived. His pathway west is puzzling. He claimed to have been in the Rosebud fight, saying that he and his band had arrived on that field just in time for the battle and had come by an entirely different route. From the east-west reach of the Rosebud, Foolish Elk apparently then exited westward to the Little Big Horn Valley. Their journey to Sitting Bull's camp took them down the Little Big Horn, arriving at the great encampment on or about June 24.[30]

This third week of June, in the Sioux Moon of Good Berries, was strikingly different from previous years. Conditions were almost idyllic and certainly memorable. "We did not know of any other soldiers hunting for us," recalled Wooden Leg. "There were feasts and dances in all of the camps. On the benchlands just east of us our horses found plenty of rich grass. Among the hills west of the river were great herds of buffalo. Every day, big hunting parties went among them. Men and women were at work providing for their families." The immensity of the camp was striking. "There were more Indians in those six camps than I ever saw together anywhere else," remembered Kate Big Head.[31]

The Cheyennes were familiar with this country, having camped along the Little Big Horn River each summer in many previous years. They continued to serve as able guides and hosts for the people in the other circles. Everyone was busy in an almost ageless way: men hunting buffalo; women gathering wild fruits, digging roots for food, drying meats, and tanning robes; and boys tending ponies and fishing. Families bathed in the river. Men talked and smoked. Councils were held. Each tribe tended to its own internal affairs, but chiefs from each of the circles also met as equals. This was the normal business of summer. The year could as well have been 1830 or 1850. The moment was a pure reflection of the simple, timeless age in the buffalo country among the people of the northern plains, before the days of interference from whites. But, like a pricked bubble, that moment quickly vanished forever. Forever.[32]

Wooden Leg recalled that the plan was to continue traveling up the Little Big Horn Valley chasing buffalo, even if doing so threatened to take them near the soldier camp somewhere south of the Tongue. But game scouts reported great herds of antelope behind them, in the uplands west of the Big Horn River. The chiefs decided that the village had enough buffalo and would turn around and move north to the mouth of the Little Big Horn. West of that confluence with the Big Horn where the antelope herds grazed was Crow Country, but the chiefs believed that they had sufficient men in the combined Sioux and Cheyenne circles for defense and thus had no reason to fear those old enemies. On June 24 they set out, with the Cheyennes again leading and passing the other circles as they traveled northward. Very quickly the Cheyennes crossed the Little Big Horn above the mouth of Reno Creek and soon came onto another vast open plain that extended for miles on the west side of the river. The journey that day was short. The Cheyennes stopped some six or seven miles from their start at a point opposite a broad arroyo on the east side of the Little Big Horn—what would become known famously as Medicine Tail Coulee. The other five bands pulled up behind them in the conventional order. The Hunkpapa camp defined the southern end of the new village, about two miles below the mouth of Reno Creek.[33]

For all the joy and ease in these days since the Battle of the Rosebud, there were signs that all was not well. Sitting Bull's belief that Rosebud was not the battle of his fantastic dream was cautionary. So was another dream. In the Cheyenne circle the elderly council chief and holy man Box Elder also had a dream. Three months earlier he had been among the elders in the Powder River camp that the soldiers had attacked. The eighty-one-year-old sage, fully blind, was the keeper of Ox'zem, a Cheyenne sacred wheel lance possessing great mystical power. In the hours after the Powder River fight Box Elder invoked the wheel lance's concealing power to protect the movements of Cheyenne wolves who trailed the Powder River soldiers, intent on recapturing the ponies taken from their village. The day after the battle the wolves succeeded in their quest and brought back five hundred animals, to the utter delight of the tribesmen and sheer consternation of the *ve'ho'e*. When Box Elder awakened from his dream on the Little Big Horn, he sent a crier through the camps, cautioning the people to keep their ponies tied up beside their lodges, a traditional means of readiness. "In my dream I saw soldiers coming," he warned. Warriors tied their best horses close to their tipis. "They recalled that, in the past, Box Elder's prophesies had always come true."[34]

The morrow was Sunday, June 25, 1876, a day of valor and infamy on the northern plains.

CONSEQUENCES

The importance of the Battle of the Rosebud became plainly apparent to history eight days later when George Armstrong Custer, commanding all twelve companies of the Seventh Cavalry, struck Sitting Bull's village on the Little Big Horn. Custer and five full companies of his regiment, 210 officers, enlisted men, and civilians, plus another 51 soldiers and civilians who accompanied Marcus A. Reno and Frederick W. Benteen, perished there. Sitting Bull's colossal village had indeed grown, both physically, with the influx of anticipated summer roamers, and emotionally, after having met and repulsed the great army column operating from the south. Crook, still blithely fishing and hunting in the Big Horns while awaiting reinforcements and resupply, learned of this catastrophe on July 10, when a courier from Fort Fetterman arrived on Goose Creek. Royall, commanding Camp Cloud Peak in the general's absence, hurriedly dispatched Captain Mills and his entire company to find Crook and deliver the devastating news. They located him eighteen miles away, descending from the mountains with pack mules loaded heavy with elk, deer, and bighorn sheep. Mills recalled Crook's look of mortification, "a feeling that the country would realize that there were others who had underrated the valor and numbers of the Sioux."[1]

Attitudes in Crook's camp instantly turned against the general. Many were already critical of his leadership on the Rosebud battlefield, but before July 10 the focus seemed limited to the costs and conduct of that fight alone, reflected in the casualties, the reputations of participating officers and regiments, and the unseemliness of fishing now instead of fighting. Anyone with a voice debated notions of victory or defeat at Rosebud. Crook indeed repulsed his attackers and held the field, which smacked of a victory. He and many viewed the action that way. Moreover, withdrawing to Goose Creek to tend his wounded and reinforce and resupply was generally respected as a logical move, at least initially, but the decision was wearing thin as the summer wore on. The Custer disaster changed everything and served to bolster the case that Crook could and should have done more, something, anything offensively that might have averted the great disaster on the Little Big Horn.

But what might that action have been? We can imagine many alternatives.

On the afternoon of the battle on June 17, at the mouth of the Rosebud Narrows, Crook implored his Crow and Shoshone scouts to lead his column through the cañon and charge the Indian village that surely lay at the other end of that defile. All evidence to that moment reinforced this simple belief. The Crows had first told Crook of their enemy's whereabouts when they arrived in his camp on Goose Creek on June 15. Sitting Bull was on Rosebud Creek, they said with absolute confidence, and on that day he was. Importantly, too, all day long the battle had played out by way of the Rosebud Narrows. When Sioux warriors fell upon Crow and Shoshone scouts and chased them from the cañon southward and westward over the heights, through the Gap, and across the foreground between the east-west reach of the stream and the Camel-Back Ridge, they reinforced the notion of a village lying somewhere down the Rosebud. This belief was reinforced yet again when Mills and Noyes traveled most of the way through the Narrows on Crook's order to find and attack the village at the other end of the cañon. Nearly all in the column were awed and even dumbstruck by the buffalo tracks scoring the dry, soft earth, tracks quickly discerned as Indian pony tracks instead. The attackers had come *up the Rosebud* from a village that simply had to be located *down the Rosebud*.

But Crook's scouts refused to go with him, partly fearing the peril of the Narrows. They offered excuses, noting that the Narrows amounted to a massive trap. It was immaterial that Mills and Noyes had just traveled that same ground barely an hour before and sensed no trap at all. The auxiliaries were adamant. A year later Crazy Horse played into this thinking. In an interview at Red Cloud Agency shortly after his surrender, he told Frank Grouard, who in turn told Robert Strahorn, that he in fact had two thousand warriors posted behind the crags of the cañon and would have swooped down on Crook had he dared to enter. "Another terrible massacre would have been the inevitable result," Strahorn penned. Horned Horse told reporter Charles Deihl much the same thing at Camp Robinson on May 24, 1877, again during the time of the surrenders. Horned Horse had come in with Crazy Horse and told Deihl that the chief purposefully retreated with the idea that the troops would follow and "then fall into their stronghold." The peril of the Narrows is a notion that dogs the Rosebud story to this day.[2]

Nothing of the sort happened, of course. Crazy Horse did not command two thousand warriors at the close of the battle or at any time, and no stronghold or trap existed in the cañon. He and some dozens of followers may have lingered on the heights of the Narrows to see whether Crook actually ventured that way and perhaps would have renewed a fight of sorts. But Crook remained strong and capable, his cavalry bruised but cohesive and ably led. Sioux and Cheyenne warriors had been strong that day too, but by midafternoon they were hungry, tired, and making their way to their camps on Reno Creek.

That evening Crook again implored his scouts to join him in an advance down the Rosebud under the cover of darkness for an attack on the village at daybreak the next morning. Again they demurred and stood by their reasoning. But suppose that the Crows and Shoshones had agreed to an advance down the stream, whether on the afternoon of June 17 or in the wee hours of June 18. Almost certainly Crook would have reengaged his enemy. On the afternoon of June 17 Crazy Horse would have responded, based on the evidence gathered after his surrender. It might have been a small fight that could well have escalated into a major battle had other warriors rallied to the chief's side. In the midafternoon the entire Sioux and Cheyenne fighting force was within meaningful recall. A second battle of the Rosebud might have played out that afternoon. In the cañon Crook's troops would have been at a distinct disadvantage in an escalating fight simply because the Indians would have spilled from the prevailing high ground. How long such a renewed fight might have ensued is pure conjecture, as is the outcome. It was the high ground that gave dominance to the position, not crags, fallen trees, or any other vestige of a so-called trap. But, again, nothing of the sort happened. Crook did not advance down the Rosebud Narrows on the afternoon of June 17.

What if Crook had pursued his opponents on June 18? Until his scouts refused again to join him, Crook was fully prepared to reapportion his existing ammunition, which remained plentiful column-wide, park his wounded on the east-west reach, likely in the care of Tom Moore's packers and perhaps an infantry company or two, and advance down the Rosebud. The Indian allies were crucial, both as trailers and as a fighting force, but the trail itself was obvious. Certainly such a movement would have been observed. We know that a handful of warriors remained on the field through the evening of June 17 to keep an eye on Crook. But while any movement on Crook's part in the wee hours of the next morning would have been seen, the general would have had all the advantage. Aside from those few warriors stalking him, the considerable force that had challenged him so heroically on June 17 had returned to Reno Creek. It would have been hours before they could have seriously opposed a movement by Crook, which they simply would not have known of. Crook's Crows and Shoshones would have followed the enormous pony trail down the Rosebud to where it diverted northwestward, out of the valley and straight to the Forks of Reno Creek. At that moment Crook and his scouts would have quickly grasped that Sitting Bull's village was not on Rosebud Creek at all but across the divide to the west. The point would have been wholly immaterial. Crook, the aggressor, would have followed that trail to the village and probably would have reached and attacked it at dawn, the classic moment in which attacks on Indian villages optimally occurred.

If Crook had attacked Sitting Bull's camp on the morning of June 18, his force would have been every bit equal in numbers to the warriors occupying that sprawling camp. In a dawn attack, which was more or less a surprise assault (even if the four warriors dogging him had somehow preceded him to the village and sounded the alarm), the advantage would not have fallen to the tribesmen but to General Crook. He would have been attacking a village filled with women, children, and the elderly. Mass chaos would have ensued. Crook himself certainly would have taken high ground, just as he did on the Camel-Back Ridge, and commanded another great battle, throwing all his troops into the fight cohesively. He would have been fiercely resisted, but in due course the warriors' allegiances, particularly in the confusion of the initial attack, would have been torn between aggressively countering the blow and defending the defenseless. The advantage in such circumstances always accrued to the army. Victory for Crook was not inevitable, but it may have been probable. The camp sprawled for miles, but this village was not yet as large as the Little Big Horn camp. Its defense would have been vigorous, the fighting bloody and devastating. Yet history suggests that Plains Indians never won village battles but instead fought and fled. Whetstone Hill, Killdeer Mountain, Sand Creek, Washita, even Powder River affirmed that point, which was doctrine in the army. But it is moot. Crook did not advance down the Rosebud in the dawning hours of June 18.

An aggressive movement on Crook's part on June 17 or 18 would have had one other and perhaps even greater effect on the larger story of the Great Sioux War. This was a village basking in the glow of the great Northern Indian Ascendancy, Sioux and Cheyenne people rallying to the cause of tribal sovereignty and sacred rights. They were strong, empowered by Sitting Bull's Sun Dance vision, and were growing stronger by the day, even as they were equally vulnerable. Sitting Bull's village overflowed with foodstuffs, day-to-day wares, cultural finery, and people, with five times as many noncombatants as warriors. Sitting Bull's warriors had taken the fight to Crook at Rosebud and Prairie Dog Creek. Here Crook would have been taking the fight straight to Sitting Bull. Win, lose, or draw, the disruption would have been catastrophic. In some likelihood, the village could not have remained cohesive. Conventional wisdom and simple facts suggest that villagers under such duress would scatter. Perhaps they would have regrouped, but perhaps not. Perhaps the Great Ascendancy might have regenerated, but perhaps not. The summer people might have continued their outward course into the buffalo country, but perhaps not, especially after another aggressive army attack on a Northern Indian village—and this time no less than Sitting Bull's village. But this disruption to the Ascendancy never occurred. Crook did not advance down the Rosebud Narrows.

Allow Crook his withdrawal to Goose Creek to tend his wounded and resupply and accept the abandonment of the Crows and Shoshones. The retrograde was completed on the afternoon of June 19. On June 20 attention turned to preparing for the retirement of the wagons and ambulances to Fort Fetterman on June 21. Certainly time was sufficient on the June 19, 20, and 21 to reequip the expedition's men with full issues of ammunition and rations. Thus Crook could have renewed the campaign immediately. While some stores still required caching on Goose Creek, Crook's vaunted mule train could easily have been reconstituted to carry essential reserves of munitions, food, and grain. Two infantry companies could have been allotted to the wagon train, and maybe one more detailed to protect the stores on Goose Creek, joining a greatly downsized cadre of lingering teamsters, packers, and miners. Crook still would have had all fifteen companies of his cavalry and two or maybe three companies of infantry. He could have renewed his offensive movement with more than 950 men, this time well supported by Moore's pack train after the departure of the wagons on June 21 or in the customary wee hours of the following day.

Crook's trail north would have been simple. Even without Indian scouts, he knew the way to the east-west reach and the Rosebud Narrows, which he could have reached on the afternoon of June 23. He could have made his way partly through the Narrows on June 23 or on the following morning and turned northwest toward the Forks of Reno Creek, following a still-obvious pony trail. He might have crossed paths with other bodies of Indians, summer roamers perhaps. Fighting might have erupted. Then again, he might have discovered Custer's Arikara and Crow scouts or been discovered by them. On June 24 they were ranging far ahead of that column as it wended its way up Rosebud Creek while Crook was perchance ranging down that same watercourse. The notion of Crook and Custer operating in concert against an enemy whose trail, whether scored by travois tracks or pony tracks, "could have been followed by a blind person," as Wooden Leg recalled, becomes yet another intriguing what-if of the Rosebud story. Even the cagey Hunkpapa warrior Rain in the Face appreciated the threat of a Crook-Custer alliance, telling an interviewer in 1905 that Crook might well have "pushed on and connected with the Long-Haired Chief. That would have saved Custer and perhaps won the day." Henry Noyes saw it this way as well, embracing the merits of supporting General Terry, who was commanding the Dakota column at this early stage of the war. But "we returned to our base on Goose Creek, and a week later heard of the massacre of Gen. Custer's party." The simple fact is that Crook did not renew his campaign after securing his wounded. He never rendezvoused with Custer. They never jointly swooped down on Sitting Bull's village. General Crook might have changed history. Instead he went fishing.[3]

ıııııııııııııııııııııııııııııııı

Contemporaries of Crook and chroniclers chasing this story ever since have struggled to understand and explain why this otherwise innovative and accomplished Indian fighter, who until that unsettling moment was one of the army's finest field generals, stopped dead in his tracks in the third week of June 1876. He made much, as did others, of the overwhelming, even daunting odds that he confronted. But Crook had faced numerically superior forces before in the Civil War, and he was no stranger to being outmanned on a battlefield. His experiences in the Far West and in Arizona, sequences of small-unit operations invariably pitting disciplined, well-armed troops against scattered but determined bodies of Indians, were challenges of another sort. Yet they too prepared him for this new circumstance, aside perhaps from the dimension of numerical odds. Indian fighting was intense to be sure, but Crook embraced it wholly and successfully. He always used to complete advantage his own sheer determination of will, capacity for self-privation, mobility, and innovative tactics to grow his confidence and reputation and achieve success. Crook had been a perpetual aggressor until then, and his enemies withered.

But Crook had never faced Plains Indians before. In Montana his enemy came to him, defiantly, haughtily, and in forceful numbers. The Sioux and Northern Cheyennes were unafraid of his disciplined soldiers and their needle guns and matched him warrior for warrior. Crook fought his enemy at Rosebud well, but it was a perplexing battle. He never controlled the field and came close to losing the fight altogether if it had not been for Royall's steadfastness at Kollmar Creek. When Crook's scouts abandoned him, they not only took away his eyes and ears in a foreign land but seemingly sapped his own aggressive tendencies. Those factors—a forceful enemy with strength in numbers, a tactically bewildering battlefield, and seemingly essential allies faithful only up to a point—were massive blows to Crook's psyche. This was no mirror of any previous experience in Indian warfare.

Matters only worsened when key subordinates and the newsmen around him inflated the numerical superiority of the enemy beyond all reason. In Crook's initial report to Sheridan on June 19 he hesitated to estimate the strength of his opponent but allowed that "they anticipated that they were strong enough to thoroughly defeat the command." He said even less on the matter in his June 20 report, but by then everyone else in the command had plenty to say, bloating the storm of warriors into the thousands. A most telling reflection of the impact of this thinking comes in a remark captured by John Finerty. Crook received a dispatch from Sheridan on or around July 10 reflecting on the Rosebud fight. This was the same day when Crook learned of Custer's demise. Sheridan told his masterful general: "Hit them again, and hit them harder!" Crook smiled grimly, Finerty recalled, and quietly remarked, "I wish Sheridan would come out here himself and show us how to do it. It is rather difficult to surround three Indians with one soldier!" By then Crook was an emotionally crippled Indian fighter, done in at the Rosebud. Custer's demise was a sad direct consequence, and inwardly Crook knew it. His actions tell us so.[4]

|||||||||||||||||||||||||||||||||

Criticism of all sort cut Crook to the quick, especially any that had army fingerprints on it. A blistering story appeared in the *Helena Daily Independent* on June 30, 1876, datelined Fort Laramie, June 25. Under the headline "CROOK DEFEATED!" the near page-length column told of the Rosebud fight in close detail, with specifics of the sort that could only have been gleaned from someone who was there. The story recounted the surprise of the attack, the many soldier rallies, the stellar fighting of the Crows and Shoshones, and small details, such as cavalry horses falling into Indian hands and Royall's horse shot from beneath him. The source of the account was carefully hidden, beyond noting that it was someone who had "just reached the Fort from

Fetterman" bearing the news. But Crook and his cronies could unmask the storyteller in a moment. This was an officer-to-officer conversation at Fort Laramie and could only have involved First Lieutenant Thaddeus Capron of Captain Samuel Munson's Company C, Ninth Infantry. Capron was among the small infantry escort accompanying Furey's wagons and the wounded from Goose Creek to Fort Fetterman, where he secured permission to continue on to Fort Laramie to visit his wife. When he departed from Laramie earlier that summer, he left behind a sickly child, and the boy had died during his absence.[5]

A deceased child and a grieving wife were reasons enough for a hurried side trip and Capron's view was pardonable if somehow out of line. But what happened next was indeed out of line and certainly beyond the pale for a junior officer necessarily surviving within the rigid structure of the Regular Army. That story in the Helena newspaper went on to castigate Crook for the "retreat" to his supply train, an action viewed by the officers at Fort Laramie with "unmeasured condemnation." Those officers furthermore "denounce[d] his retreat in the face of the savage enemy as *cowardly*" and thought the battle story "humiliating and disgraceful to the last degree."[6]

It is unclear how this story from Fort Laramie, Wyoming, first appeared in a Helena, Montana, newspaper. But it was bristling stuff and was quickly picked up by newspapers as far away as Chicago and New York. It also became an utter embarrassment for the officers at Fort Laramie, who quickly labeled it a gross and libelous falsehood and demanded an immediate retraction. Their response was covered in a long letter and resolution signed by Major Edwin F. Townsend, commanding officer at Fort Laramie, who attempted to set the record straight. "It is not the custom of officers of the army generally, or of ourselves in particular, to be guilty of such unsoldierly conduct as to criticize the action of the general commanding in any such grossly unmilitary manner, especially upon receipt of the first meagre reports of the action." Townsend's letter was sent to the Associated Press and to the *Army and Navy Journal* for publication, but the calumny died slowly. Any consequence to Capron is unknown. He was perfectly silent about the matter in his diary. In due course he returned to the campaign. The thin-skinned Crook had to be seething.[7]

As the years wore on, other carpers also weighed in, sometimes insightfully (unlike the Capron brouhaha) if still rather critically. An unnamed officer with Crook at the Rosebud wrote the *New York Herald* on the second anniversary of the battle, offering pithy commentary that again cut Crook short:

I shall always believe that all subsequent troubles with the Sioux—the Custer massacre and all—can be traced to one or two pivotal points: Leaving our pack trains on Goose Creek and making it impossible or inadvisable to follow up such a little fracas as that of the Rosebud; or our failure to seek the enemy again immediately after our return to Goose Creek, on the 19th. In either event we would have met Custer's army. The two commands would have united. The whole Sioux Nation was there and keen for a fight. There would have been one great battle and our troubles with the Sioux would have been forever ended.[8]

Anson Mills, in long hindsight, was much more charitable. Speaking to the Order of Indian Wars audience in 1917, he reflected on Crook's mortification when learning of the Custer fight: "While Gen. Crook was a cold, gray-eyed and somewhat cold-blooded warrior, treating his men perhaps too practically in war time, there yet ran through us a feeling of profound sympathy for his great misfortune, while at the same time we had a still more profound sympathy for the other gallant, more sympathetic Custer—at least, most of us." The stories of Crook and Custer on the plains and at Rosebud and Little Big Horn were already intertwined and have remained so forever.[9]

In the months after Rosebud Crook opened up as well. Several times he offered personal reflections both on that momentous battle and on that extended campaign season. At the conclusion of that tormented summer Crook sat with Robert Strahorn for a long interview at Red Cloud Agency. Strahorn probed widely into all matters related to the Sioux war, which at that moment was far from concluded. Crook, the steadfastly reticent man, had plenty to say. Instead of finding an expected thousand or fifteen hundred warriors at the Rosebud, for instance, he believed that he confronted "five or six times that number of well-armed and thoroughly agency-equipped Indians." Notwithstanding that numerical disparity, his command "thrashed these Indians on a field of their own choosing, and completely routed them from it." Those outsized numbers had by now become engrained. What ultimately mattered was that he held the field, he believed. When his troops were reinforced by additional infantry and cavalry later in the summer, he finally felt able to beat any force of Indians: "their villages disintegrated and scattered in every direction."[10]

Crook regretted the lack of support from the agents and chiefs at Red Cloud Agency in May when he sought to recruit friendly Indians for the campaign. And he bristled when Strahorn asked about Davenport and the charges leveled in his newspaper. It claimed that at the end of the campaign, when the troops were confined to one blanket per man and living on horse meat, "you had extra blankets from the hospital, and were messing with the packers, living much better than the rest of the command." Crook rejected it all. "Every officer and man in the command knows the statements to be untrue," he said. He had no extra blankets. Furthermore, "the fare allotted to the soldiers was all that I had myself, or allowed my staff officers to have." Crook got along well with his newsmen, except perhaps Davenport, who turned on the general soon after the Rosebud fight. That soured relations between the two and others in the command for decades to come.[11]

In his obligatory annual department report to General Sheridan, dated September 25, 1876, and destined for transmittal to the secretary of war for his own annual report, Crook made several key points about the Rosebud aimed at cementing his views of the battle and its consequences forevermore.

At the fight on the Rosebud, June 17, the number of our troops was less than one thousand, and within eight days after that the same Indians we there fought met and defeated a column of troops of nearly the same size as ours, killing and wounding over three hundred, including the gallant commander, General Custer himself.

I invite attention to the fact that in this engagement my troops beat these Indians on a field of their own choosing, and drove them in utter route from it, as far as the proper care of my wounded and prudence would justify. Subsequent events proved beyond dispute what would have been the fate of the command had the pursuit been continued beyond what judgment dictated.[12]

The problem with Crook's rationalizations was that by that time others, not the least Philip Sheridan, knew too much of the story.

〰〰〰〰〰〰〰〰〰〰〰

Guy Henry's return to Fort Fetterman was a painful ordeal involving seven days of wagon travel over a hot, dusty road. "My only food on this journey," he remembered, "was broth made from such small birds as could be shot, fed to me by a spoon. I was kept up by occasional teaspoonfuls of brandy, and at night was able to obtain sleep only by the aid of chloral" (chloral hydrate, a sleep-inducing sedative). The North Platte ferry cable at Fetterman had broken owing to high water, but Henry and the wounded (one and two at a time) were delicately ushered across in a small skiff and carried up the bluff to the post hospital. It was a veritable paradise for the captain and the others, with clean beds, clean clothes, bathing, dressing of wounds, and beef tea and proper food. The nineteen wounded soldiers overwhelmed the facility, but additional matrons and attendants were secured on extra duty from the garrison. In addition, resident physician Captain Joseph R. Gibson received assistance from contract surgeon Valentine McGillycuddy, who was biding his time awaiting Furey's turnaround to Crook, and Doctor Patzki, also there with Furey. Together they made the most of the challenge until the afflicted soldiers could be moved to their posts of origin. McGillycuddy coolly tallied the burden: "19 wounded. 5 legs, rest arms, heads & bodies."[13]

An unnamed officer of the Fourteenth Infantry from Camp Douglas, Utah, pausing at Fetterman en route to Goose Creek, sent a letter home that captured a sense of the place and also Henry's fragile condition. "Everything here looks like war," he wrote. "A good share of the wounded in the last fight are here. An officer has one of the ugliest wounds. He was hit above the right cheek bone, and the ball came out under the left eye. He will probably recover." The officer had the bullet's trajectory wrong, but his description was grim enough.[14]

After a week in Doctor Gibson's care, Henry was transferred by ambulance to Medicine Bow, on the Union Pacific. He continued by rail to Fort D. A. Russell at Cheyenne, his home, which he reached on July 5. Even rail travel was brutal. As the train passed the small, windswept rail town of Sherman in the Laramie Mountains, the highest point on the Union Pacific line and about halfway between Laramie and Cheyenne, "the rarefied air and the cumulative action of the chloral" that he still required caused Henry to black out for a frightfully long segment of the journey. His wife awaited him in Cheyenne. Several times she had attempted to travel to Fort Fetterman to be at her husband's side but was repeatedly forbidden to do so. By one account Henry's attending surgeon, Major John F. Randolph, allowed his bandages to be lifted so that he could glimpse his wife. His face was so traumatizing that she left the room. The story could well be apocryphal. Many small details in Henry's story read that way. For two months Henry's wound was probed and dressed daily. He eventually gained sufficient strength and nearly full use of one eye. He was granted a year's leave and went to California, where, "in that balmy climate, with plenty of red wine, which makes blood, I became myself again."[15]

Guy Henry returned to duty a year later. His eyesight was partially restored, but his battle wound, two "ugly looking bullet marks, one on each side of the head," oozed for the rest of his life. Promoted to major, Ninth

Cavalry, in 1881, Henry commanded posts across the West in the next several decades, including Fort McKinney in the lee of the Big Horn Mountains, scene of so much action in 1876. He served as inspector of rifle practice for the Department of the Platte in the mid-1880s and had a role in the Ghost Dance turmoil of 1890–91, although he was not at Wounded Knee. In 1887 Henry lectured to an audience in Omaha about his experiences in the Department of the Platte and was pressed, the report says, to tell of Rosebud. Such lectures may have sharpened his focus. In July 1895 *Harper's Weekly* published his story, "Wounded in an Indian Fight," a gripping recounting less of Rosebud than of being shot in the face and the travails of recovery. Henry retired a brigadier general and was ever after known as "Fighting Guy," hero of Rosebud Creek.[16]

Captain Avery B. Cain was a Rosebud victim of another sort. Unlike Guy Henry's wounds, Cain's wounds were psychological. He suffered from what was sometimes known as soldier's heart at that time, as shell shock and battle fatigue in other conflicts, and in the twenty-first century as Post Traumatic Stress Disorder (PTSD). As the issue is comprehended today, delayed stresses caused by exposures to combat can produce an array of symptoms: rage, guilt, flashbacks, nightmares, depression, emotional numbing. Such stresses often have associated coping mechanisms—drug use, alcohol abuse, suicide—that are themselves life-compromising and even life-ending. Elsewhere already in this complicated war, the combined Montana-Dakota column suffered the suicide of Captain Lewis Thompson of the Second Cavalry on July 19 near Fort Pease on the Yellowstone. Thompson was among those who had seen the grim toll at the Little Big Horn and was suffering from "neuralgia and nervous prostration, but improving," remembered Doctor Holmes Paulding, who accompanied and tended the Montana troops.[17]

The long-suffering thirty-six-year-old Cain was a veteran of George Sykes's Regular Infantry Division of the Army of the Potomac's Fifth Corps. With Sykes, Cain fought in nearly all of its engagements from Yorktown through Chancellorsville, actions that decimated the regiment. Hospitalized during the Gettysburg campaign, Cain returned to duty and eventually commanded the remnant Fourth Infantry, serving as headquarters guard for General Grant. In due course the Fourth was reconstituted. Cain and Company F served first in New York state and then from 1868 through 1871 at Fort Laramie, where he often commanded the post and frequently served with Captain William S. Collier of Company K, another afflicted Civil War veteran and apparent friend. From early 1871 through late 1872 Cain served on Reconstruction duty at Elizabethtown, Kentucky, where he established the Post of Elizabethtown and from time to time served with Custer. This assignment was interrupted in October 1871 when Cain's outfit and two others from Kentucky were detailed to Chicago to guard property and preserve peace and order after the great fire. Over the winter of 1872–73 Cain and Company F were posted at Little Rock, Arkansas, where he again served with Collier. In May 1873 the Fourth Infantry returned to the Department of the Platte, where Cain variously served at Fort D. A. Russell and at Fort Fetterman through June 1875, occasionally commanding Fetterman.[18]

In these postwar years a pattern of behavior emerges in the Fourth Infantry's monthly regimental returns and in various other records. Cain was repeatedly arrested, relieved from duty, and court-martialed. The courts consistently suspended him from rank and command, but he invariably returned to duty after serving little or none of his sentence. In July 1875 Cain transferred to the command of Company D, Fourth Infantry, but was almost immediately arrested, court-martialed in Cheyenne, sentenced, but again soon released. Meanwhile his company transferred to Fort Fred Steele on the Union Pacific Railroad west of Laramie. From there he joined Crook's Big Horn and Yellowstone Expedition in May 1876.[19]

The official records reveal that Cain and Collier, two colleagues of the same age in the same regiment (Cain married, Collier single), were chronic alcoholics. Their drinking was in all likelihood exacerbated if not outright precipitated by their exposures to combat. Their cases manifest themselves differently, but root issues and associated consequences were plainly apparent. At Fort Laramie in 1868 two enlisted men in Cain's company faced their own courts-martial charges for procuring three gallons of beer for him from an outlying roadhouse. A few years later a sergeant in Company C, Fourth Infantry, serving at Fetterman concurrently with the captain, observed that Cain "was on intimate terms with John Barleycorn." In trouble again in 1874, Cain took the army's infamous pledge to "abstain from the use of all alcoholic drinks." In plain violation of the abstinence pledge, three nearly back-to-back episodes of Cain reporting for duty "in a state of drunkenness" occurred at Fort Laramie in 1875.[20]

In Collier's case, meanwhile, a paper trail exposing his struggles with drink caught up with him while he was serving at Fort Bridger, Wyoming, and Camp Mouth of Red Cañon in the southwestern Black Hills. He spent the summer of 1876 protecting gold rush traffic and interdicting Indian movements from nearby Red Cloud Agency. Collier engaged warriors on the Cheyenne River during the assignment in one of the many small fights of the Great Sioux War. Cain's demons, meanwhile, surfaced again soon after the Rosebud battle. Alcohol seems not to have been involved this time, the case being even more fundamental. Cain's Company D suffered casualties in the fight, and he was called upon to charge and hold Conical Hill during a tense moment in the battle. Those stress-provoking inducements—blood, bullets, a combat adrenaline rush—evidently proved overwhelming for the captain and brought on outright insanity.[21]

Captain Gerhard Luhn and others witnessed Cain's erratic behavior. Luhn noted on July 25 that his condition was deplorable and getting worse. "He is really out of his mind . . . [and] talks all kinds of nonsense." Cain worried about his wife and especially about his men. Robert Strahorn recalled that Cain's "principal obsession was his commanding of the forces in battle. He plead and cried like a child to be permitted to lead his troops to victory. I was . . . one of his mess, and the close association naturally led to my participating in his care. He was powerfully built, in his prime, and a soldier to the last drop of his fine blood." But, Strahorn regretted, he was "becoming insane."[22]

Chambers and Patzki became involved in the problem almost immediately. By then the two had returned from Fort Fetterman, and the column was again on the move. Patski examined Cain and observed his "mental alienation," a nineteenth-century term for a psychotic disorder effecting function. Chambers ordered Cain's return to Furey's supply camp. But Cain escaped his arrest and rejoined the column that same day, determined to command his company again. The next day Cain was "acting very wildly, muttering to himself and flourishing his pistol. He is now under surveillance," remembered Bourke. The matter soon rose to Crook's attention, as the captain's "insanity was now unmistakable and violent." On August 21 on the Yellowstone, Crook ordered Captain Burrowes of the Fourth, himself suffering hypertrophy of the heart (circulation issues manifested by chest pains, dizziness, and shortness of breath) to take charge of the captain and escort him and others determined unfit for duty to Omaha on the first available steamboat. In due course Cain reached Omaha, traveling by boat from the mouth of the Powder down the Yellowstone and Missouri Rivers to Bismarck and continuing from there by rail.[23]

The Old Army had its hands full tending its alcoholics. But it had virtually no mechanisms for treating psychiatric disorders other than removing individuals from duty and sometimes ushering them to the Government Hospital for the Insane in Washington, D.C. The army was especially tolerant of long-suffering officers like Cain and Collier, men who had experienced the worst of combat and from time to time outwardly bore the stigmas of their battles but also functioned normally a greater share of the time. Thus in his post–Civil War years Cain was repeatedly arrested, court-martialed, convicted, and quietly released to duty. Doubtless Cain's wife, Anna, was a stabilizing influence, along with the comforts of home and the simple routines of garrison duty. Cain was absent on leave for the remainder of 1876 and returned to his family home in Rutland, Vermont. In March 1877 he resumed command of Company D, then stationed at Omaha Barracks. Cain and his unit transferred to Fort Laramie in May 1878, where he again occasionally commanded the post. He died there unexpectedly on March 16, 1879, of cerebral apoplexy, a stroke. Captain Collier also served there and commanded his friend's funeral escort.[24]

⁞⁞⁞⁞⁞⁞⁞⁞⁞⁞⁞⁞⁞⁞⁞⁞⁞⁞⁞⁞⁞⁞⁞⁞

Heroes of other sorts are also forever connected to the Rosebud story. Trumpeter Elmer A. Snow of Mills's Company M, Third Cavalry, shot through both arms in the fighting in the Gap, was evacuated from Goose Creek to Fort Fetterman. He eventually made his way to Fort Laramie and on March 19, 1877, was discharged from the army on a Surgeon's Certificate of Disability. He made his way home to Athol, Massachusetts, where he resided until his passing in 1892. Snow is remembered for many reasons, not least that he received a Medal of Honor in November 1877 for bravery in action in the battle. Curiously, Snow received his medal by mail and promptly wrote the army's adjutant general to thank "the People of the United States for this courteous recognition of what was simply my duty as a soldier."[25]

Snow went on to lead a good life, seemingly never allowing his infirmity to control his actions or success. John Bourke and Frank Grouard remembered him as having been shot through both wrists, but examinations by surgeons confirmed instead that an Indian bullet had entered the right elbow and passed through the left wrist joint. Splints were applied to the fractured limbs. After enduring great swelling and inflammation over the next five or six months the wrist wound healed, but the elbow wound persistently disgorged bone fragments and did not close permanently until September 1878. Snow visited the Army Medical Museum in Washington, D.C., in February 1879 and was examined and photographed by assistant surgeon George A.

Otis, curator of the museum. His left wrist was stiff, and the loss of sensation in both hands was great. But with the assistance of a wire apparatus his hand could be supported, enabling him to write. The surviving photograph taken during the visit is a grim reminder of a tough fate in a difficult battle.[26]

Equally interesting is Snow's correspondence with John Bourke, Crook's long-serving aide-de-camp. Nine letters survive in the John Gregory Bourke Papers at the Nebraska State Historical Society. All were written in the mid- to late 1880s. Many are dated June 17 on the anniversary of the Rosebud fight, the day when Bourke saved Snow's life. Bourke acknowledged receiving such a letter in 1880 from Snow, whom he then recalled simply as the "gallant young bugler-boy of Co[mpany] M." Snow was twenty-four at the time of the fight. Beyond the business of pension matters and army promotions (their respective interests), the many letters add compelling postenlistment details to the story of a one-time cavalry trumpeter who went on to father five children (naming one John G. Bourke Snow), studied law and became a successful criminal defense attorney in East Boston, and was well connected politically. His life was inexplicably cut short in 1892 at the age of forty.[27]

IIIIIIIIIIIIIIIIIIIIIIIIIIIIIIIIIIIIIIIII

Three other Medals of Honor were awarded to Rosebud soldiers, for bravery in the horrendous fighting at the Kollmar Crossing, when the fates of many of Royall's soldiers were in jeopardy as men scrambled to locate and mount their horses. John Henry Shingle, Michael A. McGann, and Joseph Robinson, respective first sergeants of William Andrews's Company I, Bainbridge Reynolds's Company F, and Guy Henry's Company D, exhibited uncommon valor in fending off attackers, controlling the men in their companies and helping oversee the mounting and extrication of their men from the swale. The battle narrative clearly places these men in the thick of the action. The citations for Shingle and McGann, which merely read "gallantry in action," understate their courage and valor in those trying moments. Robinson faced an additional battlefield crisis when Captain Henry was shot. Company D had no other commissioned officer present in the field. The burden of leading the unit fell immediately to the first sergeant, a duty that he discharged "under a heavy fire in such a manner as to bring credit upon himself, his company and his regiment." His citation (somewhat rambling) read: "Discharged his duties while in charge of the skirmish line under fire with judgment and great coolness and brought up the lead horses at a critical moment." For these three men the honor bestowed was justly deserved.[28]

Unquestionably one of the more puzzling if not the most mean-spirited episode in the fallout from the Rosebud battle occurred in Omaha in 1886. Crook had returned to the city from Arizona in April after a second and only partially successful tour there. His management of the troublesome Apache chief Geronimo was usurped by one of the general's greatest rivals, Brigadier General Nelson A. Miles. Crook's thin skin was bruised, but he was still adored in Omaha. Civic leaders there remembered him for his support for the opening of the Black Hills, his relentless campaigning against the Northern Indians in 1876, and his role in the surrenders of thousands of Indians at the Red Cloud and Spotted Tail Agencies the following spring. They also admired him for his just treatment for Standing Bear, the respected if still put-upon Ponca chief from eastern Nebraska. The city feted Crook grandly on April 29. The Arizona-bronzed general mingled with dozens of the city's luminaries and enjoyed fine food and wine, cut flowers, and cordial comments. Crook spoke too, regaling his Omaha friends with tales of the recent Apache operation.[29]

Crook took residence in a private home on Chicago Street in Omaha, within a few blocks of the Department of the Platte's offices on Farnam Street in the heart of the city. On the occasion of a visit to Omaha by Colonel William Royall, the general hosted a dinner in his home on the evening of August 7. Royall had served on Crook's staff as the Department of the Platte's acting assistant inspector general from October 1876 to September 1882 and now commanded the Fourth Cavalry in Arizona. Also present were Guy Henry, then inspector of rifle practice for the department; Captain Cyrus S. Roberts, acting judge advocate for the department; Second Lieutenant Lyman W. V. Kennon, aide-de-camp who had succeeded Bourke; and others, including spouses.[30]

At the conclusion of the meal the guests adjourned to Crook's front porch. At around 9 P.M. Royall prepared to depart. As he sidestepped Guy Henry, he said to him: "These are all your friends, I suppose."

Henry replied: "I am Genl. Crook's friend, but no more than I am your friend[,] Col. Royall."

In response to that seemingly innocuous exchange, Crook erupted. Young Kennon witnessed the general's surprising outburst firsthand and immediately jotted it down in his diary, word for word.[31]

Kennon remembered:

General Crook said: "It has come to my knowledge from Washington and elsewhere, Col. Royall, that you have been going around the country making remarks and statements of a nature disparaging to me. This does not seem to me to be generous or in good taste. For ten years I have suffered silently the obloquy of having made a bad fight at Rosebud, when the fault was in yourself and Nickerson. There was a good chance to make a charge, but it couldn't be done because of the condition of the cavalry. I sent word to you to come in, and waited 2 hours—nearer three (3) before you obeyed. I sent Nickerson three (3) times at least. Couriers passed constantly between the points where we were respectively. I had the choice of assuming the responsibility myself for the failure of my plans or of court-martialing you and Nickerson. I chose to bear the responsibility myself. The failure of my plan was due to your conduct."

Col. Royall said, "I have never had any reason to think my conduct at the Rosebud was bad. Nickerson came to me but once and then I moved as soon as I received the order. Did I not move as soon as I could after Nickerson came, Col. Henry?"

Col. Henry said, "Yes, I think you did."

Col. Royall said, "I was with the leading battalion with Col. Henry. It was the leading battalion. I went with it where the enemy was thickest. I was not responsible for the scattered condition of the cavalry."[32]

Here the conversation shifted to Royall's interviews the day before with two of Omaha's newspapers. Like Crook, Royall was well regarded in the city. He too was just in from Arizona and thus newsworthy. His undoing in Crook's eyes and almost certainly the cause of the tempest, despite the seeming cordiality of a dinner among friends, was the praise that the colonel showered on Miles in the interviews for his innovative campaigning, including the use of the heliograph, a new signaling device, and the widespread confidence that the troops were showing their commander. This simply was too much for Crook. Royall defended himself, and again Kennon captured the moment. "As to what I said in the interview with the reporter I did not mention your name," Royall asserted. "I have the interview in my pocket (produced a slip of paper folded looking like a cutting from newspaper; then returning it to his pocket). The account of the interview given in the *Bee* was garbled and incorrect. The account given in the *World* was correct. (Col. R. here mentioned an interview with the Editor of the *World*, as if he had seen and talked with him.)"[33]

The Arizona matter aside, there are many problems with Crook's tirade beyond its sheer unseemliness. Members of the press had not been kind toward Crook and the Rosebud through the years. They invariably faulted his decisions, including not pursuing his attackers more aggressively afterward and almost always directly or by inference linked Rosebud and what they referred to as the Custer Massacre. But the accusations made that evening that any real or perceived setback on Rosebud Creek was somehow Royall's or Nickerson's fault stretched all credulity. Crook certainly could not "make a charge" (an oblique reference to his burning wish to advance down the Rosebud in pursuit of Sitting Bull's village) because his cavalry was scattered, but not by any disobedience or malfeasance on Royall's part. Royall was simply and honorably following Crook's own order to attack on the left. That fight on the left, on Kollmar Creek, became a crest-hopping affair that drew his command ever westward. Indeed couriers had passed between Crook and Royall, including Nickerson, and Royall was faithfully responsive each time. The inferred time lapse seems quite immaterial. The Sioux had not withdrawn from the field after Mills and Noyes commenced their ride down the Rosebud Narrows but instead redoubled their fight on Kollmar. Royall was caught up in the maelstrom.

It is shameful that Nickerson (who was no longer on Crook's staff in 1886) should be the focus of part of the general's enmity for having dispersed the command initially and for any perceived delays in delivering messages. He too followed Crook's orders to a fault. Nickerson apparently never responded to Crook's venom and may never have known of it. The idea that therein were any grounds for courts-martial is utterly preposterous. While charges and trials were among the legacy of the Powder River battle, no judge advocate would have supported such baseless Rosebud allegations, just as judges had not supported every Powder River allegation.[34]

Royall, Nickerson, Henry, and Crook fought a good fight at Rosebud. That much seems perfectly clear. But when Crook was still convinced that he should advance down the Rosebud on the afternoon of June 17 or in the darkness of June 18, he was thwarted by his Crow and Shoshone allies. Only then did he choose to retire to Goose Creek. In the ensuing days the enormity of what he faced on June 17, real and perceived, became crippling. When Crook had opportunities to return to the Rosebud on June 21 or 22, he instead chose to await reinforcements and meanwhile went fishing and hunting. Of the men gathered on Crook's porch on August 7, 1886, three were engaged on that field, including one who was shot in the face. At the least, as one Crook scholar put it bluntly, the episode revealed "little of the 'placid equanimity,' 'honest purpose' and 'good intentions' attributed to him by Captain Bourke." Crook's tirade is also at complete odds with the praise that he heaped on Royall in his June 20, 1876, report to Sheridan, where he lauded the "able manner" in which the colonel commanded his column. What happened on the porch that evening may well be the lowest moment in General Crook's long military career.[35]

The Sioux and Northern Cheyenne people had their own long associations with the Rosebud battle and battlefield—innumerable heroes, complexities of memory, and an embrace of a place. These were sometimes like and many times unlike those of their counterparts in blue. It is especially interesting that Indian accounts seem to contain nothing of the enmity permeating so many *wašicu* stories. There was no leader comparable to General Crook who dressed down warriors for what they did or should have done at Rosebud. More fundamentally, of course, for those in Sitting Bull's camp on Reno Creek, the battle of June 17, 1876, was but part of the story. It was one inexorable step, at the time a joyous one, on a long, painful trail that altered their destiny forever. Many other battles followed Rosebud and Greasy Grass in the course of the Great Sioux War, a conflict that the Indians could not win. Spring 1877 brought massive surrenders at the agencies in Dakota and Nebraska, followed almost immediately by a tide of change that swept the Sioux Country of old. New and larger military posts emerged on the northern plains, ensuring the government's grip on the region. New railroads spanned the buffalo country, facilitating a relentless and complete slaughter of the vast northern buffalo herd. Soon thereafter cattle replaced buffalo on the range. Reservations became the home for all Indians. Yet throughout such change, many remembered the exhilaration, valor, and dignity at Rosebud. They also remembered the dead, and compelling stories emerged.[36]

Often it is said that the Northern Cheyenne people remember the Rosebud fight as the Battle Where the Girl Saved Her Brother. The heroic ride of Buffalo Calf Road Woman in the Gap early in the fight, sweeping down on the back of her pony to save her unhorsed brother from sure death and riding to safety with him to fight again that day, is a story of honor told with pride. The life-saving ride was depicted not once but twice by pictographic artists in the time of Buffalo Calf Road Woman herself and is still depicted today. More recently the slender threads of Buffalo Calf Road Woman's life have been woven into an award-winning biographical novel. Her life was a dramatic tale of both extraordinary heroism and tragedy that was cut short by her death in 1879.[37]

Buffalo Calf Road Woman's fearlessness shone again eight days later at the Little Big Horn. Kate Big Head in a story told to Thomas Marquis remembered the valor of Buffalo Calf Road Woman, whom she knew as Calf Trail Woman. Buffalo Calf Road Woman brandished a six-shooter with bullets and powder and fired many shots at the soldiers, Kate recalled. She was mounted all the while and kept close to her husband, Black Coyote. At one point in the fight she came upon a young Cheyenne warrior who had lost his pony. She was about to give him her own pony when Kate Big Head called out to them that the Cheyenne women had many horses at the river. Buffalo Calf Road Woman took the young warrior up behind her and rode with him to the river. Her fearlessness in combat, combined with extraordinary generosity, knew no bounds.[38]

Buffalo Calf Road Woman lived through the long ordeal of the Cheyennes that followed Little Big Horn, including their battle with Ranald S. Mackenzie on the Red Fork of the Powder River in November and their surrender at Red Cloud Agency the following spring. She endured the despicable removal of the Cheyennes to the Indian Territory in the summer of 1877 and their heroic trek north a year later. During that exodus, she and her husband followed Little Wolf when he and Dull Knife separated in the Nebraska Sand Hills. Dull Knife believed that he would find friends at the Red Cloud Agency, but he was captured by the army instead and imprisoned in a barrack at Camp Robinson. Little Wolf and his followers, meanwhile, skirted the Black Hills and surrendered to a much more amenable Colonel Nelson Miles at Fort Keogh on the Yellowstone River. Sadly, Buffalo Calf Road Woman died there of diphtheria in May 1879, but not before being photographed. She was not yet thirty and the mother of two. In her eyes we see a proud, resolute Northern Cheyenne woman.[39]

ııııııııııııııııııııııııııııııı

Anniversary events through the years at the Little Big Horn battlefield drew inordinate attention, invariably attracting veteran soldiers connected to that place and often veteran Indians as well. A reality in the legacy of the Great Sioux War is that Custer and the mystique of the Little Big Horn have consistently dominated the war story, relegating Powder River, Rose-bud, Warbonnet, Slim Buttes, and every other battle and skirmish almost to footnotes. But from time to time those footnotes drew attention too.

The year 1926 marked the fiftieth anniversary of the story. In the third week of June a spectacular commemoration drawing some forty thousand attendees was held at Crow Agency and nearby Little Big Horn battlefield. Among notable Seventh Cavalry survivors from 1876 who attended were retired Brigadier General Edward S. Godfrey, a lieutenant and stellar troop commander in the Seventh's hilltop defense at the south end of the field that day, and also enlisted men William Slaper and Theodore Goldin, who was a water carrier for the wounded and a Medal of Honor recipient. A battalion of the modern-day Seventh Cavalry from Fort Bliss participated, and among distinguished attendees were William S. Hart from Hollywood and George Bird Grinnell from New York City. The celebration was held partly at Crow Agency, which guaranteed the attendance of countless Crow Indians, but event planners also carefully ensured the participation of Sioux and Chey-enne veterans. Through the long week notable delegations from nearby Busby and Lame Deer on the Northern Cheyenne reservation were present, along with groups from the Standing Rock, Cheyenne River, and Pine Ridge Sioux Reservations in the Dakotas. Most of those old veteran warriors were also participants in the Rosebud battle.[40]

One unique moment in the 1926 reunion stands out. The warriors from 1876 had their own gatherings at Crow Agency. Present with the Sioux del-egation from Pine Ridge was sixty-eight-year-old Jack Red Cloud, son of the great Oglala chief Red Cloud. Jack was by then also a chief. At the Rosebud Jack was remembered as the young warrior who was humiliated for having worn his father's feather bonnet, an honor that he had no right to, and for running off when unhorsed in the Gap without taking along his horse's valu-able bridle. One of Crook's Crow scouts, Bull Doesn't Fall Down, counted coup on him and then openly berated him for his callow behavior, unwor-thy of a warrior. Bull Doesn't Fall Down also attended the 1926 event and noticed Jack among the Sioux men across the broad camp circle opposite the Crow side. At an appropriate moment and in plain sight, he walked briskly to him, pulled out a quirt, and flogged the dignified and thoroughly startled old Sioux chief. Through it all Jack sat still and proud and showed no sign of insult, although onlookers were puzzled. Bull Doesn't Fall Down explained that he had cursed and counted coup on Jack Red Cloud fifty years ago at the Rosebud. He then summoned a buggy full of gifts and presented them to Jack. The two shook hands, Jack exclaiming *Aho! Aho!* (Thank you! Thank you!), to the warm approval of his fellow Sioux. The Crows and Sioux were enemies no more.[41]

<hr />

In 1934, on the occasion of the fifty-eighth anniversary of the Battle of the Rosebud, the Billings chapter of the Daughters of the American Revolution (DAR) unveiled a monument of stone and bronze placed on a knoll at the Big Bend of the Rosebud on the Penson Ranch. The memorial occupies part of the very locale where Guy Henry and Bainbridge Reynolds positioned their companies in the earliest moments of the fight to protect Crook's right flank. The threat never materialized in that quarter, as the battle exploded farther to the west. The monument unveiled there was imposing (one of a wave of memorials orchestrated by the National DAR to mark such places in America). But that hot, bright day in 1934 was perhaps notable less for the monument itself than for the participation of "four wrinkled old men," Beaver Heart, Louis Dog, Charles Limpy, and Weasel Bear. The four had journeyed from the Northern Cheyenne reservation for the unveiling. A fifth old man, Kills Night, was unable to attend and remained home near Busby, lamenting his poor health. All were veterans of the Rosebud battle and were acknowledged as the last of the Cheyennes who fought there and at the Little Big Horn. They came dressed in historical garb. According to a reporter from the *Billings Gazette* who covered the event, they were in a talkative mood. They shared stories, adding their tales to the rich legacy of the Rosebud.[42]

Yet another manifestation of the Rosebud saga occurred that day, this one connecting most directly to the Northern Cheyennes. Unlike the Sioux and Crows, who were perpetually ensnared by the legacy of the Little Big Horn, the Cheyennes embraced Rosebud as a commensurate if not greater battle. Proximity contributed to this view. The Rosebud battlefield is located only a short distance due south of the reservation community of Busby. This awareness and enthusiasm was encouraged by such men as George Bird Grinnell, and especially Thomas B. Marquis, the long-serving agency physician at Lame Deer who assiduously published historical narratives gathered from the Cheyennes, many with a focus on the Rosebud story. In due course both men produced critically important works, Grinnell's *The Fighting Cheyennes* and Marquis's *A Warrior Who Fought Custer*. Marquis's book was not only an extraordinary as-told-to biography of Wooden Leg but also a first-person account of the Northern Cheyenne people during this most gripping time of conflict and change. For these reservation Cheyennes, languid Rosebud Creek and the Rosebud battlefield were sacred ground, virtually inseparable, in their front yard and backyard.[43]

One other individual made contributions in the same vein as Grinnell and Marquis: a full-blood Northern Cheyenne named John Stands in Timber. Stands in Timber was born in 1882 in the remote reservation community of Birney, southeast of Lame Deer on the Tongue River. Educated at the Haskell Institute in Lawrence, Kansas, Stands in Timber returned to the reservation, secured employment at the Indian school in Busby, and later farmed on his allotment near the Tongue River divide. His parents died when he was young, but he was close to his grandparents and from them heard countless stories of battles, Indian heroics, and cultural matters, all shared in the oral tradition of his people. Such stories spawned Stands in Timber's own lifelong interest in collecting and recording what he heard from family members and other elders and in visiting places of importance to them, sometimes with individuals critical to those very episodes. In 1934 he accompanied Limpy to the Rosebud battlefield monument dedication. This passionate labor continued until Stands in Timber's death in 1967.[44]

Stands in Timber was welcoming and bilingual. Through the years scholars exploring Cheyenne history sought him out. This interaction sometimes led to compelling partnerships, as with Father Peter J. Powell and especially Margot Liberty. In the mid-1950s Stands in Timber spent hundreds of hours with Liberty, who recorded and transcribed his many stories of tribal history and culture. The two jointly authored *Cheyenne Memories*, published in 1967, a book widely acclaimed not only as a classic history of the Northern Cheyenne people but an exemplary study in the larger realm of American Indian history. More recently Liberty published her entire collection of Stands in Timber interviews, *A Cheyenne Voice*. Its essence formed her earlier work, and these unadulterated words joined the rich trove of Indian accounts of the Rosebud, Little Big Horn, and other such places on the northern plains.

One additional collaboration with this notable Northern Cheyenne historian must be acknowledged. When Jesse W. Vaughn, a Windsor, Colorado, attorney, began researching his history of the Rosebud battle in the early 1950s, he wisely sought out Stands in Timber. Vaughn visited the field with the Cheyenne historian on many occasions. His trips there occurred at the about the same time when Liberty was recording and transcribing Stands in Timber's stories. Between Liberty's *A Cheyenne Voice* and Vaughn's *With Crook at the Rosebud*, we see one man's passionate interest in that place and another's unquenchable desire to discover and validate action on the ground so that he might write about it. Vaughn tells in his book, for instance, of finding horse skulls with bullet holes in them, because Stands in Timber knew the place and took him to it. He told of action occurring across a certain ridge. The old Cheyenne would occasionally lament that others dismissed these places that he took Vaughn to see, and "sure enough he found many shells there." Stands in Timber also showed Vaughn the stones placed by Cheyennes where Captain Henry was shot and the site where a cairn of rocks once marked where the young Sioux boy was killed. The rocks had disappeared when that bit of the field was plowed. He showed him that place where Chief Comes in Sight was unhorsed during his bravery run but subsequently rescued by his sister. Occasionally Stands in Timber would dispute some notion that Vaughn had about this or that aspect of the story, forcing him to reassess the sources. It was a grand collaboration—for the Rosebud story and all of the Indian wars—that is now gone. Stands in Timber was a living primary source talking face-to-face with Vaughn, a historian driven to tell a story. Ultimately, there can be no finer manifestation of their embrace of sacred ground, in one sense Northern Cheyenne sacred ground but ultimately American sacred ground.[45]

BIG HORN AND YELLOWSTONE EXPEDITION ORDER OF BATTLE

MAY 29–JUNE 21, 1876

HEADQUARTERS

Brig. Gen. George Crook, Department of the Platte, Commanding

Capt. Azor H. Nickerson, Twenty-Third Infantry, ADC and AAAG

1st Lt. John G. Bourke, Third Cavalry, ADC

Capt. William S. Stanton, Corps of Engineers, Chief Engineer

Capt. John V. Furey, Quartermaster Department, Chief Quartermaster (detached at Goose Creek since 6/16/1876)

1st Lt. John W. Bubb, Fourth Infantry, Chief Commissary of Subsistence (detached at Goose Creek since 6/16/1876)

Capt. George M. Randall, Twenty-Third Infantry, Chief of Scouts

Asst. Surg. and Capt. Albert Hartsuff, Medical Director

Asst. Surg. and Capt. Julius H. Patzki

AAS Charles R. Stephens

Thomas Moore, Chief of Pack Train

Charles Russell, Chief of Wagon Train (detached at Goose Creek since 6/16/1876)

CAVALRY BRIGADE

Lt. Col. William B. Royall, Third Cavalry, Commanding

2nd Lt. Henry R. Lemly, Third Cavalry, Cavalry Brigade Adjutant

2nd Lt. Charles Morton, Third Cavalry, Cavalry Brigade AAQM

SECOND CAVALRY BATTALION

Capt. Henry E. Noyes, Commanding Battalion and Co. I

Co. A, Capt. Thomas B. Dewees
    2nd Lt. Daniel C. Pearson

Co. B, 1st Lt. William C. Rawolle

Co. D, 1st Lt. Samuel M. Swigert
    2nd Lt. Henry D. Huntington

Co. E, Capt. Elijah R. Wells
    2nd Lt. Frederick W. Sibley

Co. I, Capt. Henry E. Noyes
    2nd Lt. Frederick W. Kingsbury

THIRD CAVALRY BATTALION

Maj. Andrew W. Evans, Commanding

2nd Lt. George F. Chase, Acting Regimental Adjutant

1st Lt. George Drew, Regimental Quartermaster

FIRST BATTALION, THIRD CAVALRY

Capt. Anson Mills, Commanding

Co. A, 1st Lt. Joseph Lawson

Co. E, Capt. Alexander Sutorius

    1st Lt. Adolphus H. Von Luettwitz (attached from Co. C since 6/12/1876)

Co. I, Capt. William H. Andrews

    2nd Lt. James E. H. Foster

Co. M, 1st Lt. Augustus C. Paul

    2nd Lt. Frederick Schwatka

SECOND BATTALION, THIRD CAVALRY

Capt. Guy V. Henry, Commanding Battalion and Co. D (WIA, 6/17/1876)

Co. B, Capt. Charles Meinhold

    2nd Lt. James F. Simpson

Co. D, Capt. Guy V. Henry

Co. F, 2nd Lt. Bainbridge Reynolds

Co. L, Capt. Peter D. Vroom

THIRD SQUADRON, THIRD CAVALRY

Capt. Frederick Van Vliet, Commanding Squadron and Co. C

Co. C, Capt. Frederick Van Vliet

    1st Lt. Adolphus H. Von Luettwitz (detached 6/12/1876)

Co. G, 1st Lt. Emmet Crawford

INFANTRY BATTALION

Maj. Alexander Chambers, Fourth Infantry, Commanding

1st Lt. Henry Seton, Fourth Infantry, Battalion Adjutant

FOURTH INFANTRY

Co. D, Capt. Avery B. Cain

Co. F, Capt. Gerhard L. Luhn

NINTH INFANTRY

Co. C, Capt. Samuel Munson

    1st Lt. Thaddeus H. Capron

Co. G, Capt. Thomas B. Burrowes

    1st Lt. William L. Carpenter

Co. H, Capt. Andrew S. Burt

    2nd Lt. Edgar B. Robertson

Source: Hedren, *Great Sioux War Orders of Battle*, 102–4.

BIG HORN AND YELLOWSTONE
EXPEDITION CASUALTIES

MAY 30, 1876, SEVENTEEN MILE CREEK

Tierney, Francis A.	Pvt., Co. B, 3rd Cavalry	Accidental gunshot, thigh and abdomen. Died on Prairie Dog Creek, June 7

JUNE 15, 1876, GOOSE CREEK

Nelson, William	Pvt., Co. L, 3rd Cavalry	Chronic diarrhea, died

JUNE 17, 1876, ROSEBUD CREEK

Killed

Allen, William W.	Pvt., Co. I, 3rd Cavalry
Bennett, Richard W.	Pvt., Co. L, 3rd Cavalry
Connors, Brooks	Pvt., Co. L, 3rd Cavalry
Flynn, Eugene	Pvt., Co. I, 3rd Cavalry
Marshall, Daniel	Sgt., Co. F, 3rd Cavalry
Mitchell, Allen H.	Pvt., Co. L, 3rd Cavalry
Newkirchen, Anton	Sgt., Co. L, 3rd Cavalry
Potts, George	Pvt., Co. L, 3rd Cavalry
Roe, Gilbert	Pvt., Co. F, 3rd Cavalry

Wounded

Henry, Guy V.	Capt., Co. D, 3rd Cavalry	Gunshot, face
Broderson, Otto	Sgt., Co. F, 3rd Cavalry	Gunshot, not in hospital, not treated by surg.
Carty, Tobias	Corp., Co. I, 3rd Cavalry	Gunshot, slight, not carried on sick report
Cook, Samuel	Sgt., Co. L, 3rd Cavalry	Gunshot, left thigh
Devine, James A.	Pvt., Co. D, 4th Infantry	Gunshot, head
Edwards, William H.	Tptr., Co. L, 3rd Cavalry	Gunshot, left thigh
Featherly, William	Pvt., Co. I, 3rd Cavalry	Gunshot, left arm
Flynn, Richard	Pvt., Co. D, 4th Infantry	Gunshot, left shoulder
Grosch, Andrew	Sgt., Co. I, 3rd Cavalry	Gunshot, left forearm
Harold, Horace	Pvt., Co. E, 3rd Cavalry	Gunshot, right shoulder
Kremer, John	Pvt., Co. L, 3rd Cavalry	Gunshot, left shoulder

June 17, 1876, Rosebud Creek, Wounded (Continued)

Loscibosky, John	Pvt., Co. I, 3rd Cavalry	Gunshot, right elbow
Meagher, Thomas	1st Sgt., Co. I, 2nd Cavalry	Gunshot, right forearm
O'Brien, James	Pvt., Co. I, 3rd Cavalry	Gunshot, left forearm
O'Donnell, Patrick	Sgt., Co. D, 2nd Cavalry	Gunshot, right forearm
Smith, Francis	Pvt., Co. I, 3rd Cavalry	Gunshot, left leg
Snow, Elmer A.	Tptr., Co. M, 3rd Cavalry	Gunshot, left wrist and right arm
Steiner, Henry	Pvt., Co. B, 3rd Cavalry	Gunshot, left shoulder
Stewart, Charles W.	Pvt., Co. I, 3rd Cavalry	Gunshot, left wrist, arm, and chest
Terry, John H.	Pvt., Co. D 4th Infantry	Gunshot, left leg
Towne, Phineas	Pvt., Co. F, 3rd Cavalry	Gunshot, abdomen

Sources: "List of Killed," "List of Wounded," Big Horn and Yellowstone Expedition, Hartsuff Report, NA; "Report of Killed, Wounded and Missing, Big Horn and Yellowstone Expedition," BH&Y Expedition Order Book, June 21, 1876, NA.

CARTRIDGES, CARTRIDGES

One question has vexed the Rosebud story almost from the start. How could Crook's command expend 10,000, 15,000, or the oft-quoted but improbable 25,000 rounds of ammunition in a half-day-long battle and account for only thirteen Indian fatalities, with a few others hauled away on ponies? Corollary questions exist. Extraction issues were exposed at the Rosebud and on other 1876 battlefields. Did the standard-issue Bloomfield Gilding Metal cartridge produced by the Frankfort Arsenal represent a signal failure in design? Was there an inherent flaw in the design of the .45 caliber Springfield breech-loading carbines and rifles? Or were there other contributing factors? These were parallel contemporary concerns centered on the weapon and its ammunition but were in reality issues of training and fire control on the one hand and the consequences of weapon and cartridge handling on the other.

In a thoughtful essay published in the *Journal of the Military Service Institution* in 1896, Captain Edward S. Godfrey of the Seventh Cavalry explored the problems of fire discipline on Indian wars battlefields. Godfrey fought at the Washita in 1868, on the Yellowstone in 1873, and at the Little Big Horn. He witnessed firsthand the problems of undisciplined fire, meaning uncontrolled shooting by troops, and put the entire blame on the command structure of the engaged force. In Godfrey's view, the burden of achieving disciplined fire on a battlefield rested almost entirely with the chiefs of platoons (nominally company sergeants, sometimes corporals), who by design were to be positioned slightly behind their men, and with company officers positioned slightly behind the noncommissioned men. Embracing this structure conceivably enabled deliberate, concentrated, well-aimed fire at an enemy. Godfrey saw few differences on the line between recruits and old-time veterans. Everyone, he observed, could easily be rattled and problematical in combat, but proper command mitigated that. Godfrey acknowledged such tertiary issues as the "veil of smoke" on a battlefield that obscured the enemy, the din of battle, and the fact that men "firing at will" rarely aimed deliberately. He was a long-serving officer, and in his experience any success on a battlefield was reliant upon strong leadership and the conscientious use of the weapons in hand. His points touched, at least in part and if only by inference, the issues of battlefield fire and casualties at Rosebud.[1]

In a similar vein, Captain Charles King, another veteran of the Great Sioux War and the Apache war almost immediately preceding it, published some years earlier than Godfrey an insightful essay in the *United Service* magazine that explored the interrelated matters of weaponry and tactics. He concluded that, while better weapons may exist in the world's arsenal, the American Springfield was not just a fine weapon but all in all an excellent one. Thus, as he said, the fundamental question in Indian warfare "becomes not so much the make of the gun as the manner of using it." King concluded that the use of the army's Springfield breechloaders included not only matters of individual weapons management and marksmanship but also appropriate battlefield tactics that gained the advantage of position. Only then could the army's superior weaponry be used to its fullest capacity. King particularly extolled the almost-from-birth fighting competency of the enemy, Indian warriors who moved from point to point in a flash, used the rolling prairie to full advantage, and, when mounted, were the oft-referenced finest light cavalry in the world. Robert Strahorn and others on the Rosebud battlefield said much the same thing, acknowledging warriors who fought skillfully and with reckless abandon. In King's view, Indian warriors were simply better marksmen and tacticians. He offered numerous examples of encounters where Indian fights opened bravely and seemingly successfully for the army—Washita, Summit Springs, Powder River, Slim Buttes, Red Fork of the Powder, Big Hole—but soon enough degenerated into indecisive and sometimes near calamitous affairs. He offered no remedies for the army's marksmanship issues or its tactical shortcomings but defended the Springfield.[2]

The army spent years grappling with Godfrey's fire discipline and King's battlefield tactics and all the while seemingly ignored simple lessons from the Civil War that were plainly revealing and entirely pertinent to combat with Indians on the frontier. The Civil War was marked with extraordinary advances in weaponry at the most fundamental level with the widespread distribution and use of rifles that were deadly at extreme ranges when their sights were properly used. Yet soldiers then habitually practiced and fired in combat with fixed sights, meaning with no adjustments for elevation or windage, almost entirely negating the deadly potential of their modern weaponry. Moreover, scholars have observed that these modern weapons increased the zone of fire but failed to increase the effectiveness of that fire because bullets were so greatly dispersed. Even when laying down what soldiers called a "rain" or "perfect shower" of lead, getting hit in Civil War combat was largely a matter of chance. With marked exceptions, the same may be said about combat in the Indian wars. Soldiers consistently overshot their enemy and then were amazed that so much lead could be expended to kill or wound so comparatively few. The simple fact was that most Civil War engagements were eminently survivable, and so was combat on the western frontier.[3]

While soldiers of the Civil and Indian wars were reasonably well introduced to the weapons they carried and on practice ranges may actually have thoughtfully aimed at targets, even adjusting their weapon's sights and practice-fired ten, fifteen, or twenty rounds per month, training was still limited and even flawed. In another day marksmanship would become an obsession to the army, but that was not the case in 1876. The army's handbook (*Description and Rules for the Management of the Springfield Rifle, Carbine, and Army Revolvers*) that accompanied these new armaments to posts around the country is ultimately revealing. According to this 1874 Ordnance Department publication, "the men should be habituated in firing with the sight fixed at the nearest mark, that of 300 yards, and should be taught that with this elevation their fire will be generally the most effective." In nearly the same breath, pages later, the manual comprehended and fully measured such matters as elevation, accuracy, drift, trajectory, and deadly space but still encouraged that soldiers be taught to use these weapons in the simplest manner possible, with fixed sights achieving a generally effective fire.[4]

Adding to this, the smoke on a battlefield that obscured everything, the din of combat, Godfrey's questionable fire discipline, and King's descriptions of an unconventional, expertly mounted foe can produce a Rosebud battlefield where soldiers pointed their carbines and rifles at Sioux and Cheyenne warriors, fired 10,000, 15,000, or 25,000 times, and killed thirteen Indians.

Sitting Bull's warriors grasped this circumstance plainly. One old-timer from the Rosebud remarked that "the soldiers never stopped to take aim at you; they just shoot here and there." And of course there's irony here. King paid utmost respect to an intimidating foe—in his view, fine combatants and exquisite marksmen one and all. But those skills were not telling at Rosebud, where only nine soldiers were killed and nineteen wounded. Fetterman, Little Big Horn, and collateral fatalities in village fights are marked exceptions to the general rule, with distinctive explanations. But most Indian wars battles were eminently survivable, despite a seemingly pervasive hail of fire.[5]

Carbine and rifle cartridges were issues unto themselves. The standard-issue army cartridge of the Rosebud era was fabricated from Bloomfield Gilding Metal, a soft alloy consisting of 95 percent copper and 5 percent zinc. Frankford Arsenal, the army's ammunition-production facility, favored this metal because it was easily drawn, straightforwardly loaded with a primer, propellant, and bullet, and readily crimped at the head and bullet. From the start the army understood that these relatively soft cartridges could be cut through at the rim upon extraction if the weapon's chamber was fouled with dirt (particularly sand), which could cause expended cases to stick. No mention was made of dirty cartridges, but the principle was the same. A clean breech obviated at least in part the probability of a stuck case. The army prescribed commonsense care for these weapons, particularly the cleaning of chambers. If a case should stick and be cut through by the extractor, a soldier needed only to "draw the ramrod and drive the shell out," which of course was a perfect solution . . . for an infantryman.[6]

In the field, however, matters got complicated. To carry on their persons a suitable percentage of the one hundred rounds issued to each Rosebud soldier or any 1876 campaigner, men routinely abandoned the parade-ground-suited McKeever cartridge box and Dyer pouch. Instead they went to the field wearing homemade thimble belts, which were current issue or surplus leather waist belts with leather or canvas loops sewn onto them. Alternatively, cavalry troopers may have worn a pair of the army's so-called Hazen Cartridge Loops, a device of twenty leather loops sewn to a central leather strip and worn on a waist belt. Using either homemade cartridge belts or the army's loops, forty or more cartridges could thus be carried by one man. Whether the loops were canvas or leather, copper cartridges touched leather to a greater or lesser extent, with a predictable consequence. The copper case chemically reacted to the tanning compositions in the leather and formed a sticky green deposit known as verdigris. If the cartridges were not wiped clean from time to time, that sticky substance became a perfect adhering agent that attracted dust and easily glued spent shells in Springfield breeches, whether the mechanisms were combat-hot or not. Hence the infamous stuck or jammed cartridge cases reported at the Rosebud, Little Big Horn, and other Sioux war battles.[7]

The spectacle of soldiers "punching and swearing at their carbines, all of which had 'stuck,'" owing to ejectors not throwing out spent cases, as John Finerty observed, resonates in the Rosebud story. To his horror, Finerty witnessed such a scene in the Gap. Unlike a trooper's infantry counterpart, the horse soldiers had no "iron wand wherewith to punch [that case] out." Finerty berated the cavalry carbine savagely. It ought to have two extractors, he screamed. It ought to have a ramrod. It ought to be abandoned altogether in favor of the infantry rifle. But Finerty missed the point almost entirely. The problem was not with the weapon, beyond the chance of a dirty breech, but almost assuredly with verdigris-encrusted cartridges. It should be noted that Guy Henry, having only barely returned to Fort D. A. Russell in his frightful condition, commented on this very matter. He told the army's chief of ordnance on August 6, 1876: "I see some papers report the carbine failed to 'eject' cartridges at Rosebud—I had no such trouble—other companies may have."[8]

That summer Major Marcus A. Reno of the Seventh Cavalry also weighed in on the matter, writing the chief of ordnance in July. His letter was published in the *Army and Navy Journal* on August 19. Reno questioned a perceived design flaw apparent, he thought, in the manner in which cartridges rested loosely instead of snugly in Springfield breeches. He also noted the issue of dust, a contributor to the problem of properly closing breeches that ultimately led to the tearing of cartridge heads upon extraction. He said nothing about verdigris.[9]

To what extent this issue factored in battle and was injurious or even fatal is not wholly known. The study of nicked and pried cartridge cases at the Little Big Horn in an attempt to quantify the issue is itself a cottage research specialty. To be sure, Seventh Cavalrymen pried jammed or stuck cartridge cases from their carbines, just as some Third Cavalrymen did at the Rosebud. In the entrenchments on the Reno battlefield at the Little Big Horn, Private William Slaper of Captain Thomas French's Company M, Seventh Cavalry, marveled as he watched his captain coolly go about extracting a jammed cartridge case from a gun in which it had stuck, pass that weapon back loaded to his man, and move on to fix another.[10]

Reno firmly asserted the deadliness of the issue. In his letter to the chief of ordnance, he reported examinations on the Custer field afterward where knives with broken blades were seen lying next to dead soldiers. This was positive proof, he was sure, of a fatal connection. A Sixth Infantryman stationed that summer at the Powder River Depot commented in a letter that "the carbines of our cavalrymen, with breeches similar to our infantry guns, are represented to be almost useless after the fifth and sixth round has been fired from them, the spring refusing to throw the shell, thus necessitating the use of the ramrod to eject it."[11]

Simple solutions existed all along, of course, although this often proved a perplexing matter for cavalrymen. Already the army had prescribed in its *Description and Rules* that a Springfield's chamber needed to be cleaned from time to time by swabbing it with a moistened rag, using warm water if possible, and wiping it consecutively with a drying rag and then a lightly oiled one. This was camp toil, certainly, and pity any field-bound trooper with no access to an infantryman's ramrod. But soldiers' cartridges needed wiping as well, to remove verdigris buildup. Officers and soldiers knew this intuitively, although doing so on the trail was apparently spotty. Perhaps Guy Henry was a stickler for so mundane a detail and thus could report to the chief of ordnance that he knew of no extraction problems at Rosebud. Likewise, in Crook's Goose Creek camp the men of Captain Elijah R. Wells's Company E, Second Cavalry, spent a day in early August "cleaning cartridges." Would that all the campaigners of 1876 had been so diligent in that simple duty.[12]

NOTES

ABBREVIATIONS

AAG	Assistant Adjutant General
ACP	Appointment, Commission, Personal
AGO	Adjutant General's Office
AHC	American Heritage Center
ARCIA	*Annual Report of the Commissioner of Indian Affairs*
BH&Y	Big Horn and Yellowstone
BHSU	Black Hills State University
BYU	Brigham Young University
CMHS	Congressional Medal of Honor Society
DPL	Denver Public Library
FLNHS	Fort Laramie National Historic Site
MHS	Montana Historical Society
MnHS	Minnesota Historical Society
NA	National Archives
NSHS	Nebraska State Historical Society
SHSND	State Historical Society of North Dakota
UCSB	University of California–Santa Barbara
USAWC	United States Army War College

CHAPTER 1. A CHAOTIC SPRING

1. Finerty, *War-Path and Bivouac*, 25–27 (quotations); Knight, *Following the Indian Wars*, 159–60.

2. "Frontier Fighters," *Chicago Times*, May 15, 1876.

3. Ibid.; "Brevities," *Omaha Daily Bee*, April 24, 1876 (first quotation); Finerty, *War-Path and Bivouac*, 27 (second quotation), 28.

4. Finerty, *War-Path and Bivouac*, 28 (first and second quotations); "Frontier Fighters," *Chicago Times*, May 15, 1876 (third and fourth quotations); "About People," *Omaha Republican*, May 9, 1876.

5. Hedren, *Ho! For the Black Hills*, 37 (quotation), 42.

6. Hedren, *Powder River*, 31; Powers, *The Killing of Crazy Horse*, 54, 217.

7. McDermott, "Fort Laramie's Iron Bridge," 141; "Sidney," *Omaha Republican*, May 20, 1876; "The Sidney Black Hills Route—Bridge Completed," *Omaha Republican*, June 23, 1876.

8. "The Battle of Rosebud Creek," *Cincinnati Commercial*, June 26, 1876 (quotation); Bourke, *On the Border with Crook*, 283–84.

9. These episodes are discussed in considerable detail in Hedren, *Powder River*, ch. 1, "The Long Road to an Inevitable Sioux War"; and Buecker, *Fort Robinson and the American West*, 77–80.

10. Hedren, *Ho! For the Black Hills*, 132 (first quotation), 150 (second quotation).

11. Ibid., 109–110, 115, 126, 130.

12. "The Far West," *Chicago Tribune*, April 21, 1876 (first quotation); "The Indians," *Sidney Telegraph*, April 22, 1876; "Indian Matters," *Weekly Rocky Mountain News*, April 26, 1876; "The Black Hills," *Chicago Tribune*, May 3, 1876 (second quotation).

13. "Red Devils at Work," *Cheyenne Daily Sun*, April 21, 1876; "The Noble Red Man," *Omaha Daily Herald*, April 25, 1876; "Indians on the War Path," *Omaha Daily Bee*, April 21, 1876; "Indian Deviltries," *Omaha Republican*, April 25, 1876; Hedren, *Ho! For the Black Hills*, 106, 126; Hedren, "Persimmon Bill Chambers," 3, 5, 7.

14. "The Bloody Red-Skins," *Omaha Daily Bee*, April 24, 1876; "Piling Up Wrath," *Omaha Republican*, April 25, 1876; "The Noble Red Man," *Omaha Daily Herald*, April 25, 1876; Hedren, *Fort Laramie in 1876*, 77–78; Hedren, "Persimmon Bill Chambers," 7–9.

15. "Indian Matters," *Omaha Republican*, April 25, 1876.

16. "Lo the Poor Indian," *Cheyenne Daily Sun*, April 26, 1876 (quotations); "The Late Indian Depredations," *Cheyenne Daily Leader*, April 26, 1876.

17. "Indian Matters," *Weekly Rocky Mountain News*, April 26, 1876; "Military Protection for the Cheyenne Black Hills Route," *Omaha Daily Bee*, April 29, 1876; Hedren, *Fort Laramie in 1876*, 78–79. The Noyes court-martial is detailed in Hedren, *Powder River*, ch. 13.

18. "Breakfast Table Talk," *Cheyenne Daily Leader*, April 29, 1876 (first quotation); "Gen. Crook at Cheyenne," *Omaha Daily Bee*, May 1, 1876; *Cheyenne Daily Sun*, May 2, 1876 (second and third quotations).

19. "Will Keep 'em Up a While," *Cheyenne Daily Sun*, May 2, 1876 (first quotation); "Indian Matters," *Weekly Rocky Mountain News*, May 3, 1876; "Give 'em Lead," *Omaha Daily Herald*, May 9, 1876; Hedren, *Ho! For the Black Hills*, 133 (second quotation).

20. "The Indians," *Omaha Daily Bee*, May 3, 1876; "Indian Deviltries," *Omaha Republican*, May 3, 1876; "An Indian Row," *Omaha Daily Herald*, May 3, 1876; Bourke, *Diaries*, 1:265; "Particulars of the Fort Hartsuff Fight," *Cheyenne Daily Leader*, May 5, 1876.

21. "Indian Depredation," *Cheyenne Daily Sun*, May 7, 1876; "The Indians," *Chicago Tribune*, May 7, 1876; "The Indian Creek Fight," *Cheyenne Weekly Leader*, May 13, 1876; "Raiding Redskins," *Weekly Rocky Mountain News*, May 17, 1876; "Gold, Indians, and Death," *Chicago Times*, June 1, 1876.

22. "Raiding Redskins," *Weekly Rocky Mountain News*, May 17, 1876; Flannery, *John Hunton's Diary*, 88; "Indian Depredation," *Cheyenne Daily Sun*, May 7, 1876; Bourke, *Diaries*, 1:265; Hedren, *Fort Laramie in 1876*, 83–84.

23. "Wars and Rumors of Wars," *Omaha Daily Herald*, May 12, 1876.

24. "Frontier Fighters," *Chicago Times*, May 15, 1876.

25. "The Victims of the Sioux," *Laramie Daily Sentinel*, May 5, 1876 (first quotation); "From the Front," *Omaha Republican*, May 20, 1876; "Gold, Indians, and Death," *Chicago Times*, June 1, 1876 (second quotation); "The Black Hills," *Chicago Inter-Ocean*, April 26, 1876 (third quotation); "Indian Matters," *Weekly Rocky Mountain News*, May 3, 1876.

26. "The Sioux War," *New York Herald*, May 3, 1876; "The Sioux War," *Chicago Tribune*, May 2, 1876; "Deadwood Alive," *Omaha Daily Herald*, June 8, 1876 (first quotation); "The Powder River Expedition," *Weekly Rocky Mountain News*, June 7, 1876 (second quotation).

CHAPTER 2. ORGANIZING A SECOND CAMPAIGN

1. "Roster of Troops Serving in the Department of the Platte, May, 1876," filed with Department of the Platte General Orders, 1876, NA; Paul, *Sign Talker*, 76 (quotation).

2. *Report of the Secretary of War, 1875*, 36; "Gen. Crook's Movements," *Cheyenne Daily Leader*, April 12, 1876.

3. Department of the Platte Special Orders No. 68, June 2, 1876, NA; *Report of the Secretary of War, 1876*, 58.

4. These circumstances are discussed in detail in Hedren, *Powder River*, with the soldier abandonment episode addressed on pp. 184–93 and the desertion issue analyzed on p. 344.

5. "The Indians," *Omaha Daily Herald*, April 15, 1876.

6. "The Army," *Omaha Republican*, April 20, 1876; "Crook's Chagrin," *Cheyenne Daily Leader*, April 5, 1876 (quotation); "The Leader and the Third Cavalry," *Cheyenne Daily Leader*, April 11, 1876; Hedren, *Powder River*, 259–60.

7. Bourke, *Diaries*, 1:33, 52; "Uncle Sam's Crook," *Chicago Times*, July 1, 1876 (quotation); [Powell,] *Records of Living Officers*, 118–20; Hutton, *Phil Sheridan and His Army*, 50–51.

8. "The Army," *Omaha Republican*, May 4, 1876; "The Army," *Omaha Republican*, April, 28, 1876; *Cheyenne Daily Sun*, April 28, 1876; Hedren, *Powder River*, 343 (quotation).

9. "The Army," *Omaha Republican*, April 20, 1876; Cullum, *Biographical Register*, 86–87; [Powell,] *Records of Living Officers*, 166; Utley, *Frontier Regulars*, 149 (first quotation), 154, 161n23; Finerty, *War-Path and Bivouac*, 62 (second quotation).

10. Department of the Platte Special Orders No. 68, June 2, 1876, NA; *Organization of the Bridge Equipage of the United States Army*, 25–29; "Breakfast Table-Talk," *Cheyenne Daily Leader*, May 14, 1876; Robrock, "A History of Fort Fetterman," 52.

11. Mears, "Campaigning against Crazy Horse,"70; *Cheyenne Daily Sun*, April 26, 28, 1876.

12. Henry to AAG, Department of the Platte, April 27, 1876, Guy V. Henry Papers, B. William Henry Jr. Collection, BHSU; Hutton, *The Apache Wars*, 146; Third Cavalry Regimental Return, April 1876, NA; Buecker, "'The Men Behaved Splendidly,'" 57–59; Brady, "What They Are There For," 410; Hallberg and Neal, "'For This Are We Soldiers,'" 65.

13. "About People," *Omaha Republican*, May 4, 1876; "The Big Horn and Yellowstone Expedition," *Omaha Republican*, May 10, 1876.

14. Hutton, *Phil Sheridan and His Army*, 306, 308–9; Stiles, *Custer's Trials*, 433–34, 435 (quotation); "Custer Sacrificed," *New York Herald*, May 6, 1876.

15. "Personal Mention," *Omaha Republican*, May 6, 1876; "Personal," *Omaha Daily Herald*, May 6, 1876.

16. "Gen. Custer," *Chicago Tribune*, May 9, 1876; Hutton, *Phil Sheridan and His Army*, 311; "General Terry's Expedition Against the Indians," *Omaha Daily Bee*, May 8, 1876.

17. Department of the Platte Special Orders No. 68, June 2, 1876, NA.

18. [Powell,] *Records of Living Officers*, 50, 56; *Journal of the American Medical Association*, November 30, 1901, s.v. "Deaths and Obituaries"; "Charles R. Stephens," Department of the Platte Personal History of Surgeons Serving in the Department, NA; Hedren, *Powder River*, 75; Gillett, *The Army Medical Department*, 18–19.

19. Department of the Platte Special Orders No. 68, June 2, 1876, NA.

20. "Military Matters," *Omaha Daily Bee*, May 9, 1876.

21. Bourke, *Diaries*, 1:264; "After the Indians," *Omaha Daily Bee*, May 10, 1876 (quotation).

22. "The Black Hills Question," *Chicago Inter-Ocean*, May 17, 1876.

23. Bourke, *Diaries*, 1:190 (first quotation); "Frontier Fighters," *Chicago Times*, May 15, 1876 (second, third, and fourth quotations); Daly, "The Powder-Stained 70's," 20.

24. Hutchins, "Captain Michaelis Reports," 30; "Crook's Campaign," *Cheyenne Daily Leader*, August 5, 1876; Balentine, *Freund & Bro.*, 334; "In the Black Hills," *Daily Alta California*, October 2, 1876. The Minnesota Historical Society possesses a Freund altered Model 1873 Springfield rifle, serial number 13894 from the 1874 first year of armory production. No other surviving Freund Springfield specimens are known. Whether the MnHS rifle belonged to Crook is unknown but not discounted.

25. Magid, *The Gray Fox*, 37; Crook to Sheridan, May 1876, Crook Papers, Henry E. Huntington Library; Bourke, *Diaries*, 1:265; Hedren, *Powder River*, 60, 298.

26. *Cheyenne Daily Leader*, May 25, 1876.

27. *Cheyenne Daily Sun*, April 8 (quotation), 25, May 2, 1876; *Cheyenne Daily Leader*, May 5, 25, 1876; Hedren, *Powder River*, 72–73.

28. "Frontier Fighters," *Chicago Times*, May 15, 1876; "Breakfast Table-Talk," *Cheyenne Daily Leader*, May 14, 1876; Finerty, *War-Path and Bivouac*, 34, 35 (quotation).

29. "Personal," *Omaha Daily Bee*, May 13, 1876; "Personalia," *Omaha Republican*, May 16, 1876; Kime, *The Black Hills Journals*, 56–57 (quotations); Powers, *The Killing of Crazy Horse*, 162; Magid, *The Gray Fox*, 226–27.

30. "Personal Paragraphs," *Cheyenne Daily Leader*, May 18, 1876; "Brave Boys Are They," *Rocky Mountain News*, August 8, 1876 (quotation).

31. Knight, *Following the Indian Wars*, 168–69; Magid, *The Gray Fox*, 22–23; Bourke, *On the Border with Crook*, 94–95; Hutton, *The Apache Wars*, 213; "Brave Boys Are They," *Rocky Mountain News*, August 8, 1876.

32. Abrams, *"Crying for Scalps,"* 4–5, 10. Another source suggests that Stanley was much younger than fifty-four, though with no specificity beyond an 1876 mention of "the young and good scenic painter." See Abrams, *Sioux War Dispatches*, 357n60.

33. Magid, *The Gray Fox*, 224.

34. Jamieson, *Crossing the Deadly Ground*, 38, citing the Sherman Papers, Library of Congress.

35. "The War on the Sioux," *Philadelphia Press*, June 8, 1876.

36. Jamieson, *Crossing the Deadly Ground*, 40; Hedren, *Great Sioux War Orders of Battle*, 39–40.

37. Hutton, *Phil Sheridan and His Army*, 285; "Wyoming," *Omaha Daily Bee*, April 28, 1876; "Indian Matters," *Omaha Republican*, April 25, 1876 (first quotation); *Cheyenne Daily Leader*, April 28, 1876 (second quotation); "General Crook and the Indians," *New York Herald*, May 10, 1876.

38. Bourke, *Diaries*, 1:266 (quotation), 267; Hedren, *Fort Laramie in 1876*, 91.

39. Bourke, *Diaries*, 1:266; Bourke, *On the Border with Crook*, 286 (quotation); "Gen. Crook's Plans," *Cheyenne Daily Leader*, May 11, 1876.

40. Fort Laramie Medical History, May 5, 1876, FLNHS; Bourke, *Diaries*, 1:267 (first quotation); Bourke, *On the Border with Crook*, 288; "Spotted Tail Reserve," *Omaha Daily Bee*, May 15, 1876 (second quotation).

41. Bourke, *Diaries*, 1:268–69.

42. Ibid., 269 (quotations), 270–71; Crook to Sheridan, May 1876, Crook Papers, Henry E. Huntington Library.

43. Olson, *Red Cloud and the Sioux Problem*, 217–18; Hyde, *Red Cloud's Folk*, 259n5; Hyde, *Spotted Tail's Folk*, 222; Bourke, *Diaries*, 1:271, 275 (quotation repeated on both pages).

44. Bourke, *Diaries*, 1:268 (quotations); "Going to War," *New York Herald*, June 9, 1876.

45. "Going to War," *New York Herald*, June 9, 1876.

46. Bourke, *Diaries*, 1:273 (quotation), 275; "How Crook Will Be Assisted," *Laramie Daily Sentinel*, May 25, 1876; Powers, *The Killing of Crazy Horse*, 164.

47. Olson, *Red Cloud and the Sioux Problem*, 219; "The Indian Country," *Chicago*

Inter-Ocean, May 18, 1876. Determining the Sioux population at the time of the Great Sioux War is challenging. Kingsley Bray's "Teton Sioux Population History" is a thoughtful analysis of the greater Sioux population, tribe by tribe, decade by decade, through most of the nineteenth century. Distinguishing agency people from committed nonreservation people, the Northern Indians or "hostiles" of the war era, is especially problematic. Interpolating from Bray's graphs, the Brulés in 1876 are estimated to have numbered some 5,300 people; the Oglalas, 4,400; the Hunkpapas. 1,750; the Miniconjous, 1,400; the Blackfeet, 1,100; the Sans Arcs, 975; and the Two Kettles, 800: a combined Teton Sioux population at the time of the war of 15,725. With this in mind, comparisons with episodes from the war become dramatic and revealing.

48. Bourke, *Diaries*, 1:273–74; Buecker, *Fort Robinson and the American West*, 8.

49. Bourke, *Diaries*, 1:284; Bourke, *On the Border with Crook*, 288; Crook to Sheridan, May 1876, Crook Papers, Henry E. Huntington Library.

50. Bourke, *Diaries*, 1:284 (quotation); Bourke, *On the Border with Crook*, 288.

51. Bourke, *Diaries*, 1:284–85; "Indian Matters at Red Cloud Agency," *Omaha Republican*, May 24, 1876.

52. Letter, Crook to Sheridan, May 1876, Crook Papers, Henry E. Huntington Library; "Crook's 'Close Shave,'" *Cheyenne Daily Leader*, May 18, 1876; "The Indians," *Omaha Daily Bee*, May 18, 1876; "The Indian Country," *Chicago Inter-Ocean*, May 18, 1876; Bourke, *On the Border with Crook*, 289; "Indian Matters," *Weekly Rocky Mountain News*, May 31, 1876; "Gen. Crook's Campaign," *New York Tribune*, June 2, 1876. The Canby story is recounted in Utley, *Frontier Regulars*, 198–206. There was yet another instance where a general officer was nearly killed by Indians: Paul (*Sign Talker*, 15–16) recounts the confrontation between Hugh Scott and Navajos in 1913.

53. "Black Hills," *Chicago Tribune*, May 30, 1876; "A Good Country," *Chicago Inter-Ocean*, May 30, 1876; Powers, *The Killing of Crazy Horse*, 166–67; Second Cavalry Regimental Return, May 1876, NA; Hedren, *Fort Laramie in 1876*, 100 (quotation), 101.

54. Fort Laramie Medical History, May 17, 1876, FLNHS; Bourke, *Diaries*, 1:286; "The Indians," *Omaha Daily Bee*, May 18, 1876 (quotation).

55. Crook to Sheridan, May 17, 1876, Special Files, Sioux War, Division of the Missouri, NA; Gray, *Centennial Campaign*, 93; DeBarthe, *Life and Adventures of Frank Grouard*, 106.

CHAPTER 3. FORT FETTERMAN

1. Magid, *The Gray Fox*, 81; Paul, *Sign Talker*, 105 (quotation); Bourke, *On the Border with Crook*, 150; "Interview in a Tent," *Laramie Boomerang*, August 27, 1891; Hedren, *Powder River*, 57–58.

2. Abrams, "*Crying for Scalps*," 11–14.

3. *Laramie Daily Sentinel*, May 12, 1876; Hedren, *Great Sioux War Orders of Battle*, 79–80, 102–4.

4. Department of the Platte Special Orders No. 68, June 2, 1876, NA; Zinser, *Indian War Diary*, May 13, 1876; "Train Topics," *Cheyenne Daily Leader*, May 13, 1876; "The Army," *Omaha Republican*, May 17, 1876.

5. Buecker, "Letters of Caroline Frey Winne," 21–22.

6. "Gold and Gore," *Chicago Times*, May 18, 1876; "Going to the War," *New York Herald*, June 9, 1876; Abrams, "*Crying for Scalps*," 14–15.

7. Finerty, *War-Path and Bivouac*, 45 (quotation); Altshuler, *Cavalry Yellow & Infantry Blue*, 325.

8. "Going to the War," *New York Herald*, June 9, 1876; "Facing the Foe," *Chicago Times*, May 20, 1876 (quotations); "Those Deserters," *Cheyenne Daily Leader*, May 24, 1876.

9. Finerty, *War-Path and Bivouac*, 46, 47 (quotations).

10. Ibid., 48; "The Indian War," *New York Herald*, May 20, 1876; Abrams, "*Crying for Scalps*," 19 (quotations).

11. Zinser, *Indian War Diary*, 3–4; Stanton, "Annual Report," 706 (quotation), 715; "Personal Mention," *Omaha Republican*, May 18, 20, 1876; "Military Movements," *Omaha Daily Herald*, May 21, 1876; Dickson, "Soldier with a Camera," 26.

12. Zinser, *Indian War Diary*, 4. A vintage typescript of Zinser's diary and other personal papers are archived at the Belleville, Illinois, Labor & Industry Museum. Following his enlistment in the Third Cavalry, Zinser spent thirty years as a traveling agent for the Belleville Stove and Range Company.

13. Zinser, *Indian War Diary*, 4–5; Fort Laramie Medical History, May 18, 1876, FLNHS; Bourke, *Diaries*, 1:286, 287 (quotation).

14. *Outline Description of the Military Posts in the Military Division of the Missouri*, 97–98; Finerty, *War-Path and Bivouac*, 59 ("Spitsbergen"); "Indians!" *Chicago Times*, July 22, 1876. Finerty's reference to Spitzbergen, an Arctic whaling and coal mining island in the Norwegian archipelago, was meant as a dismissal, a point well understood in the nineteenth century. Regarding Sheridan's campaign to construct military posts, see Hedren, *After Custer*, ch. 3.

15. Bourke, *Diaries*, 1:287; "Army of the Big Horn," *New York Herald*, May 28, 1876; "The Indian Country," *Chicago Inter-Ocean*, May 29, 1876; DeBarthe, *Adventures of Frank Grouard*, 109–10 (quotation); *Laramie Daily Sentinel*, May 28, 1876.

16. Fort Laramie Medical History, May 22, 1876, FLNHS; Hedren, *Fort Laramie in 1876*, 95; Mattes, *Indians, Infants and Infantry*, 213–14 (quotation).

17. "Fighting Folks," *Chicago Times*, May 24, 1876; Abrams, "*Crying for Scalps*," 24; Reneau, *The Adventures of Moccasin Joe*, 54.

18. "Fighting Folks," *Chicago Times*, May 24, 1876 (quotation); "Crook on the War Path," *Laramie Daily Sentinel*, May 30, 1876.

19. "The Pittsburgh Black Hills Expedition," *Wyoming Weekly Leader*, April 22, 1876; "Indian Matters," *Weekly Rocky Mountain News*, May 3, 1876; Hedren, *Ho! For the Black Hills*, 21–22; "The Battle of the Rosebud," *Pittsburg Leader*, July 21, 1876.

20. Finerty, *War-Path and Bivouac*, 53 (first quotation), 56; Abrams, "*Crying for Scalps*," 29 (second quotation), 34; "Crook's Expedition," *Chicago Inter-Ocean*, June 7, 1876; Reneau, *The Adventures of Moccasin Joe*, 54; Bourke, *Diaries*, 1:288–89.

21. "The Battle of the Rosebud," *Pittsburg Leader*, July 21, 1876.

22. Big Horn and Yellowstone (BH&Y) Expedition Order Book, NA, 1; Abrams, "*Crying for Scalps*," 37–39; "Army of the Big Horn," *New York Herald*, May 28, 1876.

23. Abrams, "*Crying for Scalps*," 39 (quotation); Zinser, *Indian War Diary*, 6; Hedren, *Powder River*, 102–3.

24. "Running Down the Redskins," *Weekly Rocky Mountain News*, June 7, 1876; "Army of the Big Horn," *New York Herald*, May 28, 1876; BH&Y Expedition Order Book, NA, 1; Finerty, *War-Path and Bivouac*, 58; "Indian Matters," *Weekly Rocky Mountain News*, May 31, 1876.

25. "At the Front," *Omaha Republican*, May 28, 1876; Pearson, *The Platte-Dakota Campaign of 1876*, 7 (first quotation); Bourke, *Diaries*, 1:290; *Frank Leslie's Illustrated Newspaper*, October 14, 1876; "Crook's Expedition," *Chicago Inter-Ocean*, June 29, 1876 (remaining quotations).

26. Finerty, *War-Path and Bivouac*, 59 (quotation); "Crook's Expedition," *Chicago Inter-Ocean*, June 29, 1876.

27. "The War on the Sioux," *Philadelphia Press*, June 8, 1876.

28. "At the Front," *Omaha Republican*, May 28, 1876; Hedren, "Garrisoning the Black Hills Road," 6–7; Hedren, *Fort Laramie in 1876*, 98–99.

29. BH&Y Expedition Order Book, NA, 1; Department of the Platte Special Orders No. 68, June 2, 1876, NA; Bourke, *Diaries*, 1:289. See appendix A, "Big Horn and Yellowstone

Expedition Order of Battle," for details on the command and its officers.

30. Abrams, *"Crying for Scalps,"* 19 (quotations); BH&Y Expedition Order Book, NA, 3; Hutchins, *Boots and Saddles at the Little Bighorn*, 3–12, 33–37; McChristian, *The U.S. Army in the West*, 191–92. Photographs of some of these troops in the field exist, and the suggested broad conformity and relative nonconformity is plainly apparent. See Hedren, *With Crook in the Black Hills*, 25, 26, 28.

31. Hutchins, *Boots and Saddles at the Little Bighorn*, 29–32; McChristian, *The U.S. Army in the West*, 114–17; Hedren, *Powder River*, 130, 390n21; McChristian, *Regular Army O!*, 446 (quotations); McChristian, *Uniforms, Arms, and Equipment*, 2:185; Hutchins, "Captain Michaelis Reports," 28. To the point of company stars and bars guidons used in the field, a Stanley sketch of troops early in the movement clearly shows staffs and flags unfurled in the column. "Signal Fires of the Sioux, near Powder River," *Frank Leslie's Illustrated Newspaper*, August 12, 1876.

32. Crook to Sheridan, May 29, 1876, M1495, Roll 2, NA; Townsend to Sheridan, May 30, 1876, Division of the Missouri, Special Files, NA; Bourke, *Diaries*, 1:290; "A Good Country," *Chicago Inter-Ocean*, May 30, 1876; *Laramie Daily Sentinel*, May 30, 1876; "Crook on the War-Path," *Weekly Rocky Mountain News*, May 31, 1876; Townsend to Royall, Fort Laramie Letters Sent, May 24, 1876, FLNHS.

33. These numbers are rather consistently reported although one source might say 100 wagons and another 105, depending apparently on whether the ambulances and pontons were counted. "The Big Horn Expedition," *Cheyenne Daily Leader*, May 27, 1876; "Going to the War," *New York Herald*, June 9, 1876; "Crook on the War-Path," *Weekly Rocky Mountain News*, May 31, 1876; "Running Down the Redskins," *Weekly Rocky Mountain News*, June 7, 1876; Essin, *Shavetails and Bell Sharps*, 116; "The Sioux War," *Cincinnati Commercial*, July 17, 1876.

34. Waggoner, *Witness*, 676–77n3; Hedren, *Powder River*, 67–68; Crawford, *Rekindling Camp Fires*, 241; "The Kanaka Scout," *Chicago Inter-Ocean*, July 21, 1876; Hardorff, "The Frank Grouard Genealogy"; DeBarthe, *Life and Adventures of Frank Grouard*. DeBarthe's biography of Grouard is criticized by some. The two were contemporaries in Buffalo, Wyoming. While DeBarthe embellished Grouard's story some and plainly misunderstood a few things, this narrative is critically important to our understanding of the scout and his time in the West.

35. Hedren, *Powder River*, 67. 117; "Going to the War," *New York Herald*, June 9, 1876; DeBarthe, *Life and Adventures of Frank Grouard*, 106 (quotation).

36. "Baptiste Pourier's Interview," in Jensen, *The Settler and Soldier Interviews of Eli S. Ricker*, 255–66.

37. "Running Down the Redskins," *Weekly Rocky Mountain News*, June 7, 1876; Crawford, *Rekindling Camp Fires*, 236.

38. "Army of the Big Horn," *New York Herald*, May 28, 1876; Williams to Crook, June 5, 1876, Crook Papers, University of Oregon; Spring, "Dr. McGillycuddy's Diary," 281–83; McGillycuddy, *McGillycuddy Agent*, 41; Moulton, *Valentine T. McGillycuddy*, 73, 76.

39. "Military Matters," *Cheyenne Daily Leader*, June 16, 1876 (quotation); Fourth Infantry Regimental Return, May 1876, NA.

40. Crook to Sheridan, May 29, 1876, Division of the Missouri, Special Files, NA; *Laramie Daily Sentinel*, May 30, 1876.

CHAPTER 4. THE NORTHERN INDIANS AND THE GREAT ASCENDANCY

1. Bray, *Crazy Horse*, 199–200; Marquis, *A Warrior Who Fought Custer*, 169, 170 (quotations), 172; "The Young Two Moon Interview," in Hardorff, *Cheyenne Memories of the Custer Fight*, 160; "Forcing of Tribe from Black Hills Country Provoked Trouble," *Billings Gazette*, July 17, 1932; Hedren, *Powder River*, 219–20. Two Moon called the place where the Cheyennes

first met Crazy Horse Charcoal Butte, but that landmark is farther on. Garland, "General Custer's Last Fight as Seen by Two Moon," 101.

2. Garland, "General Custer's Last Fight as Seen by Two Moon," 101 (first quotation), 102 (second quotation); Bray, *Crazy Horse*, 200; Hedren, *Powder River*, 220.

3. Marquis, *A Warrior Who Fought Custer*, 172; Marquis, *She Watched Custer's Last Battle*, [2].

4. DeMallie, "Teton," 794.

5. Ibid., 794–95.

6. Denig, *Five Indian Tribes of the Upper Missouri*, 25–27.

7. Hyde, *Red Cloud's Folk*, 252; Waggoner, *Witness*, 121.

8. Hedren, *After Custer*, 8–16; Waggoner, *Witness*, 106–8.

9. Hyde, *Red Cloud's Folk*, 251–53; Marquis, *A Warrior Who Fought Custer*, 156–57; Larson, *Gall*, 102; Hedren, *Powder River*, 30–31.

10. Hedren, *Powder River*, 45–47, 51; Waggoner, *Witness*, 106, 123–24; Marquis, *A Warrior Who Fought Custer*, 156–57.

11. "Interview with Flying By," in Hammer, *Custer in '76*, 209; Utley, *The Lance and the Shield*, 128; McLemore, "Fort Pease," 21–30; Stewart, "Major Brisbin's Relief of Fort Pease," 119.

12. Marquis, *A Warrior Who Fought Custer*, 156–57; Weasel Bear interview, in Hunt and Hunt, *I Fought with Custer*, 216; Utley, *The Lance and the Shield*, 128; Marshall, "How Many Indians Were There?," 210; Hedren, *Powder River*, 113–17.

13. Bray, *Crazy Horse*, 194; Hyde, *Red Cloud's Folk*, 251.

14. Marquis, *The Cheyennes of Montana*, 251; Marshall, "How Many Indians Were There?," 211.

15. Hyde, *Red Cloud's Folk*, 256; Utley, *The Lance and the Shield*, 128, 132; Vestal, *New Sources of Indian History*, 162–63; Taylor, *Frontier and Indian Life and Kaleidoscopic Lives*, 167; Stewart, *Custer's Luck*, 184; "Forcing of Tribe from Black Hills Country Provoked Trouble," *Billings Gazette*, July 17, 1932 (quotation). Gray (*Centennial Campaign*, 325) provides insights on the well-forested Blue Mountains, a component of today's Custer National Forest located south of Ekalaka, Montana.

16. Utley, *The Lance and the Shield*, 132 (first quotation); Marquis, *A Warrior Who Fought Custer*, 170–71, 172 (second quotation).

17. Utley, *The Lance and the Shield*, 133; "The Two Moons Interview," in Hardorff, *Lakota Recollections of the Custer Fight*, 133 (first quotation); DeMallie, *The Sixth Grandfather*, 151 (second quotation); Bray, *Crazy Horse*, 201 (third quotation).

18. Hyde, *Red Cloud's Folk*, 256–57; Utley, *The Lance and the Shield*, 133.

19. Marquis, *A Warrior Who Fought Custer*, 178–79.

20. Ibid., 179, 180 (quotation), 181; "Forcing of Tribe from Black Hills Country Provoked Trouble," *Billings Gazette*, July 17, 1932; Marquis, *The Cheyennes of Montana*, 252.

21. Bray, *Crazy Horse*, 201; Hedren, "Persimmon Bill Chambers," 6–7.

22. Marquis, *A Warrior Who Fought Custer*, 180–81; Powell, *People of the Sacred Mountain*, 2:948, 1363n3; Marshall, "How Many Indians Were There?," 212.

23. Marquis, *A Warrior Who Fought Custer*, 181.

24. Ibid., 181–82.

25. Beck, *Inkpaduta*, 135; "The He Dog Interview," in Hardorff, *Lakota Recollections of the Custer Fight*, 78; Marquis, *A Warrior Who Fought Custer*, 182 (quotations); "Sitting Bull's G-2 Was Efficient," in Graham, *The Custer Myth*, 6.

26. Marquis, *A Warrior Who Fought Custer*, 182–83; Powell, *People of the Sacred Mountain*, 2:949; "The Thunder Bear Narrative," in Hardorff, *Indian Views of the Custer Fight*, 87–88; Anderson, "Cheyennes at the Little Big Horn," 85–86.

27. For a look back at the manner in which Plainsmen computed Indian people per lodge, see Paul, "Counting Indians," 27. Three students of the Great Sioux War who have produced four distinct studies have carefully analyzed Indian population and lodge numbers and postulated multipliers. Based on reminiscences and surrendering tabulations, Harry Anderson ("Cheyennes at the Little Big Horn," 82, 88) concluded that a Cheyenne lodge at the time of the Little Big Horn had a population of some 7.14 people per tipi and 1.29 warriors per tipi. Surrender data in 1877 suggested an average of 1.62 adult Cheyenne men per tipi. John Gray (*Centennial Campaign*, chs. 26 and 27 and p. 313) studied population figures and the Ascendancy and concluded that Sioux tipis averaged 7 persons per lodge and 1.75 men per lodge and Cheyenne tipis averaged 8 persons per lodge and 2 men per lodge. Anderson had made a strong case in his study of the Cheyennes that there could not have been two men per Cheyenne lodge, despite an important source that suggests as much. Anderson (foreword to *The Crazy Horse Surrender Ledger* by Buecker and Paul, xii–xiii) subsequently analyzed the particulars of Crazy Horse's surrender at Red Cloud Agency in May 1877 and noted an average of 1.5 adult men per lodge in a group of 145 lodges. Robert Marshall ("How Many Indians Were There?," 218) studied many of the same sources as Anderson and Gray did plus additional accounts not used by either and concluded that there were 6.36 people per lodge and 1.47 men per lodge. The current study adds to the lodge tabulation in Marshall's analysis but embraces his multipliers, which are the most conservative of those mentioned while also being thoughtfully grounded.

28. Marquis, *A Warrior Who Fought Custer*, 183–84 (quotation); Garland, "General Custer's Last Fight as Seen by Two Moon," 102.

29. Gray, *Centennial Campaign*, 329; Bradley, *The March of the Montana Column*, 87; Marquis, *A Warrior Who Fought Custer*, 185.

30. "The Indian Battles," *New York Herald*, September 24, 1876; "Kill Eagle's Story," *New York Herald*, October 6, 1876; Dickson, "Prisoners in the Indian Camp," 5–6.

31. Marquis, *A Warrior Who Fought Custer*, 184; Gray, *Centennial Campaign*, 329.

32. Marquis, *A Warrior Who Fought Custer*, 184; Anderson, "Cheyennes at the Little Big Horn," 85–86.

33. Marquis, *A Warrior Who Fought Custer*, 184–85; Marquis, *She Watched Custer's Last Battle*, [2] (quotation); Powell, *People of the Sacred Mountain*, 2:949–50.

34. Marquis, *A Warrior Who Fought Custer*, 185 (quotation); "Forcing of Tribe from Black Hills Country Provoked Trouble," *Billings Gazette*, July 17, 1932.

35. Bradley, *The March of the Montana Column*, 91–92, 98–103; Gibbon, "Last Summer's Expedition against the Sioux and Its Great Catastrophe," 284; Gray, *Custer's Last Campaign*, 152–53.

36. Marquis, *A Warrior Who Fought Custer*, 186–88; Anderson, "Cheyennes at the Little Big Horn," 86; Powell, *People of the Sacred Mountain*, 2:950.

37. Utley, *The Lance and the Shield*, 136; DeMallie, "Lakota Belief and Ritual in the Nineteenth Century," 28.

38. Eastman, "Rain-in-the-Face," 511 (quotation); Bradley, *The March of the Montana Column*, 118–19; Schneider, *The Freeman Journal*, 47–48; Johnson, "Dr. Paulding and His Remarkable Diary," 54–55; Gibbon, "Last Summer's Expedition against the Sioux and Its Great Catastrophe," 286–87.

39. Bradley, *The March of the Montana Column*, 122; Schneider, *The Freeman Journal*, 48; Johnson, "Dr. Paulding and His Remarkable Diary," 56; Gray, *Custer's Last Campaign*, 156.

40. Marquis, *A Warrior Who Fought Custer*, 188; Bradley, *The March of the Montana Column*, 123 (first quotation), 124 (second quotation), 125–26.

41. Marquis, *A Warrior Who Fought Custer*, 190–91.

42. Utley, *The Lance and the Shield*, 137 (quotation); Vestal, *Sitting Bull*, 148–49; White

Bull Interview, Campbell Collection, Box 105, Notebook 24, 82, University of Oklahoma Libraries; Powers, *The Killing of Crazy Horse*, 173.

43. Bray, *Crazy Horse*, 202; Townsend to Sheridan, May 30, 1876, Division of the Missouri, Special Files, NA; Marquis, *A Warrior Who Fought Custer*, 190 (quotation); Powers, *The Killing of Crazy Horse*, 166–67; "William Garnett's Interview," in Jensen, *The Indian Interviews of Eli S. Ricker*, 46; DeMallie, *The Sixth Grandfather*, 170–71; "A. G. Shaw's Interview," in Jensen, *The Settler and Soldier Interviews of Eli S. Ricker*, 309; "Interview with Short Buffalo (Short Bull)," in Hinman, "Oglala Sources on the Life of Crazy Horse," 37. Much is known about the Big Road band. See the Dickson essays "Reconstructing the Little Big Horn Indian Village" and "The Big Road Roster."

44. Hyde, *Red Cloud's Folk*, 241–46; Potter, "*From Our Special Correspondent*," 13–19; Manypenny, *Our Indian Wards*, 308–10; "The Black Hills," *Chicago Inter-Ocean*, April 25, 1876.

45. Bingham Report, September 1, 1876, *ARCIA*, 22–24 (quotation on 23); Anderson, "A History of the Cheyenne River Indian Agency and Its Military Post," 430.

46. Burke Report, August 19, 1876, *ARCIA*, 38–40 (quotations on 39).

47. Howard Report, August 10, 1876, *ARCIA*, 33–36 (quotation on 35).

48. Hastings Report, August 10, 1876, *ARCIA*, 33; Merritt to Sheridan, June 7, 1876, Division of the Missouri, Special Files, NA (quotation); Olson, *Red Cloud and the Sioux Problem*, 219.

49. "Very Latest," *Omaha Daily Bee*, May 22, 1876 (first quotation); "Alarming State of Affairs at Red Cloud," *Cheyenne Daily Leader*, May 19, 1876 (second and third quotations); "The Big Horn Expedition," *Cheyenne Daily Leader*, May 27, 1876; "Crook on the War Path," *Laramie Daily Sentinel*, May 30, 1876.

50. Marquis, *A Warrior Who Fought Custer*, 191; Bear Soldier Interview, Crawford Papers, SHSND; Grinnell, *The Cheyenne Indians*, 2:96; Matson, *Crazy Horse*, 94–95.

51. Marquis, *A Warrior Who Fought Custer*, 191–92; Hassrick, *The Sioux*, 282–83; Bray, *Crazy Horse*, 203; Red Shirt, *George Sword's Warrior Narratives*, 217; Utley, *The Lance and the Shield*, 137. The Sun Dance camp was occupied for four days, June 4–7. Dance preparations occurred on June 4, and the dance followed for three days. Near Red Cloud Agency an Oglala Sun Dance was held on June 14–19. "The Red Devils," *Sidney Telegraph*, June 24, 1876.

52. Utley, *The Lance and the Shield*, 137–38; "Tales of the Tatankas," *Saint Paul and Minneapolis Pioneer Press*, May 19, 1883; Vestal, *Sitting Bull*, 149–50.

53. Utley, *The Lance and the Shield*, 138.

54. Ibid., 138–39; Sagan, "The Face of Battle without the Rules of War," 37; Powers, *The Killing of Crazy Horse*, 174.

CHAPTER 5. THE ROAD NORTH

1. Bourke, *Diaries*, 1:291 (first quotation); Daly, "The War Path," 16 (second quotation); "The Battle of the Rosebud," *Pittsburg Evening Leader*, July 21, 1876; "The Big Horn Expedition," *Chicago Inter-Ocean*, July 6, 1876; "Uncle Sam's Crook," *Chicago Times*, July 1, 1876; Finerty, *War-Path and Bivouac*, 92.

2. "Crook's Expedition," *Chicago Inter-Ocean*, June 29, 1876; "The Sioux War," *Cincinnati Commercial*, July 17, 1876.

3. Williams to Sheridan, May 29, 1876, and Crook to Sheridan, May 29, 1876, Division of the Missouri, Special Files, NA; Finerty, *War-Path and Bivouac*, 61–62; Nottage, "The Big Horn and Yellowstone Expedition of 1876," 32.

4. Bourke, *Diaries*, 1:292; DeBarthe, *Life and Adventures of Frank Grouard*, 110; "Crook's Expedition," *Philadelphia Press*, June 30, 1876; "Crook," *Weekly Rocky Mountain News*, June 28, 1876; Hartsuff Report, NA. These sources conflict on whether Meinhold and Vroom explored to the right or left of the Montana Road. I concluded that it was to the right, because that was

the general direction of the Northern Indians and would have been Crook's natural course if another or better ford of the Powder had been located.

5. Finerty, *War-Path and Bivouac*, 66 (first quotation), 67 (second quotation); Jaycox Diary, 1, MHS; Hedren, *Powder River*, 102–3; "Crook," *Weekly Rocky Mountain News*, June 28, 1876; "The Sioux War," *Chicago Tribune*, July 5, 1876 (third and fourth quotations).

6. Finerty, *War-Path and Bivouac*, 67–69; Stanton, "Annual Report," 707–8.

7. "James Forristell," *Hardin Tribune-Herald*, January 20, 1933 (first quotation); Finerty, *War-Path and Bivouac*, 68–69, 70 (second and third quotations); Stanton, "Annual Report," 707–8.

8. "The Sioux War," *Chicago Daily Tribune*, May 2, 1876; "Powder River," *Helena Weekly Herald*, June 1, 1876; "The Powder River Expedition," *Weekly Rocky Mountain News*, June 7, 1876.

9. Abrams, *"Crying for Scalps,"* 44–45 (first quotation); "Uncle Sam's Crook," *Chicago Times*, July 1, 1876; Finerty, *War-Path and Bivouac*, 77–78; "Crook," *Weekly Rocky Mountain News*, June 28, 1876 (second quotation); "The Big Horn Expedition," *Chicago Inter-Ocean*, July 6, 1876; Reneau, *The Adventures of Moccasin Joe*, 55; Zinser, *Indian War Diary*, 6, 8; "The Big Horn Expedition," *Cheyenne Daily Leader*, July 2, 1876; Bourke, *Diaries*, 1:293.

10. "Uncle Sam's Crook," *Chicago Times*, July 1, 1876 (first quotation); Meketa, *Marching with General Crook*, 7; Hedren, *Powder River*, 242–45; Stanton, "Annual Report," 708; Bourke, *Diaries*, 1:294 (second quotation); Finerty, *War-Path and Bivouac*, 74–77; William G. Magill Memoir, FLNHS (third quotation).

11. "The Sioux War," *Chicago Tribune*, July 5, 1876; "Crook," *Weekly Rocky Mountain News*, June 28, 1876; DeBarthe, *Life and Adventures of Frank Grouard*, 110; Nickerson to Royall, June 2, 1876, BH&Y Expedition Order Book, 6, NA; "Uncle Sam's Crook," *Chicago Times*, July 1, 1876.

12. DeBarthe, *Life and Adventures of Frank Grouard*, 110; Gilbert, *"Big Bat" Pourier*, 24–27.

13. "Uncle Sam's Crook," *Chicago Times*, July 1, 1876 (quotations); Luhn Diary, Luhn Papers, AHC.

14. "Uncle Sam's Crook," *Chicago Times*, July 1, 1876 (quotation); "Crook's Campaign," *Cheyenne Daily Leader*, August 5, 1876.

15. "Crook's Campaign," *Chicago Tribune*, August 1, 1876.

16. "The Sioux War," *Chicago Tribune*, August 2, 1876; "Crook's Campaign," *Cheyenne Daily Leader*, August 5, 1876 (quotation in both).

17. "The Big Horn Expedition," *Chicago Inter-Ocean*, July 6, 1876 (quotation); "Crook's Expedition," *Philadelphia Press*, June 30, 1876.

18. Abrams, *"Crying for Scalps,"* 52; "The Big Horn Expedition," *Chicago Inter-Ocean*, July 6, 1876 (quotation); Hedren, *Ho! For the Black Hills*, 23, 116.

19. "Crook," *Weekly Rocky Mountain News*, June 28, 1876 (first quotation); Stanton, "Annual Report," 709; Bourke, *Diaries*, 1:296–97; Capron, "The Indian Border War of 1876," 482 (second quotation).

20. Bourke, *Diaries*, 1:298; "The Sioux War," *Frank Leslie's Illustrated Newspaper*, August 12, 1876, 369, 372; Abrams, *"Crying for Scalps,"* 53; Bourke, *On the Border with Crook*, 293; Finerty, *War-Path and Bivouac*, 82.

21. Abrams, *"Crying for Scalps,"* 53; "Uncle Sam's Crook," *Chicago Times*, July 1, 1876 (quotations).

22. "The Big Horn Expedition," *Chicago Inter-Ocean*, July 6, 1876; "The Sioux War," *Cincinnati Commercial*, July 17, 1876 (quotation); "Gen. Crook's Expedition," *Daily Alta California*, July 6, 1876; Bourke, *Diaries*, 1:298. The assumed Foster piece is unsigned but has phraseology similar to his near-simultaneous dispatch to the *Chicago Tribune*. Adding to

the confusion, Captain Andrew Burt of the Ninth Infantry also wrote for the *Commercial*, his hometown newspaper. Burt signed many but not all of his pieces. The Hornberger-Reese bit did not appear in the *Tribune* equivalent.

23. Hedren, *Ho! For the Black Hills*, 157, 210, 212. Captain Jack Crawford knew Graves in the Black Hills and confirms this sixty-member party. Graves subsequently became a courier for Crook as the campaign lingered into the summer.

24. Finerty, *War-Path and Bivouac*, 84; "The Sioux War," *Cincinnati Commercial*, July 17, 1876; Stanton, "Annual Report," 709; "The Big Horn Expedition," *Chicago Inter-Ocean*, July 6, 1876.

25. "The Sioux War," *Chicago Tribune*, July 5, 1876 (first quotation); Stanton, "Annual Report," 709–10; Dewees letter, June 5, 1876, FLNHS; Finerty, *War-Path and Bivouac*, 85–86; Abrams, *"Crying for Scalps,"* 55 (second and third quotations); Capron, "The Indian Border War of 1876," 483 (fourth quotation).

26. Abrams, *"Crying for Scalps,"* 55 (first quotation); Capron, "The Indian Border War of 1876," 483; "The Sioux War," *Chicago Tribune*, July 5, 1876 (second quotation); "The Sioux War," *Frank Leslie's Illustrated Newspaper*, August 12, 1876, 369.

27. Abrams, *"Crying for Scalps,"* 57–60; Meketa, *Marching with General Crook*, 9; "The Sioux War," *Frank Leslie's Illustrated Newspaper*, August 12, 1876, 369.

28. "Uncle Sam's Crook," *Chicago Times*, July 1, 1876; Nickerson to Royall, June 5, 1876, BH&Y Expedition Order Book, 7, NA; Noyes, "Story of My Life," TS, 83, Noyes-Wallace Family Collection, UCSB; Shockley, "General George Crook's Fish Shooting Army," 11. Almanacs at hand variously note the sunrise for that locale as 4:38 or 4:59 A.M.

29. Stanton, "Annual Report," 710–11; "Uncle Sam's Crook," *Chicago Times*, July 1, 1876; Nottage, "The Big Horn and Yellowstone Expedition of 1876," 32; Bourke, *Diaries*, 1:301; DeBarthe, *Life and Adventures of Frank Grouard*, 114 (quotation). The ease of getting from Piney Creek to Peno Creek is plainly apparent on the "Drainage Map" accompanying Legoski's *General George Crook's Campaign of 1876*, 9. John Gray was the first to suggest that Crook had lost his way and ended up on Prairie Dog Creek unintentionally. Others seem to have accepted Gray's assertion without further consideration and also seem to have been unaware of Finerty's and Grouard's statements. See Gray, *Centennial Campaign*, 113–14; McDermott, "Gen. George Crook's 1876 Campaigns," 24; Mathews, "Crook's Fight on Tongue River," 12n17; Mangum, *Battle of the Rosebud*, 35–36; Magid, *The Gray Fox*, 230–31; Buecker, *A Brave Soldier*, 119.

30. "Uncle Sam's Crook," *Chicago Times*, July 1, 1876.

31. Capron, "The Indian Border War of 1876," 484 (quotations); Meketa, *Marching with General Crook*, 9–10; "Crook," *Weekly Rocky Mountain News*, June 28, 1876; Bourke, *On the Border with Crook*, 294; Zinser, *Indian War Diary*, 9; Hartsuff Report, NA. The precise location of this night's camp has many labels in the sources—Peno, Pine, Piney, Pewee, and Hay. Gerhard Luhn, James Foster, and others set the identity straight. Nottage, "The Big Horn and Yellowstone Expedition of 1876," 32; "The Sioux War," *Chicago Tribune*, July 5, 1876.

32. Noyes, "Story of My Life," TS, 84, Noyes-Wallace Family Collection, UCSB; Bourke, *Diaries*, 1:301 (quotation).

33. "The Sioux War," *Chicago Tribune*, July 5, 1876; Bourke, *Diaries*, 1:301–3; Buecker, *A Brave Soldier*, 119; Stanton, "Annual Report," 711; Abrams, *"Crying for Scalps,"* 60, 61 (quotation).

34. Stanton, "Annual Report," 711; Abrams, *"Crying for Scalps,"* 61; Finerty, *War-Path and Bivouac*, 88; "Crook's Expedition," *Chicago Inter-Ocean*, June 27, 1876.

35. Hartsuff Report, NA; "Uncle Sam's Crook," *Chicago Times*, July 1, 1876; Zinser, *Indian War Diary*, 9.

36. Zinser, *Indian War Diary*, 9; Bourke, *Diaries*, 1:303 (quotation); Nottage, "The Big Horn and Yellowstone Expedition of 1876," 32; *Revised United States Army Regulations*, 44–45; "The Sioux War," *Chicago Tribune*, July 5, 1876; Wilhelm, *A Military Dictionary and Gazetteer*, 486. Bourke noted that the formal escort numbered twelve men, but the *Regulations* that he cited prescribed an escort of eight men, a complement commensurate with Tierney's rank.

37. "Crook," *Weekly Rocky Mountain News*, June 28, 1876; *Book of Common Prayer*, 226 (first quotation), 227–29; *Revised United States Army Regulations*, 45; Bourke, *Diaries*, 1:303; Finerty, *War-Path and Bivouac*, 90; "Crook's Expedition," *Philadelphia Press*, June 30, 1876 (second quotation); "The Big Horn Expedition," *Chicago Inter-Ocean*, July 6, 1876 (third quotation).

Captain Henry's reading from the Episcopal prayer book was a throwback to his days at West Point, where the Episcopal Church functioned as the de facto church at the academy and was embraced as the best Christian tradition to help shape young men into officers and gentlemen. White, *American Ulysses*, 41.

In 1890 Tierney was disinterred and reburied in the post cemetery at Fort McKinney on Clear Creek near Buffalo, Wyoming. Guy Henry, now a major in the Ninth Cavalry and the officer officiating at Tierney's initial burial, supervised the reburial. The remains were escorted to the grave by a battalion of cavalry, with the body borne on an artillery caisson. The event was witnessed by the citizens of Buffalo assembled in celebration of Memorial Day. As late as the 1950s the partially filled grave on Prairie Dog Creek was still plainly visible. With the abandonment of Fort McKinney in 1894, Tierney's remains were reburied again in 1895 in the Custer National Cemetery, Crow Agency, Montana. "Fort McKinney," *Army and Navy Journal*, June 14, 1890; Vaughn, *Indian Fights*, 123; "Francis Tierney," www.findagrave.com.

38. Stanton, "Annual Report," 711; Abrams, *"Crying for Scalps,"* 61 (first quotation); Bourke, *Diaries*, 1:304; Capron, "The Indian Border War of 1876," 484 (second quotation); Nottage, "The Big Horn and Yellowstone Expedition of 1876," 31; "The Sioux War," *Chicago Tribune*, July 5, 1876.

39. "The Sioux War," *Chicago Tribune*, July 5, 1876.

40. "Uncle Sam's Crook," *Chicago Times*, July 1, 1876; "The Sioux War," *Chicago Tribune*, July 5, 1876; Reneau, *The Adventures of Moccasin Joe*, 59; Meketa, *Marching with General Crook*, 11.

41. Finerty, *War-Path and Bivouac*, 91–92 (quotations); Crawford, *Rekindling Camp Fires*, 242–43; Abrams, *"Crying for Scalps,"* 62.

42. Nottage, "The Big Horn and Yellowstone Expedition of 1876," 31; Capron, "The Indian Border War of 1876," 484; Zinser, *Indian War Diary*, 9; "The Sioux War," *Chicago Tribune*, July 5, 1876; "Crook's Expedition," *Chicago Inter-Ocean*, June 27, 1876; "Crook's Expedition," *Philadelphia Press*, June 30, 1876 (quotation).

43. "Uncle Sam's Crook," *Chicago Times*, July 1, 1876; Bourke, *On the Border with Crook*, 298; Williams to Crook, June 5, 1876, Crook Papers, University of Oregon (first quotation); "Crook's Expedition," *Chicago Inter-Ocean*, June 16, 1876; Bourke, *Diaries*, 1:304 (second quotation).

44. "Gen. Crook's Expedition," *Daily Alta California*, July 6, 1876 (first quotation); Bourke, *Diaries*, 1:304; "The Sioux War," *Chicago Tribune*, July 5, 1876; Dewees letter, [June] 9, 1876, FLNHS; Abrams, *"Crying for Scalps,"* 62, 63 (second quotation).

45. "Brave Boys Are They," *Rocky Mountain News*, August 8, 1876, in Cozzens, *Eyewitnesses to the Indian Wars*, 262–63 (first and third quotations); "Crook's Expedition," *Philadelphia Press*, June 30, 1876; "The Sioux War," *Frank Leslie's Illustrated Newspaper*, August 12, 1876, 373; Strahorn, "Ninety Years of Boyhood," Strahorn Papers, College of Idaho, 142 (second quotation).

46. Nottage, "The Big Horn and Yellowstone Expedition of 1876," 32.

CHAPTER 6. TONGUE RIVER HEIGHTS

1. Marquis, *A Warrior Who Fought Custer*, 192–93; Hedren, *Powder River*, 217–19.

2. Marquis, *A Warrior Who Fought Custer*, 193, 194 (quotation).

3. Ibid., 194, 195 (quotations).

4. Ibid., 195–96.

5. Little Hawk reminiscence in Greene, *Lakota and Cheyenne*, 23; Marquis, *A Warrior Who Fought Custer*, 196 (first quotation), 197 (second quotation); DeMallie, *The Sixth Grandfather*, 174.

6. Little Hawk reminiscence in Greene, *Lakota and Cheyenne*, 23.

7. Nottage, "The Big Horn and Yellowstone Expedition of 1876," 32 (first and second quotations); Luhn Autobiography, Luhn Papers, Box 1, Folder 2, 30, AHC; "Uncle Sam's Crook," *Chicago Times*, July 1, 1876 (third and fourth quotations); Abrams, *"Crying for Scalps,"* 63 (fifth quotation).

8. "Uncle Sam's Crook," *Chicago Times*, July 1, 1876; Meketa, *Marching with General Crook*, 13 (first quotation), 14; "The Sioux War," *Chicago Tribune*, July 5, 1876 (second quotation).

9. "The Sioux War," *New York Tribune*, July 1, 1876; "Gen. Crook's Expedition," *Daily Alta California*, July 6, 1876; "The Sioux War," *Chicago Tribune*, July 5, 1876; "The Indians," *Chicago Tribune*, June 19, 1876; "The Sioux War," *Cincinnati Commercial*, July 17, 1876.

10. Meketa, *Marching with General Crook*, 14 (first quotation); "The Sioux War," *Chicago Tribune*, July 5, 1876 (second quotation).

11. "Uncle Sam's Crook," *Chicago Times*, July 1, 1876 (quotations); "The Sioux War," *Chicago Tribune*, July 5, 1876; "Statement of Officers and Troops Composing the Big Horn [*sic*] Expedition," Division of the Missouri, Special Files, NA; Abrams, "'A Very Lively Little Affair,'" 12.

12. Abrams, *"Crying for Scalps,"* 63 (first quotation), 64 (second quotation). Artifacts recovered from the Indians' crest-line position confirm their use of .44 caliber Henry or Winchester carbines and .50 caliber breechloading rifles, likely .50–70 Springfield rifles or cut-down rifles. Many of the chroniclers noted that the Indians were armed with long-range rifles. Werts and Booras, *The Crazy Horse and Crook Fight of 1876*, 23, 99n13; "Crook's Expedition," *Chicago Inter-Ocean*, June 16, 1876; "Crook's Expedition," *Philadelphia Press*, June 30, 1876.

13. "The Sioux War," *Chicago Tribune*, July 5, 1876; "Uncle Sam's Crook," *Chicago Times*, July 1, 1876 (quotations). Regarding an official name for the episode, in the AGO's *Chronological List of Actions, &c., with Indians* the evening demonstration was recorded simply as the fight on Tongue River, June 9, 1876. That identification is similarly noted on a participant's discharge, where a soldier's engagements are customarily listed. Private George W. McAnulty discharge, February 29, 1880, Hedren, Sioux War Papers. Heitman's "Chronological list of battles, actions, etc., in which troops of the Regular Army have participated" similarly identified the action by place, Tongue River, Wyoming, June 9, 1876. Heitman, *Historical Register and Dictionary of the United States Army*, 2:442. The episode is not acknowledged in *Record of Engagements with Hostile Indians*, published in 1882. Finerty labeled it the Tongue River Bluffs battle. "Uncle Sam's Crook," *Chicago Times*, July 1, 1876. The Tongue River Heights designation embraced here reflects notations neatly printed atop a Third Cavalryman's discharge paper, noted in Hedren, *Powder River*, 394–95n31, and observed also on William Miller's discharge, William Miller Papers, FLNHS.

14. "Uncle Sam's Crook," *Chicago Times*, July 1, 1876 (first quotation); Finerty, *War-Path and Bivouac*, 97 (second quotation); Nottage, "The Big Horn and Yellowstone Expedition of 1876," 32 (third quotation); "Crook Heard From," *Cheyenne Daily Leader*, June 16, 1876; "Crook's Expedition," *Chicago Inter-Ocean*, June 16, 1876; *Army and Navy Journal*, June 24, 1876, 741; "Big Horn Expedition," *Army and Navy Journal*, July 1, 1876, 758; Bourke, *Diaries*, 1:305 (fourth quotation).

15. Meketa, *Marching with General Crook*, 14; "The Sioux War," *Chicago Tribune*, July 5, 1876; "Brave Boys Are They," *Rocky Mountain News*, August 8, 1876, in Cozzens, *Eyewitnesses to the Indian Wars*, 263; "Crook's Expedition," *Philadelphia Press*, June 30, 1876; Strahorn, "Ninety Years of Boyhood," 143 (first quotation), Strahorn Papers, College of Idaho; Bourke, *Diaries*, 1:306 (second quotation).

16. Meketa, *Marching with General Crook*, 15 (first quotation); Nottage, "The Big Horn and Yellowstone Expedition of 1876," 32 (second quotation); Luhn Papers, AHC; [Powell,] *Records of Living Officers*, 249.

17. "Crook's Expedition," *Philadelphia Press*, June 30, 1876.

18. Bourke, *Diaries*, 1:305.

19. "Crook's Expedition," *Philadelphia Press*, June 30, 1876.

20. Bourke, *Diaries*, 1:306; Meketa, *Marching with General Crook*, 15; "The Sioux War," *Chicago Tribune*, July 5, 1876.

21. "The Sioux War," *Chicago Tribune*, July 5, 1876; "The Indian Campaign," *Chicago Inter-Ocean*, June 21, 1876 (quotation); Gray, *Centennial Campaign*, 116; Mathews, "Crook's Fight on Tongue River," 12; Stanton, "Annual Report," 711.

22. Bourke, *Diaries*, 1:306–307; Strahorn, "Ninety Years of Boyhood," Strahorn Papers, College of Idaho, 143; Nottage, "The Big Horn and Yellowstone Expedition of 1876," 32; Capron, "The Indian Border War of 1876," 485; Crook to Sheridan, June 11, 1876, BH&Y Expedition Order Book, NA (quotation).

23. Bourke, *Diaries*, 1:307 (first quotation); "The Sioux War," *Chicago Tribune*, July 5, 1876 (second quotation); White, *American Ulysses*, 447 (third and fourth quotations).

24. Bourke, *Diaries*, 1:308–309; Meketa, *Marching with General Crook*, 16; Luhn Diary, Luhn Papers, AHC; Reneau, *The Adventures of Moccasin Joe*, 61; "The Battle of the Rosebud," *Pittsburg Leader*, July 21, 1876. Capron believed that Noyes bagged the cinnamon bear; Bourke identified Mills.

25. Bourke, *Diaries*, 1:308–309; Meketa, *Marching with General Crook*, 16.

26. Bourke, *Diaries*, 1:309–10.

27. McLaird, *Calamity Jane*, 49 (quotation); Etulain, *The Life and Legends of Calamity Jane*, 46.

28. McLaird, *Calamity Jane*, 37–40; Etulain, *The Life and Legends of Calamity Jane*, 42–43; John Hunton, "My Recollections of Calamity Jane," in Flannery, *John Hunton's Diary*, 111; Hedren, *Fort Laramie in 1876*, 115.

29. "Crook's Expedition," *Chicago Inter-Ocean*, June 8, 1876 (quotation); "Crook's Camp Followers," *Cheyenne Daily Leader*, June 13, 1876.

30. Email, Tom Lindmier to author, January 10, 2017; McLaird, *Calamity Jane*, 47.

31. Crawford, *Rekindling Camp Fires*, 242–47; "Crook," *Weekly Rocky Mountain News*, June 28, 1876; "Gen. Crook's Expedition," *Daily Alta California*, July 6, 1876.

32. McLaird, *Calamity Jane*, 48, citing "Calamity Jane," *Rocky Mountain News*, June 25, 1876; "Jane's Jamboree," *Cheyenne Daily Leader*, June 20, 1876; Hedren, *Fort Laramie in 1876*, 115.

33. Crawford, *Rekindling Camp Fires*, 248 (quotation), 249.

34. Bourke, *On the Border with Crook*, 299–300 (quotation); Strahorn, "Ninety Years of Boyhood," Strahorn Papers, College of Idaho, 145–47.

35. Daly, "The Powder-Stained 70's," 19; "Pony Soldier Sets Record Straight," *Buffalo Bulletin*, June 28, 1984 (quotation).

36. Mills, "Address by General Anson Mills," 6.

37. Ibid. (first quotation); "Pony Soldier Sets Record Straight," *Buffalo Bulletin*, June 28, 1984 (second quotation).

CHAPTER 7. FATEFUL INTELLIGENCE

1. Bourke, *Diaries*, 1:309–10 (quotations); "The Indian Campaign," *Chicago Inter-Ocean*, June 21, 1876; Magid, *The Gray Fox*, 234.

2. "The Sioux War," *New York Tribune*, July 1, 1876 (first quotation); William Miller Papers, FLNHS (second quotation).

3. Abrams, *"Crying for Scalps,"* 70 (quotation); Bourke, *Diaries*, 1:311.

4. DeBarthe, *Life and Adventures of Frank Grouard*, 111–12.

5. Ibid., 113.

6. "No Crows for Crook," *Cheyenne Daily Leader*, June 20, 1876; DeBarthe, *Life and Adventures of Frank Grouard*, 113, 114 (Grouard quotations); "The Sioux War," *Chicago Tribune*, May 2, 1876; Gray, *Centennial Campaign*, 117; Linderman, *American*, 155 (Plenty Coups quotation).

7. "Crook's Expedition," *Chicago Inter-Ocean*, June 27, 1876 (first quotation); Bourke, *Diaries*, 1:312–13; DeBarthe, *Life and Adventures of Frank Grouard*, 114 (second quotation); "Uncle Sam's Crook," *Chicago Times*, July 1, 1876.

8. DeBarthe, *Life and Adventures of Frank Grouard*, 114–15 (quotation); "Uncle Sam's Crook," *Chicago Times*, July 1, 1876; "The Sioux War," *Cincinnati Commercial*, July 17, 1876; Bourke, *Diaries*, 1:310–11.

9. Bourke, *Diaries*, 1:311; "Uncle Sam's Crook," *Chicago Times*, July 1, 1876; Hagan, *"Exactly in the Right Place,"* 239; Gilbert, *"Big Bat" Pourier*, 50; "The Sioux War," *Cincinnati Commercial*, July 17, 1876; Mattes, *Indians, Infants and Infantry*, 217; "Crook's Expedition," *Chicago Inter-Ocean*, June 27, 1876; Linderman, *American*, 156 (quotation); "The Indian Campaign," *Chicago Inter-Ocean*, June 21, 1876.

10. Bourke, *Diaries*, 1:312; Luhn Diary, Luhn Papers, AHC; "Uncle Sam's Crook," *Chicago Times*, July 1, 1876; "The Sioux War," *New York Tribune*, July 1, 1876 (quotation).

11. DeBarthe, *Life and Adventures of Frank Grouard*, 116; Dewees letter, June 14, 1876, FLNHS; "The Sioux War," *Cincinnati Commercial*, July 17, 1876; Daly, "The War Path," 17; Gray, *Centennial Campaign*, 119 (quotation).

12. Little Hawk reminiscence in Greene, *Lakota and Cheyenne*, 23; Marquis, *A Warrior Who Fought Custer*, 196–97.

13. Hedren, *Great Sioux War Orders of Battle*, 34–70; Porter, *Paper Medicine Man*, 40–41; Magid, *The Gray Fox*, 236–37.

14. Bourke, *Diaries*, 1:313.

15. "The Battle of the Rosebud," *New York Times*, July 13, 1876; Bourke, *On the Border with Crook*, 302–303; Bourke, *Diaries*, 1:313 (quotation).

16. "Crook's Expedition," *Philadelphia Press*, July 1, 1876; Dewees letter, June 14, 1876, FLNHS; "The Sioux War," *Cincinnati Commercial*, July 17, 1876; Meketa, *Marching with General Crook*, 16–17 (quotation).

17. DeBarthe, *Life and Adventures of Frank Grouard*, 115; "Uncle Sam's Crook," *Chicago Times*, July 1, 1876; "Crook's Expedition," *Chicago Inter-Ocean*, June 27, 1876; Trenholm and Carley, *The Shoshonis*, 253; "Battle of Rosebud Creek," *New York Herald*, July 6, 1876; "Crook's Expedition," *Philadelphia Press*, July 1, 1876; Hart, "Edmore LeClair," 8–9.

18. Michno, *Encyclopedia of Indian Wars*, 278–80; Hutton, *Phil Sheridan and His Army*, 285; Calloway, "Army Allies or Tribal Survival?," 70–71; "Crook's Expedition," *Philadelphia Press*, July 1, 1876; "Crook's Expedition," *Chicago Inter-Ocean*, June 27, 1876 (quotation).

19. Bourke, *Diaries*, 1:314 (first quotation); "Crook's Expedition," *Chicago Inter-Ocean*, June 27, 1876; "Old Crow," *Chicago Times*, June 21, 1876; "The Battle of the Rosebud," *New York Times*, July 13, 1876; "Crook's Expedition," *Philadelphia Press*, July 1, 1876 (second quotation).

20. Bourke, *Diaries*, 1:314; "The Battle of the Rosebud," *New York Times*, July 13, 1876; Linderman, *American*, 158–59; "Crook's Expedition," *Chicago Inter-Ocean*, June 27, 1876

(quotations); "The Sioux War," *Frank Leslie's Illustrated Newspaper,* September 2, 1876.

21. Bourke, *Diaries,* 1:315.

22. "Uncle Sam's Crook," *Chicago Times,* July 1, 1876; Finerty, *War-Path and Bivouac,* 103; "Old Crow," *Chicago Times,* June 21, 1876 (quotation); Powers, *The Killing of Crazy Horse,* 168.

23. "Uncle Sam's Crook," *Chicago Times,* July 1, 1876 (first quotation); "The Battle of the Rosebud," *New York Times,* July 13, 1876 (second quotation); "Old Crow," *Chicago Times,* June 21, 1876; Bourke, *Diaries,* 1:315.

24. Bourke, *Diaries,* 1:315; "The Sioux War," *Chicago Tribune,* July 5, 1876 (first quotation); "Uncle Sam's Crook," *Chicago Times,* July 1, 1876 (second quotation); "The Sioux War," *Frank Leslie's Illustrated Newspaper,* August 26, 1876; Abrams, *"Crying for Scalps,"* 73 (third quotation).

25. Bourke, *Diaries,* 1:315 (quotation); "Crook," *Weekly Rocky Mountain News,* June 28, 1876.

CHAPTER 8. ELEVENTH U.S. DRAGOONS

1. Nickerson, "Major General George Crook and the Indians," Crook-Kennon Papers, USAWC, 24 (quotations); Bourke, *Diaries,* 1:315; Powers, *The Killing of Crazy Horse,* 168; Abrams, *"Crying for Scalps,"* 76; "The Sioux War," *Frank Leslie's Illustrated Newspaper,* August 26, 1876.

2. "The Sioux War," *Chicago Tribune,* July 5, 1876 (quotation); Finerty, *War-Path and Bivouac,* 113.

3. Lemly, "The Fight on the Rosebud," 13; Nickerson, "Major General George Crook and the Indians," Crook-Kennon Papers, USAWC, 24 (quotation); Bourke, *Diaries,* 1:316.

4. Finerty, *War-Path and Bivouac,* 113; Nickerson, "Major General George Crook and the Indians," Crook-Kennon Papers, USAWC, 24; Stanton, "Annual Report," 712; "The Battle of the Rosebud," *New York Times,* July 13, 1876 (first quotation); Strahorn, "Ninety Years of Boyhood," Strahorn Papers, College of Idaho, 149; DeBarthe, *Life and Adventures of Frank Grouard,* 116 (second quotation).

5. Linderman, *American,* 160–61.

6. Lemly, "The Fight on the Rosebud," 13 (first quotation); Luhn Diary, July 15, 1876, Luhn Papers, AHC (second quotation); Luhn Autobiography, 33, Luhn Papers, AHC.

7. "The Indian War," *New York Herald,* June 24, 1876; Otis, *Circular No. 9,* 20; Hedren, *Powder River,* 108.

8. Essin, *Shavetails and Bell Sharps,* 93–96; Magid, *The Gray Fox,* 25–27, 81; Hedren, *Powder River,* 57–58; Daly, "Following the Bell," 114 (first quotation); Bourke, *On the Border with Crook,* 150 (second quotation).

9. Magid, *George Crook,* 51, 73; Magid, *The Gray Fox,* 24; Michno, *The Deadliest Indian War in the West,* 26, 69, 105, 116, 304; "Crook," *Weekly Rocky Mountain News,* June 28, 1876 (quotation).

10. Mills, "Address by General Anson Mills," 7 (quotation); Lemly, "The Fight on the Rosebud," 13; Cullum, *Biographical Register,* 88–92.

11. "Running Down the Redskins," *Weekly Rocky Mountain News,* June 7, 1876 (first quotation); Heitman, *Historical Register and Dictionary of the United States Army,* 1:293–94; [Powell,] *Records of Living Officers,* 329–30; *Ordnance Memoranda, No. 19,* 56 (second quotation); Chambers ACP File, NA; Greene, "Chasing Sitting Bull and Crazy Horse," 196 (third quotation).

12. Luhn Diary, June 15, 1876, Luhn Papers, AHC; Bourke, *Diaries,* 1:316; Mills, "Address by General Anson Mills," 7; "Crook's Expedition," *Chicago Inter-Ocean,* June 27, 1876; "The Battle of the Rosebud," *New York Times,* July 13, 1876; Kane, "Who Saved Guy Henry at the Battle of the Rosebud?," 10; Lemly, "The Fight on the Rosebud," 13; Stanton, "Annual Report,"

712; "The Sioux War," *Chicago Tribune*, July 5, 1876; Reneau, *The Adventures of Moccasin Joe*, 61; Daly, "Following the Bell," 113.

13. Dewees letter, June 14, 1876, FLNHS. The essential gear is partly described and illustrated in Hutchins, *Boots & Saddles at the Little Bighorn*, and comprehensively detailed in the army's *Ordnance Memoranda, No. 18*. The items mentioned in the text are likely those scrounged and incorporated into each individual set.

14. Bourke, *Diaries*, 1:316; "The Battle of the Rosebud," *New York Times*, July 13, 1876; Brady, *Indian Fights and Fighters*, 191 (quotation); Strahorn, "Ninety Years of Boyhood," 148, Strahorn Papers, College of Idaho; Finerty, *War-Path and Bivouac*, 111–12.

15. Luhn Autobiography, 30, Luhn Papers, AHC (first quotation); Finerty, *War-Path and Bivouac*, 112 (second and third quotations); "The Battle of the Rosebud," *New York Times*, July 13, 1876 (fourth quotation).

16. Finerty, *War-Path and Bivouac*, 112; DeBarthe, *Life and Adventures of Frank Grouard*, 115 (first and second quotations), 116 (third quotation); Essin, "Army Mule," 40.

17. Bourke, *On the Border with Crook*, 305 (first quotation); "The Big Horn Expedition," *Cheyenne Daily Leader*, July 2, 1876 (second quotation); "The Battle of the Rosebud," *New York Times*, July 13, 1876 (third quotation); Luhn Autobiography, 30–31, Luhn Papers, AHC.

18. Bourke, *Diaries*, 1:316 (first quotation); Hedren, *Ho! For the Black Hills*, 209, 212; "The Battle of the Rosebud," *Pittsburg Evening Leader*, July 21, 1876, (second quotation). Foster reported a contingent of sixteen packers, not twenty as Bourke and others have it. "The Sioux War," *Chicago Tribune*, July 5, 1876.

19. Crook to Sheridan, June 15, 1876, Division of the Missouri, Special Files, NA.

20. Linderman, *American*, 161–62, 163 (quotation). Davenport reported five Crows going forward, not nine. "Looking for Sioux," *New York Herald*, June 21, 1876.

21. Bourke, *Diaries*, 1:317; Abrams, *"Crying for Scalps,"* 74. In 1890 Frank Grouard supervised the taking up of bones from the area, including those of Nelson, for reburial in the Fort McKinney Post Cemetery at Buffalo Wyoming. As with Tierney's grave, when Fort McKinney was abandoned, Nelson was reinterred at Custer National Cemetery in 1895. Regrettably, somewhere along the way Nelson's identity was lost. He is among fifteen Fort McKinney reburials recorded simply as unknown in Custer National Cemetery records. According to one source, Nelson's original burial was near the corner of Sheridan's Alger and Brooks Streets (behind the J. C. Penney store according to Vaughn) and was still visible in the mid-1950s. Hanson, *Frank Grouard*, 189; email, Jerry Jasmer to Hedren, December 22, 2016; Vaughn, *Indian Fights*, 126.

CHAPTER 9. TRAIL TO ROSEBUD CREEK

1. Finerty, *War-Path and Bivouac*, 114 (quotation); Bourke, *Diaries*, 1:322; Abrams, *"Crying for Scalps,"* 78.

2. Bourke, *Diaries*, 1:322; Bourke, *On the Border with Crook*, 307; Strahorn, "Ninety Years of Boyhood," 149, Strahorn Papers, College of Idaho; Reneau, *The Adventures of Moccasin Joe*, 61; Meketa, *Marching with General Crook*, 19 (quotation); "The Indian War," *New York Herald*, June 24, 1876; Stanton, "Annual Report," 712; "The Big Horn Expedition," *Cheyenne Daily Leader*, July 2, 1876.

3. Stanton, "Annual Report," 716; "Battle of Rosebud Creek," *New York Herald*, July 6, 1876; Mills, "Address by General Anson Mills," 7; "Battle of Rosebud," *Highland Weekly News*, July 20, 1876; DeBarthe, *Life and Adventures of Frank Grouard*, 116.

4. Abrams, *"Crying for Scalps,"* 78; Finerty, *War-Path and Bivouac*, 114 (first quotation); "A Bull Fight," *Chicago Times*, June 24, 1876; Bourke, *Diaries*, 1:322; "The Sioux War," *Chicago Tribune*, July 11, 1876 (second quotation).

5. Stanton, "Annual Report," 712; "The Sioux War," *Chicago Tribune*, July 5, 1876; Lemly, "The Fight on the Rosebud," 13; Vaughn, *Indian Fights*, 127.

6. Stanton, "Annual Report," 716; Mills, "Address by General Anson Mills," 7.

7. Strahorn, "Ninety Years of Boyhood," 149, Strahorn Papers, College of Idaho.

8. Bourke, *Diaries*, 1:323 (quotation); Linderman, *American*, 163–64; Meketa, *Marching with General Crook*, 19.

9. Bourke, *Diaries*, 1:324 (first quotation), 325; Stanton, "Annual Report," 712; Morton Interview, Camp Papers, BYU; Strahorn, "Ninety Years of Boyhood," 149, Strahorn Papers, College of Idaho; "Braving the Braves," *Chicago Times*, July 5, 1876 (second quotation); Bourke, *On the Border with Crook*, 309; "The Battle of the Rosebud," *Pittsburg Leader*, July 21, 1876; Finerty, *War-Path and Bivouac*, 115 (third quotation).

10. Finerty, *War-Path and Bivouac*, 115–16 (quotations); Bourke, *On the Border with Crook*, 310–11; Strahorn, "Ninety Years of Boyhood," 151, Strahorn Papers, College of Idaho.

11. Hedren, *Powder River*, 72.

12. Finerty, *War-Path and Bivouac*, 118 (first quotation); Stanton, "Annual Report," 713; "Battle of Rosebud Creek," *New York Herald*, July 6, 1876; "The Sioux War," *Chicago Tribune*, July 5, 1876; Lemly, "The Fight on the Rosebud," 13; Mills, "Address by General Anson Mills," 7 (second and third quotations).

Crook's camp on June 16 in the headwaters area of the South Fork of Rosebud Creek has been located and according to historian Keith Werts still features a small marshy lake. Over the years Werts and friends explored the place many times but never found physical evidence confirming that the expedition overnighted there. Lawyer-turned-historian Jesse W. Vaughn also explored the area. While finding no physical evidence himself, he wrote of meeting in 1955 the son of the man who owned much of the land around the Rosebud forks and being given a weather-beaten McClellan saddle found "beside a spring north of the divide" (35). The saddle's pommel and cantle were present as were its rings and attachments, but one of the connecting pieces was broken. A standard reference in Vaughn's *With Crook at the Rosebud* was John Finerty's *War-Path and Bivouac*. Oddly, Vaughn did not recount the reporter's escapade with the pistol in this camp. Might this have been Finerty's saddle? Might a replacement have come from the auxiliaries or Engineer Stanton and Finerty's shot-up saddle been discarded "beside a spring north of the divide"? The whereabouts of this tell-tale relic is unknown today. Werts and Booras, *The Crazy Horse and Crook Fight of 1876*, 36, 100n23; Vaughn, *With Crook at the Rosebud*, 35–36.

13. Lemly, "The Fight on the Rosebud," 13; "Battle of Rosebud," *Highland Weekly News*, July 20, 1876; Pearson, *The Platte-Dakota Campaign of 1876*, 9 (first quotation); DeBarthe, *Life and Adventures of Frank Grouard*, 116 (second quotation); Magid, *The Gray Fox*, 239.

14. "The Battle of Rosebud Creek," *New York Herald*, July 13, 1876; Noyes, "Story of My Life," 85, Noyes-Wallace Family Collection, UCSB; Linderman, *American*, 164–65; Finerty, *War-Path and Bivouac*, 119 (quotations); Crook Report (reports identified by surname are under Campaign and Battle Reports in the bibliography), June 20, 1876, 128; "The Sioux War," *Cincinnati Commercial*, July 17, 1876; "Battle of Rosebud," *Highland Weekly News*, July 20, 1876.

15. "Braving the Braves," *Chicago Times*, July 5, 1876 (first quotation); Abrams, *"Crying for Scalps,"* 80; Nickerson, "Major General George Crook and the Indians," 25, Crook-Kennon Papers, USAWC; "The Big Horn Expedition," *Cheyenne Daily Leader*, July 2, 1876; Reneau, *The Adventures of Moccasin Joe*, 61 (second quotation); Finerty, *War-Path and Bivouac*, 121–22.

16. "Braving the Braves," *Chicago Times*, July 5, 1876; Crawford, *Rekindling Camp Fires*, 249 (quotation); Finerty, *War-Path and Bivouac*, 121.

17. Bourke, *Diaries*, 1:323; "Braving the Braves," *Chicago Times*, July 5, 1876 (first

quotation); Nickerson, "Major General George Crook and the Indians," 25 (second quotation), Crook-Kennon Papers, USAWC.

18. "Battle of the Rosebud," *New York Herald*, July 6, 1876; Lemly, "The Fight on the Rosebud," 13–14; "Battle of the Rosebud," *New York Daily Graphic*, July 13, 1876; "Description of Rosebud Fight," Luhn Diary following the July 23 entry, Luhn Papers, AHC; "The Battle of the Rosebud," *New York Times*, July 13, 1876; Finerty, *War-Path and Bivouac*, 122 (quotation).

19. "The Battle of the Rosebud," *New York Times*, July 13, 1876; "The Sioux War," *New York Tribune*, July 6, 1876; Mears, "Campaigning against Crazy Horse," 70.

20. Abrams, *"Crying for Scalps,"* 80; Stanton, "Annual Report," 713; Nottage, "The Big Horn and Yellowstone Expedition of 1876," 34; "Crook," *Weekly Rocky Mountain News*, July 5, 1876; Schmitt, *General George Crook*, 194; "The Sioux War," *New York Tribune*, July 6, 1876; "Battle of the Rosebud," *New York Daily Graphic*, July 13, 1876; "The Sioux War," *Chicago Tribune*, July 5, 1876; Dickson, "With General Crook's Campaign," 4. The time given here, 8 A.M., is a consensus appearing in nearly every account, although engineer Stanton, the expedition's official recorder, wrote 7:15 A.M.

21. Bourke, *On the Border with Crook*, 311 (first quotation); "The Sioux War," *Cincinnati Commercial*, July 17, 1876 (second quotation); "Crook," *Weekly Rocky Mountain News*, July 5, 1876; "The Battle of the Rosebud," *New York Times*, July 13, 1876 (third quotation).

22. *Ordnance Manual*, 155, 159; Hutchins, *Boots & Saddles at the Little Bighorn*, 50, 54.

23. "Baptiste Pourier's Interview," in Jensen, *The Settler and Soldier Interviews of Eli S. Ricker*, 266; Meketa, *Marching with General Crook*, 19; Zinser, *Indian War Diary*, 12 (quotation).

24. Hedren, *Powder River*, 178–79, 293–94; Noyes Report, 133 (quotation).

25. Meketa, *Marching with General Crook*, 19; Nickerson, "Major General George Crook and the Indians," 25, Crook-Kennon Papers, USAWC; "The Sioux War," *Chicago Tribune*, July 5, 1876; Zinser, *Indian War Diary*, 12; Lemly, "The Fight on the Rosebud," 14; Finerty, *War-Path and Bivouac*, 122; "The Sioux War," *Cincinnati Commercial*, July 17, 1876; "Description of Rosebud Fight," Luhn Diary following the July 23 entry, Luhn Papers, AHC.

26. Lemly, "The Fight on the Rosebud," 14.

27. Mills Report, 150–52; Royall Report, 142; Evans Report, 130–31; "Battle of Rosebud Creek," *New York Herald*, July 6, 1876. This story's many chroniclers and historians generally confuse the placement of troops along Rosebud Creek at the 8 A.M. stop. To a degree this is understandable, because the column stretched for nearly two miles east to west and occupied both banks of the creek. No one individual could see it all. A construction is possible by accepting individual contemporary statements describing where so and so was at any particular moment and generally disregarding where he thought anyone else was at that same time.

28. Noyes Report, 133; Chambers Report, 134–35; "Description of Rosebud Fight," Luhn Diary following the July 23 entry, Luhn Papers, AHC; Lemly, "The Fight on the Rosebud," 13; Mills, "Address by General Anson Mills," 8; Mills, *My Story*, 405; King, "Recollections of General Crook," 515.

29. "Braving the Braves," *Chicago Times*, July 5, 1876.

30. Mills Report, 152; Royall Report, 144; "Battle of the Rosebud," *Pittsburg Leader*, July 21, 1876 (quotation).

31. "Gen. Crook's Fight with the Sioux," *Perrysburg Journal*, July 7, 1876 (first quotation); "The Sioux War," *Cincinnati Commercial*, July 17, 1876; "On the War-Path," *Chicago Inter-Ocean*, June 24, 1876; Finerty, *War-Path and Bivouac*, 123; "The Battle of the Rosebud," *New York Times*, July 13, 1876; "The Sioux War," *Chicago Tribune*, July 5, 1876 (second and third quotations).

32. Schmitt, *General George Crook*, 194 (first quotation); Mills, *My Story*, 404 (second and third quotations); Finerty, *War-Path and Bivouac*, 123 (fourth quotation).

CHAPTER 10. ON RENO CREEK

1. Utley, *The Lance and the Shield*, 139; Bray, *Crazy Horse*, 204; Vestal, *Sitting Bull*, 152.

2. Marquis, *A Warrior Who Fought Custer*, 196 (quotation), 197; "Little Hawk Reminiscence," in Greene, *Lakota and Cheyenne*, 23.

3. Bray, *Crazy Horse*, 204–205; Gray, *Centennial Campaign*, 332–33; Marquis, *A Warrior Who Fought Custer*, 197.

4. Dixon, *The Vanishing Race*, 65–66; Hunt and Hunt, *I Fought with Custer*, 215–16; Marshall, "How Many Indians Were There?," 214.

5. Bray, *Crazy Horse*, 205; Marquis, *A Warrior Who Fought Custer*, 197; Vestal, *Sitting Bull*, 152; Utley, *The Lance and the Shield*, 139; Vestal, *New Sources of Indian History*, 163.

6. Dixon, *The Vanishing Race*, 65; "Little Hawk Reminiscence," in Greene, *Lakota and Cheyenne*, 23; Stands in Timber and Liberty, *A Cheyenne Voice*, 424, 428–29; Grinnell, *The Fighting Cheyennes*, 330.

7. "Young Two Moon Account," in Greene, *Lakota and Cheyenne*, 26.

8. "Little Hawk Reminiscence," in Greene, *Lakota and Cheyenne*, 24 (quotations); Grinnell, *The Fighting Cheyennes*, 330–31.

9. "Little Hawk Reminiscence," in Greene, *Lakota and Cheyenne*, 24, 25 (quotations); Grinnell, *The Fighting Cheyennes*, 331.

10. "Little Hawk Reminiscence," in Greene, *Lakota and Cheyenne*, 25 (quotation); Grinnell, *The Fighting Cheyennes*, 331–32; Grinnell, *The Cheyenne Indians*, 2:228; Stands in Timber and Liberty, *A Cheyenne Voice*, 270.

11. Stands in Timber and Liberty, *A Cheyenne Voice*, 270.

12. Hammer, *Custer in '76*, 205, 211; Marquis, *A Warrior Who Fought Custer*, 198; Vestal, *Warpath*, 185; "The Story of White Man Runs Him," in Graham, *The Custer Myth*, 23; "Interview with Thomas Disputed," in Liddic and Harbaugh, *Camp on Custer*, 124–25; Clark, *The Killing of Chief Crazy Horse*, 131; Hutchins, *The Papers of Edward S. Curtis*, 99, 136, 147, 148. The massive though then abandoned Northern Indian campsite sprawling up and down Reno Creek at its South Fork junction is important to the Custer story in ways partly detailed in this volume. This intrigue is additionally explored by Meketa and Bookwalter in *The Search for the Lone Tepee*. Two revealing historical maps of the Reno Creek-South Fork confluence area are presented and discussed in Donahue, *Drawing Battle Lines*, 315–20.

13. Marquis, *A Warrior Who Fought Custer*, 198; "Forcing of Tribe from Black Hills Country Provoked Trouble," *Billings Gazette*, July 17, 1932. This confluence center-point is easily located. Since the 1920s, and perhaps earlier, a local road bridge has crossed Reno Creek just below the South Fork confluence. This crossing exists today.

14. Marquis, *A Warrior Who Fought Custer*, 198; Utley, *The Lance and the Shield*, 140; Powell, *People of the Sacred Mountain*, 2:956; Porter, *Paper Medicine Man*, 42.

15. Powell, *People of the Sacred Mountain*, 2:956; Eastman, "Rain-in-the-Face," 511 (first quotation); Bray, *Crazy Horse*, 205; Sandoz, *Crazy Horse*, 315 (second quotation); Marquis, *A Warrior Who Fought Custer*, 198 (third quotation).

16. Eastman, "Rain-in-the-Face," 511 (first quotation); Dixon, *The Vanishing Race*, 66 (second quotation); "Wrinkled Cheyenne Warriors Tell of Battle with Crook and His Soldiers on the Rosebud," *Billings Gazette*, June 24, 1934; Powell, *People of the Sacred Mountain*, 2:956; Grinnell, *The Fighting Cheyennes*, 332; Killsback, "Crowns of Honor," 13–14; Vestal, *Warpath*, 186 (third quotation); Howard, *The Warrior Who Killed Custer*, 48; Powers, *The Killing of Crazy Horse*, 177.

17. Powell, *People of the Sacred Mountain*, 2:956; Powers, *The Killing of Crazy Horse*, 176–77; High Dog, "Wearing Battle Charms," in Buechel and Manhart, *Lakota Tales & Texts*, 1:297–98; Killsback, "Crowns of Honor," 7; Donovan, *A Terrible Glory*, 147.

18. Hinman, "Oglala Sources on the Life of Crazy Horse," 13–14; Jackson, *Black Elk*, 80; Joseph Black Elk, "Life of Warrior Chief Crazy Horse," in Kadlecek and Kadlecek, *To Kill an Eagle*, 80; Peter Bordeaux, "Statement," in Kadlecek and Kadlecek, *To Kill an Eagle*, 89; Powers, *The Killing of Crazy Horse*, 178–80. The story of Crazy Horse's spiritual beliefs and customs, explained within the religiosity of the Lakotas, is consciously summarized here. It is a critically important element of the story and no better told than by Tom Powers (*The Killing of Crazy Horse*, 176–81), who, moreover, places it within the context of the Rosebud battle. Crazy Horse's ear and heart stones and other battle medicines survive and are carefully described by Belitz, "Chips Collection of Crazy Horse Medicines," 101–108; and pictured in Brown, *Thunder Visions*, 15–26.

19. Vestal, *Sitting Bull*, 146–47; "The White Bull Interview," in Hardorff, *Indian Views of the Custer Fight*, 164; Bear Soldier Interview, Crawford Papers, SHSND; Werts and Booras, *The Crazy Horse and Crook Fight of 1876*, 115.

20. Powers, *The Killing of Crazy Horse*, 176 ("open and shoot").

21. "Kill Eagle's Story," *New York Herald*, October 6, 1876 (all quotations except as indicated in note 20).

22. Vestal, *Warpath*, 186–87; Garavaglia and Worman, *Firearms of the American West*, 128; Marquis, *A Warrior Who Fought Custer*, 199 (quotation), 200; Scott, "Ammunition Components from the Rosebud Battlefield"; Scott, "Systematic Metal Detector Survey and Assessment"; Miltner, "History and Archaeology of the Rosebud Battlefield"; McDermott, "Gen. George Crook's 1876 Campaigns," 48; Werts and Booras, *The Crazy Horse and Crook Fight of 1876*, 165–66; White, "Artifacts from the Battle of the Rosebud."

23. "Flying By Interview," May 21, 1907, Camp Papers, MMS 56, Box 6, BYU; Vestal, *Warpath*, 187; "Young Two Moon Account," in Greene, *Lakota and Cheyenne*, 26–27; "Little Hawk Reminiscence," in ibid., 25; Grinnell, *The Fighting Cheyennes*, 332; "Weasel Bear Reminiscence," in Hunt and Hunt, *I Fought with Custer*, 216.

24. Stands in Timber and Liberty, *A Cheyenne Voice*, 428; Stands in Timber and Liberty, *Cheyenne Memories*, 182; Fox, "The Value of Oral History," 8; Powell, *People of the Sacred Mountain*, 2:957.

25. Bray, *Crazy Horse*, 206; Powers, *The Killing of Crazy Horse*, 175.

26. Vestal, *Sitting Bull*, 153; Utley, *The Lance and the Shield*, 141; "White Bull Interview," July 23, 1910, Camp Papers, MMS 57, Box 2, Group 1, BYU.

27. "Young Two Moon Account," in Greene, *Lakota and Cheyenne*, 26; Grinnell, *The Fighting Cheyennes*, 332; Marquis, *A Warrior Who Fought Custer*, 199; "Iron Hawk Tells about the Rosebud Battle," in DeMallie, *The Sixth Grandfather*, 174. The Sioux Pass in this instance is not the same as a better-known Sioux Pass located some twelve miles straight west of the Three-Mile Reach.

28. This is a simple calculation drawn from DeLorme's *Montana Atlas & Gazetteer*, 32. Two Moon's dog-leg route was longer, nearly thirty miles.

29. Powell, *People of the Sacred Mountain*, 2:956.

30. "Interview with Thomas Disputed," in Liddic and Harbaugh, *Camp on Custer*, 125; DeMallie, *The Sixth Grandfather*, 174; Neihardt, *Black Elk Speaks*, 99; Jackson, *Black Elk*, 101; "Kill Eagle's Story," *New York Herald*, October 6, 1876; Grinnell, *The Fighting Cheyennes*, 336–37; Anderson, "Cheyennes at the Little Big Horn," 87; Stands in Timber and Liberty, *A Cheyenne Voice*, 435.

The final population calculation in chapter 4 remains telling. Using the multipliers embraced in this work, the Northern Indian village on June 17, 1876, likely numbered some 840 men. A few were too old to fight. Some remained behind to guard the village when the others rode away. A few warriors were added when Two Moon's band passed Magpie Eagle's camp. Somewhere between 750 to 800 Indian combatants in the Battle of the Rosebud seems like a defensible number.

31. Grinnell, *The Fighting Cheyennes*, 337–39; Powell, *People of the Sacred Mountain*, 2:957–59; Stands in Timber and Liberty, *Cheyenne Memories*, 184–85.

32. Stands in Timber and Liberty, *Cheyenne Memories*, 184–85; Stands in Timber and Liberty, *A Cheyenne Voice*, 416.

33. Stands in Timber and Liberty, *Cheyenne Memories*, 185; Stands in Timber and Liberty, *A Cheyenne Voice*, 427, 430; Vaughn, *With Crook at the Rosebud*, 135.

34. Grinnell, *The Fighting Cheyennes*, 333; "Young Two Moon Account," in Greene, *Lakota and Cheyenne*, 27 (quotations).

INTERLUDE: NOTES ON ROSEBUD GEOGRAPHY

1. Clausewitz, *On War*, 416.

2. Mangum, "Rosebud Battlefield Historic Base Data Study," 29.

3. Strahorn, "Ninety Days of Boyhood," 152, Strahorn Papers, College of Idaho.

4. "The Sioux War," *New York Tribune*, July 16, 1876; Clausewitz, *On War*, 421.

5. "Crook," *Weekly Rocky Mountain News*, July 5, 1876.

6. Rosebud Battlefield landmarks are documented by Mangum in "Rosebud Battlefield Historic Base Data Study." Robert O'Neill's "Rosebud" and Dave Roth and Robert O'Neill's "General Crook's Expeditions against Hostile Indians" offer a splendid array of color photographs showing many of the battlefield's critical vistas and attractions. A caution is necessary, however. These works also feature numerous battle maps that in many instances do not comport with movements detailed in this study. A generous array of battlefield photographs also fills Werts and Booras's *The Crazy Horse and Crook Fight of 1876*.

CHAPTER 11. OPENING SALVOS

1. Finerty, *War-Path and Bivouac*, 123 (first quotation); "Braving the Braves," *Chicago Times*, July 5, 1876 (second quotation).

2. DeBarthe, *Life and Adventures of Frank Grouard*, 117.

3. "A Bull Fight," *Chicago Times*, June 24, 1876 (first quotation); "Braving the Braves," *Chicago Times*, July 5, 1876 (second quotation); Pollock, "With the Third Cavalry in 1876," 105 (third quotation).

4. Finerty, *War-Path and Bivouac*, 123; Chambers Report, 135 (first quotation); Luhn Autobiography, 30, Luhn Papers, AHC (second quotation); Munson Report, 136 (third quotation).

5. Finerty, *War-Path and Bivouac*, 123 (quotation); Leermakers, "The Battle of the Rosebud," 31; Vaughn, *With Crook at the Rosebud*, 86; Werts and Booras, *The Crazy Horse and Crook Fight of 1876*, 167; Stands in Timber and Liberty, *A Cheyenne Voice*, 437. Tom Penson, first owner of the land upon which many picket pins were found and himself the prime collector of those pins and other remarkable battle artifacts, freely gave most of them away as souvenirs, especially when veterans of the fight visited later. Letter, Penny Penson Iekel to author, August 25, 2016. Crook's troops camped near but apparently not on this same ground on the evening of June 17. Some writers have asserted that the pins were abandoned the next day, but that seems unlikely. The departure on the morning of June 18 was not under duress. In any other context picket pins were useful and accountable property.

6. Lemly, "The Fight on the Rosebud," 14; Abrams, "*Crying for Scalps*," 81; "The Indian War," *New York Herald*, June 24, 1876; Nickerson, "Major General George Crook and the Indians," 25 (quotations), Crook-Kennon Papers, USAWC; "The Indian War," *New York Herald*, June 24, 1876.

7. Abrams, *"Crying for Scalps,"* 81; DeBarthe, *Life and Adventures of Frank Grouard,* 117 (quotation).

8. Schmitt, *General George Crook,* 194 (quotation); Nickerson, "Major General George Crook and the Indians," 25, Crook-Kennon Papers, USAWC; Bourke, *On the Border with Crook,* 311–12; Bourke, *Diaries,* 1:325; DeBarthe, *Life and Adventures of Frank Grouard,* 117, 119.

9. Nickerson, "Major General George Crook and the Indians," 25–26, Crook-Kennon Papers, USAWC.

10. "Crook," *Weekly Rocky Mountain News,* July 5, 1876.

11. Bourke, *Diaries,* 1:325.

12. [Hanna,] *An Old Timer's Story of the Old Wild West,* 46 (first quotation); Brady, *Indian Fights and Fighters,* 194 (second quotation); Mears, "Campaigning against Crazy Horse," 70–71 (third quotation).

13. "The Battle of the Rosebud," *New York Times,* July 13, 1876; "Battle of Rosebud Creek," *New York Herald,* July 6, 1876; Daly, "The War Path," 18 (first quotation); DeBarthe, *Life and Adventures of Frank Grouard,* 117 (second and third quotations); Bourke, *Diaries,* 1:317.

14. DeBarthe, *Life and Adventures of Frank Grouard,* 117 (first quotation); Dixon, *The Vanishing Race,* 103 (second quotation); Brown, *The Plainsmen of the Yellowstone,* 267, 268 (third quotation).

15. Linderman, *Pretty-Shield,* 230–31; Miller, *Custer's Fall,* 239–40; Ewers, "Deadlier Than the Male," 10–11; Thomas, "Daughters of the Lance," 150–51.

16. "The Big Horn Expedition," *Cheyenne Daily Leader,* July 2, 1876; Chambers Report, 135; Nottage, "The Big Horn and Yellowstone Expedition of 1876," 35; Burt Report, 139; "Crook," *Weekly Rocky Mountain News,* July 5, 1876; "Statement of Officers and Troops Composing the Big Horn [*sic*] Expedition," Division of the Missouri, Special Files, NA; Fourth Infantry Regimental Returns, June 1876, NA.

17. "The Indian War," *New York Herald,* June 24, 1876; "Crook," *Weekly Rocky Mountain News,* July 5, 1876 (quotation); "The Big Horn Expedition," *Cheyenne Daily Leader,* July 2, 1876.

18. "Crook's Expedition!" *Platte Valley Independent,* July 8, 1876 (quotation); Avery Billings Cain, Names File, Archives, FLNHS.

A Vermont native, Cain was commissioned directly from civil life into the Fourth U.S. Infantry in August 1861 and served continuously with the regiment throughout the Civil War, being promoted to captain in October 1863. The Fourth and nine other Regular Army infantry regiments formed George Sykes's stellar Regular Infantry Division in the Army of the Potomac's Fifth Corps. With Sykes's Regulars, Cain was engaged at Yorktown, Fair Oaks, Gaines Mill, and Malvern Hill in the Peninsular Campaign as well as Second Bull Run, South Mountain, Antietam, and Chancellorsville. He was hospitalized during the Gettysburg campaign and battle, an action that spelled the virtual ruin of the Regular Infantry Division. The following spring Cain participated in the skirmishes at North Anna River and Totopotomoy Creek. By late June 1864 the decimated Fourth Infantry, barely numbering the size of a prewar company in those months, was withdrawn from line service, consolidated with the comparably shredded Second Infantry, and posted to City Point, Virginia, where it served as Grant's headquarters guard. Cain commanded the consolidated unit until Lee's surrender (with Second Lieutenant Gerhard Luhn commanding a company and serving as regimental adjutant).

Following the war, the reconstituted Fourth, with Cain again commanding a company, served on Reconstruction duty in Kentucky and Arkansas and at posts in the Department of the Platte. He came to the Big Horn and Yellowstone Expedition from Fort Fred Steele, Wyoming. "4th Infantry," *Army and Navy Journal,* April 12, 1879; Reese, *Regulars!,* 133, 208, 255;

Fourth Infantry Regimental Returns, June, July 1863, NA; Leyden, "The Fourth Regiment of Infantry," 464; Newell and Shrader, *Of Duty Well and Faithfully Done*, 236; "Maj. Avery Billings Cain," www.findagrave.com; Avery Billings Cain, Names File, Archives, FLNHS.

19. Cain Report, 140; "List of Wounded," Hartsuff Report, NA.

20. Nottage, "The Big Horn and Yellowstone Expedition of 1876," 35; "Crook's Expedition!" *Platte Valley Independent*, July 8, 1876.

21. Nottage, "The Big Horn and Yellowstone Expedition of 1876," 35; "The Battle of the Rosebud," *New York Times*, July 13, 1876 (quotation); "Crook," *Weekly Rocky Mountain News*, July 5, 1876.

22. Letter, McAnulty to Cynthia Capron, October 6, 1921, Thaddeus Capron Family Papers, AHC.

23. Zinser, *Indian War Diary*, 13.

24. "The Sioux War," *Chicago Tribune*, July 5, 1876; "The Big Horn Expedition," *Cheyenne Daily Leader*, July 2, 1876; Noyes Report, 132–33 (quotation).

25. "Crook," *Weekly Rocky Mountain News*, July 5, 1876.

CHAPTER 12. SWEEPING THE GAP

1. Strahorn, "Ninety Years of Boyhood," 152–53, Strahorn Papers, College of Idaho.

2. Evans Report, 130; "Braving the Braves," *Chicago Times*, July 5, 1876 (quotation).

3. Evans Report, 130; Van Vliet Report, 149, 150 (first quotation); Zinser, *Indian War Diary*, 13; Finerty, *War-Path and Bivouac*, 125, 126 (second quotation).

4. Evans Report, 130–31; Reynolds ACP File, NA; *Official Army Register for January, 1876*, 54–55; Henry Report, 146 (quotations).

5. Mills Report, 150–51.

6. "A Bull Fight," *Chicago Times*, June 24, 1876; "Another Account of Crook's 'Bull' Fight," *Cheyenne Daily Leader*, June 27, 1876; "Gen. Crook's Fight with the Sioux," *Perrysburg Journal*, July 7, 1876 (quotation); "On the War-Path," *Chicago Inter-Ocean*, June 24, 1876.

7. Mills, "Address by General Anson Mills," 8; Andrews Report, 147.

8. "Battle of the Rosebud," *New York Herald*, July 6, 1876; Finerty, *War-Path and Bivouac*, 125 (quotation); Evans Report, 131; Andrews Report, 147; Royall Report, 142; Mills Report, 150–51.

9. Mills, "Address by General Anson Mills," 8 (first and second quotations); "Statement of Officers and Troops Composing the Big Horn [*sic*] Expedition," Division of the Missouri, Special Files, NA; "The Sioux War," *Chicago Tribune*, July 5, 1876 (third quotation); Lawson Report, 152; "The Indian War," *New York Herald*, June 24, 1876; "Battle of the Rosebud," *New York Daily Graphic*, July 13, 1876.

10. Mills Report, 152; Finerty, *War-Path and Bivouac*, 124 (quotation).

11. "A Bull Fight," *Chicago Times*, June 24, 1876. This account also appeared verbatim as "Another Account of Crook's 'Bull' Fight," *Cheyenne Daily Leader,* June 27, 1876.

12. Finerty, *War-Path and Bivouac*, 125.

13. Mills, "Address by General Anson Mills," 8.

14. Ibid., 8 (first quotation), 9 (second quotation); Brady, *Indian Fights and Fighters*, 195.

15. Bourke, *Diaries*, 1:326 (quotations); Finerty, *War-Path and Bivouac*, 125; Noyes Report, 133.

16. Noyes Report, 133; "List of Wounded," Hartsuff Report, NA; Bourke, *Diaries*, 1:326.

17. Pearson, *The Platte-Dakota Campaign of 1876*, 10.

18. Chambers Report, 135; Munson Report, 136; Burt Report, 139.

19. "James Forrestell," *Hardin Tribune-Herald*, January 20, 1933.

20. Chambers Report, 135; Burt Report, 139.

21. Finerty, *War-Path and Bivouac*, 126.

22. "The Big Horn Expedition," *Cheyenne Daily Leader*, July 2, 1876; Mills Report, 151 (first quotation); Finerty, *War-Path and Bivouac*, 126 (second and third quotations).

23. "Telegraphic!" *Sidney Telegraph*, June 24, 1876; Mills, "Address by General Anson Mills," 9; Mills Report, 151.

24. Thomas Lloyd Letter, January 20, 1877, MnHS.

25. Mills Report, 152; "List of Wounded," Hartsuff Report, NA.

26. Elmer A. Snow File, CMHS; Paul Report, 153; "Ex-Trooper Towne on the Rosebud Fight," in Brady, *Indian Fights and Fighters*, 205–206; Daly, "The War Path," 19.

27. DeBarthe, *Life and Adventures of Frank Grouard*, 119; Vestal, *Warpath and Council Fire*, 224.

28. Bourke, *Diaries*, 1:327 (first quotation); DeBarthe, *Life and Adventures of Frank Grouard*, 119–20 (second quotation); Lemly, "The Fight on the Rosebud," 18; Mills, "Address by General Anson Mills," 9; Bourke, *On the Border with Crook*, 313. In James Foster's brief recap of the episode, Snow managed to ride to the hospital where he threw himself off. "Battle of the Rosebud," *New York Daily Graphic*, July 13, 1876.

29. Bourke, *Diaries*, 1:326–27; Lemly, "The Fight on the Rosebud," 18; Beyer and Keydel, *Deeds of Valor*, 2:210; Gray, "Frank Grouard," 58.

30. "'Lo' Game," *Chicago Times,* August 1, 1876.

31. Ibid. (first through fourth quotations); Reneau, *The Adventures of Moccasin Joe*, 69 (fifth quotation). The so-called copper cartridge case was fabricated from Bloomfield Gilding Metal, an alloy of 95 percent copper and 5 percent zinc. The issue of verdigris-encrusted shells is carefully analyzed by Noyes, "A Question of Arms." The depth of the problem, with the Battle of the Little Big Horn as a case study, is investigated by Hedren, "Carbine Extraction Failure at the Little Big Horn"; and Scott et al., *Archaeological Perspectives on the Battle of the Little Bighorn*, 113–15. Extraction problems indeed existed on these Sioux War battlefields.

32. Finerty, *War-Path and Bivouac,* 127; "Another Account of Crook's 'Bull' Fight," *Cheyenne Daily Leader*, June 27, 1876; "The Indian War," *New York Herald*, June 24, 1876.

33. "The Sioux War," *Chicago Tribune*, July 11, 1876; Finerty, *War-Path and Bivouac*, 128; Lawson Report, 152; "The Murdered Van Moll," *Cheyenne Daily Leader*, December 20, 1877; "Lynched by His Comrades," *Army and Navy Journal*, December 29, 1877. Oddly, Thomas MacMillan, writing exclusively for the *Chicago Inter-Ocean* and riding with Lawson and Company A during the fight, told of Mills's charges as if they were one relatively continuous action instead of two. He did not mention the Van Moll episode even though he was among those closest to it. "On the War-Path," *Chicago Inter-Ocean*, June 24, 1876.

34. Finerty, *War-Path and Bivouac*, 128 (first quotation); "The Sioux War," *Chicago Tribune*, July 11, 1876 (second quotation); "The Murdered Van Moll," *Cheyenne Daily Leader*, December 20, 1877 (third quotation); Abrams, *Sioux War Dispatches*, 83, 360–61n31. Andrew Burt believed that Van Moll's savior was Old Crow, a point echoed in "Incidents of Crook's Fight," *Cheyenne Daily Leader*, June 28, 1876. Finerty and others identify him as Humpy. Davenport, riding with Royall and not an observer of the episode, incorrectly places Van Moll's rescue on Royall's front. "The Indian War," *New York Herald*, June 24, 1876. Lieutenant Foster, also riding with Royall, correctly locates the episode but identifies the rescuer as Old Crow. "Battle of the Rosebud," *New York Daily Graphic*, June 13, 1876. The retrospective in the *Cheyenne Daily Leader*, December 20, 1877, on the occasion of Van Moll's murder, correctly identified Humpy and called him a Shoshone. That Humpy was indeed a Shoshone is confirmed in Trenholm and Carley, *The Shoshonis*, 259; and "Sioux Slaughtering Shoshones," *Cheyenne Daily Leader*, November 3, 1876. Van Moll is buried in the Fort McPherson National Cemetery, Maxwell, Nebraska.

35. Clausewitz, *On War*, 421 (first quotation); Finerty, *War-Path and Bivouac*, 127 (second quotation)

CHAPTER 13. COMMANDING THE FIELD

1. Bourke, *Diaries*, 1:328; Finerty, *War-Path and Bivouac*, 136.

2. "Telegraphic," *Sidney Telegraph*, June 24, 1876 (first quotation); "Fighting the Fiends," *Cheyenne Daily Leader*, June 24, 1876; "Further Particulars from the Recent Indian Fight," *Omaha Bee*, June 24, 1876; "Crook's Indian Battle," *Omaha Bee*, June 26, 1876; "Military Matters," *Omaha Bee*, July 11, 1876 (second quotation); Magid, *The Gray Fox*, 249, 436n31.

3. *Army and Navy Register*, August 27, 1881 (quotation); Spring, "Prince of Packers," 44; Daly, "The War Path," 18; "Crook," *Weekly Rocky Mountain News*, July 5, 1876; "The Battle of the Rosebud," *New York Times*, July 13, 1876; Bourke, *Diaries*, 1:327; Bourke, *On the Border with Crook*, 314; Vaughn, *With Crook at the Rosebud*, 88; Vaughn-Kobold Correspondence, September 19, 1961, MHS.

4. Royall Report, 142.

5. Ibid. (first quotation); "Statement of Officers and Troops Composing the Big Horn [*sic*] Expedition," Division of the Missouri, Special Files, NA; "Another Account of Crook's 'Bull' Fight," *Cheyenne Daily Leader*, June 27, 1876 (second quotation).

6. Meinhold Report, 145 (first quotation); "Another Account of Crook's 'Bull' Fight," *Cheyenne Daily Leader*, June 27, 1876 (second quotation); Royall Report, 143.

7. "General Crook's Battle of the Rosebud," *Army and Navy Journal*, July 22, 1876.

8. Lemly, "The Fight on the Rosebud," 14 (first and second quotations); "Battle of Rosebud Creek," *New York Herald*, July 6, 1876 (third quotation).

9. "A Bull Fight," *Chicago Times*, June 24, 1876; Finerty, *War-Path and Bivouac*, 125 (quotation).

10. Chambers Report, 135; Cain Report, 140.

11. Cain Report, 140; Munson Report, 136; Nottage, "The Big Horn and Yellowstone Expedition of 1876," 35 (quotation).

12. Meketa, *Marching with General Crook*, 20 (first quotation); Nottage, "The Big Horn and Yellowstone Expedition of 1876," 35 (second quotation); Luhn Report, 141; Fourth Infantry Regimental Return, June 1876, NA; "Statement of Officers and Troops Composing the Big Horn [*sic*] Expedition," Division of the Missouri, Special Files, NA.

13. "James Forristell," *Hardin Tribune-Herald*, January 20, 1933 (first quotation); "Crook's Campaign," *Cheyenne Daily Leader*, August 5, 1876 (second quotation); "The Indians," *New York Herald*, November 10, 1876 (third quotation); Abrams, *Sioux War Dispatches*, 81, 360n26.

14. "The Red Horse Interview," in Hardorff, *Indian Views of the Custer Fight*, 75.

15. Cain Report, 140; Nottage, "The Big Horn and Yellowstone Expedition of 1876," 34–35; "List of Wounded," Hartsuff Report, NA. Luhn asserted that no man was injured on this advance and counted Terry among the casualties incurred on the initial skirmish line. The present narrative accepts Cain's accounting.

16. Nickerson, "Major General George Crook and the Indians," 27, Crook-Kennon Papers, USAWC.

17. "Battle of Rosebud Creek," *New York Herald*, July 6, 1876.

18. Andrews Report, 147; Abrams, *"Crying for Scalps,"* 83; "Battle of Rosebud Creek," *New York Herald*, July 6, 1876 (first and second quotations); "Statement of Officers and Troops Composing the Big Horn [*sic*] Expedition," Division of the Missouri, Special Files, NA; "Ex-Trooper Towne on the Rosebud Fight," in Brady, *Indian Fights and Fighters*, 205; "Battle of the Rosebud," *New York Daily Graphic*, July 13, 1876 (third quotation); Vaughn, *Indian Fights*, 133.

19. "Battle of Rosebud Creek," *New York Herald*, July 6, 1876 (first quotation); Lemly, "The Fight on the Rosebud," 14 (second quotation).

20. Finerty, *War-Path and Bivouac*, 123, 136; Bourke, *On the Border with Crook*, 314 (quotation).

21. Finerty, *War-Path and Bivouac*, 136; Vaughn, *With Crook at the Rosebud*, 95.

22. Strahorn, "Ninety Years of Boyhood," 153–54 (quotations), Strahorn Papers, College of Idaho; Knight, *Following the Indian Wars*, 188–89; Magid, *The Gray Fox*, 251.

23. Crook Report, June 20, 1876, 128–29.

24. "Fighting the Fiends," *Cheyenne Daily Leader*, June 24, 1876 (first quotation); "Crook," *Weekly Rocky Mountain News*, July 5, 1876 (second and third quotations); "The Indian War," *New York Herald*, June 24, 1876; DeBarthe, *Life and Adventures of Frank Grouard*, 120 (fourth quotation).

25. Schmitt, *General George Crook*, 195.

CHAPTER 14. SOWING THE WIND

1. Nickerson, "Major General George Crook and the Indians," 27, Crook-Kennon Papers. USAWC (first quotation); "The Sioux War," *New York Tribune*, July 6, 1876 (second quotation).

2. Mills Report, 151; *Official Army Register for January, 1876*, 53; Hedren, *Powder River*, 185–86, 194–95; Mills, "Address by General Anson Mills," 9.

3. Mills Report, 151 (quotation); Lawson Report, 153.

4. Mills Report, 151; Noyes Report, 133 (quotation); Mills, "Address by General Anson Mills," 9.

5. Finerty, *War-Path and Bivouac*, 130 (quotation), 131; Mills Report, 151; "List of Wounded," Hartsuff Report, NA.

6. "Battle of the Rosebud," *New York Daily Graphic*, July 13, 1876.

7. Ibid.; Clausewitz, *On War*, 138 (quotation), 140–41. The writer of the *Daily Graphic* piece, signed simply "Z," has been identified as Second Lieutenant James Foster. As Foster rode with Royall, this critical statement occurs with slight hindsight and reflection.

8. Bourke, *On the Border with Crook*, 315 (first quotation); DeBarthe, *Life and Adventures of Frank Grouard*, 120 (second quotation).

9. *Official Army Register for January, 1876*, 51; Altshuler, *Cavalry Yellow & Infantry Blue*, 249; 231, Hedren, *Powder River*, 187 (quotation); Finerty, *War-Path and Bivouac*, 132.

10. "The Sioux War," *Chicago Tribune*, July 5, 1876; "The Battle of Rosebud Creek," *New York Herald*, July 6, 1876; Evans Report, 131 (first quotation); Van Vliet Report, 150 (second quotation).

11. Finerty, *War-Path and Bivouac*, 30 (first quotation), 131 (third quotation); "A Bull Fight," *Chicago Times*, June 24, 1876 (second quotation); "Braving the Braves," *Chicago Times*, July 5, 1876; Bookbinder, "Inspired by Plains Indian Drawings," 163.

12. Bourke, *On the Border with Crook*, 315.

13. Ibid. (first and second quotations); Finerty, *War-Path and Bivouac*, 131 (third quotation).

14. "The Big Horn Expedition," *Cheyenne Daily Leader*, July 2, 1876; "Telegraphic," *Sidney Telegraph*, June 24, 1876; "A Bull Fight," *Chicago Tribune*, June 24, 1876; "The Battle of Rosebud Creek," *New York Herald*, July 6, 1876; "Battle of the Rosebud," *New York Daily Graphic*, July 13, 1876.

15. "The Indian War," *New York Herald*, June 24, 1876; "The Sioux War," *Chicago Tribune*, July 11, 1876 (quotations); "Battle of Rosebud Creek," *New York Herald*, July 6, 1876; "Battle of Rosebud," *Highland Weekly News*, July 20, 1876.

16. Heitman, *Historical Register and Dictionary of the United States Army*, 1:167; Andrews Report, 147 (quotation). Andrews retired from the army on November 30, 1879, "for incapacity

resulting from long and faithful service." Doubtless the hardships suffered on Crook's prolonged summer campaign contributed to his frailty. He died in Washington, D.C., on June 21, 1880, and was buried in the city's Oak Hill Cemetery. "Capt. William H. Andrews," www .findagrave.com.

17. Andrews Report, 148 (quotation); "Battle of Rosebud Creek," *New York Herald*, July 6, 1876; "Battle of Rosebud," *Highland Weekly News*, July 20, 1876; "The Battle of Rosebud Creek," *New York Herald*, July 13, 1876; "Foster's Feat," *Pittsburg Leader*, July 5, 1876.

18. "Battle of the Rosebud," *New York Daily Graphic*, July 13, 1876 (first, second, and fourth quotations); "The Sioux War," *Chicago Tribune*, July 5, 1876 (third quotation).

19. "Battle of the Rosebud," *New York Daily Graphic*, July 13, 1876 (quotations); "Battle of Rosebud Creek," *New York Herald*, July 6, 1876; "Foster's Fight," *Pittsburg Leader*, July 9, 1876.

20. "Battle of Rosebud Creek," *New York Herald*, July 6, 1876 (first quotation); "Battle of the Rosebud," *New York Daily Graphic*, July 13, 1876 (second quotation); "The Sioux War," *Chicago Tribune*, July 5, 1876; "The Sioux War," *Cincinnati Commercial*, July 17, 1876; "The Sioux War," *Chicago Tribune*, July 11, 1876 (third quotation).

21. "Crook's Column," *Chicago Tribune*, August 1, 1876.

22. "Battle of the Rosebud," *New York Daily Graphic*, July 13, 1876 (first and second quotations); "The Sioux War," *Chicago Tribune*, July 5, 1876; "The Sioux War," *Cincinnati Commercial*, July 17, 1876 (third quotation).

23. "The Sioux War," *Chicago Tribune*, July 5, 1876; "List of Wounded," Hartsuff Report, NA; "Battle of Rosebud Creek," *New York Herald*, July 6, 1876 (quotation); "Foster's Feat," *Pittsburg Leader*, July 5, 1876; "Foster's Fight," *Pittsburg Leader*, July 9, 1876; "The Battle of Rosebud Creek," *New York Herald*, July 13, 1876.

24. Andrews Report, 148.

25. "The Sioux War," *Chicago Tribune*, July 5, 1876; Vaughn, *With Crook at the Rosebud*, 81; Werts and Booras, *The Crazy Horse and Crook Fight of 1876*, 50, 64, 102n52.

26. "The Sioux War," *Chicago Tribune*, July 5, 1876; Royall Report, 143; "Battle of Rosebud Creek," *New York Herald*, July 6, 1876 (quotation); "Battle of the Rosebud," *New York Daily Graphic*, July 13, 1876.

27. "The Sioux War," *Cincinnati Commercial*, July 17, 1876; Royall Report, 143 (first and second quotations); "Sioux Indian Campaign," *Army and Navy Journal*, July 22, 1876 (third quotation); "Battle of Rosebud Creek," *New York Herald*, July 6, 1876 (fourth quotation).

28. Royall Report, 143; Meinhold Report, 145 (quotation); "List of Wounded," Hartsuff Report, NA.

29. "Statement of Officers and Troops Composing the Big Horn [*sic*] Expedition," Division of the Missouri, Special Files, NA; "Battle of Rosebud Creek," *New York Herald*, July 6, 1876; King, "An Honorable Amende."

30. "Battle of the Rosebud," *New York Daily Graphic*, July 13, 1876.

31. Royall Report, 143.

32. "Battle of Rosebud Creek," *New York Herald*, July 6, 1876 (first quotation); "Sioux Indian Campaign," *Army and Navy Journal*, July 22, 1876; "Nickerson in Battle," *Omaha Herald*, July 9, 1876 (second quotation); "The Rosebud Fight," *Washington Evening Star*, undated, Mrs. George Crook Scrapbook, USAWC (third quotation).

CHAPTER 15. REAPING THE WHIRLWIND

1. "Battle of the Rosebud," *New York Sun*, July 6, 1876 (quotation); "Battle of Rosebud," *Highland Weekly News*, July 20, 1876; Lemly, "The Fight on the Rosebud," 14. There is a strong likelihood that the unnamed writer whose story first appeared in the *New York Sun* was Henry Lemly, Royall's adjutant. Wording in the two noted accounts is strikingly similar.

2. "Battle of the Rosebud," *New York Daily Graphic*, July 13, 1876; "The Sioux War," *Cincinnati Commercial*, July 17, 1876 (quotation).

3. "Battle of Rosebud Creek," *New York Herald*, July 6, 1876.

4. Andrews Report, 143.

5. Ibid.

6. "Battle of the Rosebud," *New York Daily Graphic*, July 13, 1876; Abrams, *"Crying for Scalps,"* 83; "Sioux Indian Campaign," *Army and Navy Journal*, July 22, 1876 (quotation); "Battle of Rosebud Creek," *New York Herald*, July 6, 1876; Lemly, "The Fight on the Rosebud," 15. The *New York Daily Graphic* essay cited consistently herein was also reproduced in part as "Conduct of Our Officers and Men," *Army and Navy Journal*, July 22, 1876.

7. "The Sioux War," *Chicago Tribune*, July 5, 1876; Lemly, "The Fight on the Rosebud," 15 (quotation); "Battle of the Rosebud," *New York Sun*, July 6, 1876.

8. Lemly, "The Fight on the Rosebud," 15; "Battle of the Rosebud," *New York Daily Graphic*, July 13, 1876 (quotation); "Battle of Rosebud Creek," *New York Herald*, July 6, 1876.

9. "The Sioux War," *Chicago Tribune*, July 5, 1876; "The Sioux War," *Cincinnati Commercial*, July 17, 1876 (first quotation); "Battle of the Rosebud," *New York Daily Graphic*, July 13, 1876 (second quotation); Stands in Timber and Liberty, *A Cheyenne Voice*, 402; Werts and Booras, *The Crazy Horse and Crook Fight of 1876*, 139.

10. Andrews Report, 143 (quotation); "The Sioux War," *Chicago Tribune*, July 5, 1876.

11. "Battle of Rosebud Creek," *New York Herald*, July 6, 1876; Andrews Report, 144; "Battle of the Rosebud," *New York Sun*, July 6, 1876.

12. "Sound on the Goose," *Chicago Times*, July 12, 1876 (first quotation); "Reap the Whirlwind," www.wikipedia.org (second quotation); "The Rosebud Fight," *Washington Evening Star*, no date, Mrs. George Crook Scrapbook, USAMHI.

13. "Sioux Indian Campaign," *Army and Navy Journal*, July 22, 1876; Werts and Booras, *The Crazy Horse and Crook Fight of 1876*, 138–39, 142.

14. "The Sioux War," *Chicago Tribune*, July 5, 1876.

15. "The Sioux War," *Cincinnati Commercial*, July 17, 1876.

16. Henry, "Wounded in an Indian Fight."

17. Abrams, *"Crying for Scalps,"* 83.

18. "Battle of the Rosebud," *New York Daily Graphic*, July 13, 1876 (quotation); "The Sioux War," *Chicago Tribune*, July 5, 1876.

19. "The Big Horn Expedition," *Cheyenne Daily Leader*, July 2, 1876; "The Battle of the Rosebud," *Bozeman Times*, July 6, 1876; Linderman, *American*, 166 (first quotation); Trenholm and Carley, *The Shoshonis*, 251 (second quotation).

20. "Sioux Indian Campaign," *Army and Navy Journal*, July 22, 1876; Patzki Certificate, July 2, 1876, B. William Henry Jr. Collection, BHSU; "The Sioux War," *Cincinnati Commercial*, July 17, 1876; Hartsuff to Henry, April 18, 1890, B. William Henry Jr. Collection, BHSU (first quotation); Abrams, *"Crying for Scalps,"* 83 (second quotation).

21. Morton ACP File, NA; Finerty, *War-Path and Bivouac*, 129; Henry, "Wounded in an Indian Fight," 627 (quotation); Brady, *Indian Fights and Fighters*, 198; Abrams, "Henry's Fall," 43.

22. "The Indian War," *New York Herald*, June 24, 1876 (first quotation); Henry, "Wounded in an Indian Fight," 627 (second quotation).

23. Linderman, *American*, 166.

24. David, *Finn Burnett*, 340 (quotation); Hebard, *Washakie*, 185; [Bruce,] "Pawnee Trails and Trailers," 17; Trenholm and Carley, *The Shoshonis*, 251; "Battle of Rosebud Creek," *New York Herald*, July 6, 1876; Abrams, *"Crying for Scalps,"* 118–19 and 119n1; "The Indian War," *New York Herald*, June 24, 1876; Abrams, "St. George Stanley & the Great Sioux War," 9; DeBarthe, *Life and Adventures of Frank Grouard*, 120. The episode is thoughtfully analyzed

by Kane, "Who Saved Guy Henry at the Battle of the Rosebud?," 10. Kane also accepts Tigee as the captain's savior. Interestingly, Henry himself asserted that a Shoshone scout saved him, oddly naming the great chief Washakie, perhaps to enhance his story. Washakie was not yet present on this campaign but was still on the Shoshone Reservation in Wyoming. Henry, "Wounded in an Indian Fight."

25. Finerty, *War-Path and Bivouac*, 129.

26. Abrams, "Henry's Fall: Mystery Solved," in Abrams, *"Crying for Scalps,"* 133–34; Mangum, *Battle of the Rosebud*, 79; "Battle of the Rosebud," *New York Daily Graphic*, July 13, 1876 (first quotation); "What They Are There For," *Winners of the West*, May 30, 1934; "Indian Maid's Vengeance in Early Montana Days," *Billings Gazette*, September 20, 1911 (second and third quotations).

27. Henry, "Wounded in an Indian Fight," 627; Hart, "Edmore LeClair," 9 (first quotation); "Battle of the Rosebud," *New York Sun*, July 6, 1876 (second quotation); Hallberg and Neal, "'For This Are We Soldiers,'" 68.

28. "Battle of Rosebud Creek," *New York Herald*, July 6, 1876; "Gen. Crook's Fight with the Sioux," *Perrysburg Journal*, July 7, 1876; Lemly, "The Fight on the Rosebud," 15 (quotation).

29. "Battle of the Rosebud," *New York Daily Graphic*, July 13, 1876 (quotations); "Crook Defeated," *Helena Daily Independent*, June 30, 1876; "Crook and Custer," *New York Herald*, July 12, 1876.

30. Chambers Report, 135; "The Big Horn Expedition," *Cheyenne Daily Leader*, July 2, 1876; Burrowes Report, 137–38; Burt Report, 139 (first quotation); Nottage, "The Big Horn and Yellowstone Expedition of 1876," 35 (second quotation); "The Indian War," *New York Herald*, June 24, 1876 (third quotation); Vaughn, *With Crook at the Rosebud*, 105.

31. "The Battle of the Rosebud," *Pittsburg Evening Leader*, July 21, 1876.

32. Evans Report, 131.

33. "The Death of Crawford," *Army and Navy Register*, February 13, 1886 (Crawford and Evans exchange); Zinser, *Indian War Diary*, 13 (Zinser quotation).

34. "The Sioux War," *Chicago Tribune*, July 5, 1876; "Battle of the Rosebud," *New York Daily Graphic*, July 13, 1876 (quotations); "Sioux Indian Campaign," *Army and Navy Journal*, July 22, 1876; "The Indian War," *New York Herald*, June 24, 1876; "The Big Horn Expedition," *Cheyenne Daily Leader*, August 2, 1876; Henry, "Wounded in an Indian Fight," 627; Hedren, *Great Sioux War Orders of Battle*, appendixes B and C.

35. "List of Killed," "List of Wounded," Hartsuff Report, NA; Altshuler, *Cavalry Yellow & Infantry Blue*, 345; Royall Report, 144 (quotation).

36. Bourke, *Diaries*, 1:331; "Incidents of Crook's Fight," *Cheyenne Daily Leader*, June 28, 1876; "The Indian War," *New York Herald*, June 24, 1876.

37. "Battle of the Rosebud," *New York Sun*, July 6, 1876; "Battle of Rosebud Creek," *New York Herald*, July 6, 1876.

38. Lemly, "The Fight on the Rosebud," 15; "The Sioux War," *Chicago Tribune*, July 11, 1876; "Ex-Trooper Towne on the Rosebud Fight," in Brady, *Indian Fights and Fighters*, 206; "Battle of the Rosebud," *New York Sun*, July 6, 1876 (quotation); Mangum, *Battle of the Rosebud*, 81; "Battle of Rosebud Creek," *New York Herald*, July 6, 1876. Daniel Pearson, an officer riding with the Second Cavalry, related a slightly cleansed version of Roe's killing, doubtless as heard at an evening campfire. "One of the recruits handed an Indian his carbine in token of surrender. The Indian, acting with dispatch, grasped the carbine, smashed the soldier's face with the stock and then dashed away." Pearson, *The Platte-Dakota Campaign of 1876*, 10.

39. "The Sioux War," *Chicago Tribune*, July 5, 1876 (quotations); "The Sioux War," *Chicago Tribune*, July 11, 1876; "Battle of Rosebud Creek," *New York Herald*, July 6, 1876; "Ex-Trooper Towne on the Rosebud Fight," in Brady, *Indian Fights and Fighters*, 206.

40. "Ex-Trooper Towne on the Rosebud Fight," in Brady, *Indian Fights and Fighters*, 206, 207 (quotations); McChristian, *Regular Army O!*, 554–55.

41. "List of Wounded," Hartsuff Report, NA; "Ex-Trooper Towne on the Rosebud Fight," in Brady, *Indian Fights and Fighters*, 207–8; Towne, "Fighting at Powder River and Rosebud Creek," in Greene, *Indian War Veterans*, 108 (quotation).

42. "Battle of the Rosebud," *New York Daily Graphic*, July 13, 1876; Royall Report, 143–44; "The Sioux War," *Chicago Tribune*, July 5, 1876 (first quotation); "The Battle of Rosebud Creek," *New York Herald*, July 13, 1876 (second quotation); "The Sioux War," *Cincinnati Commercial*, July 17, 1876; Mangum, *Battle of the Rosebud*, 82.

43. Lemly, "The Fight on the Rosebud," 15 (quotation); "Battle of the Rosebud," *New York Daily Graphic*, July 13, 1876; "The Indian War," *New York Herald*, June 24, 1876.

44. Beyer and Keydel, *Deeds of Valor*, 2:208, 210; Shingle File, CMHS; McGann File, CMHS; Potter, "McGann's Medal of Honor," 11; Robinson File, CMHS; "Military Matters," *Cheyenne Daily Leader*, March 19, 1880; Andrews Report, 148.

45. "The Indian War," *New York Herald*, June 24, 1876; "Battle of Rosebud Creek," *New York Herald*, July 6, 1876; "The Battle of Rosebud Creek," *New York Herald*, July 13, 1876.

46. Hart, "Edmore LeClair," 9.

47. "The Indian War," *New York Herald*, June 24, 1876; "The Big Horn Expedition," *Cheyenne Daily Leader*, July 2, 1876; "Battle of the Rosebud," *New York Daily Graphic*, July 13, 1876; "The Sioux War," *Chicago Tribune*, July 5, 1876; "Foster's Fight," *Pittsburg Leader*, July 9, 1876; Vaughn, *With Crook at the Rosebud*, 105; Mattes, *Indians, Infants and Infantry*, 219; Henry Report, 146 (quotation).

48. "Battle of the Rosebud," *New York Sun*, July 6, 1876; Lemly, "The Fight on the Rosebud," 15 (quotation).

49. "List of Wounded," "List of Men Killed," Hartsuff Report, NA; Andrews Report, 148; Bourke, *Diaries*, 1:328; "The Indian War," *New York Herald*, June 24, 1876; "Why the Column Fell Back," *New York Times*, July 13, 1876.

50. Lemly, "The Fight on the Rosebud," 15.

CHAPTER 16. WARRIORS HEROIC

1. Medicine Crow, "Custer and His Crow Scouts," 109–10; McGinnis, "When Courage Was Not Enough," 467; "Wrinkled Cheyenne Warriors Tell of Battle with Crook and His Soldiers on the Rosebud," *Billings Gazette*, June 24, 1934; Stands in Timber and Liberty, *A Cheyenne Voice*.

2. Vestal, *Sitting Bull*, 153 (quotation); Utley, *The Lance and the Shield*, 141.

3. "Young Two Moon Account," in Greene, *Lakota and Cheyennes*, 27 (first quotation); Grinnell, *The Fighting Cheyennes*, 339; Marquis, *A Warrior Who Fought Custer*, 199 (second and third quotations), 200.

4. Vaughn, *With Crook at the Rosebud*, 83; Stands in Timber and Liberty, *A Cheyenne Voice*, 418; "Wrinkled Cheyenne Warriors Tell of Battle with Crook and His Soldiers on the Rosebud," *Billings Gazette*, June 24, 1934.

5. "The Battle of Rosebud Creek," *New York Herald*, July 13, 1876 (quotations); Hedren, *Powder River*, 174.

6. Hyde, *Red Cloud's Folk*, 263–64.

7. Bear Soldier Interview, Lewis Crawford Papers, SHSND.

8. Marquis, *A Warrior Who Fought Custer*, 201 (quotation); Stands in Timber and Liberty, *Cheyenne Memories*, 204–5. Today a red granite memorial marks the relative location of Lame White Man's death at the Little Big Horn. "Lame White Man," www.findagrave.com.

9. Sandoz, *Crazy Horse*, 319 (quotation); Neihardt, *Black Elk Speaks*, 101; DeMallie, *The*

Sixth Grandfather, 175; Miller, *Ghost Dance*, 289; Andrist, *The Long Death*, 265; Bray, *Crazy Horse*, 209. The root source of Crazy Horse's memorable exhortation is often and rightly debated. The first known appearance of the lines in a Rosebud context occurs in Neihardt's book, where Iron Hawk remembered "voices crying in our language: 'Take Courage! This is a good day to die! Think of the children and helpless at home!'" Sandoz subsequently repeated virtually the same wording, without provenance, but attributed the words to Crazy Horse. The expression does not appear in the associated Hinman interviews. Neihardt's *Black Elk Speaks*, first published in 1932, is likely Sandoz's source. Miller suggests that most of the words were recalled and repeated years later by Frank Kicking Bear, son of the traditionalist Kicking Bear, a cousin and close ally of Crazy Horse, who attributed them to Crazy Horse. No direct interview of Kicking Bear is known. Young Kicking Bear also suggested that Crazy Horse uttered those same words as he lay dying at Camp Robinson on September 6, 1877. Andrist, who is occasionally referenced as a secondary source, twisted the final line somewhat and also used it without attribution.

Interestingly, identical words again attributed to Crazy Horse are also known in a Little Big Horn context. Jesse Lee, a Ninth Infantry officer who was not present at the Rosebud or Little Big Horn but was intimately associated with the great chief in the months before his death, set down these lines in 1914: "It was Crazy Horse's voice that rang out when some of the advance warriors recoiled from Custer's fire, 'Come on! Die with me! It's a good day to die! Cowards to the rear!'" Lee, "The Capture and Death of an Indian Chieftain," 325. The same words commonly attributed to Crazy Horse were apparently also uttered by the Oglala warrior Low Dog, who purportedly called out to his own followers: "This is a good day to die: follow me." "Low Dog's Story of Custer's Fight," *Army and Navy Journal*, August 13, 1881; "The Low Dog Interview," in Hardorff, *Indian Views of the Custer Fight*, 65, citing the *Leavenworth Times*, August 14, 1881; "Low Dog: His Account," in Tillett, *Wind on the Buffalo Grass*, 86.

Similarly, the Oglala Iron Hail, better known subsequently as Dewey Beard, recalled shouting "It's a good day to die!" as he rode to the sound of gunfire on the Little Big Horn battlefield. Miller, "Echoes of the Little Bighorn," 38; Tillett, *Wind on the Buffalo Grass*, 94; Burnham, *Song of Dewey Beard*, 32. In 1931 Moving Robe Woman remembered the Miniconjou chief Red Horse shouting above the din at the Little Big Horn: "There is never a better time to die!" "Moving Robe Woman Interview," in Hardorff, *Lakota Recollections of the Custer Fight*, 95. The most it may be possible to say is that these memorable lines appear in keeping with the larger than life image of the endearing and charismatic Crazy Horse.

10. "Noted Oglala Medicine Man Kept Crazy Horse's Secret," *Rapid City Daily Journal*, February 11, 1951 (quotation); Fielder, *Sioux Indian Leaders*, 17.

11. Grinnell, *The Fighting Cheyennes*, 340; Stands in Timber and Liberty, *A Cheyenne Voice*, 418; Linderman, *Pretty-Shield*, 230–31.

12. "Little Hawk Reminiscence," in Greene, *Lakota and Cheyenne*, 25; Powell, *People of the Sacred Mountain*, 2:957; Grinnell, *The Fighting Cheyennes*, 340 (quotation).

13. Stands in Timber and Liberty, *A Cheyenne Voice*, 418 (first quotation), 431 (fourth quotation); McGinnis, "When Courage Was Not Enough," 471; Killsback, "Crowns of Honor," 5 (second and third quotations); Stands in Timber and Liberty, *Cheyenne Memories*, 188; Sandoz, *Crazy Horse*, 319.

14. Stands in Timber and Liberty, *A Cheyenne Voice*, 402 (quotation), 423; Powell, *People of the Sacred Mountain*, 2:957, 962, 1000; Grinnell, *The Fighting Cheyennes*, 336; Vestal, *Warpath and Council Fire*, 224; Stands in Timber and Liberty, *Cheyenne Memories*, 188–89; Grinnell, *The Cheyenne Indians*, 1:157, 2:44; "The Young Two Moons Interview," in Hardorff, *Cheyenne Memories of the Custer Fight*, 161.

15. Agonito and Agonito, "Resurrecting History's Forgotten Women," 8–9; "Buffalo Calf Road Woman," www.wikipedia.org; Grinnell, *The Cheyenne Indians*, 2:44; Stands in Timber

and Liberty, *Cheyenne Memories*, 181, 189; "The Young Two Moons Interview," in Hardorff, *Cheyenne Memories of the Custer Fight*, 161, 161n22; Powell, *People of the Sacred Mountain*, 2:964–65; Musgrave, "Woman Warrior," 2; Hantz, "The Girl Who Saved Her Brother"; Killsback, "Crowns of Honor," 15. Another ledger art depiction of this episode was created by the Oglala artist Amos Bad Heart Bull, who as a child may have been in the Reno Creek camp and created in the years surrounding the turn of the twentieth century a sizable folio of art documenting important episodes of Oglala Sioux history, including the Rosebud Battle. Bad Heart Bull and Blish, *A Pictographic History of the Oglala Sioux*, 189, plate 104.

For an understanding and appreciation of traditional painting and ledger art relatively contemporary with Rosebud and Little Big Horn, see Bottomley-O'looney, "The Art of Storytelling"; Szabo, *Howling Wolf and the History of Ledger Art*; and McLaughlin, *A Lakota War Book from the Little Bighorn*.

16. "Young Two Moon Reminiscence," in Greene, *Lakota and Cheyenne*, 28 (quotation); Grinnell, *The Fighting Cheyennes*, 334.

17. Vaughn, *With Crook at the Rosebud*, 83.

18. Stands in Timber and Liberty, *A Cheyenne Voice*, 418.

19. Bad Heart Bull and Blish, *A Pictographic History of the Oglala Sioux*, 190, plate 105; Marquis, *A Warrior Who Fought Custer*, 199 (first quotation), 200; Sandoz, *Crazy Horse*, 318; Powell, *People of the Sacred Mountain*, 2:996, 1366n33; "William Garnett's Interview," in Jensen, *The Indian Interviews of Eli S. Ricker*, 84; Killsback, "Crowns of Honor," 14–15; Powers, *The Killing of Crazy Horse*, 186 (second quotation).

20. Sandoz, *Crazy Horse*, 318; Bray, *Crazy Horse*, 12, 70, 153; Powell, *People of the Sacred Mountain*, 2:996, 1366n33; Bad Heart Bull and Blish, *A Pictographic History of the Oglala Sioux*, 190–96, plates 105–11; Agonito, *Lakota Portraits*, 205 (quotation).

21. Hyde, *Red Cloud's Folk*, 264 (first and second quotations); Department of the Platte Letters Received, September 1, 1877, NA; Buecker, "Lt. William Philo Clark's Sioux War Report and Little Big Horn Map," 15 (third quotation); "Crook," *Weekly Rocky Mountain News*, July 5, 1876 (fourth quotation); Donovan, *A Terrible Glory*, 150.

22. Howard, *The Warrior Who Killed Custer*, 49 (first quotation); Vestal, *Warpath*, 188 (second quotation); McGinnis, "When Courage Was Not Enough," 467.

23. Powell, *People of the Sacred Mountain*, 2:960; "Iron Hawk Speaks," in Neihardt, *Black Elk Speaks*, 100–101; Stands in Timber and Liberty, *Cheyenne Memories*, 186, 207; Vaughn, *With Crook at the Rosebud*, 131.

24. "Wrinkled Cheyenne Warriors Tell of Battle with Crook and His Soldiers on the Rosebud," *Billings Gazette*, June 24, 1934; "Charles Limpy," www.findagrave.com; Stands in Timber and Liberty, *A Cheyenne Voice*, 417; Stands in Timber and Liberty, *Cheyenne Memories*, 187–88; Powell, *People of the Sacred Mountain*, 2:995.

25. Stands in Timber and Liberty, *A Cheyenne Voice*, 417, 426, 427 (quotation); Stands in Timber and Liberty, *Cheyenne Memories*, 188–90; Powell, *People of the Sacred Mountain*, 2:995.

26. Stands in Timber and Liberty, *A Cheyenne Voice*, 417–18, 438; Stands in Timber and Liberty, *Cheyenne Memories*, 188 (quotation); Powell, *People of the Sacred Mountain*, 2:995; Vaughn, *With Crook at the Rosebud*, 132; Grinnell, *The Fighting Cheyennes*, 334.

27. "Wrinkled Cheyenne Warriors Tell of Battle with Crook and His Soldiers on the Rosebud," *Billings Gazette*, June 24, 1934.

28. Stands in Timber and Liberty, *A Cheyenne Voice*, 403–4.

29. Charles A. Eastman, "The Sioux of Yesterday and To-Day," 234, in McDermott, "Crook and the Rosebud," [14] (quotation); "Chief Ogallala Fire," www.findagrave.com; "Chief Ogallala Fire Joins Ancestral Warriors," *Leadville Herald Democrat*, January 10, 1916.

30. "Young Two Moon Reminiscence," in Greene, *Lakota and Cheyenne*, 28; Grinnell, *The*

Fighting Cheyennes, 334. The army casualty lists do not record the death of any trumpeter at Rosebud. "List of Killed," Hartsuff Report, NA

31. Stands in Timber and Liberty, *A Cheyenne Voice*, 409, 419, 436; Stands in Timber and Liberty, *Cheyenne Memories*, 187. Grinnell tells this story differently, suggesting that Scabby (Scabby Eyelid) struck a soldier with his whip, got pulled from his horse, and struggled but then got separated from the tussle, with neither man seriously hurt. Grinnell furthermore places Scabby in the Red Fork fight of November 25, 1876, where he was seriously wounded and died two days later. Grinnell, *The Fighting Cheyennes*, 335, 365.

32. Crawford, *Rekindling Camp Fires*, 251–52.

33. Stands in Timber and Liberty, *A Cheyenne Voice*, 402, 432; Marquis, *A Warrior Who Fought Custer*, 201, 202 (first and second quotations); "Crook," *Weekly Rocky Mountain News*, July 5, 1876 (third quotation); Thralls, "The Sioux War," 574–75 (fourth and fifth quotations); "J. M. Thralls' Interview with Two Moons," in Hardorff, *Cheyenne Memories of the Custer Fight*, 112.

34. "Iron Hawk Speaks," in Neihardt, *Black Elk Speaks*, 100 (first quotation); Howard, *The Warrior Who Killed Custer*, 49 (second quotation).

35. Miller, *Ghost Dance*, 209 (first quotation); "Hamlin Garland's Interview with Two Moons," in Hardorff, *Cheyenne Memories of the Custer Fight*, 100 (second quotation).

CHAPTER 17. EVENING ON THE ROSEBUD

1. "Crook," *Weekly Rocky Mountain News*, July 5, 1876 (first, second, and third quotations); Hartsuff Report, NA (fourth quotation); Otis, *Circular No. 9*, 20.

2. "Crook," *Weekly Rocky Mountain News*, July 5, 1876 (first quotation); Henry, "Wounded in an Indian Fight," 627 (second quotation).

3. Altshuler, *Cavalry Yellow & Infantry Blue*, 164–65; Patzki Report, Guy V. Henry Papers, B. William Henry Jr. Collection, BHSU (first and second quotations; the Patzki document is not sourced though it is probably from Guy Henry's ACP File, NA, a matter not confirmed); "What They Are There For," *Winners of the West*, May 30, 1934 (third quotation).

4. "What They Are There For," *Winners of the West*, May 30, 1934 (first quotation); "Battle of the Rosebud," *New York Sun*, July 6, 1876 (second quotation); "Battle of the Rosebud," *New York Daily Graphic*, July 13, 1876; Henry Report, 146; Henry, "Wounded in an Indian Fight," 627 (third quotation).

5. Henry, "Wounded in an Indian Fight"; Hartsuff Report, NA (quotation); Mears, "Campaigning against Crazy Horse," 71; "The Sioux War," *New York Tribune*, July 6, 1876.

6. Magid, *The Gray Fox*, xii; "Crook," *Weekly Rocky Mountain News*, July 5, 1876; Finerty, *War-Path and Bivouac*, 132; Mills, "Address by General Anson Mills," 9; Brady, *Indian Fights and Fighters*, 199–200.

7. Brady, *Indian Fights and Fighters*, 202; Finerty, *War-Path and Bivouac*, 132 (quotation).

8. Finerty, *War-Path and Bivouac*, 133 (quotation); "Brigadier General Anson Mills," *Washington Herald*, March 3, 1907.

9. "Brigadier General Anson Mills," *Washington Herald*, March 3, 1907; Mills, "Address by General Anson Mills," 9 (quotations); Finerty, *War-Path and Bivouac*, 133.

10. Mills, "Address by General Anson Mills," 9–10; Finerty, *War-Path and Bivouac*, 133 (first quotation), 134 (second quotation); DeBarthe, *Life and Adventures of Frank Grouard*, 121; Mills Report, 151; Noyes Report, 133–34 (third quotation).

11. Mills, "Address by General Anson Mills," 10.

12. Powers, *The Killing of Crazy Horse*, 188.

13. "Telegraphic," *Sidney Telegraph*, June 24, 1876; Bourke, *On the Border with Crook*, 315.

14. Abrams, *"Crying for Scalps,"* 84 (quotation); Luhn, Autobiography, 31, Luhn Papers,

AHC. Evidence in several groupings of military artifacts recovered from Conical Hill shows a preponderance of nearly identically flattened .45–70 cartridge cases, suggesting that the flattening action was deliberate. Schug, "Rosebud Battle Artifacts Inventory."

15. Lemly, "The Fight on the Rosebud," 15, 16 (quotation); "Baptiste Pourier's Interview," in Jensen, *The Settler and Soldier Interviews of Eli S. Ricker*, 267; "The Indian War," *New York Herald*, June 24, 1876.

16. Lemly, "The Fight on the Rosebud," 16 (first four quotations); "Baptiste Pourier's Interview," in Jensen, *The Settler and Soldier Interviews of Eli S. Ricker*, 267 (fifth and sixth quotations): "The Indian War," *New York Herald*, June 24, 1876; "On the War-Path," *Chicago Inter-Ocean*, June 24, 1876; "Indian Maid's Vengeance in Early Montana Days," *Billings Gazette*, September 20, 1911.

17. "Baptiste Pourier's Interview," in Jensen, *The Settler and Soldier Interviews of Eli S. Ricker*, 267; DeBarthe, *Life and Adventures of Frank Grouard*, 121–22.

18. Nickerson, "Major General George Crook and the Indians," 28 (first and second quotations), Crook-Kennon Papers, USAWC; "Sioux Indian Campaign," *Army and Navy Journal*, July 22, 1876; Strahorn, "Ninety Years of Boyhood," 154 (third quotation), Strahorn Papers, College of Idaho; "Battle of the Rosebud," *New York Sun*, July 6, 1876; "Crook," *Weekly Rocky Mountain News*, July 5, 1876 (fourth and fifth quotations); "Adenda: Why Crook Did Not Meet Terry, Gibbon and Custer," in Thompson, *George Armstrong Custer's "Winners of the West,"* 194; "Battle of the Rosebud," *New York Times*, July 13, 1876.

19. Bourke, *On the Border with Crook*, 311; Hyde, *Red Cloud's Folk*, 265–66; Reneau, *The Adventures of Moccasin Joe*, 62 (first quotation); Fontaine Narrative, *Walla Walla Bulletin*, March 13, 1921, TS, Lewis Crawford Papers, SHSND (second quotation); McDermott, "Gen. George Crook's 1876 Campaigns," 41–42; "Crazy Horse's Report of the Rosebud Fight," *Cheyenne Daily Leader*, May 22, 1877; Vestal, *Warpath and Council Fire*, 228–29.

20. Noyes Report, 134; "Why the Column Fell Back," *New York Times*, July 13, 1876 (first quotation); Zinser, *Indian War Diary*, 14 (second quotation); "John P. Slough," *Hardin Tribune*, July 1, 1921.

21. "Indian Arms and Ammunition," *Chicago Inter-Ocean*, July 10, 1876; "Indian Arms and Ammunition," *Cheyenne Daily Leader*, July 14, 1876; "Crook," *Weekly Rocky Mountain News*, July 5, 1876; Lemly, "The Fight on the Rosebud," 18; "A Bull Fight," *Chicago Times*, June 24, 1876 (first quotation); "Braving the Braves," *Chicago Times*, July 5, 1876 (second quotation); Finerty, *War-Path and Bivouac*, 135; "The Indian War," *New York Herald*, June 24, 1876 (third quotation); "Why the Column Fell Back," *New York Times*, July 13, 1876.

22. Finerty, *War-Path and Bivouac*, 137.

23. Noyes Report, 134 (first quotation); Bourke, *Diaries*, 1:328; Meketa, *Marching with General Crook*, 20; Finerty, *War-Path and Bivouac*, 137 (second quotation); Luhn Autobiography, 31, Luhn Papers, AHC.

24. Henry, "Wounded in an Indian Fight," 627 (first quotation); Hartsuff Report, NA; "Crook," *Weekly Rocky Mountain News*, July 5, 1876; Bourke, *Diaries*, 1:328 (second quotation).

25. "List of Wounded," Hartsuff Report, NA (first quotation); Henry, "Wounded in an Indian Fight"; "Sioux Indian Campaign," *Army and Navy Journal*, July 22, 1876; Bourke, *On the Border with Crook*, 317; Bourke, *Diaries*, 1:328 (second quotation). The strain among the physicians working the Rosebud hospital was palpable, a detail apparent in the accounts. It is worth recalling, however, the even greater burden shouldered singly by acting assistant surgeon Henry R. Porter, the only surviving physician at the Little Big Horn battle, who for nearly three days tended fifty-nine soldiers whose wounds ranged from slight to severe and ultimately mortal. Stevenson, *Deliverance from the Little Big Horn*, 71–78, with a nod to Randy Kane for the observation.

26. Bourke, *Diaries*, 1:329 (first quotation); Abrams, *"Crying for Scalps,"* 84; Finerty, *War-Path and Bivouac*, 134 (second quotation); "Crook," *Weekly Rocky Mountain News*, July 5, 1876 (third quotation); Strahorn, "Ninety Years of Boyhood," Strahorn Papers, College of Idaho, 155; "The Sioux War," *Chicago Tribune*, July 5, 1876 (fourth quotation).

27. Crook Report, June 20, 1876, 129; "Report of Casualties," Crook to Adjutant General, June 20, 1876, Adjutant General's Office Letters Received (Main Series), 1876, NA (first quotation); "Chicago Headquarters," *Chicago Tribune*, July 18, 1876; Finerty, *War-Path and Bivouac*, 134 (second quotation); Hartsuff Report, NA (third quotation); "Further Particulars from the Recent Indian Fight," *Omaha Bee*, June 24, 1876; "Battle of the Rosebud," *New York Times*, July 13, 1876; "The Indian War," *New York Herald*, June 24, 1876. McDermott identified several additional men with lesser wounds not tallied by Hartsuff or Crook: "Gen. George Crook's 1876 Campaigns," 54–55n42.

28. Mills, "Address by General Anson Mills," 10 (quotations); Brady, *Indian Fights and Fighters*, 347; Brady, "What They Are There For," 411.

29. Finerty, *War-Path and Bivouac*, 130 (first and third quotations); Hutton, "'Correct in Every Detail,'" 232 (second quotation); "Colonel Guy V. Henry," *Army and Navy Register*, May 16, 1891; Brady, *Indian Fights and Fighters*, 346; Hallberg and Neal, "'For This Are We Soldiers,'" 68. An unsigned but carefully researched account of the captain's life, written by someone who knew him and appearing in *Winners of the West*, organ of the National Indian War Veterans organization, offers this version of Henry's great utterance: "'It's all right, Jack,' gurgled out from the bleeding lips; 'it's what we're here for.'" "What They Are There For: A Sketch of General Guy V. Henry, a Typical American Soldier," *Winners of the West*, May 30, 1934.

30. Lemly, "The Fight on the Rosebud," 17.

31. Finerty, *War-Path and Bivouac*, 47 (first quotation); "Military Matters," *Cheyenne Daily Leader*, February 17, 1881 (second quotation); "Thomas C. MacMillan," *Chicago Eagle*, November 24, 1917.

32. Henry, "Wounded in an Indian Fight," 627.

33. Finerty, *War-Path and Bivouac*, 136; "Why the Column Fell Back," *New York Times*, July 13, 1876; Letter, Ashkey to Camp, August 26, 1913, Ellison Papers, DPL; U.S. Army Register of Enlistments, M233, 1871–77 H-O, NA, www.ancestry.com; "Incidents of Crook's Fight," *Cheyenne Daily Leader*, June 28, 1876.

34. "James Forristell," *Hardin Tribune-Herald*, January 20, 1933 (first quotation); "Why the Column Fell Back," *New York Times*, July 13, 1876 (second quotation); Bourke, *Diaries*, 1:331; Strahorn, "Why Crook Did Not Meet Terry, Gibbon and Custer," in Brininstool, *The Custer Fight*, 35; Bourke, *On the Border with Crook*, 317–18; "Crook," *Weekly Rocky Mountain News*, July 5, 1876; Henry, "Wounded in an Indian Fight," 627; Strahorn, "Ninety Years of Boyhood," Strahorn Papers, College of Idaho, 155. Luhn asserted that a picket line was stretched across the grave and that horse's hooves cut the ground and obscured it. "Luhn Autobiography," 31, Luhn Papers, AHC. Crook had forbidden picket ropes at the start, although perhaps this line was in the medical kit. Forristell asserted that Crook reburied these dead when passing this ground again in August in a more suitable location away from the stream. That action is not confirmed and is doubted, especially when Crook's trail in August did not in fact pass the battlefield.

35. "Veteran Recalls Hardships of Indian Fighting in the West," *National Tribune*, October 3, 1940 (first quotation); Reneau, *The Adventures of Moccasin Joe*, 62 (second quotation). The location of the Rosebud mass burial has vexed researchers since 1876. The remains were never recovered. In 1931 human remains may have been located but were not exhumed. In later years a depression near the Kobold house was assumed to be the burial site. Vaughn noted

that that ground had been disturbed to a depth of four feet, but no remains were encountered. Present-day consensus holds that the burial site is on the north side of the Rosebud, not at all near the Kobold house but slightly east of the mouth of Kollmar Creek, as described in the narrative. Werts and Booras, *The Crazy Horse and Crook Fight of 1876*, 177–79; Vaughn, *With Crook at the Rosebud*, 125–26; Vaughn, *Indian Fights*, 139.

36. Chambers Report, 135; Munson Report, 137; Burrowes Report, 138; "Luhn Autobiography," 31, Luhn Papers, AHC; Luhn Diary, June 17, 1876, Luhn Papers, AHC.

37. Bourke, *Diaries*, 1:328; "On the War-Path," *Chicago Inter-Ocean*, June 24, 1876 (quotation).

38. Bourke, *Diaries*, 1:328; Lemly, "The Fight on the Rosebud," 16–18; "Battle of Rosebud Creek," *New York Herald*, July 6, 1876; "Indian Maid's Vengeance in Early Montana Days," *Billings Gazette*, September 20, 1911; Gilbert, *"Big Bat" Pourier*, 51; "On the War-Path," *Chicago Inter-Ocean*, June 24, 1876.

39. Bourke, *On the Border with Crook*, 316 (first quotation); Lemly, "The Fight on the Rosebud," 17 (second quotation); DeBarthe, *Life and Adventures of Frank Grouard*, 122 (third quotation).

40. Crook Report, June 19, 1876, 214; Crook Report, June 20, 1876, 129 (quotation).

41. "Crook," *Weekly Rocky Mountain News*, July 5, 1876; "A Bull Fight," *Chicago Times*, June 24, 1876; "Fighting the Fiends," *Cheyenne Daily Leader*, June 24, 1876; "Why the Column Fell Back," *New York Times*, July 13, 1876; "On the War-Path," *Chicago Inter-Ocean*, June 24, 1876; Finerty, *War-Path and Bivouac*, 137 (quotation).

42. Bourke, *On the Border with Crook*, 316 (first quotation); "The Battle of Rosebud Creek," *New York Herald*, July 13, 1876 (second quotation); https://en.wikiquote.org/wiki/Arthur_Wellesley,_1st_Duke_of_Wellington (third quotation); Powers, *The Killing of Crazy Horse*, 190; Reneau, *The Adventures of Moccasin Joe*, 62 (fourth quotation). Wellington's quotation was popularized in a contemporary and oft-reprinted book, *Memorable Battles in English History* (1862), by William Henry Davenport Adams, an English writer and journalist.

43. "A Bull Fight," *Chicago Times*, June 24, 1876 (quotation); "Another Account of Crook's 'Bull' Fight," *Cheyenne Daily Leader*, June 27, 1876.

44. "The Battle of Rosebud," *New York Times*, July 13, 1876.

45. "The Battle of Rosebud Creek," *New York Herald*, July 13, 1876; "The Battle of the Rosebud," *Bozeman Times*, July 6, 1876 (quotation); Knight, *Following the Indian Wars*, 189; Vaughn, *With Crook at the Rosebud*, 124.

46. "The Sioux War," *New York Tribune*, July 6, 1876 (first quotation); "Crook's Expedition," *Platte Valley Independent*, July 8, 1876 (second quotation); Bourke, *Diaries*, 1:328; "On the War-Path," *Chicago Inter-Ocean*, June 24, 1876; "Fighting the Fiends," *Cheyenne Daily Leader*, June 24, 1876; Finerty, *War-Path and Bivouac*, 126; "The Battle of Rosebud," *New York Times*, July 13, 1876; Nottage, "The Big Horn and Yellowstone Expedition of 1876," 34; Luhn Autobiography, Box 1, Folder 8, 10, Luhn Papers, AHC; "The Indian War," *New York Herald*, June 24, 1876. For a smattering of additional calculations and estimations, see McDermott, "Gen. George Crook's 1876 Campaigns," 50n8; and Abrams, *Sioux War Dispatches*, 103. Strahorn's estimation inflated greatly over the years. In the early 1930s he told Custer scholar E. A. Brininstool that the body of Indians at the Rosebud was "estimated all the way from 2,000 to 3,000 to 4,000." Strahorn, "Why Crook Did Not Meet Terry, Gibbon and Custer," in Brininstool, *The Custer Fight*, 35.

47. "The Sioux War," *Chicago Tribune*, July 5, 1876.

48. "Braving the Braves," *Chicago Times*, July 5, 1876 (first quotation); Abrams, *"Crying for Scalps,"* 85; "The Indian War," *New York Herald*, June 24, 1876; "The Indian War," *Cincinnati Commercial*, June 24, 1876 (second quotation); "Crook's Command," *Chicago Tribune*,

June 24, 1876; "Crook," *Weekly Rocky Mountain News*, July 5, 1876; Crook Report, June 20, 1876, 129 (third quotation); "The Sioux War," *Chicago Tribune*, July 5, 1876; Bourke, *Diaries*, 1:327–28 (fourth quotation).

49. "A Bull Fight," *Chicago Times*, June 24, 1876; "On the War-Path," *Chicago Inter-Ocean*, June 24, 1876; Vaughn, *With Crook at the Rosebud*, 132.

50. Bourke, *Diaries*, 1:328 (quotation); Finerty, *War-Path and Bivouac*, 138–39; "Why the Column Fell Back," *New York Times*, July 13, 1876.

51. Hartsuff Report, NA; Otis, *Circular No. 9*, 20–21; "Frontiersman Tom Cooper," *Wyoming Tribune*, February 20, 1903.

CHAPTER 18. RETURN TO GOOSE CREEK

1. Lemly, "The Fight on the Rosebud," 17; Luhn Diary, June 17, 1876, Luhn Papers, AHC; Bourke, *Diaries*, 1:329; Finerty, *War-Path and Bivouac*, 138; Abrams, *"Crying For Scalps,"* 87.

2. Bourke, *Diaries*, 1:329; Stanton Report, 713.

3. Finerty, *War-Path and Bivouac*, 139; "A Bull Fight," *Chicago Times*, June 24, 1876; Crawford, *Rekindling Camp Fires*, 252; Reneau, *The Adventures of Moccasin Joe*, 62 (quotation).

4. Bourke, *Diaries*, 1:329 (first quotation); Hartsuff Report, NA; Otis, *Circular No. 9*, 20 (second quotation); "Why the Column Fell Back," *New York Times*, July 13, 1876. Tom Cooper, one of Tom Moore's packers, recalled that the litter and travois were borne by cavalry horses, while all other sources consistently suggest the use of mules. "Frontiersman Tom Cooper," *Wyoming Tribune*, February 20, 1903.

5. Bourke, *Diaries*, 1:329–30; Otis, *Circular No. 9*, 20.

6. Bourke, *Diaries*, 1:332; Henry, "Wounded in an Indian Fight"; Brady, "What They Are There For," 412; Linderman, *American*, 171 (quotation); Noyes, "Story of My Life," 86, Noyes-Wallace Family Collection, UCSB.

7. Abrams, *"Crying for Scalps,"* 87 (first and third quotations); Bourke, *On the Border with Crook*, 318; Bourke, *Diaries*, 1:330; "The Battle of Rosebud Creek," *New York Herald*, July 13, 1876; Crawford, *Rekindling Camp Fires*, 252–53; Finerty, *War-Path and Bivouac*, 139; Letter, Ashkey to Camp, February 1, 1914, Ellison Papers, DPL (second quotation). Davenport's vivid description of this ruthless killing and dismemberment in the *New York Herald* made compelling newspaper copy throughout the land: for example, "The Gentle Indian," *Saint Paul and Minneapolis Pioneer Press*, July 18, 1876; "A Savage Spectacle," *Cheyenne Daily Leader*, July 18, 1876; and "The Gentle Savage," *Virginia City Madisonian*, August 10, 1876, all echoing Davenport.

8. Mills, "Address by General Anson Mills," 10 (quotation); Powers, *The Killing of Crazy Horse*, 190.

9. Bourke, *Diaries*, 1:332, 333 (quotations); Bourke, *On the Border with Crook*, 318; Vaughn, *With Crook at the Rosebud*, 150.

10. Bourke, *Diaries*, 1:332–33; Bourke, *On the Border with Crook*, 318; "The Battle of Rosebud Creek," *New York Herald*, July 13, 1876; Reneau, *The Adventures of Moccasin Joe*, 62; "The Battle of the Rosebud," *Pittsburg Evening Leader*, July 21, 1876.

11. Stanton Report, 713; Bourke, *On the Border with Crook*, 318; Finerty, *War-Path and Bivouac*, 140; "The Battle of Rosebud Creek," *New York Herald*, July 13, 1876; Reneau, *The Adventures of Moccasin Joe*, 62 (Howard's diary).

12. "Why the Column Fell Back," *New York Times*, July 13, 1876; "Indian Maid's Vengeance in Early Montana Days," *Billings Gazette*, September 20, 1911; "On the War-Path," *Chicago Inter-Ocean*, June 24, 1876; "Military Movements," *Omaha Bee*, July 8, 1876; "The Indian War," *Omaha Republican*, July 9, 1876; "A Bull Fight," *Chicago Times*, June 24, 1876; DeBarthe, *Life and Adventures of Frank Grouard*, 122 (first quotation); Linderman, *American*,

171 (second and third quotations); Bourke, *Diaries*, 1:333; "Crook's Expedition," *Chicago Inter-Ocean*, June 27, 1876.

13. Bourke, *Diaries*, 1:333; Henry, "Wounded in an Indian Fight," 627; "Why the Column Fell Back," *New York Times*, July 13, 1876; Finerty, *War-Path and Bivouac*, 140 (quotation).

14. Bourke, *Diaries*, 1:333; Hartsuff Report, NA; Stanton Report, 713 (quotation), 714; Meketa, *Marching with General Crook*, 21.

15. Bourke, *Diaries*, 1:333–34; Bourke, *On the Border with Crook*, 318–19.

16. Stanton Report, 714; Bourke, *Diaries*, 1:334 (quotation); Bourke, *On the Border with Crook*, 319.

17. Crook Report, June 19, 1876, 213–14; BH&Y Expedition Order Book, NA, 4–5; Telegram, Crook to Sheridan, June 19, 1876, via Fort Fetterman, June 23, 1876, Division of the Missouri, Special Files, NA (quotation); Telegram, Nickerson to AAG, Division of the Missouri, June 19, 1876, via Fort Fetterman, June 23, 1876, Division of the Missouri, Special Files, NA; Crawford, *Rekindling Camp Fires*, 255; "The Indians," *Omaha Daily Bee*, June 23, 1876; "The Indian Campaign," *Omaha Republican*, June 24, 1876; "Red Blood," *Omaha Daily Herald*, June 24, 1876; "The Recent Fight with the Sioux," *New York Times*, June 26, 1876; "Indian Affairs," *Army and Navy Journal*, July 1, 1876; McGillycuddy Notebook, June 22, 1876, NSHS.

18. "The Chase after Indians," *New York Daily Graphic*, June 24, 1876; "Crook Fighting the Sioux," *Daily Alta California*, June 24, 1876; Telegram, Hawkins to AAG, Division of the Missouri, June 23, 1876, Division of the Missouri, Special Files, NA; Fourteenth Infantry Regimental Return, May, 1876, NA.

19. Nottage, "The Big Horn and Yellowstone Expedition of 1876," 34; Burt Papers, FLNHS; Mattes, *Indians, Infants and Infantry*, 218; "The Indian War," *Cincinnati Commercial*, June 24, 1876 (quotation).

20. Crawford, *Rekindling Camp Fires*, 254–55; Knight, *Following the Indian Wars*, 189, 192–93; Powers, *The Killing of Crazy Horse*, 191; Hedren, *Powder River*, 244.

21. Stanton Report, 714; Finerty, *War-Path and Bivouac*, 146; Bourke, *Diaries*, 1:339 (quotation); "The Sioux War," *New York Tribune*, July 6, 1876; Henry, "Wounded in an Indian Fight," 627. The name Camp Cloud Peak becomes common in the BH&Y Expedition Order Book, where it was also first used on June 20.

22. Bourke, *Diaries*, 1:343; "The Sioux War," *New York Tribune*, July 6, 1876; "The Indian War," *Laramie Daily Sentinel*, June 24, 1876; *Report of a Board of Officers to Decide upon a Pattern of Ambulance Wagon for Army Use*, 12; http://www.civilwarhome.com/ambulancewagons.html.

23. Royall Report, 142; Noyes Report, 132; Evans Report, 132 (quotation); Hartsuff Report, NA; "Plucked from the Rosebud," *Chicago Times*, July 18, 1876.

24. Crook Report, June 20, 1876, 127–30 (quotation on 130).

25. Bourke, *Diaries*, 1:340; Abrams, *"Crying for Scalps,"* 92–93; Bourke, *On the Border with Crook*, 319; Finerty, *War-Path and Bivouac*, 143; Hebard, *Washakie*, 189–90; letter, Crook to Irwin, June 20, 1876, BH&Y Expedition Order Book, NA (quotation). Stanley asserted that the Shoshones departed on June 22.

26. Bourke, *Diaries*, 1:339; Nickerson, "Personal Recollections of Two Visits to Gettysburg," 21; "Why the Column Fell Back," *New York Times*, July 13, 1876 (first quotation); Finerty, *War-Path and Bivouac*, 141 (second quotation).

27. King, *Campaigning with Crook*, 170; Juarez, *The Tarnished Saber*, 76–77; "The Battle of Rosebud Creek," *New York Herald*, July 13, 1876; Stanton Report, 714–15; Gray, *Centennial Campaign*, 198.

28. Bourke, *Diaries*, 1:339; Abrams, *"Crying for Scalps,"* 93; Knight, *Following the Indian Wars*, 193; Gray, *Centennial Campaign*, 198; "The Sioux War," *Frank Leslie's Illustrated*

Newspaper, August 12, 1876 (first quotation); Abrams, "St. George Stanley," 10; "The Battle of the Rosebud," *Pittsburg Evening Leader*, July 21, 1876 (second quotation); Gilbert, *"Big Bat" Pourier*, 51–52; McLaird, *Calamity Jane*, 57; Hedren, *Fort Laramie in 1876*, 115.

29. Bourke, *Diaries*, 1:341 (quotation); Shockley, "General George Crook's Fish Shooting Army," 11.

CHAPTER 19. EIGHT DAYS

1. Bourke, *Diaries*, 1:341; Magid, *George Crook*, 42–43; Magid, *The Gray Fox*, 154–55.

2. Bourke, *Diaries*, 1:341; Zinser, *Indian War Diary*, 16; Finerty, *War-Path and Bivouac*, 146 (quotation); Shockley, "General George Crook's Fish Shooting Army," 11–12.

3. Bourke, *Diaries*, 1:341–42; Bourke, *On the Border with Crook*, 321; Finerty, *War-Path and Bivouac*, 147; Schuyler letter, June 27, 1876, Schuyler Papers, Henry E. Huntington Library; Hedren, *Ho! For the Black Hills*, 201.

4. Bourke, *Diaries*, 1:341; Finerty, *War-Path and Bivouac*, 147; Schuyler letter, June 27, 1876, Schuyler Papers, Henry E. Huntington Library (quotation); Hedren, *Great Sioux War Orders of Battle*, 38–42.

5. "The Battle of Rosebud Creek," *New York Herald*, July 13, 1876 (quotations); Magid, *The Gray Fox*, 259.

6. Glusing letter, January 7, 1877, Chris Kortlander Collection (quotations); "Braving the Braves," *Chicago Times*, July 5, 1876.

7. Burgan, "Remembering Camp Cloud Peak," 12; Vaughn, *With Crook at the Rosebud*, 157; Miller, *Military Sites in Wyoming*, 121–22. The stone survives and is a showpiece in today's Bozeman Trail Museum, Big Horn, Wyoming.

8. Bourke, *Diaries*, 1:342–43; Finerty, *War-Path and Bivouac*, 147–48; "The Big Horn," *Weekly Rocky Mountain News*, July 12, 1876 (quotations).

9. "The Sioux War," *Chicago Tribune*, July 11, 1876 (quotation). Bourke places the receipt of the mail and newspapers on June 26. Bourke, *Diaries*, 1:343. Strahorn is equally specific that this occurred on June 25. The point plays either way.

10. Finerty, *War-Path and Bivouac*, 148.

11. Endorsements, June 25, June 26, 1876, BH&Y Expedition Order Book, 10–11, NA.

12. Tall Bull interview, Camp Papers, MSS 57, Box 4, BYU; Tall Bull Interview, in Hardorff, *Cheyenne Memories of the Custer Fight*, 75; "Interview with He Dog," in Hammer, *Custer in '76*, 205 (quotation); Vaughn, *With Crook at the Rosebud*, 147, citing John Stands in Timber; Donovan, *A Terrible Glory*, 152.

13. Marquis, *A Warrior Who Fought Custer*, 201; "Crook," *Weekly Rocky Mountain News*, July 5, 1876.

14. "Iron Hawk Tells about the Rosebud Battle," in DeMallie, *The Sixth Grandfather*, 176 (first quotation); "Kill Eagle's Story," *New York Herald*, October 6, 1876; "Standing Bear Tells about the Dead Soldiers," in DeMallie, *The Sixth Grandfather*, 177 (second quotation); Jackson, *Black Elk*, xii–xiv.

15. Grinnell, *The Fighting Cheyennes*, 336; Powell, *People of the Sacred Mountain*, 2:999; Buecker, "Lt. William Philo Clark's Sioux War Report and Little Big Horn Map," 17; Hyde, *Red Cloud's Folk*, 265.

16. "Standing Bear Tells about the Dead Soldiers," in DeMallie, *The Sixth Grandfather*, 177 (quotations); "Respects Nothing's Interview," in Jensen, *The Indian Interviews of Eli S. Ricker*, 304; American Horse reminiscence, in Greene, *Lakota and Cheyenne*, 48.

17. "Standing Bear Tells about the Dead Soldiers," in DeMallie, *The Sixth Grandfather*, 177 (quotations); Stands in Timber and Liberty, *A Cheyenne Voice*, 422–23, 437; Jackson, *Black Elk*, 102. Private James Forristell of First Lieutenant Samuel Swigert's Company D, Second Cavalry,

recollected years later that when Crook resumed his campaign in August his route took him past the Rosebud Battlefield, where the general paused long enough to "make a change in the burial places of our dead comrades," suggesting at the least an opportunity to cover the dead if not relocate them entirely. "James Forristell," *Hardin Tribune-Herald*, January 20, 1933. This action is doubted.

18. "Standing Bear Tells about the Dead Soldiers," in DeMallie, *The Sixth Grandfather*, 177 (quotation); "Respects Nothing's Interview," in Jensen, *The Indian Interviews of Eli S. Ricker*, 304; American Horse reminiscence, in Greene, *Lakota and Cheyenne*, 48.

19. "The Two Moons Narrative," in Hardorff, *Indian Views of the Custer Fight*, 108, 108n4; "Two Moons Interview," in Jensen, *The Indian Interviews of Eli S. Ricker*, 322; "Tales of the Tatankas," *Saint Paul and Minneapolis Pioneer Press*, May 19, 1883; "Kill Eagle's Story," *New York Herald*, October 6, 1876 (first and second quotations); Marquis, *A Warrior Who Fought Custer*, 202–203 (third quotation).

20. Buecker, "Lt. William Philo Clark's Sioux War Report and Little Big Horn Map," 17; "The Custer Fight," *Colorado Banner*, June 21, 1877; "Doves and Devils," *Chicago Times*, May 26, 1877, in Hardorff, *The Surrender and Death of Crazy Horse*, 223; Bourke, *Diaries*, 2:287 (quotation).

21. White Bull Interview, Campbell Collection, Box 105, Notebook 24, 82, University of Oklahoma Libraries; Hardorff, *Indian Views of the Custer Fight*, 25n5, 108n4; Marquis, *A Warrior Who Fought Custer*, 202–203; Grinnell, *The Cheyenne Indians*, 2:160; "The American Horse Interview," in Hardorff, *Cheyenne Memories of the Custer Fight*, 28n5; Killsback, "Crowns of Honor," 9–10; Stands in Timber and Liberty, *Cheyenne Memories*, 186, 187, 207; Stands in Timber and Liberty, *A Cheyenne Voice*, liv, lvi, 419, 436; Hardorff, *Hokahey!*, 90–91.

22. "The Julia Face Interview," in Hardorff, *Lakota Recollections of the Custer Fight*, 188; "Iron Hawk's Interview," in Jensen, *The Indian Interviews of Eli S. Ricker*, 316; "Black Elk Tells about the Bear Medicine Ceremony," in DeMallie, *The Sixth Grandfather*, 178–79.

23. Marquis, *She Watched Custer's Last Battle*, [2]; Marquis, *A Warrior Who Fought Custer*, 203; "Interview with He Dog," in Hammer, *Custer in '76*, 205; "Account of the Custer Fight as Given by 'Feather Earring,'" in Graham, *The Custer Myth*, 98; "The Day Custer Fell," *Utah Journal*, October 17, 1885; "The American Horse Interview," in Hardorff, *Cheyenne Memories of the Custer Fight*, 28; American Horse reminiscence, in Greene, *Lakota and Cheyenne*, 48; "The Young Two Moons Interview," in Hardorff, *Cheyenne Memories of the Custer Fight*, 152.

These tipis of the dead along the middle reach of Reno Creek are a much-studied footnote of the Custer story but, foremost here, objects related to the Battle of the Rosebud. See Smalley, "The Lone Tepees along Reno Creek"; Meketa and Bookwalter, *The Search for the Lone Tepee*; and Liddic, *Vanishing Victory*, 40–42. In the context of the Custer story, as Smalley notes, "suggesting that there was only one lone tepee and that everyone referred to that single location greatly confuses the story." "The Lone Tepees along Reno Creek," 9.

24. Marquis, *A Warrior Who Fought Custer*, 203; Tall Bull interview, Camp Papers, MSS 57, Box 4, BYU; "The Tall Bull Interview," in Hardorff, *Cheyenne Memories of the Custer Fight*, 75 (first quotation); Eastman, "Rain-in-the-Face," 511 (second quotation); Weasel Bear interview, in Hunt and Hunt, *I Fought with Custer*, 216 (third quotation); Powell, *People of the Sacred Mountain*, 2:999; "Respects Nothing's Interview," in Jensen, *The Indian Interviews of Eli S. Ricker*, 304.

25. Marquis, *A Warrior Who Fought Custer*, 204 (first quotation); Utley, *The Lance and the Shield*, 143; Powell, *People of the Sacred Mountain*, 2:999–1000; "Interview with He Dog," in Hammer, *Custer in '76*, 205 (second quotation).

26. "Henry Oscar One Bull," in Miller, "Echoes of the Little Bighorn," 30; Utley, *The Lance and the Shield*, 142.

27. Marquis, *A Warrior Who Fought Custer*, 204; Young Two Moon account, in Greene, *Lakota and Cheyenne*, 67; Powell, *People of the Sacred Mountain*, 2:1004 (first quotation); "The Story of Waterman," in Graham, *The Custer Myth*, 109 (second quotation); "The Story of Left Hand," in Graham, *The Custer Myth*, 111. Wooden Leg recollected that six Arapahos joined the camp; Young Two Moon remembered seven. Waterman and Left Hand named the same five, including themselves.

28. "Crow King's Story of the Fight," in Graham, *The Custer Myth*, referencing the *Leavenworth Weekly Times*, August 18, 1881; Marquis, *A Warrior Who Fought Custer*, 207 (quotation); Marshall, "How Many Indians Were There?," 215; Stewart, *Custer's Luck*, 311; Burdick, *The Last Battle of the Sioux Nation*, 39. At one point Gall stated that he was among those in the Rosebud fight, but his biographer dispels that claim. Larson, *Gall*, 109–111.

29. "The Hollow Horn Bear Interview," in Hardorff, *Lakota Recollections of the Custer Fight*, 178–79.

30. "Interview with Foolish Elk," in Hammer, *Custer in '76*, 197–98; Marshall, "How Many Indians Were There?," 214.

31. Marquis, *A Warrior Who Fought Custer*, 204 (first and second quotations; Marquis, *She Watched Custer's Last Battle*, [2] (third quotation).

32. Marquis, *A Warrior Who Fought Custer*, 205; Marquis, *The Cheyennes of Montana*, 255; Marquis, *She Watched Custer's Last Battle*, [2]; Dixon, *The Vanishing Race*, 171.

33. Marquis, *A Warrior Who Fought Custer*, 204–207; Marquis, *The Cheyennes of Montana*, 255; Powell, *People of the Sacred Mountain*, 2:1004–1005; Bray, *Crazy Horse*, 212–13; Utley, *The Lance and the Shield*, 142–43.

34. Powell, *People of the Sacred Mountain*, 2:1008 (quotations); Hedren, *Powder River*, 215; Powell, "Ox'zem," 34–36; Vestal, *Sitting Bull*, 155.

CHAPTER 20. CONSEQUENCES

1. Mills, "Address by General Anson Mills," 11.

2. "Northern Indians," *Denver Daily Tribune*, May 20, 1877 (first quotation); "Crazy Horse's Report of the Rosebud Fight," *Cheyenne Daily Leader*, May 22, 1877; "The Custer Fight," *Colorado Banner*, June 21, 1877; Buecker, "Lt. William Philo Clark's Sioux War Report and Little Big Horn Map," 17; Robinson, "Crazy Horse's Story of Custer Battle," 228, reprinting the *Chicago Times* account of May 27, 1877 (second quotation).

3. Marquis, *A Warrior Who Fought Custer*, 207 (first quotation); Eastman, "Rain-in-the-Face," 511 (second quotation); Noyes, "Story of My Life," 86 (third quotation), Noyes-Wallace Family Collection, UCSB.

4. Crook Report, June 19, 1876, 214 (first quotation); Finerty, *War-Path and Bivouac*, 181 (second and third quotations); Magid, *The Gray Fox*, 270.

5. "Crook Defeated," *Helena Daily Independent*, June 30, 1876 (quotations); Meketa, *Marching with General Crook*, 25; Hedren, *Fort Laramie in 1876*, 126–28.

6. "Crook Defeated," *Helena Daily Independent*, June 30, 1876 (emphasis in the original).

7. "General Crook's 'Defeat,'" *Chicago Inter-Ocean*, July 12, 1876; "A Montana Account of Crook's Defeat," *New York Herald*, July 12, 1876; "A Base Slander Refuted," *Cheyenne Daily Leader*, July 20, 1876 (quotation); "The Officers at Fort Laramie," *Army and Navy Journal*, August 5, 1876; Hedren, *Fort Laramie in 1876*, 134–35.

8. *Army and Navy Journal*, July 6, 1878, quoting an undated *New York Herald* article; "Brevaties," *Helena Weekly Herald*, July 18, 1878.

9. Mills, "Address by General Anson Mills," 11.

10. "The Fellows in Feather," *Chicago Times*, November 4, 1876 (quotations). See also "General Crook Speaks," *Army and Navy Journal*, October 21, 1876, for a similar interview.

11. "The Fellows in Feather," *Chicago Times*, November 4, 1876.

12. Crook Report, September 25, 1876, 500.

13. Henry, "Wounded in an Indian Fight," 627 (first quotation); Patzki Certificate, July 2, 1876, Guy V. Henry Papers, B. William Henry Jr. Collection, BHSU; "Crook's Supply Train," *Cheyenne Daily Leader*, June 28, 1876; "The Big Horn Expedition," *Chicago Inter-Ocean*, June 28, 1876; "Crook's Wounded," *Laramie Daily Sentinel*, June 29, 1876; "The Army," *Omaha Republican*, July 8, 1876; Brady, "What They Are There For," 412; "What They Are There For," *Winners of the West*, May 30, 1934; Moulton, *Valentine T. McGillycuddy*, 78; Spring, "Dr. McGillycuddy's Diary," 284 (second quotation).

14. *Cheyenne Daily Leader*, July 15, 1876 (quotation); "The Far West," *Chicago Tribune*, July 7, 1876.

15. "Personal Paragraphs," *Cheyenne Daily Leader*, July 7, 1876; Brady, "What They Are There For," 412; "What They Are There For," *Winners of the West*, May 30, 1934; Randolph Certificate, September 12, 1876, Guy V. Henry Papers, B. William Henry Jr. Collection, BHSU; Henry, "Wounded in an Indian Fight," 627 (quotations); Special Orders No. 219, October 21, 1876, AGO, NA.

16. "A Battle-Scarred Veteran," *Army and Navy Journal*, May 25, 1878 (first quotation); "A Cavalry Charger," *Colorado Transcript*, August 22, 1894; Potter, "'Uncle Sam's Sharpshooters,'" 96–97; "Personal Items," *Army and Navy Journal*, December 17, 1887; "Service Record of Gen. Guy V. Henry," *Seventh Regiment Gazette*, September 1, 1896 (second quotation), McDermott Papers, BHSU. Henry died in 1899 and is buried in Arlington National Cemetery.

17. Willey and Scott, *Health of the Seventh Cavalry*, 287–302; McChristian, *Regular Army O!*, 570–71; Schneider, *The Freeman Journal*, 70 (quotation).

18. Fourth Infantry Regimental Returns, 1868–1875, NA; Crackel, "Custer's Kentucky," 150–53; Lindmier, *Drybone*, 203.

19. Fourth Infantry Regimental Returns, 1875–1876, NA; Avery Billings Cain, Names File, Archives, FLNHS; Adjutant General's Office, General Court-Martial Orders No. 5, January 22, 1876, in *General Court-Martial Orders, 1876* (hereinafter cited as AGO, General Court-Martial Orders No. 5).

20. Avery Billings Cain, Names File, Archives, FLNHS; Ward, "Fort Fetterman," 361 (first quotation); AGO, General Court-Martial Orders No. 5, January 22, 1876 (second and third quotations).

21. Hedren, "Drunk on the Black Hills Road," 443–47.

22. Luhn Diary, July 25, 1876, Luhn Papers, AHC (first quotation); Strahorn, "Ninety Years of Boyhood," 173–74 (second and third quotations), Strahorn Papers, College of Idaho.

23. Luhn Diary. July 28, 1876, Luhn Papers, AHC; BH&Y Expedition Order Book, 29–31, NA; Bourke, *Diaries*, 2:47 (first quotation), 49 (second quotation), 57 (third quotation), 58, 84; "From the Front," *Omaha Bee*, September 11, 1876.

24. Fourth Infantry Regimental Returns, September 1876-March 1877, NA; "St. Elizabeths Hospital," www.wikipedia.org. For a discussion of the problems of alcohol in the Old Army, see Hedren, "Drunk on the Black Hills Road," 448–51. Cain is buried in Evergreen Cemetery, Rutland, Vermont. Collier was cashiered by general court-martial in 1880, as a consequence of his own problems with alcohol.

Psychiatrist James S. Brust, MD, observed that Cain's mental illness likely now would be labeled bipolar disorder, with mood swings, delusions, and hallucinations that eventually remit, allowing the individual's return to normal. A striking parallel is the bipolar illness of Mary Todd Lincoln, a case carefully analyzed by Brust that informed this discussion. See Brust, "A Psychiatrist Looks at Mary Lincoln."

25. Elmer A. Snow, Names File, Library, FLNHS; Elmer A. Snow File, CMHS; *American Decorations*, 101 (quotation).

26. Elmer A. Snow photograph and marginalia, 1879, National Library of Medicine, Washington, D.C.

27. E. A. Snow letters, Bourke Papers, RG 2995, NSHS; Bourke, *Diaries*, 4:168 (quotation), 185–86; Porter, *Paper Medicine Man*, 248–49. Snow is buried in Highland Cemetery, Athol, Massachusetts.

28. John Henry Shingle File, Michael A. McGann File, Joseph Robinson File, all CMHS; *American Decorations*, 67 (first quotation), 90 (third quotation), 98; [Potter,] "McGann's Medal of Honor"; "A Medal of Honor," *Army and Navy Journal*, March 13, 1880 (second quotation); "Military Matters," *Cheyenne Weekly Leader*, March 25, 1880.

29. "Feted for His Laurels," *Omaha Daily World*, April 29, 1886.

30. Vaughn, *With Crook at the Rosebud*, 166; "More Troops for Utah," *Omaha Bee*, August 7, 1886; "William B. Royall," in Price, *Across the Continent with the Fifth Cavalry*, 298; [Powell,] *Records of Living Officers*, 120; Kennon diary, August 7, 1886, Crook-Kennon Papers, USAWC; Robinson, *General Crook and the Western Frontier*, 287.

31. Kennon diary, August 7, 1886, Crook-Kennon Papers, USAWC, with thanks to Paul Magid for providing a copy of the original at the War College. Transcriptions can also be found in Robinson, *General Crook and the Western Frontier*, 287–88, and Vaughn, *With Crook at the Rosebud*, 166–67. They are identical to the original in most respects aside from punctuation and a paragraph that Robinson summarized. A portion was also reproduced in Schmitt's *General George Crook*, 196.

32. Kennon diary, August 7, 1886, Crook-Kennon Papers, USAWC.

33. Ibid. (quotations); "From the Apache Land," *Omaha Daily World*, August 6, 1886; "Talks with Travelers," *Omaha Bee*, August 7, 1886.

34. Juarez, *The Tarnished Saber*, 78–79; Robinson, *General Crook and the Western Frontier*, 288.

35. King, "Needed: A Reevaluation of General George Crook," 227, 228 (first quotation); McDermott, "Gen. George Crook's 1876 Campaigns," 46–47; Magid, *The Gray Fox*, 258–59; Crook Report, June 20, 1876, 130 (second quotation).

36. For a look at this transformative time of battles, forts, railroads, buffalo, cattle, and consequences, see Hedren, *After Custer.*

37. Stands in Timber and Liberty, *Cheyenne Memories*, 181; Agonito and Agonito, *Buffalo Calf Road Woman.*

38. Marquis, *She Watched Custer's Last Battle*, [7]; Thomas, "Woman Warriors of the Greasy Grass," 52; Monaghan, "Cheyenne and Lakota Women at the Battle of the Little Bighorn," 14–15; Hantz, "The Girl Who Saved Her Brother," 67–68.

39. Agonito and Agonito, "Resurrecting History's Forgotten Women," 9; "Buffalo Calf Road Woman," www.wikipedia.org; Hantz, "The Girl Who Saved Her Brother," 68–70.

40. The Little Big Horn anniversaries of 1886 and 1926 are thoughtfully explored and lavishly illustrated in Upton, *The Battle of the Little Big Horn and Custer's Last Fight*, with photos of Jack Red Cloud and other Sioux veterans on 114–32. In "Burying the Hatchet," McChristian focuses on the 1926 event, with important details on the participating Indian and white survivors.

41. Medicine Crow, "Custer and His Crow Scouts," 109–10.

42. "Wrinkled Cheyenne Warriors Tell of Battle with Crook and His Soldiers on the Rosebud," *Billings Gazette*, June 24, 1934 (quotation); Vaughn, *With Crook at the Rosebud*, 144–45.

43. Weist, Editor's Introduction to *The Cheyennes of Montana* by Thomas B. Marquis, 18–19.

44. Stands in Timber and Liberty, *A Cheyenne Voice*, xxxii–xxxv; Stands in Timber and Liberty, *Cheyenne Memories*, 188.

45. Stands in Timber and Liberty, *A Cheyenne Voice*, 401 (quotation), 402, 417, 431; Vaughn, *With Crook at the Rosebud*, 45, 92, 107, 131, 137; Stands in Timber and Liberty, *Cheyenne Memories*, 188.

APPENDIX C. CARTRIDGES, CARTRIDGES

1. Godfrey, "Cavalry Fire Discipline," 255.

2. King, "Arms or Tactics," 495 (quotation), 497; "Crook," *Weekly Rocky Mountain News*, July 5, 1876.

3. Hess, *The Union Soldier in Battle*, 25 (quotations), 55, 150; Hess, *Civil War Infantry Tactics*, 222.

4. McChristian, *An Army of Marksmen*, 27–33; *Description and Rules for the Management of the Springfield Rifle, Carbine, and Army Revolvers*, 29–33 (quotation on 32).

5. Stands in Timber and Liberty, *A Cheyenne Voice*, 403.

6. *Description and Rules for the Management of the Springfield Rifle, Carbine, and Army Revolvers*, 22 (quotation); Frasca and Hill, *The .45–70 Springfield*, 235–35; Reuland, *Cartridges for the Springfield Trapdoor Rifles & Carbines*, 2–5.

7. McChristian, *The U.S. Army in the West*, 114, 181, 201, 216–19; Mills, *My Story*, 314; Noyes, "A Question of Arms," 11–12.

8. "'Lo' Game," *Chicago Times*, August 1, 1876 (first and second quotations); *Laramie Daily Sentinel*, June 28, 1876; Henry to Chief of Ordnance, August 6, 1876, Guy V. Henry Papers, B. William Henry Jr. Collection, BHSU (third quotation).

9. Noyes, "A Question of Arms," 9; "The Carbine in Reno's Fight," *Army and Navy Journal*, August 19, 1876, in Hutchins, The Army and Navy Journal *on the Battle of the Little Bighorn*, 80–81.

10. McChristian, *The U.S. Army in the West*, 114; Stewart, *Custer's Luck*, 421; "A Trooper's Account of the Battle," in Brininstool, *Troopers with Custer*, 55.

11. "The Carbine in Reno's Fight," *Army and Navy Journal*, August 19, 1876, in Hutchins, The Army and Navy Journal *on the Battle of the Little Bighorn*, 81; "The Custer Fight," *New York Herald*, August 1, 1876 (quotation); "Victims of Treachery," *Chicago Times*, August 3, 1876; Hedren, *Great Sioux War Orders of Battle*, 92–93.

12. *Description and Rules for the Management of the Springfield Rifle, Carbine, and Army Revolvers*, 22, 27–28; Reneau, *The Adventures of Moccasin Joe*, 69 (quotation); McChristian, *The U.S. Army in the West*, 115. In an otherwise rather insightful analysis of the army's breechloaders in combat, including at the Little Big Horn, Philip Shockley, a weapons scholar, dismissed the issue of verdigris while laying principal blame for failures on the army's copper cases: "Troopers cleaned and oiled their carbine barrels and gun locks." Shockley, *The Trap-Door Springfield in the Service*, 12–13.

BIBLIOGRAPHY

MANUSCRIPTS AND ARCHIVAL COLLECTIONS

American Heritage Center, University of Wyoming, Laramie, Wyoming
    Capron, Thaddeus, Family Papers
    Luhn, Gerhard, Papers
    Throssel, Richard, Papers
    Vaughn, Jesse W., Papers

Bennington Museum, Bennington, Vermont
    Cain, Avery Billings, Papers

Black Hills State University, E. Y. Berry Library, Spearfish, South Dakota
    Henry, B. William, Jr., Collection
    McDermott, John D., Papers

Brigham Young University, L. Tom Perry Special Collections,
    Harold B. Lee Library, Provo, Utah
    Camp, Walter Mason, Papers

College of Idaho, N. L. Terteling Library, Caldwell, Idaho
    Strahorn, Robert E., Papers

Congressional Medal of Honor Society, Mount Pleasant, South Carolina
    McGann, Michael A., File
    Robinson, Joseph, File
    Shingle, John Henry, File
    Snow, Elmer A., File

Denver Public Library, Western History Collection, Denver, Colorado
    Ellison, Robert S., Papers

Fort Laramie National Historic Site, Archives, Fort Laramie, Wyoming
    Burt, Andrew S., Papers
    Dewees, Thomas, Letters
    Fort Laramie Letters Sent, 1876
    Fort Laramie Medical History, 1876
    Magill, William H., Memoir
    Miller, William, Papers
    Names File

Greene, Jerome A., Arvada, Colorado
    Collections

Hedren, Paul L., Omaha, Nebraska
    Sioux War Papers

Henry E. Huntington Library and Art Gallery, San Marino, California
Crook, George, Papers
Schuyler, Walter, Papers

Kortlander, Chris, Custer Battlefield Museum, Garryowen, Montana
Glusing, Hinrich, Letter

Minnesota Historical Society, Saint Paul, Minnesota
Lloyd, Thomas, Letter

Montana Historical Society, Helena, Montana
Jaycox, William W., Diary
Rosebud Papers, Vertical Files
Vaughn-Kobold Correspondence, Vertical Files

National Archives, Washington, District of Columbia
Adjutant General's Office Letters Received (Main Series), 1876, Microcopy 666, Roll 271
Adjutant General's Office Special Orders, 1876, Record Group 94
Chambers, Alexander, Appointment, Commission, Personal File, 5006 ACP 1874, Record Group 94
Department of Dakota Field Records, Big Horn and Yellowstone Expedition Letters, Telegrams, and Endorsements Sent, 1876, Record Group 393, Entry 1342 (this is an unexplained misfile by the National Archives, perhaps dating to the army's original transfer of papers)
Department of the Platte General Orders, 1876, Record Group 393, Entry 3740
Department of the Platte Letters Received, 1877, Record Group 393, Entry 3731
Department of the Platte Personal History of Surgeons Serving in the Department, 1866–1902, Record Group 393, Entry 3931
Department of the Platte Special Orders, 1876, Record Group 393, Entry 3741
Division of the Missouri, Special Files, Sioux War, 1876, Microcopy 1495, Roll 2
Fourteenth Infantry Regimental Returns, 1876, Microcopy 665, Roll 155
Fourth Infantry Regimental Returns, 1863, Microcopy 665, Roll 45
Fourth Infantry Regimental Returns, 1868–75, Microcopy 665, Roll 46
Fourth Infantry Regimental Returns, 1876–77, Microcopy 665, Roll 47
Morton, Charles, Appointment, Commission, Personal File, 285 ACP 1876*, Record Group 94
Reynolds, Bainbridge, Appointment, Commission, Personal File, 1231 ACP 1879, Record Group 94
Second Cavalry Regimental Returns, 1876, Microcopy 744, Roll 19
Third Cavalry Regimental Returns, 1876, Microcopy 744, Roll 31

Nebraska State Historical Society, Lincoln, Nebraska
Bourke, John Gregory, Papers
McGillycuddy, Valentine, Notebook

State Historical Society of North Dakota, Archives, Bismarck, North Dakota
Crawford, Lewis, Papers

United States Army War College, Library and Archives, Carlisle, Pennsylvania
Crook-Kennon Papers
Crook, Mrs. George, Scrapbook

University of California Santa Barbara, Special Collections, Davidson Library, Santa Barbara, California
Noyes-Wallace Family Collection

University of Oklahoma, Western History Collections, Libraries, Norman, Oklahoma
Campbell, Walter Stanley, Collection

University of Oregon, Special Collections, Knight Library, Eugene, Oregon
Crook, George, Papers

CAMPAIGN AND BATTLE REPORTS

Andrews, William H. Report, June 20, 1876. In *Battle of the Rosebud: Prelude to the Little Bighorn*, by Neil C. Mangum, 147–49. El Segundo, Calif.: Upton & Sons, 1987.

Burrowes, Thomas B. Report, June 20, 1976. In *Battle of the Rosebud: Prelude to the Little Bighorn*, by Neil C. Mangum, 137–38. El Segundo, Calif.: Upton & Sons, 1987.

Burt, Andrew S. Report, June 20, 1876. In *Battle of the Rosebud: Prelude to the Little Bighorn*, by Neil C. Mangum, 138–39. El Segundo, Calif.: Upton & Sons, 1987.

Cain, Avery B. Report, June 20, 1876. In *Battle of the Rosebud: Prelude to the Little Bighorn*, by Neil C. Mangum, 140. El Segundo, Calif.: Upton & Sons, 1987.

Chambers, Alexander. Report, June 20, 1876. In *Battle of the Rosebud: Prelude to the Little Bighorn*, by Neil C. Mangum, 134–35. El Segundo, Calif.: Upton & Sons, 1987.

Crook, George. Report, June 19, 1876. In *With Crook at the Rosebud*, by J. W. Vaughn, 213–14. Harrisburg, Pa.: Stackpole Company, 1956.

———. Report, June 20, 1876. In *Battle of the Rosebud: Prelude to the Little Bighorn*, by Neil C. Mangum, 127–30. El Segundo, Calif.: Upton & Sons, 1987.

———. Report, September 25, 1876. In *Report of the Secretary of War, 1876*, 498–502. Washington, D.C.: Government Printing Office, 1876.

Evans, Andrew W. Report, June 20, 1876. In *Battle of the Rosebud: Prelude to the Little Bighorn*, by Neil C. Mangum, 130–32. El Segundo, Calif.: Upton & Sons, 1987.

Hartsuff, Albert. Report, Big Horn and Yellowstone Expedition, Montana, and Battle of the Rosebud, June 17, 1876. Record Group 94, Entry 624, File F. National Archives, Washington, D.C.

Henry, Guy V. Report, June 20, 1876. In *Battle of the Rosebud: Prelude to the Little Bighorn*, by Neil C. Mangum, 146–47. El Segundo, Calif.: Upton & Sons, 1987.

Lawson, Joseph. Report, June 20, 1876. In *Battle of the Rosebud: Prelude to the Little Bighorn*, by Neil C. Mangum, 152–53. El Segundo, Calif.: Upton & Sons, 1987.

Luhn, Gerhard L. Report, undated [June 20, 1876]. In *Battle of the Rosebud: Prelude to the Little Bighorn*, by Neil C. Mangum, 141. El Segundo, Calif.: Upton & Sons, 1987.

Meinhold, Charles. Report, June 20, 1876. In *Battle of the Rosebud: Prelude to the Little Bighorn*, by Neil C. Mangum, 144–45. El Segundo, Calif.: Upton & Sons, 1987.

Mills, Anson. Report, June 20, 1876. In *Battle of the Rosebud: Prelude to the Little Bighorn*, by Neil C. Mangum, 150–52. El Segundo, Calif.: Upton & Sons, 1987.

Munson, Samuel. Report, June 20, 1876. In *Battle of the Rosebud: Prelude to the Little Bighorn*, by Neil C. Mangum, 136–37. El Segundo, Calif.: Upton & Sons, 1987.

Noyes, Henry E. Report, June 20, 1876. In *Battle of the Rosebud: Prelude to the Little Bighorn*, by Neil C. Mangum, 132–34. El Segundo, Calif.: Upton & Sons, 1987.

Paul, Augustus C. Report, June 20, 1876. In *Battle of the Rosebud: Prelude to the Little Bighorn*, by Neil C. Mangum, 153. El Segundo, Calif.: Upton & Sons, 1987.

Royall, William B. Report, June 20, 1876. In *Battle of the Rosebud: Prelude to the Little Bighorn*, by Neil C. Mangum, 142–44. El Segundo, Calif.: Upton & Sons, 1987.

Stanton, William S. "Annual Report of Captain W. S. Stanton, Corps of Engineers, for the Fiscal Year Ending June 30, 1876." In *Report of the Chief of Engineers, 1876*, part III, 704–18. Washington, D.C.: Government Printing Office, 1876.

Van Vliet, Frederick, Report, June 20, 1876. In *Battle of the Rosebud: Prelude to the Little Bighorn*, by Neil C. Mangum, 149–50. El Segundo, Calif.: Upton & Sons, 1987.

NEWSPAPERS

Army and Navy Journal (New York, New York), 1876–81, 1890.
Army and Navy Register (Washington, D.C.), 1881, 1886, 1891.
Billings Gazette (Montana), 1911, 1932, 1934.
Bozeman Times (Montana), 1876.
Buffalo Bulletin (Wyoming), 1984.
Cheyenne Daily Leader (Wyoming), 1876–77, 1880–81.
Cheyenne Daily Sun (Wyoming), 1876.
Cheyenne Weekly Leader (Wyoming), 1880.
Chicago Eagle (Illinois), 1917.
Chicago Inter-Ocean (Illinois), 1876.
Chicago Times (Illinois), 1876–77.
Chicago Tribune (Illinois), 1876.
Cincinnati Commercial (Ohio), 1876.
Colorado Banner (Boulder, Colorado), 1877.
Colorado Transcript (Goldin, Colorado), 1894.
Daily Alta California (San Francisco, California), 1876.
Denver Daily Tribune (Colorado), 1877.
Frank Leslie's Illustrated Newspaper (New York, New York), 1876.
Hardin Tribune (Montana), 1921.
Hardin Tribune-Herald (Montana), 1933.
Helena Daily Independent (Montana), 1876.
Helena Weekly Herald (Montana), 1876, 1878.
Highland Weekly News (Hillsborough, Ohio), 1876.
Laramie Boomerang (Wyoming), 1891.
Laramie Daily Sentinel (Wyoming), 1876.
Leadville Herald Democrat (Colorado), 1916.
Leavenworth Weekly Times (Kansas), 1881.
National Tribune (Washington, District of Columbia), 1940.
New York Daily Graphic (New York), 1876.
New York Herald (New York), 1876.
New York Sun (New York), 1876.
New York Tribune (New York), 1876.
Omaha Daily Bee (Nebraska), 1876, 1886.
Omaha Daily Herald (Nebraska), 1876.
Omaha Daily World (Nebraska), 1886.
Omaha Republican (Nebraska), 1876.
Perrysburg Journal (Ohio), 1876.
Philadelphia Press (Pennsylvania), 1876.
Pittsburg Evening Leader (Pennsylvania), 1876.

Platte Valley Independent (Grand Island, Nebraska), 1876.
Rapid City Daily Journal (South Dakota), 1951.
Rocky Mountain News (Denver, Colorado), 1876.
Saint Paul and Minneapolis Pioneer Press (Minnesota), 1876, 1883.
Sidney Telegraph (Nebraska), 1876.
Utah Journal (Logan City, Utah), 1885.
Virginia City Madisonian (Montana), 1876.
Washington Herald (District of Columbia), 1907.
Weekly Rocky Mountain News (Denver, Colorado), 1876.
Winners of the West (Saint Joseph, Missouri), 1934.
Wyoming Tribune (Cheyenne, Wyoming), 1903.
Wyoming Weekly Leader (Cheyenne, Wyoming), 1876.

BOOKS AND ARTICLES

Abrams, Marc H., ed. *"Crying for Scalps": St. George Stanley's Sioux War Narrative*. Brooklyn, N.Y.: Abrams Publications, 2011.

———. "Henry's Fall: Mystery Solved." *Last Stand Magazine* 2 (August 2009): 43.

———, ed. *Newspaper Chronicle of the Indian Wars*. Vol. 5, *Jan. 1, 1876–July 12, 1876*. Brooklyn, N.Y.: Abrams Publications, 2010.

———, ed. *Newspaper Chronicle of the Indian Wars*. Vol. 6, *July 13, 1876–Aug. 24, 1876*. Brooklyn, N.Y.: Abrams Publications, 2010.

———, ed. *Newspaper Chronicle of the Indian Wars*. Vol. 7, *Aug. 26, 1876–Dec. 31, 1876*. Brooklyn, N.Y.: Abrams Publications, 2010.

———, ed. *Newspaper Chronicle of the Indian Wars*. Vol. 8, *Jan. 4, 1877–Aug. 31, 1877*. Brooklyn, N.Y.: Abrams Publications, 2010.

———. *Sioux War Dispatches: Reports from the Field, 1876–1877*. Yardley, Pa.: Westholm Publishing, 2012.

———. "St. George Stanley & The Great Sioux War." *Research Review: The Journal of the Little Big Horn Associates* 23 (Winter 2009): 2–10, 29–31.

———. "'A Very Lively Little Affair': The Skirmish at Tongue River Heights, 9 June 1876." *Crow's Nest: Journal of the Custer Association of Great Britain* 13 (Autumn–Winter 2013): 7–17.

Adjutant General's Office. *General Court-Martial Orders, 1876*. Washington, D.C.: Government Printing Office, 1877.

Agonito, Joseph. *Lakota Portraits: Lives of the Legendary Plains People*. Guilford, Conn.: TwoDot, Globe Pequot Press, 2011.

Agonito, Rosemary, and Joseph Agonito. *Buffalo Calf Road Woman: The Story of a Warrior of the Little Bighorn*. Guilford, Conn.: TwoDot, Globe Pequot Press, 2006.

———. "Resurrecting History's Forgotten Women: A Case Study from the Cheyenne Indians." *Frontiers: A Journal of Women Studies* 6 (Autumn 1981): 8–16.

Altshuler, Constance Wynn. *Cavalry Yellow & Infantry Blue: Army Officers in Arizona between 1851 and 1886*. Tucson: Arizona Historical Society, 1991.

American Decorations. Washington, D.C.: Government Printing Office, 1927.

Anderson, Harry H. "Cheyennes at the Little Big Horn: A Study of Statistics." *North Dakota History* 27 (Spring 1960): 81–93.

———. Foreword to *The Crazy Horse Surrender Ledger*, by Thomas R. Buecker and R. Eli Paul, ix–xv. Lincoln: Nebraska State Historical Society, 1994.

———. "A History of the Cheyenne River Indian Agency and Its Military Post, Fort Bennett, 1868–1891." *South Dakota Report and Historical Collections* 28 (1956): 390–551.

Andrist, Ralph K. *The Long Death: The Last Days of the Plains Indians.* New York: Macmillan Company, 1964.

Annual Report of the Commissioner of Indian Affairs, 1876. Washington, D.C.: Government Printing Office, 1876.

Bad Heart Bull, Amos, and Helen H. Blish. *A Pictographic History of the Oglala Sioux.* Lincoln: University of Nebraska Press, 1967.

Balentine, F. J. Pablo. *Freund & Bro. Pioneer Gunmakers to the West.* Newport Beach, Calif.: Graphic Publishers, 1997.

Beck, Paul N. *Inkpaduta, Dakota Leader.* Norman: University of Oklahoma Press, 2008.

Beyer, W. F., and O. F. Keydel. *Deeds of Valor.* 2 vols. Detroit: Perrein-Keydel Company, 1906.

Bookbinder, Judith. "Inspired by Plains Indian Drawings: The Mystery of Lieutenant Adolphus von Luettwitz's Drawings of the Plains Indian War." *Great Plains Quarterly* 36 (Summer 2016): 161–85.

Book of Common Prayer, and Administration of the Sacraments, and Other Rites and Ceremonies of the Church. Philadelphia: J.B. Lippincott & Company, 1860.

Bottomley-O'looney, Jennifer. "The Art of Storytelling: Plains Indian Perspectives." *Montana The Magazine of Western History* 62 (Autumn 2012): 42–55.

Bourke, John G. *The Diaries of John Gregory Bourke, Vol. One, November 20, 1872–July 28, 1876.* Edited by Charles M. Robinson III. Denton: University of North Texas Press, 2003.

———. *The Diaries of John Gregory Bourke, Vol. Two, July 29, 1876–April 7, 1878.* Edited by Charles M. Robinson III. Denton: University of North Texas Press, 2005.

———. *The Diaries of John Gregory Bourke, Vol. Four, July 3, 1880–May 22, 1881.* Edited by Charles M. Robinson III. Denton: University of North Texas Press, 2009.

———. *On the Border with Crook.* New York: Charles Scribner's Sons, 1891.

Bradley, James H. *The March of the Montana Column: A Prelude to the Custer Disaster.* Norman: University of Oklahoma Press, 1961.

Brady, Cyrus Townsend. *Indian Fights and Fighters.* New York: Doubleday, Page & Company, 1904.

———. "What They Are There For." *Scribner's Magazine* 34 (October 1903): 409–14.

Bray, Kingsley. *Crazy Horse: A Lakota Life.* Norman: University of Oklahoma Press, 2006.

———. "Teton Sioux Population History, 1655–1881." *Nebraska History* 75 (Summer 1994): 165–88.

Brininstool, E. A. *The Custer Fight.* Hollywood, Calif.: By the Author, 1933.

———. *Troopers with Custer: Historic Incidents of the Battle of the Little Big Horn.* Harrisburg, Pa.: Stackpole Company, 1952.

Brown, Franz K. *Thunder Visions: The Crazy Horse Wotawe of the Lakota Medicine Man Woptuha.* Hot Springs, S.Dak.: By the author, 2010.

Brown, Fred R. *History of the Ninth U.S. Infantry.* Chicago: R. R. Donnelley & Sons Company, 1909.

Brown, Mark H. *The Plainsmen of the Yellowstone: A History of the Yellowstone Basin.* New York: G. P. Putnam's Sons, 1961.

[Bruce, Robert.] "Pawnee Trails and Trailers." *Motor Travel* (March 1930): 17–20.

Brust, James S. "A Psychiatrist Looks at Mary Lincoln." In *The Mary Lincoln Enigma: Historians on America's Most Controversial First Lady,* ed. Frank J. Williams and Michael Burkhimer, 237–58. Carbondale: Southern Illinois University Press, 2012.

Buechel, Eugene, and Paul I. Manhart. *Lakota Tales & Texts.* 2 vols. Chamberlain, S.Dak.: Tipi Press, 1998.

Buecker, Thomas R. *A Brave Soldier & Honest Gentleman: Lt. James E. H. Foster in the West, 1873–1881.* Lincoln: Nebraska State Historical Society Books, 2013.

———. *Fort Robinson and the American West, 1874–1899.* Lincoln: Nebraska State Historical Society, 1999.

———. "Letters of Carolyn Frey Winne from Sidney Barracks and Fort McPherson, Nebraska, 1874–1878." *Nebraska History* 62 (Spring 1981): 1–46.

———. "Lt. William Philo Clark's Sioux War Report and Little Big Horn Map." *Greasy Grass* 7 (May 1991): 11–21.

———. "'The Men Behaved Splendidly': Guy V. Henry's Famous Cavalry Rides." *Nebraska History* 78 (Summer 1997): 54–63.

Buecker, Thomas R., and R. Eli Paul. *The Crazy Horse Surrender Ledger.* Lincoln: Nebraska State Historical Society, 1994.

Burdick, Usher L. *The Last Battle of the Sioux Nation.* Stevens Point, Wisc.: Worzalla Publishing Company, 1929.

Burgan, Scott. "Remembering Camp Cloud Peak." *The Log: Official Publication of the Sheridan County Historical Society and Museum* 4 (Spring 2012): 12–13.

Burnham, Philip. *Song of Dewey Beard: Last Survivor of the Little Bighorn.* Lincoln: University of Nebraska Press, 2014.

Calloway, Colin G. "Army Allies or Tribal Survival? The 'Other Indians' in the 1876 Campaign." In *Legacy: New Perspectives on the Battle of the Little Bighorn,* ed. Charles E. Rankin, 63–81. Helena: Montana Historical Society Press, 1996.

Capron, Cynthia J. "The Indian Border War of 1876." *Journal of the Illinois State Historical Society* 13 (January 1921): 476–503.

Carroll, John M., ed. *The Battle of the Rosebud Plus Three.* Bryan, Tex.: By the author, 1981.

———. *The Medal of Honor: Its History and Recipients for the Indian Wars.* Bryan, Tex.: By the author, 1979.

Carroll, John M., and Byron Price, eds. *Roll Call on the Little Big Horn, 28 June 1876.* Ft. Collins, Colo.: Old Army Press, 1974.

Chronological List of Actions, &c, with Indians from January 15, 1837 to January, 1891. Reprint ed., Fort Collins, Colo.: Old Army Press, 1979.

Clark, Robert A. *The Killing of Chief Crazy Horse.* Glendale, Calif.: Arthur H. Clark Company, 1976; reprint, Lincoln: University of Nebraska Press, 1988.

Clausewitz, Carl von. *On War.* Trans. and ed. by Michael Howard and Peter Paret. New York: Alfred A. Knopf, Everyman's Library, 1993.

Cozzens, Peter. "The Earth Is Weeping." *Cowboys & Indians* (January 2017): 118–20.

———, ed. *Eyewitnesses to the Indian Wars, 1865–1890.* Vol. 4, *The Long War for the Northern Plains.* Mechanicsburg, Pa.: Stackpole Books, 2004.

Crackel, Theodore J. "Custer's Kentucky: General George Armstrong Custer and Elizabethtown, Kentucky, 1871–1873." *Filson Club History Quarterly* 48 (April 1974): 144–54.

Crawford, Lewis F. *Rekindling Camp Fires: The Exploits of Ben Arnold (Conner).* Bismarck, N.Dak.: Capital Book Company, 1926.

Cullum, George W. *Biographical Register of the Officers and Graduates of the U.S. Military Academy at West Point, New York, since Its Establishment in 1802.* Vol. 4. Cambridge, Mass.: Riverside Press, 1901.

Daly, Henry W. "Following the Bell." *American Veteran* (February 1928): 111–18.

———. "The Powder-Stained 70's." *American Legion Monthly* (October 1926, 18–21): 80–85.

———. "The War Path." *American Legion Monthly* (April 1927): 16–19, 52.

David, Robert Beebe. *Finn Burnett, Frontiersman.* Glendale, Calif.: Arthur H. Clark Company, 1937; reprint, Mechanicsburg, Pa.: Stackpole Books, 2003.

Davis, E. Elden, ed. *The Indian Campaign of 1876: A Pittsburg Perspective, Articles from the Pittsburg Leader.* Howell, Mich.: Powder River Press, 1991.

DeBarthe, Joe. *Life and Adventures of Frank Grouard.* Edited by Edgar I. Stewart. Norman: University of Oklahoma Press, 1958.

DeMallie, Raymond J. "Lakota Belief and Ritual in the Nineteenth Century." In *Sioux Indian Religion: Tradition and Innovation,* ed. Raymond J. DeMallie and Douglas R. Parks, 25–43. Norman: University of Oklahoma Press, 1987.

———, ed. *The Sixth Grandfather: Black Elk's Teaching Given to John G. Neihardt.* Lincoln: University of Nebraska Press, 1984.

———. "Teton." In *Handbook of North American Indians: Plains,* vol. 13, part 2, ed. Raymond J. DeMallie, 794–820. Washington, D.C.: Smithsonian Institution Press, 2001.

Denig, Edwin Thompson. *Five Indian Tribes of the Upper Missouri.* Edited by John C. Ewers. Norman: University of Oklahoma Press, 1961.

Description and Rules for the Management of the Springfield Rifle, Carbine, and Army Revolvers. Springfield, Mass.: National Armory, 1874; reprint, Philadelphia: Ray Riling, 1960.

Dickson, Ephriam D., III. "The Big Road Roster." In *Proceedings of the Brian C. Pohanka 21st Annual Symposium, Custer Battlefield Historical & Museum Association* [CBHMA], *Held at Hardin, Montana, on June 22, 2007,* edited by Ronald H. Nichols, 47–57. Hardin, Mont.: CBHMA, 2008.

———. "Prisoners in the Indian Camp: Kill Eagle's Band at Little Big Horn." *Greasy Grass* 27 (May 2011): 3–11.

———. "Reconstructing the Little Big Horn Indian Village: The Oglala Tribal Circle." In *Proceedings of the Brian C. Pohanka 20th Annual Symposium, Custer Battlefield Historical & Museum Association, Held at Hardin, Montana, on June 23, 2006,* edited by Ronald H. Nichols, 65–72. Hardin, Mont.: CBHMA, 2006.

———. "Soldier with a Camera: Private Charles Howard's Photographic Journey through Eastern Wyoming, 1877." *Annals of Wyoming* 77 (Autumn 2005): 22–32.

———. "With General Crook's Campaign: A Soldier's Letter Home, 1876." *Little Big Horn Associates Newsletter* 40 (June 2006): 4–5.

Dixon, Joseph K. *The Vanishing Race: The Last Great Indian Council.* Garden City, N.Y.: Doubleday, Page & Company, 1913; reprint, New York: Bonanza Books, 1976.

Donahue, Michael N. *Drawing Battle Lines: The Map Testimony of Custer's Last Fight.* El Segundo, Calif.: Upton & Sons, Publishers, 2008.

Donovan, James. *A Terrible Glory: Custer and the Little Bighorn, The Last Great Battle of the American West.* New York: Little Brown & Company, 2008.

Eastman, Charles A. "Rain-in-the-Face: The Story of a Sioux Warrior." *Outlook,* October 27, 1906, 507–12.

Essin, Emmett M. "Army Mule." *Montana The Magazine of Western History* 44 (Spring 1994): 30–45.

———. *Shavetails and Bell Sharps: The History of the U.S. Army Mule.* Lincoln: University of Nebraska Press, 1997.

Etulain, Richard W. *The Life and Legends of Calamity Jane.* Norman: University of Oklahoma Press, 2014.

Ewers, John C. "Deadlier Than the Male." *American Heritage,* June 1965, 10–13.

Fielder, Mildred. *Sioux Indian Leaders.* Seattle: Superior Publishing Company, 1975.

Finerty, John F. *War-Path and Bivouac, or The Conquest of the Sioux.* Chicago: Donohue & Henneberry, 1890.

Flannery, L. G. (Pat). *John Hunton's Diary, Vol. 2, 1876–'77.* Lingle, Wyo.: Guide-Review, 1958.

Fox, Richard A., Jr. "The Value of Oral History: White Eagle's Account." In *Proceedings of the 9th Annual Symposium, Custer Battlefield Historical & Museum Association, Held at Hardin, Montana, on June 23, 1995*, edited by Bob Reece, 1–27. Hardin, Mont.: CBHMA, 1996.

Frasca, Albert J., and Robert H. Hill. *The .47–70 Springfield*. Northridge, Calif.: Springfield Publishing Company, 1980.

Garavaglia, Louis A., and Charles G. Worman. *Firearms of the American West, 1866–1894*. Albuquerque: University of New Mexico Press, 1985.

Garland, Hamlin. "General Custer's Last Fight as Seen by Two Moon." In *The Custer Myth: A Source Book of Custeriana*, by William A. Graham, 101–3. Harrisburg, Pa.: Stackpole Company, 1953.

Gibbon, John. "Last Summer's Expedition against the Sioux and Its Great Catastrophe." *American Catholic Quarterly Review* 2 (April 1877): 271–304.

Gilbert, Hila. *"Big Bat" Pourier*. Sheridan, Wyo.: Mills Company, 1968.

Gillett, Mary C. *The Army Medical Department, 1865–1917*. Washington, D.C.: Center for Military History, United States Army, 1995.

Godfrey, Edward S. "Cavalry Fire Discipline." *Journal of the Military Service Institution* 19 (September 1896): 252–59.

Graham, W. A. *The Custer Myth: A Source Book of Custeriana*. Harrisburg, Pa.: Stackpole Company, 1953.

Gray, John S. *Centennial Campaign: The Sioux War of 1876*. Ft. Collins, Colo.: Old Army Press, 1976.

———. *Custer's Last Campaign: Mitch Boyer and the Little Bighorn Reconstructed*. Lincoln: University of Nebraska Press, 1991.

———. "Frank Grouard: Kanaka Scout or Mulatto Renegade?" *Westerners (Chicago) Brand Book* 16 (October 1959): 57–59, 62–64.

Greene, Jerome A., ed. "Chasing Sitting Bull and Crazy Horse: Two Fourteenth U.S. Infantry Diaries of the Great Sioux War." *Nebraska History* 78 (Winter 1997): 187–201.

———, comp. and ed. *Indian War Veterans: Memories of Army Life and Campaigns in the West, 1864–1898*. New York: Savas Beatie, 2007.

———, comp. and ed. *Lakota and Cheyenne: Indian Views of the Great Sioux War, 1876–1877*. Norman: University of Oklahoma Press, 1994.

Grinnell, George Bird. *The Cheyenne Indians: Their History and Ways of Life*. 2 vols. New York: Cooper Square Publishers, 1962.

———. *The Fighting Cheyennes*. Norman: University of Oklahoma Press, 1956.

Hagan, Barry J. *"Exactly in the Right Place": A History of Fort C. F. Smith, Montana Territory, 1866–1868*. El Segundo, Calif.: Upton & Sons, Publishers, 1999.

Hallberg, V. R., and J. B. Neal. "'For This Are We Soldiers': Guy V. Henry and a Concept of Duty." *Journal of the West* 43 (Spring 2005): 63–71.

Hammer, Kenneth, ed. *Custer in '76: Walter Camp's Notes on the Custer Fight*. Provo, Utah: Brigham Young University Press, 1976.

[Hanna, Oliver Perry.] *An Old Timer's Story of the Old Wild West, Being the Recollections of Oliver Perry Hanna, Pioneer, Indian Fighter, Frontiersman, and First Settler in Sheridan County, WY*. [Big Horn, Wyo.]: Privately printed, 1984.

Hanson, Margaret Brock, ed. *Frank Grouard, Army Scout: True Adventures in the Early West*. Cheyenne, Wyo.: Frontier Printing, 1983.

Hantz, Joan. "The Girl Who Saved Her Brother." In *We, The Northern Cheyenne People: Our Land, Our History, Our Culture*, ed. Richard Little Bear, 67–70. Lame Deer, Mont.: Chief Dull Knife College, 2008.

Hardorff, Richard G., ed. *Cheyenne Memories of the Custer Fight.* Spokane, Wash.: Arthur H. Clark Company, 1995.

———. "The Frank Grouard Genealogy." In *Custer and His Times: Book Two*, ed. John M. Carroll, Jay Smith, and Nancy Allan, 123–33. Ft. Worth, Tex.: Little Big Horn Associates, 1984.

———. *Hokahey! A Good Day to Die! The Indian Casualties of the Custer Fight.* Spokane, Wash.: Arthur H. Clark Company, 1993.

———, ed. *Indian Views of the Custer Fight: A Source Book.* Spokane, Wash.: Arthur H. Clark Company, 2004.

———, ed. *Lakota Recollections of the Custer Fight: New Sources of Indian-Military History.* Spokane, Wash.: Arthur H. Clark Company, 1991.

———, ed. *The Surrender and Death of Crazy Horse: A Source Book about a Tragic Episode in Lakota History.* Spokane, Wash.: Arthur H. Clark Company, 1998.

Hart, Sheila. "Edmore LeClair, Son of a Mountain Man." *Wind River Mountaineer* 5 (January–March 1989): 8–11.

Hassrick, Royal B. *The Sioux: Life and Customs of a Warrior Society.* Norman: University of Oklahoma Press, 1964.

Hebard, Grace Raymond. *Washakie.* Cleveland: Arthur H. Clark Company, 1930; reprint: New York: AMS Press, [1982].

Hedren, Paul L. *After Custer: Loss and Transformation in Sioux Country.* Norman: University of Oklahoma Press, 2011.

———. "Carbine Extraction Failure at the Little Big Horn: A New Examination." *Military Collector and Historian* 25 (2, 1973): 66–68.

———. "Drunk on the Black Hills Road in 1876: Army Reprisals against Doctor Reynolds, Lieutenant Taylor, and Captain Collier." *South Dakota History* 41 (Winter 2011): 436–55.

———. *Fort Laramie in 1876: Chronicle of a Frontier Post at War.* Lincoln: University of Nebraska Press, 1988.

———. "Garrisoning the Black Hills Road: The United States Army's Camps on Sage Creek and Mouth of Red Canyon, 1876–1877." *South Dakota History* 37 (Spring 2007): 1–45.

———. *Great Sioux War Orders of Battle: How the United States Army Waged War on the Northern Plains, 1876–1877.* Norman, Okla.: Arthur H. Clark Company, 2011.

———, ed. *Ho! For the Black Hills: Captain Jack Crawford Reports the Black Hills Gold Rush and Great Sioux War.* Pierre: South Dakota State Historical Society Press, 2012.

———. "Persimmon Bill Chambers: The 'Scourge of the Black Hills.'" *Annals of Wyoming* 81 (Autumn 2009): 2–10.

———. *Powder River: Disastrous Opening of the Great Sioux War.* Norman: University of Oklahoma Press, 2016.

———. *With Crook in the Black Hills: Stanley J. Morrow's 1876 Photographic Legacy.* Boulder, Colo.: Pruett Publishing Company, 1985.

Heitman, Francis B. *Historical Register and Dictionary of the United States Army, from Its Organization, September 29, 1789, to March 2, 1903.* 2 vols. Washington, D.C.: Government Printing Office, 1903; reprint, Urbana: University of Illinois Press, 1965.

Henry, Guy V. "Wounded in an Indian Fight." *Harper's Weekly*, July 6, 1895, 627.

Hess, Earl J. *Civil War Infantry Tactics: Training, Combat, and Small-Unit Effectiveness.* Baton Rouge: Louisiana State University Press, 2015.

———. *The Union Soldier in Battle: Enduring the Ordeal of Combat.* Lawrence: University Press of Kansas, 1997.

Hinman, Eleanor H. "Oglala Sources on the Life of Crazy Horse." *Nebraska History* 57 (Spring 1976): 1–51.

Howard, James H., trans. and ed. *The Warrior Who Killed Custer: The Personal Narrative of Chief Joseph White Bull*. Lincoln: University of Nebraska Press, 1968.

Hunt, Frazier, and Robert Hunt. *I Fought with Custer: The Story of Sergeant Windolph*. New York: Charles Scribner's Sons, 1950.

Hutchins, James S., ed. *The Army and Navy Journal on the Battle of the Little Bighorn and Related Matters, 1876–1881*. El Segundo, Calif.: Upton & Sons, Publishers, 2003.

————. *Boots & Saddles at the Little Bighorn: Weapons, Dress, Equipment, Horses, and Flags of General Custer's Seventh U.S. Cavalry in 1876*. Ft. Collins, Colo.: Old Army Press, 1976.

————, ed. "Captain Michaelis Reports on Army Weapons and Equipment on the Northern Plains, 1876–1879." In *Guns at the Little Big Horn, A Man at Arms Special Publication*, 27–31, 34–37. N.p.: Andrew Mowbray, 1988.

————, ed. *The Papers of Edward S. Curtis Relating to Custer's Last Battle*. El Segundo, Calif.: Upton & Sons, 2000.

Hutton, Paul Andrew. *The Apache Wars: The Hunt for Geronimo, the Apache Kid, and the Captive Boy Who Started the Longest War in American History*. New York: Crown, 2016.

————. "'Correct in Every Detail': General Custer in Hollywood." In *Legacy: New Perspectives on the Battle of the Little Bighorn*, ed. Charles E. Rankin, 231–70. Helena: Montana Historical Society Press, 1996.

————. *Phil Sheridan and His Army*. Lincoln: University of Nebraska Press, 1985.

Hyde, George E. *Red Cloud's Folk: A History of the Oglala Sioux Indians*. Norman: University of Oklahoma Press, 1937.

————. *Spotted Tail's Folk: A History of the Brulé Sioux*. Norman: University of Oklahoma Press, 1961.

Jackson, Joe. *Black Elk: The Life of an American Visionary*. New York: Farrar, Straus & Giroux, 2016.

Jamieson, Perry D. *Crossing the Deadly Ground: United States Army Tactics, 1865–1899*. Tuscaloosa: University of Alabama Press, 1994.

Jensen, Richard E., ed. *The Indian Interviews of Eli S. Ricker, 1903–1919, Voices of the American West, Volume 1*. Lincoln: University of Nebraska Press, 2005.

————, ed. *The Settler and Soldier Interviews of Eli S. Ricker, 1903–1919, Voices of the American West, Volume 2*. Lincoln: University of Nebraska Press, 2005.

Johnson, Barry C., ed. "Dr. Paulding and His Remarkable Diary." In *Sidelights of the Sioux Wars*, ed. Francis B. Taunton, 47–68. London: English Westerners' Society, 1967.

Journal of the American Medical Association, November 30, 1901 (s.v. "Deaths and Obituaries").

Juarez, Angelo D. *The Tarnished Saber: Major Azor Howell Nickerson, USA, His Life and Times*. Chatham, Mass.: Nickerson Family Association, 2001.

Kadlecek, Edward, and Mabell Kadlecek. *To Kill an Eagle: Indian Views on the Last Days of Crazy Horse*. Boulder, Colo.: Johnson Books, 1981.

Kane, Randy. "Crook after the Rosebud: The Fateful Decision Not to Move North." *Greasy Grass* 29 (May 2013): 36–42.

————. "Who Saved Guy Henry at the Battle of the Rosebud?" *Greasy Grass* 30 (May 2014): 8–11.

Keenan, Jerry. "'Rosebud, Oh Rosebud'—Crook, Custer and Conjecture." In *Proceedings of the 6th Annual Symposium, Custer Battlefield Historical & Museum Association, Held at Hardin, Montana, on June 26, 1992*, edited by Ron Nichols, 37–42. Hardin, Mont.: CBHMA, 1993.

Killsback, Leo. "Crowns of Honor: Sacred Laws of Eagle-Feather War Bonnets and Repatriating the Icon of the Great Plains." *Great Plains Quarterly* 33 (Winter 2013): 1–23.

Kime, Wayne R., ed. *The Black Hills Journals of Colonel Richard Irving Dodge*. Norman: University of Oklahoma Press, 1996.

King, Charles. "Arms or Tactics?" *United Service* 2 (April 1880): 492–98.

———. *Campaigning with Crook and Stories of Army Life.* New York: Harper & Brothers, 1890.

———. "An Honorable Amende." *Harper's Weekly*, April 25, 1891.

———. "Recollections of General Crook." *Youth's Companion*, October 19, 1899, 515.

King, James T. "Needed: A Re-evaluation of General George Crook." *Nebraska History* 45 (September 1964): 223–35.

Knight, Oliver. *Following the Indian Wars: The Story of the Newspaper Correspondents among the Indian Campaigners.* Norman: University of Oklahoma Press, 1960.

Larson, Robert W. *Gall: Lakota War Chief.* Norman: University of Oklahoma Press, 2007.

Lee, Jesse M. "The Capture and Death of an Indian Chieftain." *Journal of the Military Service Institution.* 54 (May–June 1914): 323–40.

Leermakers, J. A. "The Battle of the Rosebud." *Westerners New York Posse Brand Book* 2 (2, 1955): 25, 27–28, 30–31, 43.

Legoski, Robert J. *General George Crook's Campaign of 1876, June 5 through August 3: Newspaper Accounts of the Day.* Sheridan, Wyo.: By the author, 2000.

Lemly, H. R. "The Fight on the Rosebud." In *The Papers of the Order of Indian Wars*, ed. John M. Carroll, 13–18. Fort Collins, Colo.: Old Army Press, 1975.

Leyden, James A. "The Fourth Regiment of Infantry." In *The Army of the United States: Historical Sketches of Staff and Line with Portraits of Generals-in-Chief*, ed. Theo F. Rodenbough and William L. Haskin, 452–65. New York: Argonaut Press, 1966.

Liddic, Bruce R. *Vanishing Victory: Custer's Final March.* El Segundo, Calif.: Upton & Sons, Publishers, 2004.

Liddic, Bruce R., and Paul Harbaugh, eds. *Camp on Custer: Transcribing the Custer Myth.* Spokane, Wash.: Arthur H. Clark Company, 1995.

Linderman, Frank B. *American: The Life Story of a Great Indian.* New York: John Day Company, 1930.

———. *Pretty-Shield.* New York: John Day Company, 1932; reprint, Alexandria, Virg.: Time-Life Books, n.d.

Lindmier, Tom. *Drybone: A History of Fort Fetterman, Wyoming.* Glendo, Wyo.: High Plains Press, 2002.

Magid, Paul. *George Crook: From the Redwoods to Appomattox.* Norman: University of Oklahoma Press, 2011.

———. *The Gray Fox: George Crook and the Indian Wars.* Norman: University of Oklahoma Press, 2015.

Mangum, Neil C. *Battle of the Rosebud: Prelude to the Little Bighorn.* El Segundo, Calif.: Upton & Sons, 1987.

Manypenny, George W. *Our Indian Wards.* Cincinnati: Robert Clarke & Company, 1880.

Marquis, Thomas B. *The Cheyennes of Montana.* Algonac, Mich.: Reference Publications, 1978.

———. *She Watched Custer's Last Battle.* Hardin, Mont.: Hardin Tribune-Herald Print, 1933.

———. *A Warrior Who Fought Custer.* Minneapolis: Midwest Company, 1931.

Marshall, Robert A. "How Many Indians Were There?" In *Custer and His Times: Book Two*, ed. John M. Carroll, Jay Smith, and Nancy Allan, 207–24. Fort Worth, Tex.: Little Big Horn Associates, 1984.

Matson, William B. *Crazy Horse: The Lakota Warrior's Life & Legacy: The Edward Clown Family.* Layton, Utah: Gibbs Smith, 2016

Mattes, Merrill J. *Indians, Infants and Infantry: Andrew and Elizabeth Burt on the Frontier.* Denver: Old West Publishing Company, 1960.

McChristian, Douglas C. *An Army of Marksmen.* Fort Collins, Colo.: Old Army Press, 1981.

———. "Burying the Hatchet: The Semi-Centennial of the Battle of the Little Bighorn." *Montana The Magazine of Western History* 46 (Summer 1996): 50–65.

———. *Fort Laramie: Military Bastion of the High Plains.* Norman, Okla.: Arthur H. Clark Company, 2008.

———. *Regular Army O! Soldiering on the Western Frontier, 1865–1891.* Norman: University of Oklahoma Press, 2017.

———. *Uniforms, Arms, and Equipment: The U.S. Army on the Western Frontier.* Vol. 2, *Weapons and Accouterments.* Norman: University of Oklahoma Press, 2007.

———. *The U.S. Army in the West, 1870–1880: Uniforms, Weapons, and Equipment.* Norman: University of Oklahoma Press, 1995.

McDermott, John D. "Fort Laramie's Iron Bridge." *Annals of Wyoming* 34 (October 1962): 136–44.

———. *Red Cloud's War: The Bozeman Trail, 1866–1868.* 2 vols. Norman, Okla.: Arthur H. Clark Company, 2000.

McGillycuddy, Julia. *McGillycuddy Agent: A Biography of Dr. Valentine T. McGillycuddy.* [Stanford, Calif.:] Stanford University Press, 1941.

McGinnis, Anthony R. "When Courage Was Not Enough: Plains Indians at War with the United States Army." *Journal of Military History* 26 (April 2012): 455–73.

McLaird, James D. *Calamity Jane: The Woman and the Legend.* Norman: University of Oklahoma Press, 2005.

McLaughlin, Castle. *A Lakota War Book from the Little Bighorn: The Pictographic "Autobiography of Half Moon."* Cambridge, Mass.: Houghton Library of the Harvard Library, Peabody Museum Press, 2013.

McLemore, Clyde. "Fort Pease: The First Attempted Settlement in Yellowstone Valley." *Montana Magazine of History* 2 (January 1952): 17–31.

Mears, David T. "Campaigning against Crazy Horse." In *Proceedings and Collections of the Nebraska State Historical Society,* 68–77. Vol. 15. Lincoln, Nebr.: Jacob North and Company, 1907.

Medicine Crow, Joe. "Custer and His Crow Scouts." *In Little Bighorn Remembered: The Untold Indian Story of Custer's Last Stand,* by Herman J. Viola, 105–23. New York: Random House, Times Books, 1999.

Meketa, Ray. *Marching with General Crook, or, The Big Horn and Yellowstone Expedition against Hostile Indians in the Summer of 1876, Including the Battle of the Rosebud and the Black Hills March.* Douglas, Alaska: Cheechako Press, 1983.

Meketa, Ray, and Thomas E. Bookwalter. *The Search for the Lone Tepee.* N.p.: Little Horn Press, 1983.

Michno, Gregory F. *The Deadliest Indian War in the West: The Snake Conflict, 1864–1868.* Caldwell, Idaho: Caxton Press, 2007.

———. *Encyclopedia of Indian Wars: Western Battles and Skirmishes, 1850–1890.* Missoula, Mont.: Mountain Press Publishing Company, 2001.

Miller, David Humphreys. *Custer's Fall: the Indian Side of the Story.* New York: Duell, Sloan & Pearce, 1957.

———. "Echoes of the Little Bighorn." *American Heritage,* June 1971, 28–39.

———. *Ghost Dance.* New York: Duell, Sloan & Pearce, 1959.

Miller, Mark E. *Military Sites in Wyoming, 1700–1920: Historic Context.* Laramie: Wyoming Department of State Parks & Cultural Resources, 2012.

Mills, Anson. "Address by General Anson Mills, U.S. Army Ret., On 'The Battle of the Rosebud.'" In *The Papers of the Order of Indian Wars,* ed. John M. Carroll, 1–12. Fort Collins, Colo.: Old Army Press, 1975.

————. *My Story.* Washington, D.C.: By the author, 1918.

Monaghan, Leila. "Cheyenne and Lakota Women at the Battle of the Little Bighorn. *Montana The Magazine of Western History* 67 (Autumn 2017): 3–21, 89–90.

Montana Atlas & Gazetteer. Freeport, Maine: DeLorme Mapping, 1994.

Moulton, Candy. *Valentine T. McGillycuddy: Army Surgeon, Agent to the Sioux.* Norman, Okla.: Arthur H. Clark Company, 2011.

Musgrave, Judy. "Woman Warrior." *Log: Official Publication of the Sheridan County Historical Society and Museum* 4 (Spring 2012): 2, 6.

Neihardt, John G. *Black Elk Speaks: Being the Life Story of a Holy Man of the Oglala Sioux.* Lincoln: University of Nebraska Press, 1988.

Newell, Clayton R., and Charles R. Shrader. *Of Duty Well and Faithfully Done: A History of the Regular Army in the Civil War.* Lincoln: University of Nebraska Press, 2011.

Nickerson, Azor H. "Personal Recollections of Two Visits to Gettysburg." *Scribner's* 14 (July 1890): 19–28.

Nottage, James H. "The Big Horn and Yellowstone Expedition of 1876 as Seen through the Letters of Captain Gerhard Luke Luhn." *Annals of Wyoming* 45 (Spring 1973): 27–46.

Noyes, C. Lee. "A Question of Arms: Ordnance 'Causes' and Consequences of the Little Big Horn." *Greasy Grass* 32 (May 2016): 8–19.

Official Army Register for January, 1876. Washington, D.C.: Adjutant General's Office, 1876.

Olson, James C. *Red Cloud and the Sioux Problem.* Lincoln: University of Nebraska Press, 1965.

O'Neill, Robert F. "Rosebud." *Blue & Gray Magazine* 31–5 (2015): 6–30, 39–50.

Ordnance Manual for the Use of the Officers of the United States Army. [Philadelphia]: J. B. Lippincott & Company, 1861; facsimile reprint, n.p.: Ordnance Park Corporation, 1970.

Ordnance Memoranda No. 18, on Horse-Equipments, Cavalry Equipments and Accouterments, Saddlers' and Smiths' Tools and Materials, and Standard Supply Table of Ordnance Stores for the Cavalry Service. Washington, D.C.: Government Printing Office, 1874; reprint, n.p., n.d.

Ordnance Memorandum No. 19, on Infantry-Equipments, and Materials and Supplies Necessary for Efficient Outfit of Infantry-Troops in Field and Garrison. Washington, D.C.: Government Printing Office, 1875; reprint, n.p., n.d.

Organization of the Bridge Equipage of the United States Army, with Directions for the Construction of Military Bridges. Washington, D.C.: Government Printing Office, 1870.

Otis, George A. *Circular No. 9. A Report to the Surgeon General on the Transport of Sick and Wounded by Pack Animals.* Washington, D.C.: Government Printing Office, 1877.

Outline Description of the Military Posts in the Division of the Missouri. Chicago: Headquarters Military Division of the Missouri, 1876; facsimile edition, Fort Collins, Colo.: Old Army Press, 1972.

Paul, R. Eli. "Counting Indians." *Wild West*, December 2005, 27.

————, ed. *Sign Talker: Hugh Lenox Scott Remembers Indian Country.* Norman: University of Oklahoma Press, 2016.

Pearson, D. C. *The Platte-Dakota Campaign of 1876.* New York: Republic Press, 1896.

Pollock, Oliver C.C. "With the Third Cavalry in 1876." In *Indian War Veterans: Memories of Army Life and Campaigns in the West, 1864–1898*, ed. Jerome A. Greene, 103–7. New York: Savas Beatie, 2007.

Porter, Joseph C. *Paper Medicine Man: John Gregory Bourke and His American West.* Norman: University of Oklahoma Press, 1986.

Potter, James E., ed. *"From Our Special Correspondent": Dispatches from the 1875 Black Hills Council at Red Cloud Agency, Nebraska.* Lincoln: Nebraska State Historical Society Books, 2016.

———. "'Uncle Sam's Sharpshooters': Military Marksmanship at Fort Omaha and Bellevue, 1882–1894." *Nebraska History* 97 (Summer 2016): 91–106.

[Potter, Tracy.] "McGann's Medal of Honor." *Past Times* 6 (October 1999): 1, 10–11.

Powell, Peter J. "Ox'zem: Box Elder and His Sacred Wheel Lance." *Montana The Magazine of Western History* 20 (April 1970): 30–41.

———. *People of the Sacred Mountain: A History of the Northern Cheyenne Chiefs and Warrior Societies, 1830–1879, with an Epilogue 1969–1974.* 2 vols. San Francisco: Harper & Row, Publishers, 1981.

[Powell, William H.] *Records of Living Officers of the United States Army.* Philadelphia: L. R. Hamersly & Co., 1884.

Powers, Thomas. *The Killing of Crazy Horse.* New York: Alfred A. Knopf, 2010.

Price, George F. *Across the Continent with the Fifth Cavalry.* Reprint, New York: Antiquarian Press, 1959.

Rankin, Charles E., ed. *Legacy: New Perspectives on the Battle of the Little Bighorn.* Helena: Montana Historical Society Press, 1996.

Record of Engagements with Hostile Indians within the Military Division of the Missouri from 1868 to 1882, Lieutenant-General P. H. Sheridan, Commanding. Washington, D.C.: Government Printing Office, 1882; reprint, Bellevue, Nebr., Old Army Press, 1969.

Red Shirt, Delphine. *George Sword's Warrior Narratives: Compositional Processes in Lakota Oral Tradition.* Lincoln: University of Nebraska Press, 2016.

Reese, Timothy J. *Regulars! A History of Gen. George Sykes' U.S. Regular Infantry Division of the Fifth Army Corps, 1861–1864.* Revised ed. Burkittsville, Md.: By the author, 2006.

Reneau, Susan C. *The Adventures of Moccasin Joe: The True Life Story of Sgt. George S. Howard.* Missoula, Mont.: Blue Mountain Publishing, 1994.

Report of a Board of Officers to Decide upon a Pattern of Ambulance Wagon for Army Use. Washington, D.C.: Government Printing Office, 1878.

Report of the Secretary of War, 1875. Washington, D.C.: Government Printing Office, 1875.

Report of the Secretary of War, 1876. Washington, D.C.: Government Printing Office, 1876.

Reuland, Walter P. *Cartridges for the Springfield Trapdoor Rifles & Carbines, 1865–1898.* Laramie, Wyo.: Walter P. Reuland Heritage Concepts, 1993.

Revised United States Army Regulations of 1861. Washington, D.C.: Government Printing Office, 1863; reprint, Yuma, Ariz.: Fort Yuma Press, 1980.

Robinson, Charles M., III. *General Crook and the Western Frontier.* Norman: University of Oklahoma Press, 2001.

Robinson, Doane. "Crazy Horse's Story of Custer Battle." In *South Dakota Historical Collections, Vol. 6*, 224–28. [Pierre]: South Dakota State Historical Society, 1912.

Robrock, David P. "A History of Fort Fetterman, Wyoming, 1867–1992." *Annals of Wyoming* 48 (Spring 1976): 4–76.

Roth, Dave, and Bob O'Neill. "General Crook's Expeditions against Hostile Indians, March–June, 1876." *Blue & Gray Magazine*, 31–5 (2015): 50–65.

Sagan, Scott D. "The Face of Battle without the Rules of War: Lessons from Red Horse & the Battle of the Little Bighorn." *Daedalus* 146 (Winter 2017): 25–43.

Sandoz, Mari. *Crazy Horse: The Strange Man of the Oglalas.* New York: Hastings House Publishers, 1942.

Schmitt, Martin F., ed. *General George Crook: His Autobiography.* Norman: University of Oklahoma Press, 1946.

Schneider, George A., ed. *The Freeman Journal: The Infantry in the Sioux Campaign of 1876.* San Rafael, Calif.: Presidio Press, 1977.

Scott, Douglas D. "Ammunition Components from the Rosebud Battlefield and Their Relationship to the Battle of the Little Bighorn." In *Proceedings of the Brian C. Pohanka 28th Annual Symposium, Custer Battlefield Historical & Museum Association, Held at Hardin, Montana, on June 27, 2014*, edited by Rodney G. Thomas, 102–25. Hardin, Mont.: CBHMA, 2015.

———. *Custer's Heroes: The Little Bighorn Medals of Honor*. Wake Forest, N.C.: AST Press, Publisher, 2007.

Scott, Douglas D., et al. *Archaeological Perspectives on the Battle of the Little Bighorn*. Norman: University of Oklahoma Press, 1989.

Shockley, Philip M. "General George Crook's Fish Shooting Army." *Gun Report* 12 (February 1967): 8–14.

———. *The Trap-Door Springfield in the Service*. Aledo, Ill.: World-Wide Gun Report, 1958.

Smalley, Vern G. "The Lone Tepees along Reno Creek." In *Proceedings of the 12th Annual Symposium, Custer Battlefield Historical & Museum Association, Held at Hardin, Montana, on June 26, 1998*, edited by Ron Nichols, 1–11. Hardin, Mont.: CBHMA, (1999).

Spring, Agnes Wright. "Dr. McGillycuddy's Diary." In *The Denver Westerners 1953 Brand Book: IX*, ed. Maurice Frink and Francis B. Rizzari, 277–307. Denver: Westerners, 1954.

———. "Prince of Packers." *True West*, September-October 1970, 24–25, 42–46.

Stands in Timber, John, and Margot Liberty. *Cheyenne Memories*. New Haven, Conn.: Yale University Press, 1967.

———. *A Cheyenne Voice: The Complete John Stands in Timber Interviews*. Norman: University of Oklahoma Press, 2013.

Stevenson, Joan Nabseth. *Deliverance from the Little Big Horn: Doctor Henry Porter and Custer's Seventh Cavalry*. Norman: University of Oklahoma Press, 2012.

Stewart, Edgar I. *Custer's Luck*. Norman: University of Oklahoma Press, 1955.

———. "Major Brisbin's Relief of Fort Pease." In *Great Sioux War, 1876–77: The Best from Montana The Magazine of Western History*, ed. Paul L. Hedren, 115–21. Helena: Montana Historical Society Press, 1991.

Stiles, T. J. *Custer's Trials: A Life on the Frontier of a New America*. New York: Alfred A. Knopf, 2015.

Szabo, Joyce M. *Howling Wolf and the History of Ledger Art*. Albuquerque: University of New Mexico Press, 1994.

Taylor, Joseph Henry. *Frontier and Indian Life and Kaleidoscopic Lives*. Washburn, N.Dak.: Washburn's Fiftieth Anniversary Committee, 1932.

Thomas, Rodney G. "Daughters of the Lance: Native American Women Warriors." *Journal of the Indian Wars* 1 (No. 3, 2000): 147–54.

———. "Woman Warriors of the Greasy Grass." In *Proceedings of the Brian C. Pohanka 14th Annual Symposium, Custer Battlefield Historical & Museum Association, Held at Hardin, Montana, on June 23, 2000*, edited by Ron Nichols, 47–55. Hardin, Mont.: CBHMA, 2001.

Thompson, Mary Ann. *George Armstrong Custer's "Winners of the West" on the Battle of the Little Big Horn and Related Matters*. El Segundo, Calif.: Upton & Sons, Publishers, 2007.

Thralls, J. M. "The Sioux War." In *Collections of the Kansas State Historical Society, 1923–1925*, Vol. XVI, ed. William Elsey Connelley, 573–76. Topeka: Kansas State Printing Plant, 1925.

Tillett, Leslie, ed. *Wind on the Buffalo Grass: The Indians' Own Account of the Battle of the Little Big Horn River & the Death of Their Life on the Plains*. New York: Thomas Y. Crowell Company, 1976.

Trenholm, Virginia Cole, and Maurine Carley. *The Shoshonis: Sentinels of the Rockies*. Norman: University of Oklahoma Press, 1964.

Upton, Richard, comp. and ed. *The Battle of the Little Big Horn and Custer's Last Fight Remembered by Participants at the Tenth Anniversary, June 25, 1886, and the Fiftieth Anniversary, June 25, 1926.* El Segundo, Calif.: Upton & Sons, Publishers, 2006.

Utley, Robert M. *Frontier Regulars: The United States Army and the Indian, 1866–1891.* New York: Macmillan Publishing Company, 1973.

———. *The Lance and the Shield: The Life and Times of Sitting Bull.* New York: Henry Holt and Company, 1993.

Vaughn, J. W. *Indian Fights: New Facts on Seven Encounters.* Norman: University of Oklahoma Press, 1966.

———. *With Crook at the Rosebud.* Harrisburg, Pa.: Stackpole Company, 1956.

Vestal, Stanley. *New Sources of Indian History, 1850–1891.* Norman: University of Oklahoma Press, 1934.

———. *Sitting Bull: Champion of the Sioux.* Norman: University of Oklahoma Press, 1957.

———. *Warpath: The True Story of the Fighting Sioux Told in a Biography of Chief White Bull.* Boston: Houghton Mifflin Company, 1934.

———. *Warpath and Council Fire: The Plains Indians' Struggle for Survival in War and in Diplomacy, 1851–1891.* New York: Random House, 1948.

Waggoner, Josephine. *Witness: A Húŋkpapȟa Historian's Strong-Heart Song of the Lakotas.* Ed. Emily Levine. Lincoln: University of Nebraska Press, 2013.

Ward, J. O. "Fort Fetterman." *Annals of Wyoming* 4 (January 1927): 358–63.

Weist, Thomas D. Editor's Introduction to *The Cheyennes of Montana,* by Thomas B. Marquis, 9–22. Algonac, Mich.: Reference Publications, 1978.

Werts, Keith T., and Stevan C. Booras. *The Crazy Horse and Crook Fight of 1876: New Discoveries at the Battle of the Rosebud.* Spokane Valley, Wash.: Werts Publishing, 2011.

White, Ronald C. *American Ulysses: A Life of Ulysses S. Grant.* New York: Random House, 2016.

Wilhelm, Thomas. *A Military Dictionary and Gazetteer.* Philadelphia: L. R. Hamersly & Company, 1881.

Willey, P., and Douglas D. Scott, eds. *Health of the Seventh Cavalry: A Medical History.* Norman: University of Oklahoma Press, 2015.

Zinser, Louis. *Indian War Diary: Expedition of 1876.* Vienna, W.Va.: Old West Shop, n.d.

SPECIAL REPORTS

Belitz, Larry. "Chips Collection of Crazy Horse Medicines." TS [photocopy]. 2010. In author's possession.

Hedren, Paul L. "Where Are They Now? Burial Places of Officers, Physicians, and Other Notables of the Great Sioux War." TS. 2017. In author's possession.

Mangum, Neil C. "Rosebud Battlefield Historic Base Data Study." TS [photocopy]. 1984. In author's possession.

Mathews, George. "Crook's Fight on Tongue River, June 9, 1876." TS [photocopy]. N.d. John D. McDermott Papers, E. Y. Berry Library, Spearfish, South Dakota.

McDermott, John D. "Bibliography for Rosebud Battlefield State Park." TS [photocopy]. 2000. In author's possession.

———. "Crook and the Rosebud." TS [photocopy]. N.d. John D. McDermott Papers, E. Y. Berry Library, Spearfish, South Dakota.

———. "Gen. George Crook's 1876 Campaigns." TS Report. Sheridan, Wyo.: Frontier Heritage Alliance for the American Battlefield Protection Program, 2000.

Miltner, Thomas Andrew. "History and Archaeology of the Rosebud Battlefield, June 17, 1876." M.A. thesis, University of Montana, 2013.

Schug, Karl. "Rosebud Battle Artifacts Inventory, October 13, 2017." TS. In author's possession.

Scott, Douglas D. "Systematic Metal Detector Survey and Assessment of Fire Effects of the Rosebud Battlefield State Park, Montana." TS Report. Grand Junction: Colorado Plateau Cooperative Ecosystem Studies Unit, 2016.

White, Thain. "Artifacts from the Battle of the Rosebud, June 17, 1876." TS [photocopy]. 1961. Archives, Montana Historical Society, Helena.

INDEX

References to illustrations appear in italics.

CPSIA information can be obtained
at www.ICGtesting.com
Printed in the USA
LVHW091650030921
696895LV00001B/1/J